THE AUTHOR Christopher Tadgell taught architectural history for almost thirty years before devoting himself full-time to writing and research, travelling the world to see and photograph buildings from every tradition and period.

Born in Sydney, he studied art history at the Courtauld Institute in London. In 1974 he was awarded his PhD for a thesis on the Neoclassical architectural theorist, Ange-Jacques Gabriel. He subsequently taught in London and at the Kent Institute of Art and Design in Canterbury, with interludes as F.L. Morgan Professor of Architectural Design at the University of Louisville and as a Member of the Institute for Advanced Study, Princeton. He has lectured at academic institutions around the world, including the universities of Princeton, Harvard, Columbia and Cornell, the Graham Foundation in Chicago, and Cambridge University and the Courtauld Institute in the UK. He is a Trustee of the World Monuments Fund, a Fellow of the

ARCHITECTL
of seven books de
seminal architect
settlements in th
to the technologically complex and stylistically sophisticated buildings of the second half of the twentieth century. In a synthesis of extraordinary range, it brings together the fruits of a lifetime of teaching and travelling the world, seeing and photographing buildings. Each stand-alone volume sets the buildings described and illustrated within their political, technological, social and cultural contexts, exploring architecture not only as the development of form but as an expression of the civilization within which it evolved.

The series focuses on the story of the Classical tradition from its origins in Mesopotamia and Egypt, through its realization in ancient Greece and Rome,

TRANSFORMATIONS
Baroque and Rococo in the age of absolutism and the Church Triumphant

Society of Antiquaries and a member of both the British and American Societies of Architectural Historians.

His *The History of Architecture in India* (1990, several reprints, Phaidon) is the definitive one-volume account of the architecture of the subcontinent, while many publications on French architecture include the standard account in *Baroque and Rococo Architecture and Decoration* (ed. Blunt, 1978, Elek). He has contributed many articles on Indian and French architecture to *The Grove Dictionary of Art* and other major reference books.

to the Renaissance, Neoclassicism, Eclecticism and Modernism. This thread is supplemented with excursions to cover the development of architecture in Central America, India, South-East Asia and the Islamic world.

For students of architecture and art history, for travellers and for readers who want to understand the genesis of the buildings they see around them, each volume provides a complete, readable and superbly illustrated reference.

ARCHITECTURE IN CONTEXT is dedicated to my wife Juliet, without whose support – spiritual and material – it would never have been realized.
CT

TRANSFORMATIONS

Baroque and Rococo in the age of absolutism and the Church Triumphant

Christopher Tadgell

Routledge
Taylor & Francis Group

LONDON AND NEW YORK

ARCHITECTURE IN CONTEXT VI

First published in paperback 2017

First published 2012
by Routledge
2 Park Square, Milton Park, Abingdon, Oxon, OX14 4RN

and by Routledge
711 Third Avenue, New York, NY 10017

Routledge is an imprint of the Taylor & Francis Group, an informa business

PUBLISHER'S NOTE
This book has been prepared from camera-ready copy provided by the authors.

Series design: Claudia Schenk
Image processing and drawings: Mark Wilson
Editorial and production assistants: Beth Jackson and Nancy Wilson

BRITISH LIBRARY CATALOGUING-IN-PUBLICATION DATA
A catalogue record for this book is available from the British Library

LIBRARY OF CONGRESS CATALOGING-IN-PUBLICATION DATA
A catalogue record for this book has been requested

ISBN: 978-0-415-50010-4 (hbk)
ISBN: 978-1-138-03895-0 (pbk)

Printed in Great Britain by Ashford Colour Press Ltd

CONTENTS

NOTES

In the text, AIC1 indicates a reference to *Antiquity*, volume 1 in this series; AIC2 to volume 2, *The East*; AIC3 to volume 3, *Islam*; AIC4 to volume 4, *The West*; AIC5 to volume 5, *Reformations*; AIC7 to volume 7, *Modernity*.

BIRTH, DEATH AND REIGN DATES

Birth and death dates are normally given; however, reign dates are given for kings, emperors, popes and other potentates.

SOURCES OF ILLUSTRATIONS FROM
CONTEMPORARY PUBLICATIONS

DR = Domenico de Rossi, *Studio d'architettura civile*, from 1702

VB = Colen Campbell, *Vitruvius Brittannicus*, from 1715

BI = Jan Kip and Leonard Knyff, *Britannia Illustrata*, 1708

AF = Jean Mariette, *L'Architecture françoise*, 1727

DDM = Jacques-François Blondel, *De la distribution des maisons de plaisance et de la décoration des édifices en général*, 1737

RP = Jean Marot, *Recueil des plans, profils et élévations des plusieurs palais, chasteaux, églises, sépultures, grottes et hostels bâtis dans Paris*, undated, but probably from the late-1650s

SK = Salomon Kleiner, *Wahrhafte und eigentliche Abbildung*, 1737

DYNASTIC CONFLICT IN THE AGE OF ABSOLUTISM

The last phase of sectarian conflict in Europe, the first phase of the Thirty Years' War, was succeeded by a continent-wide conflict for political hegemony which resulted in an essentially new order: the Austro-Spanish Habsburg ambition of restoring a truly catholic empire, supporting a truly Catholic Church in Europe and the new world of the Americas, was denied by French arms and the aspiration of 'nations' to sovereignty within defensible boundaries – or, at least, of rulers over of territory whose inhabitants may, or may not, have been distinguished linguistically.

Of the linguistic entities which were yet to coalesce, the most significant were the Italians and the Germans. Of the former, Rome was resurgent spiritually and temporally with more enthusiastic support from Habsburgs than Bourbons: Savoy was wooed from allegiance to Spain by France but the Spanish king retained his dominions in Milan and Naples. Of the Germans, the most significant were Bavaria, Saxony, Brandenburg, the Palatinate, Hesse and Württemberg: their allegiance to the emperor was honoured mainly in the breach and among them reverence for the pope was often divisive.

Of the polities which were national entities in the main, England and Scotland were emerging from traumatic civil war, Sweden would briefly win dominance in the Baltic from Denmark, Portugal would be free of declining Spain and so too would the united Protestant provinces of the Dutch Netherlands, which maintained economic preeminence through several generations. Bent on obviating any vestige of fissiparous feudalism at home and encirclement by the Spanish abroad, however, France claimed the century and its king asserted absolutism with his predominance over both branches of Habsburgs and the papacy.

0.1a

0.1b

>0.1 WAR: from the initial triumph of (a) the Spanish against the Dutch at Breda in 1625 (Diego Velázquez, 1634; Madrid, Prado) and (b) the Emperor Ferdinand II ('über seine Feinde', 1629, engraved by Egidius Sadeler) to (c) the turning of the tide by the Swedish King Gustaf II Adolf (at the Battle of Breitenfeld, 1631, Johann Walter; Strasbourg Historical Museum).

WAR: FROM 1618 TO 1635

The condition for war was the erosion of the compromise reached at Augsburg (1548–55) with which neither Catholics nor Protestants were satisfied, especially as the Calvinists were excluded (AIC5, page 61). Emperor Maximilian II had largely honoured its spirit with religious tolerance but this was reversed by his mentally unstable son Rudolf II (1576–1612). The context of increasingly bitter hostility was exacerbated by the conversion of the Palatinate, Nassau, Hesse and Brandenburg from Lutheranism to Calvinism. The latter's adherents banded together in the League of Evangelical Union led by the Elector Palatine (1608). The Catholics responded with their League (1609) under the auspices of the Bavarian Duke Maximilian.

The brief reign of Rudolf's childless brother Matthias (1612–19) was destabilized by League rivalry and the issue of succession. The heir apparent, Ferdinand of Styria, was an ardent Catholic of the Jesuit school bent on restoring the old order. His confirmation as Crown Prince of Bohemia in 1617 countered the will of the Hussite populace and nobility who sought to join the Evangelical Union: his representatives were ejected from a window of Prague castle and he was rejected in favour of the Elector Palatine Frederick V, who had the armed support of the Dutch. Revolt led to war in Bohemia and renewed conflict in the Netherlands.**0.1**

From general sectarian conflict to territorial war

After the intervention of Spain in support of their Austrian cousins and the Catholic League, the defeat of the Protestants by the combined Catholic forces under the Count of Tilly on the White Mountain (near Prague, 1620) opened the protracted phase in the war, which favoured the Catholics. Frederick was replaced by Maximilian of Bavaria: the Evangelical Union disintegrated and Catholic supremacy had been restored in Habsburg domains by 1623. And Spanish forces prevailed against the Dutch, whose support for Frederick was incompatible with the truce initiated in 1609 (AIC5, page 97).

Catholic triumph aroused the Lutherans of Scandinavia: they were first mobilized by Christian IV of Denmark and Norway (1588–1648) who was enriched by tolls at the outlet of the Baltic and suzerainty over several major Hanseatic ports. Though nominally supported by Protestant England and Catholic France, however, he was defeated by the imperial army under the Bohemian magnate Albrecht von Wallenstein and forced to withdraw. The emperor issued the Edict of Restitution which recognized Catholic claims to disputed territory and bishoprics (1629): harvesting of the fruits of victory, this was checked by the advent of a phenomenal new power.

0.1c

The Lutheran mantle passed to Christian's rival, the great Swedish Vasa king Gustav II Adolf (1611–32) who had married the daughter of the Brandenburg elector Johann Sigismund (1572–1619) – though the latter was one of the principal German converts from Lutheranism to Calvinism (1613). Bent on avenging the Protestants, he retained the armed support of the Dutch. Bent on Swedish hegemony in the Baltic and the reduction of imperial pretensions, he had the material support of the French. His devastating progress through Germany culminated in the defeat of the erstwhile victorious imperial general Tilly in 1632. However, both Tilly and King Gustav fell that year. Ruthlessly ambitious, Wallenstein won the return bout in 1634 but the emperor made the fatal mistake of sacrificing him to paranoia when he had regained the upper hand. The ensuing Peace of Prague (1635) delayed the implementation of the Edict of Restitution, confirmed Protestant rulers in their holdings of 1627, granted amnesty to

0.2a

›0.2 RULERS OF FRANCE: (a) Louis XIII (Simon Vouet, c. 1625; Paris, Louvre); (b) Cardinal Richelieu (Armand Jean du Plessis, Duc de Richelieu, Philippe de Champaignec, 1637; Paris, Louvre).

Bishop of Luçon in 1608 (consecrated as a minor, under special dispensation from the pope), Richelieu represented the First Estate (the clergy) of Poitou at the Estates General of 1614: he opposed taxation of the Church and promoted the implementation in France of the reforms decreed by the Counter-Reformation Council of Trent (AIC5, pages 77f). Thereafter chosen by Queen Anne of Austria to administer her religious affairs, he was appointed Secretary of State (for foreign affairs) in 1616 and worked closely with the chief minister, Concino Concini, the protégé of the queen-mother, Marie de' Médici. She had been regent for her son, Louis XIII, until he attained his majority in 1614 but continued to assert her unpopular rule until 1617: in that year Concini was assassinated, the queen banished and Richelieu dismissed. He re-emerged as mediator between the king and his mother in 1619. His success in restoring her to the royal council led to his promotion in the king's service and his elevation to cardinal (1622); his role in suppressing the Huguenot rebellion recommended his appointment to the royal council from which he soon emerged as the king's chief minister (1624). Now alienated from his former patroness, he successfully countered the conspiracies she entered into with her younger son, Gaston of Orléans. He remained in supreme power until his death in 1642.

Sweden's supporters but proscribed alliance between German states or any of them with foreign powers and prescribed the forging of an imperial army from all German forces. That alarmed the French.

0.2b

FRANCE AND RENEWED WAR

While the empire was being torn apart, France was subject to an adroit regime of consolidation. The king, Louis XIII (1610–43), was less than effectual but his chief minister, Cardinal Richelieu (1585–1642), sought to reinforce the centralized power of the French monarchy by crushing internal opposition, primarily from the old feudal nobility (*noblesse d'épée*), and exert it to counter the traditional Austro-Spanish Habsburg enemy abroad.**0.2** He elevated the class of professional administrators (*noblesse de robe*) from the ranks of the high bourgeoisie or the gentry rather than the old aristocracy: outstanding amongst these was the secretary of state François Sublet de Noyers (1589–1645), superintendent of finances and royal buildings, who determined that Paris would eclipse Rome culturally as his master prepared for the Bourbons to eclipse the Habsburgs politically.

To secure the realm from the machinations of the old magnates within, Richelieu ordered the disbanding of private armies and the slighting of all castles except those needed by the crown for frontier defence. Without, beyond the south-eastern border, he connived with the Protestant Swiss to defeat Spanish aims in northern Lombardy and subsidised the Dutch in their conflict with Spain. At home, however, he saw the Protestants as a danger to his unifying cause, not least because they too had significant military forces and were supported by the English. Enforced reintroduction of Catholicism into predominantly Protestant areas provoked rebellion. English help failed to further the Huguenot cause: the fall of their major stronghold of La Rochelle after a long siege (1628) led to the curtailment of their right to hold arms but not to their freedom of worship.

In the war so far, the Spanish army had acquitted itself as the most formidable in the field but the kingdom, ruled by the rash and over-ambitious Count-duke of Olivares, was in sad decline under Philip IV (1621–65).**0.3** Hostile to France, the regime had subsidized the Huguenot revolt to distract Richelieu from Lombardy and the Netherlands. Though officially non-belligerent in the German War, moreover, alliance with the Swedes in 1631 committed him to help pay for Gustav Adolf's anti-imperial campaign. Finding ready allies among the Protestant princes of the south and west, naturally antipathetic to the imperial cause, the threat of a united German force at the emperor's command prompted him to open the last phase of the war in support of his allies, leaderless after the death of their king.

Back to war: the last phase

France opened hostilities with Spain in May 1635: the aggressor met disaster initially but the enemy advance was halted before Paris a year later. War was declared on the Empire but was pursued indecisively until the death of Ferdinand II. Seeking peace, the new Emperor Ferdinand III (1637–57) countered a central provision of the Prague settlement – and ceded the strength renewed by it – in granting the German states freedom to make their own foreign policy. Neither this nor even the death of Cardinal Richelieu in 1642 and of Louis XIII a year later effected relief to the ruinous war effort. Louis de Bourbon, Prince de Condé, finally overcame the indomitable Spanish army at Rocroi in 1643. That was followed two years later with Swedish victory over the imperial forces near Prague and French victory over the Bavarians. The war dragged on for three more years, catastrophically for the Empire.

Richelieu was succeeded by his protégé, the Italian clerical adventurer Giulio Mazarini (1602–61), who had been made cardinal at French instigation in 1641: two years later, he began to rule France for the young Louis XIV in concert with the queen-regent, Anne of Austria. Two years further on, threatened with popular uprising against taxa-

›0.3 PHILIP IV OF SPAIN (Diego Velázquez, 1639; London, National Gellery).

King of Castile and Léon, Aragon, Naples and Sicily, Portugal and much of the New World, Philip was born in 1605 to Philip III and his wife Margaret of Austria (sister of Emperor Ferdinand II). His sister Anne (of Austria) was married to Louis XIII and he was first married (at the age of ten) to Louis's sister Élisabeth (1602–44): their promising son Baltasar Carlos died aged seventeen (1646), their daughter was to become Queen of France (wife of their nephew Louis XIV). In 1646 he married his niece Maria Anna of Austria (1634–96), daughter of his younger sister Maria Anna and Emperor Ferdinand III. The inbreeding did not secure a sound male heir for Spain: the only surviving son of Philip's second marriage, the future Carlos II, was chronically ill, mentally unstable and expected to die imminently throughout his thirty-five year reign with serious consequences for the stability of Europe – as we shall see.

A highly cultured man, great connoisseur of art, patron of Velázquez – the greatest painter of Spain's Golden Age – Philip was not a success politically. This was due in part to a deeply withdrawn piety and lack of mundane confidence which led him to depend on unsound ministers - particularly Olivares for the first twenty years of the reign. With the latter's encouragement, in the main it was due to retracing the disastrous course of religious intolerance in the Netherlands which had beggared his grandfather, Philip II (AIC5, pages 94ff), and supporting his Austrian Habsburg cousins in the war resulting from their repressive policies. Throughout, moreover, he attempted to maintain hegemony over vulnerable Italian domains, recalcitrant Spanish provinces and rebellious Portugal. His resources were depleted by the incessant warfare and persistence in a naive view of the value of treasure – of the bullion imported from the Americas with escalating inflationary consequences – rather than the economics of industry.

0.4
›0.4 PEACE: the Treaty of Westphalia, 1648 (Spanish and Dutch delegates at Münster, Gerard ter Borch c. 1649; Amsterdam, Rijksmuseum).

Excluding a comprehensive settlement with Spain, the so-called Peace of Westphalia (1648) was based on three main treaties: the first concluded at Münster (May 1648) to end the Eighty Years' War between Spain and the Dutch Republic with recognition of the latter's independence; the two complementary ones concluded by the Emperor with Sweden at Osnabrück and with France at Münster (both October 1648). Cardinal Mazarin was the prime author.

tion to pay for the German war but backed by victories in the field, the regime turned to diplomacy. After protracted negotiation the Truce of Ulm suspended hostilities with Bavaria in March 1647, leaving the emperor isolated. The imperial forces were decisively defeated by the French under the Vicomte de Turenne and the Prince de Condé in March 1648. Peace, under negotiation with the Spanish since Rocroi, was henceforth concluded in treaties signed at several towns in Westphalia between all parties: the contending German powers apart, these were principally France, the Empire, Spain, the Dutch Republic, Sweden and Denmark. All were on the verge of bankruptcy: vast swathes of Europe, especially the German states and the kingdom of Bohemia, were devastated and depopulated.**0.4**

As Philip IV had lost Portugal in the last decade of the conflict and conceded Dutch independence at its end, the Habsburgs emerged from the war reduced to Austria and Bohemia – with the rump of Hungary – on the one hand, Spain and its American colonies on the other. The empire had long been defunct as a supranational power but now the contrary principle of individual state sovereignty was enshrined in international agreement, state boundaries were set and within them subservience to the constituted authority was demanded to the exclusion of religious or secular affiliations abroad. While this assertion of state sovereignty weakened the head of the house of Habsburg as emperor, it strengthened him as archduke of Austria and king of Bohemia – though that strength would be tested for nearly another half-century by the Ottoman Turks.

FRANCE: CENTRALIZED POWER CHECKED AND REASSERTED

With the eclipse of the emperor and the fragmentation of Germany, the balance of power tipped steeply in France's favour though Cardinal Mazarin's regime was immediately challenged by the uprising known as the Fronde. Popular discontent with taxation to pay for the war prompted the *parlements* – courts of appeal – to challenge the royal prerogative extended by Richelieu. Moreover, members of the *noblesse d'épée*, heading armed bands hardened by war in Germany and unsettled back into civil society, saw their chance to reassert their feudal rights. The latter were joined by major figures, including the great general Condé whose repatriated army had been instrumental in mollifying the *parlements.* Turenne, at first favourable to Condé's cause – like many who hated their upstart Italian ruler – was ultimately the instrument of its destruction: the Paris mob, initially hostile, turned back to the royal regime against the chaos of princely rebellion. The royal family had left Paris in the face of insurrection and Mazarin had fled the country in 1651 and 1652: they now returned and, capitalizing on the craving for order, enforced the lapsed proscription of private militias and advanced the cause of royal absolutism.

Settlement had yet to be achieved between France and Spain, at war since 1635. The Spanish army, hitherto seemingly invincible, had ceded its prestige to the forces led by Turenne and Condé: the war drew to a close in 1659 with Turenne having gained the upper hand. Mazarin's final triumph was the ensuing Peace of the Pyrénées which gained France important provinces to the north-east and south-west – and a Spanish princess as queen on unfulfilled conditions depriving her of her Spanish inheritance.**0.5**

With the Peace of the Pyrénées, completing the series of settlements favourable to the Bourbons but lamentable for the Habsburgs, France emerged supreme in Europe. Mazarin's secular state interest – *realpolitik* – had triumphed over religious affiliation and the ideal of catholicism, the pursuit of which had ruined the Habsburgs: there was to be no recurrence of general religious war in Europe but dynastic conflict was endemic. And the first generations of

The Augsburg principle of *cuius regio, eius religio* (AIC5, pages 71f) was reaffirmed and extended to Calvinists, who were to be deemed equal before the law with Lutherans and Catholics. More than three hundred German states were recognized as sovereign: imperial taxation or war would henceforth require the assent of their assembly in the imperial diet. Apart from thus crucially weakening the emperor, France was confirmed in possession of the strategic eastern cities of Metz, Toul and Verdun – and representation in the imperial diet. In addition to the United Dutch Provinces, Switzerland, Savoy, Tuscany, Parma and several smaller Italian states were recognized as independent of the Habsburgs.

The Catholic Duke Maximilian of Bavaria retained the Upper Palatinate and its electoral vote. The Lower Palatinate, with a new electoral vote, was accorded to the deposed Frederick V's son, the Protestant Charles Louis who had supported the French. Dismissing Denmark as the principal power in the north, Sweden held western Pomerania and therefore controlled the outlets of the Elbe, Oder and Weser: this, and the prince-bishopric of Bremen, also gave it voices in the imperial diet but freedom of trade was promoted. Eastern Pomerania went to Brandenburg who also secured Cleves and several bishoprics, notably Magdeburg, Halberstadt and Minden. However, full settlement to conflict between the Baltic powers in the 'First Northern War' was not achieved until 1660 – to Sweden's advantage.

0.5

›0.5 PEACE OF THE PYRÉNÉES concluded between the France of Louis XIV and the Spain of Philip IV: the meeting of the kings and the presentation of the Infanta María Teresa on the Île des Faisans in the River Bidassoa where it forms the frontier between their kingdoms, (1659, anon.; Le Mans, Musée de Tessé).

Nearly a decade after Westphalia, an inconclusive end to the Franco-Spanish war seemed unavoidable: Mazarin turned to diplomacy. On the death of Emperor Ferdinand III in 1657, he proposed Louis XIV as his successor: Archduke Leopold (son of Ferdinand III and Philip IV's sister Maria Anna) was chosen instead but he mollified France with a promise of neutrality unless imperial lands were threatened. Also in 1657 the devious cardinal secured an alliance with regicide Oliver Cromwell's Puritan English Commonwealth against Spain in the expectation of colonial gains. Then came Turenne's advance at arms and peace.

The Pyrénées watershed was established as the frontier between Spain and France, the latter gaining Roussillon – and most of Spain's other holdings on the French side – in return for the renunciation of claims to Catalonia. The settlement in the north was less clear cut but France gained the important province of Artois from Spanish Flanders. Spain recognized all France's gains at Westphalia: France renounced support for Portuguese independence. Spain sent his daughter María Teresa to France as queen: she was constrained to renounce her claim to her father's throne in return for a dowry settlement which was not paid.

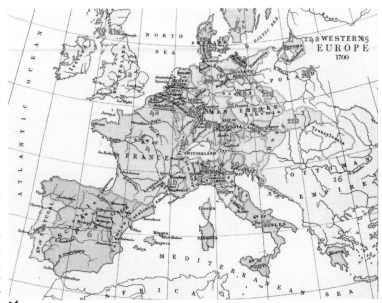

0.6

›0.6 EUROPE AFTER THE WESTPHALIAN SETTLEMENT AND THE PEACE OF THE PYRÉNÉES: map with (1a–c) the conjoined kingdoms of England, Scotland and Ireland; (2) the United Provinces of the Protestant northern Netherlands and (3) the Catholic southern Netherlands adhering to Spain with the rump of Burgundy, the Franche-Comté (3a); (4) France with Artois (4a) and Roussillon (4b) detached from Spanish control; (5) Portugal; (6) Spain and the Spanish dominions in Italy, (6a) Sicily, (6b) Naples, (6c) Milan; (7) the Duchy of Savoy; (8) Papal States, (9) Tuscany, (10) Venice; (11) the Empire with the Archduchy of Austria (11a), the Kingdoms of Hungary (11b) and Bohemia (11c), Silesia (11d) and the principal sovereign German powers of Saxony (11e), Bavaria (11f), Württemberg (11g), the Upper and Lower Palatinates (11h, i), Hanover (11j) and Brandenburg (11k); (12) Denmark; (13) Sweden with Swedish Pomerania (13a); (14) the Commonwealth of Poland and Lithuania (14a); (15) Muscovy; (16) the Ottoman Balkans.

that would be perpetrated by King Louis XIV (1638–1715), who assumed his personal rule after the wily cardinal's demise in 1661.[0.6]

DUTCH EXPANSION

The most effective rival of France in power, economic and naval if not military, was the most unlikely state in Europe: the inextensive United Provinces of the Protestant Netherlands whose 'Golden Age' matured when their 'Eighty Years' War' of independence from Spain – and Spanish Flanders – was terminated by the first of the treaties signed at Münster in 1648. The French had connived at the dissection of Habsburg Burgundy by the Dutch. Now – and increasingly as their belligerence left them chronically short of money – they were jealous, wary indeed, of the commercially astute Calvinists who dominated maritime trade after extending the war to displace the Catholic Iberians in the key stations of their world-encircling colonial empire.

0.7.1a

›0.7 THE GOLDEN AGE OF DUTCH PAINT-ING: 1 Rembrandt van Rijn: (a) the civic militia guard (Kloveniers), 'The Company of Frans Banning Cocq and Willem van Ruytenburch' ('The Night Watch', 1642; Amsterdam, Rijksmuseum) commissioned by eighteen of the participants to hang in their Amsterdam meeting hall (Kloveniersdoelen) where, as a celebration of a daytime venture, it astonished for its startling *chiaroscuro* and for the introduction of movement to the traditionally static group portrait; (b) portrait of Aeltje Uylenburgh (1632; Boston, Museum

0.7.1b

0.7.1c

of Fine Arts); (c) 'Landscape with a Stone Bridge' (late-1630s) – and an impending storm about to engulf the enlightenment of wilderness.

The Dutch East India Company was established in 1603 (AIC5, pages 545ff). The pivot was the Cape Colony of southern Africa, founded in 1652 in place of a Portuguese way station. Two years earlier, however, the Portuguese won back Brazil which had been taken from its Spanish masters in 1630: they proceeded down the coast to Rio de Janeiro (settled by 1590) and from thence inland. In compensation, the Dutch made do with Surinam, north of the Amazon basin. Of less obvious importance, as yet, their dominance in the northern continent beckoned from the foundation in 1614 of New Amsterdam at the Atlantic mouth of the Hudson River.

Amsterdam, not Paris, was the financial hub of Europe: with the first full-time stock exchange, it was the first centre of capitalism. Its capitalists insured themselves and provided for their retirement in tall, narrow, canal-fronting houses, unostentatiously decorated in the main but

2 Willem van der Velde the Younger, the Battle of Texel, commemorating the engagement in August 1673 of the Dutch fleet, commanded by Michiel de Ruyter, Adriaen Banckert and Cornelis Tromp, with the combined English and French fleets under Prince Rupert of the Rhine, Jean II d'Estrées and Edward Spragg – which were deployed to assist a French invasion force under the terms of Charles II's secret Treaty of Dover with his cousin Louis XIV (c. 1675; Amsterdam, Rijksmuseum).
3 Pieter de Hooch, 'Interior with Women beside a Linen Chest' (1663; Amsterdam, Rijksmuseum).

0.7.2

0.7.3

4 Jan Vermeer, 'View of Delft' (c. 1660; The Hague, Mauritshuis).

0.7.4

enriched with the superb range of marine, topographical, genre, portrait and history paintings of their native school.**0.7** That would remain supreme but the society it served – and depicted – was small relative to its British maritime rivals, over-extended abroad and divided at home between Republicans and the royalist supporters of the house of Orange. Extraordinarily, as we shall see, the latter inherited Britain but then the British took primacy. They had already taken New Amsterdam in 1667, renamed it New York and held it despite being beaten by the Dutch in the second bout of their recurrent trade war.

BRITAIN: RESTORATION AT HOME, EXPANSION ABROAD

Spain – or, rather, Spanish missionaries – continued to expand in America, from Mexico north-east into Texas and north-west into California. Contracted in Europe, on the other hand, the Spanish Habsburgs sustained their presence in Italy but Italy had lost its importance to the Atlantic powers. Of these, England was now emerging from a generation of civil war which had culminated in the execution of King Charles I in 1649 (AIC5, page 102).

After a decade of increasingly unpopular Puritan commonwealth Britain reverted to monarchy: the restored king, Charles II (1660–85), was Louis XIV's cousin and was rather to be his client than his rival – though the British parliament would have different ideas. The king's preference for tolerance of Catholicism countered parliamentary opinion but his rejection of Puritanism was extremely popular.**0.8**

The Portuguese ceded Bombay and its dependencies to the British crown as part of the dowry of Charles II's queen Catherine of Braganza in 1661. Sixty years earlier the English East India Company had been chartered by Queen Elizabeth: it was floated on the stock market with the award of monopoly in the spice, cotton, indigo, tea and opium trade in competition with the flagging Portuguese and advancing Dutch. That was the first major move in capitalizing on colonial enterprise which, of course, was to have its cycles of spectacular boom and bust (see below). The groundwork began with the founding of the first trading post at Surat in 1608; the east coast of India was reached within two years and the most important English bases were established at Madras and Calcutta by 1635 and 1690 respectively.

The first British colonial empire was founded in 1607 with Jamestown in Virginia – named after Queen Elizabeth by Sir Walter Raleigh, the claimant of the north American continent's Atlantic seaboard for the crown (1584). Religious fundamentalism and opposition to quasi-Catholic Stuart monarchy, rather than rapacity, motivated the first main wave of colonists in Massachusetts to the north (1620). Like the other European maritime powers, Britain already had substantial holdings in the Caribbean: like them, too, it imported slaves to labour on the highly lucrative plantations of sugar there, tobacco and cotton on the northern mainland where the expansion of Virginia, Massachusetts and New York was followed by the foundation of Delaware, Pennsylvania and Georgia (between 1682 and 1733).

0.8a

›0.8 THE STUART RESTORATION: (a) Charles I with Queen Henrietta Maria, the Prince of Wales, later Charles II, and Mary, Princess Royal, later wife of William II (Stadtholder of the Netherlands) and mother of William III, by Anthony van Dyck, 1632; (b) Charles II enthroned, by John Michael Wright, 1661; (c) 'The Sea Triumph of Charles II', by Antonio Verrio, c. 1674 (Royal Collection Trust /© Her Majesty Queen Elizabeth II 2013).

Defeated by the Parliamentary forces of Oliver Cromwell at Worcester in 1651, the erstwhile Prince of Wales, contender for the fallen throne, escaped across the Channel where he spent nine years of exile in France and the Netherlands. After the death of Crom-

0.8b

0.8c

THE ASCENDANCY OF LOUIS XIV

By 1660 France was a powerfully centralized autocracy, the vestiges of feudalism having been dismissed with the Fronde. In 1660 France was on the verge of overtaking the cultural hegemony of Rome. And from 1661 France was an ambitious young absolute monarch bent on military and cultural glory. As he himself would maintain, famously, Louis XIV embodied the state, but for nearly twenty years he ran it with the excellent guidance of Mazarin's protégé Jean-Baptiste Colbert.**0.9**

Like Richelieu, Colbert pursued the reform of every branch of administration. Like Sublet de Noyers, he was also bent on propelling France to pre-eminence in European culture: he saw the completion of the royal Parisian palace of the Louvre as the occasion for the visible attain-

well and the accession of his weak son to the unpopular Puritan Protectorate, anarchy threatened until the armed opposition forced the resignation of the republican parliament and secured its replacement with a royalist one. Charles II, deemed the legitimate king since the execution of his father in January 1649, was invited to return and was duly crowned in April 1661.

A new settlement devised by the Earl of Clarendon reinforced the position of the re-established Church of England as much against the Puritans who had disestablished it as against Catholics: the king preferred tolerance but acquiesced in a series of measures furthering the prescription of conformity. Widely welcomed, however, was the restoration of theatre and other sources of enjoyment proscribed under the Protectorate. Inevitably, the Puritans blamed this for the visitation of the plague in 1665 and the destruction of much of London by fire in the following year; the conformists blamed the Catholics, at least for the fire. This was unfounded, of course, but the dynasty would succumb to the political conflagration ignited by its Catholicism.

›0.9 POWER AND ITS ADMINISTRATION AT THE OUTSET OF THE SIÈCLE DE LOUIS XIV: (a) the king's assumption of personal rule in 1661 (c. 1680, Charles Le Brun, vault of the Hall of Mirrors,

0.9a

ment of this goal but the king preferred to manifest the achievement at Versailles, conceived as the ultimate expression of the centralization of power at the expense of the upper aristocracy imprisoned there. Not by the emasculated nobility, thus, ultimately efficient bureaucracy was halted in the enforcement of the royal will only by the courts, especially the venal old *parlements* – to which we shall return.

Seeking to free France from dependence on imports – especially of expensive luxuries – Colbert promoted the development of commerce and industry under the auspices of the state, both for prestige and as a major source of revenue to supplement reformed taxation. The endeavour was successful in the main but escalating harassment of the Huguenots, which culminated in the revocation of the Edict of Nantes in 1685, sent many of the kingdom's most productive artisans abroad. That followed the demise of Colbert but, meanwhile, the great minister had failed to overcome the estates of vested interest who opposed the institute an equitable system of taxation: the secular magnates had been paid in tax privileges for surrendering their feudal rights to raise arms in assertion of local power and it was deemed impious to exact revenue from the servants of God. Thus those who could afford to pay most paid little and the chronic weakness of the royal finances, pressed to bankruptcy by virtually incessant war, ultimately caused catastrophe.

Colbert's promotion of industry at home was complemented by the expansion of commerce and colonialism abroad. Settlement in New France, centred on Québec (founded 1608) and expanding from fur-trading bases in the St Lawrence basin, had been regulated by Richelieu: explorers from there penetrated across the Great Lakes and down the Mississippi where the colony of Louisiana was established in 1682. In the Caribbean, meanwhile, the Compagnie des Îles d'Amérique settled colonies in Guadeloupe, Martinique and Saint Lucia (1635–50): the largest

Versailles); (b) Jean-Baptiste Colbert, Marquis de Seignelay and Seigneur de Sceaux, and (c) François-Michel Le Tellier, Marquis de Louvois (both Robert Nanteuil, c. 1665, 1675).

Three years after the demise of his mentor, Cardinal Mazarin, Jean-Baptiste Colbert (1619–83) was superintendent of royal buildings, the first of the several official appointments which would propel him to the head of the king's highly restricted 'cabinet' of ministers: he had emerged from the ranks of the bourgeoisie – like Sublet de Noyers under Richelieu – and was instrumental in the founding of academies of the arts and sciences. He was Controller-General of Finances from 1665, launching a ruthless campaign of eradicating corruption, fraud and tax evasion – but made little progress in limiting the privilege of avoidance. As Secretary of State for the Navy from 1669 he held important ancillary offices including superintendence of colonization and commerce.

Promoting commerce and industry, Colbert attempted to order the economics of the state as he was ordering its government. Abroad, the West and East Indies trading companies – the Compagnies des Îles d'Amérique and des Indes – were founded on his initiative, north America explored. At home the roads and canals were improved. Glass, textiles and tapestry were among the luxury products sponsored to meet the vast needs of the court (see page 241). The traditional guilds were regulated and their activities protected at huge bureaucratic cost and ultimate stultification: protection of trade with extreme tariff barriers invited retribution – commercial and military. Contrary to his better judgement, Colbert acquiesced in the king's determination to rescind the rights of the Huguenots.

The most important post not entrusted to Colbert was Secretary of State for War: from 1666 that was filled by François-Michel Le Tellier, Marquis de Louvois, who dedicated himself to reorganizing and enlarging the army to further the king's aggressive ambitions – of course at a cost which undermined the financial reforms promoted by Colbert. He welded the inherited agglomeration of regiments, 'owned' by their colonels, into a disciplined standing army (300,000 strong by the end of the century): its infantry, cavalry and artillery were integrated under a rigorous hierarchy of command devolved in virtue of merit at least in principle. He could not obviate the venality of military office entirely, but he repressed absenteeism, fraudulence in provisioning and pillaging. He was relatively humane to the men, founding the Hôpital des Invalides (1670). He oversaw the realization of the Marquis de Vauban's system of frontier forts – having commissioned the splendid series of their models (see pages 258f). He succeeded Colbert as Superintendent of Buildings to indulge the king's other favourite exercise in lavish expenditure (see below).

0.9c

gain, Saint-Domingue (modern Haiti, the western half of Hispaniola), followed in Colbert's first year of power. Also in 1664, the Compagnie des Indes was established to tap the legendary riches of the real Indies – and founded factories on the east coast of India. As in England, experience of Asia informed art, not least in equipping the style known as Rococo with its *chinoiserie* motifs.

Virtually incessant war promoted the development of a model army from the ill-disciplined horde inherited from the late Valois and their era of civil strife. Two centuries earlier, at the end of the Hundred Years' War, the Valois had been the first in the European field with a professional standing army (AIC4, pages 241f): in this, as in the reformation of the state whose ambitions were to be served by that army, the example was recalled by the servants of the Bourbons – the Marquis de Louvois, in particular. Moreover, military colleges were founded to promote merit instead of venality. That complemented a bureaucratic hierarchy, central and provincial, which was supposed to be proof against inefficiency and corruption. Both these objectives were insufficiently realized, but the French army was Europe's most formidable fighting force within a decade of the Peace of the Pyrénées.

France's ally Sweden had emerged from the Baltic war as the dominant power in the north where Russia was yet to be challenged. The Austrian Habsburgs were threatened with extinction by the Ottomans: the Spanish Habsburgs faced extinction through the genetic decadence of Louis XIV's brother-in-law, the hopelessly inbred Carlos II (1665–1700). Thus the way was opened to France for aggrandizement. Louis XIV's Spanish queen, María Teresa, could take her father's throne on the demise of her impotent brother because the dowry condition for the renunciation of her claim had never been met. Control over Spain's military, naval and colonial resources was of major interest, of course, but France's most pressing aim was the acquisition of Spanish Flanders and Franche-Comté (the rump of old Burgundy) which would remove the eastern frontier to the Rhine – long claimed as the natural boundary.

The wars of Louis XIV: initial aggression

Louis XIV sent armies into both the Spanish Netherlands and the Franche-Comté in 1667 in assertion of tenuous claims to the devolution of the late Philip IV's Flemish territories to María Teresa. At the time the United Provinces and England were preoccupied with a renewed bout of their trade war: New York was the main gain of the latter but their substantial loss was much of the home fleet to surprise Dutch attack in the Thames. Peace – relaxing trade restrictions and leaving the English with New York but not valuable spice islands in the East Indies – was hastily concluded as Louis XIV threatened the Dutch who needed English support. This was provided in concert with Sweden in 1668. France withdrew with minor gains (under the Peace of Aix-la-Chapelle, 1668) and major grievance over the Anglo-Dutch alliance.

Louis returned with a pre-emptive strike against the Dutch in 1672: advance into Holland was rapid but the defenders flooded their country and forced the invaders to withdraw. William III of Orange, Stadtholder of the Netherlands (from 1672), assembled another anti-French coalition which even included the Empire and Spain and the leading northern Protestant powers. The English were ambivalent: they saw the Dutch as their main rivals and their king had a secret accord with his French cousin – as we shall see.

Stalemate ensued and the French turned their attention to Flanders. This alarmed the English: peace was concluded with the Dutch in 1674; three years later Charles II sent his niece Mary to marry his nephew William III. The French were enjoying victories against the Spanish in Flanders and the Franche-Comté but, faced with a new Anglo-Dutch alliance, agreed to settle with depleted satisfaction (at Nijmegen, 1679): among the most notable provisions were France's surrender of gains in Flanders but retention of Franche-Comté. And Louis returned to the fray on the dubious interpretation of the Westphalian settlement in terms of the reunion of disputed territory: he annexed several imperial Rhenish cities and occupied Strasbourg in 1681 as a major bridgehead on the Rhine.

While despoiling the emperor in the west, France aided his Hungarian and Ottoman enemies in the east. However, the balance of power was dramatically redressed with the crushing defeat of the Ottomans before the walls of Vienna in September 1683 by the German troops of Emperor Leopold I (1658–1705) reinforced most significantly by those of John III Sobieski, King of Poland.**0.10** The allied armies, led by Prince Eugène of Savoy, who had distinguished himself in the battle for Vienna, chased the enemy back east into the Balkans and liberated most of Hungary, removing the main obstacle to comprehensive post-Westphalian reconstruction in the devastated imperial domains.

›0.10 THE SIEGE OF VIENNA, 1683: (Frans Geffles; Vienna Museum, Karlsplatz).

0.10

Vienna secure, the emperor turned west in league with the major Catholic powers. Louis was constrained to accede to the Treaty of Regensburg in 1684: France retained Strasbourg and several of the annexed Flemish towns on her border in return for abandoning the so-called *réunion* policy. And the balance of power was again altered dramatically by the eclipse of the Stuarts in Britain. Within three years of Charles II's death, parliament deposed his Catholic brother and successor James II (VII of Scotland) in favour of his daughter Mary II and her cousin and husband William III (reigned jointly until 1694 and he alone until 1702). Jacobite attempts to regain the throne and reclaim England for Catholicism were obviated finally in 1745 but, meanwhile, the principles of the 'Glorious Revolution' formed the basis of modern constitutional monarchy beholden to parliament. And parliament, hitherto dominated by rural magnates, was now also to represent new wealth accrued from colonial plantation and trade. On the continent, on the other hand, absolutism was ascendant.**0.11, 0.12**

Absolutism and constraint

Asserted by Louis XIV, absolute autocracy was the aspiration of monarchs throughout Europe in the aura of his ascendency: it might be complete in Russia, where there was no effective institutional check on the tsar's exercise of power, but not elsewhere, even in France. There, the personal power of the king contrasted with the limited power of his cousin in England or the Stadtholder of the Netherlands or even the king of Spain where the assemblies (*cortes*) of the constituent kingdoms were assertive in legislature. And in Catholic countries there was the influence of Rome exerted – to varying degrees – through their ecclesiastical establishments.**1.10**

The centrifugal motive of the French monarchy, determined to eradicate the dissipations of feudalism, had to contend with the metropolitan and provincial *parlements*: venal courts of appeal, devolved in the later Middle Ages from the royal council through the primary body in Paris, these jealously guarded their customary rights of consultation and deliberation, of registering, or refusing to register, royal decrees. Registration could be enforced by a *lit de justice*, a formal royal session of the Parlement de Paris in which the members were less concerned with furthering freedom than preserving fiscal privilege. And that would destroy them and the entire *Ancien Régime*.

Quite contrary was the new order of England's 'Glorious Revolution' which King William III and Queen Mary II were constrained to endorse before the proclamation of their accession in 1689. It was defined in the terms of the Declaration of Rights drafted at the beginning of the year and enacted in December: in defence of the 'ancient rights' of the king's subjects (provided they were not Catholics), it asserted most particularly the illegality of government without parliament meeting in regular session, of raising money or armed forces in peacetime without its consent, of curbing

›0.11 THE GLORIOUS REVOLUTION: (a) King James II and Queen Mary of Modena at their coronation banquet with members of parliament in Westminster Hall (1685, engraved record by Francis Sandford, 1687) before the former fell foul of the latter and ended in exile; (b) 'William and Mary Presenting the Cap of Liberty to Europe' (c. 1710, Sir James Thornhill, Royal Hospital Greenwich, Great Hall).

In general King Charles II avoided confrontations which might upset the Restoration but ultimately his foreign connections alienated his erstwhile supportive parliament. His cousin Louis XIV's War of Devolution was stalled by parliament's rapid endorsement of transition from war to alliance with the Dutch in 1668, as we have seen. Two years later the perceived inadequacy of his parliamentary grants prompted Charles to reach a secret accord with his cousin promising conversion to Catholicism in return for financial and military aid (should the latter be needed in the Catholic cause).

Charles proposed a Declaration of Indulgence for Catholics and Protestant dissenters (1672) but parliament rejected it and advanced repression on the pretext of unsubstantiated allegations of a 'popish plot' to assassinate the king. That culminated in the introduction to parliament of a bill excluding the Catholic Duke of York from the succession to the throne: the measure crystallized the basic division of sentiment in British politics between 'Whigs' and 'Tories' – those in favour and against the bill respectively, the heirs to the Parliamentarians and Royalists in the late Civil War. Several dissolutions of parliament staved off the threat until the king's unexpected death in 1685. Apart from the endurance of the Restoration, largely popular not least due to its merriment, his legacy was the flourishing of the arts and sciences, particularly with the chartering of the Royal Society (amongst whose founding members were Sir Isaac Newton and Richard Boyle) and the patronage of Sir Christopher Wren.

Charles was discreet about his religious convictions but converted to Catholicism on his deathbed as he had promised his cousin. His brother was vigorous in the cause of tolerating nonconformity to the tenets of the established church: some relief for alternative Protestant sects was carried in parliament but his policy of Catholic emancipation and accord with France was anathema to the majority. His raising of a standing army and commissioning of Catholic officers in an extraor-

0.11a

dinary exercise of the royal prerogative was alarming, especially as he dissolved parliament for objecting. His marriage to the Catholic princess Mary of Modena (at the instigation of Louis XIV) and the birth of their son James in mid-1688, displacing his Protestant daughter Mary from the succession, was unacceptable to the Whigs and even many Tories. Mary and her husband William III, who secured the acquiescence of the Emperor in face of their common French enemy, were invited to invade in defence of parliament and the rule of law. James was quickly defeated in England, less so in Scotland and Ireland – where William's victory at the Battle of the Boyne reopened a sore that still runs.

The accession of William and Mary as joint monarchs was proclaimed (February 1689) after they were constrained to endorse a declaration of rights which James was deemed to have abrogated: in particular to be governed through their freely elected representative in parliament. Adherents of the Roman rite were denied the ballot, offices of state, commissions in the army and the throne. The succession would be through the issue of the joint monarchs or, if they remained childless, Mary's sister Anne. Under the latter, the hitherto distinct realms of England and Scotland were united in the single parliamentary regime of 'Great Britain' (1707).

Queen Anne died without issue. Her half-brother claimed the throne as James III (the 'Old Pretender') in opposition to the succession of George I of Hanover (1714–27). His challenge was defeated in 1715 but his son Charles Edward (the 'Young Pretender') renewed it unsuccessfully in 1745.

freedom of election or speech and penalizing petitioners. Absolutism was rejected and the principles of constitutional monarchy established in law. And those are the principles of the modern polity – monarchical or republican, honoured in practice or in the breach.

0.11b

THE WARS OF LOUIS XIV
REPRISED

Raising his sights, Louis invaded the Palatinate in 1686 to impose a Catholic successor to the Protestant electorate. Following the revocation of the Edict of Nantes the previous year – withdrawing religious tolerance in France – this provoked the Protestant powers of the north, led by William of Orange, to join the Catholic powers of the south, led by the emperor, in the League of Augsburg to which England adhered when William became king in 1688.

Faced with exceptional unity of opposition in all directions on land and sea, the French war effort achieved no decisive military triumph at the cost of bankruptcy. The League had no major military victories to its credit either, except over the French fleet en route to invade England at La Hogue (1692). General antipathy to the war was sharpened by famine (1693). The League disintegrated: France signed separate peace treaties at Rijswijk in 1697 with the western allies on the one hand and the empire on the other. The aggressor again gained little from either, renounced his cause in the Palatinate (which had extended to the Bavarian succession), recognized William III as king of England in place of his cousin James, restored most of the former *réunions* to the empire or Flanders, but kept Strasbourg.

The final great conflict of Louis XIV's costly reign supervened in 1700 with the long-awaited death of Carlos II of Spain. Exhausted by the late war, France had attempted to pre-empt the issue with diplomacy: a covert partition agreement with the emperor was recalled and variants were promoted with the other major powers. Free of threat from the east and no longer cowed by France in the west, Emperor Leopold asserted his claim as the head of the house of Habsburg to which the Spanish monarchy belonged. However, French diplomacy won the day in Spain itself. The dying

›0.12 LOUIS XIV, c. 1701 in the model of absolutist state portraiture set by Hyacinthe Rigaud (Paris, Louvre).

king was persuaded to prefer the Bourbons though their claim derived from his sister who had died in 1685: thus the royal will specified Louis XIV's grandson, Philip Duc d'Anjou, as heir to his undivided empire and stipulated that if this was not realized the whole succession would devolve on the emperor's son, Archduke Charles. Louis agreed. Leopold acquiesced, reluctantly.

Britain and the United Provinces had little option but to accept the will of the late Spanish king but the implications alarmed their joint ruler, William III. Alarm increased when Louis called on the *parlement* of Paris to reaffirm Philippe d'Anjou's rights to the French crown with all its potential for upsetting the balance of power. Alarm increased further when French forces were again deployed to threaten Dutch defences and the French maritime interest tried to limit Anglo-Dutch access to Spanish colonial ports. Alarm turned to anger in 1701 when the exiled King James II died and France recognized his son as the legitimate claimant to the British thrones instead of William III. The latter again assembled a Grand Alliance of the northern Protestant and central Catholic powers – including the emperor, of course. The War of the Spanish Succession ensued in 1701.

Conflict over Spanish succession

Hostilities dragged on for more than a decade. Commanded by John Churchill (later Duke of Marlborough) and Prince Eugène of Savoy, who met to save Vienna from the advancing French at Blenheim in 1704, the allied armies had gained the upper hand by 1708. France, devastated by the following severe winter, was on the verge of bankruptcy again. Overtures for peace met unacceptable terms: war was renewed until Marlborough mauled the French at Malplaquet in 1710. But the parliamentary election of that year returned the anti-war party to power in England and Marlborough was withdrawn.

Peace was finally concluded between the disintegrated allies and France at Utrecht and Rastatt in 1714: French hegemony was countered in favour of a new balance of power. France lost its conquests east of the Rhine but kept

Franche-Comté and Strasbourg. The allies recognized Philippe d'Anjou as Philip V of Spain but denied him the succession to France. The Spanish Habsburgs' Flemish and Italian dominions – principally the duchy of Milan and the kingdoms of Sardinia and Naples – were ceded to the Austrian Habsburgs.

Britain retained her early gains of Gibraltar and Minorca – securing her access to the Mediterranean. France recognized the late King James's second daughter Anne as the legitimate British monarch, instead of his Catholic son, and ceded Nova Scotia, Newfoundland and the Hudson Bay to her. Britain also won favourable treatment in trade with the Portugese empire – whose title to Brazil was confirmed – and enhanced freedom of trade with the Spanish colonies, especially the monopoly for the importation of slaves.

The elector of Brandenburg became king of Prussia and received the Palatinate. The Duke of Savoy was also raised to royal status as king of Sicily which he was later constrained to exchange with the emperor for Sardinia.

Relatively liberal politics, the Protestant ethic, the suspension of Anglo-Dutch naval rivalry under the joint rule of William III, the relaxation of trade restrictions with the Iberian colonial empires under the settlement of 1714 and the union of England and Scotland in 1707 were the main conditions for Britain's advancement to the status of a great power, economically and politically. Primarily maritime, that power would be deployed to build her own colonial empire, particularly at the expense of the French. However, the surprising prowess of her army under John Churchill in the late war left her in position to maintain a balance of power on the continent, to counter the dominance of any one power, particularly to curb any further attempts at hegemony by the French.

THE BALTIC AND RUSSIA

By 1660, at the close of the brief reign of Charles X Gustav, the Swedes had ejected the Danes from the southern provinces of Skåne and Halland, completing their Baltic coast.

›0.13 COMBATANTS IN THE GREAT NORTHERN WAR: (a, b) Peter the Great of Russia (Étienne Maurice Falconet, 1782; Saint Petersburg) and his vic-

0.13a

ПЕТРУ ПЕРВЬОМУ
ЕКАТЕРИНА ВТОРАЯ
ЛѢТА 1782.

On the eastern side of the Baltic they had held Estonia and Finland (1561–81) from where they expanded further east and south into Karelia, Ingria and Livonia under Gustav II Adolf. That discomforted Russia. There the new dynasty of Michael Romanov (1613–45) was then re-establishing order in Muscovy after the chaos attending the demise of the Rurik dynasty in the late-1590s (AIC5, pages 86f). The next tsar, Alexis I (1645–76), was preoccupied to the south where his rule was extended to eastern Ukraine (beyond the Dnieper) at the expense of Poland-Lithuania, and in monitoring the advance of his Cossacks into Siberia.

Alexis was succeeded by his sons Feodor III (1676–82), Ivan V (1682–96) and Peter I (1682–1725): the first two were negligible, Peter formidable.**0.13** After the demise of his co-regnant brother, he began with a comprehensive programme of westernized modernization after extended travels incognito in western Europe (1697): of the army on French lines, of the navy on Anglo-Dutch lines – and of the rigorously centralized state over which he was ultimately to assert himself as Autocrat of all the Russias. He first deployed his navy against the Turks in the Black Sea to win access to the Mediterranean. After initial success he turned to confront the Swedes in the Baltic to win an exit to the wider maritime world from his new, western-orientated, capital of Saint Petersburg (founded 1703; see pages 749ff).

The War of the Spanish Succession had important consequences in the north. Fighting for survival, France could no longer support her erstwhile allies Sweden and Poland. As events unfolded in western Europe, Swedish preeminence in the Baltic was confronted by a formidable new coalition: the rising powers of Prussia, Saxony and Hanover were joined by Denmark-Norway and backed by Russia in the Great Northern War (1700–21).**0.14** Initially successful against Peter (at Narva, 1700), the young Swedish King Charles XII (1682–1718) turned on Augustus of Saxony-

0.13b

0.13c

Poland (1694–1733, elected king of Poland as Augustus I in 1697) who was threatening Livonia: successful again, he dethroned Augustus as king of Poland in favour of Stanisław Leszczyński (1704–09). Charles then returned to the offensive with Peter but lost his exhausted army to the Russians at Poltava in 1709. By 1718, when he was killed fighting the Norwegians, he had lost most of his empire: the pretension of his dynasty to absolutism in Sweden died with him.

tory against the Swedes at the Battle of Poltava, 1709 (c. 1717, Louis Caravaque; Saint Petersburg, Russian Museum); (c) Augustus I/II of Saxony-Poland, Frederick I of Prussia and Frederik IV of Denmark meeting at Potsdam after Poltava to forge a new anti-Swedish alliance which would include Russia and Hanover (Samuel Theodor Gericke, post-War location obscure).

0.14

›0.14 THE BALTIC BEFORE THE GREAT NORTHERN WAR: map with (1) Denmark with Norway (1a); (2) Sweden and Finland (2a); (3) the Commonwealth of Poland and Lithuania; the Baltic states of Karelia (4), Ingria (5) and Livonia (6); (7) Russia.

›0.15 THE NEW GENERATION OF RULERS: (a) King Philip V of Spain (1701, Hyacinthe Rigaud; Madrid, Prado); (b) Emperor Charles VI (c. 1707, Francesco Solimena; private collection); (c, d) George I of Britain (1717, Godfrey Kneller; London, National Portrait Gallery) and 'Prime Minister' Sir Robert Walpole (1740, studio of Jean-Baptiste Van Loo; private collection); (e, f) Louis XV (c. 1717, Hyacinthe Rigaud; New York, Metropolitan Museum of Art) and Cardinal Fleury (c. 1728, studio of Hyacinthe Rigaud; London, National Gallery).

0.15a

0.15b

0.15c

0.15d

0.15e

0.15f

Augustus the Strong regained Poland. Brandenburg-Prussia gained Pomeranian control over the Oder estuary. But the Swedish will to deny Russia dominance in the Gulf of Finland – which might threaten the free flow of trade in materials needed by timber navies – was shared by the major European powers. France and Britain cooperated in the attempt to constrain the forceful tsar. Unopposed by the Austrians, however, Peter was not prepared to be constrained in realizing his ambition to open a window on the west: he returned Finland to Sweden but kept most of Karelia, Ingria and Livonia in the Treaty of Nystadt (1721). He was less successful in a return bout with the Turks.

CHANGE OF CAST IN THE WEST

Having secured the throne of Spain for his second grandson Phillipe, Louis XIV was succeeded in 1715 by his first grandson's five-year-old son Louis XV: as his mother had died with his father in the smallpox epidemic of 1711–12, regency during the minority devolved on the scion of the royal family's collateral branch, Philippe, Duc d'Orléans.**0.15** Across the channel in the newly united kingdom of Britain and Ireland (1707), Queen Anne was succeeded in 1714 by her distant German cousin George of Brunswick-Lüneburg, Elector of Hanover, in accordance with the Act of Settlement (1701) which disbarred all her closer Catholic relatives. He was immediately confronted with – and overcame – rebellion in favour of the late queen's half-brother who pretended to the crown as James III; the problem would recur.

During the late war, meanwhile, Emperor Leopold I was succeeded by his two sons Joseph I (1705–11) and Charles VI (1711–40) under whom the development of Baroque Vienna would reach its apogee: that was attendant on the further repulsion of the Turks from the Balkans in which the younger emperor was initially – but not ultimately – successful in alliance with Russia.

Seeking exit from the Black Sea into the Mediterranean, inevitably at Ottoman expense, Russia at the time was ruled by the German coterie surrounding Empress Anna (1730–40), daughter of Peter's brother co-ruler Ivan V: her uncle had been succeeded in 1725 by his second wife Catherine, then by his ephemeral grandson Peter II. The benign reign of Tsarina Elizabeth (1741–62), daughter of Peter I and Catherine I, saw expansion into the Baltic, oversaw the founding of universities and academies of arts and sciences. She brought her father's new capital of Saint Petersburg to the apogee of Baroque opulence, as we shall see.

The problem of succession in France, should the boy king die, was of concern to the great powers as Philp V of Spain revived his claim. Britain, the United Provinces and Austria united in recognizing the counter-claim of the Duc d'Orleáns. Married hastily at the age of twelve to Maria Leszczyński, the daughter of the dispossessed king of Poland, Louis XV long survived the Regent but his reign, marking the apogee of French-led European civilization, was not successful politically or militarily.

Abandoning Versailles for the delights of Paris, the Regent's dissolute coterie lacked the will to confront vested interest in fiscal privilege and promote essential changes in the nature of the state. Prompted by disenchantment with a rigid authoritarian regime which had expended vast resources of men and money for incommensurate reward – despite a Bourbon on the Spanish throne – the demand for reform would escalate with the diversification of urban economic activity and intellectual enlightenment: it extended, not least, to approbation of constitutional developments in the Anglo-Saxon world.

When Louis XV matured he tried reform at two reprises: the first time, in the late-1740s, he failed in the determination to follow it through against the opposition of the

0.16a
›0.16 LAW AND THE LAW OF DIMINISHING RETURNS: (a) political cartoon (published 1720); (b) William Hogarth, 'Emblematical Print on the South Sea Scheme' (engraved after the painting of 1721).

The Royal Exchange had been founded in 1565 as the centre of commercial activity in the City of London but stockbrokers were barred from it as uncouth and resorted to taverns or, later, coffee houses. With colonial expansion went the proliferation of opportunities to speculate, of course – to capitalize on the profits of plantation and trade, real or prospective. A major phase of boom in the acquisition of futures was promoted by the Scots financier John Law whose system was based on the recognition that the wealth of nations was to be measured in the products of trade and industry, not gold: the latter's real value lay in backing the means of exchange – money which could be printed on paper. He proposed the establishment of a national bank in Edinburgh to capitalize on the idea by fostering credit through the introduction of banknotes backed by bullion or land.

His idea rejected at home, Law sought his fortune abroad where the Regent of France might be excused for welcoming him as the author of means literally to paper over the void in the kingdom's finances – which, in any case, were short of precious metals in the aftermath of war. In 1716 he was appointed Contrôleur Général des Finances, inaugurated a central bank (not in principle but in practice as it was capitalized on government bills), promoted credit at low interest, floated shares in commercial ventures to the benefit of the treasury and introduced paper money nominally exchangeable for gold. An extravagant sense of security in that promise inflamed speculation from 1720: the promise inevitably proved false, the bubble burst – particularly the 'Mississippi Bubble' inflated by the greed for shares in the state-sponsored and guaranteed conglomerate accorded the monopoly of trade with Louisiana. The same thing was happening in London in 1720 to the South Sea Company set up in 1711 to monopolize trade with South America and capitalized on shares oversold to reduce the national debt.

As in England, many private investors were ruined in France. The state finances, in a state of partial recovery on Law's promise, returned to the near bankruptcy of the immediate post-war era. Law fled the country (disguised as a woman). Fleury failed to panic but applied his native frugality to reform with the perseverance of Philibert Orry who succeeded Law as Contrôleur Général des Finances and retained his best ideas. He boosted the royal credit at its nadir by initiating regular payment of interest on the national debt: that and forced labour from the peasantry helped pay for improvements to the infrastructure of roads and canals (toll free, as Law had recommended), boosting commerce and industry (on the basis extended by Law) and tax receipts from the non-privileged members of the population engaged in them (whose lot Law had sought to alleviate). By the end of the 1730s, deficit had turned into credit and the chafers at peace had the means to reverse the sage old Cardinal's recuperative policy.

0.16b

venal Paris *parlement* – and the church – whose propriety rights he was bound to respect; he died in 1774 as the last initiative was on the point of realization despite the *parlement*. However, he began his reign with a great minister: André-Hercule de Fleury, bishop of Fréjus (1653–1743, cardinal from 1726).

The king's septuagenarian tutor and confidant, Fleury promoted peace for nearly twenty years in unusual alliance with the Whig Sir Robert Walpole, First Lord of the Treasury (or 'prime minister' 1721–42), who faced similar problems of reconstruction and retrenchment in Britain. Both had to contend with war debt compounded by the ruinous bursting of speculative colonial and commercial investment bubbles: the earlier one in London was inflated on similar misunderstood modern principles to those introduced to Paris by the radical Scottish financier John Law. Walpole was his own Chancellor of the Exchequer. Law had held the equivalent position in France (1716–23) under the Regent: under Fleury, the sound conservative Philibert Orry restored the royal finances despite the young king's bankrupt inheritance from his great-grandfather and the lethal legacy of Law.**0.16**

THE END OF PEACE

British recognition of Orléans neutralized France when the Jacobites opposed George I of Hanover as the successor to Queen Anne in 1714. With regency France, Britain and its allies countered Spain's attempts to recover its Italian possessions – lost to Austria at Utrecht – until 1734: then the oldest son of Philip V and his queen Elisabetta Farnese, Charles, Duke of Parma, wrested the kingdoms of Naples and Sicily from Emperor Charles VI. In this he took advantage of the emperor's distraction in conflict with the Turks and in the war of the Polish succession to the Saxon elector Frederick Augustus I/II. Saxony, backed by

Austria and Russia, promoted the late ruler's son Augustus II/III: instead France engineered the election of Louis XV's father-in-law, the ex-Polish king Stanisław Leszczyński. In fact Fleury, limiting his king's objectives, was little interested in the Polish question but used it as an excuse for war with Austria primarily over Lorraine (Lotharingia). Hostilities were mainly in the west where, in addition to the Italian reverse, the Empire lost its nominal suzerainty over the duchy to France. In Poland, however, the Austrians and the Russians consorted with Saxony to secure the counter-election of Augustus II/III (1733–63) after the dismissal of Stanisław (1736): the latter was compensated with Lorraine which would revert to France on his death.

The ousted Lotharingian duke, Francis Stephen, was given Tuscany whose last Medici duke had died in 1737: he had married the emperor's daughter Maria Theresa the year before. Her claims to Austria, his to the imperial title, were disputed in the most serious European war since the settlement of the Spanish succession. Charles VI had secured the Austrian succession for his daughter with the Pragmatic Sanction (1713): abrogating the Salic prescription of male inheritance in Austria, this was accepted by all the major powers as the archduchess would be the legitimate ruler in Bohemia and Hungary. Yet Maria Theresa's accession in Austria in 1740 was rejected by France, Spain, Bavaria, Saxony-Poland and Prussia. The new ruler of the latter, Frederick II (1740–86), seized the initiative unprovoked and sent the army honed by his father (the 'soldier-king' Frederick-Wilhelm I, 1713–40) to seize the rich province of Silesia from Maria Theresa. War ensued.**0.17**

0.17a

0.17c

Austrian succession

Already at war with Spain over colonial trade, Britain supported the Habsburgs who were confronting Spain in Italy – ultimately with little advantage to either. Allied to the Dutch, who feared Spain's ally France, the British

›0.17 OPPONENTS AT WAR OVER THE AUSTRIAN SUCCESSION: (a, b) Maria Theresa, Archduchess of Austria, Queen of Bohemia and Hungary and her husband, Emperor Francis I (c. 1744, Martin

could do little when Frederick II summarily invaded Silesia (December 1740) and the Bavarian elector Charles Albert claimed the imperial title as Charles VII against the Habsburg candidate, Maria Theresa's husband Francis Stephen (January 1742).

Bavaria had the support of France where the war party had gained ascendancy in the late conflict over Poland. Spain followed, bound to his Bourbon nephew. That led France to engage in Spain's hostilities with the British who inflicted heavy losses on both at sea. On land the advance of the Franco-Bavarian forces was halted before Vienna and the new emperor driven back to oscillation between Munich and Frankfurt. At Dettingen (mid-1743) Anglo-Hanoverian troops sent the French back across the Rhine but they turned north, worsted Anglo-Dutch forces and entered Austrian Flanders (1743–44): thus occupied, they failed to overawe the imperial electors on the death of Charles VII (January 1745) and prevent Francis Stephen's election. Frederick, having secured Silesia despite several reverses, did not object. Meanwhile, at Fontenay, the French were again victorious over the Dutch and British: the latter withdrew to deal with the Jacobites at home; the enemy held Flanders.

Three years of negotiation between the exhausted parties produced the Peace of Aix-la-Chapelle: the Pragmatic Sanction was confirmed; Frederick kept Silesia to the extreme chagrin of Austria; Britain withdrew from its Caribbean conquests; Louis XV withdrew from Flanders – to the consternation of his generals and people but with an eye to a fundamental shift in alliance which would free him from the traditional Habsburg hostility the better to confront the British.

The War of the Austrian Succession closed exactly a century of pan-European warfare motivated primarily by extended Bourbon–Habsburg rivalry: the theatres were mainly European though there were important colonial conflicts, especially in the western hemisphere. Within a decade extended Anglo-French rivalry introduced the truly worldwide war of a new era – ironically enough, the era of the so-called Enlightenment which will open our next volume.

0.17d
van Meytens; Vienna, Kunsthistorisches Museum); (c) Augustus II/III of Saxony-Poland (c. 1735, Hyacinthe Rigaud; Dresden, State Collection); (d) Frederick of Prussia (1739, Antoine Pesne; Berlin, Gemäldegalerie).

CROSS-CURRENTS OF PAINTING IN A MODERNIST ERA

The *Instructiones fabricae et supellectilis ecclesiasticae* of Carlo Borromeo, issued in 1577, ushered in an era of reform in the arts at the service of the Church, rejecting forms descended from pagan antiquity – sculptural or architectural. Among several significant devotional tracts emerging from the ranks of the Counter Reformation orders, moreover, the *Spiritual Exercises of S. Ignatius of Loyola* promoted the senses to primacy in the comprehension of the divine, obviously obviating the sophisticated metaphysical contortions of late Mannerism (AIC5, page 294). It took a generation for the Church to recognize radical response. By the end of the century two seminal artists were exploring it from different directions. Michelangelo Merisi da Caravaggio (1571–1610) took his departure primarily from Leonardo da Vinci and was guided rather by his observation of life than the conventions of Classic art. Annibale Carracci (1560–1609) returned to Raphael but was bent on effecting a synthesis drawn from the achievements of all the High Renaissance masters – Florentine, Roman, Parmesan and Venetian – in accord with venerable Classical procedure (AIC5, pages 3ff).

Not damned or celebrated as a revolutionary, Annibale has been celebrated or damned as a revivalist of tradition – the tradition of Italian Renaissance painting culminating in Raphael – precisely as tradition itself has been defended or defamed. Like all the artists who furthered Classical tradition, he promoted idealism through selection and synthesis (AIC1, page 380, AIC4, page 830): he emulated – rather than imitated – the masters of the past, seeking to exceed them in virtue of his personal genius, and if posterity has not ranked him above Raphael or

›**0.18 CARRACCI IN BOLOGNA:** (a) Ludovico's 'Madonna and Child with S. Francis, S. Joseph and Donors' (1591; Cento, Galleria d'Arte Moderna); (b, c) Annibale's 'Madonna and Child in Glory with Six Saints' ('San Ludovico Altarpiece', c. 1588), 'Assumption of the Virgin' (variously dated between 1587 and 1590; both Madrid, Prado).

Ludovico's altarpiece at Cento is unprecedented in his œuvre for the freedom with which the brush enriches the impasto, enhancing the vitality of the conception: observation from nature – particularly in the portraiture of the donors, of course, but also in the emotive modulation of the iconic ideal – prevails over overt dependence on conventional precedent.

Transforming a model provided by Correggio, Annibale's San Ludovico altarpiece is novel in the proximity of heaven and earth: the reciprocal glances of the Madonna and the saints to the left (S. Louis of Toulouse, S. Francis and S. Clare) are vital in establishing the connection, of course, but it is forged tangibly along the dramatic diagonal of the Correggiesque S. John's gesture followed by the glance of the Roman patrician Alexis (who abandoned his world to devote himself to the poor). The work is celebrated for reconciling Raphaelesque idealism (particularly in the

0.18b

0.18c

Michelangelo, its devotees of Classicism have rarely set him much lower.

Annibale and his older brother Agostino (1557–1602) probably followed the lead of their slightly older cousin Ludovico (1555–1619) in setting out on their reformatory path. Like Caravaggio, they returned to nature in rejection of the abstruse artificiality of late Mannerism but with Classicists' eyes not obviously focused on commonality, drawing masterfully and prolifically to record and then to refine. The ideal is synthetic: the *disegno* of the Florentine tradition, recording penetrating study of the antique and the modern masters; the *colore* of the Venetians modulated by the sensitive, softening *sfumato* of Correggio. Determined in its eclecticism, the ideal was a tangible artistic one rather than a Platonic abstraction. It will be recalled, however, that the ancient Classical artistic ideal had originally been perceived in the light of Plato's cave; it will also be recalled that ancient Greek 'eclecticism' originated with the school of philosophers dedicated to effecting a synthesis from all that was best in all previous schools (AIC1, pages 377, 441ff).**0.18**

To further their principles, the three Carracci founded their Accademia degli Incamminati ('insiders') in 1582. Its method, to which drawing from life and the antique was central, would be forever standard to the academic tradition in the graphic arts – though its relative lack of interest in theorizing was not. The precedent – institutional if not practical – was the Accademia delle Arti del Disegno, founded in Florence under the auspices of Grand Duke Cosimo I de' Medici (1563). The parallel was the Roman Accademia di San Luca (1593), re-established under the directorship of Federico Zuccari by Pope Clement VIII on the basis of Sixtus IV's Compagnia di San Luca (AIC4, page 655, AIC5, page 82).

Initially Correggiesque in inspiration, Ludovico

had assimilated Tintoretto's painterliness, sombre palette, dramatic lighting and startling perspectives into an heroic, emotive style by the mid-1590s: he stayed in Bologna but failed to sustain his reforming impetus into the new century. Also Correggiesque in sensibility, but bent towards Veronese rather than Tintoretto, Annibale and his brother effected a calmer, more Classical synthesis drawn from Leonardo, Raphael, Andrea del Sarto or Fra Bartolomeo, forging figures into balanced asymmetry on the *contrapposto* formula derived by his Renaissance predecessors from the work of the ancient Greek master Polykleitos (AIC1, page 402, AIC4, pages 826f).

With Agostino, Annibale left Bologna in 1695 for Rome – where the pope was still retaining mediocre services but the Farnese were alive to new genius. Annibale excelled, raised to a new dimension of gravitas in mass and gesture by his first-hand experience of Michelangelo and Raphael – the Sistine Chapel and Vatican Stanze frescoes, of course, but also the Transfiguration (AIC5, page 20). His dramatic trajectory from the naturalistic

conception of the Madonna and Child, of course) with Veronesian *colore* – the latter perhaps at the initiation of Annibale's Venetian phase.

Transposing Correggiesque sensuality, Titianesque freedom of brushstroke – and form – elides the natural and the supernatural in the mystery staged by Annibale in his astonishing Prado 'Assumption': realistically coarse, naturalistic in their astonishment, the disciples – charging the base of intersecting diagonals – witness the fusion of their world and the celestial in the bodily propulsion of the accelerating Virgin: hitherto the Virgin was usually portrayed as a passive object of beatification.

›0.19 ROME, PALAZZO FARNESE: (a, b) gallery, views, (c) central panel with Triumph of Bacchus.

Drawn from the *Metamorphoses* of Ovid, the theme is the power of love illustrated in vivid narratives without abstruse allegory. Given the scale of the vault (18.3 x 6.1 metres) the scope of the scenography invited complexity of form: rather than an all-embracing *quadratura* (chosen for lesser exercises by several Bolognese then working in Rome), Annibale preferred to construct a *quadratura* context for *quadri riportati* (respectively, spatial recession defined illusionistically by simulated architecture and simulated easel pictures); the immediate precedent was Pellegrino

0.19c

Tibaldi's Ulysses cycle of c. 1555 in the Palazzo Poggi of the Carracci's native city; the ultimate inspiration was Michelangeo's Sistine ceiling and Raphael's innovative mixture of the media in both the Vatican Loggie and in the Psyche Loggia of the Villa Farnesina (AIC4, page 822, AIC5, pages 9, 19, 119, 272).

Highly complex in its illusionism, the scheme builds to a climax in the centre in unambiguous respect for the laws of physics: the articulation of the walls with a Corinthian Order of pilasters, between which oval niches alternate with rectangular panels, is echoed in syncopation in the cove behind Michelangelesque ignudi perched on the entablature; the niches become medallions (in simulated bronze) and herms (in simulated masonry) take over from the pilasters to support a simulated cornice. The 'structure' is revealed as open to the sky in the corners but concealed by the major *quadri riportati* images suspended from it on the cardinal axes and across the centre. These, shared in execution by Annibale with his brother, are informed by prolific drawing after antique sculpture. The great central 'Triumph of Bacchus and Ariadne' retains the format of a frieze, as do 'Aurora' and 'Galatea' below it to either side, but 'Polyphemo Innamorato' and 'Furioso' at the ends (in the context of the 'open' architecture) operate in penetrating depth on dynamic diagonals.

expression of excitement to Classical rhetoric, with transposed but undiminished dynamics elicited from Venetian *colore* disciplined by Roman *disegno*, is well demonstrated by comparison of the Dresden and S. Maria del Popolo 'Assumptions' of 1587 and 1601.[0.18b, 0.20b] Meanwhile, commissioned by the Farnese to fresco the gallery of their great Roman palace in 1597, his response ranks with the greatest ever conceived in the medium.[0.19]

0.19a

0.19b

0.20a

0.20b

0.20d

In Rome after uncertain experience, Caravaggio's somewhat androgynous early work was attracting the attention of certain princes of the Church by the middle of the decade – the middle of the period of transition to full-blooded reform in pontifical circles. Cardinal Francesco del Monte introduced him to the Contarelli and his first great commission followed the century's end: the cycle of paintings dedicated to S. Matthew in the family's chapel in S. Luigi dei Francesi. The response, predicated on recognition of the senses as ineluctable agents of spiritual revelation – particularly of the sensual impact of light as the

›**0.20 CARAVAGGIO**: (a) presumed self-portrait as Bacchus (c. 1595; Florence, Uffizi); (b) 'Musicians' (c. 1595; New York, Metropolitan Museum of Art); (c) 'Calling of S. Matthew' (from 1599; Rome, S. Luigi dei Francesi); (d, e) 'Crucifixion of S. Peter' and 'Conversion of S. Paul' (1600–01; Rome, S. Maria del Popolo,

0.20c

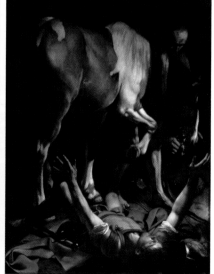

0.20e

Cerasi Chapel); (f) 'Death of the Virgin' (c. 1605; Paris, Louvre); (g) 'Raising of Lazarus' (1609; Messina, Museo Nationale).

In Rome from c. 1590, Caravaggio fled a manslaughter charge in 1606, and was peripatetic in the south – Naples, Messina and Malta in particular – for the last four years of his short life.

Never was human coarseness more shocking to conventional religious sensibilities than when it stained the figures of S. Peter being crucified or, above all, of the dead Virgin. On the other hand, nowhere is the penetration of light to divine purpose more apparent than in the great canvases recording the calling of S. Matthew, the conversion of S. Paul or the raising of Lazarus.

0.20f

immediate manifestation of God – promised truly radical reform to the next pontificate, that of Paul V Borghese. His reign would embrace transformation in architecture on the grandest scale: his nephew, Cardinal Scipione, was one of Caravaggio's most enthusiastic patrons.[0.19]

TENEBROSO

The ideal empyrean – Classical or Christian, in *quadratura* or *quadro riportato* – was not Caravaggio's element. Into the shadows of terrestrial life – so often dismissed as nasty, brutal and short – he shone penetrating light to purposes as divine as any idealist had ever achieved: for this he is as celebrated as once he was damned for his indecorous modelling of the holiest of personages after peasants or vagabonds. Back beyond Loyola, this may be seen as a permutation of Thomas à Kempis's *Imitation of Christ* in identifying the common worshipper with the actors in his holy tableaux (AIC4, page 257). Though revolutionary in his uncompromising naturalism, his debts are clear and by no means narrow in their range: to Leonardo for the *chiaroscuro* which was essential to his style; to Venetian *colore* for the freedom of technique which naturally matched his impetuosity, though he rejected rich chromaticism in the maturity of his Roman period; to Roman *disegno* – particularly to Michelangelo – for firmness of figure, though he would renounce the eponymous technique of preliminary drafting and might defy structural logic for compositional or expressionistic purpose.

Caravaggio painted straight onto the canvas, apparently without detailed study in drawing. His reference to common humanity was virtually unique in his time and place: though criticized for disregard of decorum, his naturalism was naturally conditioned by his personal conception of faithfulness, not to his life model, but to his subject. As his brief career acceler-

0.20g

ated in its development away from Classical convention – of composition as well as propriety – he seems
to have relied more on his memory, retaining the
characteristics of his erstwhile models to heighten the
immanence of the sacred event he was staging. At the
same time, to convey the transcendence of its tragedy
he subjected the morphology of his cast to an idiosyncratic repertory of expressionistic poses which projected
the composition of the scene as a whole away from the
realities of nature towards austere abstraction. And
the stark effect depended utterly on the lighting in an
increasingly ombrageous context: ostensibly natural or
manifestly supernal, it was as theatrical as limelight in
its direction to the isolation of the leading players in
the semblance of their stage or, ultimately, in a lowering spacelessness.

LATE ANNIBALE

In the tragically short span of time left to him after the triumphant achievement of his great Ovidian cycle, Annibale capitalized on his review of the dynamics of the *contrapposto* formula – as deployed for monumental gravitas by both Michelangelo and Raphael – in the conception of both figural part and spatial whole. The mode is already marked in the 'Assumption' from the first year of the new century which shares the Cerasi Chapel in S. Maria del Popolo with the contemporary initial works of Caravaggio's early maturity – already in clear contrast to the latter's modernism. Further, the contemplative stasis of his early religious *sacra conversazione* was also reviewed in a manner as spiritually moving as any of Caravaggio's late, profound, un-Classical tragedies.**0.21a**

Rationally conceived in terms of Classical *contrapposto*, the actors in Annibale's late masterpieces are alive with emotions articulated after the antique but staged in modern colour and light – the irrational agents of atmosphere.**0.21b** Innovatively, he applied the same methods to the construction of landscape and the representation of its mood, not as a background to history painting, but as an end in itself – though ostensibly the scene of a religious or mythological event.**0.21c**

En route to Egypt, the path taken by the diminutive Holy Family in the most celebrated of Annibale's panoramas is overlooked by a formidable agglomeration of Classical, medieval and vernacular buildings. Inspiration – rather than precise precedent – for this architectural eclecticism may be found in the organic growth of the hill town, typical of the Roman Campagna, but the forging of design principle from evolutionary practice was radical: the various forms are balanced asymmetrically in carefully calculated *disegno* by the complementary distribution of horizontals and verticals to either side of the

0.21a

›0.21 ANNIBALE CARRACCI IN ROME: (a) 'Pietà' (c. 1600; Naples, Museo Nazionale di Capodimonte); (b) 'Assumption' (1601; Rome, S. Maria del Popolo, Cerasi Chapel); (c) ideal landscape with the 'Flight into Egypt' (1604; Rome, Galleria Doria Pamphilj).

Michelangelo's iconic essay on the theme of the Pietà is recalled with Leonardesque *sfumato* in Annibale's Capodimonte essay on the subject: rarely, however, has the discipline of Roman *disegno* been more rigorous in the delineation of the essential in the iconography, nor the atmosphere generated in accordance with the Venetian tradition of *colore* more highly affecting emotionally; the combination is unsurpassed. Early commentators (Gian Pietro Bellori in particular) noted how the pain of the scene is elucidated at the human level, without sentimentality, by the child angel responding to the prick of the crown of thorns. The motif of the partially open sepulchre was not to be ignored – even by Caravaggio.

centre of gravity – the domed rotunda to the right of true centre. For the broad context, moreover, he developed an informal order from nature – rather than imposing a formal one on it – by placing the ostensible subject at the crux of diagonals, adjusting the scale and shape of the elements and effecting balance between large and small, near and far, simple and complex, clear and obscure on the *contrapposto* principle (compare the analysis of Raphael's 'Madonna of the Meadows', AIC4, page 830). 'Picturesque' pluralism and Arcadian idealism, furthered by Annibale's Bolognese followers, were certainly not lost on the great French masters Nicolas Poussin, Claude Lorrain and their followers in their transformations of the Roman Campagna, as we shall see.

The fluidity of movement in lowering space in the Prado 'Assumption' cedes to the compression of bulky, statuesque, theatrically gesticulating figures into the intensely crowded composition of the S. Maria del Popolo 'Assumption'. And the immediacy of the Virgin's explosive apparition links earth and heaven in a way that could hardly differ more starkly from the artist's earlier, Correggiesque-Venetian, evocation of the phenomenon.

›0.22 **PETER-PAUL RUBENS**: (a) 'Landscape with Rainbow' and (b) 'Battle of the Amazons' (c. 1635 and 1618 respectively; both Munich, Alte Pinakothek); (c) 'Assumption of the Virgin' (1626; Antwerp, Onze-Lieve-Vrouwekathedraal).

Conceived *en plein air* about his country house, Rubens's landscapes are free and painterly in the record of the transitory, brilliantly atmospheric in the tradition of Venetian *colore* seemingly undisciplined

0.21b

0.22c

0.21C

0.22a

RUBENS

Nothing better illustrates the complexity of the transformations in early 17th-century painting than comparison between Annibale's masterly late landscape, Rembrandt's lowering, highly naturalistic essay,[0.17C] and the late masterpiece in the same genre of the third and youngest of our three seminal masters of the Baroque era, Peter Paul Rubens (1577–1640).[0.22] Like Annibale, he may be seen as eclectic but the elements of his style are transfused in the forge of protean imagination. He was widely travelled in response to the demand of princely patrons and, later, in quasi-diplomatic capacities (AIC5, page 97). Like the Florentines and Romans, like the Carracci, he was an avid draughtsman of form and composition: he drew from the antique, from the Roman High Renaissance masters and through them explored the mean between the extremes on which their syncretic ideal was based (see page 30). He also studied the Venetians, naturally, and drew from nature – sensual but neither rough nor over-

by Roman *disegno*: they are nevertheless organized in accord with the ancient *contrapposto* principle, like those of Annibale, but on the serpentine elision of intersecting diagonals rather than on their conjunction. And the dynamism introduced by Annibale to the iconography of the Assumption – in his more naturalistic, less hieratic, less sculptural pre-Roman, essays – was obviously not lost on the Flemish genius in his dramatic response to Titian's Venetian masterpiece in S. Maria Gloriosa dei Frari (AIC5, page 13).

Rubens's ecstatic, corporeal Virgin was propelled on the direct diagonal trajectory linking earth with heaven. At least as characteristic of that dynamic is ovoid swirling inspired by Leonardo: indeed, the 'Battle of the Amazons' incorporates diverse figures in violent conflict inspired by his record of Leonardo's lost 'Battle of Anghiari' and, without pure geometric device, they are disposed on the scale of that work with no less organic unity (AIC5, page 6).

0.22b

refined – to revise the Classical parameters in preference for a heavy, muscular, Herculean male canon and a full-figured, plump, Junoesque female canon: the Farnese Hercules and Michelangelo were his guides.**0.5**

A master of illusionistic vault painting, informed by both Raphael, Correggio and Veronese (AIC5, pages 624, 19, 32, 225), his compositional method was modern too, of course: in place of the pure geometry at the base of the Raphaelite ideal he generated swirling movement about elliptical conjunctions learned from Leonardo's Anghiari and, like Annibale, exploited the dynamics of the diagonal. Not unidealized, the vitality of his vision was realized in colour and light rather than line – and that he learned from the Venetians. His influence was vital, especially on his Flemish compatriots: in particular his principal assistant Anthony van Dyck (1599–1641) who emerged from Genoa to London at least to equal the master in penetrating portraiture and its radiant clothing.**0.8** Detailed consideration of his work – and that of the other great artists mentioned below – is beyond us in this sketched outline of the major trends in 17th-century painting.

CARAVAGGESCHI AND INCOMPARABLE MODERNS

Annibale's death in 1609 did not entail the demise of his influence on Roman art: on the contrary, the Classical strand in his style would prevail. After his departure from Rome, on the other hand, Caravaggio lost favour there but the masterpieces of his late years in the south exerted prime influence on Spain through Naples – on Jusepe de Ribera (1591–1652) in particular but even on the incomparable Iberian genius Diego Velázquez (1599–1660). He began his career under indirect influence from Caravaggio, learned more from the Venetians in the Spanish royal collection on taking up a court position in Madrid

›0.23 THREE OF THE ERA'S GREATEST PAINTERS AT WORK: (a) Diego Velázquez addressing 'The Family of Philip IV' ('Las Meninas', 1656; Madrid, Prado); (b) Jan Vermeer and his 'Allegory of painting' (c. 1667; Vienna, Kunsthistorisches Museum); (c) Rembrandt van Rijn in his studio (c. 1629; Boston, Museum of Fine Art).

Velázquez's free brushwork captures the incidence of raking daylight on naturalistically haphazard disposition. The caste includes, primarily, the king and queen (mirrored from our position as observers) posing for their court painter and visited by their daughter Margarita Teresa with her maids (*las meninas*). Enigmatic, one of several possible points of the exercise seems to be the demonstration of the artist's paradoxical purpose in conjuring the illusion of life in art: recording the enduringly significant (the rulers of Spain and their servant, the painter, in the dim light

0.23b

of their ordered world) but also elevating transitory insignificance (the momentary conjunction of incidental figures illuminated in the shadow of stability) to permanent importance. More, of course: the illusion in the mirror reflects the reality of the situation before the artist but from that same point of view the reality of everything else is illusory.

Apart from Vermeer's precision posing, the drops of sparkling light suggest refraction through a primitive lens but there is no evidence that he actually possessed one – indeed the inventory of his effects does not include such an object. The lighting effects are off-set by the brilliant primary colours – especially yellow, vermilion and expensive lapis lazuli blue for individual elements or reflected onto the base colours of their neighbours for the compound effect noted by Leonardo da Vinci. Apart from genre scenes and portraits, his limited œuvre (of only some thirty-four surviving authenticated works) includes two cityscapes.[0.7.3]

True to life down to the details of the grim, monochrome room's crumbling plasterwork, the Rembrandt is unprecedented in depicting the artist overawed by – or contemplating heroically – the challenge before him. Unsurpassed in exploring the human predicament with unrelenting realism, Rembrandt is at his most poignant in his records of his own psychological state – as in this early work which launched the trajectory to the devastating images of his final years.

0.23a

in 1623: he graduated to supremacy in painting light to reveal the vitality of texture in raiment and the psychology of the figure within it – particularly Philip IV and his familiars.[0.1, 0.3, 0.23a]

As in the south, in the north supreme genius emerged from the shades of brute realism to achieve heights of luminosity in penetrating domesticity and depths of poignancy in the study of humanity. Johannes Vermeer and Rembrandt van Rijn, complementary in range and palette, are incontestably *sui generis*. Speculation has the former peering into the *camera obscura* for precision distribution and refined focus on life observed at home or abroad: be that as it may, he realized his vision objectively rather than through the eyes of others.[0.7.3, 0.23b] Peering out beyond the circle of the Dutch Caravaggeschi, Rembrandt's observations ranged widely from Raphael to Rubens and his powers of assimilation were overwhelming – not least in representing himself.[0.7.1, 0.23c]

0.23c

A major body of Caravaggeschi took *tenebroso* and rough realism – the dramatic lighting of the sacred and the profane, of the elevated but more particularly of the debased – to France and the Netherlands. Tavern scenes, plebeian musicians and card sharpers did not go unobserved by Italians familiar with Caravaggio's early works but shadowing low life fascinated foreigners. Risking the invidious one might single out Bartolomeo Manfredi (1582–1622) from the natives, Valentin de Boulogne (1591–1632) and the brothers Antoine, Louis and Mathieu Le Nain (1600–48, 1603–48 and 1607–77) among the French, David Teniers (1610–90) among the Flemish, Hendrick ter Brugghen (1588–1629) and Gerard van Honthorst (1592–1656) among the Dutch in their Golden Age of excellence in all genres (see pages 10f) and, probably through them, Georges de la Tour (1593–1652) in Nancy.

THE PROMOTION OF THE ANCIENTS IN THE ORBIT OF ROME

Meanwhile the influence of the Carracci was predominant in Rome where ecclesiastical commissions remained prolific. The main recipients came to Rome from the Carracci's Bolognese academy, notably Domenico Zampieri (Domenichino, 1581–1641), who assisted the master at the Palazzo Farnese, Francesco Albani (1578–1660) and Guido Reni (1575–1642). The latter had transferred to the Academy about the time Annibale left for Rome (in 1595) and went there himself to join the Farnese team only in 1601: he travelled still with some Mannerist baggage which survived even in Caravaggesque *chiaroscuro*.**⁰·²⁴ᵃ** Based in Rome from 1607, after the fashion for Caravaggio had faded, he found favour with the Borghese clan of Pope Paul V who, though avid patrons of Moderns ranging from Caravaggio to the phenomenal young Neopolitan sculptor Gian Lorenzo Bernini, endorsed his

0.24a

›0.24 GUIDO RENI: (a) 'Crucifixion of S. Peter' (1604; Rome, Vatican Museum); (b) 'Aurora' (1613; Rome, Casino dell'Aurora, Palazzo Pallavicini-Rospigliosi).

The dramatic lighting derives from Caravaggio but, instead of harsh diagonals and the energy involved to generate them, the discipline of the picture plane is sustained in the Bolognese manner against vague landscape (compare AIC5, page 295). The figures, though hardly idealized, are by no means as coarse as those of Caravaggio.

Idealism, not coarse realism, was required of altarpieces and of the mythological cycles commissioned by the princes of the papal entourage to grace the vaults of their garden loggias or casinos. In that context it achieved its apogee in the glorious case of Guido's Aurora, poised in measured movement parallel to the picture plane, as in a frieze, but ineffable in the light of the colour which transubstantiates marble into flesh and raiment to effect the synthesis between Classical idealism and naturalism.

0.24b

0.25

›0.25 GUERCINO: 'Aurora' (from 1622; Rome, Casino Ludovisi).

Escaping *quadro riporato*, this foreshortened chari-oteer hurtles through sky revealed above the *quadra-tura* of Agostino Tassi's partly ruined parapets. Start-lingly theatrical, dramatically lit, the painterly illusion is uncompromising in its vigorous would-be realism but particularly ungainly for the horses viewed in all their parts *di sotto in sù*: the contrast with Guido's elegant conception could hardly be greater. The work stunned but the Roman patrons reeled from the shock: over the following decade a rather different sense of reality per-suaded Guercino to change 'to satisfy … those who com-mission paintings and have the money to pay for them'.

transmogrification into Classicism. That culminated in the Aurora fresco on the vault of a casino on the Quiri-nal which invites comparison with Annibale's more virile, sensual evocation of a similar scene: both emulate Rapha-el's Classicizing initiative, the one aimed at surpassing an imagined standard of antique painting or tapestry design, the other at the ethereal transcendence of its source in the sculptured frieze of a Roman sarcophagus with lumi-nous colour.**0.24b** Both may be compared with the radi-cal departure from *quadro riportato* to three-dimensional *quadratura* illusionism for the Casino Ludovisi Aurora of Giovanni Francesco Barbieri (Guercino, 1591–1666).**0.25**

Guercino was the most Caravaggesque of the Bolognese, at least at the start of his Roman career, but he succumbed to the change in the taste of patronage and learned from the success of Annibale's Classicizing followers. Of these the mantle would ultimately pass to Carlo Maratta (1625–1713). On Guido's return to Bologna shortly after he had completed his splendid Aurora, how-ever, it was Domenichino who assumed the leadership of the Ancients. *Disegno* was his forte, naturally in preparing religious pieces but also in the genre of the poetic land-scape. In the latter, he furthered the idealizing of the con-text overwhelming the subjects in the master's late works.

0.26a

0.26b

In the former, emulating Annibale in imbuing antique sculptural form with stylized vitality (psychological more than physiological, perhaps, if often with diminished individuality), he reached his apogee in the apse vault of S. Andrea della Valle – where his formidable pendentive Evangelists competed with the stunning illusionism of Parmesan Giovanni Lanfranco (1582–1647), who emulated Correggiesque illusionism (AIC5, page 32). **0.26, 0.27**

Domenichino's ascendancy was challenged by Lanfranco, Lanfranco's by Pietro da Cortona (1596–1669).

›0.26 DOMENICHINO: (a, b) landscapes with Flight into Egypt (c. 1606, Oberlin, Allen Art Museum; c. 1623, Paris, Louvre); (c, d) Rome, S. Andrea della Valle, choir vault and detail of 'S. John the Baptist revealing Christ to Ss. Peter and Paul'.

Domenichino's first essay in the Arcadian genre is clearly a paraphrase of the master's recent work. Over the next two or three decades he would elaborate the formula, introducing craggier eminences on bolder diagonals as the foil to – but not the path of – figures more purely refined in their Classicism. With greater severity than Annibale preferred, that rationalist ideal was already furthered in S. Andrea della Valle's rigor-

0.26d

0.26c

0.27

ous *quadro riportato* fresco cycle but the frieze of actors, oratorical in their gestures, front a depth of field which provides the essential context for their witness of Christ.

›0.27 GIOVANNI LANFRANCO: dome fresco of the Virgin in Glory (from 1625; Rome, S. Andrea della Valle, over the assertive pendentives of Domenichino).

In competition with the disappointed Domenichino – who failed to extend his S. Andrea commission – and in dramatic contrast with his *quadro riportato* approach, Lanfranco introduced Rome to the illusion of the empyrean alive with the host of heaven which his compatriot Correggio had conjured on a grand scale in the dome of Parma's cathedral (AIC5, page 31). Henceforth the quintessentially Baroque *quadratura* mode would be vital to the service of the Counter Reformation church in vault embellishment – though Domenichino's Classicism might still be preferred for altarpieces.

Excelling at illusionism (see page 65), he was promoted to leadership of the profession in Rome as principal of the Accademia di San Luca (for four years from 1634; see below). Formed in Florence, devoted to the study of Raphael and the antique no less than Domenichino, he was familiar with masters of Venetian *colore* in the collections of his eminent patrons, informing his modification of the antique sculptural ideal as he restaged the sensual vitality of Annibale's Farnese vault in convincing depth – if also in the setting of restored antiquity.**0.28** Reconciling the Ancient and the Modern, his sculptural equivalent is Bernini – if the latter may be thought of as equivalent to anyone (see pages 67ff).

›**0.28 PIETRO DA CORTONA:** 'Rape of the Sabines' (c. 1629; Rome, Pinacoteca Capitolina).

Cortona took the *quadratura* mode of Lanfranco to its apogee in denying the physical constraint of masonry vaulting. In his easel pictures his depth of field is not necessarily more profound than Domenichino's but the full-blooded actors in its setting respond naturalistically – no less than oratorically – to the dynamic of its diagonals.

›**0.29 CLAUDE LORRAIN:** (a) 'S. Paula Romana Embarking at Ostia' (c. 1640; Madrid, Prado); (b) 'Rest on the Flight into Egypt' (1666; Saint Petersburg, Hermitage).

Dedicated to studying Ovid, Claude devoted his life to evoking the Arcadia of *Metamorphoses* through numerous variant idealizations of the landscape of the Roman Campagna: in doing so he raised the art form of the Classical landscape, invented by Annibale and developed by Domenichino, to the level set for history painting though the dramatis personae were usually inferior in scale – and even execution. His chosen environment rarely rose from monotony to the rugged physical features imagined by the mature

The Roman Classicists had their affiliates abroad, especially in France. There Simon Vouet (1590–1649) mastered both strands of reformatory style after having spent his extended formative years 1613–27 mainly in Rome – where the alternatives presented by Domenichino and Lanfranco in S. Andrea della Valle were fully to be realized before his return home. He was in the van as a Classicist and the younger Laurent de La Hyre (1606–56) was a distinguished follower. The greatest of the school, Nicolas Poussin (1594–1665) and Claude Lorrain (1600–82), stayed in Rome, however: Domenichino's approach to both genres, religious and landscape, appealed greatly to the former, his Arcadian landscapes particularly to the latter.**0.29**

No less eclectic than Annibale, Poussin's sources of inspiration in the schools of *colore* and *disegno* are complex and again beyond our limited scope here. At the outset of his Roman career in 1624 he worked in Domenichino's studio and emulated his style in his sole major altarpiece, the Martyrdom of S. Erasmus commissioned for S. Pietro's basilica (1628). Moving on in the light of the Titians in Rome, however, his

0.29b
Domenichino: if drama was sought it was found in the highlighting of distant views penetrated on the usual diagonal through the region's peculiar trees and its ample supply of ruins; typically, however, he looked into the light of radiant morning or melancholy evening, through the silhouettes of trees and ruins, to idealize the unremarkable in the atmospherics of mood.

›0.30 NICOLAS POUSSIN: (a) 'The Arcadian Shepherds' (c. 1630, Chatsworth, Devonshire Collection); (b) 'Landscape with a Man Killed by a Snake' (c.

'Arcadian Shepherds' (1629) might well be compared not with Domenichino's landscapes, but with his 'S. John the Baptist revealing Christ to Ss. Peter and Paul' in S. Andrea della Valle: as we have seen, the principles there are set against the landscape at significant remove, unlike the younger man's naturalization from the antique in vivid colour – which, ironically, enhances melancholy mystification. Progressive in this respect, the Arcadians might also be compared with Cortona's near-contemporary 'Rape of the Sabines'.

In his maturity Poussin took the genre of the Arcadian landscape to an apogee scaled also only by Claude: if the latter's works tinge the poetic pastoral mode with the elegiac, Poussin takes the elegiac to the epic in recalling that death haunts paradise. Much of his mature work is also well characterized as severe in its stoicism: drained of Modernist spontaneity but colour-coded in Raphael's manner, his idealized sculptural figure types are moulded in light and shadow without recourse to the *chiaroscuro* of Leonardo and his followers – let alone Caravaggio.

0.30a

0.30b

Sculptural form, disciplined by precise *disegno*, was interpreted in glowing colour by Philippe de Champaigne (1602–74) fully in tune with the order of Richelieu's regime:**0.2b** in his later work – especially for the Jansenists of Port-Royal – an austere, near-monochromatic stoicism supervened. Following his similar trajectory simultaneously, Poussin retained the colour: beyond the evolution of his two stupendous series of 'Sacraments', foremost examples range from the 'Holy Family on the Steps' (1648) to the 'Judgement of Solomon' (1649).

0.30c

Poussin's homage to Solomon is to be contrasted with Rubens' 'Judgement of Paris' (c. 1632): the statuesque figures in the one are organized as a frieze parallel to the base plane in standard Classical mode; ripe in luscious flesh, the protagonists of the other are distributed to capitalize on the dynamic of the diagonal in thoroughly Baroque mode. These two images could hardly be bettered as the standard representatives of the contrasting ideals of the Ancients and the Moderns, the intellect behind the former asserting *disegno* and Classical principle over *colore* and modern licence, the spectacular genius behind the latter promoting the opposite. Confused with politics in an era of French preponderance, when the arts

1648; London, National Gallery); (c) 'The Holy Family on the Steps' (1648; Cleveland, Ohio, Museum of Art).

Poussin's Classical imperative, derived from Raphael and antique sculpture, was inspired by his early association with Philippe de Champaigne in Paris. After 1624 it was informed by his experience of Annibale in the Roman context of Domenichino's studio: like Cortona, however, he transformed it in the light of Venice, where he stayed on his way to Rome, and of the Venetians encountered in the collections of the patrons who employed him primarily to supply them with cabinet pictures. Supplanting his earliest Roman essays in frieze-like composition against space, early examples of his painterly, richly chromatic mode include the Chatsworth Arcadian Shepherds. There is literary conceit furthered from the inspiration of the Venetian poesie (AIC5, page 34): the mythological idyll from which the participants emerge, in freedom from restraint, is transmuted atmospherically by the morbid revelation of death in its midst. In the superbly idealized Arcadian context of the solemn essay on the theme (now in the National Gallery, London), its features plotted mathematically, the menace is manifest in the brute realty of the fate of the figure succumbing to the snake.

In the early 1630s, studies of antique sculpture commissioned by one of his principal patrons (Cassiano dal Pozzo, Cortona's patron too) returned Poussin to strict *disegno* in practice and principle – to the High Renaissance symbolic use of colour, to an earlier renaissance of Aristotelian rhetorical device. Ovid is supplemented, if not supplanted, by the Old Testament, then by the New and by the Stoics: the moody cedes to the cerebral. The statuesque forms of a Classical frieze, their chiselled features softened in *sfumato*, recur in the laconic works of his maturity, absolute in their clarity of form and restriction to the essentials of symbolism, restrained in equilibrium. In the masterpiece now in the Museum of Art in Cleveland, the Madonna and Child (after Raphael's 'Madonna of the Fish', AIC5, page 24) form the apex of a group disposed geometrically in concentrated intensity on a step against the space implied by the development of the flight. Leading to heaven from the world of Christ's newly revealed humanity, however, the superimposition is crucial: those steps are surrogate for the central figures as an allegory of the Madonna's key role in effecting the salvation promised by her son.

The perfect symmetry of Solomon in judgement is disturbed by the startling colours as much as by the jagged oratorical gestures of the appellants and the potential violence of the soldiers. Clearly, Poussin has observed Raphael's 'Death of Ananias' (tapestry cartoon of 1515) and the High Renaissance master's own 'Judgement of Solomon' (Vatican Loggia, 1518), though there judgement is cast asymmetrically.

As we have noted, Rubens was hardly less impressed with the High Renaissance masters than Poussin but the trajectories of these two supreme artists could hardly be more spectacular in their divergence: the latter in his emulation of Classical achievement in the judicious balance of his Old Testament monarch, the former in transmogrifying the Raphaelesque ideal (the Three Graces of c. 1503 in particular) in his brilliantly spontaneous, highly 'picturesque' representation of mythological Paris diagonally disposed in contemplating judgement between three lusciously constituted ladies in their luxurious sylvan setting.

0.31a

served the purposes of state even more determinedly than they had traditionally served the purposes of the Church, the debate exercised the Académie royale de peinture et de sculpture (constituted in 1648) for thirty years from 1671 (see below): it extended to architecture.**0.30, 0.31**

0.31b

GENNES

PARME

ANCÔNE

LORETTE

NAPLES

NOUVELLE
CARTE
D'ITALIE
la Feuille exc.
Amsterdam.

VERONE

FLORENCE

ROME

MER MEDITERRANÉE

1.1a

PART 1 SEMINAL ITALIANS

1.1b–e

1 INCEPTION OF THE HIGH BAROQUE IN ROME

As we anticipated at the outset of our brief coverage of the major trends in early 17th-century painting, the development of the style known as Baroque must be seen against the background of the crisis in Catholicism provoked by the Reformation and confronted by the councillors convened at Trent in 1543. Recognizing the need to reorder its house from within, they regulated all aspects of the life of the Church but left prescription for the actual building to the Cardinal-archbishop of Milan, Carlo Borromeo – nephew of the last Tridentine pope, Pius IV (AIC5, pages 77ff).

The most militant of the Counter-Reformation orders, the Jesuits, responded to the requirements of reform with

›1.1 ITALY: (a) map by Daniel de La Feuille (1706) with overviews of the major cities; (b–e) insignia of the Papal States, the Republic of Venice and the kingdoms of Sardinia (Piedmont) and Naples (Sicily).

›1.2 PANORAMA OF BAROQUE ROME.

The view from S. Trinità ai Monte of the west-south-west sector of the city spans from the great basilica of S. Pietro in the Vatican and the church of Ss. Ambrogio e Carlo al Corso (respectively background and middle distance, right) to the church of S. Agnese in Piazza Navona (background, left).

the prototype for the grand congregational church in plan and elevation: matching Carlo Borromeo's prescriptions in providing a clear acoustical environment for large numbers, the Gesù was conceived by Vignola as a theatre with the sanctuary as stage for the priest to perform the holy mystery of the Eucharist viewed through the proscenium arch beyond the domed crossing by the congregation in the auditorium (AIC5, pages 184f). The example was followed by the other reforming orders. And the prescribed plan form was to prevail at the very centre of Catholic Christendom. The extension of S. Pietro was entrusted to Carlo Maderno (1556–1629) who had emerged from association with Michelangelo's successor, Giacomo della Porta (AIC5, pages 296ff): he was currently engaged on his first independent ecclesiastical commission, the façade of S. Susanna.**1.3**

>1.3 MADERNO AND THE ROMAN CHURCH:
(a) S. Susanna, façade (1603); (b–e) basilica of S.
Pietro, east front, plan and section, nave attic window
detail (the extended structure was completed by 1614,
except for the towers which were projected over double-bay extensions to either side of the vast front); (f)
S. Andrea della Valle, dome (constructed by 1624).

Domenico Fontana was responsible for renovating
an ancient basilica on S. Susanna's site c. 1570. Furthering the work within Fontana's fabric in the main,
Maderno received the contract for the façade in 1597
and completed its construction in 1603.

A competition for the façade of S. Andrea was held in
1599 but lack of funding inhibited progress until 1608,
when Maderno took charge: his design, establishing
the rhythm of the Order, was only partially realized
until the late-1660s when Carlo Fontana and Carlo
Rainaldi were responsible to indeterminate degrees
for revising the project. The dome, the second largest
in Rome, had been realized by 1625, when Lanfranco

Achieving S. Pietro: the basilican extension

Shortly after his elevation in 1605, Pope Paul V took the controversial decision to convert Michelangelo's (and Bramante's) centralized masterpiece
into a basilica. Transforming the Greek cross into a Latin cross in conformity with post-Tridentine dogma (AIC5, pages 77ff), Maderno projected
three great arcaded bays extending the building to a narthex in the east
in accordance with its unorthodox counter-orientation. Articulated after

began the great fresco in its interior. For the exterior, reference to S. Pietro's dome was unavoidable: the enhanced aspiration effected by Porta's elongated departure from Michelangelo's hemisphere is furthered by increasing the relative height – and hence the vertical accents – of the drum.

the style of the original cross arms, with the doubled Corinthian pilasters projected by Bramante to support the great tunnel vault, the arcades rise to the full height of the Order as at S. Andrea in Mantua. Here, however, the aisle bays are groin-vaulted and interconnected: on each side the two outer bays open into recessed chapels, the pair of inner ones lead to the enclosed rectangular halls of sacristy and choir.

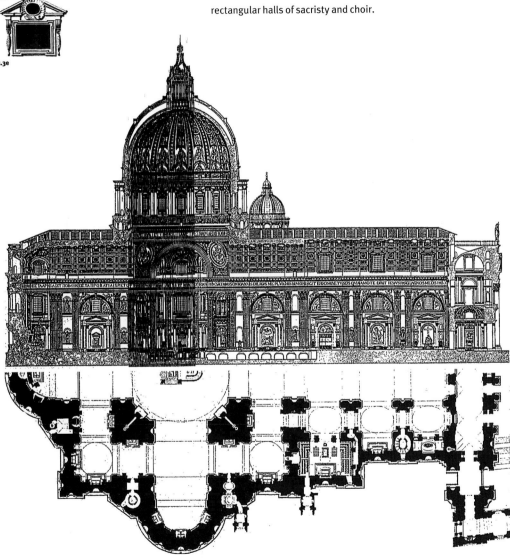

1.3e

1.3c, d @ 1:1500

We have seen how Michelangelo overrode Bramante's differentiation of the parts, amalgamating the subsidiary spaces into a continuous ambulatory and imposing a giant Order on the envelope – in response to Bramante's initiation of the interior articulation (AIC5, pages 159f). The colossal Order expressed the grandeur of the predominant space inside and was, therefore, as appropriate as Bramante's expression of the subordinate ones outside. The pilasters of the north, west and southern perimeters were to cede to the columns of a prostyle portico of ten columns doubled by those of a temple front before the central three bays. Maderno retracted and contracted this for the articulation of his seven-bay scheme, preserving the integrity of the central temple front as the culmination of a progression from pilasters to half columns in concert with the projection of the intermediate bays – and providing the central benediction loggia which Michelangelo's columns could not accommodate.

Nowhere is the conception of scale more overwhelming than in the basilica as Maderno left it, inside and out. And the cost was considerable: the extension partially masked the stupendous dome projected by Michelangelo, denying it full appreciation from the precinct in front where the faithful congregated for papal benediction. In recompense, as it were, Maderno provided a solution to the problem of elevating a dome to dominance over a basilican nave at S. Andrea della Valle by raising the height of the drum – to the advantage of élan over gravitas. To preserve the impact of the Vatican domes, at least from afar, Maderno set the bases of twin towers to the sides of his new nave elevation: found to be unstable, these were never to be realized above the level of the main cornice and, consequently, the façade was left seeming too long for its height despite the vertical accents introduced by the progressive projection of the bays and their articulation with the most colossal Order deployed in Rome since antiquity.

The motive of the colossal Order goes back at least to Raphael at the Villa Madama, as we know, but it was the key to the conception of scale in the forthcoming era identified as 'Baroque'. Even in designing for God, Classical architects made their buildings comprehensible to

1.3f

1.4a

›1.4 ROME, CONSERVATIVE CHURCH DESIGN: (a) S. Maria in Vallicella, façade (Fausto Rughese, 1605); (b, c) S. Carlo ai Catinari (begun by Rosato Rosati in 1611), façade (added by Giovanni Battista Soria from 1627), plan.

The Oratorian church, built to the Gesù formula from 1575 by Martino Longhi the Elder (AIC5, page 290), was equipped with its façade by the otherwise unknown Rughese. His competent exercise was too early to have been informed by Maderno's achievement in advancing the formula of Vignola as revised by Porta. On the other hand Soria, who provided the Barnabites with the façade of S. Carlo long after the completion of S. Susanna, is doubtless rightly seen as a self-conscious Classicist opposed to Maderno and his mentors.

Unusually for a mother church of a Counter Reformation order, the plan of S. Carlo departs from the Gesù formula to approximate a Greek cross: the entrance axis is slightly longer than the transept; naturally there is a dome in the centre and minor domical corner chapels. This belongs to the widespread sub-Bramantesque type developed from Alessi's S. Maria in Carignano, Genoa, by Giuseppe Valeriano in Genoa and Naples and by Lorenzo Binago for his Milanese church of S. Alessandro (AIC5, pages 261, 275f).

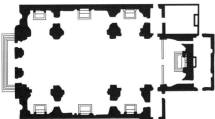

1.4b @ 1:1000

1.4c

the mind of man, using his proportions and appealing to his sense of logic in insisting that a column, like a post, held up a roof over his head: the size varied according to the prestige of the dedicatee but the scale was always human. However, it was the renaissance of humanism, precisely the implications of the elevation of man, which exercised the councillors at Trent as they deliberated on the service of God: the style of their Counter Reformation, celebrating the mystery of the divine, was calculated to move the emotions before engaging the mind.

The projection of successive wall planes in concert with progression in the plasticity of an applied Order, generating vitality in S. Pietro's new façade, was to be a key 'Baroque' technique. Maderno first deployed it for the church of S. Susanna (1603), evidently under the inspiration of Vignola's unexecuted scheme for the Gesù façade (AIC5, page 185).[1.3] Furthering the latter at ground-floor level – with more plasticity, more clarity and, consequently, enhanced effects of *chiaroscuro* – the Order progresses from pilaster to half columns to full column through three gradations of plane, defining three amplifications of increasingly open bay and accenting the axis of entry. The orchestration of forces leads to a climax as in the movement of a symphony and the eye moves with it.

Maderno's invigorating achievement was ignored by his conservative contemporaries, Classicists dedicated to deploring egregious complexity in the works of post-Michelangelesque Mannerists like Giacomo del Duca. Initially represented by Porta's S. Maria ai Monte and S. Luigi dei Francese – the former of the standard 'basilican' type, the latter a 'palace' variant with full upper storey – the subsistence of the purist tradition may be traced from Fausto Rughese's S. Maria in Vallicella (1605) to variants by G. B. Soria for S. Maria della Vittoria, S. Gregorio Magno or S. Carlo ai Catinari in the second quarter of the century.[1.4]

`1.5`

›1.5 MILAN, FABIO MANGONE AT THE COL-
LEGIO ELVETICO: first court (from 1608).

›1.6 MILAN, SELECT WORKS OF FRANCESCO
MARIA RICCHINO: (a) Collegio Elvetico, façade
(1627); (b–e) S. Giuseppe (1607–30), section, plan,
exterior, interior; (f) Ospedale Maggiore, portal (c.
1640); (g) Seminario, portal (from 1652); (h, i) Palazzo
di Brera (from 1651, ex-Jesuit college, now the Pinacoteca di Brera), façade, cortile.

In Rome before 1603, at the instigation of Cardinal
Archbishop Federico Borromeo, Ricchino was doubtless privy to the ideas of his compatriot Maderno for
the façade of S. Susanna – realized after his return to
Milan. However, the latter's method of generating movement in terms of stepped progression was varied for S.
Giuseppe. Ricchino's over-riding interests there were
vertical unity and external/internal coherence. In furthering the latter he was original in achieving a dominant
axis through the fusion of centralized spaces with a progressive Order but he avoided Mannerist ambiguity by
preserving the integrity of his two Greek crosses in plan.
In pursuit of vertical unity outside, he produced interlocked aedicules which, in clarifying Alessi's approach
at S. Maria presso S. Celso, takes its departure from the
base level of Tibaldi's S. Fedele, follows through to the
top and obviates ambiguity (AIC5, pages 271, 274).

MILANESE DIGRESSION

Conservatism also marked early 17th-century Milan, not
least in homage to the austere ideal of Carlo Borromeo
and his nephew Federico: endowed by the latter with the
chair of architecture at the Accademia Ambrosiana, Fabio

`1.6a`

`1.6f`

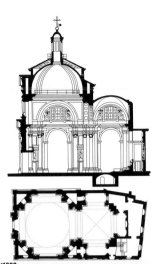

1.6b, c @ 1:1000

1.6e

Ricchino developed his aedicular façade formula in several other contexts, notably the façades of the Milanese cathedral (where he followed Mangone in 1629), the Ospedale Maggiore and the Seminario: at the Ospedale the planar projection and expression of the Order are simplified; at the Seminario their vitality is asserted in development of the Milanese theme of the atlante, which derives at least from the Palazzo Omenoni of nearly a century earlier (AIC5, page 267).

Mangone (1587–1629) was most prominent in the field as architect to the cathedral from 1617. Best represented by the court of the Collegio Elvetico, he worked there with his contemporary, Francesco Maria Ricchino (1584–1658), who had embarked in a different direction – also prominently represented at the Collegio Elvetico.[1.5]

While the façade of S. Susanna was rising in Rome, in Milan Maderno's compatriot Ricchino was working in a similar mode on S. Giuseppe, both outside and in: the

1.6d

dominant entrance-altar axis, opened between the columns of the projecting portal bay, was achieved by aligning two Greek crosses and forging them through the progression of the Order from pilaster to column at the salient points. An alternative to that procedure is Ricchino's Collegio Elvetico façade (1627), which claims primacy among proto-Baroque works for generating movement by drawing curve from elliptical counter curve.**1.6**

Seminal in his ecclesiastical and institutional aedicular façades, Ricchino was relatively conservative in his dependence on recent Lombard precedent for his many palazzo designs. However, in eliminating the complexity to which Pellegrino Tibaldi was inclined, he achieved a monumentality in the Palazzo di Brera which cedes little to the Roman school of Sangallo and his followers (AIC5, pages 146, 273). In Rome itself, meanwhile, the specific circumstances of Maderno's two main secular commissions prompted innovation.

1.6g

He resorted to various centralized forms for his many lost churches, including the ellipse. He was innovative in impressing elliptical convexity on a palace front. In contrast, his late work for the Jesuits is relatively austere without but recalls Tibaldi's superimposed 'serlian' ranges for the galleries of its splendid court (AIC5, page 273).

1.6i

1.6h

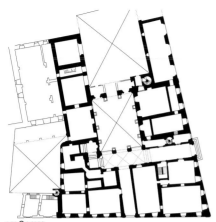

1.7a @ 1:1000

›1.7 MADERNO AND THE ROMAN PALAZZO:
(a, b) Mattei di Giove (from 1598 to c. 1616), plan and
cortile; (c, d) Palazzo Barberini (from 1628), plan and
entrance front.

The Mattei work was unexceptional in the severity of
its external brickwork: in sharp contrast, the embellishment of the court with fragments of antique sculpture
emulates the richest of villa fronts – open courts like
those of the Medici and Borghese.

1.7b

BACK TO ROME: ADVENT OF THE BARBERINI

Maderno's first exercise in palazzo design was launched at
the outset of his Roman career in 1598 for Mattei di Giove:
the main novelty of the biaxial plan was in the circulation, particularly the staircase which departed from, but
arrived on, the lateral axis in its assent from base to piano
nobile. Thirty years later, at the end of his career, Maderno transformed the concept of the Roman palazzo for
the Barberini clan of Pope Urban VIII (1623–44) and his
nephew Cardinal Francesco: the exceptional elevated site,
expansive enough for a vast complex to be set in a garden,
prompted the development of a hybrid palazzo-villa with
entry through an open court centred on three storeys of
loggias.**1·7** The outer range of the receding undercroft leads
to two ingenious staircases, the main one serving the piano
nobile and the huge salone, whose embellishment is itself
of seminal significance.

Maderno was assisted – and succeeded – in the completion of work on the Palazzo Barberini by the three artists
who would take the Baroque style to its apogee in Rome:
the Neapolitan Gianlorenzo Bernini (1598-1680), whom we
are soon to encounter as a sculptor of unmatched genius;
Pietro Berrettini from Cortona, whose Roman painting
we have seen before he emerged as an illusionist of unsurpassed genius in the palazzo's salone; and Francesco Castelli
(1599–1667), a Maderno relative from the Milanese orbit
of Borromeo (and calling himself Borromini), who had
entered his kinsman's Roman workshop as a draftsman by
the mid-1620s and emerged as an architect of radical genius.

Bernini's specific contribution to the Barberini project
is difficult to determine: preoccupied with the interior
embellishment of S. Pietro to the pope's great satisfaction, he was appointed to supervise execution of work
at the palace on Maderno's demise at the beginning of

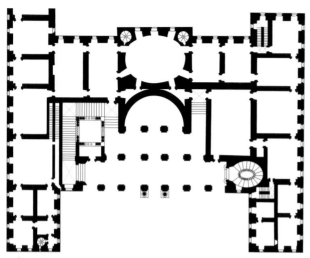

1.7c @ 1:1000

Undertaken initially for the pope's nephew Cardinal Francesco, the Barberini complex is unique among Roman palazzi in its extroversion. Instead of the typical rectangular block, defined by a network of streets and enclosing a cortile with superimposed loggias, these are exposed as the entrance front between lesser projecting wings: it may be seen as amplifying the scheme of the Villa Farnesina or amending that of the Palazzo Farnese but clearly acknowledges the inspiration of the Villa Mondragone at Frascati (AIC5, page 286). Planning was under way at least as early as 1626, when Francesco consigned the site to his brother Taddeo. Maderno's kinsman from the north, Francesco Borromini was assisting the master at S. Pietro by the mid-1620s and, as his principal draftsman, produced a study of the loggia (now in the Albertina, Vienna). Borromini remained in post when the pope appointed Bernini to succeed

1.7d

the deceased Maderno: then the two young geniuses were free to make modifications.

Access arrangements are as novel as the semi-open plan. The main block rises over an arcaded undercroft in which the ranges are progressively reduced from seven bays to one: the latter is closed with an apse; the front range leads left to the rectangular cage of the grand staircase and right to an elliptical variation on Bramante's Belvedere spiral which is usually attributed to Borromini.

1.8a
>**1.8 BORROMINI AT THE PALAZZO BARBER-INI:** (a) spiral staircase, (b, c) windows (Domenico de' Rossi, *Studio d' architettura civile*, from 1702, *DR*).

In designing the windows of the attic flanking the central loggias, Borromini began with Maderno's take on Michelangelo's ideas for the attic of S. Pietro (AIC5, page 161): the pediment is canted out over the supporting consoles to the sides: in the centre it curves into a mini tympanum to enclose the shell motif inherited from his predecessors. The garden front frames have 'ears'.

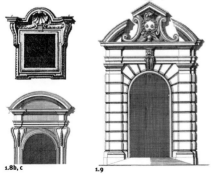

1.8b, c   1.9
>**1.9 CORTONA AT THE PALAZZO BARBERINI:** court portal (*DR*). See also page 65.

1629. That had been under way for barely three months but planning had proceeded for at least three years. The most important surviving drawings – including one of the loggia façade – are attributed to Borromini as Maderno's principal draftsman from the outset, but there is no evidence that either he or his new master effected strategic change.

Initiation of the High Baroque in the circle of the Barberini

Free to modify even under his old master, Borromini is credited with the spiral staircase serving the Barberini's principal apartment (to the south). He is also credited with seminal variations to the attic window in the bays linking the central reception rooms with the two residential wings.[1.8] Flanked by these windows, the upper arches of the loggia are framed in a manner which suggests greater depth than is actually present: to correct the distortion of the view *di sotto in sù*, the imposts are tilted (from outside to in) after the example of Bramante in the false choir of S. Maria presso S. Satiro in Milan (AIC4, page 811). Maderno applied the principle at the foot of his innovative Mattei staircase and it well served the ingenious purposes of both Borromini and Bernini in their maturity (see, for example, pages 69, 100f).

Cortona is credited with a portal in the Barberini's rear court: its pediment, starting on a segmental course but broken and superseded by a triangular apex, anticipates the form usually associated with Borromini.[1.9] In this the latter promoted the uninterrupted fusion of segmental and triangular geometry after he developed his hybrid pediment/tympanum for the Barberini attic windows. Variations on these exercises were to recur throughout his career for the frames of windows and doors: beyond that, multiform pediments and obtuse-angled projections – especially rounded off through concave elliptical curves – are hallmarks of his style. Varied idiosyncratically, these are the hallmarks of Cortona's architectural style too.

Cortona was first in the Roman field with a flattened ellipse as a major façade motif when he embarked on his independent architectural career with a villa for the Sachetti in 1630. And that must be seen in the light of his recent studies in reconstructing the Temple of Fortuna at Palestrina for the Barberini – to whom he was introduced by the Sachetti.[1.10, 1.11]

>1.10 CORTONA AND THE PIGNETO SAC-
CHETTI, c. 1630, destroyed: 17th-century engraving.

Cortona had been taken into the Sachetti house-hold on the strength of his studies after Raphael. His first venture into architecture is dependent on Raphael's teacher: the central three-storey block with its huge niche is clearly derived from Bramante's Belvedere with its 'rhythmic bays' and double-height *nicchione* (which framed the huge antique *pigna*; AIC4, pages 854f). To either side, however, arcaded wings describe an elliptical curve flattened towards the centre in the manner which would be characteristic of Cortona's mature work: they embrace open arcaded pavilions with screened apses derived from antique thermae.

Feigned perspective is another trait shared by Maderno's protégés. However, it is in this medium that Cortona eclipsed his colleagues with his main contribution to the Barberini complex: the stupendous fresco in the salone with which, in 1633, he opened his career as an illusionist ceiling decorator of seminal importance.[1.12]

Working for the Barberini on their great Roman palazzo, Maderno and his three assistant geniuses – Bernini, Borromini and Cortona – evolved a range of techniques which would transform architecture, primar-ily for the Counter Reformation Church. We need now to define these techniques.

>1.11 CORTONA AND THE TEMPLE OF FOR-
TUNA AT PALESTRINA: drawing of c. 1631 as engraved in 1638 by Sebastiano Fulcro.

The great late Roman Republican sanctuary of Fortuna Primigenia at Palestrina (AIC1, page 522) was developed as a palace in the 11th century by the Col-onna. In 1630 it was bought by the Barberini for the papal nephew Taddeo who embarked on the refection of the palace. With much greater antique grandeur in mind – perhaps for a villa – Taddeo's brother Cardinal Francesco immediately called on Cortona for graphic reconstruction of the ancient complex. In elaborating a more comprehensive view than had hitherto been seen in the light of archaeological research, Cortona's imagination drew on anonymous earlier 17th-century drawings in the Barberini collection which were prob-ably informed – in part at least – by the records of Pirro Ligorio's antiquarian activities rather than those of Palladio (AIC5, page 228).

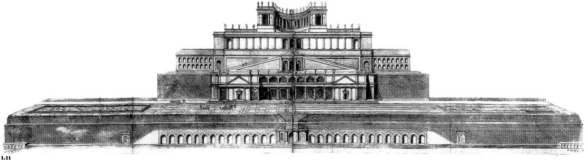

›1.12 CORTONA AND THE FRESCOED EMPY-REAN IN THE PALAZZO BARBERINI: salone vault, 'The Triumph of the Barberini Pontificate' (1633–39).

The ceiling takes its departure from Annibale Caracci's stunning achievement at the Palazzo Farnese which, as we have noted, drew its inspiration from the combined sources of Raphael and Michelangelo. As there, all the elements of the highly complex illusion are painted: the sculpture and the architecture as well as the spaces they determine – of this world and of heaven – and the figures in apotheosis.

The architectural framework remains but it is supplemented with figures who have renounced the subservience of herms: *quadratura* overwhelms *quadro riportato*. The coves open to the illusionistic extension of land-based space, the ceiling to the empyrean: all zones team with figures acting out complex allegorical dramas but, apart from the personification of Catholicism, the star parts are played by those supporting the laurel cartouche which frames the Barberini bees in exalted representation of Urban VIII as motivator of the Church Triumphant.

1.12

2 THE STYLE OF THE CHURCH TRIUMPHANT

The glorification of the Roman Church initiated by the Barberini Pope Urban VIII on his election in 1623 and culminating in the 1660s under Alexander VII Chigi is to be seen as the apotheosis of Counter Reformation motives – but in accordance with the transformation of the ideals of the major Counter Reformation orders. Militants dedicated single-mindedly to the cause of exorcizing perceived heresy, at first they ceded nothing in austerity of style to the Cistercian, Franciscan, Dominican: further, indeed, they ceded little to the arch-Protestant reformers who had confronted decadence in the Church establishment at their several reprises since self-denying monastic rule had taken root in Europe (AIC4, pages 10, 36ff, 58, 166, etc.). By the third decade of the 17th century, however, heroic militancy issued in celebration as the containment of the Protestant threat seemed like triumph to the Catholic establishment in Rome. The austere directive of the Trentine era was relaxed: the embellishment of the theatre of Grace was to envisage the scene of divine motivation. To reinforce the Catholic faith, the faithful were to be overawed by the resplendent vision of the empyrean to which that faith would lead through intercession – not least in the churches dedicated to the canonized heroes of the struggle, the scions of the new orders whose apotheosis was the main motive for the marshalling of all the arts to promote the development of the requisite new style.

Despite this sense of purpose – because of it, indeed, from the Protestant point of view – the style was abused with a term for the bizarre probably primarily derived from the Portuguese for a mis-shaped pearl: *barocco*. The altar rails of the Certosa di S. Martino at Naples are bizarre but strict regularity characterizes the design of Baroque ornament in the main – even despite mesmerizing flo-

1.13b

›**1.13 COMPLEXITY IN DESIGN AND ELABORATION OF FORM IN RICH MATERIALS:** (a, b) Certosa di S. Martino, Naples (Cosimo Fanzago from 1631, interrupted in 1656, continued by Bonaventura Presti and others from the mid-1660s, completed in the 18th century), general view over chapel floor (executed by Presti, probably with his own elaborations) and altar rail detail (by Giuseppe Sammartino, c. 1760?).

1.13a

1.14a, b

**›1.14 BERNINI AT THE VILLA BORGHESE,
ROME:** (a) Apollo and Daphne, (b) Goliath (both c. 1623; Rome, Borghese Gallery).

**›1.15 BERNINI IN THE PIAZZA BARBERINI,
ROME:** the Triton Fountain (1642).

1.15

ridity, as S. Martino's gorgeous floor demonstrates.**1.13** As Bernini's sculpture demonstrates, moreover, Baroque form is essentially dynamic.

Paul V's reign saw the burgeoning of Baroque styles in painting and architecture. His nephew Scipione – the collector of Caravaggio's early works – commissioned the seminal works of Baroque sculpture from Bernini, the young Neapolitan genius whom we have just encountered in the later stages of work for the Barberini – the followers of the Borghese. The latter's patronage, thus, introduced Baroque principles to Rome on both the grandest and the most intimate of scales: the completion of S. Peter's basilica and the sculpture groups commissioned for the family villa on the Pincio. Bernini was to play a crucial role in the culmination of the former because of his astonishing achievement of the latter.

Bernini could endow cold stone with the warmth and softness of flesh: from hair to silk or velvet no texture seemed beyond his power to simulate. The supreme master of mounting dramatic display, however, he was never to be matched in endowing inert material with vitality, indeed with the immediacy of momentary action. The difference between the Baroque and the other main phases of Renaissance art may well be characterized by comparing his virile statue of David in the process of felling Goliath with those of his major predecessors, Donatello and Michelangelo – the former resting after the event, the latter shot through with anxiety immediately before it (AIC4, page 684, AIC5, page 5). The symbolism is axiomatic: commissioned at the end of the Borghese era, when the radical was still confronted with the reactionary, Bernini's determined David represents all that would motivate the new era in both the secular and ecclesiastical fields. The divinely inspired dynamic directing him to the kill has its salutary secular counterpart in the Triton Fountain of the Piazza Barberini.**1.14, 1.15**

Apart from the manipulation of scale to evoke grandeur, the display of rich materials to radiate glory is the most obvious of the High Baroque techniques evolved in Rome. More significant, perhaps, is the orchestration of complexity in plan and elevation to assert profundity.[1.16] Most significant is the mobilization of kinetic force to generate power: progressively articulated through projecting planes or undulating with the changing curvature of elliptical moulding, mass is infused with vitality, volumes are fused to forge dynamic axes.[1.17, 1.18] Certainly not least significant are the staging of scenographic spectacle: the illusionistic extension of space horizontally and vertically; the fusion of all the arts to illusionistic purpose in the projection of a unified iconographic theme – *concetto* – especially for the celebration of the militant Church.[1.19]

No Baroque technique was invented by Baroque artists. Elliptical planning was their forte. As we know, however, Vignola had followed Serlio and Peruzzi in applying the oval to the design of the small scale church as an alternative to the Latin cross of grander congregational import: both, of course, provided clear sight lines along a dominant axis. On the other hand, the arrangement of scenographic vistas through enfilades of diversified space was derived by Palladio from his study of the antique Roman thermal complex. Moreover, Classical Antiquity provided object lessons in the breach of rule for emotional effect: the Colossal Order - denying the normal measure of human space as Raphael, Sangallo, Michelangelo and even Palladio found it expedient to do – is one manifestation; the denial of structural logic in effecting a sense of movement in mass by moulding it elliptically is another. And the imaginative restoration of antique monuments, especially by Giovanni Battista Montano, provided endless source of inspiration to Baroque architects at home and abroad.

1.16a

›**1.16 COMPLEXITY IN ELEVATION AND MANIPULATION OF SCALE:** (a) Cappella S. Cecilia, S. Carlo ai Catinari (Antonio Gherardi, from c. 1695); (b) imaginative reconstruction from the antique (Giovanni Battista Montano).

1.16b

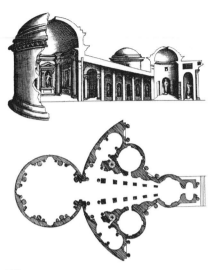

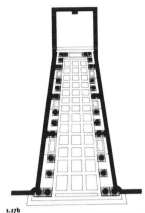

1.17b

1.17c

1.17d

1.18c

1.17a

›1.17 FEIGNED EXTENSION OF SPACE: (a) imaginative reconstruction from the antique (Montano); (b, c) gallery of the Palazzo Spada (Borromini, from 1652, reduces the size of the columns progressively, enhancing the effect of perspective diminution, to create the illusion of greater depth than the actual context provided), plan and view from court; (d) Lateran tomb of Cardinal Chaves (Borromini, from c. 1655).

›1.18 GENERATION OF MOVEMENT: (a, b) imaginative reconstructions from the antique (circle of Montano); (c) monument to Pope Alexander III, S. Giovanni in Laterano (Borromini, after 1655).

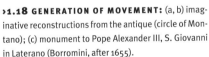

TEMPIVM HONORIS   ET VIRTVTIS

1.18a

1.18b

Maderno's progressive movement in mass at S. Susanna and S. Pietro was drawn from the ingredients provided by Vignola in his scheme of advancing planes for the Gesù façade, as we have seen (AIC5, page 185). And various Renaissance masters provided at least two of his assistants at the Palazzo Barberini with their means for enriching the evolution of the new century's style. Michelangelo, for example, promoted complex geometry in planning and multiplica-

tion of form in elevation (AIC5, page 163). Bramante, after
Mantegna, inspired stunning illusionism: the latter on the
vertical plane, the former on the feigned extension of sanctuary space (AIC4, pages 698, 810). Correggio – if not Giulio
Romano – took the technique to its apotheosis (AIC5, pages
32, 127). Raphael, who offered various means to that end,
combined the arts to effect iconographical unity of space
on the scale of the Chigi chapel: to subtract a painting or
a sculpture would leave a physical and spiritual void there
but the architecture, the paintings and the sculptures have
independent validity (AIC5, pages 12f). That can not be said
unequivocally of Buontalent's grotto in the Boboli gardens –
but the situation is ambivalent in that extraordinary exercise
(AIC5, page 207). It is certainly not true of Cortonesque vault
decoration or the scenographic spectacles of Bernini.

Among the Counter Reformation Orders promoting
the church type developed by Vignola, the Theatines and
Oratorians led the advance from austere ideals to splendour in interior embellishment. As we have seen, the former retained Domenichino for the choir of S. Andrea della
Valle (from 1624) and commissioned Giovanni Lanfranco
to introduce Rome to the illusion of heaven in the dome
of their crossing (see above, pages 56). Pietro da Cortona
rehearsed the theme in the dome of S. Maria in Vallicella
for Oratorians twenty years later. He had already developed it on the expansive scale of the Barberini salone vault,
with reference to Annibale Carracci's stupendous work for
the Farnese.**0.19**

Cortona is justly credited with perfecting the fusion of the
arts in the grandest manner of illusionist vault decoration.
Hardly had he finished his great work for the Barberini
when he was called to Florence to work for the Grand Duke
of Tuscany at the Palazzo Pitti. In the extended enfilade
of the principal reception rooms there, he advanced from
untrammeled fresco into mixed media: he reconstituted

1.19a

1.19b

1.19c

›1.19 **CORTONA AND THE FRESCOED EMPY-
REAN FURTHER ENRICHED:** (a–d) Florence,
Palazzo Pitti, Sala di Marte, Sala di Venere, Sala di
Apollo, Sala di Saturno; (e) S. Maria in Vallicella, the
'Trinity in Glory' (from 1647).

1.19d

architecture and sculpture in association with painting with
stunning variety. Each successive room is dedicated to a
Classical deity whose attributes flatter the duke by association. Each has a different frame of real architecture, necessarily rich but light and therefore supported by sculpture,
which also frames the supernatural realm evoked illusionistically in paint: as foremost in the realm of Apollo, the
Olympian empyrean is distinguished from, but fused with,
the realm of the duke through the indissoluble fusion of
the arts. The formula was exported by the master's assistant
Romanelli to France and thereafter applied to the embellishment of palaces throughout Europe – as we shall see.
Meanwhile Cortona himself had taken it back to Rome for
the Oratorians.[1.19]

While engaged on his stupendous Pitti campaign, Cortona was retained by the Oratorians to decorate their mother church in Rome. By the mid-1660s, when he had reached the nave vault, the architecture extracted from simulation in fresco had achieved more integrated sculptural substance as framework for the scene of divine glory – the 'Vision of S. Fillipo'. The Jesuits followed a decade later, calling on their Brother Gaulli to evoke the very image of the Church Triumphant on the nave vault of Il Gesù in exultant graduation from their original aesthetic ideals: more dramatically even than Cortona's beatific exercise for the Oratorians, their splendid vision of the 'Adoration of the Name of Jesus' extends from two to three dimensions – in fact from paint to sculpture – as the soul of the devotee is drawn up from the space of the church by the heavenly host as it surges through the assertive architectural framework into the empyrean.[1.20]

1.19e

1.20a

>1.20 THE JESUIT FATHERS AND ROMAN HIGH BAROQUE ILLUSIONISM IN VAULT EMBELLISHMENT: (a) Il Gesù, framework and 'Adoration of the Name of Jesus' (Fra Giovanni Battista Gaulli, from 1674); (b) S. Ignazio, 'The Glory of S. Ignatius' (Fra Andrea Pozzo, from c. 1690).

In the light of Cortona's splendid evocation of the Church Triumphant for the Oratorians, the general of the Jesuit Order appointed in 1664 – Padre Giovanni Paolo Oliva – opted to renounce austerity for opulence first at Il Gesù, naturally. Cortona was retained for the chapel of S. Francis Xavier at the end of his life (1669). Within two years Gaulli (known also as Baciccio) had been commissioned to embellish the crossing, which he completed in 1675. He turned to the apse in 1680 but meanwhile began his major work, on the nave vault: Cortona set the precedent but the 'Adoration of the Name of Jesus' is distinguished by its particularly dramatic, iconographically essential, progression from dark to light. As we shall see, Bernini was the pre-eminent master of dramatic lighting in church embellishment and Gaulli entered his circle soon after arriving in Rome from Genoa.

Unlike his older brother at Il Gesù – or Cortona at the Oratory – Fra Pozzo at S. Ignazio renounced sculpture in resorting to a totally comprehensive exercise in *quadratura* – with its strictly limited viewpoint. The walls of the church are propelled heavenwards to frame the allegory of the missionary work of S. Ignatius and his Jesuits in apotheosis.

1.20b

Projecting heaven beyond the fabric of the church along the scenographic lines drawn for the optical illusion of recession in space on the two-dimensional plane of a stage backdrop, Cortona and the Jesuits complete the exposition of Baroque techniques. The axis of progression from the entrance of the church to the high altar is now surpassed by the axis leading from earth to heaven through the window of the vault, fusing the space of this world and the next. Greatly enhancing the illusion in facilitating that transition, the fusion of the arts was first comprehensively deployed by Bernini in the elaboration of a *concetto*, as we are about to see. On the other hand, Fra Pozzo provided a strictly architectural alternative to sculpted angels. Either way, the architecture creates the space of this world but also opens the window of heaven: there painting invariably translates the illusory reality of our three-dimensional state into the illusion of the supreme reality of an empyrean which knows no dimensions of space or time.

If Baroque art is best characterized as rhetorical in motive, its techniques may be considered, unpejoratively, as essentially theatrical: certainly they were used to overwhelm the senses and, if not to promote the suspension of disbelief, to promote the suspension of reason inimical to faith – to play directly on the emotions and enhance the illusion of heightened reality. But the theatre of the proscenium arch – the theatre of heightened illusion – was new when the Baroque first flourished early in the 17th century and they developed together – not least through the efforts of the Farnese and the Borghese (see above, pages 32f, 67).[1.17, 1.21]

Light was to play a crucial part. Indeed, beyond the transmogrification of either Daphne or David, the high theatricality of the era's motive is well demonstrated by the dramatic lighting which enhances the emotional impact of divine inspiration in the image of Bernini's Blessed Ludovica

1.21a

1.21b

>1.21 THE 17TH-CENTURY THEATRE AND THEATRICAL ILLUSIONISM: (a, b) Teatro Farnese in the Palazzo della Pilotta, Parma (G.B. Aleotti, from 1618, reconstructed following damage in World War II), auditorium and stage with proscenium arch; (c) scenographic perspective of the Teatro Regio, Turin, in the Bibiena manner (Piero Domenico Oliviero, c. 1740).

1.21c

›1.22 BERNINI AND THE APOTHEOSIS OF THEATRICALITY: (a) Rome, Blessed Lodovica Alberttoni (from 1671); (b) S. Maria della Vittoria, Cornaro Chapel (from 1647).

The Cornaro Chapel, commissioned by Venetian Cardinal Federico in 1645, is conceived as a theatre: the *concetto* is a divine drama seen through the proscenium in the centre by the Cornaro patrons in the boxes on the sides. The audience discusses the performance of a holy mystery, the vision of S. Teresa of Ávila, in reaction to the astonishing spectacle of the saint floating in ecstasy through the light of benediction to union with Christ. Actors and audience are sculpted in the same creamy-white marble, in contrast to the splendid colours of the architecture; beyond the proscenium, the rays of benediction directed to the action are bathed in real light filtered through yellow glass – enhancing the extraordinary expression of the saint – but the supernatural goal is evoked in paint. Sumptuous though it is, the architecture would be meaningless without the participants in the other media: they are bound together in sight and emotion by the theme.

Albertoni viewed through the proscenium arch of her family's chapel in S. Francesco a Ripa (1670s). And theatricality is nowhere more comprehensively sustained than in the miraculous performance which the same supreme entrepreneur staged for the Cornaro in the 1640s – in painting, sculpture and architecture – at S. Maria della Vittoria.[1.22]

1.22a

1.22b

3 ROMAN BAROQUE AT ITS APOGEE

All three of the seminal Baroque masters worked for the Church, of course, and each produced at least one unsurpassed masterpiece on a relatively small scale. Cortona's one complete exercise, Ss. Luca e Martina, is the earliest of these: his later contribution to the front of S. Maria della Pace is also of first-rate significance and his work on both S. Maria in Via Lata and Ss. Ambrogio e Carlo al Corso is highly distinguished. Borromini produced two unrivalled gems, S. Carlo alle Quattro Fontane and S. Ivo alla Sapienza: he was commissioned to complete the important Pamphili church of S. Agnese in Agone in Piazza Navona but he was dismissed before his ideas were fully implemented; he also failed to complete his relatively minor, but highly inventive, projects for S. Maria dei Sette Dolori and S. Andrea delle Fratte. Bernini's parish church of S. Maria Assunta at Ariccia would rate among the best had it been produced by anyone else, but it is totally eclipsed by his late excursion into the genre for S. Andrea al Quirinale. Both Bernini and Borromini were responsible for stupendous schemes of decoration in Rome's premier basilicas, at the Vatican and Lateran respectively. And the supreme talent which Bernini brought to that task also took tomb and chapel design to its apotheosis.[1.22]

The masterpieces of neither Cortona nor Borromini are grand in scale, rich in materials, particularly theatrical in lighting or expanded illusionistically in space but each is highly complex: Cortona's Ss. Luca e Martina in its enclosing fabric, if not its plan; Borromini's S. Carlo and S. Ivo in both plan and fabric. Bernini's S. Maria Assunta at Ariccia is restrained in articulation but his S. Andrea al Quirinale could hardly be more different: extending theatrical spectacle beyond the stage of the Cornaro Chapel in S. Maria della Vittoria, it is exemplary in its propitious opulence.

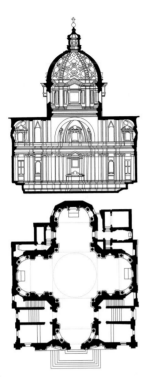

In planning his early masterpiece, Ss. Luca e Martina, Cortona varied a canonical centralized theme. As we shall see, both Borromini and Bernini were more adventurous in their semi-centralized exercises, but neither exceeds the leader of Rome's painting profession in the sculptural quality of his enclosing fabric – the penetration of depth in mass.**1.23a–f**

1.23a, b @ 1:1000

›1.23 PIETRO DA CORTONA AND THE ROMAN CHURCH: (a–f) Ss. Luca e Martina (begun before 1635), section, plan, exterior from west, interior details of reliquary crypt, upper church crossing and apse; (g–i) S. Maria della Pace (from 1656), plan and engraved view of context, elevation; (j, k) S. Maria in Via Lata, façade and vestibule (from 1658); (l, m) Ss. Ambrogio e Carlo al Corso, dome (1668–72), interior to sanctuary, dome interior (for exterior see page 53, top right).

1.23c

Cortona's ecclestical works

The plan of Cortona's church of Ss. Luca e Martina is virtually a Greek cross with apsidal ends: the entrance and sanctuary arms are slightly longer than the others to accommodate doors to ancillary spaces in the corners (not all of which were fully realized). The walls of the latter were designed to back the piers with paired pilasters which seem to press the façade into its characteristically Cortonesque flattened convex bulge: elliptical in the intermediate bays, this is interrupted by the orthogonal central bay. The ground-floor projection is covered by the portal frame but the fenestration of the upper level leaves room for engaged columns: the intermediate bays have pilasters over inset columns before the deeply recessed wall plane but this asserts itself by sending its stringcourse out beyond the columns to the entablature of the portal. In general, the two-storey scheme may be seen as a variant of the 'palace' type but it could hardly be more remote from Giovanni Battista Soria's Classical example.**1.4c**

1.23d

Plasticity is sustained throughout the enclosing fabric. The columnar Ionic Order of the lower façade zone is carried through to the interior, but the rhythm of its disposition is varied in its projection between pilasters at the crossing, as well as its recession behind pilasters in the apses: planes advance and recede as in Ammannati's Florentine church of S. Giovannino and Michelangelo's nearby Ricetto, which it is impossible to imagine that Cortona did not see on his way from his birthplace to Rome as a young apprentice painter (AIC5, pages 108 and 200). However, cutting back through layered

Cortona received the commission for his first church in the early 1630s, not because he had yet made his name as an independent architect but because he was president of the painters' Accademia di San Luca and because his current principal patron, Cardinal Francesco Barberini, was protector of the academy. Since the reign of Sixtus V, the devotions of the academicians had been centred on the ancient church dedicated to the patron saint of painting and built over the Early Christian martyrdom site near the Forum associated with S. Martina: their ambition to rebuild was frustrated for nearly half a century.

In mid-1634 Cortona was permitted to prepare a tomb for himself in the renovation of S. Martina's reliquary crypt. An apsidal chapel, with detached vestibule at the perpendicular junction of the access corridors, was advanced in 1635: its rich embellishment took another decade. At the behest of Cardinal Francesco, work began early in 1635 on the reconstruction of the upper church but there was hiatus while Cortona was in Florence between 1641 and 1647: it was completed in 1650. Thereafter the design of the exterior was revised to incorporate canted side bays: unfortunately this was not followed and the façade, lacking its pediment on Cortona's death in 1669, was finished by others with an undetermined degree of respect for the master's final

1.23e

1.23f

intentions. The same is true of the internal vault embellishment, with its innovative combination of ribs and coffering: the latter deriving from antique shell vaulting in homogeneous concrete, the former from the centring over which masonry is laid.

Ribs and coffering recur in the vault of S. Maria della Pace which Cortona executed from 1657 – the year after renovation to the late-15th-century church was instigated by Pope Alexander VII Chigi, whose family chapel there had been embellished by Raphael. Most significantly, the project entailed the construction of the façade and the carving of a piazza from the tene-

membranes – as into an onion – he exceeds his painted architecture in the extremely intricate patterns of the coffering of the vault. Superimposed on these, moreover, the broken pediments of the clerestory windows are framed by laureate ribs: the virile plays over the inert but the inert is vivified.

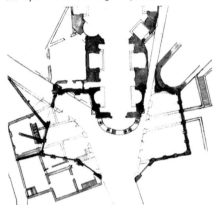

1.23g

The façade of Ss. Luca e Martina was finished after Cortona's death with a highly sculptural cartouche instead of a double pediment like that with which S. Maria della Pace was ultimately endowed.**1.23g–i** The principles of articulation developed for the former, and the profile of convex curvature, were applied to the upper storey of the latter against the broad concave recession of the embracing wings: the triangular pediment encapsulates a segmental one and the papal cartouche invades the entablature. The encapsulation recalls Michelangelo's Porta Pia, from which Cortona drew the Doric consoles and Ionic volute caps for Ss. Luca e Martina's dome. Further, the gravitas of Baldassare Peruzzi's Palazzo Massimo is recalled by the Tuscan Order of doubled columns defining S. Maria's semi-circular portico: recalled too, perhaps, is Peruzzian scenography (AIC5, pages

1.23h

1.23i

152f). The site was a peninsula defined by an alley and a narrow street. As vehicular traffic was confined to the latter, turning space was required in front of the portico at the expense of several houses: the result of the exercise clearly resembles a theatre in the round.

While working on S. Maria della Pace, Cortona was engaged to endow S. Maria in Via Lata with a vestibule and façade of the 'palace' type.**1.23j, k** Facing the ancient arterial Corso on the supposed site of S. Paul's imprisonment, the site prompted development of depth behind the façade rather than exuberance before it: superimposed Orders screen loggias on both levels in dramatic *chiaroscuro* – and with the gravitas of the S. Maria della Pace portico. As there, the lower vestibule recalls Peruzzi's Palazzo Massimo loggia – not least in the way the Order disappears behind the concavity of its apses in the layered manner typical of its author. The upper Order recalls the antique fastigium, here transposed from the celebration of pagan imperium to the proclamation of apostolic apotheosis (AICI, pages 601f).

Cortona's work on the corner of the Corso and Via Lata was completed in 1663. Five years later he had moved further along the antique artery to complete the early 17th-century church of Ss. Ambrogio e Carlo with sanctuary and dome.**1.23l, m** Large in scale, great in remove from the observer, the latter avoids Mannerist flourishes but retains the inset columns of Ss. Luca e Martina's energetic general ordonnance for its eight bays, both inside and out. The ribbed dome recalls Maderno at S. Andrea della Valle but columns in antis reverse the latter's ordonnance and the projection of grouped pilasters in support of an interpolated attic recalls Rosato Rosati's S. Carlo ai Catinari.**1.3f, 1.4c** The exercise may be seen as a sage commentary on its author's own work for Ss. Luca e Martina with its single pilasters and blind attic.

1.23j

ments before it to cope with the entrance and egress of coach traffic whose proliferation was prompted by papal patronage. The scheme was finished in 1661.

Ss. Ambrogio e Carlo al Corso – dedicated to Milan's patron saint and its canonized archbishop Carlo Borromeo – was built for the Arciconfraternita dei Lombardi. Begun in 1612 by Onorio Longhi (1568–1619) and continued by his son Martino the Younger, the main volumes rose over an aisled plan unusual post-Vignola: work stopped at the crossing in 1636. A dome was projected but doubt was entertained about the strength of the basilican structure at the crossing until Cortona was retained to reinforce the piers while completing the tribune from 1668: his scheme for the dome was begun forthwith and followed faithfully to completion after his death the next year – except for the coffering which varies the theme of the nave vault.

1.23k

1.23l

1.23m

BORROMINI'S CHURCHES

If Cortona's complexity is sculptural, Borromini's is essentially architectural: typically, he generated radical forms from elementary geometry. Seen as abandoning the anthropomorphic armature of Vitruvian order, he was deplored as an iconoclast by 'Ancients' committed to academic regulation, and lauded as a prophet by 'Moderns' inspired by the flight of individual genius. Few now would deny that the little interior he devised for S. Carlo alle Quattro Fontane – S. Carlino – and the rather larger one with which he distinguished S. Ivo alla Sapienza are among the most vibrant spaces ever produced.**1.24**

›1.24 FRANCESCO BORROMINI AND THE ROMAN CHURCH: (a–h) S. Carlino (from 1634), original project drawing for the conventual complex, lateral section through church and cloister, cortile, interior from entrance to altar, details of vaulting, exterior project drawing and general view; (i, j) S. Maria dei Sette Dolori (from 1641), plan and interior; (k–q) Oratorio di S. Filippo Neri (1637–40), façade and project drawing (*DR*), plan with (1) church, (2) oratory, (3) court, (4) sacristy, lateral section, interior oratory detail, Sala di Ricreazione fireplace and façade detail; (r, s) Collegio di Propaganda Fide (after 1647, on the complex as a whole see page 109), chapel, interior project drawing and detail; (t–w) S. Ivo alla Sapienza (1643–48, decorated from 1659), engraved axonometric section and original plan drawing, exterior and interior of dome, project for west front and detail; (x) S. Andrea delle Fratte (c. 1655), tower; (y, z) S. Agnese in Agone, project plan and elevation, foundation record of twin-towered façade with dome (after 1653).

The conventual complex of S. Carlino, at the junction of Via del Quirinale and the Strada Felice (endowed with four fountains, now Via delle Quattro Fontane) was begun in 1634, with some help from the Barberini, for

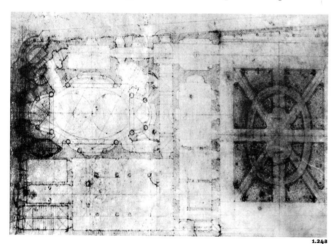

1.24a

S. Carlino: Trinitarian geometry and the ellipse

The preliminary planning drawings reveal the complex of equilateral triangles and circles which generate the core ellipse and its extrusions. In concert, syncopated rhythm modulates movement in the enclosing fabric: the Classical module governs the proportions of the Order, of course, but its orthodox extension to the intercolumniations cedes to the Trinitarian geometry – heterodox in Classical terms but essentially Christian and archetypical of Gothic practice. Yet an antique precedent for this type of complexity in volume and vaulting is to be found in the Piazza d'Oro of Hadrian's Villa at Tivoli (AIC1, page 632).

1.24b

1.24d

1.24e

1.24f

the Discalced Spanish Trinitarians – an extremely poor Order dedicated to redeeming Christian slaves from the Moors. The mendicants' accommodation and cloister – a witty miniature variation of the grand serliana schemes of Milan (see page 60) – were built first. The church was under construction by 1638 but not completed with its façade until after the architect's death some thirty years later: the original project drawings show that the undulating exterior and interior were evolved together, organically, in plan and the lower storey of the façade had been built accordingly from 1665; the upper storey seems to have been completed after 1667 at the whim of Borromini's nephew, Bernardo Castelli – the oval cartouche recalls the altarpiece designed earlier by Bernini for S. Lorenzo in Lucina.

Borromini's concept is wilfully ambiguous: though the volume is bifocal, the articulation responds to the logic of quatrelobe centralization. The dominant entrance/altar axis and the transept both terminate in apses, the former semi-circular, the latter elliptical in response to the elongation of the plan; between these cross arms are piers supporting the pendentives which carry the oval dome over the corners. The Corinthian columns of the altar and entrance apses wilfully become Composite in the elliptical sides: thus, while the geometry denies consistency of intercolumniation to the two forms of apse, the concerted change of Order disconcerts the piers. Hence the vibrant rhythm: different in the curvature of

1.24c

plan and elevation, the apses assert themselves as two pairs, each articulated with four columns (b/A/b and b'/A'/b'). On the other hand, the altar and entrance bays provide caesuras in the articulation between four sets of three bays, each also defined by four columns though in pairs of the two styles (b/c/b', b'/c/b, etc.). Despite this, the continuity of the entablature throughout the whole indented perimeter may be seen (after Wittkower, *Art and Architecture in Italy, 1600–1750*) as forcing the syncopated integration of the two alternating systems (b/A/b/c/b'/A'/b'/c, etc., and A/b/c/b'/A'/b'/c/b, etc.).

Though its plan is essentially oblong (with curved ends), S. Maria dei Sette Dolori is related to S. Carlino in internal ordonnance: as there, too, semi-circular and semi-elliptical recessions terminate the main and cross axes respectively.**1.24d, j** However, the introduction of the antique fastigium motif over the apses produces an undulating cornice below compartmentalized vaulting in which dazzling complexity is not promoted in form or coffering. In contrast, S. Carlino's coffering is hardly less dazzling than the contrapuntal rhythms of its general ordonnance: in each pair of apses – semi-circular and semi-elliptical – it is varied in trapezoidal graduation to effect the illusion of similar depth; above all, in the diminishing tiers of the main dome an ingenious web of octagons and hexagons asserts the cross.

The façade of S. Maria dei Sette Dolori – in which the elliptical curve counters the interior elevation – was never embellished. The façade of S. Carlino was completed after Borromini's death but the plan is original – indeed the only element foreign to the master's repertoire is the crowning cartouche. The composition of the two storeys – each with a minor Order combined with a major one spaced in the b/c/b rhythm of the interior – provides the consummate demonstration of the alternative to stepped progression for the generation of movement in mass: serpentine undulation thrusts the centre forward in a convex curve to accommodate the niche of S. Carlo and his asymmetrical guardian angels above the entrance; this is countered to resonant effect with a concave curve in the centre of the upper storey but that is again countered, and crescendo achieved, with the interpolation of an oval pavilion.

1.24g

1.24h

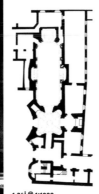

1.24i @ 1:1000

Long before the front elevation of S. Carlino was begun, but while it was in the general planning stage, Borromini revised the standard Roman ecclesiastical façade formula in secular terms for a block of public facilities provided by the Oratorians beside their Chiesa Nuova (S. Maria in Vallicella): the fit was inexact.**1.24k-q** The seeds planted at the Barberini palace site came to fruition here, in whole and in part: the concavity may be seen to derive from curving out the canted corners of the attic windows; coffering recurs in false perspective; the segmental and triangular elements of Cortona's theatre portal emerge in fusion for the pediment. Behind this screen, the main volume

1.24j
The S. Maria dei Sette Dolori scheme was produced in 1641 for its Augustinian community but Borromini delegated its execution to Antonio del Grande under pressure of other work, not least for the Oratorians. For the block next to their church, S. Maria in Vallicella (Chiesa Nuova), they had commissioned accommodation incorporating a library and concert hall – the oratory itself. Before Borromini replaced him in 1637, Paolo Maruscelli had determined the disposition: beyond the

1.24l

1.24k

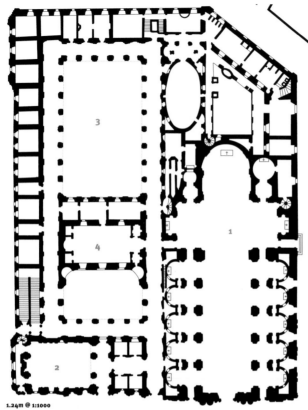

1.24m @ 1:1000

1.24n

block containing the public facilities, which naturally addressed the piazza, he extended a cloistered court to the depth of the site and divided it with a sacristy in line with the cross axis of the church. Also perpendicular to the latter but comparable in extent, the new block had clearly to be subordinate yet Borromini chose to endow it with a competitive façade: a church/palace hybrid (of brick rather than stone) centred not on the oratory at ground level within but on the court beyond. A reduced variant – or, rather, preliminary version – forms the Filamarino altar in Santi Apostoli, Naples.

The proposition that the generation of concave form was internal to Borromini's œuvre is not necessarily contradicted by the possibility that he knew of Francesco Maria Ricchino's Collegio Elvetico built ten years earlier than the Oratorian façade (ten years after he had left Milan for Rome): unlike Ricchino – but like Antonio da Sangallo at the concave end of the Palazzo della Zecca – Borromini deploys superimposed pilaster Orders (a variation on the Ionic and a more regular Corinthian); like Ricchino, however, he heightens the impact of elliptical curvature by countering concavity with convexity in the central portal bay of the ground floor. He does it again

1.140

extends laterally: a rectangular room with a canted pilaster across each corner, it is vaulted over a network of broad, flat diagonal ribs whose trajectory is curtailed by the oval frame of an illusionist fresco. In the context of Michelangelo's Capitoline type of ordonnance, that skeletal formula was expanded and enriched in the next decade for remodelling the chapel of the Collegio di Propaganda Fide: paired ribs over paired pilasters span from curved corners to contracted bays in the centres of the long sides, producing an hexagonal frame for the rays of divine wisdom emanating from the Holy Spirit.**1.24r, s**

1.24p   **1.24q**

in the elliptical Sala di Ricreazione with the extrordinary convex fireplace – a huge tent-like confection hung with a mock-Doric valence whose metopes are emblazoned with Oratorian symbols.

1.24r   **1.24s**

1.24u

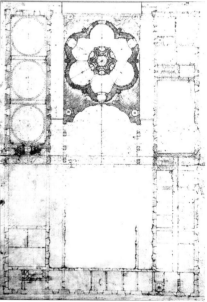

1.24t

S. Ivo: Trinitarian geometry and the hexagon

While work was in progress at S. Carlino, Borromini was commissioned to insert a chapel into the court of S. Ivo alla Sapienza, built by Giacomo della Porta late in the previous century.**1.24t–w** As we have seen, S. Carlino's elliptical plan was generated from two tangential circles inscribed in two contiguous equilateral triangles: the stellar plan of S. Ivo encapsulates one circle in two overlapping equilateral triangles, forming the six-pointed star symbolizing wisdom (*sapienza*). The points of the star, truncated for the entrance and the chapels flanking the sanctuary, cede to apses for the latter and the chapels flanking the former. These alternately concave and convex forms are generated by commensurate circles described alternately about the points of one triangle and the centres of the hexagonal sides clipping

1.24V

From 1643 Borromini was busy at the site of the Sapienza. Dedicated to the University of Rome by Pope Eugenius IV in the 1430s, the complex had been redeveloped in the second half of the 16th century by Pirro Ligorio and Giacomo della Porta. The latter's plans for a circular chapel unrealized, Borromini was commissioned to insert an alternative into the designated space at the head of the cloister: building took five years, embellishment another ten.

the other: framed in elevation by a freely interpreted Corinthian Order of pilasters – again in alternating rhythms below the staunchly binding entablature – these aspire to the formation of the extraordinary faceted dome in disdain for the intermediacy of a drum. The star of wisdom spangles the vault at its angles and rings the oculus of the lantern but the sleight of hand required to effect transition from the convex bays to the contrary arc of the culminatory circle is masked by Chigi insignia and cherubim.

Through those cherubim, sculpture becomes architecture less obviously than on the façade of S. Carlino but the transmutation is quite phenomenal in the superstructure. A drum partially encloses the dome to counter its lateral thrust – in the manner familiar to Milan – but it is hexafoil: like those of the Milanese cathedral's crown, flying buttresses rise from clustered pilasters in the groins to support the lantern. That is a tempietto with concave bays on which wisdom turns in elevation to the Tower of Babel and resolves its discord in the cross-crowned orb.

1.24W

The inspiration for S. Ivo's lantern may well have ranged from a fantastical reconstruction of the Biblical monument to the *capricii* on antique themes published by Giovan Battista Montano: its drum comes directly from records of antique survivals like the Temple of Venus at Baalbek (AICI, page 600). Another variation on that theme, with columns replaced by cherubic caryatids as later on the façade of S. Carlino, provides the most arresting element of the tower of Borromini's unfinished church of S. Andrea delle Fratte: with its several zones progressing from the rectangular to the cylindrical, the tower itself recalls an antique funerary type widely popular in the Mediterranean littoral. The drum enclosing the dome recalls the Conocchia mausoleum of Capua but varies it by contrasting curve with counter-curve (AICI, pages 646ff).**1.24X**

The mellifluous form finally given to S. Carlino's façade is a further variation on the antique: it echoes forms preserved in remote Petra but not now in the field surveyed by the progenitors of Baroque Rome. The superimposition of the elliptical dome over the counter-elliptical recession in the façade of S. Agnese in Agone in Piazza Navona is another variant on a grander scale and still further variation would have informed the towers there – had Borromini been allowed to complete the project above cornice level.**1.24y, z**

Commissioned in 1646 by Pope Innocent X to transform the interior of the antique Lateran basilica, Borromini responded again by deploying a repertory of techniques derived from the more heterodox reaches of the antique. As we have noted, purely architectural illusionism played its part in the stunning diversity of form devised for the monuments of the many popes displaced from the aisles by the renovation work: as always with Borromini, complexity of form and crisp detail – much of it in white stucco – is preferred to the chromaticism of rich materials, except for the grey marble aedicules designed to accommodate the

1.24X
Innocent X accorded the commission for S. Agnese to Girolamao Rainaldi and his son Carlo in 1652: they devised an octagon overlaid with the apsidal arms of a Greek cross and preceded by an elongated vestibule behind a planar façade which was soon seen as encroaching too far on to the piazza. By the middle of 1653, when construction had surpassed the niches in the canted corners, they had been displaced by Borromini: he demolished the basic structure of the façade to pursue a concave alternative with reduced vestibule but lateral extension for twin towers; inside,

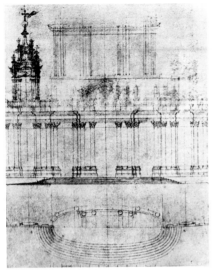

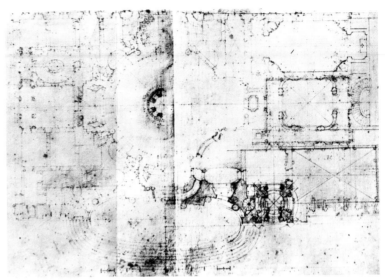

he regulated the core octagon with columns attached to the great piers but stressed the syncopation of its great and small arches below the enhanced drum of the dome. Early in 1657, two years after the death of the patron, construction had reached the cornice of the façade and the oculus of the dome but Borromini was constrained to resign. Reinstated, Carlo Rainaldi revised what he could, especially the embellishment of the interior, the elevation of the towers and the articulation of the lantern (see page 111).

Bernini was involved by 1666 and called for the orthodox replacement of the heterodox compound pediment devised by Borromini for the façade. For the loss of the virile towers, S. Andrea delle Fratte offers considerable compensation.

apostles in the piers.[1.25, 1.17d, 1.18c] The contrast with Rainaldi's approach to the completion of S. Agnese is marked: with the exercise on which Bernini was currently preoccupied in S. Pietro it could hardly be greater.[1.26]

BERNINI V. BORROMINI

Perfectly meeting the aspirations of Pope Urban VIII (1623–44), Bernini was accorded the greatest commission of the era – the embellishment of the interior of S. Pietro after its completion to Maderno's plans. His connivance at perceived extravagance attracted much opprobrium on the demise of the Barberini regime and he was temporarily eclipsed under Innocent X Pamphili (1644–55) by Borromini. Proving unwilling to direct the creative flow to definitive outcome, at least at the centre of the pope's personal concerns on the Piazza Navona, Borromini had lost favour before the end of the Pamphili pontificate and was in part supplanted by Bernini. The new pope, Alexander VII Chigi (1655–70) preferred Bernini – if certainly not to the total disadvantage of Pietro da Cortona.

›**1.25 ROME, S. GIOVANNI IN LATERANO RENOVATION,** 1646: (a) elevation project, (b) nave to east.

Much restored and rebuilt over more than a millennium from its foundation by Emperor Constantine, the cathedral of Rome at the Lateran was again dilapidated more than two centuries after its restoration by Martin V following the return of the papacy from Avignon: Innocent X conceived the project to commemorate the church jubilee of 1650. Instructed to preserve the venerable structure in working to that strict deadline, Borromini removed every third column of the main arcades and encapsulated the remaining pairs in piers. Three alternatives were devised for these: the pope rejected secondary open bays with flat lintels in

1.25b

favour of magnificent marble aedicules incorporating antique columns from the old aisles and housing the Apostles (after designs of Carlo Maratta from 1703). A vault was projected on the cross-ribbed lines of the Propaganda Fide chapel but Pius IV's splendid coffered ceiling (attributed to Pirro Ligorio) was retained. So too were the old crossing and sanctuary which had not been touched when the Holy Year dawned. After that, Borromini directed his extraordinary ingenuity to varying the articulation of the displaced peripheral papal monuments.**1.17d, 1.18c**

BERNINI'S ECCLESIASTICAL WORKS

Bernini's career as a papal architect began under Urban VIII with the commission to embellish the crossing within the basilica of S. Pietro; it culminated under Alexander VII with the commission to order the congregational space in front of the basilica and embrace the faithful gathered there for benediction in body or in spirit. In both theatres the constraints – exerted by existing building and by ideology – were formidable and Bernini's response demonstrates conclusively (if demonstration were needed) that it is constraint which makes great architecture.**1.26**

›1.26 BERNINI IN S. PIETRO: (a) tomb of Urban VIII (1628–47), (b) tomb of Alexander VII (1671–78), (c) the crossing and its baldacchino over the supposed site of S. Peter's grave (from 1624), (d) *cathedra Petri* (from 1656), (e) Holy Cross chapel portal (*DR*).

The construction of the nave, completed to Maderno's controversial plans in 1614, reiterated Michelangelo's respect for Bramante's ordonnance and coffered vaulting: high-relief sculptures of the Christian virtues had been introduced to the spandrels of the new arcade in 1599. A generation later Urban VIII commissioned Bernini to complete the programme of enrichment in this context and exercise his originality in providing the monumental baldacchino over the supposed site of S. Peter's entombment: this materialized between 1624 and 1633. By then, too, Bernini had transformed the crossing piers which accommodated receptacles for the four great relics of the Vatican basilica: a fragment of the True Cross; the lance, wielded by S. Longinus before his conversion, which pierced the side of Christ; the veil with which S. Veronica had mopped Christ's brow as he hauled the cross up the hill to Calvary; the head of S. Peter's brother, S. Andrew. Each of these is represented with its saint in a niche in the base of its pier – Bernini himself contributing the image of S. Longinus – and above in the hands of an angel in the richly chromatic aedicules incorporating the antique Solomonic columns from the Constantinian basilica.

1.26a, b

Achieving S. Pietro: the apotheosis of embellishment

Bernini was commissioned in 1624 by Pope Urban VIII to embellish the great Vatican basilica, as transformed by Maderno but articulated by Michelangelo in the colossal style introduced by Bramante: he was also to glorify the last resting place of the dedicatee at the crossing in the context of shrines for the church's most sacred relics. More than thirty years later he was commissioned by Pope Alexander VII to devise a high altar in the apse enshrining the supposed chair of S. Peter. He responded in general with a rich revetment of coloured marbles. If in this he followed lines first drawn over a century earlier, his originality in meeting the specific requirements of the crossing and the apse was liberated to prodigious effect.

Throughout the great volume, according to the time of day, light streams from the clerestory windows in shafts, caressing the texture of the marble, enhancing its colour, selecting a saint in his niche or a pope on his monument as a spotlight selects an actor on a stage to special dramatic effect. In the apse at the end, however, the natural light is filtered through yellow glass to become the radiance of the Holy Ghost and the rays are materialized with cherubs in gilded stucco as the culmination of the entire decorative scheme, glorifying the reliquary of the chair of S. Peter held supreme by the Fathers of the Church. Light, real and simulated, charges form and its ambience with life. But form is made to move as well in the identity of sculpture and architecture.

The torsion of the Solomonic columns of the aedicules in which the four great relics were enshrined – recycled, or at least restyled, from the Constantinian basilica – was resoundingly amplified in the forging of supports for the baldacchino. Deposited by angels under the great dome over the tomb of the apostle, its cross and orb raised high over volutes, its valence swarming with the papal bees and cherubs, this phenomenal exercise in architectural sculpture is made of heavy bronze. However, the malleable nature of the material – and the venerable allusion to the temple of Jerusalem – has inspired Bernini to lend an unprecedented sense of mobility to monumental structure: at once it aspires to float into the dome or progress down the nave like a portable canopy: in any case, it complements the Order of its context triumphantly.

Bernini augmented his work in S. Pietro with the tombs of his two great papal patrons: Urban VIII and Alexander VII. His work on the former spanned nearly twenty years, the latter took half that time. The *concetto* of death curling back the canopy to reveal the later pope's sepulchre is the more startling but neither has ever been surpassed in the richness of materials or equalled in the brilliance of sculpture and integrity of iconography.

1.26d

Work on the apse began with the tomb of Urban VIII in 1628, and extended thirty years later to the *cathedra Petri* at the behest of Alexander VII: held above the altar by the colossal bronze statues of saints Augustine, Jerome, Ambrose and Gregory the Great, the ancient chair encapsulated in bronze has been associated with the throne of the Carolingian emperor Charles the Bald and dated to 877. The dazzling spectacle was finally revealed in 1666.

1.26e

1.26c

Of the three Roman High Baroque masters of church architecture on the small scale, Bernini was last in the field with his glorious S. Andrea al Quirinale, begun in 1658 for the Jesuit novitiate. Apart from his early work on S. Bibiana, notable for its aedicular façade, this was preceded by S. Tommaso di Villanova at Castel Gandolfo and S. Maria Assunta at Ariccia. As these works admirably demonstrate – the former built over a Greek cross, the latter over a circle – Bernini preferred centralized geometry: in stark contrast to Borromini, however, he was essentially conservative in his Classicism of form and ordonnance. Subtle in plan on the other hand, S. Andrea set a standard of opulent theatricality which was exceeded only on the exceptionally grand scale of his embellishment to S. Pietro.**1.27**

Panelled in pink marble and articulated with canonical Corinthian pilasters, S. Andrea is oval but the shallow site forced Bernini to use the figure against the purpose which originally recommended it to Vignola: the long axis runs counter to the canonical predominance of the approach to the altar and is sealed with a pilaster at either end, to

›1.27 BERNINI'S CHURCHES: (a) S. Bibiana, façade (c. 1625); (b–d) Castel Gandolfo, S. Tommaso di Villanova (1656–61), exterior, interior and detail of altar; (e–h) Ariccia, S. Maria Assunta (1662–24), plan, perspective view of context, section, detail of interior; (i–n) Rome, S. Andrea al Quirinale (from c. 1658), plan and section, lateral, longitudinal and vertical interior axes, exterior.

The restoration of S. Bibiana's church was ordered by Urban VIII following the recovery of her relics from the foundations of her Early Christian sanctuary in 1624. Bernini collaborated (as sculptor) with Pietro da Cortona (as painter) on the interior embellishment: in his first bold move as architect he superimposed the double-height aedicule on the arcaded 'palace' type of façade most nearly represented by Giovanni Battista Soria's academic exercise for S. Gregorio Magno al Celco – rather than Maderno's invigoration of the basilican form for S. Susanna.

In 1658 Alexander VII canonized Thomas of Villanova (1488–55), a particularly pious servant of the early Counter Reformation. Bernini was commissioned to mark the event with a chapel detached from the main papal complex at Castel Gandolfo: as with Giovanni da Sangallo's S. Maria delle Carceri at Prato, the Greek-cross geometry is strict in plan – each arm is half the square of the crossing but the latter extends beyond the ideal cube in elevation – and the ordonnance is severe. However, relief from the strict tectonic discipline is provided by the angels of the high altar, the evangelists of the pendentives and, above all, the coffering of the dome overlaid with ribs – in the Cortonesque manner – between garlanded putti upholding medallion images of events in the saint's life.

Alexander VII's nephew, Cardinal Flavio Chigi, commissioned Bernini to build a parish church at Ariccia in 1662, the year after he had acquired and renovated the Albani palace there. Opposite the castle, this min-

1.27d

1.27c

1.27b

iature Pantheon was set in a semi-circular context like the faux antique 'Temple of Honour and Virtue':[1.18a] it was to address a piazza but the contours of the site inhibited strict axial alignment. Internally, a ring of chapels is gauged from the cylindrical mass which provides direct support for the hemispherical dome, as in the great antique model: the sequence is offset by the slightly larger sanctuary apse and corresponding entrance vestibule – to the subtle subversion of logic at the service of liturgy. The Corinthian articulation is purely Classical but, again, relief is mainly provided by the coffering of the dome overlaid with ribs rising from the Chigi crest and angels or putti affixing garlands to broken pediments in festive preparation for the drama to which the church is dedicated – the assumption of the Virgin into the dome of heaven.

The church of the Jesuit novitiate on the Via Pia (now Via del Quirinale) was rebuilt at the instigation of Alexander VII but with funds initially provided by the nephew of the late Pope Innocent X, Prince Camillo Pamphili. So that service could continue uninterrupted, the old church was retained and Bernini moved east to a restricted new site – its longer axis parallel to

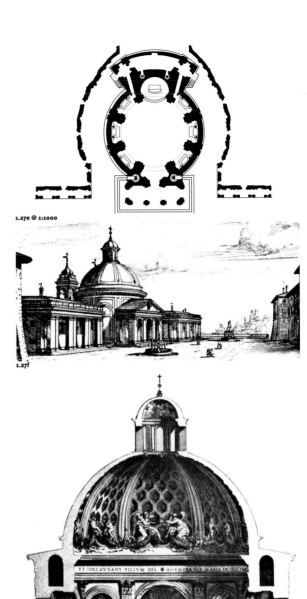

1.27e @ 1:1000

1.27f

1.27g

1.27h

neutralize it; the short axis extends from the convex portico into the concave sanctuary. The oval body is revealed beyond the concave forecourt and its entablature embraces the great pedimented aedicule which frames the projecting portico: there is a precise Montano precedent.**1.18b** But the greatest significance of Bernini's work may be seen as extra-architectural – extra-terrestrial even.

The theme of the saint's martyrdom and apotheosis – the *concetto* – is dramatically extended through the space of the church itself. Through the proscenium which frames the sanctuary, echoing the portal but enveloped in gorgeous marble, the congregation witnesses the saint's martyrdom in the painting over the altar. Through the oculus of the sanctuary dome (invisible from the auditorium), putti sent from heaven with the rays of glory lead

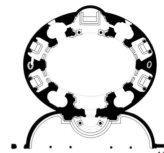

1.27i @ 1:1000

the street. Thus disposing his ellipse, Bernini followed the precedent he had set himself in the chapel of the Collegio de Propaganda Fide but there the entrance was from a vestibule at the opening of the long axis. To assert the opposite here, the ring of perimeter chapels is interrupted for the apsidal sanctuary and correspondingly widened entrance vestibule as at Ariccia – but with rectangular and elliptical variety, varied in lighting. The model was presented to the patrons in September 1658: construction was completed in 1661.

1.27k

1.27l

1.27j

the saint's soul from his painted crucifixion to epiphany in the great sculpture on the pediment of the proscenium and pave the way across the celestial dome to the lantern of the Holy Ghost. Never was the idea of the church as the theatre of Grace more consistently sustained. Never was the image of the Church Triumphant more resplendently displayed.[1.28]

1.27n

1.17m

Vatican environment

Nicholas V had begun the formal ordering of the space before the Constantinian basilica with the benediction loggia attributed to Alberti (c. 1450)
but he did not progress far with his plans to redevelop the Borgo between
new piazzas in front of the basilica and beside the Castel Sant'Angelo (AIC5,
page 139). Nothing was done to ameliorate the situation until one of the
projected new arteries was realized by Alexander VI as the Via Alessandrina
(Borgo Nuovo): to be lined with the palazzi of the papal entourage – after the
incomplete example of the town of Pienza – its formal order would provide
a fitting processional way for visitors to the pontiff but the old main artery
(Borgo Vecchio) and the areas at either end were incompletely ordered. The
open ground before the basilica and the benediction loggia sloped downwards towards the obelisk erected by Domenico Fontana for Sixtus V (in
1585): it was constrained at an oblique angle by the latter's S. Damaso wing
of the palace to the north. Above all, it was constrained by the façade of the
basilica which seemed too long for its height in the absence of the towers
intended for its flanks. All these considerations informed Bernini's scheme,
commissioned by Alexander VII in 1656, for an elliptical piazza linked to the
basilica by a trapezoidal forecourt.

 The theme of extending the arms of the mother church to embrace
the faithful – the rationale or *concetto* of the entire pontifical project as
articulated by Bernini himself – was resoundingly achieved by the ellipse
defined by twin colonnades: each has a central passage through doubled
rows of Doric columns which appear as one from the twin focuses of the
geometry. The columns were immense but the height to which they raised
the entablature – uncanonically Ionic to avoid minor vertical accents inimical to the felicity of embrace – cleared the view of the papal benediction
whether administered from the basilica's loggia or a window of the Sistine palace wing. A similar segmental range was projected to close the
piazza to the east, screening it from the unreformed Borgo either on the
perimeter of the ellipse or beyond another trapezoidal forecourt: neither
was ever to be realized to the advantage of the surprise which must have
overwhelmed the unsuspecting pilgrim on emergence from constriction to
expansion, from dark to light, before the unfortunate construction of the
Via della Conciliazione in the 20th century.

1.28b

1.28a

In elevation, the canted wings of the forecourt are diminished with the rising ground to enhance the apparent height of the basilica's façade – to compensate for its adventitious width. At the head of the corridor in the northern wing, at its junction with the narthex of the basilica, is a vestibule which closes the lateral axis with an equestrian statue of Constantine at the moment of his enlightenment. The emperor is backed by a windswept curtain whose deflected momentum encouraged ascent through the adjacent triumphal serliana up the Scala Regia, the route taken by monarchs to visit the pontiff. The constraints imposed by existing building on the design process as a whole were at their tightest where a new staircase was required to match the gravitas of the new approach: to reach the level of the Sala Regia at the head of the pontifical apartments, the flights had to turn on themselves at a landing in an increasingly narrow gap between the palace and the Sistine Chapel adjacent to Maderno's nave.

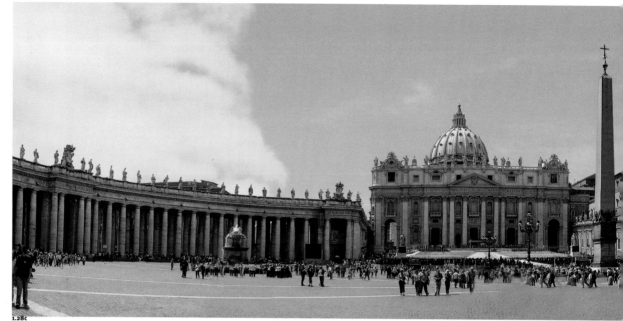

1.28c

In his scheme for the Scala Regia, Bernini is usually seen as having staged a false-perspective exercise – of the type deployed by Borromini at the Palazzo Spada**1.17c, d** – to give the illusion of greater length to the lower flight by diminishing the height of the ascending columns. Yet it would seem odd that he – or anyone else – would wish to increase the apparent length, and therefore the apparent arduousness, of a ceremonial staircase. In fact he had limited control over its elevation in whole or part and diminished the

>**1.28 BERNINI AT THE VATICAN:** (a–e) Piazza San Pietro, views before and after opening of the Via della Conciliazione, general view, engraved views of scheme with and without central colonnade; (f–h) Scala Regia plan, section, perspective view.

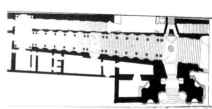

1.28f

1.28d

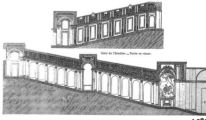

1.28g

height of the columns as they ascended the lower flight because he had no choice. Naturally the ascent had to be in felicitous gradations from the base level of the basilica's narthex and its vestibule to the Sala Regia on the piano nobile of the adjoining palace: the height of the lower portal was determined by the former, the upper one by the latter; there could, of course, be no discrepancy in the height of the tunnels where they joined the median landing, side by side, and the upper flight could hardly have been lower at

1.28h   1.28e

that end than at the top. Thus he had to diminish the height of his lower colonnades progressively. On the other hand, because the chasm in which he was operating narrowed, his main concern was with apparent width at the median landing – with countering its diminution – and this he addressed by setting the columns progressively closer to the wall. It was in fact to counter the unwanted sense of extra length (resulting from the diminution of the columns) and to enhance the desired sense of greater width (resulting from the diminution of the space between column and wall) that Bernini sought to confuse the eye with light introduced not only at the median landing but from half way up the side of the lower flight.

URBI ET ORBI

Maderno's basilica, with the giant Order of its façade projected forward and achieving a resounding climax in its progression from pilasters to columns in the centre, was enhanced by its reformed precinct as the dominant element in an enormous exercise of urbanism: Bernini's projection of the triumph of the Counter-Reformation Church on the vertical plane of the baldacchino, covering the apostle's tomb, was complemented on the horizontal plane extending from the apse of the *cathedra Petri*, out through Maderno's temple front to the greatest piazza the world had seen since Classical antiquity – embracing the faithful emergent from their tortuous path to the grace of benediction. Thus, far surpassing a Roman prospect, it is the culmination of a stupendous axis, the conceptual axis of the Catholic Church.

Baroque dynamics, generated in mass and projected through space, brooked no arrest of progress to the ultimate goal: the Baroque concept of the dynamic axis is the antithesis of the diversified context of 16th-century urbanism, where the incident of square or fountain, statue or obelisk, is at least as important as the central line: that proved impossible to generate in the urban fabric of the Rome of Sixtus V, and delightful incident continued to be staged to enhance inherited space – not least by Bernini.[1.29] However, the

1.29e

1.29d

>**1.29 BERNINI, CIVIC AND DOMESTIC WORK:** (a–d) Piazza Navona, general view, Fontana dei Quattro Fiumi and detail of Ganges, Fontana del Moro; (e) Piazza della Minerva, obelisk from the adjacent monastery garden erected in 1667 for Alexander VII by Bernini on the back of the elephant symbol of divine wisdom and strength; (f) Piazza d'Espagna, Fontana della Barcaccia; (g) Ponte Sant'Angelo (Hadrianic bridge refurbished and embellished with angels by Bernini from 1667 for Clement IX); (h, i) Palazzo Montecitorio (1650–54, completed from 1694, extended to the rear from 1871 for the new Italian kingdom's chamber of deputies), plan and piazza front; (j) Palazzo Chigi (from 1664), 17th-century engraving of façade in its original form.

1.29b

1.29a

1.29g

conditions inimical to this served to enhance the impact of Bernini's Vatican scheme – emergence into its expansive ellipse from the restriction of the irregular Borgo would have been a *coup de théâtre* of the first magnitude.

1.29f

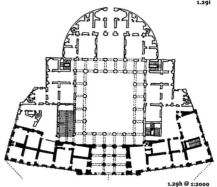

1.29i

THE SEMINAL MASTERS AND THE PALAZZO

Beyond the axis of the faith, Bernini produced seminal palace façade designs. So too did Cortona. And each made a major contribution to international developments in projects for the king of France – as we shall see in context. All their works were either unrealized, unfortunately altered or lost altogether but all were articulated with colossal Orders. If the application of the colossal Order to the exterior of a vast volume like that of S. Pietro accords fully with the Albertian ideal of *concinnitas* – and Vitruvian propriety – its adaptation to secular building is problematical: one has only to compare Bramante's Palazzo Caprini with the typical Baroque approach – as best represented by Bernini's designs for both Rome and Paris variously inspired by Michelangelo – to see immediately that man

1.29h @ 1:2000

Innocent X commissioned Bernini to build the Palazzo Montecitorio for the Ludovisi in 1650 but interrupted the work four years later after quarrelling with the intended recipient: completion waited until after 1694, when Innocent XII entrusted it to Bernini's protégé, Carlo Fontana. The gigantic stones which displace rustication at base level and the colossal Order, which far surpasses the secular precedents provided by Sangallo or Michelangelo in scale, survive from Bernini's scheme, as does the tripartite division of the piazza front into a slightly projecting central block flanked by canted wings with barely projecting end bays.

Alexander VII's nephew Flavio Chigi bought the Palazzo Colonna-Ludovisi on Piazza Santi Apostoli in 1661. Bernini was commissioned to reform the façade in 1664. The result was again tripartite in composition but the orthogonal wings are entirely rusticated in subservience to the colossal Composite Order of the main block: as in few of its rare predecessors, this encompasses two full storeys. The building was doubled for the Odescalchi in the 18th century.

›1.30 CORTONA AND THE ROMAN PALAZZO:
(a, b) projects for a Chigi fountain palace (1659).

Two years before Flavio Chigi settled on the Piazza Santi Apostoli, his brother Agostino had bought the incomplete former Palazzo Aldobrandini on the Piazza Colonna. Pietro da Cortona seems to have been invited to provide a scheme for the head of the piazza, perpendicular to the unresolved flank of the palace front. Involving considerable expropriation and demolition of properties intruding on to the site, realization was preempted by the sale of the major sector to the Ludovisi by the Barnabites in December 1659.

Cortona offered at least two variants with a fountain in the basement supporting a colossal Order which rises through piano nobile and mezzanine to an attic in the manner of the Palazzo dei Senatori on the Campidoglio (AIC5, pages 164ff). One, with alternatives of single or double pilasters, is orthogonal with a triad of lightly projecting arcaded bays above the fountain and similar single-bay projections to each side: a related half-elevation may have been for the perpendicular return along the north side of the piazza where the palace façade remained undressed. The more spectacular variant accommodates the fountain in a typically Cortonesque flattened elliptical recession with an Order of Doric columns culminating in a triumphal arch: the concave curve is to be found in Borromini's S. Agnese in Agone but Cortona provided his own precedents at S. Maria della Pace, even the Villa Pigneto Sacchetti; the columnar ordonnance extending to the triumphal-arch motif derives from his reconstruction studies of the Temple of Fortuna Primigenia at Palestrina (see page 64).

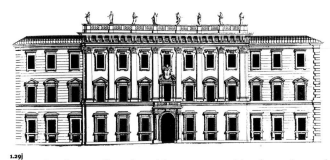

1.29j

has been eclipsed on his own ground by forces beyond him, and protean strength overwhelms discretion (see also pages 280ff, and AIC4, page 857).**1.30**

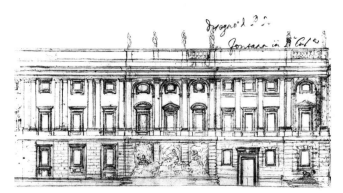

1.30a

1.30b

Borromini's involvement in the secular field is limited. His most important commission was the Pamphili palace on the Piazza Navona but he fell from favour with Innocent X before his design was resolved – indeed because

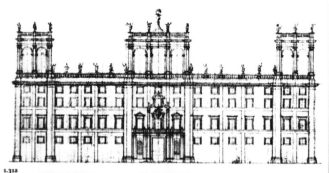

1.31a

1.31b

1.31c

›1.31 BORROMINI'S PALACES: (a, b) Palazzo Pamphili, unexecuted façade project (from 1646), gallery with vault by Cortona; (c, d) Collegio di Propaganda Fide, façade of extension to existing building (evolved 1646–62), general view and detail; (e) Palazzo Falconieri, river front of city palace with belvedere (from 1646).

At the Propaganda Fide – where the façade extends from the ecclesiastical to the domestic – heightened impact is drawn from compressing concavity into the

1.31d

portal bay between orthogonal ranges – and countering the concavity of the latters' aedicular windows with the convexity of the more complex central one. The alternating aedicular variations on the entablature theme first stated in the Palazzo Barberini attic (and in the portal attributed to Cortona there) are notable: so too is the inverted tapering of the polygonal columns of the portal (in the manner of Michelangelo); so too, again, is the conflation of capital and entablature over the colossal pilasters rising through the blind bays of the ground floor and mezzanine.

Orazio Falconieri commissioned Borromini to remodel his mid-16th-century palace on the Via Giulia when he acquired the neighbouring site in 1645: he ordered the extended street front with novel falcon-headed herms and repeated the portal, designed stunning stucco embellishment for the interior and extended wings towards the river flanking a court overlooked by a belvedere. Completing an ordonnance ascending from low and abstract to high and complex, in reverse of the normal progression from piano nobile to attic, the belvedere stands out as an affront to the Palladian principles from which its conception departs.

›1.32 BORROMINI, VILLA FALCONIERI, FRASCATI, refection of existing building begun by Borromini c. 1665, completed after his death by Ciro Ferri, heightened in the early 18th century by Ferdinando Fuga: general view.

The Falconieri scheme may be seen as a simplified variant of their palazzo riverfront development, with the belvedere reduced to a rather more conventional loggia: the transition begins with the unexecuted Pamphili scheme.

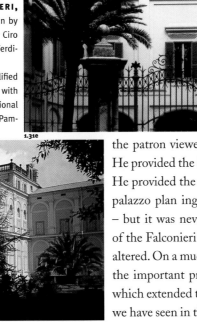

1.31e

1.32

the patron viewed the process as intolerably protracted. He provided the Spada with their illusionistic colonnade. He provided the Carpegna with an extensive trapezoidal palazzo plan ingeniously resolved around an oval court – but it was never realized. He augmented the palazzo of the Falconieri and built them a villa at Frascati – later altered. On a much larger scale, however, he did complete the important project for the Jesuit Propaganda Fide – which extended to the remodelling of Bernini's chapel, as we have seen in the ecclesiastical context.[1.31–1.33]

LESSER MASTERS

Needless to say, at a time of lavish building to celebrate the Church Triumphant and to assert the pretensions of the families who would preside over it, Bernini, Borromini and Cortona led an extensive profession – not without acrimonious rivalry, as the history of S. Agnese demonstrates. Borromini's rival there was Carlo Rainaldi (1611–91), whose father Girolamo (1570–1655) was a pupil of Domenico Fontana. The latter's Ticinese compatriot, Carlo Fontana worked in both rival studios and was mentored by Bernini. Also from a northern dynasty, Martino Longhi the Younger (1602–60) has already been encountered with his father at Ss. Ambrogio e Carlo al Corso.

Longhi, Rainaldi and Fontana all preferred comprehensive deployment of the column to Maderno's carefully graded progression in the plasticity of the Order. Longhi at Ss. Vincenzo e Anastasio sets his columns marching relentlessly forward to a crescendo which may well be

>1.33 ROME, VILLA PAMPHILI (near the Porta S. Pancrazio): engraving (by Giovanni Battista Falda, *Li Giardini di Roma*, c. 1680) of executed project attributed to Alessandro Algardi (begun 1645).

The executed Pamphili scheme, palazzo-like in its elevation, renounces the usual loggia at terrace level for superimposed belvederes in variance of the Villa Aldobrandini type (AIC5, page 288): they overlook a formal garden with dominant central axis flanked by zones of vegetation clipped into lace-like patterns – a *parterre de broderie* which must be seen in the light of current French practice.

1.34

›1.34 MARTINO LONGHI THE YOUNGER'S VARIANT ON THE ROMAN CHURCH FAÇADE: Ss. Vincenzo e Anastasio (from 1646 to c. 1650).

The façade was added to the Hieronymite church rebuilt from c. 1640 and attributed to Gaspare de' Vecchi: the multiplication of the pediments and the penetration of the cartouche down into the entablature precede Cortona's S. Maria della Pace exercise by a decade. The reliefs in the panels flanking the portal were not executed. Cardinal Mazarin, *de facto* ruler of France during the minority of Louis XIV, paid at least for Longhi's work.

1.35a

1.35c

›1.35 CARLO RAINALDI AND THE CHURCH: (a–c) S. Agnese in Agone, post-Borrominean exterior and interior, detail of the patron, Pope Innocent X Pamphili in his benediction loggia over the entrance; **1.35b**

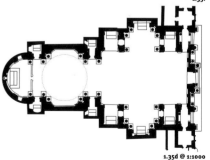

likened to that of the coda of a great organ fugue.[1.34]
In his aedicular exercise for S. Maria in Campitelli, on
the other hand, Rainaldi projects columns, then retracts
them and then projects them further in a complex manner not far removed from Cortona's Ss. Luca e Martina
or the upper storey of S. Maria della Pace or Ricchino's
S. Giuseppe.[1.35] Fontana is more straightforward, as we
shall see.[1.40a]

1.35d @ 1:1000

1.35e
(d–f) S. Maria in Campitelli (1663–67), plan, façade, interior.

S. Maria in Campitelli was rebuilt from 1663 at the instigation of Alexander VII to accommodate a miraculous image of the Virgin transferred to it in 1657 from a sanctuary which proved inadequate to contain the devotees. Rainaldi progressed from an elliptical plan to two near-Greek crosses and an apse: the transition from the vaulted nave to the transept arms and on to the domed sanctuary is effected with freestanding columns of a grand Corinthian Order. Binding the lateral to the longitudinal but asserting the predominance of the latter with the assistance of the theatrical lighting, those columns obscure the Lombard origin of the plan type in works well known to Girolamo – like the Madonna di Campagna at Piacenza, if not Ricchino's S. Giuseppe in Milan (AIC4, page 847, and see above, page 59).

›1.36 ROME, S. ANDREA DELLA VALLE: façade planned by Maderno, completed by Carlo Rainaldi and/or Carlo Fontana after 1660.

1.36

Carlo Rainaldi was commissioned to complete the façade of S. Andrea della Valle, which had been left with only the bases of the lower Order on Maderno's death in 1629: he was responsible for devising the aedicular aspect dependent on the complex faceting of the superimposed pediments.**1.36** Execution, with clarification of the supporting role of sculpture, seems largely to have been directed by Carlo Fontana.

1.37a

S. Maria in Campitelli is perhaps the most distinguished church produced at the outset of the second High Baroque generation. It is a masterly exercise in theatrical scenography, realizing a rich vista through distinct spaces, distinctly lit: the nave is the darkened auditorium and the sanctuary is the stage, bathed in brilliant light from the dome reflected in the stucco rays of glory. Others extended their vistas to the vertical axis in gradations of real space, sometimes combined with scenographic illusion: prominent examples include Antonio Gherardi's Cappella Ávila in S. Maria in Trastevere and the Cappella S. Cecilia in S. Carlo ai Catinari (of the mid-1680s and mid-1690s respectively).[1.16, 1.37] Spectacular chapels were endemic to the era and the inspiration of their authors was naturally diverse: for one more example, Giovan Antonio de' Rossi (1616–95) developed a proscenium perspective under the influence of Michelangelo's Sforza exercise at S. Maria Maggiore to stage a brilliant stucco cast for the Lancellotti at the Lateran.[1.38a]

In the secular field, variations on the Farnese formula were legion – if usually no more fundamental than the design of pediments or the distribution of rustication.[1.38b] However, theatricality well served the patricians waiting in ample wings for their call to the centre of the pontifical stage. The combination of scenographic vista through screened spaces on the horizontal plane and the illusionistic extension of a celestial axis is nowhere better illustrated – or more influential – than in the gallery of the Palazzo Colonna: it was devised by Antonio del Grande and frescoed by Filippo Gherardi from 1675 – under the inspiration of the work executed by Borromini and Cortona for the Pamphili. Del Grande's façade on the Piazza Santi Apostoli – altered in the 18th century and again in the 19th – conformed to the orthogonal norm still well represented by the same architect's Palazzo Doria-Pamphili façade opposite the Collegio Romano.[1.39]

1.37b

›1.37 ANTONIO GHERARDI AT S. MARIA IN TRASTEVERE, ROME: Cappella Ávila (mid-1680s), (a) section and plan (DR), (b) interior of dome.

›1.38 GIOVAN ANTONIO DE' ROSSI: (a) Cappella Lancellotti, S. Giovanni in Laterano (from c. 1675); (b) Palazzo d'Aste (from 1658).

1.38a

›1.39 ANTONIO DEL GRANDE: (a) Palazzo Doria-Pamphili, original entrance façade (completed 1660); (b) Palazzo Colonna, gallery (1654–65, embellishment completed 1678).

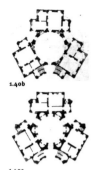

1.40b

1.40c

1.40a

EPILOGUE

By the 1680s a reaction may be detected to High Baroque exuberance: the pitch attained by the masters of the mid-century could not be sustained even had their followers equalled them in genius. In the van was Carlo Fontana: he

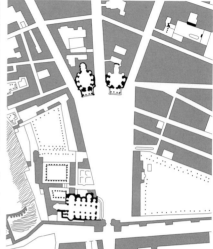

1.40f

1.40d

1.40e

›1.40 CARLO FONTANA AND THE MODIFICA-TION OF THE HIGH BAROQUE IN ROME: (a) Palazzo Montecitorio (ex-Ludovisi), cortile project for completion of the complex to accommodate the Curia Innocenziana (from 1694); (b–d) projects for a hexagonal pavilion and a portal (c. 1690); (e) S. Marcello, façade (from 1682); (f–h) Piazza del Popolo, plan and general view with S. Maria in Montesanto and S. Maria dei Miracoli (left and right respectively, 1662–79), interior of S. Maria in Montesanto.

The 'portal' churches of S. Maria in Montesanto and S. Maria dei Miracoli, at the northern source of Rome's three major arteries in the Piazza del Popolo, were commissioned by Alexander VII from Carlo Rainaldi in 1658. In place of the existing buildings, the initial project was for a pair of rotundas asserting a measure of regularity over the irregular trapezoidal piazza at the tripartite issue. Work began in 1662 on a revised project with Classical prostyle porticoes in place of attached columns – probably at the instigation of Carlo Fontana, who had been assisting Rainaldi for at least a year. Most significantly, in 1665 the Montesanto church was elongated on an elliptical plan to fill its deeper site. Work slowed after the death of the pope in 1667. It resumed in 1671 under Fontana with reference to Bernini who seems to have recommended disguising the disparity between elliptical and circular domes by giving them perimeters of twelve and eight sides.

1.40g

1.40h

was Bernini's executive architect but his independent work, much more extensive in drawings than buildings, matched the mood of the moment for moderation – if not in his unexecuted project to complete Bernini's Montecitorio complex and other published fantasies, this may be seen in the façade of S. Marcello.**1.40a–e** The curve of S. Marcello is the basic elliptical one employed by Borromini but, obviating excitement, it is echoed rather than countered for the portico. That may recall Bernini's S. Andrea al Quirinale proscenium but instead of the saint ascending vigorously over the pediment in sculpture, there is a rigid pictureless frame. The churches on the Piazza del Popolo are twinned illusionistically – probably by Fontana following Bernini – but curve and broken pediment cede to temple-front orthodoxy for their porticoes. And Classical values were ascendant within a decade of Fontana's death.**1.40f–h**

Of the several architects to emerge with or without note from Fontana's studio, Alessandro Specchi may be singled out for rejecting his master's Classicizing incentive and indulging in voluptuous curvature for his most celebrated

›1.41 ROME, EARLY 18TH-CENTURY CIVIC WORKS: (a) Ripetta quai (1704, engraved record of 1748); (b, c) Scalinata della Trinità dei Monti (Spanish Steps, 1723), bird's-eye perspective drawing and general view; (d–f) Piazza S. Ignacio (1727), plan, views;

1.41a

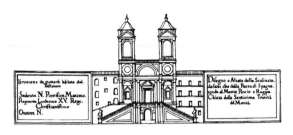

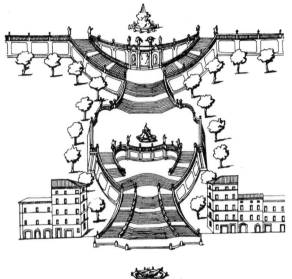

1.41b

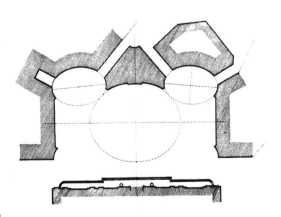

1.41d

project, the Ripetta quai opposite S. Girolamo degli Schiavoni (from 1704). His approach is seen as influencing Francesco de Sanctis in the design of the Spanish Steps before Santissima Trinità dei Monti (from 1723).**1.41a–c** The first of these is a rare example of monumental inventiveness in Rome in the first two decades of the 18th century but the work of de Sanctis opened a richer phase which also lasted for two decades.

Baroque theatricality is overtly preferred by Filippo Raguzzini (c. 1680–1771) in the little piazza in front of S. Ignacio (1727): it is a veritable stage set but may also be seen as a cortile opened inside out.**1.41d–f** Raguzzini's

1.41e

1.41f

1.41i

1.41h

1.41g

contemporary Gabriele Valvassori (1683–1761) enlivened the traditional enclosed cortile with elaborations on Borrominesque pediment themes for the Doria-Pamphili and he carried the same derivative inventiveness over to the main street front of their enormous palace (from 1730) in reaction against the work of Antonio del Grande facing the Collegio Romana.**1.41g–i** The contrast could hardly be greater than with the contemporary work of Ferdinando Fuga (1699–1782) on the façade of the Palazzo della Consulta with its selective application of a canonical Order in the context of Raphaelesque abstraction relieved by Michelangelesque window frames (from 1732).**1.41j, k**

While the Palazzo della Consulta was rising, Fuga's contemporary Nicola Salvi (1697–1751) took the Roman palazzo front to its apotheosis in the triumphal arch from

(g–i) Palazzo Doria-Pamphili (renovated from 1730), Via del Corso façade detail, cortile, Galleria dei Specchi interior (with frescoes by Aureliano Milani); (j) Palazzo della Consulta (1732–35), façade; (k) Fontana di Trevi (1732–62).

which Neptune emerges in command of the waters of the Fontana di Trevi (from 1732). He referred to Cortona's unexecuted Chigi scheme for a concave palace façade accommodating a fountain. There the colossal Order rose from a high basement as it was to do in the dominant approach to palace design after the Louvre schemes of

1.41j

1.41k

the Roman Baroque had been tamed by the French. Salvi retains a reduced basement but it is largely concealed by the rockery of the fountain: thus his Order seems to recall Michelangelo at the Campidoglio or S. Pietro's basilica and the upper windows push their pediments up through the entablature in a Mannerist manner.

Fuga's most prominent contribution to Rome's great corpus of churches was the principal façade of S. Maria Maggiore (1741) which translates the loggia from its more familiar secular context to transform the traditional closed basilican form.**1.42** Of the period's other ecclesiastical exercises, usually elegant if generally unexceptional in comparison with the High Baroque masterpieces, special note might be made of the reorientation of Michelangelo's S. Maria degli Angeli – in the great hall of the Baths of Diocletian – by the young Luigi Vanvitelli (1700–73; see AIC1, page 640, and AIC5, page 62). Working on an entirely different scale and in the most sumptuous materials, he responded admirably to the commission from João V of Portugal for a chapel to be installed in the Lisbon church of S. Roque (1748) – as we shall see in context (page 907).

Though strong in *chiaroscuro*, Fuga's S. Maria Maggiore façade pales in comparison with the greatest masterpiece of the era, the winning entry in the 1732 competition for the design of the east front of S. Giovanni Laterano by the Florentine Alessandro Galilei (1691–1737). Maderno's stupendous development of Michelangelo's ordonnance at S. Pietro is revived with stunning impact. The most obvious divergence is in the ratio of solid to void, with superimposed loggias as vigorous in their *chiaroscuro* as the Colosseum arcades – or, as we shall see, Bernini's first Louvre project. The inset minor Order, derived by Maderno from the Campidoglio palaces, is reiterated in Composite rather than Ionic terms. In contrast, the major Composite Order is as crushing in scale and austere in style as S. Pietro's

›1.42 ROME, S. MARIA MAGGIORE: portico (from 1735).

The portico was originally built for Pope Eugenius III in the middle of the 12th century. It was replaced in 1575 by Martino Longhi the Elder. In response to Clement XII's commission to replace this, Fuga projected the new western portico in 1735 and oversaw the completion of construction in 1741.

1.42

Corinthian but, the progressive development of plasticity rejected, it marches through planes as unvaried in contour as the French academic Classical ideal which we shall see emerging from the taming of the Roman Baroque projects for the Louvre. The reformative French also appreciated the Cappella Corsini which Galilei installed within the basilica for Pope Clement XII, who commissioned the competition for the façade. It is certainly grand in scale and rich in ordonnance but as pure in its formal geometry and as true in its deployment of the Corinthian repertory of architectural detail as an antique temple: except for its sculptural embellishment, it heralds a new age.**1.43**

Several of the techniques forged so spectacularly into the Baroque style of Rome were to find devotees elsewhere in Italy but the full panoply is rare beyond the locus of the Church Triumphant – at least until secular princes acquired a taste for commensurate grandeur. Few Roman masters of the style emigrated north. Fontana went south: so too, later, did Fuga and Vanvitelli.

The Venetians developed their idiosyncratic scenography from their Palladian inheritance. The Milanese developed on the lines set by Ricchino and their influence is detectable as far as Bologna – in limited instances. The Tuscan Cortona was exceptional in his Florentine venture but the Florentines were rarely Baroque: the Mannerism of Buontalenti's school subsisted in tired decline there, at least in detail – as in the most prominent exercise of the early 17th century, the Cappella dei Principe attached to S. Lorenzo (AIC4, page 710, left). Not without a lively note from Buontalenti himself, virtuoso variations on Borrominian themes were played to north and south by Guarino Guarini, a Theatine monk from Modena who studied in Rome, but only Turin is the residual legatee – as we shall see in the second of the following selective surveys of regional Baroque developments north-east and north-west of the Italian peninsula.

›1.43 ROME, S. GIOVANNI IN LATERANO: (a) portico (from 1733), (b) Cappella Corsini (from 1734).

Clement XII held a competition for the design of the east front and chose Alessandro Galilei's entry: work was begun in 1733. The pope also commissioned Galilei to design and build his Corsini family mortuary chapel: work began in 1734.

1.43b

1.43a

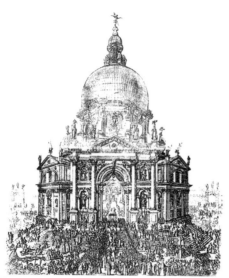

4 VENICE

The Venetians, always masters of colour, light and atmosphere in their kaleidoscopic environment, took naturally to scenography, to staging dramatic effects of light and shade drawn from rich sculptural relief and to illusionism. Andrea Palladio, inspired by the vistas through varied spaces on the axes of antique thermae (AIC5, pages 228ff), was a pioneer of theatrical perspective at the Teatro Olimpico and established the Venetian mode for the scenographic evolution of space in his great churches. The legacy proved daunting to most in the generation of and after Vicenzo Scamozzi but an heir of unrivalled talent had emerged from the latter's studio by 1630. Baldassarre Longhena (1598–1682), conservative in his early secular works, proved himself the consummate master of spectacle in the great church of S. Maria della Salute commissioned ex voto for relief from the plague of 1630: in that work, he established an alternative to the centralizing preferences of the High Baroque Roman masters – before their lesser contemporaries diversified their approach along scenographic lines.**1.44a–h**

1.44a

S. Maria della Salute

At the head of the Grand Canal, on a site second in prominence only to the island of Palladio's S. Giorgio Maggiore, S. Maria della Salute is highly eclectic – as might well be expected of a burgeoning master's first important work – but the borrowed elements are assimilated brilliantly. The archetypes of centralized planning – octagon, circle, square and Greek cross – are linked into one magnificent axial vista articulated in grey over white in Palladio's mode. The immediate precedent is the Redentore which was also built ex voto for relief from the plague (AIC5, pages 242f): the vista apart, the apsidal crossing and columnar screen are retained but Palladio's rectangular nave cedes to the octagon of Michele Sanmicheli's Veronese votive church of the Madonna di Campagna (AIC5, page 137) – and its several Lombard precedents which themselves descend from S. Vitale at Ravenna (AIC1, pages 784f, AIC4, page 796). Unity is imposed throughout, from portico to sanctuary, by the assiduous Composite Order on its high Palladian

1.44d

1.44C

1.44f

>**1.44 LONGHENA AND THE VENETIAN CHURCH:** (a–h) S. Maria della Salute (from 1631), general view from canal and consecration record (17th-century engraving), interior of octagon to the east and dome detail, sanctuary and dome detail, plan and section;

1.44g, h @ 1:1000

1.44e

pedestals and by the minor Corinthian pilasters which carry the consistent arcading; diversity is provided by the light, clear and uniform in the great octagon, clear but peripheral in the chapels beyond the dim ambulatory, diffused under the dome of the sanctuary, absent altogether under the intervening triumphal arches which echo the entrance, and uniform again in the monks' choir.

The application of an orthogonal three-bay antique motif as a frontispiece follows the precedent set by Antonio da Sangallo in his polygonal project for S. Giovanni dei Fiorentini (AIC4, page 851): a temple front rather than a pedimented triumphal arch, however, that was typologically far less exuberant in sculptural relief. Sangallo's project also clearly inspired Longhena for the buttressing of his dome with a rondo of great scrolls:

instead of a repetitive succession of semi-circular exedrae below, however, he projects his rectangular chapels and gives them minor façades dominated by their great thermal windows in the manner common to Palladio's churches (AIC5, pages 238ff).

The prominent part allotted to sculpture at S. Maria della Salute – to saints in the niches and on the pediment of the hybrid triumphal arch/temple front, to fames in the spandrels there and over the high altar, to the prophets supported by the columns of the octagon – was well in accord with

(i) S. Maria dei Derelitti (Ospedaletto), façade (1674);
(j) S. Maria Gloriosa dei Frari, tomb of Doge Giovanni Pesaro (c. 1659).

1.44i

1.44j

the Venetian tradition, not least in the High Renaissance permutation effected by the Florentine Sansovino (AIC5, pages 217ff). Longhena took it further. In his later works he promoted sculptural form from prominence to predominance, even over architecture: at the extreme, movement is not elicited in the articulation of mass but in the application of forceful figures in high relief in place of an Order – as in the façade of S. Maria dei Derelitti and the stupendous tomb of Doge Giovanni Pesero in S. Maria Gloriosa dei Frari.**1.44i, j** Many followed the lead.

Longhena worked prolifically in all genres for public and private clients – in Venice and the Veneto. He had risen to the top of his profession in Venice with the post of *proto* to the Procuratori di San Marco in 1640: from two years earlier he was engaged on the completion of the Procuratie Nuove on the south side of the Piazza San Marco to Scamozzi's revision of Sansovino's design. In addition to his prestigious commissions for tombs, he was called upon by the nobility for palaces which rivalled the greatest work of the 16th-century master in scale.

The work which won Longhena prime favour with secular clients was the relatively modest Palazzo Belloni Battagia (from 1648): it was innovative in the distinction of aedicular bays on the piano nobile and their separation with boldly emblazoned armorial panels. The larger scale of the subsequent major commissions for the Palazzo Bon and Ca' Pesaro recommended return to Sansovino's *chiaroscuro* mode of palace façade design – open with loggias on all floors in the traditional Venetian manner rather than predominantly solid in the Roman or Florentine manner – but with still greater sculptural relief. Long in building beyond the master's demise, these conformed to the time-honoured Venetian conventions in the planning of canalside palazzi: even the staircase, elsewhere the occasion for extroverted display, remained in its traditional

›1.45 LONGHENA AND THE VENETIAN BAROQUE SECULAR TRADITION: (a) Palazzo Belloni Battagia (begun in 1648 for the Belloni), canal front;

1.45a

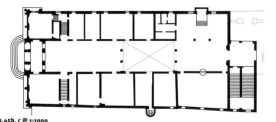

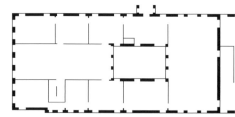

1.45b, c @ 1:1000

1.45d

1.45f

1.45e

(b–f) Palazzo Bon/Rezzonico (begun for the Bon on the canalside in 1649, completed a century later for the Rezzonico), plans of ground and main floors, canal front, entrance atrium and salone detail; (g) Ca' Pesaro (c. 1660–1710), canal front; (h–j) S. Giorgio Maggiore, monastery staircase (from 1643), views from above and below, cortile.

The form of Longhena's S. Giorgio staircase, with intermediate landings between the opening flight and the parallel ramps attached to the side walls, derives from the mid-16th-century project for the Toledo Alcázar initiated by Alonso de Covarrubias (AIC5, pages 697 and 724): the form was to reach its apotheosis in the Escalier des Ambassadeurs at Versailles from 1672.

Giorgio Massari completed the Palazzo Bon with its top storey from 1752. The piano nobile on the canal front of the Ca' Pesaro had been completed by the end of the 1670s: the upper storeys were completed by 1710 under the direction of Gian Antonio Gaspari.

1.458

1.45h

1.45j

1.45i

tunnel. For the monks of S. Giorgio, however, Longhena branched flights out around the sides of an open cage in the manner invented by the Spaniards more than a century earlier and soon to reach its apotheosis.**1.45**

In the most prominent works of Longhena's more significant followers, his sometime colleagues Giuseppe Sardi (1624–99) and Alessandro Tremignon (1635–1711), architecture provides the theatre for lavish sculptural display but the generation of momentum is rare in either of the Roman Baroque manners: examples range from Heinrich Meyring's encrustation of Tremignon's S. Moisè to

›**1.46** ALESSANDRO TREMIGNON AND ARRIGO MERENGO (HEINRICH MEYRING): S. Moisè (1668), façade.

The applied ornament, mannered rather than Baroque, obscures the essential Palladianism of the architecture.

1.46

1.47a

1.47b

Sardi's Scalzi or S. Maria del Giglio façades.**1.46, 1.47** In the next generation, the contribution of Domenico Rossi (1657–1737) to the Gesuiti was exceptional in its Roman Solomonic exuberance though the opulent embellishment of the interior as a whole was fully in accord with the Venetian *colore* tradition.**1.48**

›1.47 GIUSEPPE SARDI: (a, b) S. Maria di Nazareth (degli Scalzi, from 1670), façade and interior (from 1683); (c, d) S. Maria del Giglio (or Zobenigo, from 1678), exterior and interior.

The Giglio church (named after the lily of the Annunciation but also called Zobenigo after its 9th-century founder) was rebuilt by Sardi to a Barbaro commission between 1678 and 1681: the façade displays maps of the theatres of naval war in which the patron served the Republic as admiral.

The church of the Discalced Carmelites, begun in 1670, is attributed to Longhena; Sardi added the façade after the master's death in 1682. The exuberant embellishment of the interior is due largely to the Carmelite brother Giuseppe Pozzo.

1.47c

1.47d

1.48a

1.48b

›1.48 DOMENICO ROSSI AND GIORGIO MAS-SARI: (a, b) S. Maria Assunta (the Gesuiti, from 1715), façade and interior; (c, d) S. Maria del Rosario (the Gusuati, from 1725), façade and interior.

The Jesuits were associated with Venice from 1523, when S. Ignatius Loyola embarked there for pilgrimage to Jerusalem: they acquired the old hospital and conventual complex of the Crucifix through the offices of Pope Alexander VII. Too small for their expanding purposes, the church was demolished in 1715 and rebuilt over a plan of the Gesù type for its new dedication in 1728. The flagrant exuberance of the Trinity altar in the sanctuary apse is in marked contrast with the façade which is Baroque only in the scale of its engaged Order: the plane of the wall, if not the continuity of the entablature, are sustained in the manner soon to be associated with the Classicizing masters of late-Baroque Rome. The furthering of this process, with the aid of reference back to Palladio's S. Giorgio Maggiore, led to the application (from c. 1730) of a temple front to the Dominican church of the Gesuati on the Zattere by Giorgio Massari (1687–1766).

1.48c

1.48d

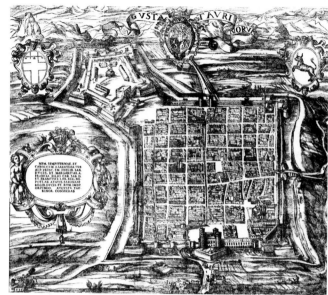

1.49a

5 PIEDMONT

Atlante, bold and rippling with protean muscle, were to be favourite Baroque devices, especially north of the Alps (AIC5, page 266). They infiltrated Milan but failed in procreativity there: Milan was to be no more Baroque than Florence. Scenography was not foreign to Genoa after

›1.49 TURIN, PHASES OF DEVELOPMENT: (a) the antique inheritance of Duke Emanuele Filiberto and its High Renaissance protection (c. 1572; north to the right); (b, c) plan and engraved aerial perspective from the east, showing southern enlargement commissioned by Carlo Emanuele I from Carlo di Castellamonte (c. 1620) with reformed palace and piazzas in the right foreground and the eastward extension of the original grid to the new walls bequeathed by Francesco Paciotti and Ascanio Vittozzi; (d) plan showing the eastward extension commissioned by Carlo Emanuele II from Amedeo di Castellamonte (c. 1673); (e) plan showing addi-

1.49c

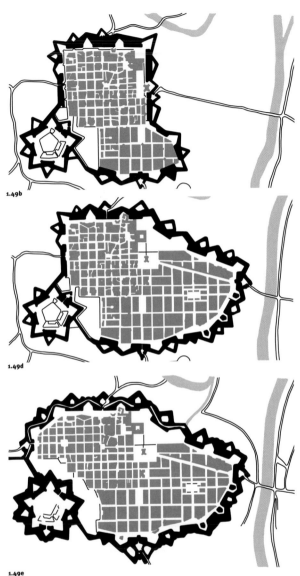

tional westward extension commissioned by Vittorio Amedeo II from Filippo Juvarra (1714); (f) Piazza San Carlo (1674) with Carlo di Castellamonte's uniform façades of residential buildings and the twin churches of S. Cristina and S. Carlo (right and left, 1639 and 1619 respectively, façades 1715 and 1836).

the development of the Strada Nuova: the projection of vistas through colonnade courts and the multiple flights of screened staircases was furthered in the 17th century as the most spectacular feature of a conservative tradition (AIC5, pages 262f). Neighbouring Piedmont was much more receptive to ingenious novelty.

DUCAL PLANNERS

Restored to his Savoyard domains by the French king in accordance with the Peace of Cateau-Cambrésis (1559), Duke Emanuele Filiberto (1553–80) moved his capital in 1563 from Chambéry, on the French side of the Alps, to the old Roman site of Turin, on the north-western plain of Italy: rather than the late-medieval Castello, he chose to move into the bishop's palace on the northern side of a putative piazza.[1.49a]

Pellegrino Tibaldi was called from Milan in 1577 to honour the town's earliest martyred patron saints (Solutore, Avventore, Ottavio) with the new church of the Santi Martiri but did not take on wider responsibility.[1.50] That was entrusted by the new duke, Carlo Emanuele I (1580–1630), to the military engineers Francesco Paciotti (1521–91) and Ascanio Vittozzi (1539–1615). The former, active throughout Italy, conceived the sophisticated defence system dependent on a pentagonal citadel. The latter furthered that project, enlarged the palace, reformed the Piazza Castello before the old residence, opened the southern axial Contrada Nuova, extended the old grid lines south and east to the new walls and began the renewal of the urban fabric with housing over shopping arcades on the main perpendicular thoroughfares.

Vittozzi's successor as architect to Carlo Emanuele I, Carlo di Castellamonte (1560–1641), also served his short-lived successor Vittorio Amedeo I (1630–37) and the latter's wife, Christine Marie of France, as regent during the minority of her son Carlo Emanuele II (1637–75): he extended the town about the formal axis from the Piazza Castello to the southern entrance (Contrada Nuova, now Via Roma) through the Piazza San Carlo (1638) and transformed the palace.**1.49b, c** He was succeeded as principal ducal architect by his son Amedeo who began in that capacity with the refacing of the ducal palace (from 1646) and laid out the Contrada del Po as the axis of the second phase of Turin's expansion which was to stretch east from the Piazza Castello to the great river.**1.49d, e**

1.49f

With its portal churches, the Piazza San Carlo was unique in Italy for its time in the uniformity of its perimeter: uniformity of façade on all squares and main arteries was a ducal obsession which inhibited the development of distinct palazzi even by otherwise self-assertive patrons and architects. The twin-portal churches precede their equivalents on Rome's Piazza del Popolo by a quarter of a century though their Baroque façades were provided later, first for Carlo di Castellamonte's S. Cristina in the early 18th century by Filippo Juvarra – to whom we shall return.**1.49f**

›1.50 TURIN, CHURCH OF THE SANTI MARTIRI, from 1577: interior towards sanctuary.

Construction in accordance with Pellegrino Tibaldi's plans, with serlianas in the main bays, was undertaken by the Milanese master-mason Giovanni Battista Ripa. The apse was altered by Carlo Giulio Quadro, who designed the dome and bell-tower (from 1706); the high altar is due to Filippo Juvarra (c. 1730).

1.50

(a, b) Paris, S.-Anne-la-Royale (c. 1663, unfinished until 1720, destroyed 1823), section and plan; (c) Lisbon, S. Maria della Divina Provvidenza (c. 1656), half plan and section; (d, e) Prague, S. Maria Altötting (1679), section and plan.

All the planning is complex in its geometry, usually elliptical in whole or in part. The ellipses, generated by interlocking circles, generally overlap to effect the fluid transition between spaces.

The Somaschi church in Messina would have been hexagonal with a ring of elliptical ambulatory spaces. S.-Anne-la-Royale in Paris was an elongated Greek cross with elliptical arms and side chapels producing an undulating perimeter. The sections of both reveal the intended complex layering of volumes to effect a rich vertical scenography through wilfully distinct zones which would have been enhanced dramatically by the lighting. The Somaschi project is the more bizarre, with a circular zone of transition to what would normally be the drum of a dome but which, instead, is a hybrid construct with parabolic ribs tracing a domical profile in a hexagonal cage. In both centralized projects the fenestration, too, is richly varied, ranging from regular pedimented rectangles to serlianas symmetrical about both axes and other less precisely defined forms with semi-circular extrusion to the cill.

The longitudinal plan of the Lisbon church is wholly composed of ovals generated by interlocking circles, except for the residual semi-circle of the sanctuary apse, and vertical momentum is initiated by extraordinary Solomonic pilasters: its publication was to prove highly influential on spatial conception, especially in

1.51c

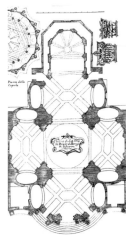

1.51a, b

GUARINO GUARINI AND TURIN

A full-blooded Baroque had been introduced to the seat of the dukes of Savoy by Guarino Guarini (1624–83), who was invited to supplant Amedeo di Castellamonte on the project to enshrine the Holy Shroud in a chapel attached to Turin cathedral. A Theatine padre, Guarini had studied in Rome from 1639 to 1647 – when Borromini was making his individual mark – and worked for his order in Lisbon (c. 1656), Messina (1660) and Prague (1679?) as well as for the French crown in Paris (1663); he was called to Turin in 1666. His engraved church designs were published in 1686, fifty years before the treatise for which they were prepared, *Architettura Civile*, which compounded their considerable impact through the agency of Bernardo Vittone – as we shall see. However, the early works have left little material trace and even their histories are usually obscure. For instance, whether Guarini actually visited Lisbon to oversee the construction of his S. Maria della Divina Provvidenza is unknown: thus, even more regrettably, it is unknown whether to do so he passed through Córdoba or Salamanca and gained first-hand experience of the type of ribbed dome which was to be his leitmotif (see AIC3, pages 206f).[1.51]

Five Turinese church projects are attributed to Guarini – in conception at least. The Immacolata Concezione, based on aligned circles, and S. Maria della Consolazione, based on an elongated octagon entered from the long side opposite an hexagonal sanctuary, were both executed by others.[1.52d, 1.53] S. Filippo Neri was begun over multiple octagons but the structure was unsound and had to be demolished: we shall return to its replacement.[1.52b, 1.58g] The two most important survivors were ducal commissions: the church of S. Lorenzo, which served as the palatine chapel, and the Cappella della Sacra Sindone (Holy Shroud) attached to the cathedral as a shrine for

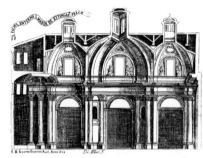

1.51d, e
Germany. Guarini varied this longitudinal theme for S. Maria Altötting in Prague by dispensing with transepts but retaining elliptical forms for the three nave zones, though the central one is larger and given canted corners.

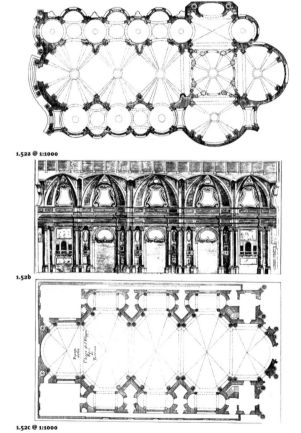

1.52a @ 1:1000

1.52b

1.52c @ 1:1000

›1.52 GUARINI'S TURINESE CHURCHES: (a) unnamed project; (b–c) S. Filippo Neri, interior elevation and plan; (d) Immacolata Concezione, plan; (e–j) S. Lorenzo (1668–87), section, plan, exterior, dome, general view of interior to sanctuary and 'transept'; (k–o) Cappella della Sacra Sindone (from 1657), section, plan, exterior, interior and detail of dome.

Guarini returned to a longitudinal theme again in several of his Turinese projects. In an unnamed one he retained the elliptical sanctuary and transepts of the Lisbon scheme but generated the nave from interlocking circles. For S. Filippo Neri the three elliptical zones of the nave all have canted corners like the central zone of S. Maria Altötting in Prague.

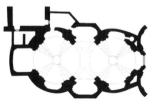

1.52d @ 1:1000

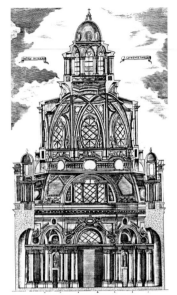

that exceptionally holy relic owned by the dynasty. Both rise over planning of Borrominian geometric complexity and in both Guarini stages complex lighting effects through the dramatic, essentially un-Classical, revision of the ribbed dome.[1.52e–o] It is possible that the earlier work was inspired by the ribbed vaulting of Borromini's Propaganda Fide chapel. The stellar net has its equivalent in the major works of the Córdoban Caliphate (AIC3, pages 206f) but they did not admit the illumination through voids in the diaphragm which was essential to Guarini's mature achievement. Moreover, in the absence of proof that he actually knew the Córdoba mosque – or similar works inherited from the Arabs in Sicily – coincidental invention must not be ruled out.

1.52i
1.52j

Guarini's mature churches

Guarini's exterior of S. Lorenzo, the chapel royal, was never realized. The interior is dominated by serlianas, bent round elliptical curves on both levels of the main arcaded axes and retaining similar three-dimensional curves on the diagonals though there they are gauged from the canted piers which would normally have supported the pendentives – the real and the apparent are both denied here. Within these, the altars offer no respite from complexity developed largely under the inspiration of Borromini's decorative detail.

There are two ribbed domes or, rather, hybrid domical drums: the major one, over the congregational space, is extruded from an eight-pointed star drawn from an octagon with semi-elliptical sides; the lesser one is extruded from a hexagonal star drawn from a circle inscribed in the elliptical sanctuary. In both the skin is stripped from the bones so that light penetrates from above in contrast to the shadowy side chapels and the oval space beyond the sanctuary reserved for the high altar. The process is most complex in the main 'dome': concealed and revealed sources, ranging from the octagonal double lantern through semi-circular or polygonal voids to oval occuli, dissolve the sense of enclosing fabric interposed between the soul and heaven.

1.52n

1.52m

The Cappella della Sacra Sindone was begun by Carlo di Castellamonte in 1657 in the void between the cathedral and the palace at the level of the latter's piano nobile. Guarini, who assumed responsibility after a decade of slow progress, can hardly have regretted the legacy of a circular plan but, with obvious Trinitarian motive, he overlaid it with an equilateral triangle – the former centred on the shrine and its stellar pavement, the latter locating twin entrances from the transepts below and the link with the palace beyond the axis of the high altar. The existing structure of the cylindrical body, articulated with Corinthian pilasters, did not inhibit the assertion of the triangle with three great arches separated by three pendentive zones over three cylindrical lobbies, each with triangular ribbed vaulting springing from columns between three portals – serving the steps, the chapel and a sacristy. The coffered pendentives and the coffered exedrae defined by the great arches all have similar oval windows. Above these, in the drum, are glazed arcades separated by Borrominian aedicules. Above that, from largely concealed sources no longer in the context of ribs, the diffused lighting infil-

1.520

trates the amazing conical structure which stands for the dome. Instead, there are six tiers of flattened arches which spring from the reinforced centres of the pairs below and are framed by continuous mouldings extruded from the arches of the drum: the membrane dissolves completely, except for a star at its crown – and the radiance of the dove of the Holy Spirit at the apex. The practical necessities of fulfilling the internal objectives inform the exterior but Guarini's ingenuity ensures that this is hardly apparent.

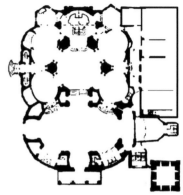

1.53a

1.53b

1.53c

The differentiation of space through light, encouraging movement out of the dark along a vertical or horizontal axis, leads on the one hand back to Gothic aspiration and the Theology of Light (AIC4, pages 263ff) and emerges, on the other, from the theatre and scenography. The alternation of light and dark planes is an essential technique for enhancing the effect of recession in the restricted context of the stage. It was equally essential to construct a passage for the soul to salvation, to elucidate the infinite path from the darkness of this world to the glory of the next.

›1.53 TURIN, S. MARIA DELLA CONSOLAZIONE AS REALIZED AFTER GUARINI: (a) plan, (b) hexagonal sanctuary, (c) Juvarra's high altar with Consolata icon.

The medieval church on the site, a basilica over a subterranean sanctuary, was entered conventionally from the west: access was moved to the south flank when Guarini's spatially ambitious scheme was developed between 1678 and 1704 under the direction of Antonio Bertola. The aisled basilica ceded to the bi-apsidal hall with the stairs to the patron's shrine in the crypt (east) opposite a major altar: opposite the entrance (south) Guarini's hexagon is the shrine of the Consolata image. From 1729 Juvarra opened a domed sanctuary apse to the north of the hexagon and inserted a new high altar for the accommodation of the holy image. In the 1730s too, Juvarra added the sacristy whose illusionist paintings are set in an elegantly stuccoed vault which may well be compared with his work in the secular field – not least the Sala di Diana at La Venaria Reale (see pages 152f). The subsidiary elliptical chapels which flank the hexagonal shrine chamber were added between 1899 and 1904.

›**1.54 TURIN, PALAZZO CARIGNANO,** from 1679: (a) façade, (b) plan, (c, d) androne, staircase, (e) prince's salone (late-17th century).

The work, commissioned by Prince Emanuele Filib-

In his *Architettura Civile*, published posthumously by Bernardo Vitone, Guarini specifically disclaims subservience to the Vitruvian tradition. That implicitly aligns him with the heterodox followers of Michelangelo, notably Bernardo Buontalenti and Borromini. Beyond that, he was unusual for his time in admiring Gothic architecture because its prime quality, lightness drawn through skeletal virility, counters the solidity of the Roman mural tradition. Thus it is possible that his rib vaulting was inspired by some network spun in the late Gothic era – but there is no more evidence that he crossed the Alps than that he crossed Iberia to Lisbon.

1.54a

The dramatic use of curve and light distinguishes Guarini's most important secular work too. The double-S curve in the façade of his Palazzo Carignano is certainly Borrominesque – as is the love of brick: even the elliptical loggia in the central caesura recalls the tabernacle in the central concavity of the façade of S. Carlo alle Quattro Fontane. However, the sense of buckling under compression exerted by the side blocks erto of Carignano, was furthered by Michelangelo Garove after Guarini's death in 1683 but not extended beyond half the side wings until the 19th century – when the court was enclosed. In Guarini's accomplished façade design, the superimposition of freely interpreted pilaster Orders follows Borromini's Oratorio di S. Filippo Neri but the elaboration of the moulded brickwork far exceeds it. The pediment, too, exceeds Borromini in convolution, varying the tripartite but continuous form he developed for the oratory in terms of Pietro da Cortona's broken Palazzo Barberini composition (see page 63).

1.54b @ 1:1000

1.54c

1.54d

1.54e

The prince's apartment on the ground floor was decorated in the last years of the 17th century while Garove was in charge of works: the design of the gilt panelling and mirror frames is unattributed.

›1.55 TURIN, DUCAL RESIDENCE (Reggia): (a) Amedeo di Castellamonte's grand project for the precinct and the Piazza Castello (engraving of 1674), (b) façade from the forecourt (from 1646).

is Cortonesque or even Berninesque. Twin staircases curve round each side of the oval *sala terrena* up to the vestibule before the oval salone whose bulge enlivens the façade; convex to accommodate the foot until the oval half-landing, the steps are concave thereafter to encourage ascent and only the landing is bathed in light to give one pause.[1.54]

1.55a

1.55b

CASTELLAMONTE AND GAROVE

Amedeo di Castellamonte (1610–83), busy with his urban projects and reforming the ducal palace in Turin, was commissioned by Carlo Emanuele II to build a vast palace outside the capital at Venaria Reale where a new town was to be devoted to silk spinning. The scheme as a whole was not to be realized but the ideal was engraved in 1674: there are French equivalents, as we shall see. Amedeo integrated the whole by centring access to the palace compound on a circular piazza at the head of the town's axial artery and continuing the line through to the ducal garden. The first phase of the work comprised the Reggia di Diana which, begun in 1659 beyond two projected courtyards, remains the core of the much expanded complex.[1.55, 1.56]

1.56a

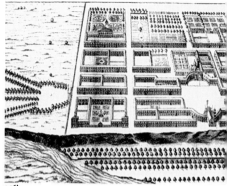

1.56b

›**1.56 LA VENARIA REALE OF CARLO EMA-NUELE II,** from 1659: (a, b) Castellamonte's grand projects for town and palace (engravings of 1682 respectively from east and north), (c) Fontana di Diana, (d, e) palace, east front, engraved and from entrance loggia, (f) Sala di Diana.

La Venaria Reale: inception

La Venaria Reale was built 10 kilometres south-west of Turin in an area favoured by the ducal court for hunting. There was to be housing for the ducal entourage in the village but living, working and commercial space was also designed for the silk weavers and dealers whose activities were seen as important to the official drive to boost the economy.

The first phase of building conducted by Amedeo di Castellamonte (from 1659) embraced the semi-circular Piazza dell'Annunziata (the precinct between village and palace with its open silk-spinning booths and shops), the entrance court with the chapel of S. Rocco contiguous to its south and the detached ducal residence, the Reggia di Diana, beyond the main court to its west. The outer court was framed by the three wings of a two-storey loggetta and a single-storey screen to the front (facing east): entrance was through a triumphal arch and a second portal under a clock tower gave access to the precinct of the palace itself. The last was built by Castellamonte from 1660. It consisted of a central block with a triple-height central salon – the Sala di Diana – and wings with the ducal apartments on the main floors. A gallery was projected from the south-west corner of the duke's apartment along the south side of the forecourt: its realization was to transform the aspect of the palace for Duke Carlo Emanuele II's regal heir.

1.56f

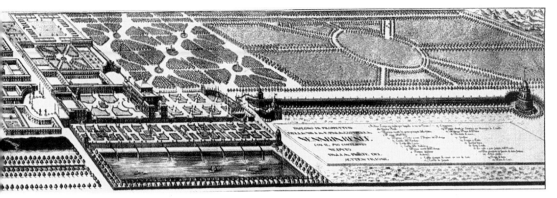

FANUM DIANÆ

1.56c

FACCIATA DEL PALAZZO REGIA DI DIANA

1.56d

1.56e

1.57a

1.57b

Renewed war with France intervened before realization of the ambition for La Venaria Reale was far advanced. Meanwhile Castellamonte had died in 1683 and been replaced by Michelangelo Garove (1648–1713) who, trained as a military engineer, worked extensively on fortifications and the second enlargement of Turin. He also practised widely in the capital for the duke and private patrons. Apart

1.57c

1.57e

1.57d

>1.57 LATE-17TH-CENTURY TURINESE PAL-
ACES: (a) Graneri della Roccia, cortile; (b, c) Falletti
di Barolo, façade and androne; (d) Asinari di San Marzano, androne; (e) university cortile.

The banded column was a leitmotif in the secular work of Guarini's Turinese followers: Michelangelo Garove's university cortile is the most
spectacular example of the style; Baroncelli's Graneri
court is another. Baroncelli's Palazzo Falletti di Barolo
has an unusually distinguished façade with a central
frontispiece over the androne: it was built in the westward extension of the town in which uniformity was not
as rigorously pursued as in the earlier developments to
the south and east of the Piazza Castello.

>1.58 JUVARRA IN THE ECCLESIASTICAL
FIELD: (a) ideal twin-towered cathedral project for
presentation to the Accademia di S. Luca (Rome 1707);
(b–e) Basilica di Superga (from 1716), interior, section, plan and exterior; (f) S. Cristina, façade (1715);

1.58a

from completing several of Guarini's projects – notably the
Palazzo Carignano and the adjacent Collegio dei Nobili
– his most spectacular works include the university and
the Palazzo Asinari di San Marzano, the former distinguished by its grand courtyard, the latter by its extraordinary permutation of the androne: the carriage tunnel/
entrance vestibule which, in lieu of an assertive façade,
is the first distinguishing feature of the Turinese palazzo
where individuality cedes to the uniformity of streetscape
preferred by the regime. Other notable examples by other
notable architects with extensive private practices in the
last decades of the century include the Palazzo Graneri
della Roccia and Palazzo Falletti di Barolo of Gian Francesco Baroncelli (from 1685 and 1692 respectively).[1.57]

JUVARRA AND THE CHURCH

After Guarini, building activity was desultory in the seats
of Savoy until well into the new century – until Vittorio
Amedeo II celebrated his acquisition of the kingdoms
of Sicily (1713) and Sardinia (1720), and his consequent
elevation in regal grandeur. Drawn from Sicily in 1714,
his architect was Filippo Juvarra (1678–1736) who had
emerged from the Roman studio of Carlo Fontana after
presenting the Accademia di San Luca with a stunning
centralized cathedral project.[1.58a] His first Turinese
work, S. Cristina (1715), is indebted to his Roman master. His contemporary S. Filippo Neri replaced Guarini's
incomplete exercise but recalls Borromini's work for the
Roman headquarters of its Oratorian patrons. Following soon after, his major works for the house of Savoy
were the votive church of the Superga, the central urban
Palazzo Madama, the extension of La Venaria Reale and
the grand rural retreat at Stupinigi.

Begun on its eminence in 1716, the Superga scheme recalls
the academic cathedral project. Its Greek-cross plan may be

1.58b

seen as a revision of Borromini's S. Agnese in Agone about an octagonal crossing with circular dome: the pier elevations also pay reduced homage to the Vatican basilica but the synthesis is reformed within a circle.**1.58b–e** In contrast to the Baroque complexity of Guarini's vertical perspectives – for which Juvarra would demonstrate his own facility – the domed rotunda recalls the Classical simplicity retained by Bernini at Ariccia and preferred by Fontana, except for the Borrominesque fenestration of the drum's interior. It is flanked by Borrominesque towers but these are set back from the front: that projects into a huge square portico, as in the ideal scheme of 1707. Opposite the portico, beyond the main space, a smaller rotunda for the sanctuary completes a horizontal scenographic exercise which might have been worthy of a follower of Baldassare Longhena had the articulation of the three elements been more subtly coordinated.

(g–i) S. Filippo Neri (1715–30), interior towards sanctuary, portico, west front; (j–l) Madonna del Carmine (1732–35), side chapel vertical perspective, interior towards sanctuary, exterior.

Overlooking the Piedmontese capital from an eminence to the east, the church of the Superga was founded by Vittorio Amedeo II in fulfillment of a vow to the Madonna on the liberation of Turin from the French in 1706: ten years later Juvarra was to hand with an ideal project. Initially formulated to mark his admission to the Roman Accademia di S. Luca in 1707, that was based on an octagonal plan with Greek-cross axial arms countered by the extension of the diagonals into apsidal chapels – in subtle revision of Borromini's inheritance from Carlo Rainaldi at S. Agnese in Agone. The main volume of the Superga rises over a more complex synthesis of Greek cross, octagon and circle: in elevation the canted corners of the octagon are eclipsed by the rim of the drum which is carried directly by the ring of freestanding columns concentric with the cylindrical perimeter, thus the primary allegiance

1.58c

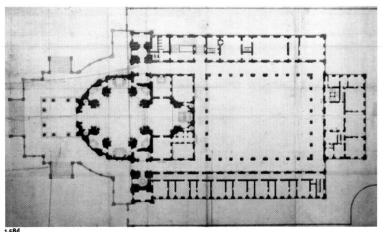

1.58d

is to the type of the Pantheon rather than the Vatican basilica. Internally, the articulation of the drum incorporated Borrominesque broken pediments over the windows between the columns based on those below: logic of structure is at once confirmed and denied. Outside, logic is unchallenged: the Orders are deployed consistently in pairs to express support from base level via the doubled ribs of the dome to lantern. As in the 1707 project, the dome is elevated in the manner of Borromini's superseded scheme for S. Agnese: the towers derive from the same source but they flank the eastern quadrants of the rotunda rather than a concave façade. Further, the prominently projecting portico seems to develop – in depth if not breadth – from Michelangelo's unrealized temple-front scheme for S. Pietro which ceded to Maderno's extensions.

Without crossing, but with a domical presbytery bay, S. Filippo Neri reiterates Alberti's S. Andrea in Mantua, to which Juvarra added the dome (from 1732; AIC4, page 749). The triumphal-arch ordonnance of the three great nave bays is retained, but the Serlian motif there seems to pay homage to the first great church of ducal Turin, Pellegrino Tibaldi's Santi Martiri. Guarini had doubled his Order of engaged columns on the canted corners of his three great bays: as part of his fabric survived to inform reconstruction, that is distantly echoed at the junction of Juvarra's nave and sanctuary. Moreover, the kidney-shaped clerestory windows, the oval medallions and the tribune balconies are indebted to the original Theatine master. On the other hand, there is much in the stucco decoration of the vault which recalls Fontana or even Rainaldi in the Piazza del Popolo churches.

1.58e

As we have noted in passing, Juvarra's first work in Turin was the façade of Carlo di Castellamonte's church of S. Cristina (1715): the lightly concave design revises Fontana's S. Marcello al Corso façade principally with the omission of the aedicular window and the interpolation of sculpture into the broken pediment.**1.58f** Next, for S. Filippo Neri (from 1715, revised 1730), he replaced Guarini's incomplete structure with a single great hall, rather than aligned octagons, revised the ordonnance but preserved the memory of the padre's fenestration.**1.58g–i** His most dramatic conception was for the Carmelites (Madonna del Carmine, from 1732): in another variant on the medieval hall-church type – not without its parallels in Germany – he elevated the chapel arcades to the full height of the nave and furthered their vertical perspective with lanterns to admit striations of clerestory light through elliptical galleries behind sculpture groups.**1.58j–l** He also provided the culmination to the scenography of S. Maria della Consolazione: Guarini conceived the juxtaposition of the ovoid and hexagonal spaces but not their execution, as we have noted; Juvarra produced

1.58f

The Madonna del Carmine plan follows the Albertian formula and, as at S. Filippo Neri, there is a domical presbytery. That rises to a lantern conventionally enough – though the proportions are exceptionally elevated – on ribs rising from single pilasters. Between the nave bays the triumphal-arch motif is honoured in the breach, literally. The elliptical chapel

1.58g

1.58h

1.58j

1.58k

vaults are opened to clerestory and lantern through diminishing oculii: the vertical perspective is staged within arcades which, crossed where the chapel vaulting cedes to a gallery, are also open to the full height of the main space in an entirely novel interpretation of the medieval – or post-Renaissance German – hall church.

the high altar and the sacristy, the former in the rich materials employed throughout the main spaces – contrary to Guarini's norm.[1.53]

1.58i

1.58l

JUVARRA AND THE PALACE

1.59b

La Venaria Reale was severely damaged by French troops in 1693. Vittorio Amedeo II (1675–1720) had begun renovation and expansion by the end of the century. The work was entrusted to Garove, now principal ducal architect, but there could be little progress until the end of the War of the Spanish Succession. Then Vittorio Amedeo determined to rebuild on the scale of his French rival's absolutist palaces in

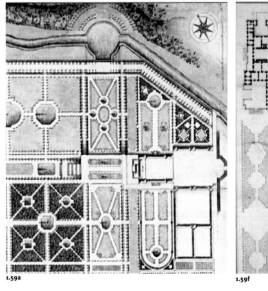

1.59a

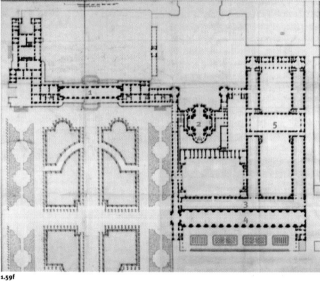

1.59f

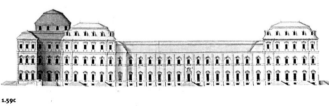

1.59c

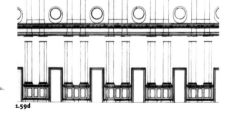

1.59d

celebration of his triumph over the French at the Battle of Turin six years earlier and his elevation to kingship with the acquisition of Sicily (1713) and then Sardinia (1720). Garove was retained to develop his earlier plans for the exercise but died before work was far advanced in 1713.

In 1716 the commission to complete the enlargement of La Venaria was given to Juvarra. Sicilian, the latter proved to be a master of scenography in ephemeral works of royal celebration and stage-set design – as well as the highly imaginative projector of ideal buildings.**1.63b, 1.58a** He returned to his native Sicily where he met the island's new king, designed a great quadrangular palace for him at Messina and was called to Turin to replace the late Garove – all in 1714.**1.59**

1.59e

1.59g

1.59h

La Venaria Reale: expansion

Amedeo di Castellamonte had projected one gallery along the south side of his forecourt: Garove revised this and projected a matching wing to close the court on the north as well. Twin galleries would have extended east from augmented ducal apartments to a chapel and a theatre in enlarged pavilions left and right of the revised entrance to a single great forecourt. The range between Castellamonte's inner and outer courts was demolished, the duke's apartments on the south flank of the main block were reformed and the adjoining great gallery wing begun by 1709 but there was little work on the original palace before Garove died in 1713 and it survived to be renovated.

Appointed to Garove's place, Juvarra focused his attention on revising the fenestration of the gallery wing, on its internal decoration, on a grand new votive church of S. Uberto to its south-east and on a vast stable block to the latter's south. Called on to match his patron's pretensions to entering the select company of Europe's kings, Juvarra resorted appropriately to variations on the triumphal-arch motif throughout his several works on the site: the façade of the great stable block, the exterior and interior of the church of S. Uberto and the interior of the great gallery.

As in the so-called rhythmic bays of Bramante's Vatican Belvedere –

1.59i

1.59k

1.59l

and its followers – the triumphal-arch motif is applied to enliven the great gallery's articulation: the overlapping series responds to the alternating arcaded and trabeated bays introduced in revision of Garove's repetitive fenestration. Unlike its counterpart at Versailles (as we shall see), light streams in from both sides, enhanced by clerestory oculii – elliptical instead of Garove's roundels. The illusionist vault painting of the French and Roman prototypes is also rejected in favour of stuccoed reliefs in grand cartouches between transverse coffered arches. The portals are enlivened with broken pediments on canted columns in the manner which Juvarra – at least as much as any of his contemporaries – established as the late-Baroque norm.

In contracted and expanded form respectively, the triumphal-arch motif distinguishes the central and side bays of the double-height pronaos of the huge building containing the great orangery in parallel to the great stables (from 1722) – rarely if ever to be matched in size (140 x 34 x 15 metres). To the east of the church complex Benedetto Alfieri added secondary stabling, a riding school and carriage house which enclosed two exercise courts.

The triumphal-arch motif also distinguishes the façade of the church on both levels and is echoed beyond the semi-circular exedrae which flank the portal. In a composition extruded from Borromini's S. Agnese in Piazza Navona, these were to be the bases of twin towers which were conceived as pivots in the links between the palace, the service buildings and the church. The latter is framed by three ranges of accommodation for its servants – as in the Superga. The link between the grand gallery and the church through the southern range, projected by Juvarra, was effected by Alfieri for Carlo Emanuele III in the mid-18th century: his is the Torre del Belvedere and the entrance screen to the palace court with the clock tower over the portal.

Inside the church, the triumphal-arch motif spans the four canted piers of the domed crossing: conceived on a scale matching the new king's pretensions, that is octagonal with Greek-cross extensions and circular chapels on the diagonals like the centralized scheme for S. Pietro as revised by Bernini, and like Rainaldi's S. Agnese as revised by Borromini. The sumptuous internal embellishment is disciplined by the colossal Corinthian Order which screens the sanctuary apse in the Palladian manner of Il Redentore. The work was completed up to the drum of the dome: not realized, the latter is evoked illusionistically with simulated coffering.

1.59j

1.60a

›1.60 TURIN, PALAZZO MADAMA: (a) elevation of Juvarra's ideal scheme, (b) great staircase.

The Roman palazzo formula is adjusted to give extra elevation to the volume of the great staircase above the piano reale: the lack of the projected wings further enhances the effect. The imperial staircase type is rejected in favour of twinned parallel flights rising from a central vestibule. The stucco embellishment is free-ranging: coffering derived from Cortona is supplemented with the scallop shells which give Rococo its name and, beyond that, stylized naturalism.

›1.61 TURIN, DUCAL PALACE EMBELLISH-MENT DIRECTED BY JUVARRA: (a, b) Reggia, gallery (now armory museum) and Scala delle Forbici (1720); (c, d) Villa della Regina, royal apartments, details of chinoiserie interior decoration.

Juvarra was fully aware of the French *genre pittoresque*: he was masterly both in translating the fashionably arabesque – grotesque – designs of Claude Audran or Jean Bérain into faux Chinese and, beyond that, in framing lacquer panels in exotic cabinets. As we have seen at La Venaria and in the vault of the Palazzo Madama staircase, he was also masterly at effecting a synthesis between rocaille and High Baroque – Cortonesque – motifs. As a prelude to the embellishment of the infinitely grander Madama exercise, he deployed the repertory of scroll mouldings and the scallop shell in the subsidiary staircase of the Reggia – with relief panels including one with an amusing play on scissor imagery in reference to the configuration of the ramps.

1.60b

1.61a

1.61c

1.61b

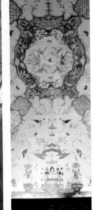
1.61d

His churches spanned Juvarra's Piedmontese career: so too did his palaces. As we have seen, at the heart of the capital was a roughly quadrangular castle with four corner towers dating largely from the 14th century. It had been the residence of the duchess dowager since 1634: Marie-Jeanne, Vittorio Amedeo II's half-Bourbon mother, decided to replace it with a modern palace in 1718. As regent from 1675 to 1680 she had furthered her pro-French policy by marrying her son to Louis XIV's niece and she sought to emulate the French king's residence. As Savoy's first architect, the Sicilian Juvarra responded with a vast scheme encapsulating the old castle: this may be seen to follow procedure at Versailles but otherwise generic propriety recommended reference to the Italian projects for the completion of Louis XIV's urban seat. In strict contrast to the most original palace in the city, Guarini's Carignano, the regular rectilinear massing of the Madama recalls the Roman palazzo projects of both Bernini and Cortona (see page 107 and pages 246f) – but with the insertion of an open colonnaded loggia addressing the piazza. Only that front block had been completed when the patroness died in 1724: it was entirely occupied by a staircase which varies the imperial type developed in the Toledo Alcázar with grandeur hitherto matched only by the ambassadors' staircase at Versailles but with sculpted medallions and Cortonesque coffering instead of illusionist painting.[1.60]

After his Madama exercise, Juvarra's ducal works extended to several other palace projects: the grand unrealized one for Rivoli; a virtuoso staircase and considerable interior schemes in the Turin residence.[1.61] His work for the crown and church was not entirely inimical to private practice: in Turin his limited corpus of palazzi is well represented by his work for Martini di Cigala and Birago di Borgaro.[1.62]

›1.62 TURIN, JUVARRAN PALAZZI: (a, b) Birago di Borgaro (from 1716), street front, androne; (c, d) Martini di Cigala (1716), street front, androne.

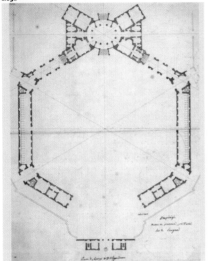

›1.63 STUPINIGI, PALAZZINA DI CACCIA,
1729–33: (a) entrance front (engraved 1773), (b) plan,
(c, d) salone, (e) antechamber vault detail, (f) fantasy,
(g) garden front.

A hunting lodge only in name, this extensive complex just outside Turin eclipsed even La Venaria Reale in the splendour of its embellishment. If the diagonal cross plan has Roman, French and Austrian antecedents, the basic formula of a villa centred on a salone is Palladian. Nothing could be further from that source, however, than the undulating, vibrantly lit, multi-tiered confection from which Stupinigi devolves: yet, through Juvarra's unrealized projects for a new cathedral (c. 1729), even that has an antique origin in works like the so-called Temple of Minerva Medica (AIC1, page 624). Germanic influence on the transmogrification is apparent in the enhanced skeletal structure and low-slung vaults yet the result has its Italian extension in the stage sets of the Bibiena dynasty.

Juvarra's work on the Palazzo Madama and the Reggia at La Venaria notwithstanding, his most celebrated legacy in the secular field is the stupendous Palazzina di Caccia at Stupinigi beyond the western outskirts of the capital. As we have often seen, the linking of diversified forms was a major Baroque technique in both the religious and secular fields. Juvarra develops it under the influence variously of Bernini and Borromini. In particular, in planning his Savoyard patron's so-called hunting lodge (from 1729) he was clearly aware of Fontana's scheme for completing the Palazzo Montecitorio to accommodate the Curia.**1.40a, 1.63** From that common source, indeed, others were busily involved in similar exercises, not least Germain Boffrand for the Duc de Lorraine and Fischer von Erlach for Count Althan (as we shall see).

At Stupinigi, as in the earlier Austrian and French works, diagonally disposed wings converge on a vast salone: entrance and garden exit are centred on the splayed fronts, apartments are fitted into the acute-angled sides. However, rather than the Classical rotunda which we shall find in Boffrand's project for the Duc de Lorraine, Juvarra's elliptical central space is richly diversified: four great piers, defining a central rectangle, carry undulating apsidal galleries derived from interlocking circles as in Borromini's S. Carlo alle Quattro Fontane; the whole is shot through with light from varied sources. Nor does French academicism have anything to do with the exterior, especially in Boffrand's radical reformulation with its stark contrast between the public centre and the private sides. Instead Juvarra preferred

1.63c

1.63f

1.63g

1.63d

1.63e

an elementary exercise in the Baroque tradition of fusing the parts: the central volume, with its elaborate pyramidal roof rising high over its complex skeletal structure, is subjected to the division between the two main storeys of the wings – partly in respect of its own internal layering – but the central portico's Ionic Order of pilasters, the only canonical element in a largely abstract ordonnance, echoes through the wings.

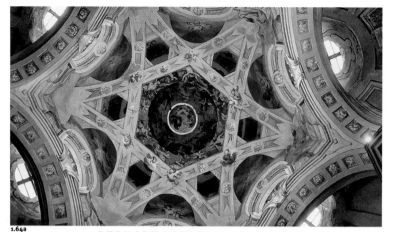

1.64a

1.64b

BERNARDO VITTONE

Not Juvarra, Guarini's most devoted heir in Turin was Bernardo Vittone (1704–70) who dominated Piedmontese architecture in the next generation, after he had returned from studying in post-Borrominian Rome and had been entrusted with preparing Guarini's *Architettura Civile* for publication in 1737. In a vigorous career as a church builder in particular, he forged some of the most extraordinary spaces in the whole Baroque repertory, linking them variously vertically and horizontally, and slashing into them with light to spectacular effect – as, for instance, in S. Bernardino at Chieri or S. Maria di Piazza in Turin. His debut at the Santuario di Vallinotto, in 1738, is unthinkable without knowledge of Guarini's idiosyncracies – but it certainly does not avoid indebtedness to Juvarra. The hexagonal plan is expanded with alternating semi-circular and elliptical chapels and the high altar is even removed into a semi-ambulatory beyond the oval sanctuary – as in Guarini's S. Lorenzo. Here, however, the stellar ribs are detached from the surface of the dome to fly freely as they had done in the most extreme German – or even English – late-Gothic fantasies but without ceding the tensile strength of Guarini's permutation.**1.64**

›**1.64 VITTONE AT LARGE:** (a, b) Santuario di Vallinotto (1738), dome detail, half-plan and section; (c, d) Chieri, S. Bernardino (1740), interior to sanctuary and detail of vaulting; (e) Bra, S. Chiara (1742), half elevation–half section and plan; (f) Rivarolo Canavese, S. Michele Arcangelo (1758), half elevation-half section and plan; (g–i) Turin, S. Maria di Piazza (1750s), half plan and section, interior to sanctuary and vault detail.

1.64e

1.64f

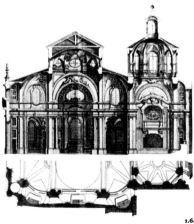

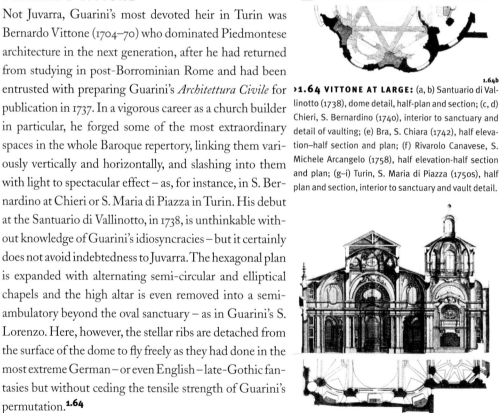

1.64g

1.64c

1.64d

1.64h

1.64i

1.65b

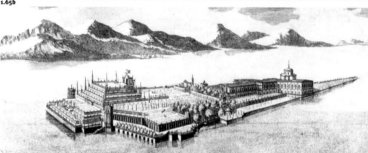
1.65a

›1.65 ISOLA BELLA (LAKE MAGGIORE): (a) engraved overview (from Marc'Antonio Dal Re, *Ville di delizia*, 1743), (b, c) general views from the lake, (d) main axis towards 'proscenium' and terraces, (e) palazzo terrace.

The embankment and terracing of the island were initiated in 1620 for Carlo II Borromeo by Angelo Crivelli: the aptly named Pietro Antonio Barca took over in 1671. The complex acquired its punning name from the natural quality of the place and Isabella, the wife of Carlo III Borromeo.

1.65c

1.65d

1.65e

EXCURSION TO ISOLA BELLA

Scenography, stage-setting in fact, was the motive pursued in the evocation of Cythera for the Borromeo on the Isola Bella in Lake Maggiore.[1.65] The culmination of the assertive central axis from the unfinished palace, the stage is raised on ten terraces alternately sprouting obelisks and statues at the corners: the proscenium masks it from immediate view with giant shells and aquatic deities in tiered niches surmounted by the unicorn of the Borromeo crest. Stepped terraces, with varied perspectives to be discovered by the venturer, were essential to the Italian Mannerist garden: so too was allusion to the antique – as we have seen. Speculatively or coincidentally, the accumulation of terraces here matches the most probable form of the hanging gardens of Babylon.

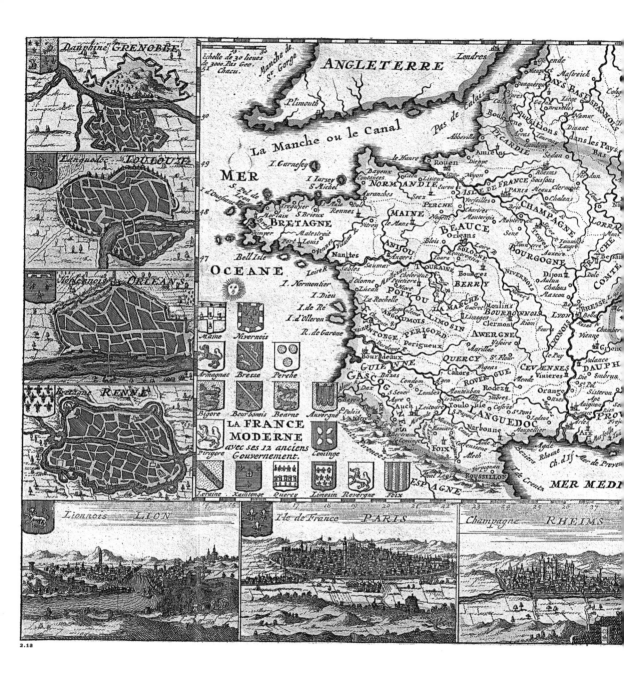

>**2.1 FRANCE:** (a) map by Daniel de la Feuille (1706) with overview of principal citie; (b) insignia of the kingdoms of France and Navarre.

PART 2
SEMINAL FRENCH

2.1b

1 FROM RICHELIEU TO MAZARIN

Countering Mannerist excess, the reassertion of Classical values in the first decade of the reign of Louis XIII – by Salomon de Brosse in particular (AIC5, pages 362ff, 390ff) – appealed to secular builders of the new administrative and professional class: they were to the fore with new projects when the king was relatively quiescent and the old nobility was engaged on much renovation of *ci-devant* feudal seats after the damage wrought in the conflicts of the past century (AIC5, pages 386ff): the Code Michaud of 1629 forbade their fortification. In refortification of the Church, however, Classical stricture was not unopposed by the proponents of the style currently being developed in Counter-Reformation Rome: naturally, matters came to a head in the genre where hitherto planning and even internal elevation remained largely conservative of Gothic forms – not only for the completion of late-medieval works or the reconstruction of churches damaged during the civil wars of religion. Instead, recently established Counter-Reformation orders were bent on innovation for their burgeoning urban foundations. To place the issue in context we must look briefly at the cultural climate in France after Louis XIII had asserted his majority.

Under the ministry of Cardinal Richelieu from 1624, most important commissions came from the *noblesse de robe* rather than the feudal *noblesse d'épée* who had dominated patronage in the 16th century. Serious-minded, committed to order, the new class also provided the administrators like the Surintendant des Bâtiments, François Sublet de Noyers and architectural theorists like Roland Fréart de Chambray, a mathematician whose *Parallèle de l'architecture antique avec la moderne* (1650) was to be a pillar of antique authority, not least in eulogizing Vitruvius yet presenting the three Greek Orders (Doric, Ionic, Corinthian) as para-

2.2a

›2.2 ROLAND FRÉART DE CHAMBRAY, PARALLÈLE DE L'ARCHITECTURE ANTIQUE AVEC LA MODERNE, 1650: (a) frontispiece, (b) Corinthian Order from the Roman Baths of Diocletian.

Fréart draws on a wide range of treatises on the Orders in his quest for 'la beauté véritable et essentielle'. He is not original in defining it in terms of Albertian *concinnitas* (AIC4, pages 734f). He published a French edition of Palladio's *Quattro libri*, according it first rank, but differed from it, from Vignola and the post-Albertian tradition, in preferring the three original Greek Orders to the discredit of the two additional Roman ones (Tuscan and Composite).

He and his generation depended on Vitruvius for their identification of Greek achievement, rather than on personal experience, and distilled from him that Doric, Ionic and Corinthian comprehend all that is both beautiful and necessary in architecture because they meet the full range of building modes: the Ionic providing for the mean between the extremes of Doric solidity and Corinthian delicacy. The excessive development of the Roman Orders was superfluous to the Greek originals, 'la fleur et la perfection des ordres, puisqu'ils contiennent non seulement tout le beau, mais encore tout le nécessaire de l'architecture, n'y ayant que trois manières de bâtir, la solide, la moyenne et la délicate, lesquelles sont toutes parfaitement exprimées en ces trois ordres'.

Through fear of challenging habitual approbation, he maintained, the Moderns pay too much deference to the Vitruvian Orders and, besides, have abused the originals. Small minds, disdainful of following the best examples bequeathed by antiquity, turn to fantasy in the belief that apprentices copy, masters are novel: given to the gratuitous elaboration of cornices and the superfluous application of masks, cartouches, etc. ('les petits esprits qui ne peuvent arriver à la connaissance universelle de l'art ... rampant incessamment autour de ces minuties: ... leurs idées sont tellement basses et disgraciées qu'elles ne produisent rien que des mascarons, de villains cartouches et de semblables grotesques ridicules'). Such degenerate licentiousness is to be reversed by returning to the source of the Orders and there drawing upon the ideas of the original masters in all their purity: that lies in the basic principles of proportion founded in geometry which have been denied by the complexity of latter-day conjecture – as indeed by the excessive embellishment of the Corinthian Order in the Baths of Diocletian, for example.

2.2b

gons of beauty which contain 'all that is necessary in architecture'.[2.2] Together, bureaucrat and theorist attempted to bring architectural practice into line with theory – Palladian discipline in particular – for the first time in France to purify the native tradition from the excesses of Mannerism and protect it from the licence of both Roman and Flemish Baroque as the contemporary Dutch were doing (see pages 236f, and AIC5, pages 549f).

The queen-mother, Marie de' Medici, was building lavishly at the Luxembourg on the southern outskirts of Paris: her second son Gaston was to embark on an even more ambitious scheme at Blois (AIC5, pages 867f, and see below, pages 232ff). But Louis XIII was not one of France's great builders: his only major project, promoted by Sublet, was the completion of the Cour Carré of the Louvre and the decoration of the Grande Galerie linking it with the Tuileries, both as a palace and a centre for the arts pre-eminent in Europe. Fréart was dispatched to Rome in 1639 to bring Nicolas Poussin back for the decoration of the Grande Galerie, but also perhaps to found an academy of the arts.

Reluctant to return to France, Poussin ensured his repatriation was short and his scheme remained unresolved, though he was persuaded to pursue its evolution from Rome until the end of 1643. Meanwhile, in 1624, Sublet endorsed the quadrupling of Lescot's Louvre (AIC5, pages 336ff) and commissioned Jacques Lemercier (1585–1654) whom he considered the leading Classicist after de Brosse. The latter was out of favour – indeed subject to legal proceedings – due to troubles with his patroness, Marie de' Medici, over the construction of her Luxembourg palace. Lemercier, Premier Architecte du Roi since 1618, had spent much of the decade to c. 1615 in Rome while Maderno was active but seems to have gravitated to the more conservative practitioners (see pages 56f). Initiating his royal career back in Paris, however, his response to the problem of designing

2.3c

2.3d

2.3a

›2.3 FURTHERING THE LOUVRE: (a, b) Grande Galerie (Choiseul snuffbox, Louis-Nicolas van Blarenberghe) and Poussin's scheme for its decoration (from 1638), (c, d) Lemercier's extension to Lescot's Cour Carrée and his Pavillon de l'Horloge (from 1624).

For his Pavillon de l'Horloge, which binds the original block of the new Louvre to his repetition of it to the north, Lemercier wanted an extra storey to raise the square dome above Lescot's ordonnance. No full Order being admissible over the Corinthian or Composite, caryatids have generally been endorsed in principle but academic Classicists find Lemercier's examples over-scaled and their double pediments over-complex.

2.3b

a high new central pavilion between his reproduction of Lescot's wing and the original is alien to academic stricture: it was not to be repeated and the court remained undefined for nearly half a century.

Sublet also fostered the career of Étienne Martellange (1569–1641). Like Lemercier, he had been in Rome during the formative years of the Baroque but had not been seduced by it. Searching, on the contrary, for an alternative to the florid anti-Classical style of the late-16th century, especially in ecclesiastical architecture, both recalled Antonio da Sangallo's formula for the Roman church façade – or its post-Tridentine revision by Giacomo della Porta – as the basis for their own work. Martellange was a Jesuit but his confreres had other ideas for their major Parisian foundation – and their works elsewhere.**2.3-2.5**

Stylistic conflict in the Church Militant

Of the several mendicant orders which were to make significant contributions to the Parisian ecclesiastical heritage, the Jesuits were to the fore as usual. In France from the middle of the 16th century, banished by the Parlement de Paris in 1594, reinstated in 1603, they prospered with the support of Henri IV: first at La Flèche, where they established a college at the king's instigation (from 1604), building began to the designs of the royal architect Louis Métezeau but was amplified by Étienne Martellange as a shrine for the heart of the assassinated king.

Dedicated to S. Louis under the auspices of Louis XIII – and to S. Paul – the church of the Jesuit Parisian headquarters was built to overawe the rue Saint-Antoine – the artery through the fashionable Marais quarter developed for the upper echelons of society from the nucleus of Henri IV's Place Royale (AIC5, pages 381f). At Sublet's behest, Martellange was awarded the commission and proceeded to emulate the Roman Gesù – whose authorities asserted the right to vet all their order's planning but allowed latitude for local building traditions. Thus the plan is an elongated version of the Gesù type, with linked side chapels instead of aisles and the crossing of the limited transepts is crowned with a largely masonry dome – for the first time in Paris. However, the elevation is quasi-Gothic with more generous tribunes (for the brothers and their charges) than the Roman model, much higher clerestory and the dome is elongated into a *tour-lanterne*. As was now to be the norm, the windows were void of stained glass – for the illumination of reason.

Martellange may be credited with the conception of S.-Paul-S.-Louis's executed volume and its internal articulation with colossal pilasters: that reiterates the system he had adopted for the chapel at La Flèche. However, his façade, marked by the influence of Salomon de Brosse's S.-Gervais in its determination to Classicize un-Classical height, was rejected by the Parisian fathers – apparently for lack of the drama they had sought in the inception of the Roman Baroque. They turned instead to another Jesuit priest, François Derand. He too referred to S.-Gervais for his façade but projected the central bay, increasing the plasticity of the Order from half-columns on the side bays to three-quarter ones in the centre, in the manner of Carlo Maderno, and applied ornament liberally, in the manner of the Flemish – like the portal of the college at La Flèche on which work was continuing.

Derand's work was bitterly condemned by Martellange, both for the profusion of ornament and the Roman conception of movement. By the 1620s, as we have seen, the progression from pilaster to column in concert with the projection of the plane of the wall was the standard French-Classical solution to the essentially French problem of binding pavillons and corps de logis together (AIC5, page 340). As we have seen, the Roman conception of movement was dependent on transition through varying degrees of plasticity in the Order and that was unacceptable to academic Classicists because it involved the 'mutilation' of the column. The Jesuits retained Derand for S.-Paul-S.-Louis but all his façade columns had been given full plasticity when work began in 1629. The near-contemporary work for the Jesuits at Blois, S.-Vincent-de-Paul, was not alone in similarly transforming Philibert de l'Orme's formula for 'Classicizing' Gothic elevation. At the beginning of the next decade, however, the Jesuits turned back to Martellange for their church of the Novitiate in Paris and he responded with a manifesto of academic Classical principles: the elevation was more Roman than French and, though the nave projected slightly, strictly canonical pilasters were used across the whole façade in the manner of Giacomo della Porta.

2.4a

2.4b

**›2.4 LA FLÈCHE, PRYTANÉE NATIONAL MILI-
TAIRE:** (a) outer portal, (b) interior.

The château, founded by the Duchesse d'Alençon in
the 16th century, was assigned to the Jesuits by Henri
IV in 1604 to accommodate the Collège Royal Henri-Le-
Grand. Considerable works were undertaken by the
Jesuits at the outset of their tenure, especially the outer
portal and the church built by their brother Étienne
Martellange from 1607 which ultimately enshrined the
hearts of the king and queen. Following the expulsion
of the Jesuits in 1674 the college was developed as a
military academy.

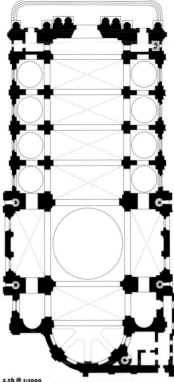

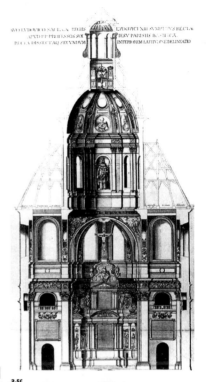

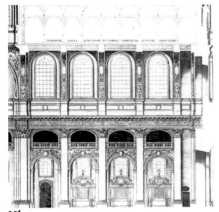

2.5d

2.5b @ 1:1000

2.5c

2.5a

›2.5 PARIS, THE JESUIT CHURCH: (a–f) S.-Paul-
S.-Louis (projected from the mid-1620s, construction
to 1641), reconstruction of original façade plans of
Martellange (1) and Derand (2), plan as executed, lateral section through crossing, nave elevation, interior
to sanctuary, façade; (g) Jesuit church of the Novitiate,
façade (17th-century engraving recording lost work).

2.5e

2.5f

2.5g

DIGRESSION TO FLANDERS

When, in the era of Richelieu, François Sublet de Noyers
and his circle deplored the ostentation of Flemish architecture they meant the style of Cornelis Floris de Vriendt and
Hans Vredeman de Vries – and its roots in the Mannerist
School of Fontainebleau – as well as the late Mannerism
perpetrated by the works of Jacques Androuet du Cerceau
in both print and building (AIC5, pages 368ff). Specifically
in contemporary Flanders, it meant the works of Rubens
in print and building – his own house (from 1618) informed
by his *Palazzi di Genova* (published in Antwerp in 1622)
– and developments in façade design represented by the
church of S. Carolus Borromeus in Antwerp (from c. 1620)

DESIGN: (a) Bruges, S.-Walpurga (S.-Walburgakerk, designs date from 1619, construction began a decade later); (b) Louvain, S.-Michel (former Jesuit church, from c. 1650).

As with Jesuit churches in general, the architect belonged to the order: Willem Van Hees (1601–90), architect of S.-Michel, was a novice in Antwerp when Pieter Huyssens was working on S. Carolus Borromeus but derived his elevated approach from Jacob Francart's works in Brussels and Mechelen (AIC5, pages 534f). In articulation, however, he followed Huyssens: the latter, who usually expressed the traditional basilican form in section and elevation, was clearly aware of developments in early Baroque Roman in his designs for S.-Walpurga in Bruges but the progression in the Order of the latter is constrained – countered – by the rusticated banding of his near contemporary S.-Loup at Namur.

2.6b

2.6a

or the Augustinian church of Brussels (both of c. 1620; AIC5, pages 540f). In France, thus, the *richesse* of Derrand's S.-Paul-S.-Louis was rejected in favour of the Classical restraint of Martellange and Lemercier. In Flanders, on the other hand, Maderno was not ignored but floridity flourished: Baroque progression in the plasticity of the Order was deployed by Pieter Huyssens in several works of the 1620s but it competes with applied ornament.**2.6**

2.7a

2.7b

2.7c

›**2.7 SELECT FLEMISH SECULAR WORKS IN THE AGE OF HIGH BAROQUE:** (a) Bruges, Provost House of S. Donatian (from 1662), façade on the Burg; (b) Mechelen, De Corenbloem (Lucas Faydherbe, mid-17th century); (c) Brussels, Grand Place (from c. 1700), guild houses on the north-west side.

The reconstruction exercise in Brussels was one of self-conscious historicism: it may well be compared with its equivalent in Antwerp (AIC4, page 424).

At mid-century, the church of the Brussels Beeguinage (Begijnhofkerk) is still best categorized in terms of late Florid Mannerism but the apogee of the Baroque-Mannerist mélange is marked by S.-Michel in Louvain.**2.6b**

Church façades influenced the design of the narrow street fronts typical of Flemish domestic and guild buildings. Even as late as the end of the century, however, it is the latter, rather than the former, which distinguishes the reconstruction of the Grand Place in Brussels after its destruction by the French in 1695 – though precedents for relieving repetitive Orders with porticoes supported by atlante include the Provost House of S. Donatian in Bruges (from 1662).**2.7**

JACQUES LEMERCIER

Lemercier's main ecclesiastical exercise was the chapel of the Sorbonne commissioned by Richelieu before 1629 but begun in 1635.**2.8** Meanwhile he also built churches for the cardinal at Rueil and Richelieu. Rueil is lost. His Richelieu church is a simple basilica: its Roman type of façade, articulated solely with pilasters, is closer in its proportions to Sangallo and early Vignola than to della Porta – or Martellange's Novitiate.**2.9**

The great work at the Sorbonne, Paris's second important domed church, is adapted from the semi-centralized composition of Rosato Rosati's S. Carlo ai Catinari in Rome (from 1612, see page 57). For the west front, addressing the public domain, Rosati's articulation was revised and full columns applied on the lower level, pilasters above: neither of these gestures towards the Baroque has been well received by the academic Classicists. However, the most original feature of the scheme has generally been applauded for regularity and gravitas worthy of the greatest of the Romans: this is the north elevation with its lunette and precocious temple-front portico giving access

2.8a

2.8b

2.8c

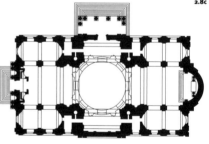

2.8d @ 1:1000

2.8e

2.8f

›**2.8 PARIS, CHAPEL OF THE SORBONNE,** from 1635: (a, b) exterior from west and north, (c, d) lateral section and plan, (e, f) longitudinal cut-away perspective and interior.

›**2.9 RICHELIEU, CHURCH OF NOTRE-DAME,** from 1631: (a) overview in urban context, (b) west front, (c) interior.

from the college court to the rotunda under which the patron was to be interred. As in the works of Martellange, but contrary to the practice then developing in Rome, the masonry of the vaults is not denied by illusionist painting and sculpture is subjected to architecture: that aesthetic was to endure with greater rigour as the century – and the next – progressed.

The church at Richelieu was built to accommodate the parishioners of the cardinal's eponymous town. Regularly planned on a new site for imported inhabitants, the latter was an exercise in ancestral invention dominated by an

2.9b

2.9c

2.9a

2.10c

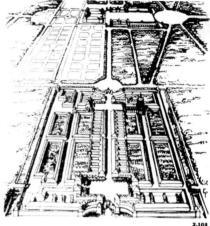

2.10a

›2.10 RICHELIEU: (a) site plan with château in background, (b, c) château, overview from the east and main residential complex (late-17th-century engravings by Gabriel Perelle), (d) southern town gate.

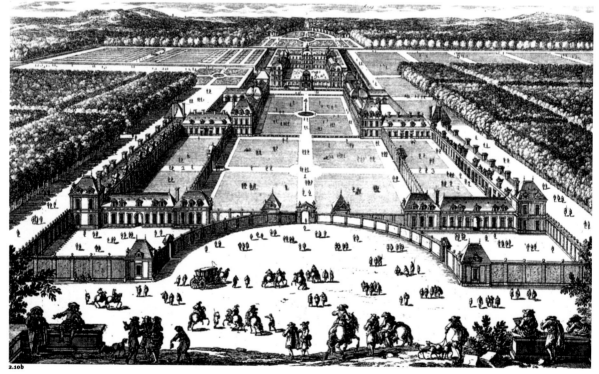

2.10b

2.10d

The property was acquired by the Thouars viscounts, vassals of Poitiers, in the 9th century: after several vicissitudes, it was settled on Louis II de la Tremoille, Prince de Talmont, Vicomte de Thouars, by Charles VIII towards the end of the 15th century. The medieval château was rebuilt from 1635 by Henri de la Trémoille, Duc de Thouars, and his wife Marie de la Tour d'Auvergne: it has now definitely been credited to Lemercier. The forecourt is defined by galleries with terrace roofs: the vigorously rusticated corps de logis – clearly related to the work at Richelieu – projects into three pavillons in the usual manner, the central one with a square dome, the doubled side ones with pitched roofs.

immense château. Striving to meet the cardinal's pretensions for his seat, where seminal importance follows court succeeding court to diminishing breadth in a formal landscape, Lemercier did not match de Brosse's conception of coherence. Indeed the variety of roof forms he used for the pavillons and the disparity between them and the corps de logis asserts differentiation and this is hardly countered by turrets at the junctions on the garden front or the accommodation of the cardinal's collection of antique sculpture in niches on the court front.[2.10] Similar massing with a square-domed central pavillon prompts the attribution of the contemporary château of Thouars to Lemercier but the forecourt is framed only with single-storey arcades and the articulation is more consistent in its assertive rustication.[2.11]

Rustication which might be called late Mannerist – with or without prejudice – recurs in considerable complexity at the château of Tanlay and, more modestly again, at Cany-Barville or Cheverny – *inter alia*. And the counterpart of the style is nowhere better represented than in the splendid suite of interiors at Cheverny too. [2.12–2.15]

2.11

2.12

2.13

2.14C

>**2.12 TANLAY, CHÂTEAU,** begun on medieval foundations after 1560 by François d'Andelot, brother of the Hugenot leader Gaspard de Coligny; interrupted by the Wars of Religion; completed to revised plans between 1643 and 1650: entrance front.

>**2.13 CORMATIN, CHÂTEAU:** salon detail (c. 1640).

>**2.14 CHEVERNY, CHÂTEAU,** finished from 1624: (a) exterior from the south, (b) staircase, (c) antechamber chimneypiece, (d) salon.

The estate, forfeited by the Hurault counts through fraud, was bestowed by Henri II on his mistress, Diane de Poitiers, but she preferred the Château de Chenonceau and sold Cheverny back to the expropriated heir. A descendant, Philippe Hurault, called for a new château from Jacques Bougier of Blois who had emerged from the studio of Salomon de Brosse.

2.14a

2.14b

2.14d

2.15b

2.15d

The work was undertaken by Louis Gouffier, Duc de Roannais and governor of Poitou (died 1642).

2.15a

2.15c

›2.16 PARIS, CHURCH OF THE FEUILLANTS,
from 1601: façade (from 1623, after Jean Mariette,
L' architecture françoise, 1727 – AF).

Reformed Cistercians on strict Bernardine lines,
the Feuillants issued from the abbey of Notre-Dame
des Feuillants near Toulouse and brought to Paris a
conservative late-medievalism which they adapted to
the Counter-Reformation church plan type: the side
chapels were lower and wider than in Vignola's masterpiece, the clerestory much higher, but Mansart could
make do with the upper two storeys of the S.-Gervais
model plus a Mannerist attic.

2.16

FRANÇOIS MANSART

In the first decade of Richelieu's ministry the mantle of the
early Classical masters had passed from de Brosse to François Mansart (1598–1666) and he set himself to perfecting
the work of his predecessors. In his châteaux of Balleroy,
Blois, Maisons and his later churches, the development of
his style is marked by the elimination of inessentials, clarity and restraint in ornament but richness in planar variation, respect for rules but flexibility within them. Though
his planning is conservative in retaining the traditional
alignment of rooms in single file (*en enfilade*), in a way
typical of his individualism his work reveals a command
of techniques usually identified as High Baroque: vigorous contrast in the contours of walls and the profiles of
masses, colossal scale, alignment of varied spaces for rich
vistas, vertical perspectives and dramatic lighting. As we
know, such techniques were concurrently being evolved
in Rome to serve the Counter-Reformation ideal of the
Church Triumphant. While the protégés of Sublet de
Noyers, who knew Rome, were bent on promoting the
purity of French Classicism by opposing them, Mansart,
who never visited Rome, seemingly sought to invigorate
the native tradition by drawing on the same sources as his
Italian contemporaries – the fantastic reconstructions of
antique buildings and church fittings by Giovanni Battista
Montano in particular (see pages 68f).**2.16**

Needless to say, perhaps, rule came first. From his earliest work on the façade of the church of the Feuillants (1623),
Mansart followed the logical and coherent approach to
ordonnance furthered by de Brosse and Métezeau after
the examples set by Lescot and de l'Orme – though the
Mannerism of the latter's late Tuileries style is also recalled
by the complex superimposition of elements at the top.

While working on his first Parisian project, Mansart
was also engaged with the transformation of the château

2.17

›2.17 BERNY, CHÂTEAU, from 1623: contract perspective provided by François Mansart.

The property was bought by Nicolas Brûlart de Sillery, chancellor of France, in 1615 but it seems to have been his father Pierre who decided on major alterations to the 16th-century château. He turned first to a member of the Métezeau clan (Clément II was active at the time) and then, at the end of 1623, unexpectedly to Mansart. The contract was for the rebuilding of the central pavillon and corps de logis with quadrant colonnades (surmounted by lavatory pavillons) linking the new work to the renovated side pavillons. Court and garden fronts were to match in simple articulation with quoins and plain panels between the windows: niches were introduced at a later stage.

›2.18 BALLEROY, CHÂTEAU, from c. 1625: (a) plan, (b, c) general views.

The patron was Jean de Choisy, who rose from the ranks of the bourgeoisie (his father was a wine merchant) to be chancellor to the king's brother, the Duc d'Orléans. Mansart doubtless came to him from neighbouring Berny and was passed on by him to Gaston d'Orléans at Blois.

Apart from the massing as a freestanding pyramidal block, the most important feature of the building is the staircase: carried only on the wall around an open cage (except for a token forward column at base level) it is a triumph of the stereotomy at which French medieval masons excelled – but its precedents (notably one from the early 16th century in the Toulouse Capitole) are lost.

at Berny in his native Normandy. He was impressed with the discrete entity of de Brosse's late secular works but constrained by existing building: he tied the truncated wings to the rebuilt main block with quadrant arcades but the roofs – and the turrets in the corners of the entrance front – assert the autonomy of the parts in the manner of Jacques Androuet du Cerceau and his medieval ancestors.

Unconstrained in his design of the château at Balleroy, where he had moved on from Berny c. 1625, Mansart eliminated the wings altogether, defining the court with a balustraded terrace flanked by lodges, and established a clear pyramidal hierarchy between the central pavillon and the corps de logis. Dispensing with ornament almost entirely, but retaining assertive keystones, he gave a new monumentality to the approach developed under Henri IV by contrasting smooth grey stone quoins with rough brown stone infill. Neither the massing nor the austerity of articulation was unique in its time though, ironically, the nearest examples of the former are furthest from the latter.**2.17, 2.18**

Mansart's design for the high altar of the Parisian church of S.-Martin-des-Champs (c. 1624), like Berny, incorporates quadrant curves framing a frontispiece. That responds to the context as much as to external inspiration but his altar of the Virgin in Notre-Dame in Paris (c. 1628) suggests that he was already consulting Montano. Four

2.18b

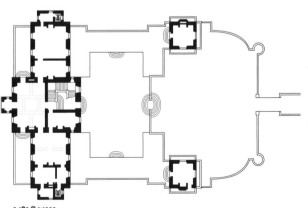

2.18a @ 1:1000

2.18c

2.19

2.20

›2.19 CANY-BARVILLE, CHÂTEAU, from c. 1640: entrance front.

The architect employed by Pierre le Marinier is unidentified: unsubstantiated local tradition attributes it to a Mansart but that is most improbably François. The form, a single corps de logis with corner pavillons but without the wings inherited from the medieval court, is modern in its compactness – except for the variety of its roofs. The contrast between brick and stone was long familiar too but here the norm is reversed: the quoins and window frames are of striking red brick and the infill is plastered.

›2.20 BEAUMESNIL, CHÂTEAU, from 1630: view from the north-west.

The property had been acquired by Jacques le Conte, Marquis de Nonant, early in the 17th century: he demolished the medieval château and began its replacement shortly after 1630. The massing without aisles (the lateral extensions are 19th century) has prompted speculation about the involvement of Mansart who was working in the vicinity at Berny and Balleroy but this is dismissed by stylistic considerations. The work is most plausibly attributed to the master-mason Jean Gaillard of Rouen who is recorded in documents relating to the construction.

›2.21 MONTANO AND MANSART: (a) project for an altarpiece (Montano, *Diversi ornamenti capricciosi per depositi o altari*, 1625); (b) Paris, cathedral of Notre-Dame, Altar of the Virgin (engraving after Mansart's project of c. 1628).

›2.22 PARIS, TEMPLE DE LA VISITATION S.-MARIE, 1632–34: (a) plan at contract stage (as reconstructed by Smith and Braham, *François Mansart*), (b) part-elevation, part-section (contract drawing of 2/1633), (c) elevation (engraved Pierretz), (d, e) exterior and interior detail.

The order of the Visitation of Holy Mary was founded in 1610 by François de Sales, bishop of Geneva, who was a refugee in Annecy from the Calvinists, author of the mystical *Introduction to the Devout Life* for the laity, and the aristocratic widow Jeanne-Françoise de Chantal: the mission was to care for the sick and to offer education to women.

2.21a

2.21b

years later, he was bringing a range of Baroque techniques to bear on the transformation of a prime French High Renaissance ecclesiastical model. Three years further on he was applying the same techniques to a secular project: reconstructing the château of Blois, his first great royal commission, his first resounding masterpiece. There he was greatly constrained: early in the next decade, at Maisons, the most enlightened of his private patrons, René de Longueil, president of the council, gave him the unique opportunity to build and rebuild unconstrained in his incessant quest for perfection.**2.19–2.24**

2.22d

2.22e

The inception of French 'Baroque-Classicism'

For the Temple de la Visitation S.-Marie (1632–34) Mansart adapted Philibert de l'Orme's centralized scheme for the chapel at the Château d'Anet (AIC5, page 332), giving semi-oval perimeters to the subsidiary spaces: centralization was not uncommon in votive works – and Protestant temples – or private and conventual chapels (as here) but rare in the planning of churches for Counter-Reformation orders in France. The expanded sanctuary is crowned by an oval dome with a lantern, large enough virtually to constitute a second dome, ringed with fleshy mouldings which recall Salomon de Brosse at the château of Coulommiers. The dome over the central rotunda, pene-

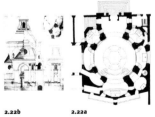

2.22b   2.22a   2.22c

trated by clerestory windows, is cut off to reveal a distinct second dome bearing the lantern. As this second dome receives no direct light, it acts as a foil to the bright zones above and below it, dramatizing the vertical perspective.

Working from 1634 on the reconstruction of the château of Blois for the king's brother, Gaston d'Orléans, Mansart retained the general distribution developed by de Brosse – for the Luxembourg in particular – from his

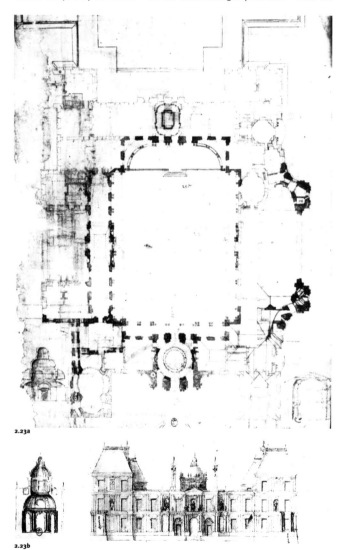

2.23a

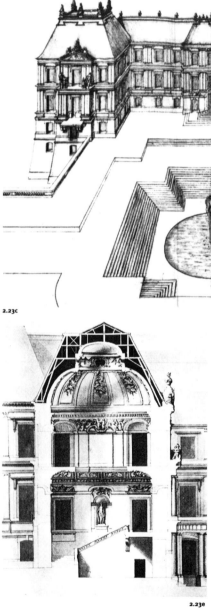

2.23c

2.23e

2.23b

›2.23   BLOIS,   CHÂTEAU   OF   GASTON
D'ORLÉANS, from 1634: (a–c) Mansart's project

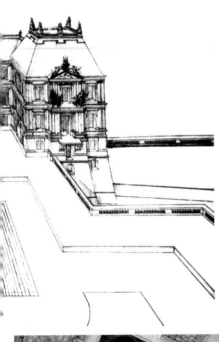

2.23d

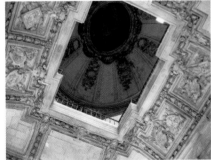

2.23f
drawings (1635–38), plan with section through chapel, entrance elevation with section through central pavilion, overview from garden, (d) model, (e, f) staircase pavilion, section and detail of vault, (g) court front.

The king's brother's pension and huge domain as Duc d'Orléans funded the project but it was suspended when he ceased to be heir presumptive on the birth of the dauphin – the future Louis XIV – in 1638.

›2.24 PARIS, PAVILLON DES MARCHANDS-DRAPIERS: façade (Jacques Bruant, from 1655).

du Cerceau inheritance (AIC5, pages 390f): a rectangular forecourt defined by a screen with entrance pavillon and side wings inferior to the corps de logis of the main residential complex at its head. Further, he perfected a formula to be followed as long as the French retained their concern with the distinction of tall pavillons – at least until the intervention of the Italians for the completion of the Louvre in the 1660s – as the surviving façade of Jacques Bruant's Pavillon des Marchands-Drapiers (c. 1655) amply demonstrates. Yet, as at the Visitation, here too he anticipates the achievements of the Roman High Baroque.

As we have seen, the principle of varying the plasticity of the Order in concert with variations in the plane of the wall, exploited by Carlo Maderno at S. Susanna and therafter a characteristic Roman Baroque way of producing movement in a façade, was not new to France. It had provided Lescot and de l'Orme with the key to the solution of the essentially French problem of binding pavillons and corps de logis together into a consistent whole, at once effecting the transition from one mass to another in the interest of unity and expressing distinctions between the masses in the interest of variety. Developed by de Brosse to ensure the subordination of all the parts in a hierarchically ordered whole, this approach to ordonnance was fundamental to Mansart's conception of scale and monumentality. At Blois, where the site was irregular and the internal requirements more complex than any faced by de Brosse, Mansart showed extraordinary virtuosity in varying the expression of his canonical Orders to generate vitality and achieve clarity in the definition of the parts within a completely consistent whole.

2.23g

If Mansart's Blois might be compared with contemporary works in Rome, its significance lies more properly in a specifically French context. And, as we have seen, into that context Mansart had already introduced curved façades, varied interior spaces, vertical perspectives and dramatic vistas without necessary recourse to direct influence from contemporary Roman practice. All these reappear to enliven plan, section and elevation at Blois. The entrance pavillon in particular, with its cut-off dome surmounted by a drum and second dome, was based on his earlier experiments at the Visitation involving the contrast of illuminated and shaded forms but the principal staircase, in which the lighting from diagonally placed sources is concealed from the main flight by the first-floor gallery, has no precedent. The great interior enfilades derive from the French tradition but Mansart showed his

2.24

›2.25 MAISONS (NOW MAISONS-LAFITTE), CHÂTEAU from 1642: (a) site plan, (b) garden front, (c) entrance to outer forecourt (destroyed), (d, e) plans of ground and first floors, (f) entrance front, (g, h) entrance vestibule and staircase, (i, j) Salle des Fêtes, general view and detail of chimneypiece, (k, l) boudoir vault and floor.

The patron, René de Longueil, was a protégé of Richelieu but rose to be Surintendant des Finances in 1650. His survival in that position does not seem to have been

originality with an exercise in landscaping, precedented in scale only in his own work at Balleroy, in which the château was to operate as the climax of converging vistas in the manner developed later by Le Nôtre.**2.25**

If the Blois project may be seen to have begun with reference to de Brosse's Luxembourg, that master's consolidated massing at Blérancourt was preferred by Mansart less than a decade later for the château of Maisons – though an outer court is framed by detached service wings. In the realization of the main block's subtle articulation in accord with the complex layering of planes, Longueil's forbearance of his architect's perfectionism was of prime exemplary significance to the masters of the French academic Classical tradition and their disciples. Nowhere else is the balance between Gallic delight in variety and Latin will to unify more triumphantly effected. Just as the creator of the finest Doric temple of antiquity invigorated the rigorous system within which he worked by cross-fertilizing it with Ionic – though that was unfamiliar to the mid-17th century – Mansart invigorated the rigor-

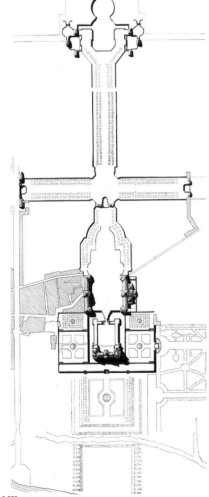

2.25a

2.25b

2.25c

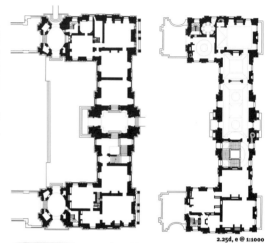

2.25d, e @ 1:1000

ous system of his own time by the restrained use of such Baroque devices as playful sculpture, the contrast of curve and counter-curve and the subtle variation of the form of the Order in response to the complex projection and recession of planes to produce movement in the façades.

Inside the Maisons corps de logis, the traditional single file of state rooms is retained but the staircase is off-centre to the right of the entrance vestibule: less disruptive there than at the Luxembourg, for example, its

2.25f

2.25h

2.25g

2.25i

2.25j

recommended by the sumptuousness with which he received the court at his château in the following year. The omen should not have been lost on his ultimate successor, Nicolas Fouquet – whose pretension and precipitation we shall soon encounter.

2.25k

2.25l

ramps are hung from the wall, as at Balleroy except for a supporting spur at ground-floor level. Less dramatically lit than at Blois, it is more exquisitely restrained in detail – principally wreathed medallions and putti playing on austere panels between Ionic pilasters. These are offset to carry a cornice whose shallow curvature gives its line to the gallery where resolution is found for the urgent impulse of the ascending balustrade's unstable interlocking arcs. Opening the vertical perspective, the gallery links the two sides of the bel-étage. To the left momentum is terminated beyond the arcaded screen of the Salle des Fêtes by the king in the festive Ionic context of a chimneypiece festooned with garlands of plenty borne by caryatids. Beyond, the Chambre de Parade has a rich, uncanonical Composite Order but the cabinets which complete the apartment in the left wing set an Ionic standard complementing the Doric of the vestibule below – and that, the apotheosis of the exterior Order, set the standard for what the 18th century would call 'le goût antique'.

Outside the château was the culmination of a vast landscaping exercise dominated by extended open vistas across the fields and the forecourts, past the service lines whose Orders were proportioned to enhance the apparent size of the main block, and beyond through terraces patterned to reflect the symmetry and order of the building itself. The gardener Claude Mollet (c. 1564–c. 1648) was involved but it is difficult not to credit the conception to Mansart himself as it developed his approach at Balleroy and Blois.

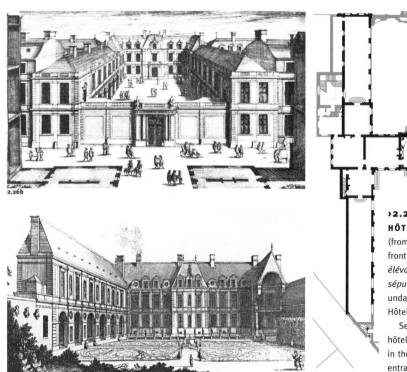

2.26b

2.26c

2.26a @ 1:1000

›2.26 **MANSART AND THE EARLY PARISIAN HÔTEL PARTICULIER:** (a–c) Hôtel de la Vrillière (from 1635), plan, overview from entrance, garden front (after Jean Marot, *Recueil des plans, profils et élévations des plusieurs palais, chasteaux, églises, sépultures, grottes et hostels bâtis dans Paris*, Paris, undated, but probably from the late-1650s – RP); (d) Hôtel de Chavigny (from 1642), detail of garden front.

Secrétaire d'État Louis Phelypeaux de la Vrillière's hôtel is among Mansart's earliest important essays in the genre of the *hôtel particulier*. Beyond the low entrance screen, the usual three wings around the court were differentiated only by the height of the roofs of the central one, where the central pavilion contained the front door, the adjoining two bays of the left wing where the staircase was located and the matching bays of the right wing. There was a service court behind the left wing but the main range of rooms extended from the central block to the full width of the garden. The main exit to the garden was in the pavilion centred on the front court but it was echoed by a

While working at Blois, Mansart was demonstrating his mastery of the formula for the Parisian hôtel inherited from the du Cerceau family through de Brosse – largely in the renovation of existing courtyard houses. Conservative of the enfilade tradition here too, until unconstrained in the late-1640s, he simplified the roof line and proved himself particularly adept at dramatizing staircases, siting them to avoid interference with ground-floor communication, and at conjuring symmetry from disparate axes. This is admirably demonstrated by the plan of the Hôtel de la Vrillière.**2.26** That complex was given the dignity of a Doric Order: otherwise articulation was confined to rusticated coins and the simple frames of the generous windows unless the master was working in an already rich context – as we shall see.

2.26d

second door to the left, redressing symmetry between the gallery wing on the right and an extraordinary niche projecting from a truncated return on the left.

Mansart's next important domestic work, for Secrétaire d'État Léon Bouthillier, Comte de Chavigny, is remarkable for the subtle variation of the ordonnance of the existing hôtel to which it was added – evoking a semblance of symmetry with variation of the system of superimposed Orders currently being developed at Maisons. As there, too, it is traditional in the single enfilade of its main range, doubled only on the return into short wings projecting from the garden side.

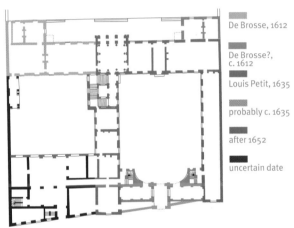

De Brosse, 1612

De Brosse?, c. 1612

Louis Petit, 1635

probably c. 1635

after 1652

uncertain date

2.27a @ 1:1000
›2.27 PARIS, HÔTEL DE LIANCOURT, from 1635 in enlargement of the Hôtel de Bouillon (destroyed): (a) base plans with stages of development, (b) lateral section through forecourt, (c) garden front.

On the death of the Duc de Bouillon in 1623, the property was acquired by Roger du Plessis, later Duc de Liancourt: the work of rebuilding and enlargement was begun in 1635 to the direction of the architect Louis Petit under the supervision of Lemercier.

Mansart's achievements in the genre of the hôtel particulier were not lost on his contemporaries, Jacques Lemercier and the younger Louis Le Vau (1612–70) in particular. The former may be represented by the Hôtel de Liancourt, where he was commissioned to extend the scheme initiated by de Brosse for the Duc de Bouillon – and began in clear awareness of the problems just solved by Mansart for the Hôtel de la Vrillière.[2.27]

If not at the Hôtels Martin and d'Aumont, Le Vau first appears at the Hôtel Bautru (1634), where he worked in the astylar brick and stone mode of Henri IV but already revealed facility in internal communication between apartments. Later in the decade at the Hôtel de Bretonvilliers he faced axial problems similar to those resolved by Mansart for the Hôtel de la Vrillière. His flair for innovative planning was admirably demonstrated on the quayside corner site of the Hôtel Hesselin (from 1641). The year before he was evolving his masterpiece in the genre, the Hôtel Lambert on an open site at the eastern end of the Île Saint-Louis. His planning there is unconventional, his external ordonnance is in marked contrast with Mansart's refined coherence in its response to external rather than internal considerations: above all his flair for Baroque spectacle is brilliantly displayed in the ellision of the spaces within and in their decoration which progresses towards unity from Mannerist complexity (see page 192). And it was his capacity for theatre which was to be the making of Le Vau in the era of Cardinal Mazarin, the opening of which coincided with the completion of the Hôtel Lambert.[2.28]

2.27b

2.27c

Prosp: des Pallais de Bautru

›**2.28 LOUIS LE VAU AND THE HÔTEL.**

1. APPRENTICESHIP: (a) Bautru (from c. 1634), court front; (b–e) d'Aumont (originally Scarron, built c. 1634?, renovated c. 1649, passed in 1656 to d'Aumont for whom renovations were planned by Mansart), plan, street front, lateral section through court, garden front (RP).

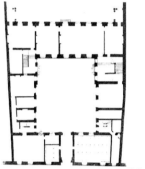

2.28b @ 1:1000

2.28a @ 1:1000

Louis Le Vau and the advance of Parisian hôtel planning

Le Vau is first definitely documented at the Hôtel Bautru: there he retained the traditional diversification of mass and roofline. That would appear to be regressive if the Hôtel Scarron (later d'Aumont) is to be dated to earlier in the 1630s: except for domed turrets on its garden side, the latter's roofline is unified overall like the contemporary work of Mansart for the Hôtel de la Vrillière. There Mansart kept the entrance to the main corps de logis in the centre but placed the staircase in a side wing. Le Vau did this too for Bautru and Scarron but associated the latter's entrance with it in the right wing, at the junction of the main enfilade from which exit to the garden remained in the centre of a symmetrical front. Ingeniously reformed by Mansart for d'Aumont (c. 1665), the main access was to the right: to the left there was a subsidiary stair and a hint at doubling the enfilade – an innovation in convenient planning which would be Le Vau's greatest claim to credit.

Early in the 1640s the entrance was restored to the centre for the hôtel in the Faubourg Saint-Germain of Jean Tambonneau, president of the Chamber of Accounts. The articulation was restricted to the superimposed Orders of the novel Palladian frontispiece. The corps de logis was doubled and the roof simplified by the suppression of corner pavilions.

2.28c

2.28d

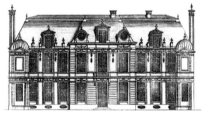

2.28e

2. TOWARDS MATURITY: (f) Tambonneau (land acquired in 1639, construction dated to c. 1642 not without question), overview from entrance; (g–j) Hesselin (from 1641), plan of ground floor (RP), river front (with Sainctot's house left), longitudinal and lateral court views.

The date of Michel-Antoine Scarron's commission for what was to become known as the Hôtel d'Aumont is disputed but he amassed the land between 1619 and 1630 and the building has clear similarities to the Hôtel Martin of c. 1631 (also attributed to Le Vau, not without doubt as he was hardly out of his teens at the time). An alternative reading of the incompletely surviving documents suggests Scarron embarked on an initial campaign c. 1634 and reformation fifteen years later.

Tambonneau's Palladian frontispiece is, of course, significant: until Le Vau paid this overt homage to the Vicentine master, *Il Quattro libri* had been admired in France for its principles of order rather than its details of practice. Le Vau reiterated the temple-front motif several times and passed it on to his French successors.

2.28f

The most important of the Tambonneau developments, the departure from a single enfilade, had already been essayed in part in a duplex exercise on the Île Saint-Louis. Next to a house on the Quai de Béthune on the Île Saint-Louis which he had already begun for Nicolas Sainctot (1640) Le Vau was commissioned to build another for Louis Cauchon, financier and Conseiller du Roi, heir to his uncle Louis Hesselin on the condition that he took the latter's name. For the Hôtel Hesselin he doubled the entry range facing the side street, to effect a greater degree of privacy and convenience for the rooms than the traditional enfilade permitted; the exterior was astylar (in sympathy with the existing work for Sainctot) but the court front of the doubled wing is articulated with colossal Doric pilasters, masking structural morphology. Le Vau is also credited with designing the château of Saint-Sepulchre, near Troyes, for Hesselin (1644): the doubling of the block to accommodate apartments, obviating the traditional enfilade, supports the attribution and his patronage circle certainly wanted châteaux.

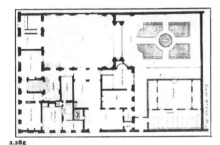

2.28g

2.28h

2.28i

2.28j

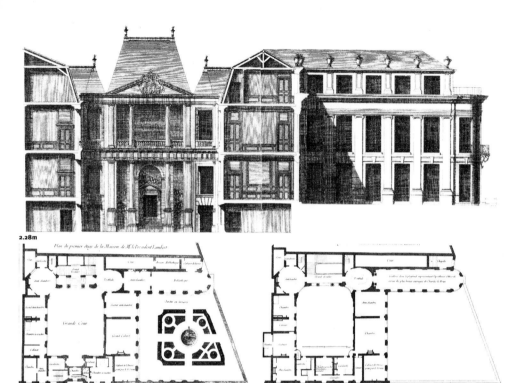

2.28m

2.28k   2.28l

Jean-Baptiste Lambert, financier, Secretaire du Roi, died young within three years of commissioning his house on its superb site facing upriver at the tip of the Île Saint-Louis. Completion was undertaken (from 1644) by his brother Nicolas, for whom the second floor was decorated. The legatee sought to employ his brother's architect for his château of Sucy-en-Brie (c. 1660) but, like several other commissions from the years of preoccupation with grand works for Mazarin's most important paladins – or the crown – Le Vau delegated the work to his younger brother François.

The planning of the Hôtel Lambert departs from tradition in arranging the main rooms no longer at the head of the court but wrapped around it – en enfilade in each range except on the street side where the corridor makes a tentative, but important, appearance. The external ordonnance is astylar only on the street range: Palladian loggias are superimposed on the staircase pavilion and a colossal Order is addressed to the view from the river. Bolder than for the Hôtel Hesselin, Le Vau's objective on this prominent site was to devise backdrops for court and garden which

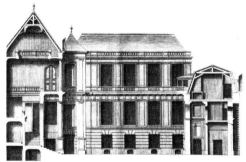

2.28n

3. MASTERY: Lambert, from 1641: (k, l) plans of ground and first floors, (m, n) lateral and longitudinal sections, (o, p) interior of gallery wing and its vault (engraved by Matthys Pool), (q, r) Cabinet de l'Amour (c. 1646) and Cabinet des Muses (c. 1646 and 1650 respectively, both engraved by Picart, c. 1705).

2.28p

2.28o

2.28q

2.28r

responded to closed and open aspects rather than to the constitution of the buildings behind them. The fenestration responds, of course: the garden front introduces the porte-fenêtre (the 'French window' rising from base level) for ease of transition between inside and out. The staircase – opposite the entrance once more – is contrived to double back on itself with maximum effect on the visitor ascending from dark flights to a wide, bright landing which commands an extensive vista through the oval vestibule and sumptuous gallery up the river beyond.

The cross-section through the main rooms of the apartments reveals tectonic panelling framing large areas left void for tapestry. Engravings record that the smaller rooms, most notably the Cabinet de l'Amour, were first decorated (c. 1646) in the traditional tiered form: arabesques in pilasters separate rectangular panels framing paintings, the largest between a median cornice derived from the projecting chimneypiece (*à l'italienne*) and its repetition in support of the panelled ceiling. Later (in the second phase of decoration, possibly involving modification to the structure, c. 1650), the fireplace of the Cabinet des Muses is reduced in bulk following the introduction of flues to the thickness of the wall ('cheminée à la moderne') in Mansart's near-contemporary Hôtel de Jars (1648; see below): the cornice is elevated over tall windows and mirrors (inserted in the 18th century with the new-fashioned mantelpiece) to support an Italianate coved ceiling; the arabesques play a more vital role in walls inset with just one suite of large pictures; the ceiling, painted by Eustache Le Sueur, is an illusionist evocation of Apollo entrusting the horses of his sun chariot to Phaeton. That follows the intervention of Charles Le Brun on his return from Italy: his semi-illusionist decoration of the gallery, dedicated to Hercules, is about to be considered in establishing the context.

›**2.29 CARDINAL MAZARIN:** in the gallery of his Paris residence, the Hôtel Tubeuf (Robert Nanteuil, 1659).

The gallery vault was the work of Francesco Romanelli.

2.29

THE ASCENDANCY OF MAZARIN

The pattern of patronage radically altered after the deaths of Richelieu and Louis XIII in quick succession between December 1642 and May 1643. The queen, Anne of Austria, assumed the regency for her infant son, Louis XIV, but her confidant, the defunct cardinal's agent, the Italian adventurer Mazarin – protégé of the Barberini, the Sacchetti and the Colonna – acceded to power. He dismissed Sublet de Noyers and his circle – and their antipathy to the Baroque – appointed a cipher instead but set the tone himself. Lemercier went on working at the Louvre as Premier Architecte du Roi but was soon eclipsed by the more versatile Le Vau in the service of the more ostentatious ministers of the crown.

Mazarin was certainly no less ambitious than Sublet in promoting Paris as the cultural capital of Europe, attempting to woo the leading Italian masters. He called in vain on Bernini to transform his Paris house, the Hôtel Tubeuf, acquired shortly after Pierre Le Muet (1591–1669) had been engaged to extend Jean Thiriot's original project (AIC5, page 401): he made do with Mansart, who provided a new staircase, superimposed galleries on the garden and left his patron with the determination not to use him again. The cardinal returned to Le Muet and, failing Bernini, moreover, imported Cortona's pupil, Giovanni Francesco Romanelli (1610–62), for the decoration of his new galleries.[2.29] And Romanelli returned to apply his master's fusion of luxuriant stucco sculpture and architecture with simulated easel pictures and illusionist scenes of heaven to the vaults of queen-mother's summer apartment on the ground floor of the Louvre in 1655. However, ceilings incorporating illusionist panels in steep perspective were not new to France.[2.30, 2.31]

>2.30 SIMON VOUET AND ILLUSIONISM: (a, b) Château de Chilly, Gallery, 'The Rising of the Sun and of the Moon' (1638; engraved record by Michel Dorigny); (c, d) Paris, Hôtel Séguier, chapel vault detail, library, 'Allegory of Architecture' (respectively 1638 and 1640; engraved record by Dorigny); (e) Saint-Germain-en-Laye, Château Neuf, queen's bedroom vault, 'Temperance' (from 1637).

2.30c

2.30d

2.30a

2.30b

Trompe-l'oeil at the French court

Francesco Primaticcio and Niccolò dell'Abbate had decorated the ceiling of the chapel of the Parisian Hôtel de Guise and the vault of Fontainebleau's Galerie d'Ulysse with semi-illusionism (AIC5, page 325). Nearly a century later, Simon Vouet reviewed the medium on his return to Paris from Italy in the light of his experience of later 16th-century and contemporary interiors in Bologna. Among his earliest works of this type was the gallery of the Château de Chilly, c. 1631, where the scheme as a whole followed the precedent set by Primaticcio and Niccolò. However, the overall effect of the heavy network of stucco ornament must have been closer to Paolo Veronese and the principal frescoes, depicting the rising of the sun and of the moon, were indebted to the great contemporary treatments of similar subjects by Guido Reni and Guercino – the former for motifs, the latter for conception *di sotto in sù*. **2.30a,b, 0.24b, 0.25**

2.30e

Vouet's most important commission for illusionist vault paintings came in the late-1630s from the queen, Anne of Austria, for her bedroom in the Château Neuf of Saint-Germain-en-Laye: they were set in richly framed compartments in the Venetian manner. His next patron was Pierre Séguier, protégé of Richelieu and one of the chief paladins of Mazarin's era as chancellor: his commission was for the decoration of the chapel and library in his Paris residence, the former Hôtel de Soissons. **2.30e** The mixture is as at the château at Chilly but more of Veronese is apparent in the *di sotto in sù* frescoes of Séguier's library, which Vouet decorated in the 1640s. **2.30d** For the chapel of 1638 he produced a single, unified scheme of consistent illusionism inspired by the Hôtel de Guise chapel. Whereas the latter was dominated by a continuous relief-like frieze of figures, however, Vouet disposed his assembly freely behind a balustrade which suggested the termination of the walls and the opening up of the room to the sky. **2.30c** Contrary was the ceiling of the gallery of the Hôtel de la Vrillière, painted by Vouet's collaborator François Perrier in the mid-1640s (revised in the 18th century; see page 326): over a full entablature unsupported by pilasters or columns, but with niches on the inner wall responding to the windows, semi-illusionist scenes were viewed through a painted framework of simulated architecture and stucco recalling in many of its details Mansart's treatment of the stone vault above his staircase at Blois.

2.31a

It is tempting to see Mazarin's choice of Romanelli for the decoration of his Hôtel Tubeuf galleries as a rejection of the work of Mansart and Perrier in favour of the latest Italian developments and this was doubtless not unconnected with the rift between him and his architect. The long narrow vault there was hardly suited to a single unified exercise based upon a fixed-viewpoint perspective or to the fusion of the arts dependent on the

2.31b

2.31c

›**2.31 GIOVANNI FRANCESCO ROMANELLI AT THE LOUVRE:** (a–c) vaults of the summer apartment of the queen-mother (regent until 1651; 1655).

highly plastic type of stuccowork developed by Cortona.**2·29** Romanelli therefore divided it into panels and treated them as easel pictures with relatively simple interlocking frames, except for the central panel which showed the 'Fall of the Giants' in clumsy perspective.

Though Romanelli returned to Italy on the completion of his work at the Hôtel Tubeuf in 1648, he was called back in 1655 to decorate the queen-regent's new summer apartment at the Louvre.**2·31** If the nature of the field in the Galerie Mazarine seems to have suggested a modification of the Baroque character of Cortona's work, the smaller, more compact rooms of the Louvre apartment presented no such problems of unity. With the possibility of a fixed viewpoint, Romanelli could choose either illusionist or non-illusionist scenes, or both, and indulge in much more of Cortona's rich variety of forms and contours.

About the time Romanelli returned to Italy, the young French painter Charles Le Brun (1619–90) returned to France from his studies with Cortona at the Palazzo Pitti in Florence.**2·28q** He was soon taken up by Le Vau and set to work decorating the gallery of the Hôtel Lambert. Faced there with a long, low, narrow vault – like Romanelli in the Galerie Mazarine – architect and painter divided the field with painted architecture resting on the continuous cornice derived from the real Order of the entrance and supported along the sides by the stucco figures associated with simulated bronze reliefs of the Labours of Hercules. More imaginatively than Romanelli, Le Brun feigned the sky at the ends as the scene for suitable mythologies and – like Raphael at the Farnesina – represented tapestries suspended as *velaria* across the central sections.

Theatrical illusionism hardly stopped – or started – with vaults. Mazarin had been a devotee of the stage since his earliest youth with the Jesuits and he promoted Italian opera and ballet at court. Giacomo Torelli (1608–78), the leading set designer of the age, was imported to stage them in 1645: fourteen years later, in 1659, Gaspare Vigarani (1588–1663) and his son Carlo (1637–1713), the leading theatre designers, were called in to build a permanent theatre at the Tuileries (see page 235). Torelli initially enchanted the court there but fell from favour two years later because of his association with the late cardinal's evidently corrupt finance minister Nicolas Fouquet, whose extreme opulence provoked his fall from the king's favour – as we shall see in lavish detail.

The extravagant spectacle of Torelli's productions – dramatically lit, using the richest of materials, relying on the fusion of the arts for sumptuous vistas and fantastic feigned architecture – was to inform the taste of the young king no less than Romanelli's decoration of his mother's apartments. After the week-long series of fêtes, 'Plaisirs de l'Île enchantée', mounted by Carlo Vigarani for the king in the court of his father's hunting lodge at Versailles in May 1664, the first fruit was the fairytale palace which emerged from the earliest embellishments there. The spectacle was to be reflected in the court fêtes, triumphal entries and *pompes funèbres* throughout the reign.**2.32**

The ostentation of Mazarin's style greatly increased the bitterness felt by the bourgeoisie over the employment of Italians: the disaffection of the very class promoted by Richelieu to the disadvantage of the old *noblesse d'épée* was seen by the latter as the opportunity to reassert itself. The outbreak of the Fronde insurrection in 1648 marked a devastating reversal of the cardinal's fortunes and temporarily terminated the development of French Baroque: its most brilliant phase would open with his final triumph in 1653.

Meanwhile the fortunes of François Mansart suffered a sharp reverse. In 1645, the queen-regent had engaged him for one of the most important commissions of the era: the church and convent-palace of the Val-de-Grâce founded in thanks for the birth of her son. Mansart was evidently directed to emulate her dynastic seat, El Escorial in Madrid, but he furthered his development of vistas through interrelated spaces of richly varied forms. His predecessors and contemporaries sustained the French obsession with Classicizing the essentially medieval basilica. At

2.32a

2.32b

›2.32 COURT THEATRE: (a) Richelieu in audience with the king and queen in the theatre-gallery of the Palais-Cardinal; (b) Versailles, fête at the 'Palais d'Armide' (c. 1664).

Richelieu called on Jacques Lemercier for the inception of a permanent theatre building in his Parisian palace in 1635: the length of the auditorium sustains the tradition of mounting theatrical entertainment ad hoc in the ubiquitous gallery; in compensation height seems to have been evoked illusionistically here. At Mazarin's instigation, Giacomo Torelli was imported as the foremost master of illusionism on stage. His efforts – like everything else – were disrupted by the Fronde. A permanent court theatre awaited the reassertion of control: then the cardinal called on the Vigaranis to install it in the north wing of the Tuileries, with the elaborate stage mechanism for which they were celebrated – hence 'Salle des Machines' (see below, page 235).

›2.33 THE PARISIAN CHURCH AT MID-CENTURY: (a) S.-Sulpice (from 1646), interior; (b) S.-Roch (from 1653), interior.

A 12th-century parish church on the site of S.-Sulpice was replaced from 1646, after its priest, Jean-Jacques Olier (1608–57), constituted the clerical congregation in the name of the saint. The obscure Christoph Gamard produced the first plans but he was superseded by Daniel Gittard: Louis Le Vau is also traditionally credited with involvement but his precise role – if any – is undefined. S.-Roch was begun to the plans of Lemercier in the last year of his life.

The S.-Sulpice complex was to be slightly smaller than the cathedral of Notre-Dame: like that of S.-Roch, the basilican plan is traditional – essentially Gothic – with chevet and a complete set of side chapels beyond ambulatory and aisles; both are Gothic in section but the greater height of S.-Sulpice is achieved internally by raising the tall clerestory over arcaded bays defined by colossal Corinthian columns – in the manner of Étienne Martellange but without triforium tribunes.

Work stopped at S.-Roch in 1660 with the choir, the transept and the innermost bay of the nave nearing completion: it was taken up again at the outset of the new century – as we shall see. At S.-Sulpice ambition had achieved only the choir by 1678: work largely lapsed for forty years, until Gilles-Marie Oppenord was commissioned to complete it in the third decade of the new century. The façade was added by Nicolas (Giovanni Niccolò) Servandoni who won a competition for its design in 1732 – as we shall see in due course.

2.33a

2.33b

the Val-de-Grâce, in contrast, he recalled Palladio's most mature exercise in scenographic planning, the Venetian Redentore, and endowed it with a Baroque façade in which the powerful Corinthian Order clearly develops Maderno's Roman theme.

Mansart's inability to draw the creative process to a practical conclusion led to his dismissal from the queen's commission. Construction had reached the main entablature of the church's nave and west front when he was replaced by Lemercier in 1646. The originality of the aborted project is in stark contrast to the result – and to the conservative contemporary churches of S.-Sulpice and S.-Roch.[2.33, 2.34]

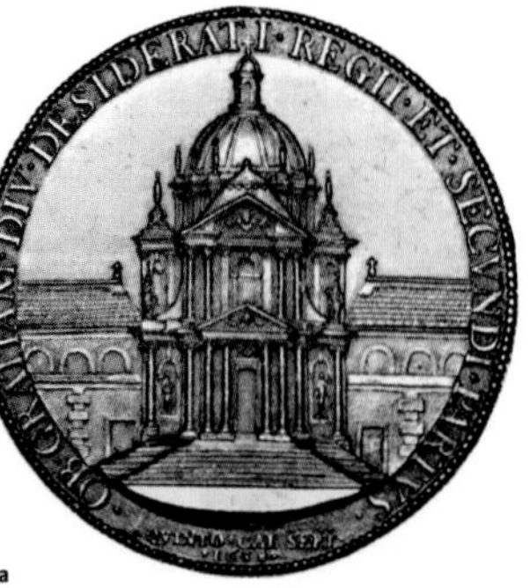

2.34a

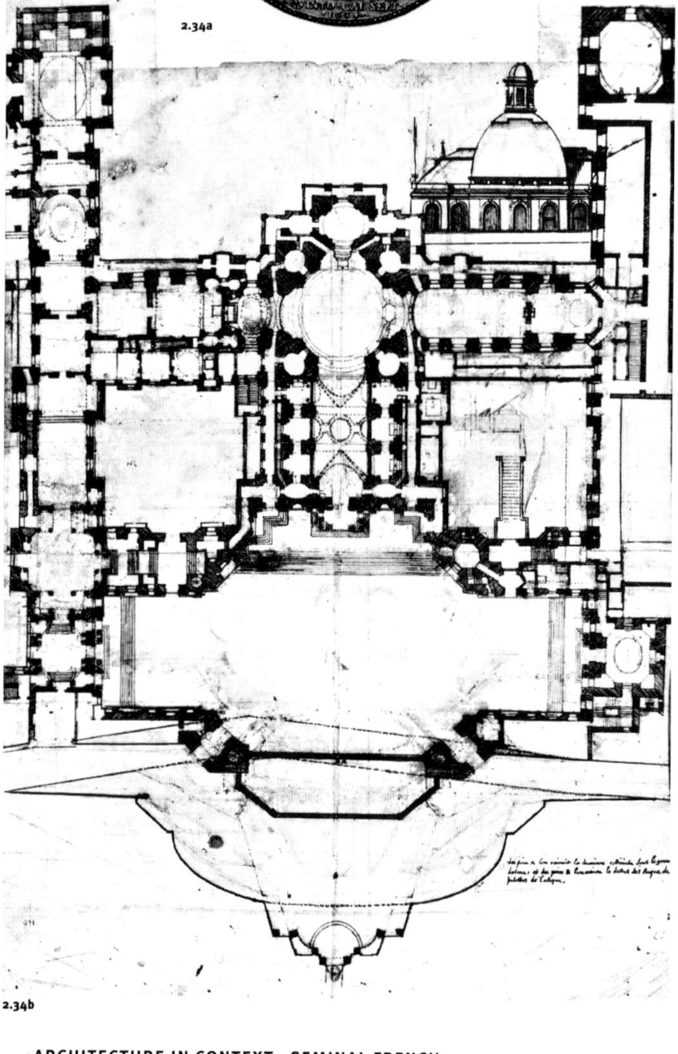

2.34b

›2.34 MANSART AND PARISIAN ECCLESIASTICAL PROJECTS ASSOCIATED WITH THE QUEEN-REGENT: (a–h) Val-de-Grâce, foundation medal, general project plan (1645) and church plan as built (from 1646), reconstruction of projected longitudinal section (after Smith and Braham), section through crossing as projected and as built, interior to east, west front; (i) Minimes, façade project (anonymous drawing after 1657).

In 1624 Queen Anne commissioned a Parisian abbatical seat for the principal of the priory of the Val-de-Grâce de Bièvres: due to her problems with her husband attendant on her apparent infertility, progress was slow. After the birth of her son in 1638 and her accession to the regency on the death of her husband five years later, the project was revived and revised, ex voto. New acquisitions were converted to conventual use and in 1645 Mansart was commissioned to build a new church and extended the project to an adjoining palace (for which there is no recorded royal request). His magnificent drawings show that the nave was to be vaulted as a distinct entity before a double dome flanked by absidal transepts and choir. The evolution of all these elements was halted by his dismissal and so too were the exercises in vertical scenography for the dome: completion was entrusted to Lemercier and

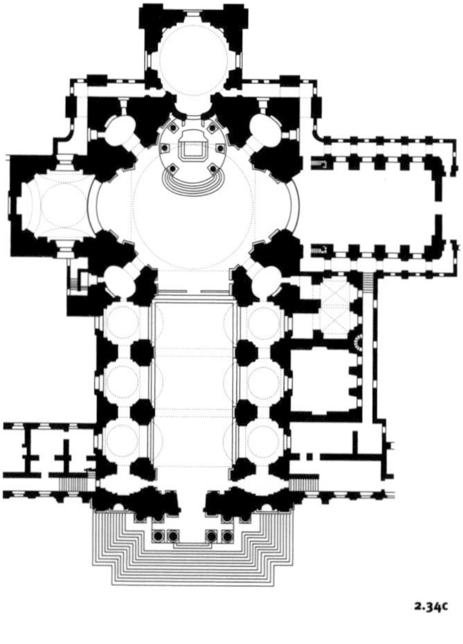

2.34c

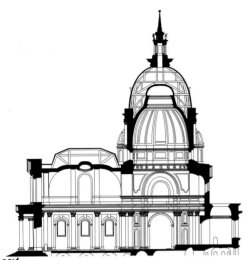

2.34d

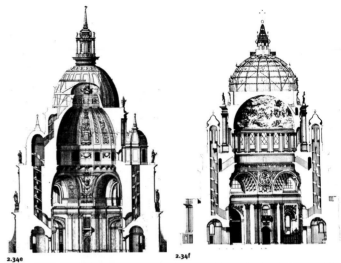

2.34e

2.34f

achieved after his death in 1654 by Pierre Le Muet (to 1667). Lemercier seems to have respected one of Mansart's ideas for the portico and a centralized chapel beyond the hemicyclical choir but simplified the tunnel vaulting of the nave. He had begun construction of the dome in 1650 but Le Muet furthered the work on the conventional hemispherical form only between 1658 and 1665. The elliptical baldacchino on its six Solomonic columns is credited to Gabriel Le Duc but is clearly endebted to Bernini who was in Paris when it was devised in 1664.

Mansart's Palladian plan may be compared with the conventional Classicizing basilican approach of, for instance, the Jesuits at S.-Paul-S.-Louis (1629), Pierre Le Muet and Libéral Bruant at Notre-Dame-des-Victoires (the choir from 1629, the transept and first nave bay from 1642 respectively), Gittard (?) at S.-Sulpice (1645), Lemercier at S.-Roch (in inception, at least, 1653).

On axis with the Place des Vosges to the south, the church of the Minimes (a mendicant order affiliated with the Capuchins) was begun in 1611: the apsidal chapels date from twenty years later. At the instigation of the queen-mother (who contributed funds), Mansart was commissioned to complete the southern entrance end in 1657. He responded with an oval vestibule set back beyond a façade, screened with a colonnade, which was itself set back from the street front between

2.34g

twin pavillons: in the contract project the screen was suppressed in favour of columns in antis flanking the portico of advanced columns – in the manner of Philibert de l'Orme, which he had perfected – and the oval vestibule, surmounted by a monks' choir, was endowed with a dome between small belfries. The intervention amounted to the provision of a 'westwork' of Romanesque lineage but with a dome brought forward from the crossing in place of a tower: innovative in general, so too in particular was the alternating rhythm of the blind drum's articulation, echoed in the disposition of the dormers in the dome – as was the centrality of the enlarged pier supporting the clock. The peregrinations of the design process generated only the completion of the lower level to Mansart's design before his death in 1666. The superstructure was begun to a reduced and varied design by Pierre Thévenot in 1672: it largely disappeared at the end of the 18th century.

In the 1650s Mansart was given another chance by the queen: she chose him to add a façade to the existing church of the Minimes. Work began in 1657 but his ambition for the project outran even the royal resources and the upper storey was completed after his death with alterations.**2.34i**

2.34i

2.35b

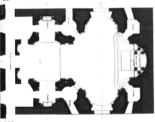

2.35a

2.35c

›2.35 FRESNES, CHÂTEAU: (a–c) chapel (late-1640s, destroyed), plan, longitudinal and lateral sections (*AF*).

Otherwise, he had to rely on the patronage of the more fastidious members of the *noblesse de robe* such as the secretary of state Henri de Guénégaud who gave him the opportunity at the château of Fresnes to carry out a reduced version of the scheme for the church of the Val-de-Grâce. In the Chapel of the Assumption he may be likened to Bernini in the contemporary Cornaro chapel of S. Maria della Vittoria: both mount a dynamic performance of the dedication theme through the fusion of the arts, infusing the space with vitality. At Fresnes expressive statues of the apostles surrounded the empty tomb at the altar: they look up to a painting of the Virgin ascending in the canopy over the altar and to the Holy Ghost waiting to receive her in the lantern (see also page 75).**2.35**

Also for Henri de Guénégaud, Mansart transformed the Hôtel de Nevers (from 1648) and for his cousin Jean-François, Seigneur des Brosses, he built the Hôtel de Guénégaud des Brosses (c. 1653). The dominant element of the former was a porte cochère modelled on Remy Collin's stable court portal at Fontainebleau (AIC5, page 378): instead of mannered rustication, however, the deflected horizontal coursing approached the 18th-century academic ideal of noble simplicity. Approached at the Hôtel de Jars too (1648), that ideal was achieved for the second Guénégaud hôtel – or would be through the agency of François's nephew Jules Hardouin-Mansart, as we shall see. It is confined to bold rustication and plain rectangular window frames: the former appears as quoins on the side pavilions but on the central frontispieces it is masked by shallow panels punctuated by the fenestration, its implied continuity suggesting greater strength than is actually revealed. The mode was developed for the front pavillons added to the Hôtel Carnavalet at the beginning of the next decade. Traditional French composition in varied masses subsists but the elements are assimilated by the articulation and roofline. Traditional enfilade planning subsists for the Hôtel de la Bazinière too but not without interpolated Baroque drama – and that was furthered elsewhere.**2.36**

2.36c　　　　　　　　　　　　　　　**2.36d**

›**2.36 MANSART'S LATER PARISIAN HÔTELS:**
(a, b) de Jars (from 1648), ground-floor plan and portal (RP and DDM respectively); (c) de Nevers, portal (c. 1650, DDM); (d–g) de la Bazinière (from 1653), portal, first-floor plan and ground-floor right wing, section through cabinet; (h) de Guénégaud des Brosses (from c. 1653), court front; (i) Carnavalet, east front.

To centralize the fragment of the hôtel project realized after 1572 for Louis de Gonzague, Duc de Nevers – one of a pair of corps de logis, a side and central pavillon – Mansart built an *avant-cour* dependent on the pavillons and dominated by the porte cochère. Unlike this project, on its prominent left-bank site down river from the Pont Neuf, the Hôtel de Guénégaud des Brosses, on its corner site in the rue des Archives, was one of Mansart's few unconstrained exercises. The continuous horizontal coursing of the Nevers portal is deflected to form a voussoir in the centre as in the recent portal of the Hôtel d'Aumont attributed to Le Vau: the rump of the latter's work there survives, so too does much of the garden front (attributed to Bruant) but Mansart's stairs are lost.

The staircase of the Hôtel de Guénégaud des Brosses is placed at the head of the right wing on the court, its doors on both levels aligned with the main enfilades. Countering the constraint of rectangular geometry in its narrow context, however, Mansart developed a thoroughly Baroque dynamic from the semi-elliptical curvature of the lower flight. He did this even more dramatically in the near-contemporary Hôtel de la Bazinière where it opened a sequence of staircase, vestibule and reception spaces alternatively oval and rectangular. At the same site, yet again, this scenographic approach was applied vertically for the celebrated cabinet added to the garden front for which one of the richest sheets of Mansart's frenetic drawings happily survives.

2.36b　　　　　　　　　　　　　　　**2.36a**

The absolute simplicity of the Hôtel de Guénégaud des Brosses was anticipated by the Hôtel de Jars, dating from the end of the previous decade: however, the Ionic portal provides traditional, if unostentatious, relief and a somewhat impractical complexity is introduced to the garden front by roof terraces and cabinets projecting from the first floor over columns. The planning was more advanced than in the later work and improvement to ducting entailed the elimination of deeply projecting chimney breasts: that prompted change to the treatment of walls, lost here but well represented in the record of the Hôtel Lambert's Cabinet des Muses (from 1649; see above). The doubling of the block between court and garden, with the stairs in the front range to the side of the entrance vestibule, acknowledged the achievement of Le Vau in the planning of works like the Hôtel Hesselin – with greater clarity but not greater luminosity in excessively deep rooms. That was dependent upon the load-bearing wall dividing the two ranges in its continuity between staircases. Doubling to this extent required the form of *toit-brisé* – the type of roof breaking from steep to shallow pitch which carries Mansart's name.

2.36g

2.36e, f @ 1:1000

old structure

added before 1652

built in 1650s

2.36h

2.36i

Meanwhile, during the Fronde, while Roland Fréart de Chambray saw his chance to publish Sublet de Noyers' principles in 1650, Antoine Le Pautre looked for a different outcome to the cardinal's difficulties and dedicated his *Desseins de plusieurs palais* to his eminence in 1652. Despite the title it included one church: the chapel of the Cistercian abbey of Port-Royal-des-Champs as projected before the patroness demanded the elimination of its opulence in execution (from c. 1646), in keeping with the austere ethic

›2.37 PIERRE PUGET: Toulon, Hôtel de Ville, portal.

A pupil of Pietro da Cortona, and assistant at the Palazzo Pitti from 1640 to 1643, Puget subsequently spent much time in Toulon where the portal he applied to the Hôtel de Ville in 1656 was supported by powerful figures, freer in their modelling and more fluid in their composition than anything yet seen in Paris.

›2.38 ANTOINE LE PAUTRE, DESSEINS DE PLUSIEURS PALAIS, 1652: (a, b) Port-Royale-des-Champs, as built and half section-elevation of published project; (c) second palace design, perspective view; (d, e) fourth palace design, ground- and first-floor plans, perspective view.

The order of strictly reformed Cistercians, detached from the abbey of Cîteaux under Angélique Arnauld, established the abbey of Port-Royal-des-Champs on the southern outskirts of Paris in 1625 and espoused the austere teachings of Jansenius on Predestination and Grace which, deemed heretical, earned them suppression in 1664. The church was extended into a nuns' choir from a domed Greek cross for the public, as was not unusual for conventual chapels: unusual – and rejected by the patroness – was the portico inspired by Jacques Lemercier's work at the Sorbonne but minus the pediment.

The grandest of the château projects, with its vast domed central vestibule serving twin longitudinal staircases leading to twin apartments for the king and the patron, may have been designed to tempt Mazarin: the de facto ruler of France had yet to devote his enormous wealth to the building of a suitable country seat in lieu of the Vincennes château, where he had commissioned a relatively modest wing from Le Vau.

2.38a

2.38b

2.38e

of her Jansenist community. The secular fantasies show no restraint whatsoever: vast and crushing in scale and weight, powerful in massing, energetic in sculptural detail, drawing the maximum effect from the contrast of concave and convex forms, rich in internal vistas, there is nevertheless a sense of self-conscious Mannerism about most of them. In France analogy is to be found mainly in the work of Le Vau – though he was unable to handle disparate elements as convincingly. One has to look across the Channel to Sir John Vanbrugh for worthier homage. The main French artist to share Le Pautre's enthusiasm for anthropomorphic order was the Provençal Pierre Puget.[2.37, 2.38]

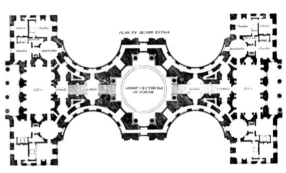

2.38d

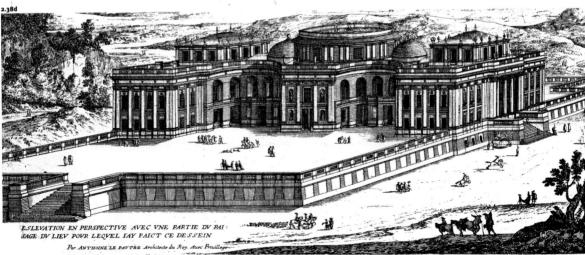

ESLEVATION EN PERSPECTIVE AVEC VNE PARTIE DV PAI-
SAGE DV LIEV POVR LEQVEL IAY FAICT CE DESSEIN
Par ANTHOINE LE PAVTRE Architecte du Roy. Auec Priuillege.

2.38c

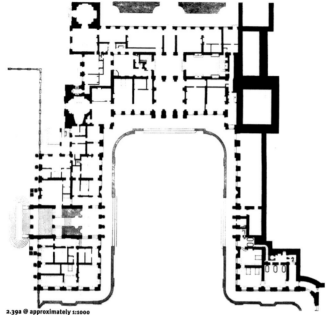

2.39a @ approximately 1:1000

2.39c

›2.39 ANTOINE LE PAUTRE AND SAINT-CLOUD, CHÂTEAU: (a, b) plan (*AF*) and model (after 1658), (c) cascade (drawn by Adam Perelle).

The splendid site on an eminence overlooking the Seine was developed from 1570 by Jérôme de Gondi, scion of the Florentine banking family who had come to France in the train of Catherine de' Medici (to whom they owed the settlement): Henri III conducted operations against Paris from their château and was assassinated there. After various vicissitudes and a sumptuous fête held by the Gondi heir in 1658 for Louis XIV and his brother, Philippe, Duc d'Orléans, the latter bought the property. He employed Le Pautre to incorporate the Gondis' south-facing residence into a vast new open courtyard scheme entered from the east: after the architect's death in 1679, work was continued under the master-mason Jean Girard until the intervention of Jules Hardouin-Mansart – to whose contribution we shall return. Again as we shall see, André Le Nôtre reformed the garden but retained Le Pautre's celebrated cascade (of 1664).

If his book did not succeed in attracting the patronage of Mazarin to its author, Le Pautre was called upon c. 1658 to rebuild the 16th-century Hôtel d'Aulnay at Saint-Cloud for Philippe, Duc d'Orléans.**2.39** A year earlier he received from Catherine de Beauvais the commission for one of

2.39b

2.40d

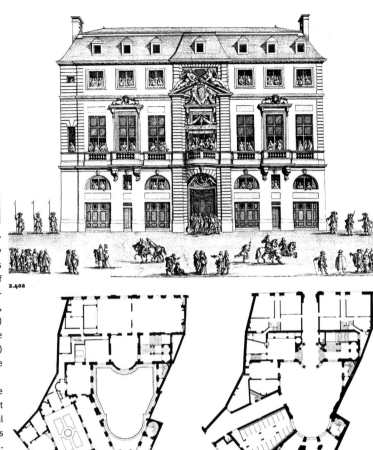

2.40a

›2.40 THE PARISIAN HÔTEL IN THE MID-1650S: (a–d) de Beauvais, street front (engraved by Marot c. 1660 with the queen-mother watching Louis XIV entering Paris with his bride, Marie-Thérèse of Spain), ground- and first-floor plans, court; (e) chimneypiece (after Jean le Pautre, *Alcôves à la Romaine*, Paris, c. 1670); (f) Roland, ground-floor plan; (g–i) Amelot de Bisseuil ('Hôtel des Ambassadeurs de Hollande'), entrance front, court detail, gallery; (j–l) Aubert de Fontenay ('Hôtel Salé'), court front, staircase views; (m, n) de Lauzun, interiors.

The Beauvais site was constrained by the acute alignement of streets: the curved façades of the court were suggested by existing foundations; the portal on the rue Saint-Antoine, with contrasting curves, is Roman. Le Pautre's resourcefulness in fitting individually symmetrical spaces into the fabric recalls Vignola but his realization of convenience in the parallel arrangement of the principal rooms in the main block, here displaced to the front on the rue Saint-Antoine and entered from a covered carriageway, is worthy of Le Vau. So too is the richly relieved, dramatically lit staircase which opens to the left of the circular porch beyond the passage from the porte-cochère. The load-bearing partition wall is sustained to either side of this passage: flexibility is introduced by non-loadbearing partitioning, particularly of the first-floor corridors in the extension over the stables and secondary access. Leading to the garden, these skirt the Grand Cabinet beyond which the oblique gallery provides dignified access to the chapel at the head of the main entrance axis.

2.40b, c @ 1:1000

the most dazzling exercises in virtuoso planning ever to be realized in Paris. His ingenuity was inspired by a wildly irregular composite site: alive to the advantages attendant on doubling the block containing the principal rooms, he proved himself to be Le Vau's equal both as an innovator of *commodité* and as *metteur-en-scène* in the unsurpassed entrance sequence from circular porte-cochère, sideways to colonnaded staircase and up to the main suite of reception rooms.**2.40a–e**

2.40e

The distinguished contemporaries of the Hôtel de Beauvais in the Marais included the lost house of the obscure M. Roland by the equally obscure Girard Desargues – influential not least for its extraordinary staircase, extraordinarily placed.**2.40f** Notable among survivors are Pierre Cottard's work for Amelot de Bisseuil and the Hôtel Aubert de Fontenay ('Hôtel Salé', 1656), once attributed to Le Vau, now to one Jean Boullier de Bourges. The former preserves splendid interiors, an exquisite forecourt and a portal which offers considerable compensation for the loss of Mansart's addition to the former Hôtel de Nevers.**2.40g–i** Beyond a generous court screened only at ground-floor level, the extravagantly pedimented frontispiece of the opulent 'Salé' exercise opens into a grand vestibule and sumptuous, scenographic staircase which serves the doubled block between court and garden.**2.40j–l**

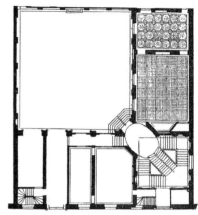

Ingenious distribution was prompted not by an awkward perimeter but by the pure rectilinearity of Roland's site. Cottard was more conventional for Amelot de Bisseuil (the reason for the popular association of his house with the Ambassadeurs de Hollande is unclear): 15th-century housing for retainers was rebuilt over a two-courtyard plan from 1655; the inner court is articu-

2.40h

2.40i

2.40g

2.40j

lated with colossal Corinthian pilasters instead of the outer court's atlante over astylar panels. The vault of the important gallery, dedicated to Psyche, was painted by Simon Vouet's pupil Michel Corneille (1601–64) and is illusionist in various modes, including simulated relief over medallions supported by putti and framed by the Composite Order of pilasters.

Pierre Aubert de Fontenay was a financier who enriched himself through marriage but especially as farmer-general of the salt tax (*gabelle*) from 1630 to 1658: that is the source of the disparaging nickname for his opulent house built by Jean Boullier de Bourges (to the direction of an unknown architect?) from 1656 to 1660; it was occupied by its proprietor for less than a year before he fell due to association with the corrupt finance minister Nicolas Fouquet (on whom see page 235). It was modern in the doubling of the enfilade which permitted the expansive development of the splendid staircase in the centre of the forward range without disruption to the circulation in general.

2.40k

2.40l

2.40m 2.40n

2.41c

Le Vau continued as a prolific builder of mansions in Paris, progressing from commissions from budding bureaucrats, financiers and commercial entrepreneurs to members of the new nobility–whose rank he aimed to join. The Hôtel de Lauzun, in the sphere of his activity on the Île Saint-Louis and attributed to him on stylistic grounds, is among the most spectacular survivors from the mid-1650s.**2.40m, n** Its principal enfilade is unsurpassed among its contemporaries but its scenographic staircase, rebuilt in the 20th century, had its equivalent at the Hôtel de Lionne (1662) where it was developed from a vestibule parallel to the entrance front: that is lost but the 'Hôtel Salé' provides ample compensation.

On Mazarin's return after the Fronde, Mansart had not regained official favour. On the death of Lemercier early in 1654, Le Vau succeeded him as Premier Architect du Roi charged with the completion of the Louvre – we shall review that complex exercise in the next chapter. Having been granted the government of the château of Vincennes after the Fronde and seeking an architect to reform twin forecourt wings projected for Louis XIII, the cardinal had chosen Le Vau from a shortlist – which included Mansart and Le Muet – presented to him by his secretary, Jean-Baptiste Colbert.

2.41a

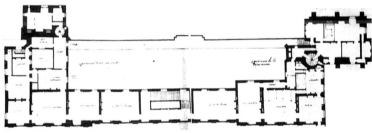

2.41b @ 1:1000

›2.41 LE VAU AND THE CHÂTEAUX OF MAZARIN AND HIS PALADINS: (a–c) Vincennes, entrance portal project, plan and court view of east wing (from 1654); (d, e) Le Raincy (from c. 1645), plan, general view from garden (RP); (f) Meudon (from 1640, revised 1652 and later), general view from garden (engraved by Perelle); (g–r) Vaux-le-Vicomte (from 1657), entrance and garden fronts, great central salon detail, plan, cabinet details, dining room, Salon des Muses vault details, king's bedroom, overview with garden and southern terraces.

Easier to work with than Mansart, less fastidious, Le Vau was highly successful with the most ostentatious members of Mazarin's circle: for his Intendants des Finances, Jacques Bordier, Abel Servien and Nicolas Fouquet at Le Raincy, Meudon and Vaux-le-Vicomte respectively, he demonstrated his skill in planning to meet new standards of comfort and convenience. At Vaux-le-Vicomte in particular he was a master of spectacle, working with Charles Le Brun for the interiors and André Le Nôtre for the garden.**2.41**

2.41e

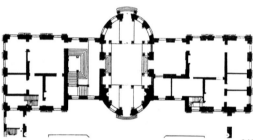

2.41d

2.41f

2.41i

Vaux-le-Vicomte and its predecessors

At the château of Vincennes the traditional enfilades of Mazarin's twin rectangular blocks survive from the scheme first formulated for Louis XIII: the colossal Order is Baroque in scale and weight but hardly more Baroque in practice than it had been in the hands of Jean Bullant in the 16th century; the portal is a solid Classical exercise. At Le Raincy, Le Vau demonstrated his skill in the distribution of the major and minor rooms of the apartments in doubled corps de logis to meet new standards of comfort and convenience. His massing was less happy. A great oval central pavillon dominated the composition and projected the main reception room into the garden but disrupted the plan and interrupted the inconsistently articulated façades on both sides with its curved projections. At Meudon he modified this device, curving only the corners of the pavillon on either side of the flat frontispiece which was bound to the corps de logis by continuous superimposed Orders.

Joint Surintendant des Finances from 1653, Nicolas Fouquet commissioned his château at Vaux three years later: three years further on he was paying for it as sole Surintendant. The main block (of rusticated masonry in contrast to the brick service buildings) is unencumbered by wings and

2.41g

2.41h

the domed central pavilion projects only from the garden front, but with its curvature emphasized by a huge dome and inconsistent in its ordonnance, it is hardly less disruptive than at Le Raincy. On the court side, the single-storey rusticated Doric portico and its extended frieze ill accords with the colossal Ionic of the uncanonically twinned bays of the side pavilions. Le Vau was certainly no match for Mansart in his experiments with combining Baroque techniques and the traditional French approach to composition. Indeed, his attempt to integrate disparate masses with a free combination of regular and colossal Orders fails to understand Baroque incentive, particularly to control movement introduced into façades by curvature or to produce it by varying the plasticity of a consistent Order. Given his vigorous approach to massing, indeed, his free use of the Orders – essentially decorative in the tradition associated with the du Cerceau rather than architectonic – actually inhibited the production of the dramatic climax which was the principal aim of Baroque composition.

Vaux's triple-arched portal leads to a square Doric vestibule. The provision of twin staircases in tunnel-like cavities to either side of the vestibule obviates impediment to lateral circulation: little was required as the upper floor contained secondary apartments. On the main floor, as at Le Raincy but not at Maisons, the traditional enfilade is rejected in favour of apartments of rooms grouped flexibly in parallel (with a load-bearing party wall) to either side of the salon and vestibule: without interrupting circulation, the scheme was thus able to incorporate permanent facilities for dining and bathing, in addition to the cabinets which had been the most private rooms in the grand house at least since the middle of the previous century.

Across the main axis, beyond the repeated arcades of the vestibule, the great oval salon is articulated with a cool Composite Order surmounted by a rich attic incorporating caryatids and atlante below a vault which was to have been painted by Charles Le Brun. Unusually, the latter was in sole charge of the château's interior decoration. For the royal apartment, he drew on his first-hand experience of Pietro da Cortona's work at the Palazzo Pitti in Florence. In the earlier rooms the architectural and sculptural elements framing the paintings are themselves feigned in paint and in the smaller cabinets arabesques are contained in rectangular panels also framing paintings, the largest over a median cornice – as at the

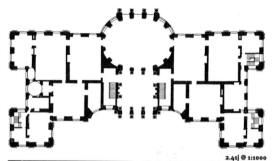

2.41j @ 1:1000

2.41k 2.41l

2.41m

Hôtel Lambert. In the king's bedroom Le Brun progressed with Cortona to the opening of an illusionist sky above rich white and gold stucco coves with winged fames supporting trompe-l'oeil medallions and panels whose

2.41n

2.41o

2.41p

›ARCHITECTURE IN CONTEXT »SEMINAL FRENCH

frames curl into volutes to ease the transition from the walls. Exuberant as it was in its combination of the arts, Cortona's work at the Palazzo Pitti carefully observed the inviolability of the frames and, decisively contrasting the white and gold stuccowork, ensured that each element of the design was self-contained. It was on precisely this principle, and with decreasing importance placed on the profusion of stucco motifs and illusionism, that Le Brun would forge for Louis XIV the style of decoration which was to reach its apotheosis in the Grands Appartements at Versailles.

In the design of the garden, André Le Nôtre developed a geometrical formula which he and his followers throughout Europe were to find applicable to a wide range of sites: the precedent was provided by Mansart's collaborators at Maisons in advance from the scheme at Richelieu. The first principle was an open axis through and beyond the site, sealed to the sides with banks of trees (*bosquets*) and apparently extended to infinity beyond a lateral canal. Further, the house was integrated with its context not only by extending its axes through the terraces but by echoing its principal forms there too. At Vaux, thus the *parterres de broderie* which cover much of the foreground respond to the side pavilions of the château, the dome of the central salon is reflected in the central pool of the main axial avenue, the château itself in the large rectangular pool further along, and the broad axial swathe, defined by banks of trees throughout, disappears over a hill at the far end of the site beyond the grand canal. The rationalism of the formula is seen as Cartesian but it was not necessarily directly indebted to Réné Descartes (died 1650): writing in Holland remote from the French establishment, he was the supreme representative of mathematics as the first principle of Creation which was fundamental to 17th-century French Classicism.

2.41r

2.41q

2.42c

2.42a @ 1:2500

2.42b

Fouquet entertained the king and his court to an extravagant fête at Vaux-le-Vicomte in summer 1661 – before the work was quite complete. He did not achieve the expected result: he was arrested by his young royal guest who was conscious of having nothing quite so magnificent and saw that royal funds had paid for it. His fall was due to Colbert and Colbert would replace him as Surintendant des Finances. His architect, decorator and gardener were confined to royal duties: ultimately to transform the hunting lodge the king had inherited from his father at Versailles; first to augment the Tuileries as the main royal residence pending completion of the Louvre.

As principal architect to the king since 1654, Le Vau had been entrusted with the completion of the Louvre: when funds were available on the conclusion of the Peace of the Pyrénées in 1659 he began where Lemercier had left off at the Pavillon de Beauvais, in the north-west corner of the enlarged Cour Carrée. In that year, however, he was instructed to work with the Italian engineer Carlo Vigarani on the installation of a theatre at the Tuileries with the auditorium in a northern block matching Jean Bullant's southern pavilion and the stage in a pendant to Androuet II du Cerceau's gallery (see AIC5, page 379). Naturally a pendant to the Pavillon de Flore was also required and that, together with the 'modernization' of the whole, was pursued from early 1664. And Le Nôtre, trained at the Tuileries, was commissioned to reform the garden.**2.42**

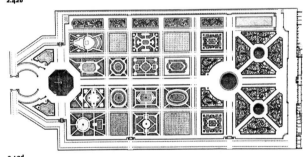

2.42d

2.42e

›**2.42 LE VAU, VIGARANI AND LE NÔTRE AT THE TUILERIES FROM THE EARLY 1660S:** (a, b) plan and extended front to garden (with Salle des Machines, left), (c) longitudinal section through Salle des Machines (1659, *AF*), (d, e) site plan and perspective.

2.43e

2.43a

The embellishment of the king's apartment in the Louvre had begun with his bedroom in 1654, soon after Le Vau had succeeded Lemercier: the scheme, primarily sculptural, was directed by Gilles Guérin.**2.43** At that stage Le Brun had a minor role in an adjacent cabinet. He emerged as a major royal decorator with his contribution to the theatrical state entry of the king and his bride into Paris in 1660 – the first of the series of spectacles translated for the king from the stage of Giacomo Torelli to the streets of his capital and the terraces of his gardens. Early the following year a fire in the Petite Galerie of the Louvre – which links the Pavillon du Roi with the Grande Galerie – prompted Le Vau to double its wing and gave Le Brun the opportunity to redecorate its gallery on the first floor. Now to be dedicated to Apollo in honour of the young 'Sun King', the height and breadth of the space permitted a much greater variety of shapes and depth of relief than in the Galerie Mazarine or the Galerie d'Hercule of the Hôtel Lambert, if not in the king's bedroom at Vaux: modulating the latter to suit the format of the former, there Le Brun began forging for Louis XIV the style of decoration which was to reach its apotheosis in the Grands Appartments at Versailles – 'Baroque tamed by the French Classical spirit'.

2.43b

2.43d

›2.43 LE BRUN AND THE ADVENT OF THE 'SUN KING': (a) Apollo Enthroned (preliminary sketch of the late-1650s presumably for the projected painting of the vault of the oval salon at Vaux-le-Vicomte; (b) triumphal arch in the Place Dauphine erected for the state entry of the king and queen into Paris on 26 August 1660; (c–e) Louvre, Chambre du Roi, ceiling, and Galerie d'Apollon in the Petite Galerie, ceiling, general view and detail.

The fête celebrated the king's assertion of his majority and glorified his marriage to the eldest daughter of Philip IV of Spain which sealed the Peace of the Pyrénées – and its cession of Artois and Roussillon to France. The entry set off from the provisional Place du Trône near Vincennes and progressed through numerous triumphal arches to its culmination at the Louvre: Le Brun's obelisk-crowned arch was the last and most magnificent in the series. Appropriately enough, the queen-mother and Cardinal Mazarin watched the procession from the balcony of the Hôtel de Beauvais (as we have seen).

2.43c

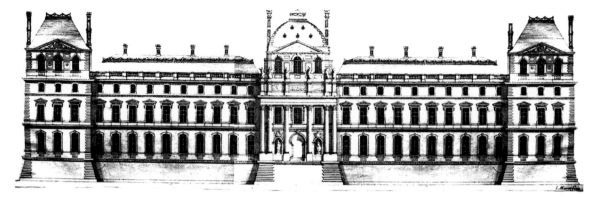

2.44a

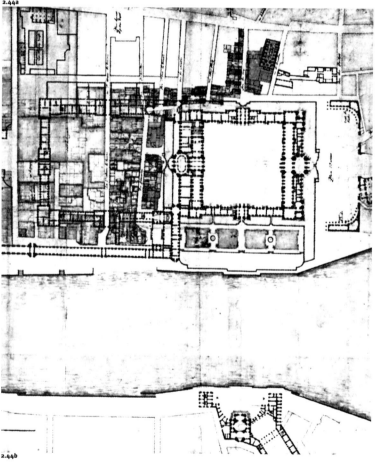

2.44b

2.44d

**›2.44 LOUIS LE VAU, PROJECT FOR COMPLE-
TION OF THE LOUVRE AND THE COLLÈGE DES
QUATRE-NATIONS (L'INSTITUT DE FRANCE),**
c. 1663: (a) elevation of the completed south wing in
its original form, (b–d) 'fifth' plan (with new forecourt
beyond doubled west range) incorporating the definitive designs for the east front and the Collège des Quatre-Nations, reconstruction of the east front, view from
south-east showing the completed south wing with the
southern pavilion of the east front partially realized
(van der Meulen, c. 1665); (e–g) detail of river front and
general views of L'Institut from the Louvre.

Mazarin's will provided for the foundation of a college for well-born students from four of the provinces
('nations') annexed by France under the terms of the
Treaties of Westphalia and the Pyrénées (territories
in Flanders and Artois, Alsace, Roussillon and Savoy):
the cardinal's important library was bequeathed to the
establishment and he was to be interred in the chapel
as his predecessor, Richelieu, had been interred in
Lemercier's Sorbonne chapel. In accordance with the

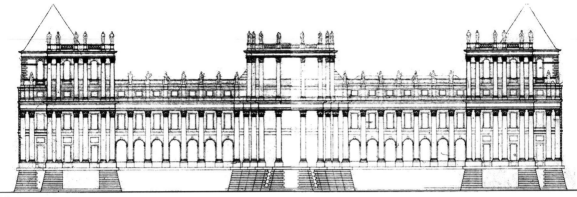

donor's preference, Colbert engaged Le Vau: the work, with the concavity of its façade developed beyond French precedent, was finished by François d'Orbay in 1672, two years after the principal architect's death.

Early in 1661, about the time of the fire which prompted him to double the Petite Galerie, Le Vau had turned his attention from the north side of the Cour Carrée to the continuation of Pierre Lescot's south wing. There, by the end of 1663, he had inserted a central pavillon with an extraneous frontispiece of colossal attached Corinthian columns reminiscent of Bullant's one at the Château d'Écouen. Rising from ground level – actually over a battered plinth in a dry moat – that Order was to extend across the east front, embracing the greatest of Le Vau's oval salons. And, in an unprecedented exercise in town planning, it was to be echoed across the river on the slightly smaller scale of the frontispiece of the Collège des Quatre-Nations, opposite the central pavillon of the south wing.**2.44**

Mazarin died a month after the fire which threatened his apartment at the Louvre, six months before the disgrace of Fouquet, but the influence of his taste survived the demise of his regime. It is apparent in his memorial, the Collège des Quatre-Nations – now the Institut de France – for which he had willed substantial funds. It is also apparent in the confirmation of Guarino Guarini as the architect for the other building provided for in the cardinal's will, S.-Anne-la-Royale. This was to be the church of the Theatine order, which Mazarin had introduced to

France in 1644: had it been completed it would have been the only unequivocally Baroque building in Paris. For this very reason it fell victim, before it was far advanced, to the change of artistic climate following the promotion of Mazarin's erstwhile assistant, Jean-Baptiste Colbert. As we are about to see, this in turn provoked a severe reversal in Le Vau's own fortunes. The interiors of Le Brun and the gardens of Le Nôtre are, indeed, the chief legacies of the Baroque era of Mazarin briskly terminated not by the king's assumption of personal power but by the fall of Fouquet organized by Colbert. For while Le Brun and Le Nôtre brought to the era of Colbert precisely that combination of sumptuousness and order which the prestige and power of the new monarchy required, Le Vau emerged from his discomfiture only by changing his style.

2.44g

2.45a

›2.45 **LOUIS XIV AND THE STATE PROMO-TION OF ARTS AND SCIENCES:** (a, b) introduced by Colbert to the Gobelins and at the Académie royale des sciences; (c) 'Prelude to the Academy of Architecture', frontispiece to the *Traité des manières de dessiner les ordres de l' architecture antique* (Abraham Bosse, 1664).

As Surintendant des Bâtiments, Colbert was heir to Sublet de Noyers and the rationalist school of architectural criticism promoted at his behest in the absolutist *Parallele de l' architecture antique et de la moderne* of Roland Fréart de Chambray. At his accession he was presented with the *Traité des manières de dessiner les ordres de l' architecture antique* of Abraham Bosse (1602–76), whose proclamation of the rationalist ethic could hardly have been more prominent – or germane. That work was a suite of allegorical plates, hierarchically ordered but without text. The official dogma

2 LOUIS XIV AND FRENCH ASCENDANCY

Commissaire Ordinaire des Guerres from 1641, Jean-Baptiste Colbert distinguished himself during the Fronde and managed the exiled Mazarin's affairs. Having done so scrupulously, he was retained as the cardinal's closest adviser and began the examination of the parlous state of the royal finances which led him to Nicolas Fouquet. He was confirmed as Côntroleur-Général des Finances in 1665. He had been appointed Surintendant des Bâtiments early the previous year: that post, created for the Duc de Sully in 1602, was reformed and strengthened by its new incumbent who used the position to promote a coherent

French style which would rival the mode of the Roman Baroque masters. As we have seen (above, pages 14f), he went on to power in all the departments of state except war – which fell to the Marquis de Louvois to reform.

Colbert was the supreme example of the type of statesman to emerge through Richelieu's policy of promoting the bourgeoisie. Thus he enrolled Charles and Claude Perrault in place of the Fréarts on his assumption of Sublet de Noyers's role. Unlike Sublet, his taste was flexible and responded to extra-artistic considerations. He was credited with protecting the arts not through any particular fondness for them but because, as a statesman, he recognized that they immortalize great empires. As in all spheres of activity, regulation was of course essential. Hence he founded the royal academies of the arts and sciences as the arbiters of authority, in particular from our point of view, the Académie royale d'architecture in 1671 as supreme arbiter of taste: it was to be the central authority of the profession in the centralized realm of art, the centre of instruction in the *métier* and its related disciplines administered by its members – all Architectes du Roi. And he set up the state Gobelins factory to ensure that France would no longer be dependent on the importation of costly foreign artefacts: on the contrary, artists trained there took the French style abroad – the designer/engraver Daniel Marot is a prime example, as we shall see.[2.45]

Considerations of prestige seem to have prompted Colbert's first important act as Surintendant des Bâtiments, the cessation of work on Le Vau's scheme for the Louvre and its submission to the criticism of both French and Italian masters. Prestige apart, he was clearly determined to destroy the power which the Premier Architecte had gained at the expense of the Surintendant des Bâtiments under his weak predecessor: centralized control was to be exerted over all the organs of the state, art and art-

2.45b

would follow after the constitution of the Académie seven years later – as we shall see. Meanwhile the new Surintendant promoted his ambition for French archi-

2.45c

tecture by appointing André Félibien as historian of the tradition and commissioning Israël Silvestre (1621–91, engraver to the king from 1662 and drawing master to the dauphin a decade later) to record its achievements in engraved plates after the example of Jacques Androuet du Cerceau's *Les plus excellents bastiments de France* of 1576 and Jean Marot's *Architecture française* of 1670. The prints were issued individually or in limited series rather than in a comprehensive volume.

›2.46 SAINT-DENIS, MANSART'S DESIGNS FOR THE BOURBON MORTUARY CHAPEL, 1665: (a) presumed first draft of scheme in context, with four large ellipses separated by four smaller circular chapels dependent on a circular space, (b) revised scheme

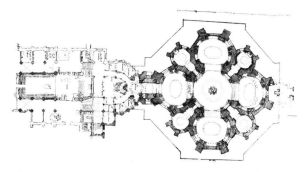

2.46a

with a large double-domed rotunda surrounded by apsidal and elliptical satellite spaces.

Leonardo and Bramante provide obvious High Renaissance precedents but Francesco Primaticcio's Valois scheme was not intermediate (AIC4, pages 814f, 836f, AIC5, page 342). The second scheme is an exceptionally grand development from the author's early excursion into centralized design for the church of the Visitation in the rue Saint-Antoine, asserting a Greek cross over a circle and exploiting the diagonals with a variety of spaces, mainly elliptical. As there, but more particularly as in the projects for the entrance pavillon and staircase at Blois, Mansart reveals a membrane between the outer shell of the dome and an oculus in the inner one in an exercise unprecedented in the scope of its vertical scenography. His Roman contemporaries, particularly Bernini, were interested in the medium too but Mansart led at Blois: we shall encounter the progeny in London and Paris in due course.

ists included. The manoeuvre had considerable artistic consequences however, for from it emerged the hybrid style of the new Louvre and Versailles. Baroque in scale, richness of materials, colour, but regulated in accordance with academic Classical principles, even when relying on the fusion of the arts in interiors: that at once satisfied the king's taste for display, responded to Colbert's ideal of order and expressed their common conception of the grandeur of the French monarchy.

The prestige of the Louvre as the principal residence of the greatest king in Europe demanded the greatest architectural talent of the age. Colbert called for a wide range of alternative proposals but hoped to commission François Mansart. The latter was encouraged to further his evolution of alternatives to Le Vau's Louvre projects. During the protracted process, Colbert favoured him with an equally prestigious project: a mortuary chapel for the Bourbon dynasty to be constructed beyond the apse of the basilica at Saint-Denis – where the Valois had failed to realize their grandiose scheme for a burial rotunda attached to the north transept (see AIC5, page 342).**2.46**

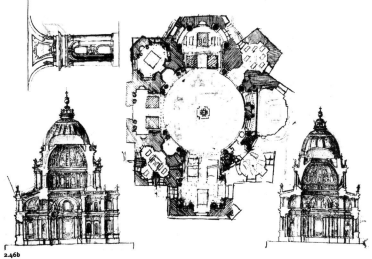

2.46b

The Bourbon chapel was Mansart's last crown commission: he died before it came to fruition but the second draft would prove highly influential. Meanwhile, unable to hold his preferred master to a definitive project for the Louvre, Colbert turned to the Italians. Bernini, Cortona, Rainaldi and the otherwise unknown Candiani responded: attracting Bernini, widely considered the greatest master in Europe, would have the added advantage of despoiling the pope.**2.47**

2.47a

2.47b

International aspiration at the Louvre

When Colbert called a halt on his scheme for the east wing of the king's Parisian seat, Le Vau had laid most of the foundations and built the southeast corner pavillon in accordance with the projected ordonnance: that was based throughout on a colossal Order rising from the ground as in the frontispiece of the south wing (see page 238). Three different approaches emerge from the surviving proposals of the French respondents: Le Vau's scheme with a colossal Order rising from a stepped podium was favoured by Mansart and Pierre Cottard; Pierre Lescot's scheme for the interior court with its superimposed Orders, first translated to the exterior by Lemercier ten years earlier, was favoured by Jean Marot; a colonnade supported by a rusticated basement was favoured as early as 1661 by Antoine-Léonor Houdin in a strictly Classical, indeed Bramantesque, interpretation of the

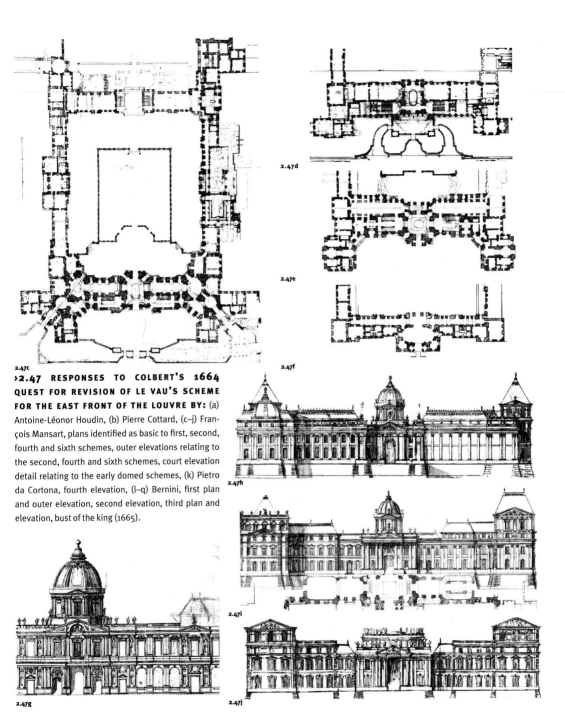

2.47c

›2.47 RESPONSES TO COLBERT'S 1664 QUEST FOR REVISION OF LE VAU'S SCHEME FOR THE EAST FRONT OF THE LOUVRE BY: (a) Antoine-Léonor Houdin, (b) Pierre Cottard, (c–j) François Mansart, plans identified as basic to first, second, fourth and sixth schemes, outer elevations relating to the second, fourth and sixth schemes, court elevation detail relating to the early domed schemes, (k) Pietro da Cortona, fourth elevation, (l–q) Bernini, first plan and outer elevation, second elevation, third plan and elevation, bust of the king (1665).

2.47d

2.47e

2.47f

2.47h

2.47i

2.47g

2.47j

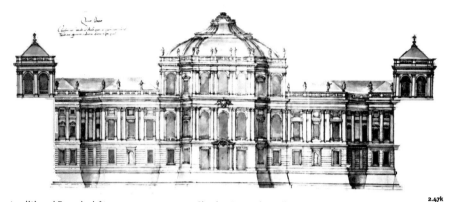

2.47k

traditional French château entrance screen. Charles Perrault, Colbert's secretary, claimed that his brother Claude also produced a colonnade scheme
which the Surintendant admired – though it did not satisfy his requirement
of conformity to existing work. That scheme is lost and so is an undefined
one of late-1664 by Louis's brother, François Le Vau.

In an incredibly complex series of drawings demonstrating precisely that
inability, or unwillingness, to bring the creative process to a practical conclusion which made it impossible for Colbert to retain him, Mansart brought
his own style to its apogee. It is not possible, considering them, any longer
to speak of Mansart as merely invigorating French Classicism: his ideas
for the Louvre are quite distinctly Baroque in scale, in vigour of massing,
in movement explicit in curved façades and Orders of varied plasticity, in
planning for dramatic vistas through richly diversified room shapes, not only
along the principal axes at right angles to one another but along the diago-

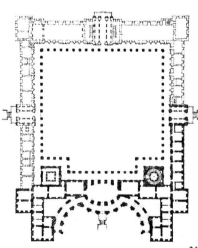

2.47m

2.47l

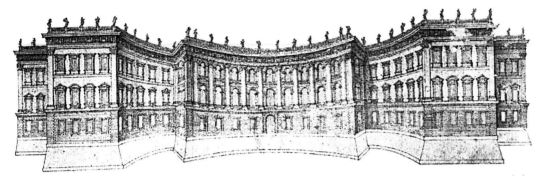

nals as well. Yet there is no specifically Roman importation in all this torrent of invention: on the contrary the colossal Corinthian Order was suggested by Le Vau's existing work, and the massing of differentiated blocks, the ordonnance based on the principle of progression in plasticity, the planning about enfilades, were all essential characteristics of the French tradition which Mansart had inherited from Salomon de Brosse, Philibert de l'Orme and Pierre Lescot, and which he had begun to develop thirty years before he turned his attention to the Louvre.

Of the Italian respondents, both Carlo Rainaldi and Pietro da Cortona attempted to work in the French idiom. Rainaldi's effort was bizarre. Cortona also wrestled unsuccessfully with a central pavillon derived from Le Vau's typical form but beside it he introduced the Roman palazzo formula developed after Bramante by Michelangelo with a colossal Order raised on a rusticated basement to embrace two storeys below a concealed roof – and that was to prove an important contribution.[1.30] Bernini, though keeping all the existing work, made no concession to its style beyond the adoption of a colossal Corinthian Order rising from a podium: the central oval pavillon was doubtless suggested by Le Vau but in setting it off against concave wings he used one of the most characteristic techniques of the Roman High Baroque – doubtless prompted by fantastic response to the antique (see page 69). Moreover, likening French to Venetian taste, he combined the loggias of Jacopo Sansovino's Biblioteca Marciana with the clustered pilasters and half columns of his colossal Order in a scheme which otherwise suggests Michelangelo's Palazzo dei Conservatori (AIC5, pages 166f, 220).

The king chose Bernini but Colbert, noting the vast amount of open arcading, called for revision of his project to meet the practical necessity of housing the king in security – and a cold climate. The concave curve remained but the Order was raised over a rusticated basement and it framed loggias only in the centre. Though this too was open to practical criticism, the king was still enthusiastic. Bernini was invited to Paris for final revisions in mid-1665 and given a quasi-royal progress through France. Colbert had little success in concentrating his attention on the internal requirements of the palace and none at all in persuading him to renounce the extravagance of refacing the existing buildings. Satisfying the demand for apparent strength, however, he straightened the broad central projection, eliminated the loggias altogether and applied the Order of half-columns and pilasters selectively in a gigantic attempt at compromise between the Roman formula, with its homogeneous mass and hidden roof, and the French approach based on the distinction of pavillons.

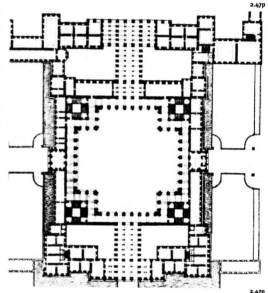

Though fêted by the king, Bernini alienated everyone else concerned. His third scheme's foundation stone was laid in October 1665 but his return to Rome was followed by a year of desultory effort on substructure during which the French opposition mobilized itself. Colbert was gravely concerned about the scheme's cost and practicality but feared that countering the king's enthusiasm for it would prompt him to forsake the capital: Versailles was in the ascendant. Totally preoccupied there by April 1667, indeed,

2.48a

2.48b

›2.48 RESPONSE OF COLBERT'S COMMIS-
SIONERS AND THEIR ASSISTANTS TO THE
PROBLEM OF COMPLETING THE LOUVRE: (a,
b) the astylar projects attributed by Charles Perrault to
Louis Le Vau and Charles Le Brun, the latter's version
of late-1667; (c, d) the Colonnade project attributed
by Charles Perrault to his brother Claude, a working
drawing attributed to the office of the Premier Architecte and plan; (e, f) Colonnade scheme overview and
plan incorporating the decision to double the south
wing (mid-1668); (g) François Le Vau's revision of the
east front in connection with the developments of mid-
1668; (h) junction of west and south range with transition from Pierre Lescot's attic to a full third Order; (i, j)
late projects for the south and east fronts with alternative roofs on the corner pavilions; (k, l) the Colonnade,
from without and within.

the king finally abandoned Bernini. The only tangible result of his expensive French excursion was the splendid royal bust which he carved while in Paris.[2.47q] Even the equestrian statue ordered at that time was out of fashion when it ultimately reached Versailles in 1685. Yet his last Louvre project was to be of fundamental importance for the development of French 'Baroque-Classicism' – as we shall see.

Le Vau had continued working on the Louvre during Bernini's visit. Alive to the interests of his brother Claude, Charles Perrault promoted the idea of constituting a council of experts for definitive design. In April 1667 Colbert commissioned Le Vau, Charles Le Brun and Claude Perrault: they were to work on the project in common so that none could claim the authorship to the prejudice of the others; that proved impossible but, naturally, the requirement entailed controversy over the allocation of responsibility.[2.48]

French resolution at the Louvre

Unable to agree on a single design, the committee submitted two: one with a colonnade or peristyle at first-floor level, the other without an Order of columns. Charles Perrault consistently refers to the scheme with the colonnade as his brother's: it is nevertheless possible that at some stage in its evolution the uncanonical doubling of its columns may have been suggested by Le Brun who had introduced the motif to his unexecuted illusionist scheme for the vault of the salon at Vaux-le-Vicomte. Perrault reported that Le Vau was responsible for the alternative without Orders: unlike the colonnade, it accorded with the existing south wing but the surviving drawings include a version of it generally attributed to Le Brun. Perrault also relates that Colbert preferred the astylar solution – it had been his persistent concern that the new work should accord with the old. The king chose the colonnade scheme on 13 May 1667: it was, naturally, the responsibility of the office of the Premier Architecte to produce the working drawings.

At first it was intended that the new east wing should be joined to the north and south wings as planned by Le Vau but in June 1668 the project

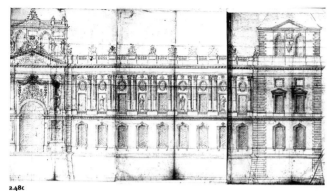

2.48c

was revised to provide for the doubling of the south wing so that the king, the queen, the royal family and their attendants could be accommodated in the most agreeable part of the château. The revised project was defended by François Le Vau, Louis's brother who had long worked for Colbert and who had been called upon to review projects of the Premier Architecte at least twice before. His principal aim was to demonstrate that the advantages to be gained by doubling the south wing – comfort, beauty and propriety – would be worth the expense. To provide all the accommodation needed by the royal family and their attendants there, Lescot's attic would be replaced on the court side with a third full storey, giving the building a height proportioned not only to its length but to its usage; rising from a full basement, the now necessarily colossal Order would be applied both to the east and the south fronts. It was objected – almost certainly by Perrault – that the display of habitation in a full storey over the head of the king was improprietous. Pragmatism had won by 1671 when Colbert invited competition for the design of a French Order for the third floor – the addition of a sixth style to the Classical canon was required as Corinthian and Composite had already been used by Lescot.

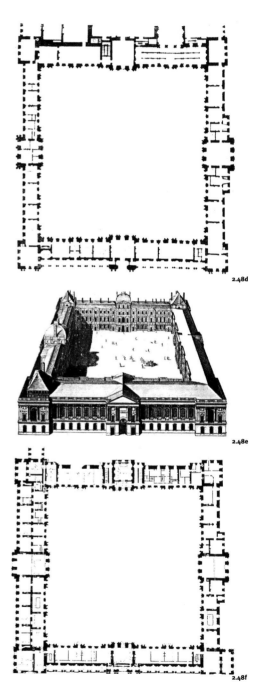

2.48d

2.48e

2.48f

2.48g

2.48h

Whatever the role of Louis Le Vau in the evolution of the 1667 project for the Louvre, his brother's involvement in the revision of that project went further than mere advocacy. In so far as his defence specifically deals with the east wing, it is closely related to a project published over his own name, in which the end pavillons – revised for the doubling of the south wing – are almost direct quotations of the corps de logis of Pietro da Cortona's 'fourth' west front. This design marks the transition from the project of 1667 to the executed one. That followed François Le Vau's approach for the side pavillons, doubling the side pilasters, but the simplified central pavillon was also derived from Cortona; there was to be only one attic storey above the king's floor but, as in François Le Vau's project, the Order embracing both these storeys was greater than that of the 1667 colonnade.

The articulation of the Louvre's east and south fronts was to provide one of the principal standards for French architects throughout the next century. With regular pavillons – derived from Cortona – and a canonical Corinthian Order disposed rhythmically right across the façade over a finely rusticated

2.48i

2.48j

2.48k

basement, it may in fact be seen as an academic Classical correction of the Roman High Baroque projects which had appealed to the king. Specifically, if Bernini's third project for the east front is submitted to the criticism spelt out in the mid-eighteenth century by Jacques-François Blondel the result is close to the realized schemes. The attribution of responsibility for the Colonnade, in particular, is controversial but the later 17th- and 18th-century commentators who reviewed all the documents opted for Perrault and, having been commissioned to produce the official French edition of Vitruvius, he was certainly the member of the commission best equipped to apply Classical theory to the correction of Baroque practice.

2.48l

2.49a

›2.49 **LOUIS LE VAU AND CHARLES LE BRUN AT VERSAILLES,** 1668–71: (a) overview c. 1668, (b, c) plans of Louis XIII's building with Le Vau's 'envelope' and its garden front, (d) first-floor plan c. 1700, (e) model of the lost Escalier des Ambassa-deurs, (f–j) Salons of Venus (first antechamber, vault and general view), Mars (guards), Mercury (inner antechamber, Apollo (parade bedroom), (k) view across entrance court, (l) Trianon de Porcelaine (1670).

The original building consisted of three corps de logis linking four pavillons around an open court. Detached service wings – of brick with stone detail, like the original work – were added to either side of a wider

ENVELOPING VERSAILLES

Louis XIV preferred Saint-Germain-en-Laye to Paris after the shock of the Fronde rebellion. From c. 1662 he turned his attention to developing his father's hunting lodge at Versailles as the scene of fête.**2·49** To Colbert's dismay, the king called on Louis Le Vau for the further expansion of the complex into a more permanent seat while the definitive scheme for the Louvre was evolving in 1667–68: the Peace of Aix-la-Chapelle (1668) confirmed Louis in the triumph to celebrate and released the means.

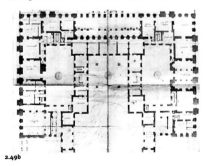

2.49b

2.49c

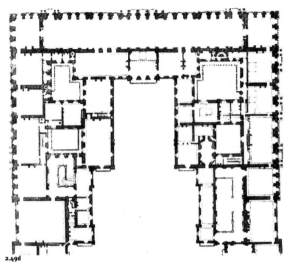

2.49d

2.49e

Wings were projected towards the burgeoning town, framing a new forecourt; the single enfilades of the main rooms were to be doubled within an envelope addressing the gardens. The style of the new work on the court side was probably dictated by Colbert to limit the cost, perhaps by the king's desire to respect the work of his father – despite his newly informed taste for the Roman Baroque. Nor, indeed, were the new outer façades essentially Baroque: the disposition of a rusticated basement supporting an Order on the main floor derives from Bramante but the panels above the windows – instead of the usual pediments – recall Pietro da Cortona's 'fourth design' for the Louvre and the frontispieces are native extrusions. In fact a French precedent for the scheme in general is to be found in Salomon de Brosse's Parlement de Bretagne (now the Palais de Justice) at Rennes which itself derives from the Roman tradition of Bramante through Francesco Primaticcio's Aile de la Belle Cheminée at Fontainebleau – including even the deep central recession (AIC5, page 320). However, contemporary French critics were disconcerted by the Italianate concealed roof.

forecourt in 1662: five years later they were heightened and joined to the original building with staircase blocks. By 1668 the main lines of the garden had been established and one of its most celebrated incidents, the Grotto of Thetis, immured in a pavilion to the north of the northern service wing.

Responsibility for the 'envelope' is sometimes questioned: though a radical departure from his style hitherto, it was conceived by Le Vau but executed largely under the direction of his assistant, François d'Orbay; it was finished in 1671 about the time of Le Vau's death. The latter produced his expansive variation on his Hôtel Lambert scheme for the king's great staircase in his last ailing year but its ordonnance was revised by d'Orbay in 1674 and, in any case, its stunning effect was due to Le Brun's illusionism – of painted spectators to the etiquette governing the graduated reception of grand envoys beneath simulated tapestries representing the king's victories in battle. History was to the fore in the staircase: in the great royal apartment which it served (from 1674), Olympian mythology was the theme – as it had been in the Galerie d'Apollon at the Louvre whose dedicatee was now to preside over the bedroom of the

2.49f

2.49j

2.49i

2.49g

2.49h

2.49k

Le Vau's 'envelope' contained grand apartments for the king and the queen, to the north and south respectively: their end pavilions framed a terrace overlooking the development of André Le Nôtre's axial garden. The extensions east – flanking the entrance court on the town side – provided for staircases to each suite: naturally the one on the king's side – the Escalier des Ambassadeurs – was of exceptional magnificence. Beyond it the state rooms were decorated by Charles Le Brun between 1671 and 1686: they display a similar combination of the arts to those at Vaux-le-Vicomte and the Galerie d'Apollon at the Louvre but the high-relief stuccowork, especially the figural elements, is reduced and the integrity of the painted zones is never violated. Illusionist panels generally occupy the centres of the vaults and glimpses of the sky are revealed beyond balustrades with spectators in the corners of the grander rooms but non-illusionist panels play an increasingly important role. The walls are covered with velvet or encrusted with 'Sun King' while Jupiter protected his council in the cabinet beyond.

Attributed to Le Vau in the absence of documentation to the contrary, the king's first private retreat from the pressure of court in his new palace was at the site of the village of Trianon which had been displaced by the northern arm of the grand canal system. Its one-storey, mansard-roofed pavillon and four detached satellites were revetted with pottery (not porcelain) panels in precocious manifestation of taste for the style of Chinese export ware. In furtherance of Le Vau's debt to Palladio, hitherto in motif, the plan is a variant on the master's villa formula.

coloured marbles in geometric patterns rather than panels in several tiers painted with arabesques as at Vaux. As usual in France, a continuous cornice marks the junction of wall and ceiling and a full Order articulates the principal spaces: that was an essential element of the final permutation of Le Brun's approach to the fusion of the arts which began with his experience of Cortona and Giovanni Francesco Romanelli nearly forty years before.

2.49l

2.50a

THEORY AND PRACTICE IN AN AUTHORITARIAN STATE

The Louvre Colonnade and the envelope of Versailles betray the influence of the Romans in their clear-cut horizontal lines, concealed roofs, sumptuous articulation and colossal scale. Setting the standard for French Classical architecture, they represented a grand compromise between the exuberant spectacle desired by the king and the academic Classicism promoted by his chief minister. Louis XIV oscillated between war and building in his quest for lasting *gloire* and certainly saw the value of Baroque techniques for promoting the idea of Absolutism Triumphant: Colbert founded the royal academies of the arts and sciences in his determination to regulate all spheres of activity in the forging of an ordered state; the Marquis de Louvois, Secrétaire d'État à la Guerre, perfected the ordering of the professional army upon which the king's foreign policy primarily depended (see page 15).

The resolution of the king's order is manifest in the systematic conception of the series of offensive defence forts constructed around the frontiers of the kingdom (from

›2.50 VAUBAN AND THE FORTIFICATION OF FRANCE: (a) Lille (from 1668); (b) Besançon (from 1687); (c) Neuf-Brisach (from 1697).

Trained under the principal royal engineer, the Chevalier de Clerville, Vauban emerged as *Ingénieur du Roi* in 1655 and quickly demonstrated his facility at directing sieges in the war with Spain. After the Peace of the Pyrénées (1659), he was deployed to construct defences but returned to siege warfare in the Flemish hostilities of 1662 – distinguishing himself at Douai, Tournai and Lille and then proceeding to rebuild or improve the fortresses held by France under the terms of the Peace of Aix-la-Chapelle (1668). Until then his fortification had remained conventional: defence in triangulated depth from a stellar nucleus. However, his expertise at siege warfare was innovative and prompted the Marquis de Louvois to call on him for a memoir on conducting sieges. His systematic method of approach depended on parallel trenches surrounding the besieged site at the limit of its firing range: the outer one to block relief, the inner one to prevent sorties and devolve into zigzag channels of assault after the defences had been breached by cannon or mine. The system was developed in the Netherlands campaign, particularly at Maastricht in 1673, and further developed over the following decade when artillery commanders were persuaded to complement vertical assault with the effects of ricochet.

2.50b

Development in depth was to be characteristic of Vauban's planning both for offence and defence – the latter, at least, far from new in principle. His first success was at Lille, where his project for fortification was preferred to that of his master, Clerville (1667). With the peace of 1668 his work on fortification intensified and he succeeded Clerville as Commissaire Général des Fortifications in 1677: two years later he published his schedule of frontier defences, listing fifteen forward installations between Dunkerque and Dinant and thirteen in secondary positions. Notable for coherent synthesis of techniques fundamental to current international practice, rather than novelty, the 'first system' was developed between Lille and Saarlouis (1668–80) and modified in the 'second system' over the following years for deployment most notably at Besançon (from 1687): in principle this involved detaching the bastions from the main line of ramparts and constructing towers in their place (for basic defence on the strength of impressive Spanish form in the fortification of Luxembourg, 1683) and projecting smaller triangular works out beyond the detached stellar line for an advanced range of fire. That was perfected in the 'third system' of modification best exemplified at Neuf-Brisach (from 1697) with its square *place* at the centre of a grid defined by octagonal ramparts projecting into pentagonal bastion towers at each point and sixteen devolved triangular outworks.

Elevated to the rank of Maréchal de Camp in 1703, Vauban's practical career was suspended and he lost some prestige when several of his most celebrated forts fell to the enemy in the War of the Spanish Succession: his achievement in advancing methods of attack was subsequently seen to overshadow even his masterly command of defensive planning.

2.50c

1668): they are due to his formidable military engineer Sébastien Le Prestre, Marquis de Vauban (1633–1707), ultimately Commissaire Général des Fortifications and marshal of France.[2.50] In the metropolis, on the other hand, the benefits of Colbert's order are nowhere more monumentally symbolized than in the great regimented schemes of Libéral Bruant for the Hôpital de la Salpêtrière and Hôtel des Invalides – though the former originated with Le Vau at the instigation of Mazarin.[2.51]

If not necessarily for a hospital – even for military heroes – the regime required compromise between Baroque éclat and Classical discipline for the architecture of state: the authors of the Louvre Colonnade and Charles Le Brun in the Grands Appartements at Versailles achieved it. So too did Claude Perrault's Arc de Triomphe du Trône with its antique form and sumptuous ornament. And that, in turn, is to be compared to the triumphal arches of Nicolas-François Blondel, first professor at the Académie royale d'architecture (from 1671): if the former promotes the claims of the Moderns, the latter champions the Ancients – and their debate was recorded by the academy's secretary, André Félibien.[2.52]

2.51a

**›2.51 LIBÉRAL BRUANT, PARISIAN GRANDS
PROJETS:** (a–c) Hôtel des Invalides (from 1670,
consecrated 1706), model (with Bruant's east-facing
complex as extended by Mansart to the west, in the
background here, see page 281), entrance range, longitudinal chapel interior (under construction 1676); (d–g)
Hôpital de la Salpêtrière (from 1656), plan, entrance
range, chapel exterior and interior (completed in 1677).

The Hôtel des Invalides was commissioned by the
king at the instigation of Louvois for the care of his
wounded soldiers. Bruant projected it over a monastic grid which some commentators see as having been
elaborated with specific reference to the Escorial –
though the formula was ubiquitous and relevance is
not immediately apparent. There is also some doubt
about the degree of Bruant's responsibility for the construction of the chapel – as we shall recall when we con-
sider the 'dome' added by Mansart (from 1677 while
work on the nave was nearing completion): in scale and
style the two parts could hardly be more different.

2.51b

2.51c

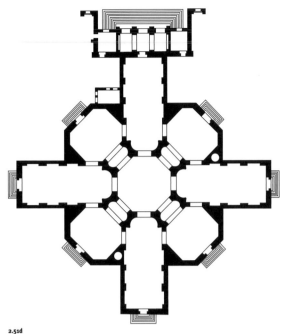

2.51d

2.51f

2.51g

First adjuncts to monastic or conventual establishments, retaining their cloistered form, hospitals were
developed as independent complexes in France from
the middle of the 16th century under the influence of
the Milanese Renaissance Ospedale Maggiore, the
pilgrims' hostel at Santiago de Compostela and the
Santa Cruz establishment at Toledo (AIC4, pages 760,
866f). The Parisian Hôtel-Dieu (attributed to Philibert de l'Orme) followed the precedent of cruciform
planning with a chapel at the crossing of the ranges
containing the wards. Instead the Hôpital Saint-Louis
(commissioned by Henri IV) was developed around a
great square court but the cruciform arrangement was
revived for the Salpêtrière. Founded by Mazarin on the
site of a gunpowder factory which had been converted
to house the insane – and the poor – building was
begun two years later under the supervision of Louis
Le Vau but most of the existing complex, expanded in
1684, is due to Libéral Bruant who assumed charge of
the project c. 1660 – when Le Vau was heavily involved
elsewhere, not least at the Louvre.

2.51e

2.52a

2.52b

Ancients and Moderns at the Sun King's service

Le Brun, Premier Peintre du Roi, head of the Académie royale de peinture et de sculpture, presented himself as the champion of the Ancients under Jean-Colbert's authoritarian regime. That was in response to Gabriel Blanchard who rejected the primacy of drawing in composition when he addressed the academy in 1671. There followed a thirty-year debate between the supporters of Colbert's protégé Le Brun and Louvoir's protégé Mignard, the champion of colour. In *Les Hommes illustres*, on the other hand, Charles Perrault presents Le Brun as the greatest of the Moderns.

Most inconsistencies in the alignment of the leading figures of the period can be explained in terms of expediency. The hero of the Ancients, Nicolas Poussin, had failed to provide a model in the Grande Galerie of the Louvre for the type of decoration which the courts of Mazarin and Louis XIV required: Raphael, at the Farnesina and Villa Madama, was hardly an adequate alternative. In taking Pietro da Cortona as his model Le Brun was more successful than any other French artist in using Baroque devices. For in Cortona's work he found an inspiration well attuned to his native ability to handle vast compositions in a free and lively manner, to cover vast spaces with a vigorous but coherent fusion of the arts. However sincere his

>2.52 CLAUDE PERRAULT: (a) Arc de Triomphe du Trône, project (1670); (b, c) frontispiece to *Vitruvius* and Plate V from *Ordonnance* (1673 and 1683 respectively); (d) section through project for the abbey church of S.-Geneviève (1670s, engraved record in the abbatical library).

The Arc de Triomphe du Trône was projected to replace a temporary structure erected at the point of Louis XIV's entry into Paris with his bride in August 1660: the work was never finished and the Place du Trône was renamed Place de la Nation after 1793.

The Académie royale des sciences, established in 1666, first pressed for the construction of an astronomical observatory at the instigation of the astronomer Adrien Auzout: Colbert readily saw the potential of the scheme for the improvement of French navigation at sea, strengthening maritime power and trade. The work, entrusted to Perrault, was completed in 1672 – three years before the founding of the Observatory at Greenwich.

The project with colonnaded aisles and apse for S.-Geneviève (late-1670s but submitted to the abbey by Charles Perrault in 1697 as the work of his brother) was inspired by its author's reconstruction of the basilica of Fano for his French edition of the ten books of Vitruvius

2.52c

(1673). An alternative version incorporates a screen before the sanctuary apse, contrary to the Counter-Reformation directive that the priest should be in full view at the high altar. The incorporation of colonnades may first have inspired developments in the articulation of the chapel at Versailles and, much later, so-called Neoclassical conceptions of the church – both of which will be considered in due course.

2.52d

admiration for Poussin and Raphael, there is more than a trace of personal ambition, of concession to the regime of Colbert, in his dogmatic stand for the Ancients in theory which was not always a happy constraint on his native talents in practice.

In 1682 Antoine Desgodetz published his *Edifices antiques de Rom dessinés et mesurés très exactiments*: it had been commissioned as an aid to architects under Colbert's auspices. For his part, Claude Perrault, the Modern, was certainly not immune to the inspiration. He compared the Colonnade of the Louvre to the peristyle of an antique temple – though the rhythm of the intercolumniations was uncanonical. And his project for the reconstruction of S.-Geneviève, in the manner of an antique basilica, was prophetic in restoring its ancient structural role to the column. However, he would use Desgodetz's research to counter received ideas, as we shall see. As we have already noted, he discussed the proposals of his colleagues – François Le Vau in particular – not primarily in the habitual terms of the proportions and details of the Orders but on grounds of decorum and plausibility – of *convenance* and *vraisemblance,* of what was true, or at least apparently true, to physical reality and of what was appropriate for modern usage, in particular the usage of the king of France.

Perrault had objected to substituting a full Order for Lescot's Louvre attic on the grounds that it was contrary to *convenance* to raise a habitable storey of stylistic magnificence over that of the king and that the height of a building should not necessarily be proportioned to its length. The matter remained unresolved until the 1750s when the Louvre was no longer a royal residence but the 'envelope' at Versailles was crowned with an attic. Though submission to the rules of proportion was a fundamental condition of a rational Order for the arts, it was above all conformity to the rules of propriety, reflecting the hierarchical order of the French monarchy, which gave the Colonnade and the new Versailles their exemplary significance.

As Colbert's principal advisers on architectural theory, the Perraults played a role similar to that of the Fréarts under Sublet de Noyers – but the similarity may be pressed too far. Charles Perrault, like Roland Fréart de Chambray, wrote a parallel of the 'Ancients' and 'Moderns'. Chambray preached the need to return to the ancient Classical authorities and learn again to apply their ideas in all their purity. Claude Perrault, the one member of the Commission with pronounced archaeological leanings, dared to suggest that blind adulation of the antique was irrational and that his own contemporaries had made great advances on it. Chambray's views reflect those of Sublet, whose policy was to provide an authoritative French school of art: Perrault's views reflect the conclusion which Colbert drew logically enough from the same policy. And although Perrault objected to the third-floor proposed for the Louvre, he entered Colbert's 1671 competition for the French Order which it would require – and won it, according to his brother.

Claude Perrault was a doctor, a member of the Académie des sciences, to whom the design of the royal observatory was entrusted. With the empiricism of the scientist and his wide-ranging experience, acquired not least through travel, he was concerned in his annotations to his translation of Vitruvius to distinguish precepts relevant to modern needs from those relating specifically to the antique. In doing so he denied the orthodox Classicist's view that there was an absolute standard of beauty reflecting the order of the cosmos and manifest in proportions as immutable as the consonances of music. These, as we have seen, were supposed to be imparted through imitation of nature – above all the human figure, the microcosm reflecting the order of the macrocosm – or of the antique masters who were credited with comprehending divine harmony (AIC4, page 739). Perrault countered that were this so, deviation from the model would be inadmissible and, noting the wide disparity in the proportions of Roman buildings as recorded by Desgodetz, he denied the infallibility of the Ancients in defence of the progressive innovations of the Moderns.

Conceding that proportions do please and recognizing the significance of the subconscious mind, especially in the association of ideas, Perrault postulated two levels of beauty: the positive in such sensible qualities as colour, texture and precision; the arbitrary in such intangibles as proportion, governed by prejudice through the elusive faculty of taste. The one acquired the force of the other through customary association. It was because views conflicted in the absence of an objective standard that rules were necessary: the framing of them was inevitably arbitrary but consensus was desirable and it was Perrault's aim in his *Ordonnance des cinq espèces de colonnes selon la méthode des anciens* to provide the basis for it.

2.53b

2.53c

2.53a

›2.53 FRANÇOIS BLONDEL AND HIS SCHOOL:
(a, b) frontispiece from *Cours d' architecture* and Porte
Saint-Martin (1672); (c) Porte Saint-Martin.

Confident in the impregnability of the frontiers fortified by Vauban and promoting the extension of Paris,
the king ordered the demolition of the ramparts protecting the conurbation north of the Seine (the Rive
Droite): work began in 1670 on their replacement with
tree-lined boulevards and a customs barrier. The fortified gates ceded to triumphal arches designed with
allegorical strength: Blondel's Porte Saint-Denis,
described by a square and centred on the circle
describing the arch, was paired with the Porte Saint-
Martin by his pupil and assistant Pierre Bullet. The
latter is the more conventional exercise: novel in the
former is the juxtaposition of obelisks which Blondel
justified in reference to antique funerary monuments.

If Colbert's conception of state order required rules for the arts, French
prestige required that those rules should be French and, therefore, Modern. Thus, ironic as it may seem that an independent-minded critical spirit
should be brought to the service of the authoritarian state, it is clear
that the very idea of an absolute standard of beauty, perceived by the
Ancients, had to be challenged if an authoritative French one were to be
established. Demonstrating in his *Ordonnance* that beauty was relative,
Perrault cleared the way for the acceptance of his definitive schedule of
proportions – and accompanied it with a French Order.

Under its first director, François Blondel, the Académie royale
d'architecture took up Perrault's challenge soon after its foundation in 1671
to determine if 'what is pleasing in architecture, and could be called good
taste, is somthing positive, or whether it pleases only because of custom and
prejudice'. Blondel was a military engineer best remembered for his contribution to Colbert's campaign of civic improvement in Paris after Vauban had
secured the frontiers: this prompted the demolition of the ramparts, their
replacement with boulevards and the rebuilding of the Portes Saint-Denis
and Saint-Martin as triumphal arches of severe Classical gravitas.[2.53]

Blondel's claim to fame also rests on the publication of the lectures he
gave to the academy school in his *Cours d' architecture* – the first course in
architecture taught under state auspices in France. Stamped with admiration
for the antique, his rationalist doctrine is certainly that of a mathematician in
sharp contrast to the empiricism of Perrault the doctor. Thus Rome's great
masterpieces are the pre-eminent models and analysis of the Orders, the
'noble elements' of architecture, is fundamental to his teaching: they demonstrate that beauty depends on proportion as the key to coherence; their rules
discipline the imagination by establishing mathematical limits to its field
of operation. Within these limits, faced with diverse circumstances, artistic
genius is led by experience to 'grace'. In pursuing the ideal proportions of
the Orders guided by the concept of the harmony of the cosmos appreciable
in music, Blondel led the academy in the search for an objective standard
of beauty. And when Perrault's ideas were debated, the polarization of the
'Ancients' and the 'Moderns' saw the majority side with Blondel in opposing
custom and prejudice with dialectic and principle – but the views of Perrault
and the 'Moderns' were to be of crucial importance to the 18th century.

2.54b

›**2.54 ARLES, HÔTEL DE VILLE,** from 1673:
(a) façade, (b) vestibule.

The building was begun to the direction of local architects but the young Mansart's intervention in 1673 was
in time to revise the façade (with the aid of his brother
Michel and local sculptors) and to devise the broad vestibule. The latter is distinguished by an extraordinary
expansion of flattened groin vaulting in diverse membranes springing from columns applied to the perimeter
but from no intermediate supports: French *stéréotomie*,
exceptional since the high Middle Ages, was not to surpass this feat in the high Classical era and its followers.

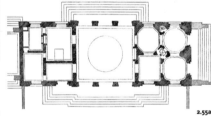

2.55a

2.55b

ADVENT OF JULES HARDOUIN-MANSART

The Escalier des Ambassadeurs which led to the king's
Grand Appartement at Versailles was the last product of
Le Brun's collaboration with Le Vau: it was begun after
the latter's death in 1670. The new Premier Architecte was
to be the young Jules Hardouin, great-nephew of François
Mansart – whose name he adopted and in whose aura he
had risen to prominence in the private sector in Paris with
specific reference to works like the Hôtel de Guénégaud des
Brosses (see pages 220f). His homage to Le Vau's new court
style in his first public work, the Hôtel de Ville at Arles, can
hardly have failed to flatter the king to whose order it was

›**2.55 ADVENT OF JULES HARDOUIN-MAN-
SART AT COURT:** (a, b) Château du Val (Saint-
Germain-en-Laye, from 1674), plan and elevation (*AF*);
(c) Château of the Maréchal Louis-François de Bouf-
flers (1644–1711), engraved elevation of the undated
building (*AF*); (d, e) Château de Clagny (from 1675,
destroyed), perspective view and detail of central elevation (contemporary records).

The hunting lodge known as the Château du Val may be seen as a simplified, thoroughly coherent revision of the single-storeyed central block of the Trianon de Porcelaine. However, its doubled plan is

2.55c

formed – and the amazing sail vaulting of its ground-floor vestibule could not have failed to impress the Bâtiments du Roi.[2.54] His own characteristic development of his uncle's *noble simplicité* in his first royal commission, the little Château du Val at Saint-Germain-en-Laye, and the much more extensive Château de Clagny (from 1675) confirmed him as the leading contender for advancement.[2.55] That was first to the Académie royale d'architecture in the year of Clagny and to the vacant position of Premier Architecte du Roi in 1681, well after the conclusion of the Peace of Nijmegen in 1678 had released funds for the king's alternative passion to war: building.

2.55e

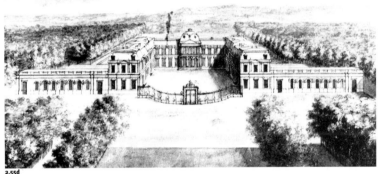

2.55d

novel – prophetic – in dispensing with a continuous load-bearing partition wall to either side of the single central salon: instead the royal apartment to the left achieves a suitable hierarchy of spaces dominated by the bedroom; the distribution of four representational rooms to the right pivots on a communal stove.

The clear-cut massing and restrained articulation of the Château de Clagny also anticipate typical developments in early 18th-century domestic architecture but it is retrospective in the single enfilades of its quasi-quadrangular distribution around an open court. The temple-front motif of the frontispiece derives from Palladio via Le Vau (see page 210). Jules Hardouin-Mansart was employed here by the king's mistress, the Marquise de Montespan.

First among Hardouin-Mansart's responsibilities, assumed in 1676 in anticipation of the necessary resources, was the vast expansion of Versailles: the following year the king announced his intention of moving the seat of government there and funds were found after the Peace of Nijmegen for this to be realized in 1682. This second transformation began with the insertion of the Galerie des Glaces between the twin salons which terminated the royal apartments on the first floor of the garden front, in place of Le Vau's recessed terrace: there, where history replaced mythology as the seat of government overwhelmed the pleasure palace, collaboration with Le Brun took French 'Baroque-Classicism' to its apogee (from 1678). The pro-

2.56a

ject extended to vast new wings, north and south, for the accommodation of the entourage – indeed of the emasculated and imprisoned grandees who might otherwise have been fomenting trouble in their provinces.

In this generation projection stopped short of a theatre and chapel in the north wing but it embraced the Orangerie (1681). It extended to many new zones in the garden and to the retreats of Trianon and Marly. On the town side its new wings for ministers framed a broad new outer court which completed the reproduction of Richelieu's telescopic form (see page 188). Beyond that, it also extended to the grand stable block and its pendant between the streets radiating out through the town from the palace gate. It was disrupted by the king's insatiable quest for military glory which provoked the War of the League of Augsburg (1688–97).**2.56**

>**2.56 HARDOUIN-MANSART AND LE NÔTRE AT VERSAILLES AND ITS SATELLITE RETREATS:** (a) exterior of garden range after insertion of Galerie des Glaces, (b, c) general view from the south-west over the Orangerie and the latter's interior (from 1681), (d) Salon de la Guerre, (e) Salon de la Paix, (f, g) Galerie des Glaces and detail of Le Brun's vault project drawing, (h, i) Grande and Petite Écuries (from 1679), overview and detail, (j, k) overview and plan of context, (l, m) main garden axis from east over the Bassin de Latone, and from north over the Bassin d'Apollon, (n) subsidiary northern axis flanked by the Bosquets de l'Arc de Triomphe and des Trois-Fontaines, (o) Bassins du Printemps, de l'Été, de l'Automne and de l'Hiver at the subsidiary axial junctions, (p, q) Bosquet des Dômes, (r) Colonnade, (s, t) Galerie des Antiquaires and Salle de Bal, (u) Bosquet de l'Encelade, (v) naval manoeuvres on the Grand Canal, (w–z) Grand Trianon (from 1687), plan and overview, entrance and garden fronts.

2.56c

Baroque-Classicism at its apogee

First noted for the *noble simplicité* of his exteriors, after his uncle's late domestic example, and for the facility of his planning, after the example of Le Vau, Hardouin-Mansart proved himself a consummate master in the appeasement of Louis XIV's taste for spectacle – and to that extent for 'Modernism' – without breaking the bounds of Classical discipline. In this too, his training by his uncle François and his early experience in the context of Le Vau and Le Brun at Versailles is clearly apparent. At Versailles he inherited the 'Roman' ordonnance adopted by Le Vau to satisfy the king's taste but the significance of his intervention can hardly be exaggerated: the vast extension of the horizontals, beginning with the suppression of Le Vau's recession for the Galerie des Glaces, and the replacement of squat rectangular windows for uplifting arched ones, are prime manifestations of his characteristic will to sustain the Classical accord of horizontals and verticals in face of the most extreme demands of Baroque scale.

2.56b

Hardouin-Mansart's models were occasionally contemporary Italian works but more often those of his French predecessors. Thus on the one hand the relationship between the Galerie des Glaces and the Salons de la Guerre and de la Paix must be compared to that between the Salone and Galleria of the slightly earlier Palazzo Colonna in Rome (see above, page 115). On the other hand the curved façades of the twin stable blocks (1679), into which all the elements were bound by a consistent articulation of the utmost simplicity, might be taken as revisions of Le Vau's Collége des Quatre-Nations. In the ancillary works at Versailles the influences are hybrid – and less determinate. The great rusticated Orangerie (1681) retains something of Jean Le Pautre's Baroque boldness of scale, without the mannerisms. The colouristic effects of Le Vau's Trianon de Porcelaine were consciously emulated in the Trianon de Marbre (the Grand Trianon, 1687) which replaced it – a unique example of such rich external revetment in France. And Marly (1679), where the principal pavilion was placed at the head of a great pool flanked by small guest pavilions in serried ranks, recalled Giacomo Torelli in its theatrical perspectives, its painted architecture and sculpture: indeed it crystallized something of the fantasy of the first Versailles during one of the king's great early fêtes.

As usual in France a continuous Classical cornice marks the junction of wall and ceiling in the Galerie des Glaces – as it had in the Escalier des Ambassadeurs and the salons of the Grand Appartement du Roi – and it was carried on a full Order. An Order was not in itself unfamiliar in French interiors, as we have seen. Moreover, Le Vau and Le Brun had themselves evolved the formula for Lambert's Galerie d'Hercule and the Galerie d'Apollon at the Louvre – the latter with sculpture and painting in which illusionism plays an important role. Apart from the tripartite division of the space and the scale, new here are the mirrors, the marble and the bronze. New too is the abandonment of Olympian allegory in the iconographical programme for the apotheosis of the king himself in Roman imperial mode – with less extreme illusionism, in the context of less exuberance of sculpture and less convolution of framework than in earlier permutations of the project when the iconography likened the exploits of the king to those of Hercules.

Hardouin-Mansart proposed rebuilding the palace court façades facing the town in a style to match his revision of the garden front: as this was rejected he extended twin new wings for the ministers in the old brick and stone style to either side of the expansive new place d'Armes. The stable blocks were to be much more 'Modern' in the restrained Classicism of their masonry-clad concave fronts facing the palace. The Orangerie was a particularly monumental expression of the *noble simplicité* which Mansart preferred after the example of the late works of his uncle François: it provided a base, extra verticality, for the vast horizontal extension to the south of Le Vau's ordonnance: that probably extended to the Orangerie's predecessor which was dislocated by the southern extensions.

2.56d

2.56g

2.56e

2.56f

›ARCHITECTURE IN CONTEXT »SEMINAL FRENCH

2.56h

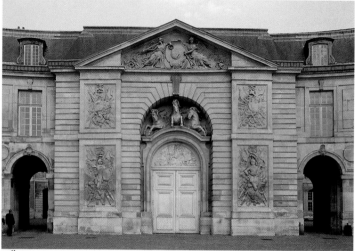

2.56i

2.56j

2.56l

2.56m

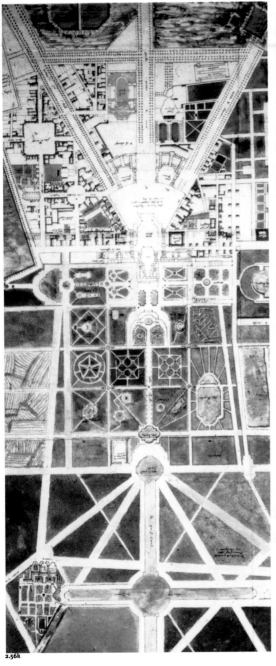

2.56k

2.56n

2.56p

2.56q

2.56o

2.56r

Though the site was marshy, Versailles provided André Le Nôtre with unrivalled scope for developing his formula of infinite axiality through wooded zones of concealed diversion – the context for the presentation of varied spectacles. Fountains within the woods and punctuating the axes were fed (from 1681) with water from the Seine at Bougival raised to an aqueduct by Arnold de Ville's current- and horse-powered timber hydraulic machine of multiple bucket-encrusted wheels and belts.

The gardens were not always solely for the entertainment of the court, as that numbered at least 4000 permanent residents (more than doubled by their servants): they were open to the public too. Therefore the king sought refuge at the château of Marly and, later, at a grander Trianon than the 'porcelain' original. The latter, clad in uniform stone progressing to marble for the ordonnance of its extraordinary open central colonnade, was developed over the foundations of its 'porcelain' predecessor under the minute scrutiny of the king and the general direction of Mansart's principal assistant, Robert de Cotte: U-shaped like the château of Clagny, but roofed *à l'italienne* (with shallow pitch concealed behind balustrades), it rambles into a lateral dependency containing the gallery.

2.56s   2.56t

Unequalled in extent and variety though they were, Le Notre's gardens were based on the formula he had applied at Vaux-le-Vicomte and was currently developing at the Tuileries. Having inherited the traditional chequerboard approach there, he brought diversity of planting in pattern and scale to bear, leaving *parterres de broderie* before the palace and carving 'rooms' from the more distant *bosquets*: he extended the axis to form the Champs-Elysées, disappearing over the western hill (see page 235). At Versailles, the *bosquets* which sealed the main axial swathe were much more extensive than at Vaux and were treated to still greater diversity of 'discoveries' than at the Tuileries, some embellished with considerable structures as the setting for fountains and statues, like the Colonnades. There was violence in the nether reaches of the garden and wilderness at Trianon.**2.56u, v**

2.56u   2.56v

2.56w

2.56x

2.56y

2.56z

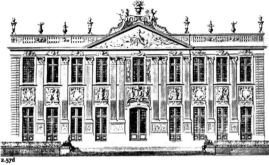

2.57c

2.57d

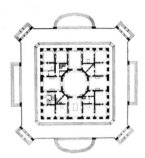

2.57b

›2.57 CHÂTEAU DE MARLY, from 1678: (a) contemporary overview (Pierre-Denis Martin, *Château de Versailles*): (b–d) plan, section and elevation (after A.A. Guillaumont, 1865).

The site was developed into a water garden with the royal pavilion at the head of the main axis and detached pavilions for the entourage ranged along both sides. As the axis continued beyond the main block, the latter was entered sideways from a guard house and addressed a feigned perspective on the face of a pendant pavilion to the other side. It emulated Palladio (via Scamozzi) in its ideal square plan, with four apartments about a double-height octagonal salon (*à l'italienne*) on the main level – if not in its trompe-l'oeil articulation with a painted colossal Corinthian Order. The guest pavilions were also decorated in trompe-l'oeil but without an Order.

2.57a

PROTOTYPES

The clear lines of the Louvre Colonnade and the garden façade at Versailles – the sustained horizontals of a strong basement surmounted by a faithfully observed Order and often a balustrade masking the roof – were to be the hallmarks of French Classical architecture from the later 1660s onwards. In his designs for two royal squares – the Place des Victoires and Place Vendôme (both initiated 1685) – Hardouin-Mansart transposed the Louvre mode for civic purpose as the nuclei of ordered development.**2.58** Equally appropriately, far less of his characteristic restraint is displayed in the first of his royal commissions for the capital, awarded in 1676 when he was starting on the expansion of Versailles: the addition of a great domed church to Libéral Bruant's Invalides project in which he furthered his great-uncle's spectacular scheme for the unrealized Bourbon funerary chapel at Saint-Denis (see page 243). Reverse attended these Parisian projects and even inhibited the completion of Versailles, though the king's new town was endowed with a relatively modest cathedral.

›2.58 PARIS, HARDOUIN-MANSART AND URBANISM: (a–c) Place des Victoires (from 1685) and Place Vendôme (realized from 1697), overview (Plan Turgot, 1734) and general view.

The Place Vendôme was developed on the site of a hôtel of that name: it was originally intended to accommodate the royal library and academies (project of 1685). Like the Place des Victoires, conceived to reconcile the alignment of several radial streets as the circular frame to the central statue of the king, it conforms to the now canonical Roman ordonnance in the Louvre version, with a rusticated arcaded basement supporting a colossal Order proportioned to an extensive open space. The later scheme was fully realized for housing, the earlier one was not, but both were to be held up by the academy as models for the French Classical square. Despite the reticence of their ordonnance they were essentially exercises in scenic architecture, designed first and foremost to glorify the king whose statue they framed. They were highly influential.

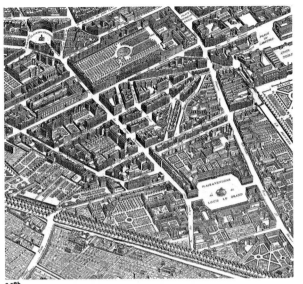

2.58b

Colbert died in 1683 and the discretion with which the great minister guided the king's absolutism was wanting in his successors. Staggering under the burden of Louis XIV's conception of his monarchy – manifest most immediately in the extravagant expansion of Versailles – France was reduced to near-bankruptcy by the almost ceaseless war waged to further that conception and the Marquis de Vauban's accomplishment in defending its elastic borders. Yet the brief moment of peace following the Treaty of Ryswick in 1697 saw the realization of the Place Vendôme and the Dôme des Invalides. Further, the Parisian cathedral of Notre-Dame was endowed with a high altar in honour of a vow made by Louis XIII. In addition, a cathedral of Notre-Dame was founded at Versailles and the palace was augmented with a grand chapel preceded by the last great state rooms.[2.59, 2.60]

2.58c

2.59a

2.59b

›**2.59 PARIS, ECCLESIASTICAL WORKS OF HARDOUIN-MANSART:** (a) cathedral of Notre-Dame, high altar (from 1699); (b–e) Dôme des Invalides, overview as originally planned in 1679 with detached quadrant arcades (engraved for Jean-François Félibien des Avaux, *Description de l' église royale des Invalides*, 1706; comprehensive plans and section were first engraved by Le Jeune de Boulancourt, *Description générale de l' hôtel royal des Invalides*, 1683), plan and section (after Blondel, *Architecture française*, 1752), exterior.

Its purpose remains undetermined but the domed Greek cross added by Hardouin-Mansart to the church of the military hospital, Les Invalides, was directly derived from his uncle François Mansart's designs for the Bourbon funerary chapel of Saint-Denis. Its High Renaissance plan is crowned by a cut-off dome with vertical perspective and dramatic lighting: its façade is subjected to a climactic movement by the breaking forward of its superimposed Orders with the plane of the wall in progressive stages, the upper Order one step behind the lower in achieving full plasticity. The eastern arm extends into an elliptical sanctuary at the junction of the 'dome' with the elongated chapel nave: within it the high altar is visible from both parts of the complex. Though Libéral Bruant included the longitudinal church in his general plan, some commentators attribute the realization of both parts to his successor.

Academic principles informed the portico of the Dôme des Invalides – though later, stricter, academic principle preferred the colossal Order of the unlayered interior volume. However, the exterior of the dome is richly embellished with gilt trophies and the sumptuous interior fittings culminated in a high altar with black Solomonic columns recalling Bernini's baldacchino in S. Pietro.

Berninesque fusion of the arts – sculpture and architecture at least – into a *concetto* distinguishes the new altar erected in Notre-Dame under the direction of Robert de Cotte (from 1708): Louis XIV and his father are spectators of divine theatre as the Virgin cradles her son's body after the descent from the Cross and raises her sight to future glory in Heaven. Bernini's sunburst glory was his most pervasive contribution to the French church.

2.59d

2.59c

2.59e

2.60a

2.60b

2.60e

›2.60 VERSAILLES, ECCLESIASTICAL WORKS **OF HARDOUIN-MANSART:** (a, b) cathedral of Notre-Dame (from 1684), exterior and interior; (c–f) palatine chapel (planning initiated in the late-1680s, construction after revisions of c. 1706), elevation, section, section, exterior, interior.

The cathedral, commissioned by the Crown as represented by the Marquis de Louvois, is a traditional basilica, essentially Gothic in plan but tunnel-vaulted: it is notable for its somewhat Vaubanesque military severity rather than grace – but that is characteristic of ecclesiastical work in Sublet de Noyers's era, especially Lemercier's Richelieu exercise. The ambulatory is interrupted by a circular lady chapel, as at S.-Roch in Paris but to a smaller scale (see page 215). The frontispiece design, with columns superimposed in the rhythm of a triumphal arch (lately amplified for the greater impact of the Dôme des Invalides), was deployed by Robert de Cotte and his followers in several works of Louis XV's early decades – as we shall see.

Authorship of the palatine chapel is ascribed to Hardouin-Mansart as Surintendant des Bâtiments du Roi (from 1699), not without doubt: that he died two years before it was finished is of little relevance but his preferred option at the project's inception was for a reduced version of his uncle's centralized Bourbon

2.60c

2.60d

funerary chapel scheme and then for an elongated volume with marble arcades on two levels. On the other hand nothing in de Cotte's work elsewhere suggests that it was his idea to translate the ordonnance of the Louvre Colonnade to provide the great height needed for the provision of the king's tribune on the level of the Grands Appartements. Ironically enough this produced an almost Gothic sense of verticality, furthered by the painter Antoine Coypel's illusionism: enhanced elevation recalling that of the double-height Sainte-Chapelle of S. Louis – naturally the dedicatee at Versailles too – was to prove as prophetic as Claude Perrault's S.-Geneviève project and these together provide the most convincing spurs to the inspiration displayed here.

2.60f

2.61

The Salon d'Hercule was the last great room of Louis XIV's reign. Long before its completion Versailles was a sad place, with the late wars of the old king going badly. Hardouin-Mansart and his successor had been called upon by subsidiary members of the royal family: now the centre of gravity would shift to Paris to which the nobility was fleeing and where there was to be plenty of patronage from the affluent new upper echelons of the bourgeoisie.**2.61**

›2.61 VERSAILLES, SALON D'HERCULE, from 1712: interior.

The Salon d'Hercule was conceived towards the end of Hardouin-Mansart's life but executed under his successor, Robert de Cotte.

JULES HARDOUIN-MANSART, ANDRÉ LE NÔTRE AND THE GRAND SEIGNEUR

During the years of desultory activity on the royal building sites, the office of the Premier Architecte du Roi had time for considerable effort on behalf of private patrons.

2.62a

2.62b

Some of these were the 'new men' of the *haute bourgeoisie* – to whom we shall return. Several were the greatest figures in the land: the Grand Dauphin at Meudon, the Duc d'Orléans at Saint-Cloud, the Prince de Condé at Chantilly. Most of them employed Le Nôtre in their parks: his stupendous efforts range from imposing formality on vast tracts of water at Chantilly to leaving the free-flowing Seine unchallenged in the panorama of Saint-Cloud and to excursion into the wilderness at Trianon.**2.62a, b**

Le Nôtre may have loosened his style but even for the grandest of clients Mansart preferred restraint, relying for decoration only on the Orders and the frames of doors and windows – indeed even only the latter in the manner of his uncle's Hôtel de Guénégaud. As 18th-century academic

2.62d

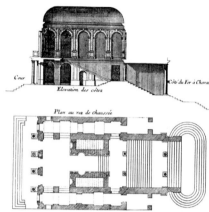

2.62c

›2.62 HARDOUIN-MANSART IN COUNTRY
AND TOWN: (a) Chantilly, 18th-century engraved
view over water garden towards the medieval and
Renaissance château complex; (b, c) Saint-Cloud,
overview, plan and section of new wing staircase;
(d) Meudon, Château Neuf, elevation and plan;

theory would specify – and as we shall have occasion to reiterate – articulation with full Orders of columns or pilasters was deemed appropriate only for royal or public building: the private house even of an aristocrat should be astylar, except perhaps for its entrance portico and the proportions derived from it.

Working in the mode on private secular commissions throughout his career, Mansart provided models of the *noble simplicité* so much admired by the 18th-century Enlightenment.**2.62c, d** His younger assistants conformed: Jacques IV Gabriel (1630–86) at the Château de Choisy provides one prominent example.**2.63**

As we have seen (see page 267), Mansart retained the traditional enfilade for his early work at Clagny but his later château at Dampierre and several Parisian hôtel projects show him also to have acquired the facility of Le Vau and Le Pautre for planning comfortable and convenient houses. He doubled the width of the corps de logis but obviated the constraint of a continuous load-bearing longitudinal party wall in planning for an extended range of facilities scaled to function: in addition to cosy cabinets, these now included dining-rooms, bathrooms, corridors and even cov-

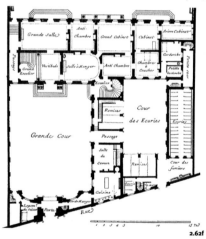

2.62f

2.62g

2.62e

(e) Dampierre, garden front; (f, g) ideal scheme for a private house (c. 1700), ground-floor plan and lateral section through entrance court.

›2.63 JACQUES IV GABRIEL AT CHOISY, after 1680, lost: garden front (*AF*).

2.63

›2.64 PIERRE BULLET AND THE DEVELOPMENT OF THE PLACE VENDÔME: plans of the contiguous Hôtel Crozat (left) and Hôtel d'Évreux (from 1702 and 1707 respectively).

The Place des Victoires and Place Vendôme were both popular with financiers: the former because it was near the Bourse, the latter as a grand arena for speculation behind the prescribed façades. The latter was the resort of Law and the richest man in France, Antoine Crozat (c. 1655–1738) – merchant-banker, proprietor of Louisiana, creditor to the government – who was rare among his peers in marrying his daughter to an aristocrat. Ennobled as Marquis de Châtel, Crozat commissioned Pierre Bullet to build adjacent houses for himself and his son-in-law, the Comte d'Évreux: both are entered from the square through the covered passage of a porte cochère which serves a double staircase in Crozat's house, a portico at the head of d'Évreux's court; as that is developed beyond the canted corner of the square, the main apartment faces the garden on the far side; the main apartment of Crozet's house faces the public space. Naturally the plans incorporate the sophistications inherited by Hardouin-Mansart from Le Vau, Le Pautre – and his uncle François.

ered access from carriage to entrance.**2.62e–g** Among his several contemporaries, Pierre Bullet was certainly no less distinguished on the most prestigious sites.**2.64**

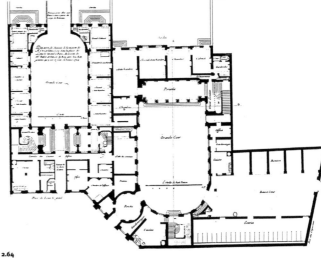

2.64

Simplicity without, comfort and convenience within were to be the hallmarks of the hôtels and châteaux produced by Mansart's assistants and their contemporaries in the early 18th century when royal patronage had flagged: Moreover, to these two basic types was now added a permutation of the château: the *maison de plaisance* which was the special – if not unique – preserve of the professional men of the *haute bourgeoisie* who had no inherited château to replace or modernize but sought retreat beyond the confines of Paris. This intermediate type, which may be seen to derive from the Château du Val via Marly, appears early in the 1680s in Pierre Bullet's work at Issy for Denis Talon, president of the parliamentary appeal court.[2.65]

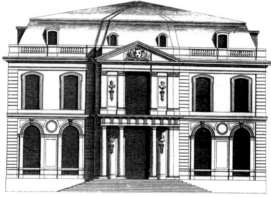

2.65a, b

Complementing the improvements in domestic distribution was the development of the non-monumental, anti-architectural mode of interior decoration called Rococo. The inclination is first licenced in the office of the Premier Architecte du Roi at the behest of the old king at Versailles but its astylar relaxation, its evolution complementing advances in conceptions of comfort and convenience, claim it for a new age.

›**2.65 ISSY, MAISON DE PLAISANCE OF DENIS TALON,** from 1681: (a, b) elevation and plan (*AF*).

Bullet's patron here was Président à Mortier of the Parlement de Paris (chief magistrate of the court of appeal). Within the strictly rectangular perimeter, typical of the distribution is the main axis of vestibule and salon, with reception rooms (one specifically for dining) to one side, private ones (including lavatory) and the staircase in the triple division of the other. Typical of the elevation is the application of Orders only to the central projection: relief of the sides is confined to quoins and the varied frames of the windows. The type proliferated in the 18th century. Bullet records his reference to Palladio.

2.66a

2.66b

>2.66 RETREATS OF AN AGEING KING: (a, b) Trianon, Salon Rond and Salon des Glaces (from 1706); (c) Marly, château, variant designs for 'cheminées à la moderne' (published by Pierre Le Pautre in *Livre de cheminées exécutées à Marly sur les desseins de monsieur Mansart*, 1699).

The *cheminée à la moderne*, with concealed flue eliminating deep projection (*à l' italienne*), was introduced in the late-1640s – as we have seen at Mansart's Hôtel de Jars and Le Vau's Hôtel Lambert. However, tall mirrors with large panes of glass were not possible until after the improvement of sheet rolling in the mid-1680s. After the lightness introduced by both these developments came insubstantiality in the design of framework, extending to the defiance of gravity at the top. Some commentators credit this development to Pierre Le Pautre (despite his homage to Hardouin-Mansart): they were not relevant to vestibules, of course.

2.66c

3 RÉGENCE AND THE EARLY YEARS OF LOUIS XV

In concert with comfortable and convenient planning and restrained external ordonnance, the office of the Surintendant des Bâtiments du Roi took the first steps towards the more relaxed, less pompous embellishment from which the style known as Rococo would develop. The exterior and interior of the château of Marly underwent several rehabilitations – as was to be expected of trompe-l'oeil façades but as fashion dictated within. Charles Le Brun had died in 1690 and his grand style was, in any case, not called for in a retreat: wood panelling replaced marble but as in the great gallery of the main palace of Versailles, the improvement of sheet-glass rolling in the mid-1680s prompted extensive revetment in light-reflecting mirrors. At the behest of the Premier Architecte and his team, especially Pierre Le Pautre (Antoine's nephew), by the end of the century these were framed with or without lightly subverted architectural members and crowned with floating masks sprouting the foliage from which the anti-architectonic Rococo would take its rampant departure.**2.66**

ADVENT OF ROCOCO

In introducing the first style of the new century, the distinction between the Rococo and the Baroque must be stressed. No matter how licentious it often appeared, the Baroque was an essentially architectural style, based on the venerable conventions of articulating structural forces with the Orders. The Rococo was an anti-architectonic style of interior decoration which denied structural forces and masked physical reality: the Orders had no place – or they were invaded, eaten away by arabesques or naturalistic floral motifs in mockery of their claim to express the forces implicit in structure. Moreover, the strict geometrical division of traditional revetment was abandoned in favour of irregular and increasingly sensuous mouldings which actually invaded the field they surrounded, breaking down the distinction between frame and framed.

The style's denigrating epithet derives from the rockery of the grotto perhaps because it was grotesque in inspiration and, ultimately, embraced shells with other aquatic motifs to supplement those stylized from vegetation. In practice members of the academic establishment were prepared to admit the mode to the relief of wood panelling, especially in the depths of private apartments, but the strictest theorists lamented its motive as a revival of Gothic imagination which they were conditioned to deplore as barbaric in its ignorance of Classical principles. Free-ranging in its approach to the representation of nature, stylized or realistic, it does indeed have close affinity with the specifically French late-medieval style known as Flamboyante (AIC4, pages 426ff) – but few now would see that as deplorable.

Rococo sprouted at the turn of the new century and was fostered for the ageing Louis XIV as relief from the ruinous quest for *gloire*: within twenty years it was flourishing in Paris under the libertarian regency of the Duc d'Orléans

›**2.67 CABINETS OF LOUIS XIV** : (a) Versailles; (b) Trianon.

2.67a

2.67b

>2.68 CLAUDE AUDRAN AND THE GRO-
TESQUE: (a) Château de Meudon ceiling scheme
(Paris, Musée des arts décoratifs), (b) 'Summer' from a
tapestry series woven at the Gobelins factory from 1707
(Paris, Mobilier national).

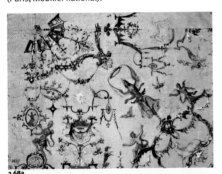

2.68a

2.67b

for the infant Louis XV. The ground was prepared by Hardouin-Mansart's office in the very different circumstances of Versailles in the mid-1680s. With Le Brun near finishing the Grande Galerie and with it the Grands Appartements, the king's attention had turned to the development of a style more fitted for withdrawing rooms. A new private suite, arranged following the death of the queen in 1683, was given wood panelling in superimposed tiers of regular geometric shapes, as usual, but painted white and gold throughout and set between tall mirrors and windows. The same desire for relative simplicity, lightness and clarity, the same tendency to develop vertical accents, characterized the decoration at Trianon and the château of Marly at the end of the decade, the increasingly elongated, but still geometrical, panelling being subjected to an Order only in the parade rooms.[2.67]

Rectilinear timber panelling was ubiquitous: its embellishment with arabesque motifs had been fashionable in various permutations since the earliest manifestation of the Renaissance in France (AIC4, pages 870ff, AIC5, pages 300ff). Le Brun's range encompassed it at Vaux-le-Vicomte but his preoccupation for the king was with grandeur. However, now that the Grands Appartements were complete – and costly materials no longer affordable – the painted arabesque was to lend a new playfulness to the private cabinets of the royal family, as in the apartments of private houses, where marble and bronze were not appropriate and painted vaults were rare. At the direction of the Premier Architecte, the leading role was played by Jean Bérain and later Claude III Audran. After the example of Le Brun, they linked the bandwork of the Northern Mannerists with the acanthus tendrils of the *grotteschi* of Raphael's followers: that had been introduced into France by the first School of Fontainebleau, in which figural elements like herms or sphinxes grow from the foliage to support medallions, simulated relief panels, baldachins, and so on.[2.68]

Audran worked primarily in two dimensions. Bérain took a new turn for the mode in three dimensions: he decorated the new, elongated panels of the regent's cabinet in 1699 and his arabesques invaded the field of framed pilaster strips flanking a fashionable tall, arched mirror. Restrained though it was as yet, such a violation had hardly been seen in France since the period of François I. In the contemporary menagerie of the Duchesse de Bourgogne,

2.69c

>**2.69 JEAN BÉRAIN AND THE GROTESQUE:**
(a) the regent, the Duc d'Orléans, in his cabinet at the Palais-Royal with his son the Duc de Chartres (?, the sitters have less plausibly been identified as the Grand and Petit Dauphins in a cabinet at Meudon); (b, c) Versailles, menagerie of the Duchesse de Bourgogne, overview and detail of salon panelling.

the king's teenaged granddaughter-in-law, virility is likewise denied to the putative Ionic pilasters of a tall mirror: moreover, the impost of its arch breaks and curls into foliage shooting from a great shell to invade the spandrels with whimsically irreverent three-dimensional realism. Similar work appeared at Marly at the same time – as we have seen. Bérain and Audran had provided the templates for the Rococo and the style is anticipated in all these works.**2.69**

In 1701 the king moved his state bedroom from the penultimate position in the enfilade of his Grand Apartement, where it faced north, to the epicentre of the château overlooking the Cour de Marbre to the east, at the very apex of the triangle of routes leading out through the town to the kingdom at large: there was high symbolism behind the move, of course, but comfort too. A full composite Order is retained but arabesques invade the pilasters of the mirrors and the panels of the doors. In the neighbouring Antichambre de l'Oeil de Boeuf, with its ravishing

The grotesque (or arabesque) from which typical Rococo ornament took its departure derives from Raphael first in paint, then in low-relief stucco – as in the mask, shell and vegetal motifs which interfere with the architecture of the mirror frame here. The mocking of architectural pretension in this way – its 'corruption' – had its antique equivalent and its early French Renaissance permutation (AIC1, page 605; AIC4, pages 87off). In their recovery of antique interior embellishment, moreover, Raphael and his team appreciated the ambivalence of the relationship between the anthropomorphic, the zoomorphic and the vegetal, which plays its seductive part in both these works of Bérain.

2.70a

›2.70 VERSAILLES, KING'S APARTMENT OF
1701: (a) Antichambre de l'Oeil de Boeuf, (b, c) Chambre, north side and model.

The new bedroom replaced the salon of the Petits
Appartements (which dated from 1679): the move may
be seen as the culmination of Versailles's transformation from the country house of the royal family – still
with a queen to claim her half – into the centre of the
king's government after the formal transfer of 1682 and
the death of his consort in 1683. The main Order of both
rooms was probably inherited from the installations
of c. 1680: the fireplaces surmounted by mirrors were
'Modern' in 1701 (the bedroom mantelpiece is later).

frieze of putti playing with garlands, the frames above
windows, mirrors and doors are filled with stylized floral
motifs and the still-rectangular panels of wainscot and
doors are dominated by filigree rosettes.**2.70**

2.70C

2.70b

2.71a

2.71b

From these beginnings the style was developed in the last important works for the Crown before the death of the king: the furniture of the chapel of Versailles and the choir of Notre-Dame, which were furthered under the direction of Mansart's chief collaborator and successor as Premier Architecte from 1708, Robert de Cotte (1656–1735).**2.71** On the sensuously curved base of the organ in the chapel at Versailles (1709–10) the palmier made its first appearance: in this context it was presumably a permutation of the martyr's palm but it quickly became a popular motif with Rococo designers. At the same time, ephemeral foliage supported the figurative reliefs of Notre-Dame's choir stalls. These were to be reflected in the cartouche-framed scenes, rimmed with shell or foliage, which were to occupy the centres of many later panels as an alternative to rosettes in interiors of the Parisian houses which were now to be the staple commissions even of the Architectes du Roi.

›2.71 THE ADVENT OF ROCOCO TO THE CHURCH: (a) Paris, Notre-Dame, choir stalls; (b) Versailles, organ case.

ROYAL ARCHITECTURE IN HIATUS

After the completion of the chapel at Versailles and the construction of the Château Neuf for the Dauphin at Meudon, Crown patronage virtually ceased for a generation. As his son, the Grand Dauphin, and his grandson,

›2.72 OYSTER LUNCHEON (1737, Jean-Francois de Troy; Chantilly, Musée Condé).

The patron of the house may have represented the *haute noblesse*, more likely the *haute bourgeoisie*. Either way, here are his sons and their friends enjoying the relief of Parisian life at a liquid luncheon. Though dining-rooms were not now uncommon, the table seems to have been set for such an occasion in the entrance hall or vestibule: there architecture was always to reign but tritons supplement – even supplant – columns as though the Classical conventions are tired and tiresome. It will be noted that the focal point of de Troy's brilliant composition is the cork flying from the latest bottle of champagne.

the Duc de Bourgogne, had died of smallpox in 1711–12 (as we have seen, page 25), Louis XIV was succeeded in 1715 by his five-year-old great-grandson Louis XV. The council of regency was presided over by the head of the collateral branch of the Bourbon dynasty, Philippe II, Duc d'Orléans. Notorious for his laxity, he hastened to abandon Versailles for the Palais-Royal in Paris. His court followed, of course. Versailles had been particularly oppressive in its melancholy in the last years of the old, bankrupt king since the tragedy of 1711–12. As we know, it had been built as a prison for aristocrats with pretensions to power: now the more resourceful of the *haute noblesse* seized their chance to escape, disclaiming the yoke of monarchical absolutism: they built themselves comfortable houses in Paris, decorated in the new playful, relaxed style – which also had its particular appeal to a very different class of society, the *haute bourgeoisie* of the financiers whose fortunes had waxed while the royal finances waned with protracted war.**2.72**

ROYAL ARCHITECTS DIVERTED

Despite the reputation of the regime which promoted them, French achievements in domestic architecture during the minority of Louis XV are of the first importance. However, the king's architects were also furthering the monumental tradition in the service of the abbots of the greater French Benedictine monasteries, of the intendants of several French provinces bent on emulating the Parisian Places Royales in particular, of the Bourbons in Spain and of the princely and ecclesiastical courts of north-eastern France and western Germany. Hardouin-Mansart had led the way – to Dijon, and especially to Nancy in 1700 on the invitation of Leopold, Duc de Lorraine. The new Premier Architecte du Roi, Robert de Cotte, was naturally to the fore but a particularly prominent part was already being played by his younger colleague, Germain Boffrand (1667–1754).

Providing the climax to the principal enfilade, the projecting oval salon was Le Vau's chief contribution to the development of the French château in the late-17th and 18th centuries. At the end of the War of the Spanish Succession in 1714, Robert de Cotte incorporated such salons in his great schemes for the king of Spain, the electors of Bavaria and Cologne, and for the prince-bishop of Würzburg (in competition with Boffrand in 1723). He preferred the Roman ordonnance of the Colonnade or Versailles for most of these foreign projects – as we shall see in their respective contexts (see pages c, 636, 842). In due course, too, we shall also see him take the Parisian *hôtel particulier* to its apogee for the prince-bishop of Strasbourg from 1720.

Boffrand was an independent spirit working for foreign princes in the first decades of the century: first at Bouchefort near Brussels for the elector Maximilian II Emanuel of Bavaria in exile for espousing the French cause in the Spanish war; later at and near Lunéville for Duke Leopold of Lorraine, who had recovered his duchy in 1698 and married the French regent's daughter. He borrowed Palladian porticoes for these works. For Lorraine, in addition, he went back to the French masters of the mid-17th century and to Bernini's Louvre, to borrow some of the basic Baroque devices which had been rejected by academic French Classicism. Of his varied projects, the second idea for the château of La Malgrange near Nancy reviews the Louvre most radically: a virtuoso exercise in planning, Baroque in its conception of unity, it is dominated by a rotunda expanding the great curved central pavilion of the Roman master's first project but extracted from his concave wings as the nexus of four diagonal ranges. Possibly informed by knowledge of Fontana's scheme for the court of Rome's Montecitorio palace (see page 116), that design is worthy of Antoine Le Pautre, who provides an orthogonal precedent in his *Desseins de plusieurs palais* (see pages 222f).**2.73**

2.73a

›2.73 BOFFRAND IN LORRAINE: (a) Bouchefort (Soignes), hunting pavilion for the Elector of Bavaria, elevation (published by its author in his *Livre d'architecture*); (b–e) the 'Versailles' of Lunéville (from 1702), plan, chapel, entrance and garden fronts; (f–k) Château de la Malgrange (1712), first project plan, garden front elevation, section through central block, second project plan, side and front elevations; (l) Nancy, palace façade ('Le Louvre de Nancy', 1717).

The palace at Lunéville was first conceived after a visit by Jules Hardouin-Mansart in 1700 but revised and executed by Boffrand: inspired by Versailles, he drew the vast plan together in the middle by reviving the massive portico of unfluted Corinthian columns which Le Vau had incorporated in the south front of the Louvre and which Jean-Baptiste Colbert had prevented him from extending around the east front. The Nancy

2.73e

2.73c

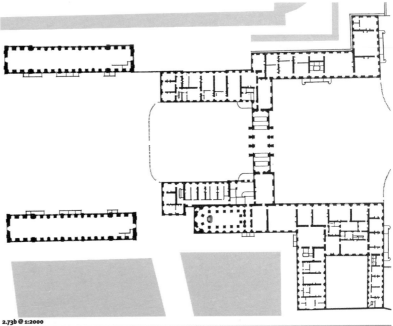

2.73b @ 1:2000

2.73d

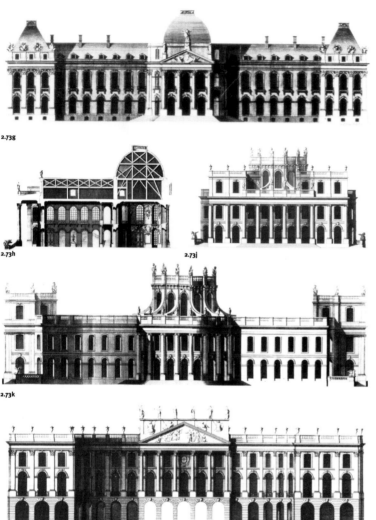

2.73g

2.73h

2.73j

2.73k

2.73l

2.73f @ approximately 1:2000

palace project, on the other hand, reviews the Roman ordonnance and concave façade of Bernini's second idea for the Louvre. Meanwhile, in his first project for the Duc de Lorraine's retreat at La Malgrange, he reiterated his Lunéville Order to bind the great projecting central pavillon (containing a vast oval salon) into the composition, expressing the distinction between the pavillons and the corps de logis by confining it to the former – as pilasters on the sides and columns only in the centre. Similarly, a colossal Order rising from the ground – as in the Louvre projects of both Bernini and Le Vau – was applied to the rotunda and the porticoes closing the triangles between the divergent wings

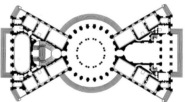

2.73i @ approximately 1:2000

of the second scheme: the vista down the main axial progression – from the vestibule and gallery inserted into the first triangle, through the great circular central space, to the heart-shaped staircase and oval salon of the second triangle – would have been as rich as Le Pautre's most extravagant scheme (see page 223).

In Lorraine Boffrand also worked for prominent courtiers such as Marc de Beauvau, Prince de Craon, for whom he followed Hardouin-Mansart at Dampierre in rebuilding the château of Haroué over its medieval foundations (from 1711). Of several other contemporary buildings associated with him, the château of Commercy was built by an inconclusively identified architect for the duke's cousin, Charles Henri Beauvau, Prince de Vaudémont, in emulation of Lunéville.

In his last important work for Lorraine, the 'Louvre' of Nancy, Boffrand used the broad concave recession of Bernini's second project to frame a vast temple-front motif raised over a basement.**2.74** It remained unexecuted; with it, however, the city had been introduced to the ordonnance of the Colonnade, as expressed in the great royal squares of

2.74a

2.74c

›2.74 NANCY, SEQUENTIAL SQUARES: (a) plan of old and new towns (after 1587 and from 1752, with site of new squares indicated in red); (b) plan embracing (1) 'Hemicycle' before the Palais du Gouvernement, (2) Place de la Carriére, (3) Place Stanislas (originally dedicated to Louis XV); (c) overview with cathedral in background behind Place Stanislas; (d–h) Place Stanislas, model from south-west and north, general view with detail of the wrought-iron screens to its outer corners and Arc de Héré; (i) Palais du Gouvernement, south front.

The new town was founded to the south of the medieval complex by Duc Charles III in 1587: the site of the

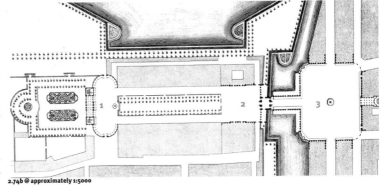

2.74b @ approximately 1:5000

2.74d

2.74g

Hardouin-Mansart. The local architect Emmanuel Héré de Corny (1705–63), like most of his contemporaries working on civic schemes in provincial capitals in the first half of the 18th century, followed that example for his Place Roy-

mid-18th-century development spanned from one to the other, from the former jousting ground across the old defence walls. Emmanuel Héré, the author, was a local pupil of Boffrand: from 1738 he was Premier Architecte to the duke (ex-king Stanisław of Poland, father-in-law to Louis XV).

The Place de la Carrière is addressed from the north by the Hôtel de l'Intendance (now Palais du Gouvernement) which was built beyond a semi-elliptical precinct (the 'Hemicycle') under Héré's direction on the site of Boffrand's projected 'Louvre': the elongated oblong space extending south from it had long been lined with housing to which Boffrand contributed the Hôtel de Beauvau-Craon and Héré a semblance of unity. The Porte Royale, which had been opened in the southern ramparts to provide access from the old town to the new, was rebuilt by Héré and now bears his name. Beyond it the great 'Place Stanislas' is addressed by the Hôtel de Ville from the south, by the residence of the intendant (called Hôtel de la Reine because Marie-Antoinette stayed there in 1769) and the opera house to the east, by a private mansion (Pavillon Jacquet) and the

2.74e

2.74f

museum (former Académie de Médecine) to the west: fountains in the open corners are framed by the superb wrought-iron screens of the local master Jean Lamour (1698–1771). The façade of the town hall varies Boffrand's variations on the Parisian formula with minimal intermediate relief. Similarly, the articulation of the four side pavillons derives from Boffrand's Hôtel de Beauvau-Craon on the Place de la Carrière.

2.74h

2.74i

ale: even the interpolation of playful Rococo ironwork, seductive as it is, does not deny the essentially Classical academicism of the ordonnance nor the Baroque grandeur of the conception which embraced three linked squares.

2.75

By mid-century, when the Place Stanislas was nearing completion, the formula was being reiterated in the many provincial capitals which commemorated Louis XV's perceived success in the War of the Austrian Succession with squares addressed by civic buildings: the Capitole at Toulouse is an example; we shall return to the enterprise.**2.75**

Jacques V Gabriel (1667–1742), Premier Architecte du Roi from 1735, in succession to Robert de Cotte, was more extensively involved in the provinces than abroad – in particular at Dijon, Rennes and Bordeaux. In the former, he provided the Palais des États de Bourgogne with a splendid new staircase (from 1731) – the final element in an extensive urban project begun to Mansart's plans in 1685. At Bordeaux, his Place Royale stands at the apogee of variations on the Parisian formula. Earlier at Rennes he renovated Salomon de Brosse's Parlement de Bretagne, removing the external staircase (AIC5, page 396), and revised a local scheme for a new royal square as the nucleus of ordered redevelopment after the medieval

›2.75 TOULOUSE, CAPITOLE: façade (from 1750 to earlier design).

The design of a new façade for the medieval town hall complex was commissioned in 1739 from the local painter/architect Guillaume Cammas (1688–1777): execution to a revised scheme was delayed until 1750. The metropolitan formula is varied to obviate monotony with concave and convex curves to the central and side projections (respectively) and with articulation in stone against a ground of the indigenous pink brickwork.

›2.76 JACQUES V GABRIEL AT LARGE: (a, b) Dijon, Palais des États de Bourgogne, staircase (1731), view from below and project section; (c, d) Rennes, Place de la Mairie (formerly Neuve or Louis XV), civic administrative complex (from 1730, engraved for Pierre Patte, *Monuments érigés en France à la gloire de Louis XV*, 1765) and model; (e) Bordeaux, Place de la Bourse (formerly Royale, from 1729).

Much of central Rennes was destroyed by a fire in 1720: rebuilding was entrusted to Isaac Robelin, a marine engineer from Brest, but the strictures of his rigid scheme were resisted by the inhabitants. Sent by the royal authorities to arbitrate in 1725, Gabriel introduced some flexibility about the nuclei of two squares

2.76b

– one dedicated to Louis XIV as the precinct for de Brosse's Parlement de Bretagne (which Gabriel modified; see AIC5, page 397), the other dedicated to Louis XV and addressed by a new civic building: Gabriel's Hôtel de

2.76a

2.76c

Ville (right) is joined to the matching block for the courts by a pavillon with frontispiece framing a niche enshrining a statue of Louis XV by Jean-Baptiste Lemoyne.

Prospering from burgeoning colonial trade by the 1720s, Bordeaux was the seat of the Intendant Claude Boucher who governed the Guyenne region in the name of the king from 1720 to 1743. His plans for regularization of the subsisting medieval situation, especially by demolishing the ramparts which defended it from the great Garonne River and replacing them with squares punctuating lines of warehouses, were opposed by the conservative jurists who dominated the civic councils. He called for support from Versailles. Jacques V Gabriel, Premier Ingénieur de Ponts et Chaussées, came and provided an elegant revision

2.76d

2.76e

fabric had succumbed to fire: it was to be addressed by a new town hall. An exquisite miniature variation on the latter's concave centre was produced by the sculptor Edmé Bouchardon for the Fontaine des Quatre-Saisons (1739) with which public work restarted in Paris after the long hiatus of the king's minority.**2.76, 2.77**

of the local plans in accordance with the metropolitan formula: the scheme of the Place Vendôme was halved for the essential aspect to the river and to the maritime world of trade; to either side were the twin blocks for the exchange (Bourse) and the office of the tax collector (Hôtel des Fermes); a central pavillon was inserted at the acute-angled apex of the access routes, on axis with the equestrian statue of the king (by Jean-Baptiste Lemoyne, 1704–78). The work begun in 1729 was finished by the architect's son Ange-Jacques Gabriel, who succeeded him as Premier Architecte du Roi in 1742.

›2.77 PARIS, FONTAINE DES QUATRE-SAISONS, from 1739.

Conceived by a sculptor for civic convenience, the public face of Classical dignity cedes nothing to the *style moderne* then at the height of its trajectory: the style is misnamed 'Louis XVI', not merely because Classicism was essential to public works – and here revived when they revived – but because the discipline of the Classical Order was restored even to intimate interiors at the end of the first decade of Louis XV's personal patronage – as we shall see.

2.77

CHURCH AND MONASTERY

Monastic building was not to the fore for much of Louis XIV's era: a major exception is the aristocratic girls' school at Saint-Cyr. Like that of the Salpetrière and the period's other public utilities, the austerity which Hardouin-Mansart imposed there was sustained when the extensive modernization of cloistered facilities supervened in the last decade of the reign. Providing an abbatical prototype at Saint-Denis for the new age of comfort and convenience in the domestic sphere, Robert de Cotte dispensed with an Order altogether despite the extended length of the façade to the principal capitular halls. Other monastic builders were not so reticent.**2.78**

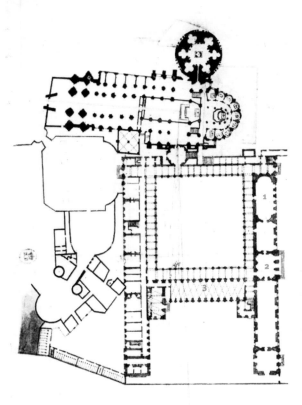

>**2.78** SELECT MONASTIC BUILDING OF EARLY 18TH-CENTURY FRANCE: (a, b) Saint-Denis, plan of abbey with (1) chapter house at the head of its formal adjuncts with the principal dormitory under, (2) grand reception suite, (3) refectory also with dormitory under, east front of main enfilade (from 1700); (c) Cluny, Benedictine abbatical cloister complex, east front; (d) Prémontré, Premonstratensian abbatical cloister complex, south front.

In 1700 Robert de Cotte was commissioned to reconstruct the monastic complex framing the cloister to the south of the great medieval church of S.-Denis and its royal necropolis (work continued until 1782): the restraint of the scheme, approved by the king for

2.78a

2.78b

2.78c

2.78d

a site of major royal significance, met academic conceptions of propriety in declining the sumptuousness with which the Benedictines usually accommodated themselves elsewhere. In accordance with the norm for abbatical work, the lay architect – here the future Premier Architecte – may have been assisted by a member of the commissioning order, Guillaume de La Tremblaye (1644–1715).

Tremblaye was responsible for several exercises of monastic reconstruction in the first decade of the century, notably for the Benedictines of S.-Étienne at Caen (from 1704): astylar, the work conforms to the approach typical of de Cotte. The metropolitan domestic style, which de Cotte promoted at Strasbourg as in Paris (as we shall see), is also represented by the early 18th-century rebuilding of the monastic complex attached to the primary Benedictine church of Cluny. On the other hand, for example, the colossal Order of Ionic pilasters which binds the semi-elliptical central pavillon to the corps de logis of the Premonstratensian community at Prémontré (from 1718) follows the example of heterodox domestic builders like Jean-Sylvain Cartaud or Germain Boffrand – to whom we shall soon turn.

2.79a

There was considerable metropolitan church building in the late years of the old king and the first of the regency: it was naturally promoted by urban expansion into new parishes, by new – and even old – conventual complexes requiring new chapels and by the provision of façades lacking to several prominent existing buildings. As head of his profession (from 1708), Robert de Cotte is first recorded providing the Parisian Visitandines with unexecuted projects for a cen-

2.79b

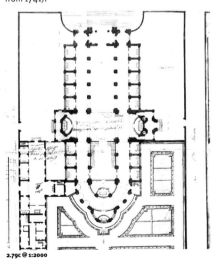

›**2.79 FROM OPULENCE TO RESTRAINT IN THE FRENCH CLASSICAL BASILICAN CHURCH:**
(a) Bordeaux, Notre-Dame (former Dominican church by Pierre-Michel Duplessy, from 1684 to 1707), facade; (b) Paris, S.-Roch, façade (c. 1728, executed from 1736); (c–e) Versailles, S.-Louis, approved project plan, entrance front and interior (Mansart de Sagonne, from 1742); (f, g) La Rochelle, cathedral of S.-Louis, foundation medal with façade, interior (Jacques V Gabriel, from 1741).

2.79c @ 1:2000

tralized chapel and unexecuted basilican façade designs for Orléans and Dijon. His first major commission was for the parish church of S.-Louis in the newly developed southern sector of Versailles, which was to be pendant to his mentor's church of Notre-Dame in the northern sector: also Classicizing the traditional basilica, he sustained the austere style of Sublet de Noyers's era, which Hardouin-Mansart had retained, and developed the latter's colonnaded façade for-

2.79d

2.79e

2.79g

2.79f

On return to Versailles in 1722, the king called for the construction of a parish church dedicated to S.-Louis. Robert de Cotte produced at least three projects of which the second was approved for execution in 1724 (funds for full realisation were not available until 1742). The plan was of the traditional – French Gothic – basilican type perpetuated by Hardouin-Mansart's Notre-Dame in the northern sector: like the latter's work on the Parisian church of S.-Roch, moreover, it incorporated a circular lady chapel off the ambulatory. De Cotte was retained to complete that Parisian church with a façade: the scheme executed shortly after his death is an amplification of Hardouin-Mansart's Versailles design along lines drawn from the Dôme des Invalides, with inset columns flanking those of the projecting frontispiece and reiterated across the aisle. Variations on this mode were the 18th-century norm: examples range from the cathedral of Nancy, Gothic in height (see page 299), to S.-Louis at Versailles by Jacques Hardouin-Mansart de Sagonne. Stark is the contrast with works of the previous generation such as Notre-Dame de Bordeaux.

mula, which he also applied to the Parisian parish church of S.-Roch (from 1728). Only the latter was executed but de Cotte's project provided the basis on which the Versailles church was built by Jules Hardouin-Mansart's grandson, Jacques Hardouin-Mansart de Sagonne (from 1742): it was followed for other prominent ecclesiastical exercises of the era, notably Jacques V Gabriel's project for the cathedral of La Rochelle.**2.79**

The arcaded, tunnel-vaulted basilican type evolved by Jules Hardouin-Mansart from the work of his predecessors – and furthered by his successors as Premier Architecte – was the French norm in the first half of the 18th century – at least for parish churches. The Abbé Jean-Louis de Cordemoy (1631–1713) did not favour it in his *Nouveau traité de toute l'architecture* (1706): he would abolish the typical heavy arcades which obstruct light and resort instead to colonnades – like Perrault (see page 246). In agreement, consciously or otherwise, were several abbatial builders in the north-east. Classicizing the medieval hall-church form, the division of nave from aisles with colossal colonnades distinguishes the

›2.80 LUNÉVILLE, S.-JACQUES, from 1686: (a) façade, (b) interior.

The basic conception is due to Jean-Nicolas Jamesson: Héré is credited with adding the towers, despite the uncharacteristic Roman Baroque style.

2.80a

2.80b

Premonstratensian abbey church at Pont-à-Mousson (from 1704). That seems to have provided the precedent for several regional exercises, not least the Augustinian abbey church of S.-Jacques at not-far-distant Lunéville and S.-Sebastien at Nancy. The former was completed by Héré: the first phase, to entablature level, was probably due to the architect Jean-Nicolas Jamesson (1686–1755), who is credited with the work for the parish of S.-Sebastien in his home town. Inspiration may have come from the Jesuits of S. Carolus Borromeus at Antwerp rather than Claude Perrault: the former has interior colonnades on two levels, like Boffrand's court chapel at Lunéville (see above) which follows the early ideas for Versailles, whereas Perrault's colossal Order revises the structural system of the typical medieval hall church – like Jamesson.**2.80**

Classicizing the medieval had been the perennial pursuit since the Renaissance: even the internal arcades inherited by Hardouin-Mansart and his colleagues from Lemercier and his predecessors are to be seen in that light – or, rather, its absence. The contrary activity, restoring or reviving Gothic for repair or reconstruction after the ravages wrought by Protestant iconoclasm in the era of the late Valois, proceeded with hardly a break from the last original medieval exercise: consistency was demanded by academic precept but, beyond stricture, the lightness of the style appealed to the enlightened followers of Perrault and Jean-Louis de Cordemoy. One of the latest and most spectacular works of the kind was undertaken in the ruins of Orléans cathedral: Jacques V Gabriel developed his neo-Flamboyante Gothic project for the west front after de Cotte had attempted the feat on the instruction of Louis XIV in 1708 – just when Cordemoy was making his point. Hawksmoor had recently set the precedent at Westminster Abbey, without Gallic flamboyance – as we shall see.**2.81**

›2.81 ORLÉANS, CATHEDRAL OF THE HOLY CROSS: (a) model from the north-west, (b) general view of west front.

The Romanesque west front survived the destruction of the crossing and adjacent bays by Huguenot insurgents in 1588: reconstruction of the main volume (from 1601) conformed to the Gothic remainder but debate ensued over the style to be adopted for the transept façades: the Ancients promoted Renaissance Classicism, the Moderns wanted Gothic and Étienne Martellange won the day for them – not least because his solution would honour the academic precept of consistency (work began on his schemes in 1626). Early in the new century the massive task of replacing the dilapidated west work was addressed by the local architect Guillaume Hénault: following the precedent of Martellange, his scheme was 'Modern' but he died in 1723 with little more than his foundations laid. Jacques V Gabriel was delegated to revise the project and oversee its execution.

2.82

›2.82 FONTAINEBLEAU, AILE LOUIS XV, from 1738: garden front.

The first major work at the site for more than a century – though anticipated in several grand projects produced by Robert de Cotte – was prompted by the need to house the king's entourage in modern comfort during the annual autumn relocation of the court there: replacing the dilapidated Galerie d'Ulysse on the south flank of the Cour du Cheval Blanc, it consisted of twin four-storey, eighteen-bay corps de logis separated by a three-bay central pavillon – all in brick with stone structural detailing. Similarity with contemporary monastic building is hardly surprising.

ROYAL ARCHITECTS DOMESTICATED

Splendid as were the late works of Louis XIV and those planned by his architects for foreign princes – or would have been had they all been realized – the most significant contribution of the period of his decline was domestic. And this was sustained well into the reign of Louis XV who – apart from work on the royal apartments at Versailles – began a great building career towards the end of his third decade (c. 1738) with the commission of an extensive new wing at Fontainebleau from his Premier Architecte, Jacques V Gabriel.**2.82**

The Parisian hôtel, far from representing a relaxation of academic discipline, was one of its most characteristic expressions: it was widely followed elsewhere, even at enhanced scale for episcopal palaces – notably by Gabriel at Blois and by Robert de Cotte at Verdun and Strasbourg (see page 324). Idiosyncratic too were the châteaux of the period: larger, naturally, they were similar in their commodious plans and similarly modest in their subjection to the principle of *convenance*. In between was the *maison de plaisance*: as we have noted, this was the special – if not unique – preserve of the new class who sought retreat beyond the confines of Paris, however liberated they may have been in their urban homes. Complemented by the invention of free-ranging ornament, all these house types were designed to satisfy the standards of comfort and convenience now demanded in private life: that enjoyed a new degree of freedom, for some, which was objectionable if flaunted over traditional convention in public. And there, on the public face of the house, articulation with the Orders was strictly regulated in accordance with the gradations of a hierarchically ordered society: it was not to serve private pretension.

Jean Mariette's superbly illustrated and widely influential publication of *L'architecture françoise* (1727) admirably demonstrated that the dichotomy between the discipline of *noble simplicité* without and the freedom of Rococo fantasy within responded to the time-honoured principles of *convenance* (Vitruvian decorum). Academic theorists of the next decade, Jacques-François Blondel (1705–74) in particular, stressed the importance of the latter in both articulation and distribution: they discounted the value of symmetry beyond centralization about the major rooms, remained proud of their predecessors' achievements in domestic planning because it was regulated yet they came to despise the contemporary development of ornament because it was unprincipled.

Boffrand – masterly in both public and private – regretted that the style of interior ornament native to the delicate *métier* of wood carving was being translated to exteriors against the grain of masonry which required strength and he predicted that the fashion would be transitory (*Livre d'architecture*, 1745). Two years earlier Charles-Étienne Briseux (1680–1754) published his treatise with the hope of rectifying the taste of the provincials and foreigners who transgressed in this way: less charitable ten years

›**2.83 ARCHITECTURE FRANÇAISE:** (a) Charles-Étienne Briseux (*L'Art de bâtir les maisons de campagne*, 1742 and 1761), temple d'architecture; (b–k) Jacques-François Blondel (*De la distribution des maisons de plaisance et de la décoration des édifices en général*, 1737 – DDM), Pavillon à l'Italienne (I, 42), plans and elevations of Maison dans La Brie (I, 31–35), Château de Saint-Remy, ground-floor plan and entrance front (I, 23, 25), foreword header (I, 1) and design for a salon chimneypiece (II, 61).

Briseux's enthronement of Architecture deified as Minerva in the broken pediment of a Baroque temple – Baroque in the impact of curve and counter-curve as in the opulence of its sculptural ornament – well represents the cross-currents of opinion on the central cause of the Académie royale d'architecture, the definition of *bon goût* (good taste): all agreed that *noble simplicité* was the definitive quality but homage to the most noble of royal endeavours, the patronage of architecture, required allegorical sculpture and the full display of the Orders, as in this imaginary shrine. To Briseux's contemporaries, that was indispensable to its function but by the date of its publication Roman High Baroque exuberance had generally been rejected – if it had generally been accepted by the academic establishment.

Architectural publication in the new century of French ascendency began with *Mémoires critiques d'architecture* (1702) in which Michel de Frémin, a highly rational layman, presents a novel functionalist view of architecture, stressing considerations of usage and siting over traditional concerns with Classical order. This was not followed by all: along with Perrault's relativity, however, it did influence the abbé Jean-Louis de Cordemoy's *Nouveau traité de toute l' architecture* (1706). Perrault's stance is taken to an extreme by Sébastien Le Clerc who, paying little attention to planning, treats the Orders not as enshrining absolute aesthetic values in their proportions but as indices of social status susceptible to subjective, not objective evaluation (1714). The balance was redressed in a paper delivered to the Académie in 1734 (published as the preface to his *Livre d' architecture*, 1745) by Boffrand.

Meanwhile, Briseux had emulated Pierre Le Muet (AIC5, page 401) in publishing a building manual (*L' Architecture moderne, ou l' art de bien bâtir pour toutes sortes de personnes*, 1728) in which practical information on technology is followed by commentary on plans related to defined urban sites for gradations of patronage with scrupulous attention to function. Jacques-François Blondel complemented this with a publication on villas (*De la distribution des maisons de plaisance et de la décoration des édifices en général*). Ten years earlier Jean Mariette's comprehensive *L' architecture françoise* dispensed with commentary altogether, allowing the public and private masterpieces of the present and recent past to speak for themselves through superbly engraved plans, sections and elevations. Blondel, who had assisted with this exercise, offered a new addition with commentary (1752): developed in his lectures at his school of architecture (from 1743), these were further elaborated after his appointment as professor of the Académie school (1762) and published as his *Cours d' architecture* (1771). The distillation of academic Classical theory, much in sympathy with his unrelated namesake and predecessor's work of the same title (see pages 265f), that belongs with a consideration of the era of retrenchment after the 'excesses' of Rococo when Briseux too had turned from Perrault back to the elder Blondel, Nicolas-François.

later still, Charles-Nicolas Cochin (1715–90) was clearly not unhappy to note that ignorant provincials and foreigners who preferred the *goût moderne* to the style of the past century ensured the superiority of France.**2.83**

Theory and function

At the opening of the new century the Académie read Palladio and concluded – surprisingly, for proponents of *noble simplicité* – that his villas were not appropriate for France where 'the convenience of the interior is commonly preferred to the appearance of the exterior' (freely translated from the Académie's minutes, 19 March 1700). Two writers within the next five years – Michel de Frémin and the Abbé Jean-Louis de Cordemoy – propounded an essentially functionalist theory of architecture: it was based ultimately on Perrault's definition of quality primarily in terms of decorum rather than the proportions and details of the Orders, of *convenance* and *vraisemblance*, of what was appropriate for modern usage and true, or at least apparently true, to physical reality (see pages 263f). The three basic concepts are *ordonnance*, *disposition* and *bienséance*, the first two providing the dignity and distribution proper to the building's purpose, the third that neither contravenes nature or custom. Cordemoy recognizes that practicality may discount symmetry but avoids dismissing the latter: inconsistency may not be implied here as symmetry is appreciable in elevation but not in planning though, ideally, the one follows the other. Primarily concerned with ecclesiastical building, he prefers the traditional aisled basilica to Vignola's Roman Gesù type: like Perrault, he values the stucturalist aesthetic of Gothic – and Greek – architecture but favours refusal to compromise the trabeated with the arcuate in response to the concerns of contemporary engineers.

Naturally any tendency to value function over appearance incited much debate in the Académie. Resolution was called for early in 1734 and was answered with consensus on basic concepts in terms consistent with fitness for purpose, with comfort and convenience as well as with the expression of status in a hierarchically ordered society: ordonnance is defined as the distribution of all the parts, internal and external, governed by scale and usage rather than in the traditional terms of articulation through the application of the Orders; imposed with or without these, proportion inflects the

2.83b

scale of dimensions appropriate to the exercise; and convenance dictates determination in accord with the customary practice of ordered society. *Bon goût* ('good taste', the definition of which was essential to the Académie's proceedings) was the faculty of satisfying these combined concerns.

Just as the Académie had come to its conclusion, Boffrand presented it with his own ideas on the subject of taste (*Dissertation sur ce qu' on appelle le bon goût en architecture*, 4/1734, published as the preface to his compendium of his own works, *Livre d' architecture*, 1745): he qualifies the Académie's slate of concepts with practical determinants of comfort, health, security – and common sense. The degree to which all these have been mastered, marking the advance of civilization, determines *bon goût* which, thus, is indeterminate by its evolutionary nature: standards admit of change and advancing sophistication of function but the mindless novelty of fashion is the enemy in corrupting architectonic principle. Grounded in the latter, the acme of *bon goût* is *noble simplicité* but that admits of the expression of character in building: integrated planning, elevation and decoration, not least in the choice of materials, express *caractère* in defining the status – even the occupation – of the occupant.

In his key work on country houses of various scales (*De la distribution des maisons de plaisance et de la décoration des édifices en général*, 1737) Jean-François Blondel followed the current trend in elevating distribution to primacy in celebrating his compatriots' advances in comfort and convenience, which the Rococo style was invented to complement: in consequence he maintains that the modern treatise was more complex than past dissertations on the Orders – as Briseux had demonstrated – and he determined to integrate considerations of aesthetics (*la beauté de l' ordonnance des dehors*), commodious distribution (*la commodité des dedans*) and stability (*la solidité de construction*) – contrary to his perception of past practice. He acknowledged the difficulty of demonstrating means of effecting ideal unity of plan and elevation (*le vrai* of the Greek temple) in meeting modern demands. Deploring surrender to fashion, at this stage in his career as a theorist he followed Perrault in relating order in architecture to the customs of its social milieu rather than to rationalist principle – to *convenance* in distinguishing public from private in the hierarchy of space and mass, as of society, and to *vraissemblance* in modifying the ideal with the practical. He

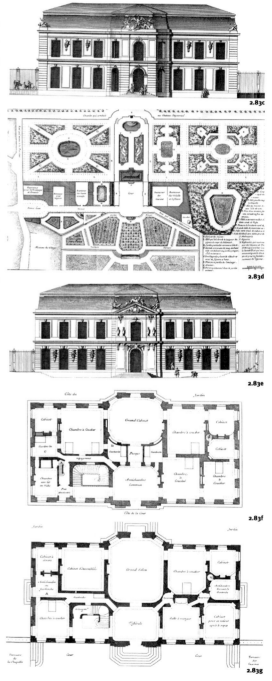

2.83c

2.83d

2.83e

2.83f

2.83g

2.83j

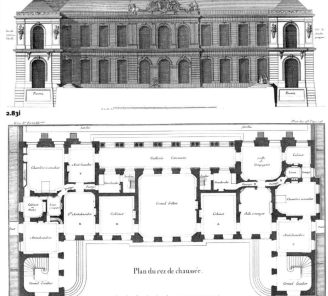

2.83i

Plan du rez de chaussée.

2.83h

By the end of the 1730s the 'excesses' of Rococo were being deplored in favour of return to the *bon goût* of rational principle founded on physical reality: Blondel was in the van. In his treatise on the *maison de plaisance* he admired the grandeur of Louis XIV's century but admitted the need to lighten it with vivid fantasy in intimate rooms (see I, 8, reproduced below, page 361) and he even adopted a thoroughly Rococo cartouche as the header to his introductory 'Réflexions préliminaires sur l'architecture' (and see the salon mirror, II, 61, for example, or the even more radical scheme for an Appartement de Parade in II, 74, reproduced below, page 332). Nevertheless, calling for return to sound architectonic principle as the armature of *noble simplicité*, he was among the first to ridicule the current conflation of marine, floral, zoomorphic and fantastic motifs in decoration ('un amas ridicule de coquilles, de dragons, de roseaux, de palmiers & de plantes, qui font à present tout le prix de la décoration intérieure, & qui ... transparent jusqu'à celle des dehors', II, page 67). In due course we shall review the succession of polemicists who espoused the cause as mid-century approached and called for reactionary reform.

2.83k

seems also to have been aware of Boffrand's view on the didactic relationship of exterior to interior without, as yet, the emotive dilation on terminology which would lead later 18th-century commentators from *caractère* to *architecture parlante*.

Assertive of French superiority from the outset of the new century, paradigms of the country house range from the *maison de plaisance* of Champs-sur-Marne (from 1701) by Pierre Bullet's son Jean-Baptiste Bullet de Chamblain (1665–1726), to the château of Champlâtreux by Jean-Michel Chevotet (1698–1772) a generation later and on to the diminutive Bagatelle at Abbeville of mid-century. Despite promoting the *maison de plaisance* in print, Jacques-François Blondel built little but his uncle and teacher Jean-Francois (1683–1756) provided an even more modest alternative to the Bullet prototype with the Villa Ami Lullin at Genthod (c. 1722): unarticulated, except with abstract pilasters over rustication, it was conceived *à l'italienne* (with its roof concealed by a balustrade).**2.84–2.86** The latter form was increasingly popular: examples range from Montmorency (1708) to Asnières (c. 1750). The earlier of these, by Jean-Sylvain Cartaud (1675–1758), is to be noted as heterodox in its display of a continuous colossal Order contrary to the purist conception of *convenance* in building for private patrons. *Hors de séries*, the stable complex at Chantilly, by Jean Aubert (c. 1680–41), is Rococo in ornamental detail too but expansively Baroque in conception – and it is certainly not insignificant that the period saw fit to devote such grandeur to the accommodation of horses.**2.87–2.89**

›**2.84 CHAMPS-SUR-MARNE, CHÂTEAU,** 1701–07: (a, b) plan and entrance elevation (*AF*), (c) garden front.

The patron was the financier Paul Poisson de Bourvallais: on his fall to corruption (1716), it passed to the Duc de la Vallière who let it to the Marquise de Pompodour (1757–60). Planning began by following the tripartite division of the elder Bullet's *maison de plaisance* at Issy but projected an elliptical salon (with its panelled Corinthian pilasters) into a semi-octagonal *avant-corps* to the garden front (in revision of Le Vau) and it extended to lateral blocks projecting from the entrance front. These accommodated three parallel ranges of the most private rooms beyond dining and billiard rooms (flanking the salon), two staircases and diverse corridors. Laterally and longitudinally, the partition walls are discontinuous.

2.84b

2.84a @ 1:1000

2.84c

›2.85 VARIANT VILLAS: (a) Ami Lullin at Genthod (now Saussure; from c. 1722), elevation; (b) Jolyot at Beaumont-sur-Vingeanne (from 1724), entrance front; (c) Bagatelle near Abbeville (from 1751, attic storey added 1763), garden front.

Ami Lullin was a pastor from nearby Geneva. The reduced version of his villa was built by Claude Jolyot, a royal chaplain who settled on the Côte-d'Or in Burgundy. The patron of the semi-suburban Bagatelle villa, Abraham van Robais, was a textile manufacturer of Dutch origin.

›2.86 CHAMPLÂTREUX, CHÂTEAU, from 1733: garden front.

The property was acquired in 1618 by Mathieu Molé, président of the Parlement de Paris (from 1641): his descendant Mathieu François, who held the same post as a member of the *noblesse de robe*, demolished the late-medieval château and retained Jean-Michel Chevotet to replace it in 1757 with funds acquired through his marriage to the daughter of a banker. Pavillons still punctuate the doubled corps de logis but the complex is freestanding, like the earlier work at Champs-sur-Marne and, as there, the entrance frontispiece has superimposed Orders supporting a pediment.

2.85a

2.85b

2.85c

2.86

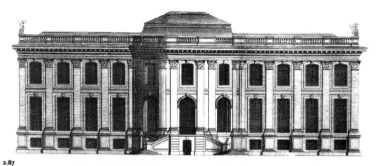

2.87

2.88

2.89b

›2.87 MONTMORENCY, CHÂTEAU CROZAT, from 1708: elevation (*AF*).

The architect Cartaud's patron was Pierre Crozat whose older brother Antoine was the even richer financier housed by Bullet on the Place de Vendôme in Paris (see page 288). The quasi-elliptical salon of Vaux-le-Vicomte becomes a true ellipse but still rises through two storeys with concealed roofs (*à l' italienne*). A continuous wall still separates the two ranges of rooms, denying the flexibility Bullet de Chamblain achieved six years earlier at Champs-sur-Marne: the traditional enfilade is preserved through both ranges but service access to the dining room – at the end of the garden range – is provided by a corridor linking it to stairs from the basement kitchens.

›2.88 ASNIÈRES, CHÂTEAU, from c. 1750: garden front.

The patron was Marc-René d'Argenson, Marquis de Voyer. The architect was Jacques Hardouin-Mansart de Sagonne, collaborating with Nicolas Pineau for the interior decoration, Guillaume II Coustou for the sculpture and Jean-Baptiste-Marie Pierre for the paintings. An enlarged *maison de plaisance* – or contracted château – the building is an excellent example of the mode *à l' italienne*.

›2.89 CHANTILLY, GREAT STABLE COMPLEX, from 1721: (a) plan, (b) general view from the south-east, (c) detail of central pavillon, (d) circular court.

The patron was Louis-Henri, Prince de Condé and Duc de Bourbon (1692–1740), son of the king's eldest legitimized daughter, president of the Council of Regency, and a beneficiary of Law's system (see page 27). His architect, Jean Aubert, had worked in the office of Jules Hardouin-Mansart – when work on the great stable blocks at Versailles was advanced – and had an extensive private practice. We shall return to his work within the château of Chantilly in due course.

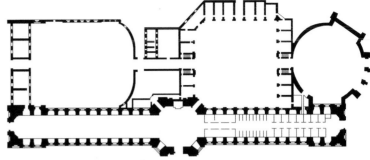

2.89a @ 1:2000

2.89d

2.89c

The early decades of Louis XV are perhaps even richer in *hôtels particuliers* than in châteaux – not only in the metropolis, but the metropolis must suffice here. Of the two basic types inherited from the 16th century and developed in the next, with the main block on the street or between court and garden, naturally the latter appealed to the grandest patrons – and those who would be grand. In Paris, the centre of social gravity had shifted west from the Marais to the other end of the Saint-Antoine axis, to the Faubourg Saint-Honoré or west of Saint-Germain on the opposite side of the river, to the area between the rue de Varenne, the rue de Grenelle and the river.

Closely followed by Bullet's work for Crozat at the Place Vendome, as we have seen, Hardouin-Mansart led the way to the development of the modern house, still in the east: his principal assistant Pierre Cailleteau (known as Lassurance, 1655–1724) took the endeavour west where he provided a prototype with his designs for the Hôtel Rothelin-Charolais (1704). Variants range from Pierre-Alexis

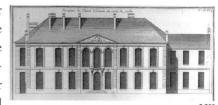

2.90a

›2.90 THE REFINEMENT OF THE PARISIAN HÔTEL in the Régence era and its immediate aftermath: (a) Estrées (Robert de Cotte, 1713), garden front; (b–d) Rothelin-Charolais (Lassurance, 1704), plan and entrance front, garden front detail; (e–g) Soubise, overview and entrance front, and Rohan, garden front (Pierre-Alexis Delamaire, from c. 1702 and 1705 respectively); (h–k) Seignelay, garden front, and Amelot de Gournay, plan and court elevation, overview (Germain Boffrand, from 1710 and 1712 respectively, engravings from *AF*); (l–n) Matignon (Jean Courtonne, from 1722), plan, entrance and garden fronts (*AF*); (o, p) Palais Bourbon (Jean Aubert?, from 1722), plan and entrance front (plans and engraved elevations from *AF*); (q, r) Peyrenc de Moras (or Biron; Jean Aubert and/or Jacques V Gabriel, from 1728), plan and garden front.

Busy in the Parisian domestic field, Lassurance is usually credited with the house at 101 rue de Grenelle for the Marquis de Rothelin: it was acquired in 1735 by Louise-Anne de Bourbon-Condé, Mlle de Charolais (1695–1758). Similarly prototypical is the same master's Hôtel Desmarets (originally de Rivié, 1704) and his later Hôtel de Roquelaure. The formula was amplified on a grand scale (from 1711) for the Duc de Noailles who married the niece of Mme de Maintenon. As with the town and country houses of his contemporaries, his *maison de plaisance* at Bellevue is comparable in its *noble simplicité*.

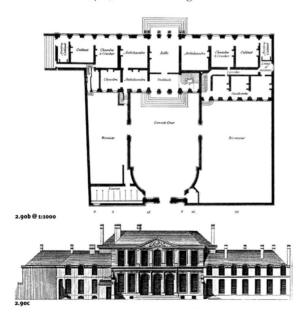

2.90b @ 1:1000

2.90c

2.90d

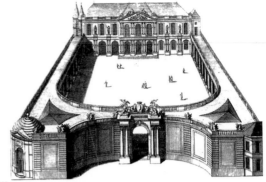

2.90e

Delamaire's Hôtel Soubise (from 1702), Boffrand's Hôtel de Seignelay (c. 1710) and Hôtel Amelot (1712), Robert de Cotte's Hôtel d'Estrées (1713), Jean Courtonne's Hôtel Matignon (1722) and Jacques V Gabriel's Hôtel Peyrenc de Moras (Biron, 1728). As its designation implies, the Palais Bourbon is exceptional (1722).**2.90**

2.90g

Pierre-Alexis Delamaire (1675–1745) went from the office of the Premier Architecte to a limited career. His extensive application of Orders to the Hôtel de Soubise court and entrance front may not have been in complete breach of *convenance*: the patron may have had illicit royal connections – possibly giving birth to another of Louis XIV's illegitimate sons, the future Cardinal de Rohan.

Boffrand, busy abroad in the first decade of the century when Lassurance was dominant, bought the site in

2.90h

Domestic planning at its apogee

The Hôtel Rothelin-Charolais in Paris and the Château de Champs-sur-Marne respectively represent the typical town and country houses of the period – at least in scale and style. With or without mansard, both types were usually of two storeys which were increasingly assimilated in height. Unlike the *maison de plaisance*, the main block of the town house was usually joined to a porte cochère by lower wings. Boffrand's Hôtel Le Brun has a relatively rare expansive site which allowed its author to provide a disengaged *maison de plaisance* in town: atypical, another example is the Hôtel Peyrenc de Moras/Biron attributed to Jacques V Gabriel and Jean Aubert. The same architect (probably) also provided the dowager Duchesse de Bourbon with an urban country house of great grandeur: the precedent for its single-storey form *à l'italienne*, with balustrades concealing the roof, was set by Hardouin-Mansart at Trianon rather than in housing for the *haute bourgeoisie*.

Distribution is typically to either side of a clearly defined central core of reception rooms, a vestibule and the salon which often reaches out to the garden. The staircase is placed to the side where it does not interfere

2.90k

2.90j

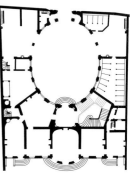

2.90i @ 1:1000

with the evolution of the plan of the building as a whole: in the château it often leads to an upper vestibule and salon, as at Champs. To either side, the parallel arrangement of the rooms of the apartments ensures that circulation will not interfere with privacy but corridors were now not uncommon, especially to serve a dining-room: beyond antichamber, bedroom and several cabinets, there were usually bathrooms and lavatories as well. Dining rooms, lavatories and corridors for servants were familiar to Hardouin-Mansart and his contemporaries, as we have seen.

The most important features of the plans of both town and country houses in 18th-century France – the convenient arrangement of apartments with facilities for dining and bathing and the projection of living-rooms into the gardens – were the legacies of Le Vau. Even a plan as extraordinarily Baroque as Boffrand's Hôtel Amelot conformed to the basic principles – though its unique elliptical court, simulating breadth in straitened circumstances, generates radial walls to pentagonal spaces for the staircase and the antichamber to the dining-room. The virtuoso planning ability needed by most Parisian architects to satisfy such diverse requirements on irregular sites was dictated by an unflagging will to uphold academic principles and ensure the symmetry of individual rooms, mask oblique junctions, preserve unimpeded the unifying enfilades through and across the building: Antoine Le Pautre had shown the way in the mid-1650s and earlier still François Mansart was adept at managing axes dislocated by the differing extent of court and garden ranges. Jean Courtonne offered a masterly exercise of that kind for the Hôtel Matignon on a site

the rue de Saint-Dominique in 1710 and sold the house to the diplomat Michel Amelot de Gournay three years later. That year he bought neighbouring blocks in the rue de Lille and developed them with astylar houses which he sold to Jean-Baptiste Colbert, Marquis de Torcy, and Charles Eléanor Colbert, Marquis de Seignelay (in 1716). Similarly Jean Courtonne (1671–1739) began speculative building before selling his incomplete project to Jacques III Goyon de Matignon: naturally, his château at Villarceaux is closely related in style.

The commission for the Palais Bourbon was initially issued by Louise Françoise de Bourbon (1673–1743), the legitimized daughter of Mme de Montespan and Louis XIV who married her to his cousin Louis de Bourbon, Prince Condé: the neighbouring Hôtel de Lassay was built by her lover, Léon de Lassay. His and her obscure Italian architect (Lorenzo de Giardini) died within months: responsibility thereafter for completing both houses as one-storey buildings (à l' italienne) is unclear: first in the field was Lassurance but he died within two years with construction at an unknown stage; next was

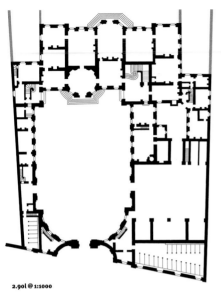

2.90l @ 1:1000

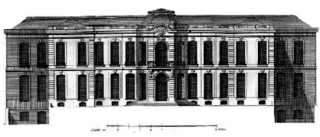

2.90n

wide enough for the partially freestanding corps de logis to be lit from the sides as well as the fronts.

In accord with the strictures of a hierarchically ordered society – and the elementary human distinction between public and private – *convenance* regulated the ordonnance of façades: as we have already noted,

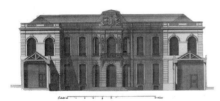

2.90m

Jean Aubert who, as we have noted, was the preferred architect of the Bourbon-Condé and signed construction specifications with Jaques V Gabriel as witness in 1726; the properties were joined in the ownership of Louis Joseph, Prince de Condé (grandson of Louise-Françoise) in 1768.

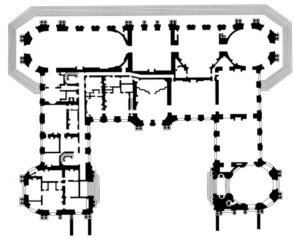

2.90o @ 1:1000

2.90p

the Orders were deemed appropriate only for royal or public buildings, private houses should be simple, unostentatious, astylar in the main. In practice architects did make sparing use of the Orders on the façades of such houses, usually to express the entrance with a portico or to link house and garden: and it was to these that the proportions of the whole necessarily conformed. Thus, articulation with a Corinthian Order throughout was admissible for the quasi-royal Palais Bourbon. Pierre-Alexis Delamaire may also have been working for a relative of royalty at the Hôtel de Soubise where the colonnade of his extraordinary forecourt enclosure derives from the monumental porte cochère and continues across the corps de logis to its fully articulated frontispiece. Boffrand's ordonnance of the Hôtel Amelot is heterodox but the Hôtel de Peyrenc de Moras and the Château de Champs are again typical, not least in eliciting relief from the varied fenestration of corps de logis and pavillons in compensation from the general absence of Orders. As we are about to see, *convenance* governed internal ordonnance too, of course.

2.90r

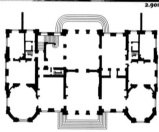

2.90q @ approximately 1:1000

Also unclear is the degree of Aubert's responsibility for the Hôtel Biron, for Abraham Peyrenc de Moras: however, the latter was a financier who enriched the Duc de Bourbon – and himself – through his subscription to Law's system and it seems likely that he would have turned first to his patron's architect.

Busy at Versailles and elsewhere on royal projects in the first decade of the century – and occasionally called in to alter existing private houses – the Premier Architecte Robert de Cotte entered the field of new domestic building in Paris with the Hôtel d'Estrées on the rue de Grenelle: it is close to the Lassurance prototype but expresses the main corps de logis as an isolated block on the garden side. He took the formula to its apogee for Cardinal Armand-Gaston de Rohan-Soubise (1674–1749), bishop of Strasbourg, for whom he had intervened in the completion of the Hôtel de Rohan in Paris – to the intense chagrin of Delamaire. He had experience in translating the Parisian house type to the grand scale required of a princely ecclesiastic at Verdun: there he took the ideal of noble simplicity to an extreme which avoided monotony only in the convexity of the main court front and its oblique approach; at Strasbourg superimposed Orders relieve the equivalent front and a colossal Corinthian frontispiece distinguishes the exposed river front.**2.91**

›2.91 ROBERT DE COTTE IN STRASBOURG: (a–c) Palais de Rohan (from 1727), river front, overview from cathedral tower, state bedroom.

The Parisian town house is amplified to approach the scale which the patron's peers, the prince-bishops of the empire, would require to satisfy their pretensions as quasi-sovereign potentates – who, as we shall see, also consulted de Cotte. The iconography of the restrained sculptural embellishment of the exterior progresses – or regresses – from the Biblical on the front facing the cathedral, to the cardinal virtues on the court and on to the more playful allegories of the seasons, the continents, etc., on the river/garden front. We shall return to the interior decoration in due course.

2.91a

2.91b

2.91c

2.92b

2.92c

›2.92 RIVALRY IN OPULENCE AT THE APEX OF REGENCY SOCIETY: (a) the Regent's Galerie d'Énée in his Palais-Royal, (b, c) the Comte de Toulouse's Galerie Dorée (1717 and 1718 respectively, DDM).

The Palais-Royal (formerly the Palais-Cardinal) had been conferred on the king's brother, Philippe d'Orléans, who had called on Hardouin-Mansart to effect alterations which included a long gallery: over an Order of Corinthian pilasters (with a Composite frieze), Antoine Coypel was employed to paint the vault illusionistically after the precedents set by Charles Le Brun at the Hôtel Lambert and, of course, Versailles. On his father's death in 1701, the property passed to the future regent Philippe II (and his wife, Louis XIV's youngest legitimized daughter) who wasted little time in moving there as his main base (along with his château at Saint-Cloud).

The regent's architect was Gilles-Marie Oppenordt (1672–1742) who was born in Paris to Dutch parentage, trained in the office of the Premier Architecte, and was in Italy as a royal pensioner (1692–1700) where he studied the Baroque, valuing Borromini no less than the Ancients – to the dismay of the Ancients. Failing acceptance into the service of the Bâtiments du Roi on return to Paris, he entered the service of Orléans c. 1708: retaining the Order of Mansart, his eclectic contribution to the decoration of the gallery – more Baroque than Le Brun's late work – includes Bérainesque putti, Berninesque fames and obelisks borrowed from Nicolas Blon-

2.92a

del's Porte Saint-Denis but he denied their architectonic monumentality in the ambiguous animate-inanimate manner essential to the proto-Rococo.

The Comte de Toulouse, legitimized son of Louis XIV, Grand Admiral of France and the bitter rival of his Orléans brother-in-law in the Council of Regency, had bought the Hôtel de la Vrillière in 1712: its gallery, originally designed by François Mansart, was transformed from 1718 by François-Antoine Vassé (1681–1736) under the supervision of Robert de Cotte with motifs relating to the patron's chief concerns – the sea and the chase. Further, de Cotte allowed Vassé to introduce Italianate out-curving pedestals (hitherto novel in France) and replace the fluted shafts of Mansart's Corinthian Order with panels infiltrated by arabesques in the way now familiar in less important rooms, reducing them to transparent fictions of support. The rest of the woodwork, especially the frames of the murals between the pilasters, is as sensuous and light-hearted as any of the period which led to the Rococo.

DECORATION DU SALLON A L'ITALIENNE ET DES PIECES SITUÉES AU MILIEU DU CHATEAU

2.93a

›2.93 GRADATIONS OF SPACE IN THE FASH-IONABLE APARTMENT: (a) section through the entrance sequence and principal reception room of a maison de plaisance (DDM, plate 8; (b) chamber (of the Duc de Choiseul with the duke attending to business of his ministry; Louis-Nicolas van Blarenberghe, 1771); (c) the cabinet or boudoir (with the young lady of the house attended by her maid; 'La Toilette', François Boucher, 1742; Madrid, Thyssen-Bornemisza Museum).

2.91c

INTERIOR DESIGN

In the most important rooms of the major patrons where the Orders were admissible – vestibules, stairwells, galleries and salons – there was still scope to develop the tradition of Charles Le Brun. An instructive comparison is offered by the Galerie d'Énée, designed in 1717 for the regent himself at the Palais-Royal by the Flemish designer Gilles-Marie Oppenordt – who spent much time in Rome and whose principal earlier works in Paris were Baroque altars – and the Galerie Dorée produced by Robert de Cotte for the Comte

2.91b

2.94a

de Toulouse, the legitimized son of Louis XIV.**2.92** With its full Order of fluted Corinthian columns, the former is still Baroque, even though the cornice is interrupted by exuberant sculpture. There is also an Order in the Galerie Dorée but the shafts of the pilasters are treated as panels decorated with arabesques, reducing them to transparent fictions of support as in the menagerie of the Duchesses de Bourgogne or the cabinet of the regent at Versailles.**2.93, 2.94**

Rococo morphology and motif

An Order was appropriate only in the entrance vestibule and principal reception room of a private house, even in the state bedroom of grandees who received there: vestigial pilasters, panelled and invaded by arabesques, often served but in lieu of an effective architectonic structure, a symmetrical geometric frame remained the basis of order.**2.93a, b** At the other end of the sequence of rooms leading from public reception to private withdrawal, the sister of our oyster eaters is dressing in the intimate disorder of her cabinet – the most characteristic domestic room of this period of comfort and convenience and the one most susceptible to the full floridity of Rococo.**2.72, 2.93c**

The rational geometry of tectonic panelling was still the basis of design in the menagerie of the Duchesse de Bourgogne at Versailles and even the cabinet of the regent. Stylized floral motifs soon rejected this discipline, however, and the formally regular pattern of panels and mirrors dissolved into undulations, especially as corners were rounded and cornices reduced to shallow coves breaking out into the ceiling.**2.93c** The process is under way in the main rooms of the Prince de Conti at Chantilly, where walls and ceiling still meet at right angles and the circular rosette still dominates.**2.94b, c** It is well advanced in the state bedroom of the Palais Rohan in Strasbourg.**2.91c**

The style was essentially free-ranging in its choice of motif. As it advanced in the 1720s, taste for the exotic grew with exploration and colonial expansion in the Indies and the Orient. Familiar grotesque 'C' and 'S' scrolls, herms, masks and sphinxes were supplemented by an increasingly bizarre array of shells, crustaceous creatures and watery elements, palm trees, bat wings, monkeys, African and Asian figures and 'Chinoiserie' dragons. They assumed a more important role not only in framing mirrors, over-

2.94b

2.94c

›**2.94 ROCOCO MORPHOLOGY AND MOTIF:** (a–c) Chantilly, Petit Château, panel of the Princesse de Conti's Singerie (monkey cage) cabinet, the prince's grand cabinet and bedroom (all from c. 1720);

2.94d

2.94e

(d) Champs-sur-Marne, château, Salon de Compagnie with its exotic embellishment (Christophe Huet, c. 1740); (e, f) Versailles, Cabinet de la Pendule in Louis XV's private suite (from 1735), queen's bedroom (1722);

doors (*dessus-de-porte*) and the increasingly large panels which filled the wall between the major accents provided by the mirrors, the windows and the doors, but on the upper edge of coves where they invade the ceiling.

2.94f

This affected reception rooms, as at Champs: unsurprisingly, its most playful manifestation appears in a cabinet – that of the Princesse de Conti at
Chantilly.**2.94a, d** However, even in the redecoration of the queen's bedroom
at Versailles after 1723 all but the most exotic of these motifs was admitted.
A somewhat less florid permutation of the style was adopted a decade later
for the young king when he called for a new apartment at Versailles.**2.94e, f**

The rounding of the corners and the reduction of the cornice to support for
an upturned fringe of foliage in coves promoted the ambivalent relationship
between walls and ceiling which was the ultimate objective of the greatest masters of the style. Boffrand led the way in curving an uninterrupted
impost up over the arches of doors, windows and mirrors to form a sort of
scalloped valance right round the room at the expense of the tectonic frame:
beginning at the Petit Luxembourg c. 1710 and in the first project for Malgrange of two years later,**2.73h** the process culminates in perhaps the most
ravishing room to survive from the period, the oval salon which he installed
for the Princesse de Soubise in her Paris hôtel about 1735. Walls, spandrels,
cove and ceiling are merged in a fusion of the arts. A crucial role is played by
vestigial pendentives, with paintings by Charles-Joseph Natoire, supported
by putti resting on the upper curves of the subsidiary frames, crowned by
stucco cartouches in the quivering cove and linked by filigree bands to the
central rosette. Glass plays an equally important part. A shimmering diapha-
nous veil of light, woven by dozens of flickering candles, refracted by the
crystal drops of the chandeliers and multiplied by the mirrors, dissolves
what little is left of substance and all sense of physical reality.**2.94g, h**

2.94g

2.94h

(g, h) Paris, Hôtel de Soubise, Salon Ovale de la Princesse (from 1735 for the wife of Hercule Mériadec de
Rohan, Prince de Soubise), orthogonal projection and
detail of vaulting.

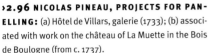

›2.95 ASYMMETRY IN DETAIL: (a) Jean-Bernard Toro, design for a cartouche (from *Dessins arabesques à plusieurs usages*, c. 1716); (b) Jacques de Lajoue, *Livre nouveau de morceaux de fantaisie* (1736); (c) Jean Mondon, *Forme rocaille* (1736).

2.95a

›2.96 NICOLAS PINEAU, PROJECTS FOR PANELLING: (a) Hôtel de Villars, galerie (1733); (b) associated with work on the château of La Muette in the Bois de Boulogne (from c. 1737).

2.95b

2.96a

2.95c

2.96b

2.97g

In all the Rococo works we have considered so far, fertility of invention has been disciplined by the strict symmetry of each individual element. By the fourth decade of the century, even while Boffrand was working at the Hôtel de Soubise, Nicolas Pineau and Juste-Aurèle Meissonnier, experimenting with asymmetry, had produced the *genre pittoresque*, the 'licentious' last phase of Rococo in France. Impetus is usually seen to have come from engraved folios of bizarre ornament, notably asymmetrical cartouches: the work of Jean-Bernard Toro, singled out in this connection, was developed by Jacques de Lajoue and Jean Mondon.**2.95**

After a period in Russia, Pineau was active in Paris from the early 1730s. In his interior designs, notably in the king's small château of La Muette on the edge of the Bois de Boulogne, he introduced individually asymmetrical elements which were not balanced by their mirror images in neighbouring panels, as they had been hitherto. He also showed a marked preference for fantastic motifs such as serpentine dragons and rich shell work, resorting less and less to the superimposed 'arabesque' motifs with which the development of the Rococo had begun. Ultimately he avoided straight lines whenever possible and relied solely on the asymmetrical play of curved frame mouldings meeting in highly plastic rocaille cartouches: his style was not ignored by the young Blondel.**2.96–2.98**

A goldsmith who is generally held primarily responsible for abandoning the last semblance of discipline in design, Meissonnier had first experimented with asymmetrical composition in silver and gold and then in decorations for court fêtes and their settings.**2.97a** Outstanding among his contemporary folio engravers, he specialized in architectural fantasies – follies, fountains, ruins – engraved as ends in themselves,**2.97b, c** but also ostensibly for execution as interior decoration.**2.97d**

2.97b

2.97c

2.97a

›2.97 JUSTE-AURÉLE MEISSONNIER, FANTASY AND THE GENRE PITTORESQUE: (a) design for a silver table centrepiece and crustaceous tureens (1735), (b, c) fantasies (from the *Livre d'Ornements*, 1734), (d–g) interior designs for the Polish Princess Czartoryski (1732), for the French Baroness de Bezenval (1740), for an unidentified Portuguese client (1740), and for the Polish Count Bieliński (c. 1745).

›2.98 JACQUES-FRANÇOIS BLONDEL: (a, b) scheme for the panelling for a state apartment (*De la distribution des maisons de plaisance*, etc., 1737, II, 74 and 62).

›2.99 PARIS, S.-SULPICE: façade project by Juste-Aurèle Meissonnier (from 1726).

A competition for the façade design was held in 1732: it was won by Giovanni Niccolò Servandoni (Jean-Nicolas Servan) with a scheme which announced the advent of Neoclassicism (to be reviewed in due course). Meissonnier had pre-empted it with a highly Baroque confection of curve and counter-curve drawn both from Bernini's S. Andrea al Quirinale and Borromini's S. Carlo alle Quattro Fontane (see pages 96f, 82f) and a roofline as sensual in its Rococo curvature as his metalwork. The reversal of Rococo fortunes – and of Borrominesque licentiousness, as academics would have it – is nowhere better demonstrated than in the rejection of that elegantly vigorous scheme in favour of Servandoni's neo-Palladian double-height temple front.

Composed of twirling consoles and asymmetrical arches, Meissonnier's fantasies defy the laws of gravity and admirably demonstrate the logical impossibility of an anti-architectonic architecture. Inevitably, the rare projects which he produced for execution are hardly Rococo at all: for instance, his design for the façade of S.-Sulpice (1726) is certainly Baroque, employing Orders before contrasted concave and convex sections of wall in the manner of Borromini, though the transept roofs anticipated his decorative mouldings with their curvature and asymmetrical palmier finials.**2.99**

The masters of Classical rule at the Académie royale d'architecture had tolerated the Rococo – indeed welcomed it for private rooms as we have repeatedly seen – until they saw the *genre pittoresque* threatening the fun-

2.97d

2.97e

2.97f

2.98a

2.98b

damental principles of architecture: then it was time to call a halt in France – if not abroad. As the 18th century advanced, moreover, Rococo ornament had spread tentatively from the interior to the exterior of buildings: licence permissible in private would certainly corrupt if displayed in public and it was precisely in that type of building upon which it was not appropriate to use the Orders that the danger was seen to be at its greatest by the critics. So persuasively did they write in favour of discipline as the key to progress – as we shall see – that the Rococo was lastingly damned as frivolous. However, promoting the freedom of the creative imagination and modern human interest over antique principle, it was, rather, a radical assertion of all that our century sees as progressive.

2.99

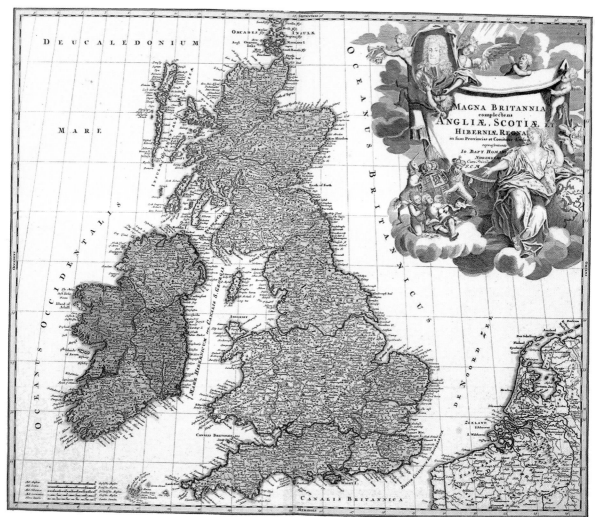

PART 3 NORTHERN
PROTESTANTS

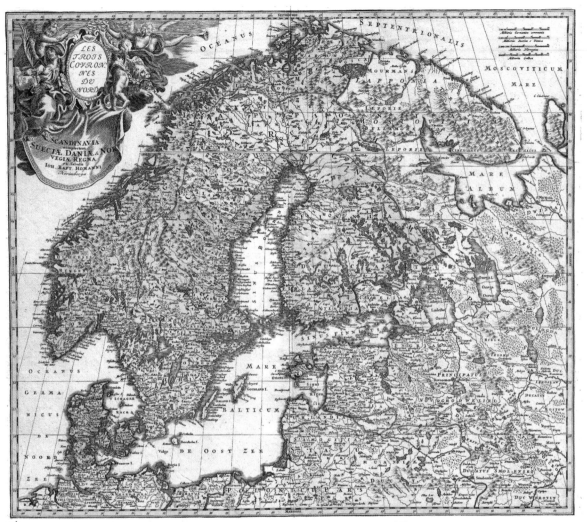

›**3.1 BRITAIN, THE NETHERLANDS AND SCAN-DINAVIA:** (a, b) maps by Johann Baptist Homann (Amsterdam, 1737); (c–e) insignia of the united realms of Britain and the Netherlands under William III and Mary II, and of the kingdoms of Denmark and Sweden.

3.1d, e

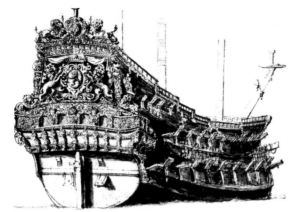

3.2a

1 THE DUTCH AND SCANDINAVIANS

›3.2 DUTCH STYLE AT SEA AND IN THE COLO-
NIES: (a) warship from the golden age (Willem van de
Velde the Elder, c. 1611–93); (b) Cape of Good Hope,
Groot Constantia (late 17th century rebuilt to the original form after a fire in 1925); (c) Curaçao, Willemstad,
representative early 18th-century commercial and
domestic building; (d) Jakarta, Batavia Kota, general
view over Sungai Ciliwung.

3.2b

Early in the 17th century Amsterdam was the dominant commercial and financial centre in northern Europe: its ships traversed the globe, its shipbuilders were unrivalled for much of the century (AIC5, page 545), the profile of its stern castle echoed through gables across the Dutch world.**3.2**

Architecture in the home provinces was dominated by Hendrick de Keyser (1565–1621), the city's chief as director of the Stadsfabryck: a decade after his death a eulogy in *Architectura moderna* (published in 1631) credited him with the reform of Dutch architecture after the excesses of the Mannerist past by reasserting the mathematical basis of design in the spirit of the ancients (AIC5, pages 416ff, 518ff).

Though still somewhat superficially mannered in modi-fication of the decorative convolutions elaborated by Hans Vredeman de Vries in particular, de Keyser's late house fronts were disciplined by a strict sense of proportion in the whole and its fenestration – and he attempted to effect a Classical sense of balance by countering the vertical thrust typical of elevation on the city's narrow plots by asserting the horizontal divisions between storeys. In his seminal church architecture, sober in accordance with the ethos of their Protestant congregations, little remains of Mannerist con-volution even in the gables: the elementary order of central-

3.2c

3.2d

3.3a

3.3b

›3.3 HAARLEM, NIEUWE KERK (from 1645): (a) exterior, (c) interior from west (Pieter Jansz. Saenredam; Haarlem, Franz Hals Museum).

The tower of the Gothic church of S. Anna was replaced in 1613 by Lieven de Key: rather more convoluted than de Keyser's norm of superimposed tempietti, this was to be retained in accordance with the city council's commission to Jacob van Campen to replace the rest of the dilapidated structure. Cross-in-square in plan, his work was the first in masonry built specifically for the Reformed church.

ized plans, focused on the pulpit, is complemented by the Classical proportioning of the elevations and the windows: elementary in its Classical mouldings too, white woodwork is profiled against red brick (AIC5, pages 61 and 550f).

JACOB VAN CAMPEN AND HIS FOLLOWERS

In the decade after de Keyser's death, Jacob van Campen of Haarlem (1596–1657) furthered the process of purification in architecture with strict geometrical order in planning, inspired by Palladio, and the reduction of ornament to the architectonic essentials: to the Orders as articulating agents of load and support and armatures of order – with respect to the canons purveyed in Palladio's *I quattro libri dell'architettura* and by Vincenzo Scamozzi rather than the Mannerism hitherto popular. He adapted the system to discipline the Dutch vernacular. In England, too, this was the endeavour of the followers of Inigo Jones: prominent among these, Nicholas Stone worked with de Keyser in Holland and married his daughter (AIC5, page 635).

Jacob van Campen preferred pilaster strips of rendered or unrendered brick on red brick rather than engaged columns on stucco simulating stone and their extensive application is foreign to the Palladian ideal: his mode is therefore perhaps best dubbed 'Dutch Classicism' rather than specifically 'Dutch Palladianism'. He applied his principles to both secular and ecclesiastical works: in the latter genre, his major legacy in his home town is the Nieuwe Kerk (1645).**3.3** Two decades earlier, he introduced his style to the burghers of Amsterdam with the Coymans house, and there too he provided them with an overtly Palladian theatre.**3.4**

Away from the whimsical to the rational along the lines drawn by de Keyser, the development of van Campen's style is sometimes related to the predominant patronage of calculating Protestant businessmen inimical to ostentatious

3.4a

3.4b

›**3.4 AMSTERDAM, EARLY WORKS OF JACOB VAN CAMPEN:** (a) house of the merchant Balthasar Coymans (1625), canal front; (b) Schouwburg (from 1637), engraved view of auditorium.

Inspired by Italian example, notably the Vicenza Teatro Olimpico, the Nederduytsche Academie was founded in Amsterdam in 1617 to promote science through lectures in the vernacular: it occupied wooden premises on the Keizersgracht. As the original founders were dramatists, the auditorium catered for theatrical performances as well as a lecture hall: too small for these purposes by 1664, it was demolished and a new theatre was built on a new site in accordance with recent developments in Italy and France.

›**3.5 THE 'DUTCH CLASSICAL' PALACE:** (a–c) The Hague, Mauritshuis (from c. 1635), ground and first-floor plans, canal front; (d, e) Huis ten Bosch ('House in the Woods', from 1645), entrance front, Orange Hall; (f) Huis Honselaarsdijk (Post after van Campen, from 1689).

The Mauritshuis plan follows a variant of the Palladian formula (AIC4, page 232), with twin apartments flanking the core reception rooms. The ordonnance is not specifically Palladian: the pilaster Order is applied to all four elevations, irregular in support of a reduced pediment on the entrance front, regular in rhythm about a temple-front motif on the waterside, where knowledge of Inigo Jones's designs for Newmarket may not be discounted (AIC5, page 622).

display, at least in the face they presented to their clients – though their progenitors were otherwise inclined. Be that as it may, there was a comparable tendency to monumental order at the court of the Stadtholder.

The Protestant Dutch could not have failed to prefer the austerity promoted by François Sublet de Noyers's bourgeois French regime to Flemish ostentation in the service of the Roman Church Triumphant. Prince of Orange and Stadtholder Frederick Hendrick (1584–1647, acceded 1625) had an equivalent to Sublet in his secretary Constantijn Huygens (1596–1687), who knew the London of Inigo Jones; indeed he attended the opening of the Banqueting House (AIC5, pages 622f). He translated Jacob van Campen from Haarlem to The Hague to inform a new official style. Assisted by Pieter Post (1608–69, also from Haarlem), he was responsible for transforming an existing house into the Noordeinde palace for Frederick Hendrick. His more celebrated first work for the ruling elite was the Mauritshuis commissioned ten years earlier (c. 1635) by Johan Maurits van Nassau-Siegen (1604–79): the paradigm of 'Dutch Classicism', elevating domestic restraint to the level of the noble seat, it was to be widely influential – especially in Denmark and Sweden.**3.5**

3.5f

3.5c

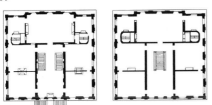

3.5a, b @ 1:1000

3.5d

The degree to which van Campen and Post shared work on Huis ten Bosch is obscure. The interiors were decorated for Amalia von Solms (1602–75). The team of artists included Gerrit van Honthorst, Pieter Soutman and Jacob Jordaens, who worked in emulation of Rubens.

Jacob van Campen's masterpiece, the Amsterdam Stadhuis (from 1648) rejected modesty for Baroque scale and embraced the French system of pavillons and corps de logis.**3.6** First mentioned in connection with the project in 1647, it is likely that he had been involved from the earlier inception. His commitment to the city authorities may explain why the position of chief architect to the Stadholder passed at this time to his erstwhile assistant, Pieter Post. Most prestigiously, the latter followed his master in applying the style evolved for Prince Johan Maurits to the design of the Huis ten Bosch (from 1645) in The Hague, the prospective seat of Frederick Hendrick, to whom it was dedicated as a monument on its completion by his widow.**3.5d, e**

3.5e

In Amsterdam provision of housing for magistrates and merchants on the expanding circuits of the canal system was dominated by Philips Vingboons who, like Post, had emerged from van Campen's circle. In particular, he

3.6c

›3.6 AMSTERDAM, STADHUIS (City Hall, now Royal Palace), begun 1648: (a) model, east front on Dam, (b) plan of main floor, (c) west front.

The building was commissioned in 1648 to accommodate the government body – the burgomaster, aldermen, treasurers, magistrates and social-service officers – of the nation's major port: it later became the royal palace. Composed in the French manner of pavillons and corps de logis, it exceeds the French and Italian norm in height. Rising from an arcaded basement, the *bel étage* and a generous mezzanine are united by a colossal Corinthian Order of pilasters in the manner of the south front of the Louvre: however, over all is another full storey and mezzanine articulated with colossal Composite pilasters.

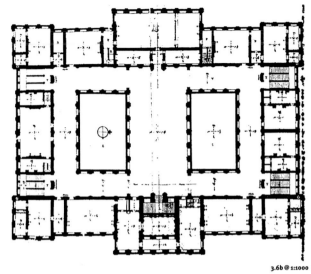

3.6b @ 1:1000

3.6a

developed the master's style in major works such as the Poppenhuis and the Trippenhuis on the Kloveniersburgwal (from 1660).**3.7a**

In general, Vingboons furthered reform to the traditional Dutch gable: though the sweep of the new urban rings was broader, the plots remained narrow and elevations high in front of elongated structures with steeply pitched roofs – in the traditional manner. However, instead of the stepped gable which survived de Keyser's Classicizing initiative, Vingboons opted to continue an undiminished central bay or bays up to the summit and turned the scrollwork of his predecessors into generous volutes to effect transition from the outer edge of the last complete storey.**3.7b** The result, derived from the solution to the problem of designing a basilican church front, matches the typical 'Baroque' sterncastle of the ships which produced – and defended – the wealth of the patrons.**3.2** Arms of the latter might embellish the typical crowning aedicule and there was usually an assertive portal: otherwise ornament was restrained outside and in. There were exceptions to the latter, notably where Catholics worshipped in secret.**3.7c,d**

3.7a

3.7b

3.7c

3.7d

›3.7 AMSTERDAM, MID-17TH-CENTURY
HOUSES: (a) Kloveniersburgwal, Trippenhuis of the
armament-dealer brothers Louis and Hendrick Trip
(Vingboons, from 1660); (b–d) Oudezijds Voorburgwal,
typical interior and general view of mid-17th-century
houses opposite the former Hartman House (Het Hart),
chapel in the attic (Ons' Lieve Heer op Solder installed
for the Westphalian Catholic merchant Jan Hartman,
who bought the property in 1661).

3.8a

As in France, the Orders were inadmissible in propri-
etorial principle beyond the realm of public building: there
were, of course, exceptions in practice but in the main
the later 17th-century Dutch promoted an austere order
drawn essentially from the proportioning of the mass and
its voids – even reducing the window frames to the bare
minimum required to support the glazing.**3.8** Prominent
examples are provided by Jacobus Roman (1640–1716), in
works ranging from the Deventer Stadhuis to the palace
of Zeist. Ultimate successor to Post as architect to the
Stadholder at the instigation of William III (1650–1702,
acceded 1672), Roman was commissioned to design the

›**3.8 THE AUSTERITY OF JACOBUS ROMAN:** (a)
Slot Zeist (from 1677), park front; (b) Deventer, Stadhuis (from 1693), entrance front; (c–g) Het Loo (from
c. 1684), engraved overview (Romeijn de Hooghe, c.
1694), entrance front, gallery, state bedrooms.

The patron at Zeist was Count Willem Adriaan van
Nassau, the son of Maurice of Nassau's illegitimate son
Louis. His cousin, the Stadtholder William III, used Jacobus Ramon for a project conceived as a modest retreat in
the Apeldoorn woods (hence the name Het Loo, 'palace
of the woods'). Nevertheless, the general distribution of
Versailles is recalled in the position of the main corps de
logis between contracting forecourts and an expansive
formal garden: the analogy was sustained inside by
Daniel Marot.

3.8b

3.8c

royal palace at Het Loo c. 1684: he was taken to England when his master was called to the throne there after the 'Glorious Revolution' of that year.

ADVENT OF MAROT AND FRENCH STYLE

After the revocation of the Edict of Nantes by Louis XIV in 1685, many Huguenots sought sanctuary abroad and took their considerable talents to the service of the French king's rivals. Of those who chose the Protestant Netherlands, the

3.9

most significant in our field is Daniel Marot – whom we encountered as a designer/engraver trained in the Parisian Gobelins (see page 242). Though engaged on his advent in 1686 primarily as a gardener for the Stadtholder, he was entrusted with the interior decoration of Het Loo: he responded with lavishness hitherto rare in Holland but conceived to emulate the otherwise-alien French court. He was similarly employed at Zeist. Thereafter, he purveyed opulence in The Hague where his work culminated in the Schuylenburch and Wassenaar-Obdam houses (from 1715 and 1716 respectively).**3·9**

Dutch sobriety was still respected in the basic design of the typical house by the followers of Roman in Amsterdam. The skyline was occasionally still convoluted in the manner of the sterncastle of a ship but buildings of greater extent than the typical house might have an expansive semi-circular gable.**3·7b, 3·10** Inside, however, Marot and his circle imported little of contemporary French fashion, sustaining the tectonic style of Louis XIV's private rooms before it was relieved by Jean Bérain with his permutation of grotesque ornament. It was not until the fourth decade of the century that some of his followers licensed the intrusion of sinuous line and florid detail: contrary to French academic conceptions of *convenance*, anyway, flagrance in external embellishment was not the Dutch norm.

›**3.9 DANIEL MAROT IN THE HAGUE:** Huis van Wassenaar-Obdam (from 1716, later Kneuterdijk), entrance front.

›**3.10 AMSTERDAM, COOVERSHOF (HEREN-GRACHT 16),** from 1723 (authorship disputed): canal front.

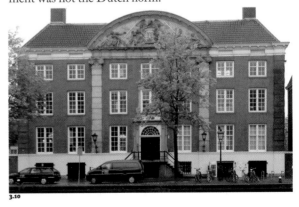

3.10

3.12a

3.11a

3.11b

3.12b

3.12c

›3.12 CHRISTIAN IV AND COPENHAGEN: (a) Rosenborg (completed c. 1624), general view from the north-east; (b, c) Børsen (from c. 1620, restored 1745, reworked inside from 1855), general view from the south and detail of central south-west entrance and spiral tower.

Hans van Steenwinckel the Younger and the otherwise obscure Bertil Lange are credited with the development of Rosenborg from the summer house commissioned by Christian IV in 1606: there were three main stages of expansion between 1613 and 1633. Sited on an island, the aspect of the single corps de logis is open: three towers project to the north, the central octagonal one for stairs, the others for rectangular withdrawing rooms on five levels; the single great tower on the southern side is crowned with a steeple formed of receding tempietti in the manner derived from the Dutch – like the rest of the embellishment.

Commissioned by Christian IV in furtherance of his wish to raise Denmark to the upper echelons of European trading nations, Børsen was built (1619–40) on Slotsholmen to the east of the castle, opposite the largely artificial island which provided the basis for the Dutch-inspired development of the king's new suburban merchant district, Christianshavn.

NORTH INTO SCANDINAVIA

Netherlanders had dominated architecture – military and domestic – in 16th-century Denmark: most spectacular at the great royal castles of Kronborg and Frederiksborg, their work continued throughout the reign of Christian IV (1588–1648). Kronborg is a grand representative of inheritance from the ubiquitous post-medieval quadrangle with four corner towers: the court at Frederiksborg was closed with a screen in the current French manner as considerable interest was shown in the pattern books of Jacques Androuet du Cerceau (AIC5, pages 368f, 553f).

As at court, so too in the manorial seat: the ubiquitous late-medieval quadrangle, defined by four ranges of similar height between corner towers, ceded to building of more open aspect based on the E-shaped plan popular in England – not without French precedents. The process may be traced from Grongad (1570) to Nørlund (from 1582) – but the old form subsisted, as at Engelsholm (from 1590).**3.11**

To clothe their buildings, the architects imported by Christian IV brought with them a Renaissance style developed with reference particularly to Sebastiano Serlio, Vredeman de Vries and Wendel Dietterlin (see AIC5, pages 143f, 420f and 490f). Frederiksborg cedes little to Floris or Vredeman in this and its multi-layered spires vary the form typical of Amsterdam. The development of both façade embellishment and the spire, furthered in the transformation of the summer pavilion of Rosenborg into a sumptuous suburban castle, culminated with the completion of Christian IV's astonishing Copenhagen commodity exchange (Børsen, from c. 1620).**3.12**

The Mannerist tendency was restrained in basic Protestant church design – as, for example, at Christian IV's new town of Kristianstadt in his province of Scania (Skåne) across the strait in modern Sweden. However, it was favoured for spires and may be especially marked

3.14a

3.14b

3.13

The square bays of nave and aisles are defined by the exceptionally slender columns which carry the rib vaulting at the same height throughout in conformity with the hall-church type popular in late-medieval Germany (AIC4, pages 436ff): buttressing is provided by the walls of the narthex, sanctuary and transepts which extend as the arms of a Greek cross.

›3.14 MALMÖ, S. PETER: (a) epitaph of Jost Ledebur (mayor of Malmö, died 1636), (b) pulpit.

›3.15 COPENHAGEN, (a) map of c. 1650 with (1) Christiansborg, (2) Amalienborg, (3) site of Kongens Nytorv, (4) Christianshavn; (b) Christiansborg slot as in 1698; (c, d) Charlottenborg (from 1672); (e) Niels Juel's house (from 1683, now the French Embassy);

3.15a

3.15b

in church fittings: the spectacular examples of the latter which distinguish S. Peter's in the Scanian capital, Malmö, are attributed to Henrik Konnicke who was obviously familiar with both Vredeman and Dietterlin.**3.13, 3.14**

With the elevation of Copenhagen to capital status as the seat of Frederik III (1648–90), who shared the pretensions of his peers to absolutism, an urban palace was required to supplant the medieval castle there: sequestered from the Church authorities and later to be known as Christiansborg, it was the nucleus around which the town developed.**3.15** The citadel, which guarded the city from the north, was improved on modern Franco-Italian stellar lines (in the 1660s) but a substantial new residence did not eventuate. Funds, depleted during the Swedish Wars and the reinforcement of the kingdom's defences, were available only for improvements to the old castle and a new suburban retreat for Queen Sophie Amalie of Brunswick Lüneburg – to the south of the citadel in the district to

3.15c

3.15d

3.15e

be known by her name. The former extended to the addition of an art and library gallery (*Kunstkammer*) inspired by Pierre Le Muet's work for Cardinal Mazarin in Paris.

The interventions in the fabric of Paris for the glorification of Louis XIV inspired the development of a grand square between the old town and Sophie Amalienborg in the first decade of the reign of Christian V (1670–99): Kongens Nytorv was addressed by a series of noble residences, beginning with the Charlottenborg of the Dutch architect Ewert Janssen (from 1672).**3.15d** The new king's Director-General of Buildings, Lambert van Haven (1630–95), was called on for a grand project for the castle but it was unrealized. Apart from restoration of Frederiksborg's fire-damaged interiors, van Haven's principal legacy is the Church of Our Saviour (Vor Frelsers Kirke, from 1682) in the new commercial district of Christianshavn: anticipating Christian IV's Holmens Kirke, it is Greek-cross in plan; like its Dutch Protestant antecedents, it is austere in its unarticulated brick style outside but not without internal stucco embellishment; it is further distinguished by the extraordinary spiral spire added in the middle of the next century.**3.15f–j**

3.15h

3.15i

(f–j) Vor Frelsers Kirke (Church of Our Saviour, from 1682), exterior, interior, detail of stucco embellishment, organ, tower (from c. 1750 by Lauritz de Thurah); (k, l) Holmens Kirke (Christian IV's naval church, converted from an anchor forge in 1619, expanded on a cruciform plan with the new arms slightly larger than the original lateral axis in 1641, eclipsed by the Vor Frelsers Kirke in the new maritime merchant district of Christianshavn, renovated 1872).

3.15g

3.15f

3.15j

3.16

›3.16 PRAESTØ, NYSØ SLOT, from 1673: entrance front.

›3.17 RANDERS, CLAUSHOLM SLOT, from 1693: entrance front.

Naturally, van Haven and his contemporary compatriots retained the 'Dutch Classical' style as the norm in their proliferating domestic work for the nobility: the major – and most splendid – example is the house of the victorious admiral Niels Juel on Kongens Nytov (from 1683).**3.15e** More representative in their restraint are the country houses of Nysø (from 1673, attributed to Janssen) or Clausholm (from 1693): the latter was built for Grand Chancellor Conrad von Reventlow by the Funenese master-builder Ernst Brandenburger with advice from the Swedish master Count Nicodemus Tessin (the Younger, 1654–1728), who had been called on for another unrealized royal castle project.**3.16, 3.17**

3.17

3.18a

3.18b

3.18c

ON TO SWEDEN

Like Denmark, Sweden naturally followed the usual northern line of transition from medieval to Renaissance over
the reigns of the first three Vasa kings, Gustav I (1523–60),
Erik XIV (1560–68) and Johan III (1568-92). Progress may
be traced from Gripsholm or Uppsala to Vadstena: the
former was modernized for King Gustav within the four
high ranges enclosing the court but retained four cylindrical
corner towers; built for King Johan (from 1570), Vadstena
has a single freestanding corps de logis to the lake side of a
quadrangular court framed by service wings.**3.18, 3.19** Traditional enclosure would persist, however, as we shall see.

Essentially a palace rather than a fortress, Johan's Vadstena acknowledges contemporary French developments,
not least in its Serlian portals, but the gables are Flemish
rather than French. French essays in Serlian portal design
remained popular but in Sweden, as in Denmark, French
Mannerist prolixity was not preferred to the convolutions
of the Flemish and their German followers (AIC5, pages
420f, 487ff). Of the latter, Franz Pahr (or Parr, died 1580)
was imported early in Johan III's reign to introduce the

›3.18 GRIPSHOLM, SLOTT, from 1537: (a) view
from Lake Malaren, (b) court, (c) Duke Karl's Chamber.

Asserting the power of the Vasa dynasty at its second
decade, fortification works began at numerous sites,
notably at medieval Gripsholm on the southern shore
of Lake Malaren which commanded the south-western
approach to Stockholm: there, as elsewhere, the master-
builders proceeded with more concern for the efficient
deployment of cannon in the lower stages of the round
towers than for Renaissance order. The main rooms were
on the upper levels of the ranges framing the irregular
courtyard but private apartments were stacked in the
corner towers – as in earlier French works like Chambord.

3.19b

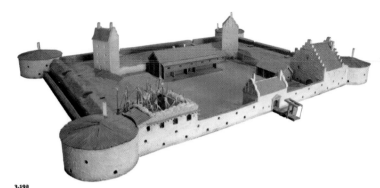
3.19a

>**3.19 VADSTENA, SLOTT:** (a) model of primitive complex, (b) entrance portal, (c) engraved view from north-west (from Erik Dahlberg, *Suecia Antiqua et Hodierna*, published from 1698), (d–f) general view from the south-west, gable and detail of court, (g, h) great hall and detail of antechamber ceiling, (i, j) chapel.

The moated quadrangular enceinte, with its four round corner towers and twin stone barracks facing the lake, was founded in 1545 as a key link in a chain of fortresses designed to control the south: the masters of current techniques for deploying artillery were imported from Leipzig. In addition to twin stone barracks on the lake side there was a timber lodge in the centre for royal visitors. Within a decade King Gustav I decided to improve the residential facilities for his

Renaissance to the Uppsala seat: joined in the royal service by several brothers, he seems to have come from Silesia via Schloss Güstrow in Mecklenburg (AIC5, page 474).

3.19c

3.19d

younger son Magnus. Apart from twin stone towers for services, emphasis shifted to building a two-storey stone palace between the barracks on the lake front (achieved by c. 1563): the portals are credited to the French stone-mason Pierre de la Roche. After 1570 King Johan added a third storey to the palace building, centred on the towering chapel: the works were conducted by the Fleming Arendt de Roy (died 1590). The roof was replaced after a fire in 1598: King Karl IX Gustav called on Hans Fleming for the gables (the eastern one was completed by 1610, the western one ten years later).

Developed over the same reigns, the castle at Kalmar is a related exercise but its regular quadrangular court, entered through a Serlian triumphal arch, is framed by ranges to full height. It was badly damaged in the Kalmar War of 1611–13 and by fire in 1642.

3.19e

3.19g

3.19h

3.19i

3.19f

3.19j

3.20a

3.20b

3.20c

›3.20 GOTHENBURG, founded 1621: (a, b) model and plan representing the canalized town within its original fortifications; (c) the granary and armoury (from 1642, known as Kronhuset after its use as a royal residence).

Developed under central supervision from the capital, the new planned towns transmitted post-Renaissance architectural principles into the provinces.

Sweden's advance to the status of a great power in the Baltic and north-central Europe under Gustav II Adolf (1611–32) and his Vasa followers in the latest phase of the Thirty Years' War was accompanied by expansion at home. New towns were founded, primarily as naval or military installations but inevitably fostering the trade of a maritime nation: the grid was rigorously imposed by the authoritarian regime but the Dutch – particularly the canalized development of Amsterdam – were followed in adapting urban order to natural features, especially on low-lying coastal sites like Gothenburg.**3.20**

Before work on the Vadstena gables was completed by Hans Fleming, the main agent of the Netherlandish style at the Vasa court was Willem Boy (1520–92) – who may have initiated the last phase of expansion at Vadstena before his departure for study abroad left the job to his compatriot Arendt de Roy (died 1589). Boy's major confirmed attributions are the modernization of the medieval castle at Stockholm, with its burgfried at the junction of ranges framing a court, and a new royal summer residence at Drottningholm. In the early Vasa age of Lutheran reformation and monastic dissolution, too, he was commissioned to convert the monastery at Svartsjö into a palace.

Little of Boy survives but early engravings reveal that King Johan was eclectic in his tastes and wide-ranging in his recruitment of talent: he retained the Gothic style for his ecclesiastical works, notably the chapel which surmounts the central pavilion at Vadstena; on the other hand, apart from Netherlandish gables and the Flemish Renaissance form of turret, at Svartsjö he opted for an Italianate domed chapel and a circular court probably derived from Serlio.**3.21**

The eclecticism promoted by King Johan was sustained well into the reign of Gustav Adolf. There was much destruction in the ecclesiastical field but Gothic persisted in the limited new building activity, often with incongruous Serlian detailing for the portal and invariably with internal sculptural embellishment provided by the altar, pulpit and memorial epitaths: apart from the king's burial chapel attached to the medieval Riddarholmskyrkan, the most prominent examples are the churches of S. Gertrude and S. Jakob in Stockholm (both from the 1570s, remodelled in the 1630s). Their rib vaults are carried by massive piers of pseudo-Classical form, Romanesque in essence: Gothic in essence, slender shafts had already become attenuated columns in the Trinity Church of the Danish king's Kristianstadt (from 1612).**3.22, 3.15**

3.21a

›3.21 STOCKHOLM AND THE LOST PALACES OF WILLEM BOY: (a) plan of the capital in 1650; (b, c) Tre Kronor and Svartsjö (both castles medieval in origin, renovated in the 1570s and recorded in engravings in Dahlberg's *Suecia Antiqua et Hodierna*).

3.21b

3.21c

3.22a

3.22b

3.22c

3.22d

3.22e

3.22f

›3.22 MEDIEVAL FORM AND SERLIAN STYLE IN THE STOCKHOLM CHURCH OF THE GUSTAVIAN ERA: (a–d) S. Gertrude (the German church, Tyska kyrkan; from 1570, transformed from 1638), tower, interiors and south portal; (e, f) S. Jakob (from 1579, transformed from 1634), south portal and interior to altar with pulpit to the left.

Gustav II's director of building works – at Stockholm, Uppsala and elsewhere – was Caspar van Panten, the first to be appointed Royal Architect. He was Dutch but German architects were still prominent in mid-century Sweden. Among them, Franz Stiemer is associated with the last great phase of work at Läckö, Caspar Vogell with Skokloster (both in the 1650s). In marked contrast to the external sobriety there, florid Mannerism – derived from Flanders but taken to the extreme by Dietterlin – was preferred by the previous generation of his compatriots: their works are best represented by the sandstone portals applied to the red-brick Schantz and Petersen houses in Stockholm by Johan Wendelstam and Christian Julius Döteber respectively (c. 1650) – and, of course, by church fittings like those in the Tyska kyrkan and the cathedral.**3.23**

3.23a

›**3.23 MANNERIST EMBELLISHMENT IN STOCKHOLM:** (a) Storkyrkan (the city's medieval parish church, dedicated to S. Nicholas, converted to Lutheranism in 1527, raised to cathedral status after the diocese of Stockholm was distinguished from the archdiocese of Uppsala in 1942), high altar retable (made in Germany of ebony and silver, c. 1650); (b, c) Petersen house, west front and portal detail (from 1645, originally for Governor Regner Leuhusen).

3.23b

3.23c

3.24a

›3.24 LÄCKÖ SLOTT: (a) general view from the west, (b) first-floor plan with (1) chapel (under), (2) Knight's Hall, (3) Hall of Peace, (4 and 4a) Austrian Hall and its antechamber, (5) state bedroom, (c, d) court portal and inner elevation, (e, f) chapel portal and interior, (g) Knight's Hall, (h) Hall of Peace, (i) antechamber to the Austrian Hall, (j, k) ceiling details from the Knights' Hall and Austrian Hall, (l) state bedroom (called after Princess Maria Eufrosyne, sister of King Karl X Gustav, patroness of the castle).

Originally an outpost of the bishop of Skara, the medieval castle was confiscated by Gustav I after the

Inevitably, the late-medieval quadrangle survived well into the 17th century as the basis for post-Renaissance modernization commissioned by the nobility whose patronage outstripped the Crown when the latter's resources were directed to fortification and armaments: the slott at Läckö is an unexcelled example (from c. 1650 and earlier). More open aspects were now known in Denmark and not ignored in Sweden, as at Rosensberg (from 1634) or Salnecker (1640) and more frequently as

3.24d

3.24b @ 1:1000

3.24c

3.24e

3.24f

Reformation of 1527. By the end of the 16th century it had been assigned to the Councillor of the Realm (Hogenskild Bielke) from whom it passed in 1615 to Field Marshall Count Jacob de la Gardie (died 1652): he began major expansion, including transformation of the outer bailey and extra elevation to the main ranges, which was furthered on an even greater scale in the next generation by Count Magnus Stenbock, Lord High Chancellor, brother-in-law of Karl X Gustav (r. 1654–1660) and regent during the minority of Karl XI. Most of the surviving interiors derive from this last phase of work, directed by the German master-builder Franz Steimer. The chapel and its portal are due to Steimer (from 1655) and his local protégé Olof Falck, under the supervision of the Augsburg master Matthias Holl: the sculptural embellishment, unusually extensive for a Protestant chapel, is largely due to the Walloon George Baselaque (died 1689).

Steimer was first commissioned to panel the Knight's Hall as the setting for a suite of paintings commemorating the Thirty Years' War (derived in the 1670s by German artists from Matthäus Merian's engravings); the same artists were responsible for the halls dedicated to the Peace of Westphalia and to the Austrian enemy but the antechamber to the latter preserves its 16th-century floral decoration.

The patron was Steward of the Realm (the highest position) in 1680 but fell the following year and lost most of his estates. Läckö passed to several generations of Councillors of the Realm before being granted in 1752 to the diplomat and chancellor Count Carl Gustaf Tessin, son of Nicodemus Tessin the Younger who we are about to encounter as principal royal architect. The redecoration of the state bedroom in French style probably dates from his time.

3.24g

3.24i

3.24j

3.24k

3.24h

3.24l

the century progressed to works like Finspång (1685). However, the enclosed court defined by ranges rising to equal height between four corner towers was even retained for new building: the slott at Skokloster is the prime example (from 1672). Neither Läckö nor Skokloster cede to the contemporary Dutch in the austerity, even the mathematical purity, of fenestration: ranging over much of the second half of the 17th century, their interiors are unrivalled.**3.24, 3.25**

›3.25 SKOKLOSTER SLOTT: (a) general view from the west, (b, c) undercroft and court, (d) main storey gallery, (e, f) King's Hall, general view and ceiling detail, (g) antechamber with chimneypiece bearing Wrangel insignia, (h, i) bedrooms.

The patron was Herman Wrangel, an army officer of Estonian origin (died 1643): the estate was granted to him by King Karl IX in 1611 in recognition of his distinguished military service. The move from the primitive stone manor house to a grand quadrangular palace was undertaken from 1654 by Herman's even more distinguished soldier son Carl Gustaf Wrangel (1613–76). The original architect was the Thuringian Caspar Vogell (c. 1660–63) whose austere work for the Duke of Saxe-Gotha, Ernst I – notably Schloss Friedenstein – the patron had encountered on campaign in Germany during the Thirty Years' War. After Vogell's death in 1663, Wrangel turned to Nicodemus Tessin the Elder and Jean de la Vallée (to whom we too are about to turn). After Carl Gustaf's death the estate passed to his daughter Margareta Juliana Wrangel and her husband Nils Brahe.

Regular geometry prevails: the court is square, the towers octagonal, the strict fenestration grid is relieved with rustication and blind arcading on all three main storeys. The plan is Italianate with the principal enfilades in each of the four perpendicular ranges served by galleries lit from the court.

The marble columns of the undercroft (from 1660) are due to the Hessian stone-mason Johan Wendelstam (died 1670). The King's Hall was completed in 1664 with the astonishing stucco ceiling of the Bavarian

3.25a

3.25c

3.25d

3.25b

3.25f

Hans Zauch in collaboration with Giovanni Antoni (or Anthoni, a stuccador of Italian extraction from Narol, Poland, died 1688). Elsewhere the ceiling stuccowork, including its application directly to beams, is due to the local master Nils Eriksson. The suite of chimneypieces, unrivalled anywhere outside early 17th-century France, is probably due to de la Vallée.

3.24e

3.24h

3.24i

3.24g

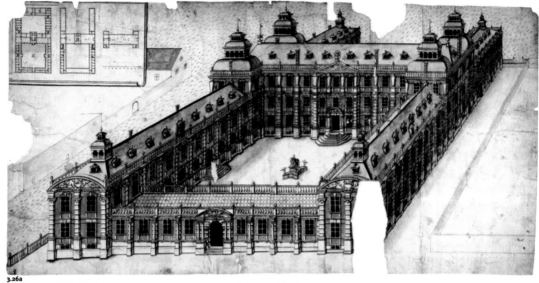

3.26a

3.26b

3.26c

FRENCH GRANDEUR: DUTCH RESTRAINT

The traditional quadrangle was retained at Skokloster a generation after the introduction to Sweden of the free-standing block with open aspect in the French manner. This is attributed primarily to the French Calvinist architect Simon de la Vallée (c. 1590–1642), a pupil of Salomon

›3.26 STOCKHOLM, THE ADVENT OF 'DUTCH CLASSICISM': (a–c) Riddarhuset (House of the Knights, or Nobles), Simon de la Vallée's project plans and perspective view (1641), and as completed (from 1652); (d) Rosersberg Palace (from 1634, *SAH*); (e) Bonde Palace (from 1662, the town hall from 1730, supreme court since 1949); (f) Scharp House (c. 1670).

The Riddarhuset was to provide a meeting place with ancillary accommodation and a residential academy for the nobility. In the manner of du Cerceau if not de Brosse (AIC5, pages 368ff, 390ff), de la Vallée projected the great hall and lesser representational rooms in a three-storey central block, the residential facilities in wings framing a screened cour d'honneur to the front and an open garden court. The reduced version favoured representation over the domestic aspect of the scheme: the corps de logis is shorn of accretions; the riverside court has become a terrace defined by twin detached corner

3.26d

pavilions. The distinctive roof form (known as *sateri* and much followed in Sweden) was developed from de la Vallée's tower caps with S-curvature to the main slope and a truncated lantern. One may only speculate on de la Vallée's role in the reduction of his scheme between its projection in 1641 and his death the following year and in effecting the transition from French Mannerism to Dutch Classicism – both of which he was involved with before going to Sweden.

The neighbouring Bonde Palace of Lord High-Treasurer Baron Gustaf Bonde (1620–67) originated with an H-shaped project of Simon de la Vallée: that was retained as the basis for a scheme articulated in the Dutch manner by his son in apparent collaboration with Nicodemus Tessin the Elder. They were also responsible for Isak Cronström's Sjofartshuset (Seafarers House, from 1660, also known under the name of Scharp). That retains its *sateri* roof behind a Dutch semi-circular pediment. The *sateri* was lost to the Bonde Palace in a fire of 1710: the attic storey was added by Johan Carlberg in renovations after a fire in 1753.

de Brosse, who furthered his career in Holland just when Jacob van Campen was introducing his Classical mode. He accepted the commission to work for Field Marshall Åke Henriksson Tott at Ekolsund in 1637 and was soon employed by the heads of the powerful Oxenstierna and Bonde families: apart from Ekolsund, Oxenstierna's Rosersberg and Bonde's Hasselby are early examples of the new type, variously reworked.

Simon de la Vallée's most sophisticated exercise in the genre of Androuet du Cerceau, as developed by Salomon de Brosse, was his project for the Riddarhuset (House of the Knights, from 1642): after his death in its initial year, the courtyard scheme was reduced to a wing built (from 1652) by Justus Vingboons (1620–98) who promoted the Dutch Classical style which he was instrumental in furthering at home in Amsterdam – distinct was the 'S' curved roof with low parapet (*sateri*). Prominent examples of his followers' work range from the Bonde Palace (begun 1662, much altered, especially at attic level) to the cubic Lillienhof and Scharp Houses (of c. 1670), which have Dutch affiliates.[3.26]

3.26f   3.26e

›**3.27 JEAN DE LA VALLÉE AND THE PARADIGM OF THE CENTRALIZED CHURCH IN STOCKHOLM:** (a–c) Katarina kyrka (from 1656), project plan and elevation, general view of exterior; (d, e) Hedvig Eleanora kyrka (from 1656, furnished by G.J. Adelcranz before consecration in 1737, dome from 1865), exterior and interior.

3.27c

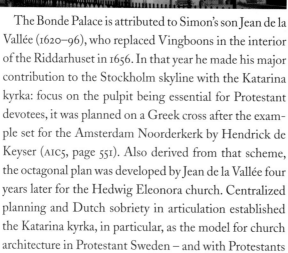

3.27a

The Bonde Palace is attributed to Simon's son Jean de la Vallée (1620–96), who replaced Vingboons in the interior of the Riddarhuset in 1656. In that year he made his major contribution to the Stockholm skyline with the Katarina kyrka: focus on the pulpit being essential for Protestant devotees, it was planned on a Greek cross after the example set for the Amsterdam Noorderkerk by Hendrick de Keyser (AIC5, page 551). Also derived from that scheme, the octagonal plan was developed by Jean de la Vallée four years later for the Hedwig Eleonora church. Centralized planning and Dutch sobriety in articulation established the Katarina kyrka, in particular, as the model for church architecture in Protestant Sweden – and with Protestants abroad, as we shall see.**3·27**

3.27e

3.28a

›3.28 NICODEMUS TESSIN AND ECCLESIASTICAL CENTRALIZATION: (a) Stockholm, Maria kyrka, side front to extended cruciform structure (begun 1580, completed c. 1620, extensions from 1675); (b, c) Kalmar cathedral (construction from 1660, interrupted by war 1675–79, completed 1703), exterior and interior; (d–g) Stockholm, Riddarkyrkan, overview from the east with the Gustavian and Caroline mortuary chapels flanking the sanctuary, vault of the Caroline chapel (Karolinska gravoret, begun in 1672 but not completed until 1743) and crypt containing the Baroque tombs of Karl X (died 1660), Karl XI (died 1697), their wives and four infant princes; (h) Karlskrona, Holy Trinity (from 1697).

Jean de la Vallée sometimes worked in association with his great contemporary, Nicodemus Tessin the Elder (1615-81). Born in Sweden's Pomeranian enclave of Stralsund and trained as a military engineer, Tessin entered Simon de la Vallée's office, was appointed Architect to the Crown in 1646, travelled through Germany, Holland, France and Italy in the first half of the 1650s and returned to develop an extensive practice within and without his mentor's circle. His first important independent work is the cathedral at Kalmar (from 1660): a Greek-cross variant, the entrance and sanctuary arms are slightly elongated there but Tessin provided the purest expression of the form for the mortuary chapel commissioned in 1672 by Karl XI to balance that of Gustav II Adolf beside the sanctuary of the Riddarkyrkan. That work was furthered by the author's son and namesake who contributed the distinguished centralized Trefaldighetskyrkan to Karlskrona (from 1697).**3.28**

3.28c

3.28b

3.28d

3.28f

3.28g

The cruciform ideal with four towers in the corners which inspired Antonio da Sangallo the Elder's church of S. Biagio at Montepulciano is not implausibly recalled by Tessin at Kalmar though, as for Stockholm's Maria kyrka façade (from c. 1675): the articulation with pilaster Orders on two levels in the Roman manner of the younger Antonio da Sangallo is assertively comprehensive (AIC5, pages 144f).

3.28e

The Caroline mortuary chapel was emulated at Turinge by the soldier and military engineer Erik Dahlbergh – the compiler of the invaluable record of notable buildings *Suecia Antiqua et Hodierna*.

Tessin the Younger's Holy Trinity at Karlskrona is octagonal with Greek-cross arms extending to Palladian porticoes: in contrast is the basilican form of the same architect's Fredrikskyrkan in the same city.

3.28h

›**3.29 STOCKHOLM, AXEL OXENSTIERNA PALACE,** from 1653: view from the east.

Foremost statesman of Gustav II Adolf's reign, close confidant of the king, chief instrument in forming a centralized administration, the patron was Lord High-Chancellor (from 1612) and held several major offices abroad, including governor of occupied Prussia in the

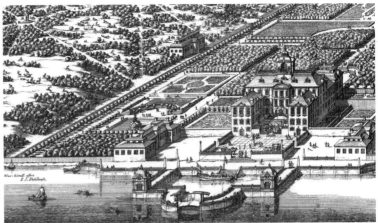

3.29

3.30

later stages of the Thirty Years' War. Jean de la Vallée built him Stockholm's first Roman Mannerist palazzo.

›**3.30 KARLSBERG SLOTT,** 1670: overview (from *Suecia Antiqua et Hodierna*).

The site's first palace was built c. 1630 in the Netherlandish Renaissance style for Lord High-Admiral Carl Carlsson Gyllenhielm (died 1650): on the death of his widow it passed to the Crown and was exchanged by the dowager Queen Hedvig Eleanora for Ulriksdal at the behest of Jakob de la Gardie, Lord of Läckö. He retained Jean de la Vallée to replace his predecessor's house with a Baroque palace, again based on an H-shaped plan with the southern court facing a waterway: flanked by wings terminating in broad pavilions with *sateri* roofs, the north court opened to extensive gardens. Lost to de la Gardie in 1683, the estate was bought by the Crown in 1688: the royal family moved there pending the rebuilding of their Stockholm seat destroyed by fire in 1697. After extensive refurbishment, they moved out in 1754.

›**3.31 NYNÄS SLOTT,** 1650s, renovated in the 1860s: general view.

The patron was Erik Gyllenstierna, chamberlain to Gustav II Adolf with whom he fought in Germany, governor of several provinces in the late stages of the war and privy councillor (1645), President of the Court of Appeal and member of the board established to reduce noble property (both c. 1655); the architect working in the Franco-Dutch Classical style was from de la Vallée's circle.

In contrast to Dutch Classical exercises, Italianate palazzi were not uncommon in Stockholm: versatile, Jean de la Vallée worked for the Oxenstierna in a Roman Mannerist style.**3.29** His most prestigious country-house project was the transformation of a pavilion at Karlsberg, to the north of the capital, for the Lord High-Admiral Magnus Gabriel de la Gardie (in the 1680s): he recalled the H-shaped plan of his father's project for the Riddarhuset – as he had done for Bonde – but not the French Mannerist articulation.**3.30** After it had been acquired by the Crown, it was modified by the elder Tessin in an elementary interpretation of the Dutch style, though the distinctive *sateri* form of roof developed for the Riddarhuset was retained. Elsewhere the mansard norm was approximated in the context of elementary Dutch Classicism – at Nynäs for example (1650s).**3.31**

3.31

3.32a

3.32b

The Crown was reasserting itself as dominant in patronage by the early 1660s and adopted Nicodemus Tessin, father and son, to build new palaces. The dowager Queen Hedvig Eleonora commissioned the father to build her a retreat in place of Willem Boy's Drottningholm (destroyed by fire soon after she bought it in 1661): he responded, appropriately, with the greatest work of his age which, unfinished on his death in 1681, was completed by the son. Meanwhile, the father had worked on many other houses for the nobility: new or renovated, variously endebted to the Vallée school, these are well represented at Mälsåker, Ericsberg, Strömsholm, Salsta and Sjöö.**3.32**

›3.32 NICODEMUS TESSIN THE ELDER AND THE GREAT HOUSE: (a) prototypical project for a manor house with alternative ordonnance; (b) Strömsholm (from 1669), entrance front; (c, d) Salsta (from 1672), entrance and garden fronts; (e, f) Sjöö (from c. 1679), entrance and garden fronts; (g–j) Drottningholm (from 1662), lake and garden fronts, interiors.

The massing of the prototype, in terms of corps de logis with central pavillon and corner towers, derives from Simon de la Vallée's Riddarhuset project: variations on the *sateri* and the colossal pilasters (borrowed from the Dutch or, indeed, from Le Vau) recall the revision of that project but the alternative is Serlian. The nearest approximation to the prototype is Strömsholm, built for Queen Hedvig Leonora: front and back are simplified variants of each alternative. A simplified variant

3.32e

3.32f

3.32c

3.32d

of the Dutch Classical alternative was adopted for both Salsta and Sjöö – though there are towers only to the entrance front and the central pavillon projects into the garden as in post-Le Vau French practice. Earlier, in the replacement of medieval Mälsåker the central pavillon projects to each front, the corner towers become the wings of an H-shaped complex but the lanterns are displaced from them to the sides of the corps de logis.

For the replacement of the waterside Drottningholm, commissioned by the queen in 1661, Tessin extruded the towers of his prototype under *sateri* roofs: pavillons rather than wings, these form an H with the recessed corps de logis. Dutch Classicism is reduced to an abstract ordonnance of pilaster strips in the main – grey sandstone against yellow stucco – but recourse to Serlio provides some relief in the centre and to the façades of

Nicodemus Tessin the Elder's initial approach to the massing of the country house was essentially French, inherited from de Brosse via Simon de la Vallée: still towers, corner pavilions were deleted from garden fronts where Dutch austerity did not go unobserved. Nicodemus Tessin the Younger (1654–1728), who trained under his father before four years of study in the circle of Bernini and Fontana in Rome and two years in Paris (1673–77–79), began where his mentor had left off and further simplified the massing and the articulation of the country house. The *sateri* prevails, side pavilions survive from the lower storeys of towers as slender pavillons.

3.32g

3.32h

3.32i

3.32j

the lower pavilions from which twin wings extend laterally to rotundas. As elsewhere in Tessin's grand domestic work, the planning is essentially French with apartments to each side of a central core of reception rooms served by a grand staircase. Beyond the latter, the decoration of these was finished by the younger Tessin after the death of his father. The formal garden, extending west from the palace in the integrated French style, was designed to accommodate the sculptures of Adriaen de Vries looted from Prague during the late stage of the Thirty Years' War.

Tessin worked for the queen at several other sites. At Ulriksdal, notably, he transformed an earlier house (bought from Magnus Gabriel de la Gardie, 1669) in an elementary Franco-Dutch Classical style.

›3.33 NICODEMUS TESSIN THE YOUNGER AND THE COUNTRY HOUSE: (a–c) Steninge (projected from c. 1690, construction from 1694), project section and elevation, general view of entrance front; (d) Rosersberg (from 1634, modernized from 1694 and again in the 1750s after acquisition by the royal family), entrance front.

The double ranges and the projecting salon of Steninge are in line with modern French developments but the twin flights of the staircase rise to either side of the vestibule in the centre of the entrance front.

The 14th-century manor on the north-eastern shore of Lake Mälaren was rebuilt from c. 1634 for Count Gabriel Bengtsson Oxenstierna who named it Rosersberg in honour of his mother. Attributed to Simon de la Vallée, it passed to the patron's son and namesake in 1656 and was thereafter modernized.

Serlian detail still pervades the initial project for Steninge slott (c. 1690) but in execution there is greater clarity: an elegant Order of pilasters rises through the piano nobile over a rusticated basement in the mode widely followed from Rome to Paris, Vienna to Berlin. Later Dutch abstraction supervenes in works like Sturefors and Rosersberg slott, the latter reworked on the basis left by Simon de la Vallée. The patron at Rosersberg was Bengt Oxenstierna, brother of Count Gabriel Bengtsson Oxenstierna, who entertained the queen there in 1666. At Steninge the patron was Karl Eriksson Gyllenstierna, chamberlain to Queen Hedvig Eleonora, who recommended Tessin and oversaw the evolution of the project (to completion of building work in 1698).**3.33**

3.33a

3.33b

3.33c

3.33d

3.34a

›3.34 STOCKHOLM, TWO GENERATIONS OF PALAZZI: (a) Nicolas Tessin the Elder's Bank of Sweden (Gamla Riksbanken, from 1675), exterior; (b–g) Nicolas Tessin the Younger's own palace, plan, engraved exterior with forecourt, general view from Slottsbacken, court and interior details.

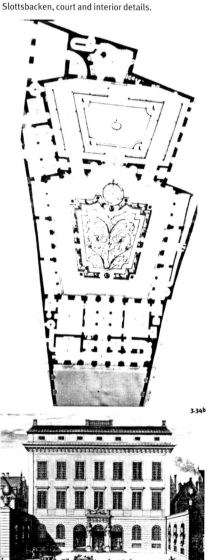

3.34b

Head of the family practice as Stockholm City Architect in succession to his father within two years of his return home, Nicolas Tessin the Younger was established in royal favour at Drottningholm and ultimately attained the highest positions at court. Schooled in Classical theory and post-Renaissance practice abroad, he rose to the occasion when commissioned to modernize the king's main seat, the Stockholm slott, even before it was destroyed by fire in 1697. Created Superintendant of the King's Works – like Jules Hardouin-Mansart – he was ennobled but long before that he had built himself the noblest of Stockholm's private palaces opposite the southern entrance to

3.34d

3.34c

3.34e

An element in a comprehensive – but unrealized – reformation of Slottsbacken (the open space to the south of the palace, east of the cathedral), Tessin's own exceptionally grand house opposite the royal ceremonial portal is eclectic. Knowledge of current developments in Vienna seems to inform the façade, though Bernard Foucquet, the sculptor of the portal, presumably knew more about Puget than Fischer (see pages 222 and 529ff): much in the interior decoration is Bérainesque. Beyond the miniature French formal courtyard garden (designed by the architect/patron), the scenae frons is a masterly Italianate exercise worthy of Scamozzi or even Torelli rather than a Roman High Baroque master – except for the Borrominesque false perspective of the upper gallery (see page 69).

3.34f

3.34g

the king's palace: less Mannerist in its façade detail, more Baroque than his father's essays of the type, it was to be a key part of a comprehensive urban scheme of Parisian scale.**3.34, 3.35**

Kungliga slottet

3.35a

As early as 1690 the younger Tessin obtained the commission to mask the medieval royal complex from Norrmalm – and the main part of the city to the north – with a massive Roman High Renaissance block taken to Berninesque extremes: a limited precedent for the approach was provided by the elder Tessin for the original Bank of Sweden (on Järntorget from 1675, superseded 1906) rather than Jean de la Vallée's more Mannerist exercise for Axel Oxenstierna (of 1653). After the fire of 1697 (which left the new north wing substantially intact), the aim was complete coherence in plan and elevation on a grandiose scale to each side of a huge quadrangle. The monumentality of the exercise emulated the French or, rather, the Roman antecedents of Bernini's third scheme for the Louvre: indeed the project was clearly motivated by determination to launch Sweden into the mainstream of European architectural developments after the emergence of France to predominance with completion of the Louvre's east front Colonnade.

3.35b

Apart from the Roman fenestration, variety is introduced in Tessin's ordonnance of each main front. In contrast to the Vignolan northern portal, the ceremonial southern entrance to the grand vestibule serving the chapel and the Hall of State (east and west in the south wing) is distinguished with Bernini's colossal Order of engaged columns but they rise from low pedestals as in Louis Le Vau's Louvre projects. The western entrance from the semi-circular forecourt to the main staircase lobby is centred on nine bays articulated with a caryatid Order surmounting rusticated Doric columns and surmounted by clustered Corinthian pilasters. A colossal Order of Corinthian pilasters rises through two storeys from rusticated basement arcades to define the nine central bays of the east front: low wings extending east

3.35d

medieval foundation, refortified by Gustav Vasa I, amplified with modern accommodation in Renaissance style by Johan III, north wing rebuilt from 1690, comprehensive rebuilding after fire damage in 1697 interrupted by war 1710–28, occupied by the royal family in 1754: (a) model of the medieval and early Renaissance complex with Tessin's new north range top left (c. 1695), (b) Tessin's project drawing for central bays of north wing (c. 1690), (c) plan of main floor of Tessin's building with (1) south entrance vestibule, (2) chapel, (3) Hall of State, (4) royal apartments, (5) gallery, (d, e) exterior from south-east and court front, (f) south entrance vestibule, (g, h) chapel, Tessin's project drawing and interior to the east as completed by Carl Hårleman, (i) western staircase, (j, k) great gallery and detail, (l, m) Carl Hårleman's project drawing for panelling in the French manner in the apartment of the crown prince and enfilade (c. 1750), (n) queen's bedroom (as completed by Hårleman, Carl Fredrik Adelcrantz and the latter's assistant Jean Eric Rehn c. 1770).

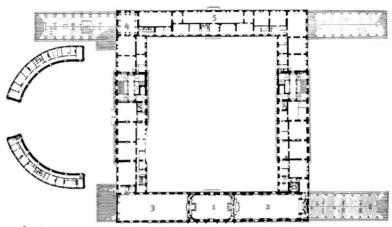

3.35c @ 1:2000

are based on cyclopean masonry in the manner promoted by Bernini (see pages 106, 248).

As at Versailles, the state apartments of the king and queen culminate in their parade bedrooms, balustraded in the French manner: they are sepa-

3.35e

3.35f

3.35h

3-35k

3-35j

3-35i

rated by a long gallery in which mirrors respond to the fenestration (on the main floor of the north wing). The latter and the grand western staircase are Tessin's principal legacies to the interior; the chapel and the Hall of State were completed to his designs but with added embellishment in the current French mode by his successors.

3-35h

3-35n

3-35l

3-35m

Work on the palace interiors extended over several generations, primarily those of Carl Hårleman (1700–53) and Karl Frederik Adelcrantz (1716–96) who were responsible for much of the refined Rococo detail in the decoration of the royal apartments. The apogee of Swedish Baroque, the negation of Dutch sobriety, the structure of the palace was completed in the main before the Crown was again impoverished by war: the Nordic War, from which Sweden emerged unvictorious and much reduced in power.

Late-Mannerist France had contributed a major ingredient to the personal eclecticism of Tessin the Elder. After the sophistication effected by his son in his determination to align Sweden with the most advanced developments abroad, Regency French was the dominant influence in the domestic field. Institutional and civic building were certainly not immune to French influence, especially as they grew grander with return to prosperity about mid century: the Stockholm Exchange (Börsen, from 1773) is the most prominent example. Otherwise, not surprisingly, major trading establishments like the Swedish East India Company continued to prefer reduced Dutch Classicism.**3.36**

›3.36 REPRESENTATIVE EXAMPLES OF 18TH-CENTURY COMMERCIAL BUILDING: (a) Gothenburg, East India Company Building (from 1748 to plans attributed to Carl Hårleman; now City Museum), canal frontage; (b) Stockholm, Exchange (Börsen, from 1773 by Erik Palmstedt after initial projects by Johan Eberhard Carlberg and Carl Johan Cronstedt).

›3.37 THE LUSTSCHLOSS OR MAISON DE PLAISANCE ON THE SWEDISH MANORIAL ESTATE: (a, b) Svartsjö slott (from 1734 as a hunting box for Queen Ulrika Eleonora), Hårleman's project drawing, east front central block; (c, d) Österbybruk (for Anna Johanna Grill c. 1750), lakeside and entrance fronts; (e) Brunneby (on the Göta Canal, from c. 1752).

Carl Hårleman had first-hand experience of modern French works like Bullet's Champs, which is clearly recalled at Svartsjö, but was of course equipped back home with the publications of Briseux and Blondel (see pages 312f). The typical plan incorporated some doubling of the enfilade in apartments flanking a projecting salon: other than the latter there is minimal projection in terms of shallow side pavillons. The canonical mansard is preferred to recollection of the *sateri* roof form. Österbybruk is based on a sketch by Hårleman whose precedent was widely followed, not least by Tessin's son Carl Gustav at Åkerö (Sodermanland, from c. 1750). The variations are numerous, often minor, sometimes grand (as at Tullgarn where Magnus Julius de la Gardie employed J.G. Destain from c. 1720). The procedure was promoted by Carl Wiinblad (1705–68) in *Drawings for Forty Houses of Stone* (1755).

3.36b

3·37a

3·37b

3·37c

3·37d

The protagonist of the modern French style was Carl Hårleman, who trained as a landscape designer before joining Tessin's studio and going on to four years of study in Paris (from 1721): he directed work at the palace after Tessin's demise in 1728, returned to Paris for a year from 1731 and succeeded the master at the head of the Swedish architectural profession a decade later. His most characteristic contribution was in the translation of the refined French type of *maison de plaisance* for the villas and manors of noble clients – most directly for the central block at Svartsjö (where he replaced Boy's slott from 1739). Brunneby is a less sophisticated provincial example. Alternatively, but certainly not discordantly, there was often a reduction of Dutch Classicism after the deduction of the colossal pilasters, as at Österbybruk (Uppland): based on a design by Hårleman, the latter is not uncharacteristically hybrid in its incorporation of a pavilion capped with a Baroque elaboration of the *sateri* rising from mansards.**3·37**

3·37e

**›3.38 DROTTNINGHOLM, CHINESE PAVIL-
ION,** from 1763: (a) Adelcrantz's project drawing, (b)
general view.

Carl Fredrik Adelcrantz attended the Design Academy (established by Carl Gustaf Tessin) while the
delayed work was proceeding at the royal palace in
the mid-1730s: he went on to study in Paris for four
years from 1739 and applied his experience of Rococo
developments thereafter as Hårleman's assistant and
successor at the royal palace. Conceived as an ephemeral fantasy, the Chinese Pavilion was given lasting
substance as a miniature *maison de plaisance* by Adelcranz from 1763: this was in line with the general flirtation with the exotic in the era of the *genre pittoresque*
but under the specific influence of the British architect
Sir William Chambers' *Designs of Chinese Buildings*
(1757).

3.38b

Sophisticated Swedish patrons were certainly not averse
to flirtation with the exotic in the manner widely popular
as western Europeans acquired greater familiarity with
the Far East. The resort of the greatest in the land seeking
complete retreat, Carl Fredrik Adelcrantz's Chinese Pavilion at Drottningholm is the most seductive example.**3.38**

BACK TO DENMARK

In Copenhagen at the beginning of the 18th century, architectural styles ranged from an extremely simple reduction of
Dutch Classicism, with limited Italianate relief, to an austere
interpretation of the Roman Baroque: Staldmestergården
(from 1703) is an example of the former, Frederiksberg
slot the latter (from 1709). The brief efflorescence of the
latter's Italian mode was due to Frederik IV (1699–1730),
who had visited Rome before his accession and returned to
Italy, including Venice, towards the end of the new century's
first decade. His instrument was Wilhelm Friederich von
Platen (1667–1732), an officer in the royal household who
had travelled in Holland, France and Italy to study art: he
was appointed building inspector in 1699, superintendent
three years later. Working to his direction were the master-
builders Christof Marselis (c. 1670–1731) and Johan Conrad

**›3.39 COPENHAGEN, EARLY PALACE BUILD-
INGS OF FREDERIK IV:** (a) Staldmestergården
(Slotsholmen, from 1703 for the staff of the royal stables, now the Ministry of Education), canal front with
Italianate portal; (b) Frederiksberg slot, engraved view
over formal garden (from 1699, enlarged from 1709 and
again from 1733).

The crown prince commissioned a villa on the Solbjerg, overlooking the capital from the south-west: the architect was probably Ernst Brandenburger. Completed with its formal garden in the French style (by 1703), that one-storey building was transformed by Brandenburger into a three-storey H-shaped Frederiksberg palace (from 1709). Inspiration may have come from Frascati – in elevated siting, if not in style.

The son of a Bavarian immigrant, Brandenburger first appears as a royal Danish master-builder on a mission to Stockholm (presumably educational). He returned to contribute to the rebuilding of Bergen (Norway) after its devastation by fire in 1702: before his assignment to the Frederiksberg project he worked at the Holmen church in Copenhagen.

Born in Poland (possibly of Dutch parentage), Christof Marselis first appears in Warsaw in the household of John III Sobieski: he went on to study in the Netherlands and Italy before entering service in Copenhagen (c. 1702) where the precise extent of his contribution to the royal building projects directed by von Platen is obscure. He left in 1716, ultimately for St Petersburg.

3.39a

Ernst (1666–1750): the former is primarily associated with the Staldmestergården, Ernst with Frederiksberg.**3.39**

Von Platen's successor Johan Cornelius Krieger (1683–1755), who first appears as a garden designer at Frederiksberg, was commissioned to sustain the Italianate for a new royal summer residence at Fredensborg (from

3.39b

1719).**3·40** That was elementary in its abstract articulation but Krieger embellished the town palace of Count Moltke with a colossal Order of pilasters and Borrominsque window frames. In transforming a 17th-century private house opposite the north entrance to the castle (from 1725) for the crown prince, on the other hand, Krieger followed the French fashion which was prevalent in Copenhagen, as in Sweden, by the third decade of the century. Meanwhile, the royal residence at Roskilde – and the several manor houses of similar style – ceded nothing in the austerity of elemental Classicism to works like the Staldmestergården in the capital.**3·41, 3·42**

›3.40 FREDENSBORG SLOT, from 1720: overview to entrance front.

With an end to the Northern War imminent, Frederik IV commissioned Krieger to oversee Brandenburger in the production of a hunting box: a Palladian variant on Marly, its central pavillon is crowned by a square dome derived from the French type but the interior (with stuccowork by Carlo Enrico Brenno) may be compared with work attributed to Peruzzi at Bologna. Construction was not completed until 1722: two years earlier a treaty between Sweden and Denmark was signed at the site which was henceforth called Fredensborg (Castle of Peace). Beyond the octagonal forecourt, the main corps de logis was altered by Lauritz de Thurah, who raised the upper storey to a new roof concealed behind a balustrade, added the four corner chimneys and extended wings for the chapel and orangery (from 1741). Nicolai Eigtved added the four corner pavilions with pyramidal roofs (from 1753). The forecourt buildings were raised by a storey and the aspect ot the palace opened between them by Caspar Frederik Harsdorff (from 1774).

›3.41 ROSKILDE, ROYAL PALACE, from 1733: court view.

The palace was built for Christian VI by Lauritz de Thura: on the site of the medieval bishop's palace, it is now again the bishop's residence.

3·41

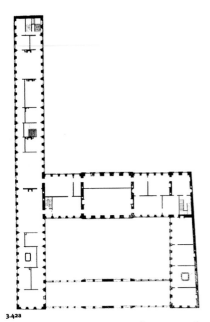

3.42a

3.42b

3.42c

›**3.42 COPENHAGEN, PRINCE'S HOUSE,** from 1725, now part of the National Museum: (a) plan, (b) engraved record of the court front of the principal corps de logis, (c) canal front.

The site of the Prince's House, facing the Frederiksholms Kanal opposite the royal palace, was developed for the Marburg merchant Wigand Michelbecker (from 1684): his house, occupied by Tsar Peter the Great in 1716, was acquired by the Crown in 1725 and thereafter rebuilt by Krieger as a residence for the future Christian VI and renovated by Nicolai Eigtved for the future Frederik V (from 1743). One of the earliest overtly French buildings in Copenhagen, it follows the Parisian norm – well represented by the works of Robert de Cotte and his contemporaries – of a court framed by three wings and closed by a lower, balustraded entrance screen (page 320). In the main corps de logis opposite the entrance, apartments with double enfilades flank a salon.

Also from the 1740s, the nearby Bachmann Palace was built in the elementary Franco-Dutch style by the Dutch architect Philip de Lange whose other prominent works include Marskalsgården (Marshal's Court, from 1729).

In town Frederik IV made do with more renovation of the old castle but embarked on rebuilding towards the end of his reign. As this proved unsound, Christian VI (1730–46) re-embarked on complete replacement (from 1732) to the designs of Elias David Häusser (1687–1745): his Christiansborg palace was destroyed by fire in 1794. After this, the royal family moved to the Amalienborg Slotsplads, the octagonal nucleus of the new district of Frederiksstad developed for Frederik V (1746–66) by his chief architect, Nicolai Eigtved (1701–54). Germans, not supplanted by the Dutch in the first half of the century, were supplemented by locals but Eigtved was trained in Dresden and a prominent role beside him was played by the Bavarian Laurids Lauridsen (Lauritz) de Thurah (1706–59) – whose Vor Frelsers spire we have already observed. However, Thurah disappeared while Eigtved was still in his prime and native talent emerged predominant: henceforth it was to be fostered by the Kongelige Dansk Kunstakademi established in the capital in 1754.**3·43**

Kongens slot

3.43b

On the Slotsholmen site of the medieval bishops' palace, the complex (devastated in conflict with the Hanseatic League in 1369) was sequestered by the Crown in 1417. It was developed as the principal royal seat after Copenhagen became the kingdom's capital in 1443.

The abortive scheme of comprehensive rebuilding for Frederik IV (from the late 1720s) incorporated the medieval tower as reformed in the 17th century. It was in the Roman Renaissance style as translated to Amsterdam by van Campen but astylar in emulation of contemporary developments in Stockholm. In contrast, J.C. Ernst's surviving Chancery is wholly Dutch Classical in style – its semi-circular pediment exceeding the model (see page 345).

3.43a

›3.43 COPENHAGEN, ROYAL RESIDENCES: (a–f) Christiansborg slot as extended by c. 1730 for Frederik IV with Chancery block left, and general view of the latter (from 1721), engraved record of the east and west (court) fronts projected for Christian VI, overview, Frederiksholm canal bridge and pavilions at the entrance to the semi-circular forecourt; (g, h) Amalienborg, overview from the west, general view towards Levetzau (or Christian VIII's) palace beyond the statue of Frederik V; (i) Eigtved's unrealized project for the Frederiks kirke.

The Christiansborg complex burned in 1794 and was replaced by a revised version which was also destroyed by fire in 1884. Part of the complex having been assigned to parliament by Frederik VI, rebuilding was designed primarily to accommodate the bicameral legislature (from 1907).

Each canted corner of the Amalienborg was developed with an identical palace for four officers of state.

3.43c

3.43d

3.43e

3.43f

Christian VI's scheme was influenced not by Bernini through Tessin's great project – or directly from Rome – but by the French academic Classical correction of the Italian schemes for completing the Louvre (which I attribute primarily to Perrault; see page 251). However, it has the enhanced elevation of the Stockholm palace's east front, with two full storeys above the rusticated basement and colossal Corinthian pilasters defining the central nine bays (as well as side pavilions). The window frames are Rococo in profile, rather than architectonic. The multi-storey tower has engaged columns in the rhythm of a triumphal arch to the main level but preserves the convoluted roof profile of its predecessor and is endebted to the Amsterdam ecclesiastical type. Nicolai Eigtved, who had supplanted Hausser by 1745, was responsible for the tower, the entrance pavilions (also articulated with an attached Order) and the approach bridge over the Frederiksholm canal: this, the pavilions and the curved forecourt wings survived the catastrophe of 1794. Developments thereafter are beyond our scope here.

The area between the old town and the citadel, acquired by Christian IV, had first been developed with the Amalienborg of Frederik III's Queen Sophie who lived there as dowager until her death in 1685: it succumbed to fire during a theatrical performance three years later. Rebuilding was delayed but in 1694 Christian V called on Tessin for the project. Too ambitious, this was

3-438

superseded by a modest villa early in the reign of Frederik V. That in turn succumbed to the project for the suburban Frederiksstad, initiated in 1748 by the king, to commemorate his dynasty's tercentenary: instigation is credited to Count Johann Hartwig Ernst von Bernstorff (1712–72, ambassador to Paris from 1744).

The first and most magnificent (inside), to the southwest, was built for the Lord High-Steward Count Adam Gottlob Moltke (died 1792) who was overseer to the whole project: finished in 1754, acquired by the Crown after the destruction of Christiansborg in 1794 – and henceforth known as Christian VII's palace – it was the royal residence until Christiansborg was rebuilt and

3-43h

was used to accommodate state guests from 1885. The north-west palace, built for the privy councillor Count Christian Frederik Levetzau (died 1760), was bought in 1794 for the king's half-brother Frederik: it passed to his son, later Christian VIII after whom it is named, and has mainly been used by crown princes. To the north-east, the palace of Count Joachim Brockdorff (died 1763) was acquired in 1765 by the Crown to house the Military (later Naval) Academy but was transformed as the residence of the future kings Frederik VII and VIII – after whom it is named. The south-western palace of privy councillor Severin Lovenskiold was acquired by the Crown in 1794 as the residence of the Prince Regent Frederik (Frederik VI, died 1839) and is called after Christian IX, its principal royal residence before it was renovated for Crown Princess (now Queen) Margrethe.

Eigtved's formal plan extended to an Amalienborg *place*: centred on a royal equestrian statue by the French sculptor Jacques-François-Joseph Saly (begun 1753), it emulated the Place Vendôme in Paris in its octagonal perimeter – if not in the style of its four identical palace buildings. Built to Eigtved's design, these are modest in the Dutch manner but, respecting the proprieties of French academic Classicism, their style is comparable to Franco-German exercises like those of Joseph Saint-Pierre in Beyreuth (see pages 717f). The domed Frederikskirke, to be built at the apex of the Frederiksstad's east–west axis from the harbour, is an extreme variation on the major Viennese or Dresden type (see pages 534ff): the sceptical king sent Eigtved's plans to Versailles for revision by Louis XV's principal architect, Ange-Jacques Gabriel but the project was first realized by the French architect Nicolas Henri-Jardin who succeeded Eigtved in 1754.

3.43i

2 BRITAIN

Patronage of architecture in Britain was disrupted by the Civil War of the mid-17th century and the resulting radical change to the state's constitution, yet there had already been radical reform of style well into the Stuart era which had continued to be characterized by the late-medieval inheritance – at least in the domestic field. A colouristic use of stone and brick overlaid with a conflation of decorative elements derived from the Classical Orders via Italian, French and Netherlandish pattern books ran at least to the coherence of symmetrical disposition: as with the French, whose masters were the prime mentors of the North as we know, the mode was first applied to redress late-medieval elevation; as with the Dutch and Flemish, whose influence was imported with trade and industry into East Anglia and Kent in particular, the convoluted treatment of gables recalls the elaboration of the sterncastles of ships (AIC5, pages 545f and see above, page 336).

Countering decorative excess in the van of similar purpose in France and the Netherlands, Inigo Jones had introduced sobriety to the early Stuart court under the influence of Palladio and Scamozzi (AIC5, pages 619f). Reference to Sebastiano Serlio prompted a secondary line in Jones's stylistic development towards abstraction in the 1630s, a decade more prosperous with peace than earlier in the Stuart era and therefore active in building for more strata of society. There was, of course, an opposite tendency – especially in funerary architecture.**3·44** However, abstraction complemented overt emulation of the antique under the guidance of Palladio and Daniele Barbaro's Vitruvius, if not also Serlio: the principal metropolitan examples range from the Tuscan temple recalled for S. Paul's, Covent Garden to the Corinthian peristyle applied to the west front of S. Paul's cathedral (AIC5, page 628).

3.44b

3.44a

›**3.44 THE PROTO-BAROQUE MONUMENT:** (a, b) to Sir Anthony and Lady Grace Mildmay (early 1620s, S. Leonard's, Apethorpe), general view and detail of dome.

3-45a   3-45b

3-45c

›3.45 SERLIO, JONES AND THE INCEPTION OF THE ASTYLAR TRADITION IN ENGLAND: (a) design for a small house (Serlio VII); (b) Lord Maltravers's House, London (Jones's project, 1638); (c) Southampton House, London (anon., 1640, demolished); (d) West Woodhay, Berkshire (anon., 1635); (e) Chevening House, Kent (anon., before 1630, late-17th-century record before extensive alteration).

Implanted by Jones on the model provided by Serlio, developed largely anonymously but in Jones's orbit, a characteristically unostentatious – even modest – domestic style had emerged in England before the hiatus attendant on civil war. A rectilinear block, the plan is usually doubled in the manner not uncommon in the Elizabethan and early Jacobean eras (as, for instance, at Burghley or even Hardwick, and Holland House, London; AIC5, pages 580ff). Brick is the usual material, slate or tile for the hipped roof rising steeply from a wooden dentillated cornice: the elevation is disciplined by a grid accommodating tall casement windows, Serlian in their proportions if not more elongated, and the central bays, at least, are surmounted by dormers. Grander works have semi-basements and external staircases.

3-45e

Restriction of articulating mouldings to the Orders of a portico or loggia and frames of voids was widely respected and the serliana was popular, but the example of Jones's lesser works, astylar villa projects in particular, impressed itself on his younger contemporaries and assistants: Nicholas Stone, who is credited with the north front of Kirby Hall (from c. 1638), *inter alia*; the anonymous author of Chevening House (before 1630), who elaborated an idiosyncratic type (AIC5, pages 632ff).**3·45**

3-45d

INTERREGNUM STYLE

The Baroque style of the Counter Reformation, contentious in the France of advancing royal absolutism, contrary in general to the ethos of the Protestant North, may be seen in England first to have appeared in ephemeral stage-set design – especially for the court masques mounted by Jones (AIC5, page 615). Apart from proto-Baroque funerary monuments, it first stood against sobriety – but also against lingering decorative Mannerism – in durable masonry at the entrance to S. Mary's church portal in Oxford (AIC5, page 630). Echoing Bernini at the very centre of Catholi-

3.46b

›3.46 HOUSING THE COMMONWEALTH GRAN-DEES AND THEIR IMMEDIATE SUCCESSORS WITH ASTYLAR RESTRAINT: (a, b) Coleshill House, Berkshire (c. 1658–62, destroyed by fire in 1952), ground-floor plan, entrance front (*VB*); (c, d) Thorpe Hall, Cambridgeshire (1653), ground-floor plan, entrance front; (e) Wisbech Castle, Cambridgeshire (c. 1658), entrance front; (f) Ashdown House, Oxfordshire (1664), aerial view; (g–j) Kingston Lacy, Dorset (1663, remodelled 1835–38), Sir Roger Pratt's project drawing, views from north-west and west, stairs; (k) Clarendon House, London (1664, demolished), late-17th-century engraved perspective.

cism, though derived from the same Biblical source as Raphael's Solomonic Order, that was naturally anathema to the Puritans of the Commonwealth interregnum – as was anything to do with theatre. And sobriety would reign in the new regime: most notably in the work of Sir Roger Pratt (1620–84), Peter Mills (c. 1598–1670), their anonymous contemporaries and followers who drew their inspiration from travel abroad and from Jones's astylar mode or its progeny.**3.46**

Naturally Pratt and his colleagues had Serlio, Palladio, Scamozzi and their English follower, Sir Henry Wotton. Sometime ambassador in Venice, Wotton had published his Vitruvian *The Elements of Architecture* in 1624, when its eclectic survey of the major theorists from Alberti to Philibert de l'Orme complemented the activities of Jones's circle: it was influential in its Restoration republication (1671). Also available was Roland Fréart de Chambray's *Parallèle de l'architecture antique avec la moderne* (1650) translated into English by John Evelyn with overtly reformative purpose (1664): as we have seen, it was a polemic promoting Palladian restraint against decorative excess associated with Flanders (see pages 176f). Limited travel and much treatise consultation would inform English architectural practice until well into the next century.

Sir Roger Pratt was a gentleman who moved to architecture while a Civil War refugee in Italy. He stayed in Rome and visited Vicenza: he listed Palladio and Scamozzi as the best authors of architecture along with Serlio (compare VII.xv, plate 33 with Coleshill). He liked Genoa from the sea but was critical of Rubens's compilation of the *Palazzi di Genoa* – presumably because of their sometimes bizarre Mannerism (AIC5, page 541). The latter was anathema to him, even in Serlian guise. Selective in general, he rejected the Palladian portico in particular as unsuitable for the English climate.

The patron of Coleshill was Sir Roger's cousin Sir George Pratt, who was a county councillor and magistrate. Contemporary records give Jones an advisory role: the scheme may be seen as translating select features from the urban works of his circle – Southampton House in particular – to the country. In the main, however, the eclectic building is credited to Sir Roger. As Summerson notes, the staircase hall recalls Longhena at S. Giorgio Maggiore, Venice (see pages 129f).

Pratt advanced the central three bays of Kingston Lacy for the privy councillor Sir Ralph Bankes: soon thereafter he introduced the pedimented frontispiece

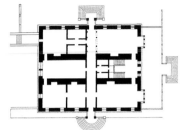

3.46c @ 1:1000

to Horseheath for Lord Arlington and for the highly influential London mansion of Lord Chancellor Edward Hyde, Earl of Clarendon (from 1664).

The patron of Thorpe was the chief justice, Oliver St John. His architect was Peter Mills, who began his career as a London bricklayer in Jones's circle. The work deployed the formula evolved by Jones: it has an enhanced piano nobile under an attic and dormers and a high basement, like one of the designs for the Prince's Lodging, Newmarket. The clarity and control of proportion is less evident in Mills's variation at Wisbech.

3.46e

3.46f

3.46d

The English country house about 1660

The great house of the type established by the few works of Sir Roger Pratt in and immediately after the Commonwealth interregnum were compact rectilinear blocks of two main storeys, astylar in articulation below galleried roofs with dormers and enormous chimneys. Pratt equated the floors in height after Jones in Whitehall. Peter Mills followed one of Jones's Newmarket projects for the grading of the floors (AIC5, pages 620, 631). According to availability and the local vernacular tradition, stone is sometimes preferred to brick (as at Thorpe) and the latter might be rendered between quoins (as at Coleshill where they were rusticated in a Continental manner foreign to Jones). Pratt's proportions tend to favour the horizontals over the verticals on oblong plans.

Pratt described the plan of Coleshill – varied at Thorpe and elsewhere – as 'double pile': two parallel ranges of rooms were divided by a continuous corridor (laterally by Pratt, longitudinally to the exclusion of axial development at Thorpe where the medieval screened hall survives to the left of the northern entrance). Unusually for the time, the sequence at Coleshill rose through twin flights in a galleried staircase hall to culminate in a 'dining room' on the first floor, above the 'great parlour'. The organization of apartments to either side of core reception rooms is ultimately Palladian, of course, but there are contemporary parallels to its augmentation in the work of Le Vau in France, which Pratt probably saw while in Paris as a refugee from the Civil War. However, the system has an

3.46h

3.46g

earlier English precedent in the loggia (i.e. southern) block of the Queen's House at Greenwich which incorporates Palladian apartments to either side of the link corridor from the spine of reception rooms and galleried hall – and with this Pratt was also personally familiar. Earlier still, as noted above, there were several less precisely ordered 'double pile' Elizabethan and Jacobean houses with apartments flanking the hall and its adjuncts (see, for example, AIC5, pages 582, 598 and 620).

3.46i

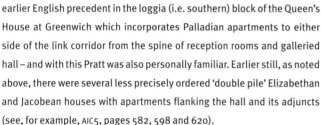

3.46k

Pratt's career was brief but his astylar approach long survived the Commonwealth, as the domestic exemplar followed even by such pillars of the restored monarchy as the privy councillor Sir Ralph Bankes and Lord Chancellor Edward Hyde, Earl of Clarendon. By then the Coleshill planar façade formula, expressing the tripartite division of the plan only in the spacing of the windows, had been relieved by the pedimented projection of the three central bays: repeated in the grander, U-shaped exercise for Clarendon in London, that was to be

3.46j

3-47a

standard for the rest of the century in England: Melton Constable, Norfolk, is a prominent early example (from 1664). Meanwhile, Hugh May (1621–84) had articulated the central projection of a 'double pile' plan with an Order of colossal pilasters at Eltham Lodge in Kent (1663). That followed the example set by Jacob van Campen in The Hague for Maurice of Nassau, and Arent van 's-Gravensande's Sebastiaansdoelen (see page 339): he expanded the formula in London for Lord Berkeley, at Cornbury for Clarendon, and probably advised the Earl of Sunderland at Althorp (all c. 1664–68). His intervention at Cassiobury for the Earl of Essex (from

3-47b

›3.47 HUGH MAY AND DUTCH CLASSI-CISM: (a) Eltham Lodge, Kent (1663), entrance front; (b) Althorp, Northamptonshire (1665), entrance front.

During the Civil War, Hugh May took refuge in the Netherlands where he certainly encountered the work of Jacob van Campen and his school. He derived his ordonnance from there but grafted it on to the English brick tradition descending from Jones and Pratt (and the vernacular, especially in south-east England): unlike the Danes and Swedes, the English rarely favoured it. U-shaped like Clarendon's London house – if not Berkeley's, which had quadrant colonnades across the inner corners of the court – Althorp is exceptional rather than typical in its Order of colossal pilasters.

1674) seems to have recalled Althorp: it is lost, as is much of his œuvre.

Later variants on the astylar norm include Belton House (1685–88), built by the master-mason William Stanton to the direction of William Winde, Stanstead Park, Uppark, and the stable block at Fitzwilliam's Milton by William Talman (1686–90), whom we shall later encounter in grander style. In addition there are many anonymous manor houses by local builders working for and with provincial gentry, especially in the south-east: representative are Squerrys Court and Bourne Park House (1681 and 1698 respectively).**3·47, 3·48**

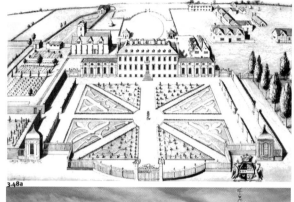

3.48a

The compact rectangular form of Thorpe or Coleshill was not considered appropriate for housing the great: as in the pre-revolutionary past, they needed a court headed by a range with state rooms and flanked by wings with subsidiary accommodation. This was shunned in the Commonwealth and, sagely, in its immediate aftermath: Clarendon soon led the way back in London (1664), the Earl of Sunderland at Althorp (1665) and the Earl of Arlington at Euston (1666).

3.48d

3.48b

3.48e

3.48c

›3.48 ASTYLAR RESTRAINT AND THE BRICK VERNACULAR AFTER THE RESTORATION: (a) Croome Court, Worcestershire (c. 1751–52), overview (pen and wash record; London, Society of Antiquaries); (b) Bell Hall, Yorkshire (1680), entrance front; (c) Uppark House, Sussex (c. 1690), view from the south-west; (d) Milton Hall, Cambridgeshire, stable block (c. 1690); (e) Bourne Park House, Kent (from 1698), entrance front; (f–h) Belton House, Lincolnshire (1685–88), plan, view from the south-west, hall.

The pedimented projection of central bays follows works like Raynham Hall, Norfolk, or Castle Ashby, Northamptonshire, which in turn follow various projects by Jones – though these may not have been fully realized (AIC5, pages 631f). Without the Palladian Order, they are common on entrance fronts but by no means universal even there: a simplified variant of Pratt's unrelieved astylar model, but even larger, was Lord Coventry's Croome Court.

Bourne exceeds Croome in length at thirteen bays: though only of four bays, the east front well illustrates the translation of Jones's unadorned astylar Maltravers model, with its grid of tall windows, into the local brick vernacular in the manner of West Woodhay. Three

3.48g

3.48h

generations earlier (1635), the garden front of the latter is of the canonical five bays: Bourne's contemporary, Stedcombe House in Devon (1697), conforms to that unpedimented formula on all four sides; even truer to type is Bell Hall.

Several works from the early Restoration years rely for relief in the main on recalling the traditional H-shaped plan: Belton House is a prominent example.

RESTORATION PALACES

Returned from exile in France towards the end of the Mazarine era, King Charles II (1660–85) would seek to emulate his French cousin Louis XIV. And French influence was not to be obviated even by the accession of the anti-French Dutch King William III, co-regnant with his cousin Queen Mary II (1689–94) – though Dutch sobriety was already pervasive in the domestic field. However, a century of British architecture was to be Palladian in the main: first in the post-Jonesian circle of Roger Pratt and Hugh May, if not in the latter's reference to the elementary Dutch translation which we have seen as hardly Palladian (see page 395); then, over half a century later, even more literally than Jones's reformatory permutation for the Banqueting House in Whitehall or the Queen's House in Greenwich (AIC5, pages 620f).

Of course there would be no clear break in stylistic fashions – no delineated watershed – but the overtly

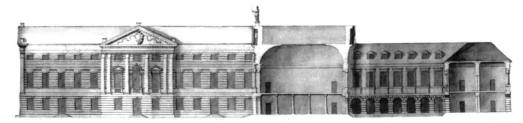

3.49a

Palladian future may be seen to have opened in 1715 with the eulogy of Jones in the anti-Baroque polemic of Colen Campbell's *Vitruvius Britannicus* (from 1715 – *VB*). Meanwhile there were two phases of flirtation with crossing largely French Mannerist and Baroque modes: the first, in which royal building was predominant, spans the reign of Charles II and extends beyond the 'Glorious Revolution' of 1688 into the era of his nephew and niece, William and Mary. Thereafter change was due to the shift in power from monarch to magnate in Parliament, but its manifestation in the concomitant shift in patronage was clear only after the turn of the new century and the completion of the great royal works begun in the first decade of Restoration by John Webb.

3.49b

›3.49 FORTUNES OF WEBB BEFORE AND AFTER THE CATASTROPHE: (a, b) Cobham Hall, Kent, project for reconstruction (1648), Peter Mill's revision for execution post-war (from 1661, as illustrated by Colen Campbell in *VB*); (c) The Vyne, Hampshire, entrance front with portico (1654); (d) Amesbury Abbey, Wiltshire (from early 1660), plan and engraved record (*VB*, 1661).

3.49c

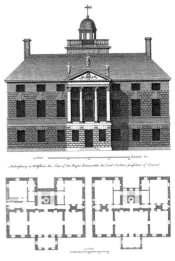

3.49d

John Webb was commissioned by the Duke of Richmond and Lennox to reface Elizabethan Cobham Hall in 1648 and responded with a portico of Jonesian grace alleviating the gravity of comprehensive rustication: the project succumbed to the catastrophic reverse of the Royalist cause in the Civil War of that time. A much reduced scheme was realised by Peter Mills (from 1661).

The Vyne was originally built for Henry VIII's Lord Chamberlain, William Sandys: Webb's additions were commissioned by the Parliamentary Speaker, Chaloner Chute. Amesbury was projected for the Duke of Somerset. Like the earlier work, the last incorporates the Palladian variant of the temple front with square pier-columns attached to spur walls but it rises from a basement: the rustication is derived from Giulio Romano via Palladian works like the Palazzo Thiene in Vicenza (AIC5, page 231).

Classicizing in the manner of Palladio's reconstruction of a Roman house, Lord Pembroke's Durham project went through three main stages before the fall of the monarchy obviated procedure: specifically, the final design suggests modification of Scamozzi's house of a Roman senator (*L'Idea dell' Architettura Universale*, 1615), with the central peristyle replaced by a great hall between the two courts. A far more elaborate version, inspired by the scenographic conception of the great imperial Roman bathing complexes but crossed with the de l'Orme-du Cerceau project for the Parisian Tuileries palace, was elaborated after Jones for Charles I's projected Whitehall Palace (AIC5, page 624).

(a) London's Champs Elysée bordering André Mollet's Saint James's Park (from the early 1660s in emulation of the 'Avenue des Tuileries' first planted beyond the western boundary of Paris for Queen Marie de' Medici from 1616; Jan Kip and Leonard Knyff, *Britannia Illustrata*, 1708 – BI); (b) the queen-mother's palace on the Strand site of Somerset House, the river range (c. 1661).

The Mollet dynasty of gardeners descends from Jacques at the Château d'Anet where the Italian formal tradition was being transplanted in the 1580s: apprenticed to his father there, Claude (c. 1564–1649) had become Premier Jardinier du Roi before 1600 (AIC5, pages 331, 377). Claude's *Théâtre des plans et jardinages*, begun in 1613 and continuously revised, was

Webb first appears as a collaborator with the master at Wilton House after a fire had gutted it in 1647: he is generally given the main credit for the Double Cube Room which remains one of the kingdom's most splendid domestic interiors (AIC5, page 636). He was imposing his own personality on the development of the reformed style before the fall of the monarchy in 1649, in particular emulating the ancients – with Scamozzi's guidance – in his design for Durham House in London, on revisions to the project for a vast royal palace at Whitehall and in the remodelling of Elizabethan Cobham Hall in Kent for the Duke of Richmond and Lennox. Not unemployed during the Commonwealth, most notably he added England's first freestanding temple-front portico to The Vyne in the new regime's median year: towards its end, he was varying the motif in the context of extensive Mannerist rustication at Amesbury.**3·49**

His attention first focused on his capital, the restored Charles II sought to expand his gardens as the theatre of court life in the manner of his cousin's Versailles.**3·50** He failed to borrow André Le Nôtre but was compensated with André Mollet: he had worked at Wilton and for the court before the revolution and his *Le Jardin de*

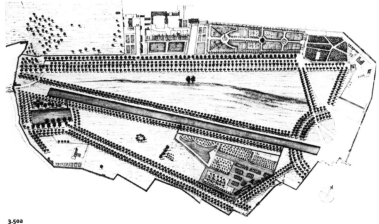

3.50a

3.50b

plaisir (1651) was the textbook of the French style which he adapted for the restored court of Saint James. At the outset of the reign, too, Webb was called on to revise his Whitehall scheme but realization required funds which were never to be found. Instead, he may have been commissioned to provide a new river frontage to the queen-mother's palace on the Strand (AIC5, page 627).

published by his son André in 1652, the year after he had published his own *Le Jardin de plaisir* (in Stockholm, where he worked for Queen Christina). André was in England from c. 1620 and crossed the Channel to serve Prince Frederick Henry of Orange from 1635.

The queen-mother's Strand palace project follows Jones's reduction of Bramante's palace façade formula for the Covent Garden 'piazzas' but with a Corinthian Order over the rusticated arcading (AIC4, page 857, AIC5, page 629). If Jones's legacy to the Greenwich site represents the High Renaissance in England at its purest, Webb's work is already Baroque at least in scale. However, the disposition of the colossal Order rising from the ground to form the frontispiece has nothing in common with Maderno at S. Pietro: instead, there is something of the Mannerism of Le Vau at the Château de Vincennes, of Bullant at the Château d'Écouen or Androuet du Cerceau at the Château de Charleval, even of Giulio Romano at the Mantuan Palazzo del Te, in the way the Order is applied directly to the rusticated wall in the centre of the court fronts (AIC5, pages 124, 355f and 368f).

3.51

At Greenwich the Elizabethan palace was to be replaced except for its adjunct, the Queen's House: the commission went to Webb.**3.51** He drew on his plans for Cobham in his design for the first phase of aggrandizement, the King Charles Block set perpendicular to the river to the west of the site: hardly Baroque in anything other than scale, the work invites comparison with the more mannered contemporary exercises of Le Vau. Building work was completed in 1669 but by then the king had moved on from Greenwich in preoccupation with the reconstruction of London after the Great Fire of 1666.

›**3.51 GREENWICH, PLACENTIA PALACE:** the King Charles Block (from 1661, *VB*).

The project for rebuilding the early Tudor palace was for a U-shaped complex with a domed central corps de logis masking the view of the Queen's House from the river. However, the king lacked the financial resources for its realization and its Continental grandeur ill accorded with the ethos of the early Restoration era: even Webb's western wing was not completed. Its pendant was added only under Queen Anne (1702–14), as its name asserts. As we shall see, the lateral block projected to connect these two wings at the head of a court was suppressed in favour of twin longitudinal ranges extended to frame – rather than obscure – the Queen's House.

3.52b

3.52c

>**3.52 WINDSOR, HUGH MAY'S BAROQUE REFURBISHMENT,** from 1674 to 1684: (a) plan of royal apartments with S. George's Hall (1), chapel (2), the King's Staircase (3), King's Guardroom (4), King's Presence and Audience Chambers (5, 6), Withdrawing Room (7), Dining Room (8), Bedroom, Dressing Room and Closet (9, 10, 11), the Queen's Staircase (12), Queen's Guardroom (13), Queen's Presence and Audience Chambers (14, 15), Ballroom (16), Queen's Dressing Room and Bedroom (17, 18), (b, c) S. George's Hall and Queen's Presence Chamber (after W.H. Pyne, *History of the Royal Residences*, 1819; except for the King's Dining Chamber and the Queen's Presence and Audience Chambers, all was lost to redecoration from 1826).

May's team of decorators included the Italian illusionist painter Antonio Verrio (c. 1636–1707) and the brilliant sculptor Grinling Gibbons (1648–1721). Verrio, who had migrated from Lecce to Toulouse in 1665 and on to Paris by 1670, was invited to England by the ambassador Ralph Montague in 1672: work for the Earl of Arlington (at Euston Hall) and the Duke of Lauderdale (at Ham House) led to royal patronage. Born in Holland to English parents, Gibbons was discovered by the diarist John Evelyn (in 1670) translating Dutch composite flower painting into timber – a bizarre, but spectacularly successful, endeavour comparable to the later English determination to translate the paint of Claude and Poussin into water, grass, trees and temples. Evelyn introduced his protégé to May.

3.52a @ 1:1000

Webb was not to be promoted to the head of his profession as Surveyor of the King's Works. That distinction was accorded instead first to the poet John Denham, unqualified except in loyalty to the king in exile, then to the polymath Christopher Wren (1632–1723) in 1669. Hugh May had been appointed Comptroller of Works in 1668: passed over for Wren, he was compensated with the Surveyorship of Windsor Castle in 1673. There, inside crenellated walls in stark contrast to the Dutch Classicism of his lodge at Eltham, he and his team evoked a Baroque palace of rich relief, illusionist painting and dramatic lighting for the first time in England.**3.52** Meanwhile the king had also called for the modernization of the 16th-century palace of Holyroodhouse in Edinburgh.**3.53**

3.53a

3.53c

3.53b

Palatial building in post-Restoration Scotland

The northern kingdom had not seen the flourishing of palace and mansion building after the court settled in London on the accession of James VI to the English throne in 1603. The restored monarchy sought to redress the situation and, at least, establish itself appropriately in its Scottish capital. The royal master-mason in Scotland, John Mylne, led the way both for the court and for those magnates with the resources – financial and psychological – to undertake new buildings or, more usually, renovations and additions to the still-prestigious towers of old ones: Panmure House (Angus, 1666)

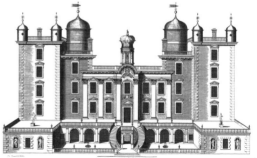

3.53d

3.53f

3.53e

3.53g

›3.53 SIR WILLIAM BRUCE, HIS CONTEMPO-RARIES AND THE GREAT HOUSE IN CAROLINE SCOTLAND: (a–c) Edinburgh, Holyroodhouse (modernization of 16th-century complex, Mylne and Bruce, from 1671), entrance, court front and morning drawing room (Royal Collection Trust / © Her Majesty Queen Elizabeth II 2013); (d) Drumlanrig Castle (Dumfrieshire, Smith, from 1675; *VB*); (e) Kinross House (Kinross, Bruce, from 1685), entrance front; (f) Newhailes (Midlothian, Smith, c. 1690), project drawing; (g) Hopetoun House (West Lothian, Bruce, from 1698), garden front.

is an example of the former, Leslie House (Fife, 1667) of the latter. Mylne's fellow master-builder, James Smith, was similarly employed: inserting a range articulated with colossal pilasters between the towers of Drumlanrig (Dumfries, 1675), for example, and working in the Jonesian-Mills mode at Newhailes (c. 1690). His grandest work, lost Hamilton Palace (1695), crossed the Mills style with that of Hugh May at Althorpe but with Palladian attached colossal columns rather than pilasters.

The commission to modernize the palace associated with the royal abbey of Holyrood was let to John Mylne in 1663: after his death four years later the project was revised by his nephew Robert. That was to the direction of Sir William Bruce who was rewarded for his loyalty to the Stuart cause with appointment as Surveyor and Master of the King's Works in Scotland on the strength of some familiarity with current developments in English architecture. The revisions were submitted to the king in 1671 and Mylne began work on the foundations of a new tower matching the main block of the early 16th-century palace: an entrance screen between them closes a forecourt framed by three-storey ranges articulated with a superimposed Order. The interiors are closely related in style to their London contemporaries.

Elsewhere Bruce worked in the astylar Jonesian mode of Pratt or Mills: Moncreiffe House (1679) is a lost example, Hopetoun House is a major (if partly rebuilt) survivor. For himself at Kinross, Bruce was hardly less austere but was innovative in adding colossal pilasters only to the corners of the projecting side blocks. France had traditionally inspired Scotland: these pilasters may have been suggested by the side pavillons of Bernini's Louvre projects.

3.54a

3.54c

3.54b

ADVENT OF WREN

Dr Christopher Wren had emerged from academe as a consultant on repairs to S. Paul's cathedral, London, with Pratt and May (1663). He was recommended by his mastery of geometry in his pursuit of astronomy, in particular, but certainly not least in virtue of his acquaintance in 1665 with the court of Louis XIV as regulated by Colbert. As we have seen, Bernini and François Mansart were the leading contenders for the commission to complete the Louvre, but Claude Perrault (a fellow polymath) was in waiting, and the king's attention had yet finally to focus on Versailles. Ultimately comparable in importance to the most prominent practitioners of his own generation, Jules Hardouin-Mansart in France and Johann Bernard Fischer von Erlach in Austria, Wren promoted a synthesis between the Classical and the Baroque, between mathematical order and visual excitement, between sense and sensibility. Like Antoine Desgodetz in France he

›3.54 WREN'S UNIVERSITY WORKS: (a–c) Oxford, Sheldonian Theatre (from 1664), entrance front (engraved by David Loggan, *Oxonia Illustrata*, 1675), general view from the north-west and interior; (d–g) Cambridge, Pembroke College Chapel (from 1663), street front, and Trinity College Library (1676), studio drawing of half-outer elevation, half-section, court front, interior; (h) Oxford, Christ Church College (1681), entrance with Tom Tower.

Wren came from a prominent ecclesiastical family: his father was Dean of Windsor, his uncle successively Bishop of Norwich and of Ely before the revolution. He was schooled at Winchester and graduated from Wadham College, Oxford, in 1651. By 1660 he was Gresham Professor of Astronomy based in London and returned to Oxford that year as Savilian Professor of the same science – and an inventor of instruments. In 1665 he visited Paris, saw all the surrounding post-Renaissance châteaux and met major talents including Bernini: he probably passed through the Netherlands but is not known to have left England again. Returning with the Val-de-Grâce, the Minimes and the Collège des Quatre-

Nations in mind, he proposed a radical renovation of S. Paul's cathedral with a dome over the crossing.

The Oxford theatre was commissioned at the behest of Archbishop Sheldon to accommodate University ceremonies. The auditorium is a reduced version of Palladio's Teatro Olimpico cavea, itself derived from the antique Theatre de Marcellus which Wren would also have known from Serlio (III.iv. fol. 21ff): the complex triangulated timber roof structure (possibly derived from medieval church practice) was masked by a representation of the sky across which a simulated velarium might be drawn in the antique manner. The façade is a variant on the superimposed temple-front motifs deployed by Palladio to cope with the composite form of the ecclesiastical basilica (AIC5, pages 238f): the arcades of the main storey reappear rusticated around the rest of the exterior below the continuation of the panelled attic ordonnance.

Attributed to Wren, Pembroke College Chapel was the bequest of his episcopal uncle. Departing from the Oxbridge Gothic tradition, the street front recalls Serlio's restoration of a temple at Tivoli (III.iv. fol. 15), even to the niches and panelling. The court front of Trinity's library recalls the superimposed Orders articulating the cortile loggias of Palladio's Convent of the Carità (now the Accademia) in Venice: the substitution of a balustrade for the original attic enhances the gravitas;

was interested in the reconstruction of ancient buildings (recorded in *Parentalia*, published 1750) but, ultimately, his purpose was to reveal their variety and widen the scope of inspiration back beyond the age of Vitruvius: he might well have prompted the same in Fischer (who probably visited him in London in 1704). Like the Ancients in the French Académie royale d'architecture, moreover, he disclaimed imagination unbridled by respect for the achievements of the Classical masters: with Perrault and the Moderns, however, he departed from the idea that the Ancients had distilled an absolute standard of beauty (see page 248).

As Wren matured as a scholar of architectural history, a critic of contemporary achievement and an extensive practitioner fired by an idiosyncratic imagination, he saw diminished relevance in Classicizing – in the sense of reproducing, even emulating, antique form. He began there, however: at Oxford in his Sheldonian Theatre (1664), at Cambridge in the fronts of his Pembroke College Chapel (1663) and Trinity College Library (1676). These come closest to various permutations of the ideal as represented by Serlio or Palladio (see also AIC5, pages 155, 229, 236).**3·54a–g** However, these Renaissance masters would not be the guide to the apogee of his career. Emulation of the masters – Ancient and Modern – implied eclecticism and, contrary to the strictures of the strictest academics, Wren did not preclude reference even to Borromini – or to English Perpendicular Gothic.**3·54h**

3.54d

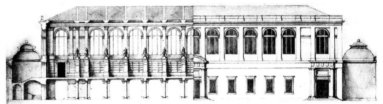

3.54e

3.54f

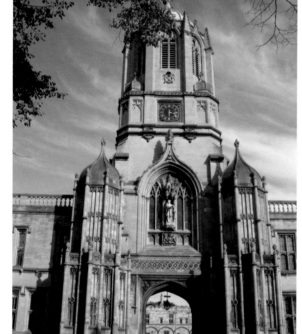

3.54h

3.54g

the outer front is abstract in its panelled articulation (AIC5, page 229).

Thomas Wolsey's college foundation of 1525 (as Cardinal College, refounded 1546 by Henry VIII as Christ Church) had been left incomplete above the base level of the gate. Wren, a graduate of the college, informs us of his resolve that the completion should 'be Gothick to agree with the Founder's work ... Yet I have not continued so busy ...'. The faceting of the piers flanking the exterior of the arch prompted an octagonal form for the new tower with a minor register of the octagonal turrets in the corners: octagonal ogee domes, not uncommon in Wolsey's day, cap all these minor and major elements. The tower itself has a Classical gravitas to its symmetry in contrast to the filigree work below, despite the ogee caps to the clerestory windows and the crocketed finials to the buttresses.

1 CITY: (a, b) the area devastated by the fire and the proposed new order; (c) Monument to the end of the Great Fire (1671, conceived to support a statue of Charles II); (d) view from Blackfriars on Lord Mayor's Day (Canaletto, before 1752; Prague, Lobkowicz Collection).

Wren submitted his plan for reconstruction on 11 September 1666, within a week of the end to conflagration: others, including John Evelyn, followed two days later when the king announced rebuilding in masonry to a comprehensive new plan. This was to be under the direction of six commissioners, three appointed by the City authorities, three by the Crown – the latter were Christopher Wren, Sir Roger Pratt and Hugh May. They failed to produce a scheme for the redistribution of property rights to match any new order but were instrumental in defining codes to be enshrined in the Parliamentary Act for Rebuilding the City of London (1667), regulating street widths and three classes of brick buildings – though these admitted varying degrees of decorative detail. Private premises apart,

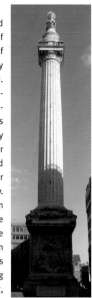

3.55.1c

3.55.1a

3.55.1b

TO LONDON

The burning of London early in September 1666 cleared the way for the progress of Wren's brilliant career. With scant delay he produced a formal masterplan for the reconstruction of the devastated area which would have obliterated the insanitary warren of narrow medieval streets. The context dictated a network of avenues linking new squares and reconstructed public buildings, with two main arteries converging at the site of the destroyed S. Paul's cathedral: inspiration was Sistine Roman rather than contemporary Parisian. However, it proved impossible in time to cope with the determination of the inhabitants to cede nothing of any former advantage in street frontage or for the authorities to sequester the situation: the old organic pattern reasserted itself.**3.55.1**

It was in replacing London's medieval ecclesiastical heritage, the cathedral and many of the parish churches, that Wren realized his opportunity. So great was the scope of the project that he would have to rely on assistance in execution and even detailed design work: that was to be provided mainly by his pupil and 'clerk' Nicholas Hawksmoor (1661–1736) who graduated to an active role in the master's office early in the 1680s.

Wren enjoyed the full confidence of the king but had to contend with an extremely conservative authority in response to the greatest ecclesiastical commission of the age, projecting the new cathedral. His approach was essentially rational, purely Classical in its predilection for the order of centralized geometry and the ordered articulation of structural forces in the context of enclosing fabric. The Church authorities were pragmatic – when not governed by emotional attachment to the Gothic past. As with the replacement of the parish churches, the story is one of compromise with that past, of the empirical acceptance of its constraint rather than of unfettered intellect.**3.55.2, 3**

3.55.1d

The London cathedral

Christopher Wren's first S. Paul's project was for comprehensive renovation incorporating a domed crossing: that was approved immediately before the fire. Incongruous in the medieval context, the idea governed his procedure throughout his evolution of the design of a wholly new building after the fire – actually after limited rebuilding was found to be impractical (1668). The first phase of the design process, producing centralized and cruciform alternatives, culminated in the surviving 'Great Model' which owed nothing to the English ecclesiastical tradition, let alone to the building it was designed to replace (1673). A sophisticated exercise in centralized planning, it consisted of a Greek cross, hemicyclical between the arms, with a great domed rotunda carried on eight piers in the centre and a smaller rotunda extending the principal axis towards the entrance portico: the latter reiterates Inigo Jones's work to the same purpose and the articulating Corinthian Order of pilasters derives from it; the transept façades recall the antique fastigium motif of apotheosis (AIC1, pages 601f). The great domed space may have been inspired by Mansart's Bourbon chapel: the alignment of self-contained spaces recalls Antonio da Sangallo's S. Pietro (AIC5, page 143, and above, page 243). Despite the subtle gesture towards the Latin cross – and the support of the king – this was rejected by the Church authorities as foreign to the Anglican conception of the nave as both processional and congregational space oriented to the high altar – and as impossible to realize in distinct stages of construction.

In fact the cathedral's arch-conservative dean and chapter wanted their old basilican plan and Wren had no option but to return to his initial Latin-

commercial or domestic, predictably the first new or restored buildings ready for occupation were the Guildhall and several livery companies. They were closely followed by the Customs House and Royal Exchange (1669 and 1671). The former, U-shaped, was articulated in van Campen's Dutch Classical mode by an unidentified architect. The new Exchange reproduced its predecessor's arcaded court (AIC5, page 603) beyond a new front range with a portal in the form of a triumphal arch supporting a three-tiered tower: it was commissioned from the City carpenter and Commission member Edward Jerman (died 1689) but realized with scant sophistication by the City mason Thomas Cartwright.

3.55.2d

2 S. PAUL'S CATHEDRAL, 1673–1711: (a–l) Great Model plan, exterior and interior, Warrant Scheme half plan, section and west elevation, executed section and half plan, section through nave, detail of crossing, views from south-east and west, interior from nave to sanctuary, spiral stair in south-west tower.

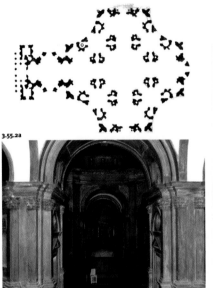

3.55.2a

3.55.2b

3.55.2c

3.55.2e

cross alternative aproach. The approved scheme was in essence a medieval body in uncomfortable Classical dress derived from Jones's portico: consciously bizarre, no doubt, it received the royal warrant (after which it is known) in May 1675. Work began immediately: as it proceeded Wren changed the design, especially of the crossing and its superstructure. Without, he replaced the peculiar domical spire with a double dome recalling the one developed by Lemercier after Mansart at the Val-de-Grâce (see pages 216f). Within, he reinforced the piers and narrowed the aisles so that the canted bays through which they issued into the crossing, below blind clerestory tribunes, were narrower than the four great orthogonal arches but framed to match: even so, resolution to the problem of imposing Classical coherence on the disparate elements of the basilican form proved elusive. Geometrical ingenuity notwithstanding, the aisles intrude awkwardly into the circumference of the great octagonal domed space. That appears central, however, because biaxial symmetry is effected in the enlargement of the westernmost nave bay and its extension laterally as a narthex, leaving three regular bays to match those of the choir.

The final scheme (from c. 1683) elevates the dome over a much higher drum than heretofore and provides it with adequate visual support throughout the length and breadth of the crossing by adopting a full second storey instead of the former attic. The upper walls are freestanding, however: they mask fly-

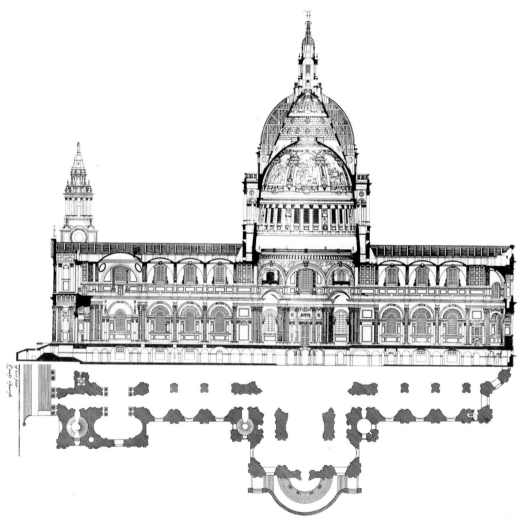

ing buttresses and act as counterweights. The enforced eclectic approach to planning naturally informed the exterior but it was complemented by a different order of willed eclecticism. After Bramante and Antonio da Sangallo at S. Pietro, but not Michelangelo, Wren articulated the walls with superimposed pilaster Orders in response to the composite nature of the basilican section; Jones at the Banqueting House is also recalled. Following the Mannerist precedent set by Raphael in the Chigi Chapel of S. Maria del Popolo (AIC5, page 13), however, he slips the frieze down into the zone of the capitals to amalgamate – rather than differentiate – parts and whole. The superim-

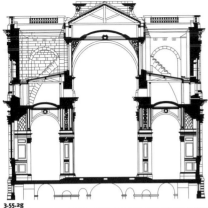

3-55.2g

posed Orders continue around both ends of the building, progressing from pilasters to columns on the west front. As in Hardouin-Mansart's Invalides, then rising in Paris, the lower Order extends beyond the temple-front motif of the upper one to engage the main mass (see pages 280f). In S. Paul's case this does express the disparate scale of nave and aisles, though the volumetric entity of the former would better have been expressed by a single large Order between towers terminating the aisles. The semi-circular porticoes of the transepts recall Pietro da Cortona at S. Maria della Pace in Rome (see page 79). Sculptural embellishment outside and in, in stone or timber, was largely due to Grinling Gibbons and his assistants (1690s). Construction was finished by the century's end, except for the dome.

3.55.2i

The evolution of the definitive dome design, achieving the great height required for monumental impact, began (c. 1685) with reference to Hardouin-Mansart's Invalides variant on his uncle's Bourbon chapel scheme (see, page 243). The internal organization survived refinement of the exterior. Again optical exigency countered physical reality: the dome is doubled with vast disparity between its internal and external shells (of masonry and timber respectively), the latter surmounted by a huge stone lantern raised on an extraordinary brick cone – the exercise is worthy of

3.55.2l

3.55.2l

3.55.2k

Nicholas Hawksmoor, who had a considerable role in realizing the post-fire projects, had entered Wren's service as his domestic clerk c. 1682 having previously served a Yorkshire justice in that capacity. He was already supervising construction work for Wren at Chelsea and Winchester, as we shall note below.

the Mansarts in its internal vertical scenography. Outside, it amplifies the pure geometry of Bramante's Tempietto, as Michelangelo had done in his version of S. Pietro's dome: but it retains piers in every fourth bay to provide bracing in Hardouin-Mansart's manner. In wilful contrast, the towers (formed finally in the early years of the new century) follow the engraved records of the Roman Baroque tradition of Borromini – or Rainaldi – with curve and counter-curve resoundingly orchestrated as at S. Agnese in Piazza Navona.

Closing the basilican section with a twin-towered front was, of course, standard medieval practice and Wren may be seen to have translated the spires of old S. Paul's cathedral into the modern idiom. He was to be at his most ingenious, even quirky, in his many variations on the same theme devised in rebuilding the London City churches after the fire on their widely varied original sites.**3·55**

The City churches

In his planning, Wren responded to the diversity of awkward sites with characteristic ingenuity. The existing arrangement was often inescapable. Classicizing was the norm in numerous variations on a limited number of themes in both plan and elevation. The latter may be antique or modern: temple-front or triumphal-arch distinguish east ends – the former on the exterior of S. Lawrence Jewry, the latter inside S. Mary-le-Bow; the west portal there follows François Mansart at the Hotel de Nevers (see page 220). Classical centralized forms, antique or Renaissance, could often be devised within more-or-less square medieval shells like S. Antolin where the nave is octagonal, or S. Mary-at-Hill, where a domed Greek cross emerged: the most splendid example is S. Stephen, Walbrook, a regular rectangular volume encapsulating colonnades defining a domed octagon in a square

3 CHURCHES: (a–c) S. Stephen, Walbrook, plan, interior (repaired post war after relatively minor damage even to the simulated masonry of the plaster and timber dome), tower; (d–g) S. Mary-le-Bow, plan, tower section and elevation (*VB*), interior (reconstituted after serious war damage); (h, i) S. Antholin, plan and 19th-century record of interior; (j, k) S. Lawrence Jewry, plan, interior (restored after extensive war damage); (l) S. Clement Danes, plan; (m, n) S. James, Piccadilly, plan, interior (repaired post war); (o–q) S. Bride, plan, pre-War interior (gutted in 1940, reconstructed in the 1950s without original galleries), tower; (r) S. Vedast, tower; (s) S. Dunstan in the East, tower; (t, u) S. Magnus the Martyr, tower, interior (north windows reduced to occuli, clerestory opened from c. 1782, repaired from 1951 after inextensive war damage).

Eighty-seven parish churches were destroyed. After the amalgamation of parishes by Act of Parliament (1670), there were fifty-one to be provisioned to the orders of a commission composed of the archbishop of Canterbury, the bishop of London and the Lord Mayor. Funds were to be raised from a tax on coal. Surveyor-General by now, Wren may have lost the chance to rebuild the City on rational lines but was best placed to rebuild the churches when approached by the parish authorities. Thirty were under construction by 1677 and the campaign was virtually over a decade later: with no relevant experience and limited post-medieval English precedent, Wren was responsible for the design but his huge commitment to the cathedral project forced

3.55b

3.55c

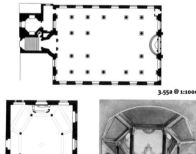

3.55a @ 1:1000

3.55h @ 1:1000

3.55i

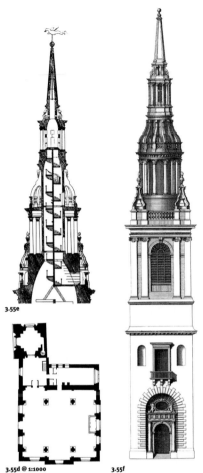

3.55e

3.55g

and the arms of a Latin cross extended towards the entrance. Not congregational, the antique temple norm was of little relevance but the Vitruvian basilican form was of primary importance in its several variations: it ran to a reduction of the Roman Basilica of Maxentius for S. Mary-le-Bow. More challenging was the ordering of the inheritance of a hall nave with just one side aisle, at S. Lawrence Jewry for example.

3.55d @ 1:1000   3.55f

delegation of the detailing and execution of the parochial buildings to a team of City surveyors led by the geometrician Robert Hooke (1635–1703). Most of the City churches were badly damaged by fire bombs in 1940 and rebuilt or restored from c. 1950, ostensibly to Wren's plans.

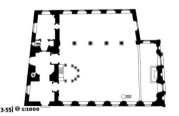

3.55j @ 1:1000

3.55k

Of the more conventional five-bay variants, S. James, Piccadilly, is important for the augmentation of the congregational space with galleries in the manner common on the Protestant Continent: they are carried on Doric piers above which Corinthian columns carry lateral tunnel vaults. At S. Bride, Fleet Street, the galleries were cut into the shafts of paired columns. For S. Magnus the Martyr galleries were omitted: the colonnades have Dutch precedents but a striking parallel in Perrault's Vitruvian basilican scheme of the late 1670s for S.-Geneviève (see pages 337, 263).

More apparent even than in the planning, certainly more memorable than most of the external ordonnance of perimeter walls, is the ingenuity with which Wren reinterpreted the Gothic spired tower in Classical terms: Netherlanders offered him guidance here, so too did the imaginative interpreters of Vitruvian form (such as Jean Martin in his French edition, 1547, or Alberti); there were the High Renaissance schemes for S. Pietro's basilica too and even Borromini (see above, pages 90f, AIC4, pages 738, 836ff, AIC5, pages 145, 749f). Generally, he combined Classical elements varied in their geometry to re-evoke sturdiness with grace: his eclectic accumulation of motifs ranges from the tetrapylon to the tholos,

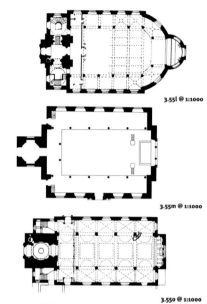

3.55l @ 1:1000

3.55m @ 1:1000

3.55o @ 1:1000

3.55n

3.55p

3.55r

3.55s

to the circular or octagonal tempietto, to the obelisk. Into the mix of the most complex example, that of S. Mary-le-Bow, is inserted a ring of flying buttresses: these recall the 'bows' which had supported the Gothic spire there and which were retained in restoration of several surviving Gothic towers (at S. Dunstan-in-the-East, for example). One or more octagonal cupolas is most usual, perhaps, as at S. Magnus the Martyr (after S. Carolus Borromeus, Antwerp) or S. Bride (with reference to Amsterdam); and there are several examples of superimposed tetrapylons, including S. Stephen, Walbrook, and S. James, Garlickhythe. Most unusual is S. Vedast's variation on the latter theme, encapsulating a cylinder in buttresses and the reversal of its curvature in the zone below: the juxtaposition of concave and convex curvature has antique precedents but Wren was probably inspired to it by Borromini, if not Montanus (see above, page 68, and AIC1, pages 646ff). Borrominian exuberance is exceptional but asserts that Wren's will to ordered articulation was not inimical to his generation of dynamic form – assuming that his was the prime responsibility for exercises of a type which would emerge as native to Hawksmoor who seems to have assumed more design responsibility in the early 1690s.

3.55q

3.55t

3.55u

Inevitably, perhaps, several of Wren's London churches acknowledge the Dutch achievement of an austere Protestant style of brickwork enriched mainly in the elevation of the single tower, usually over an entrance portico (AIC5, pages 549f): S. James's, Piccadilly is among the more prominent examples.**3·55y‑z** That Dutch mode of brick walls unrelieved even by window frames but centred on a portico is taken beyond its essential modesty to the extreme of Baroque scale for the Chelsea Hospital commissioned by Charles II for his army pensioners (from 1682): resources for royal works had been consumed by the rebuilding of London over the previous decade. The contrast with Wren's later work on the complex at Greenwich, designated as a naval hospital by William and Mary, could hardly be greater – as we shall see (pages 438ff).**3·56**

3.56c

›3.56 CHELSEA, ROYAL HOSPITAL, from 1682: (a) model, (b) court fronts, (c) chapel interior.

The project, promoted by the Paymaster-General of the Army, Sir Stephen Fox, was inspired by the king's cousin's foundation of the Hôpital des Invalides in Paris (1670, see above, page 260). John Evelyn notes the will to monastic austerity. Open to the river, the U-shaped plan of Webb's Greenwich is recalled; the wards are in the wings, the main block is divided between refectory hall and chapel to either side of the lantern-lit octagonal vestibule and between pavilions for the administration. Webb's Doric portico motif of The Vyne is also recalled (but without the square corner columns): the

3.56a

3.56b

Colossal Doric pilaster frontispieces applied to the side wings may derive from Le Vau at the Château de Vincennes, or the fantasies of Antoine Le Pautre (see above, pages 222ff). They were not to be overlooked by Wren's successors – nor was the lantern. Supervised by Hawksmoor, the work was finished in 1692.

Also supervised by Hawksmoor, construction of a similarly U-shaped complex was under way at the same time at Winchester: to be a royal palace, it was to have had a square domed pavillon in the centre of the central corps de logis in the French manner – and, indeed, like Webb's aborted plan for Greenwich. Never to be completed after the death of its royal patron in 1685, it was developed as a barracks.

›**3.57 RAGLEY HALL, WARWICKSHIRE,** from 1676: (a, b) plan and overview (*BI*).

The patron was Lord Conway. The corner pavilions may be Jacobean survivals and the plan crossed longitudinally by the hall has Elizabethan antecedents: nevertheless it was to have important descendants in the Palladian phase of developments in the second decade of the next century. The residual H-shaped plan was still current in London mansions such as those built for Sir John Denham and Lord Clarendon (before 1665) and in country houses like Belton House (as we have seen, page 396). In contrast to the Ragley plan, with minor enfilades crossing the major longitudinal axis of reception space, Hurlbutt had earlier (c. 1669) inserted an enfilade of four state rooms in Warwick Castle for Lord Brook.

THE GREAT CAROLINE HOUSE

The extended continuation of work on S. Paul's cathedral and a new campaign at Greenwich overran into the second phase of post-Restoration developments – when the magnates began to eclipse the Crown as patrons of great houses. Meanwhile – despite much optimistic attribution – Wren's private practice was necessarily limited by the huge responsibility of his commitment to the works of church and state: astylar in the mode of Kingston Lacy, but taller, Winslow Hall, Buckinghamshire (1700) is generally accepted; more prominent is the exceptional attribution of Marlborough House in London (see below). As probably there, Wren's lesser contemporaries were active in the field.

In augmenting the compact rectangular block of buildings like Coleshill, with longitudinal progression from entrance to saloon, apartments were conveniently accommodated in corner pavilions. At Ragley (from 1676), for example, Robert Hooke resorted to corner pavilions in the French manner but there is no court: four rooms deep to either side of the subdivided reception core, the plan is a reformed variant of the Elizabethan type represented at Wollaton Hall (AIC5, page 580).**3.57** However, as the Restoration allowed itself more opulence – and the king's

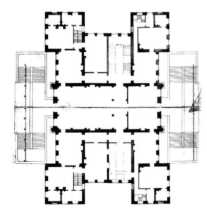

3.57a @ 1:1000

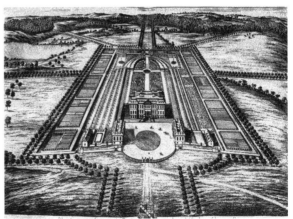

3.57b

cousin's France asserted cultural ascendancy – the aristocracy wanted more grand reception rooms aligned laterally: in a corps de logis at the head of a court flanked by wings of lesser rooms, that would emulate the grandeur of the enfilade which originated with the accumulation of antechambers in the royal palaces of the late Middle Ages. The modern ideal, however, was a pair of suites extending into the wings to either side of a gallery or great hall: that was the objective of May's work at Windsor but the medieval context obviated the symmetry of the extreme example set for Louis XIV at Versailles.

The pre-revolutionary English precedent for the enfilade of state rooms had been set at Wilton House by John Webb (and Jones?) with limited extent but great sumptuousness (AIC5, page 636). Projected for the Duke of Newcastle at Bolsover before the cataclysm, the form was realized in idiosyncratically English mannered guise there and at Nottingham in the 1670s.**3.58** Lord Brooke had been in the van of the development at Warwick in 1669. Three years later, the Duke of Lauderdale was provided with a state suite at Ham House near Richmond to the west of London: in an astylar house of the compact type with truncated wings, that was possible only by return-

3.58b

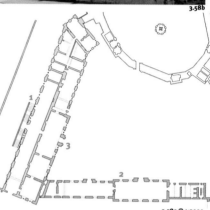

3.58a @ 1:2000

›3.58 BOLSOVER CASTLE, DERBYSHIRE: (a) plan with Gallery Range (1, designed 1630s), Riding House Range (2, begun c. 1640, completed after 1660), Newcastle Range (3, executed 1670s), (b) Gallery Range exterior, (c) Newcastle Range, court front.

The interior enfilade is gone: surviving are the retrogressive exteriors added to the complex left incompletely resolved by John and Huntingdon Smythson (AIC5, page 599). The architect here and at Nottingham was the Lincolnshire mason Samuel Marsh (died c. 1687): at Nottingham the application of a colossal Order of pilasters and columns, varied in their spacing, recalled Giulio Romano's Palazzo del Te; at Bolsover (c. 1640) the attached columns bulge idiosyncratically like cannon but the portals seem to betray knowledge of Vignola's Porte di Michelangelo – and Salomon de Brosse's Blérancourt (AIC5, pages 171 and 390). These were certainly not the only Mannerist survivals: the Plymouth citadel portal is another bizarre example for which provincial interpretation of Italian masters cannot be blamed.

3.58c

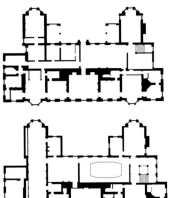

3.59c

3.59d

3.59e

3.59a, b @ 1:1000

›3.59 HAM HOUSE, RICHMOND (SURREY), LAUDERDALE EXTENSION, from 1672: (a, b) ground- and first-floor plans, (c) entrance detail, (d) garden front, (e) staircase, (f) antechamber.

The H-shaped nucleus was begun in 1610 for Sir Thomas Vavasour, the King's Marshal (died 1620). Thereafter the house was leased to Charles I's childhood companion William Murray, whose daughter Elizabeth purchased the freehold in the first year of the Commonwealth. Staunch loyalists – though dealing with the expropriating republicans – the proprietress and her husband, Lionel Tollemache, were rewarded by Charles II on his restoration with confirmation of the transaction (unlike many purchasers of sequestered property). The estate passed to their daughter and her husband John Maitland, the first Duke of Lauderdale who, rewarded by the king for his staunch loyalty, installed the pair of state apartments to either side of the hall on the ground floor in a range closing the recession on the garden side: the project is attributed to the gentleman architect William Samwell (1628–76). Dying in 1682 without issue, Lauderdale left the house to his wife's nephew, the Earl of Dysart.

ing the range back through the doubled plan.**3·59** In the next decade, however, it was accommodated in the main range of Boughton House: that was commissioned from an unidentified architect by the future Duke of Montagu who was ambassador to France in the 1670s and clearly admired the current work of Hardouin-Mansart on the great stables at Versailles and at Dampierre, if not Jacques IV Gabriel at Choisy (see page 287).**3.60a**

3.60a

: (a) London, Montagu House (from 1686, engraved elevation, *VB*); (b) Petworth Place, Sussex (from c. 1688), south front; (c) Boughton House, Northamptonshire (1680s), north front with north-eastern court entrance pavilion.

All three schemes are anonymous but John Evelyn mentions a mysterious Monsieur Puget at the service of Montagu in London: the square dome had been central to the French tradition at least since du Cerceau, particularly Lemercier, but here the immediate reference was

3.60b

3.60c

probably Hardouin-Mansart's early work (see above, pages 189, 267). The entrance pavilion at Boughton is similarly influenced.

Petworth, built for Ralph Montagu's son-in-law, Charles Seymour, Duke of Somerset, is astylar in the articulation of its corps de logis, unlike Boughton and its most obvious French models: like those of Wren's Chelsea hospital project, the frontispieces may be derived from Vincennes, and the building was to have been completed with a French square dome like the abortive palace at Winchester. Beyond that, an earlier English precedent is to be found at Stoke Bruerne (see AIC5, page 632).

›3.61 ROYAL RESIDENCES POST-1688: (a) Kensington Palace, general view from the south; (b–l) Hampton Court (from 1689), Wren's grand scheme, east elevation and block plan, definitive first-floor plan with Henry VIII's Great Hall (1), Fountain Court (2), king's state apartments (3i–x) and private suite (3xi, xii, xiii, xiv), queen's state apartment (4i–vii) and private suite (4viii–xiii, xiv),Fountain Court, Clock Court western screen, eastern and southern fronts, Grand Staircase and Queen Mary's Bedchamber (W.H. Pyne, 1819), engraved overview (Bl), King William III's Banqueting House, interior.

James II diverted his attention from Winchester to Whitehall: his hurried work was not complete on his departure into exile and the move of his successors to Kensington. Wren's work there began with a new entrance and Clock Court: his main contribution, the virtually astylar southern gallery block with its central parapet, followed Queen Mary's death in 1694.

3.61a

A pillar of the Restoration establishment, Montagu's work is one of several large-scale projects undertaken in the period of renewed prosperity following peace with the Dutch in 1674. His son-in-law Charles Seymour commissioned another at Petworth: the architect is unknown but, like his colleague at Boughton, was aware of developments in France: he crossed Anglo-Dutch vernacular with Le Vau's style at Vincennes to accommodate twin apartments *en enfilade*.**3.60b** These projects may be seen as anticipating the era in which private patronage emerged to the fore with the magnates who promoted the accession of William and Mary.

LATE STUART PALACE BUILDING

After the Glorious Revolution of 1688, the new joint monarchs forsook Whitehall, where James II had been busy building on a site inimical to his successor's health, and resorted to Kensington: there they had bought the Earl of Nottingham's house and commissioned Wren to augment it. Meanwhile the queen had initiated the development of Hampton Court as the principal royal seat on the edge of the capital in emulation of Versailles – but the king wanted it cheaply, with restrained grandeur appropriate to constitutional monarchy. A decade later, after the destruction of Whitehall by fire in 1698, the king contemplated rebuilding the main urban seat of the monarchy. Wren, increasingly inclined to delegate design to his assistants, oversaw schemes for both sites but probably left the provisional planning of Whitehall to Hawksmoor – as we shall see.

The objective at Hampton Court was to replace the Tudor palace with a modern complex in which twin royal apartments addressed a formal garden. The plan recalls the Versailles model in part but the attempt to effect a stylistic synthesis between Anglo-Dutch restraint and French 'Baroque-Classicism' is perhaps more successful inside

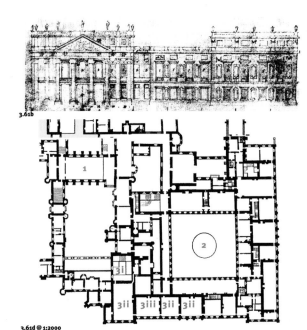

3.61b

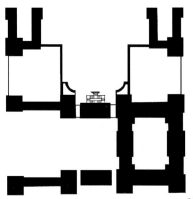

3.61c

1

2

3i

3ii 3iii 3ii 3ii

3.61d @ 1:2000

3.61e

At Hampton Court work was under way immediately after the new settlement of January 1689: it took precedence over developing Whitehall and even Kensington but was suspended on the queen's death – fortunately before the entrance courts or Great Hall succumbed. That left an amalgam of all that was most important in the Tudor complex before a court defined by a pair of perpendicular ranges containing the grand new apartments for the king and queen. As originally planned by Wren (1689) the oblong Privy Court was to be flanked by twin royal apartments (the king to the right, southwest) meeting in the middle as at Versailles (but without a Galerie des Glaces): detached wings were to frame a cour d'honneur (again as at Versailles, but apparently not at the expense of the Tudor hall). Le Vau's Versailles 'envelope' is echoed by the central block's two main storeys and attic, under a *toiture à l' italienne* of the side and central pavilions but his Louvre – and several of Mansart's variations on it – provided the main block's colossal Order rising from the ground (see above, pages 253, 238f).

In the event, the nuclear Fountain Court was reduced to a square and closed without mezzanine or attic to the west: the queen had most of the range facing the park to the east, the king all of the southern range overlooking what would be his privy garden. The apartments emulate Versailles in extent but not in opulence: most are oak-panelled in accord with King William's Dutch taste and detailed in intricate naturalistic relief by Grinling Gibbons; only the two staircase halls were painted by Verrio in his trompe l'oeil manner. Outside, brick prevails but it is offset with quoins, stone window frames

3.61f

and frontispieces with engaged columns. The variety
of the original's projection in height and depth cedes
to uniformity, the variety of fenestration to coherent
disposition. Rectangular, circular and square windows
effectively differentiate the main and subsidiary storeys
on the Fountain Court façades. The technique is less
adequate in the very different context of the extended
garden fronts to either side of frontispieces which
respond to no momentum generated by the plan: that
was the norm in France honoured in the breech on the
garden fronts at Versailles whose monotony – or sublime
consistency – is recurrent here.

3.61g

3.61h

›ARCHITECTURE IN CONTEXT »NORTHERN PROTESTANTS

3.61i

3.61j

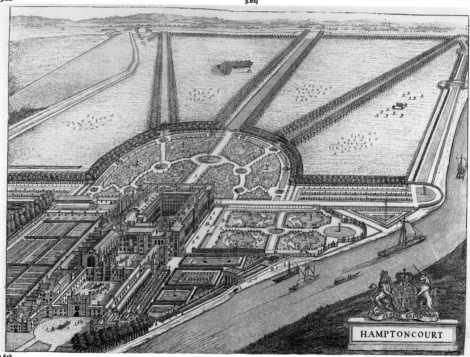

3.61k

The garden was designed by Daniel Marot for William III ostensibly on the distant advice of Le Nôtre (see above, pages 344f, and below, page 456). In the engraved overview the King's Banqueting House is shown near the centre on the river bank below the King's Privy Garden – a *parterre de broderie*.

›3.62 TALMAN AND THE COUNTRY HOUSE: (a–c) Burghley House, Northamptonshire, plan, staircase and

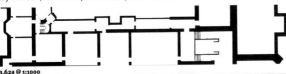

3.62a @ 1:1000

than in the extended brick and stone exteriors: the central frontispiece applied to the plane of the main southern range, in particular, seems to interrupt rather than complement the horizontals despite the forging of vertical accents from its superimposed voids.**3.61**

TALMAN AND CONTEMPORARIES

Foremost among the magnates who promoted the Glorious Revolution were the Dukes of Somerset and Devonshire. Following the former's Petworth, work began at the latter's Chatsworth within the year of the new regime's advent and the outbreak of war with France which would inhibit building for nearly a decade. The Devonshire commission was let to William Talman (1650–1719) who seems to have emerged from Hugh May's studio to undertake the relatively modest projects we have already noticed: he went on to follow the master's work at Windsor with the insertion of an enfilade at Burghley (from 1681). **3.62a–c** He succeeded May as Comptroller in 1689, at the outset of the new regime.

3.62b

3.62c

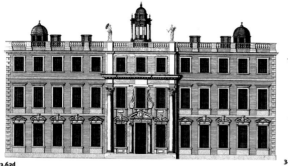

3.62d

3.62e

Talman's work for the Crown extended to Hampton Court where his involvement may explain disparity with Wren's style elsewhere, along lines characteristic of the younger man's independent works. The first of these was for Lord Dorchester at Thoresby (dating insecure) but it succumbed to fire when hardly complete. Thereafter his surviving work is best represented by Devonshire's Chatsworth, by Dyrham (from c. 1698) for the Secretary of State for War, William Blathwayt, and by the additions to Drayton (c. 1700) for Sir John Germain, a Dutch familiar of William III.

3.62f

saloon in enfilade (from 1681, decoration furthered later in the decade); (d) Thoresby Hall, Nottinghamshire (from c. 1685, destroyed, *VB*), entrance front; (e) Dyrham, Gloucestershire (c. 1698), entrance front (*VB*); (f) Drayton, Northamptonshire (c. 1702), court front; (g–p) Chatsworth House, Derbyshire (rebuilt from 1687), overview (*BI*), south front, ground- and first-floor plans (*VB*), north and west fronts, court, staircase, chapel, saloon panelling detail (with kind permission of His Grace, the Duke of Devonshire).

Unlike the Dutch Palladian variants of Hugh May's school, the design of Thoresby Hall began with Inigo Jones's astylar works and their followers: all the voids are framed with Classical mouldings and the pitched roof disappears behind a balustrade in the Italian manner, as at Kirby – or Longleat indeed – and Hampton Court. As on both fronts of the last, moreover, the frontispiece is applied without significant change of wall-plane but the young Talman engaged a pair of colossal Corinthian columns to shallow piers as the frame for three richly embellished bays. The lost building's derivatives include Wotton House (see below).

On the other hand, while retaining the *toiture à l'italienne* introduced by Le Vau to Versailles, Talman's Chatsworth and Dyrham schemes adapted the French tradition of massing in terms of pavillons and corps de logis. At Dyrham the latter is recessed throughout but the central bay of its *bel étage* is pedimented to match the central bays of the side pavilions in an astylar ordonnance descended – with some enrichment – from Sir Roger Pratt. At Chatsworth, at least at foundation level, Talman followed the French in projecting an elliptical salon from the north front: he left the centre of the south front unbroken, as the suite consisted only of four rooms with a central partition, but accented the projecting side bays with a colossal Ionic Order. In contrast, the academically correct disposition of the west

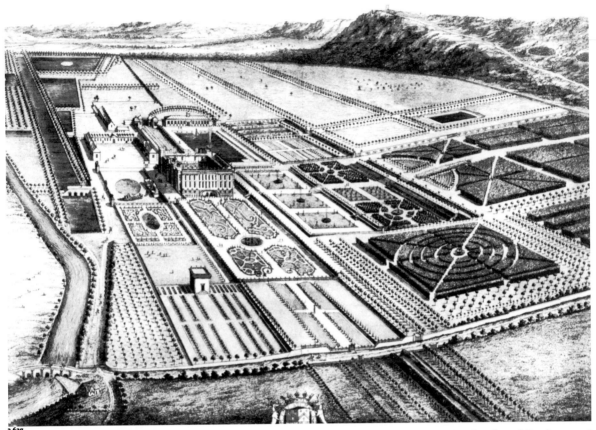

3.62g

front may be seen to reflect some knowledge of the new south front of the Louvre or Marly, as well as van Campen's Amsterdam Town Hall: it was executed by Thomas Archer after Talman's dismissal from the project in 1696 but the Ionic ordonnance and Mannerist fenestration follow through from the south. As his departure preceded the definitive arrangement of the interiors, he may not have been responsible for the sequence of the staircase hall which is screened in the manner of the anonymous Hôtel Salé in Paris but embellished on the upper walls and ceiling by Verrio. In addition to the filigree woodcarving in the Gibbons manner, the Danish master Caius Cibber contributed sculpture to the chapel and to the garden designed by London and Wise in their take on the French formal manner.

Except for their portals, the façades of Dyrham and Drayton are astylar: somewhat like a stage set, however, the latter is more richly fenestrated and embellished heraldically below an attic storey and roofs concealed behind balustrades. Contrary to the norm before Hampton Court, that was to be the new one: Chatsworth conforms but the entablature is supported by a colossal Order of Ionic pilasters on the pavilions containing the rooms to at the beginning and end of the enfilade in the south range where there is no central saloon. *Toiture à l'italienne* would prevail in France too but academic critics there would not have approved an unstressed centre.**3.62**

3.62h

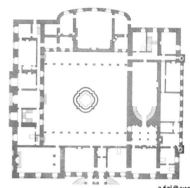

3.62i @ 1:1000

3.62k

3.62l

3.62m

3.62j @ 1:1000

3.62p

3.62n

3.62o

A disagreeable disposition lost Talman important work, such as the Duke of Chandos's Cannons and the completion of Chatsworth. The interiors there emulate the royal works, even those of May, Verrio and Gibbons at Windsor. Verrio and Gibbons were solicited from Hampton Court: they had been joined by Louis Laguerre from the circle of Charles Le Brun at Versailles (1683). The English woodcarver worked his supremely naturalistic magic on panelled chimney breasts, the Italian and French illusionists evoked a colonnaded Olympian idyll in the staircase hall as they were doing to even more overwhelming effect in the Heaven Room at Burghley. All three – and their assistants – worked widely in the relatively brief era of magnate magniloquence, their illusionism being more readily realizable and cheaper than marble and gilded stucco – except for monuments.**3.63**

Of Talman's competitors, William Winde (1645–1722) was not alone in sustaining a limited career: Buckingham House, later bought by King George III, was perhaps his most notable legacy. Looking back to Stoke Bruerne (AIC5, page 630), it may well be compared on the one

3.63

›3.63 NEW EXTON, CHURCH OF S. PETER AND S. PAUL: tomb of Viscount Cobham (1686).

Noted for his filigree woodcarving, responsible for the stalls in S. Paul's cathedral as well as much relief to the panelling of palatial interiors, Grinling Gibbons and his assistants were the foremost sculptors of tombs in the late-Stuart era: he was Master Carver to the Crown under William and Mary but his royal tombs remained unrealized.

›3.64 WORKS FROM TALMAN'S CIRCLE: (a) Newby, Yorkshire (c. 1700), garden front; (b) Wotton House (c. 1704, gutted 1820 and rebuilt inside the original façades but with a reduced attic), park front; (c, d) London, Buckingham House (from c. 1705, obliterated from 1825), engraved view of park front (VB) and Marlborough House (1707 and later), park front (VB).

Talman dressed French massing in Jonesian Palladianism for the Duke of Newcastle's unexecuted projects for Houghton (Nottinghamshire): Palladianism was yet to come. Meanwhile rectilinear profile – with a balustrade concealing a low-pitched roof – prevailed about the turn of the century.

Predominantly brick-built Newby Hall claims to have been designed under Wren's guidance (c. 1700), like

3.64a

3.64b

3.64c

3.64d

many unattributed examples of the rectilinear mode. On the other hand, the unidentified architect of Wotton is sometimes associated with Talman: the patron of the latter was Richard Grenville whose marriage would issue in the Earls Temple and Dukes of Buckingham (fourth creation) of Stowe and Wotton.

Buckingham House was built for the Tory politician John Sheffield, Marquess of Normanby, Lord Privy Seal and Lord President of the Council under Queen Anne, who was made Duke of Buckingham in 1703. Sharing the attribution with Talman, William Winde supervised construction. The precedent for quadrant colonnades linking the main block to low wings is Palladian: the English lineage descends through May's Barkley House (Piccadilly) from Stoke Bruerne (AIC5, page 630) where there was a parapet but no pediment – as in Wren's Kensington and the anonymous south front of Petworth.

Marlborough House was commissioned by Queen Anne's confidante the Duchess of Marlborough while her husband was achieving military glory against Louis XIV. Its French detailing is, therefore, ironical enough. In accordance with the patroness's wishes for it to be 'strong and plain', however, it has no central pediment, indeed no significant central projection or even a frontispiece: thus it leaves the sides dominant, contrary to French academic principle. Credited to Wren's office, the proportions were spoilt by the addition of extra storeys in the 1860s.

hand with Wotton and on the other with neighbouring Marlborough House which looks across the Channel to recent French developments in the circle of Mansart's younger contemporaries: it is French in its detailing – if not in its massing.**3.64**

EMERGENCE OF HAWKSMOOR AND ARCHER

By far the most significant of William Talman's contemporaries were Nicholas Hawksmoor (c. 1661–1736), John Vanbrugh (c. 1664–1726) and Thomas Archer (c. 1668–1743). Of these, Hawksmoor was first in the field, emerging c. 1690 from Wren's office with independent commissions inherited from the master: within five years he had embarked on his most important domestic project, Easton Neston. There he followed Talman in his roofline, in the colossal Order of pilasters rising from a truncated basement and in applying a pair of columns to form a frontispiece. Despite huge voids, however, his block is more massive, his Order more protean in its unrelieved assertion than anything in the work of his predecessors: the result

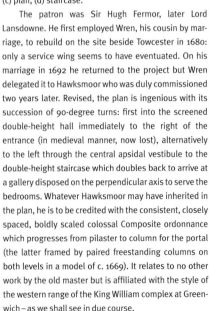

›3.65 EASTON NESTON, NORTHAMPTON-SHIRE, from 1702: (a) east front, (b) west front (*VB*), (c) plan, (d) staircase.

The patron was Sir Hugh Fermor, later Lord Lansdowne. He first employed Wren, his cousin by marriage, to rebuild on the site beside Towcester in 1680: only a service wing seems to have eventuated. On his marriage in 1692 he returned to the project but Wren delegated it to Hawksmoor who was duly commissioned two years later. Revised, the plan is ingenious with its succession of 90-degree turns: first into the screened double-height hall immediately to the right of the entrance (in medieval manner, now lost), alternatively to the left through the central apsidal vestibule to the double-height staircase which doubles back to arrive at a gallery disposed on the perpendicular axis to serve the bedrooms. Whatever Hawksmoor may have inherited in the plan, he is to be credited with the consistent, closely spaced, boldly scaled colossal Composite ordonnance which progresses from pilaster to column for the portal (the latter framed by paired freestanding columns on both levels in a model of c. 1669). It relates to no other work by the old master but is affiliated with the style of the western range of the King William complex at Greenwich – as we shall see in due course.

is undeniably Baroque in scale if not in progressing from pilaster to column with the finesse of Maderno.**3.65**

Thomas Archer was a gentleman who studied at Oxford and then travelled for four years – certainly to the Netherlands, presumably to Rome – before embarking on a limited career which benefited from the respite of war about the turn of the century. His work for the Duke of Shrewsbury at Heythrop Park (1706) – influenced by the Italian experiences of both patron and client – survives

3.66a

3.66b

›3.66 THOMAS ARCHER AT LARGE: (a–d)
Heythrop Park, Oxfordshire (1707, gutted by fire in
1831), entrance front from the north-west, garden front
from the south-east, detail of portal and east-front fenestration; (e, f) Wentworth Castle, Yorkshire (after Jean
de Bodt, from 1709), north front and detail of frontispiece; (g, h) Chettle House, Dorset (from 1710) entrance
and garden fronts; (i–k) Wrest Park, Bedfordshire, garden pavilion plan and elevation.

Working on the realization of Chatsworth while
projecting Heythrop, Archer was of course familiar
with William Talman's decentralized composition and
colossal Order rising from a plinth: he must also have
been aware of Hawksmoor's Easton Neston. As there,
the engaged columns of the garden front recall Webb at
Greenwich where, moreover, the context is rusticated:
as in Webb's additions to The Vyne and Wren's Chelsea
Hospital, however, the Order becomes freestanding for
the entrance portico though the pediment is omitted
– as at Easton Neston, again. Beyond these immediate English references are influences from abroad: Le
Pautre's fantasies (colossal Orders rising from plinths
and applied to rustication, absence of pediments,
etc.), Bernini's third Louvre project (colossal Corinthian
pilasters and engaged columns supporting a Composite cornice) and Roman High Baroque fenestration
details (Borrominian 'ears' from the Oratory façade and
elsewhere, pediments split and reversed in the manner
derived by Bernini and Fontana from Buontalenti). The
latter are purveyed by Domenico de Rossi in his lavish
coverage of all genres of Roman Baroque achievement
in *Studio d' architettura civile di Roma* (from 1702; see
above, pages 87, 94).

as a monumental shell with later interiors.**3.66a–d** The
main range of Wentworth Castle (from 1709) is complete
but there he was called on by Thomas Wentworth, Lord
Raby, to modify the scheme produced by the itinerant

3.66e

3.66f

Huguenot Jean de Bodt – who we shall encounter again in Germany.**3.66e, f** Archer followed Talman at Chatsworth, executing the west and north fronts probably on the lines established by his predecessor (see above). He is plausibly credited with Chettle but execution is due to the Bastard Brothers of Blandford after his retirement to the life of a country gentleman (1715).**3.66g, h** His bizarre, Mannerist Roehampton House survives short of the gigantic bro-

Thomas Wentworth, disappointed claimant to the Strafford inheritance at Wentworth Woodhouse in western Yorkshire (see below), bought the nearby Stainborough estate and rebuilt the front of its house: he employed Jean de Bodt whom he had encountered in Berlin when he was ambassador to Prussia. Archer took over after roofing was completed in 1714. The design of Chettle followed (but dating of execution by Blandford builders ranges from c. 1715 to c. 1730): the interior staircase is worthy of Archer in its galleried manoeuvres.

3.66g

3.66h

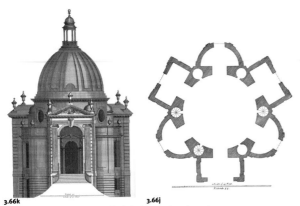

3.66k   **3.66j**

For the pavilion at Wrest Park Archer again referred to Fontana but also quaintly varied Francesco Borromini's hexagonal Sapienza (see above, pages 88, 116).

3.62i

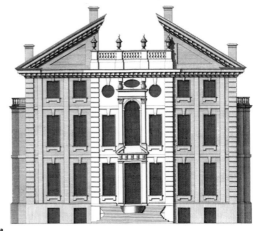

3.67a

›**3.67 THOMAS ARCHER IN TOWN:** (a) Roehampton House (built for Thomas Cary in 1712), engraved façade (*VB*); (b) Soho, Monmouth House (c. 1718).

Archer's Roman experience clearly extended to Frascati: the acute-angled pediment corners perched on the end bays of the Porta-Maderno Villa Aldobrandini there are recalled for the over-scaled broken pediments which distinguished these two houses (AIC5, page 288).

3.67b

ken pediment which dominates its engraved record: the related Monmouth House, Soho, is a lost attribution.**3.67**

In addition to the ingenious hexagonal banqueting pavilion at Wrest Park (c. 1711),**3.66i–k** Archer's extant legacy runs to three important churches: S. Philip in Birmingham, S. John in London's Smith Square and S. Paul, Deptford. The last two were commissioned in 1712 by the Anglican establishment in a campaign of parish church building: which we shall return to that in consideration of Hawksmoor's contribution and that of James Gibbs (1687–1754), the emerging talent of the next generation.

THE GREAT COLLABORATORS: HAWKSMOOR AND VANBRUGH

In contrast even to Chatsworth, the surviving domestic product of both Hawksmoor and Vanbrugh is overwhelming and highly idiosyncratic. The division of responsibility is unclear from the outset of their collaboration in the first years of the 18th century. They could hardly have been more different. A dour provincial Englishman, Hawksmoor was a highly proficient professional who trained under Wren, was his principal assistant on his greatest projects and had an independent career in the 1690s. Vanbrugh was a highly sophisticated gentleman of Flemish descent, a soldier and a major playwright – among other things – before turning to architecture as an amateur. They shared an eccentric imagination which was to exercise itself more in the moulding of mass than the articulation of form. They assisted, even superseded, Wren at Greenwich.**3.68**

The twin blocks in the centre of the Greenwich complex, called after King William and Queen Mary, were begun after 1694 when the palace was granted by the sovereigns to the Royal Hospital for Seamen. Wren's task here was the almost impossible integration of the modest Queen's House into the Baroque context of Charles II's abandoned palace, vastly different in scale and detail. Adding a second court slightly narrower than the riverside one initiated by Webb and closed with a domed corps de logis, he was clearly inspired by Versailles. Omitting a central block to leave the view open to the Queen's House, however, he split the centre of gravity of his composition, brought it forward and arranged a thoroughly Baroque optical illusion in between to place Inigo Jones's work in perspective. Baroque illusionism plays its part inside too. The Great Hall and its entrance under the dome of the King William Block were decorated by Sir Peter Thornhill with painted allegories and trompe-l'oeil architecture in a reflection of the current French pala-

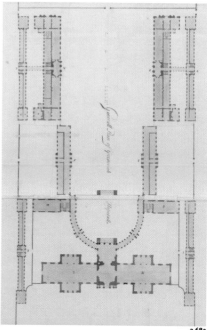

3.68a

3.68b

›3.68 GREENWICH, PALACE COMPLEX AS COMPLETED FOR THE ROYAL NAVAL HOSPITAL, from 1694 to 1708 in the main, the colonnades were built from 1704, the dome of the King William complex completed 1705, its pendant in 1735, the end pavilions of the Charles II and Queen Anne Blocks were doubled from 1711: (a, b) Wren's project of 1695, plan and court elevation of central block; (c) plan (as finally developed in the ideal, *VB*) with King Charles Block (1, as doubled from 1712 and later), Queen Anne Block (2, from 1699), King William's complex (3, the two parallel ranges north and south from 1698–99, joined by the western range from 1701), Queen Mary's complex (4, from 1698–99, here ideally matching 3); (d) axial view through William and Mary Blocks with their colonnades framing the distant view of the Queen's House, (e) general view from the river, (f) Painted Hall.

The project of 1695 inserted a domed central block at the head of receding courts, the upper one with quadrant colonnades in the Palladian manner: more particularly, the latter recall those which were to have flanked Hardouin-Mansart's Invalides (see above, page 260). Eliminating this central complex, Wren enhanced his side blocks with the twin domed towers which provide the major vertical accent at the corners of his court: he screened them with the parallel colonnades extending in perspective diminution to engage the Queen's House, apparently drawing it forward and enhancing its size. Inspiration may have come from the reconstruction of an imperial Roman avenue. Twin colonnaded porticoes open into the domed vestibules beneath the towers beyond which stairs ascend to the screened entrances of the chapel (fitted out from 1779) and painted refectory hall (east and west respectively). Beyond the main volume of the latter, a second screen distinguishes the upper hall: this screening of tripartite spaces recalls the Palazzo Colonna gallery in Rome (and its even grander derivative at Versailles).

The vault of the hall was given its illusionist painting by Sir James Thornhill (1675–1734): son of an army officer, he was apprenticed to the decorative painter Thomas Highmore but learned more from studying under Verrio and Laguerre. The work at Greenwich took him seven years from 1707. On its completion he was awarded the commission for painting the inner dome of S. Paul's cathedral with scenes from the mission of the patron saint framed in illusionist architecture – to Wren's dismay.

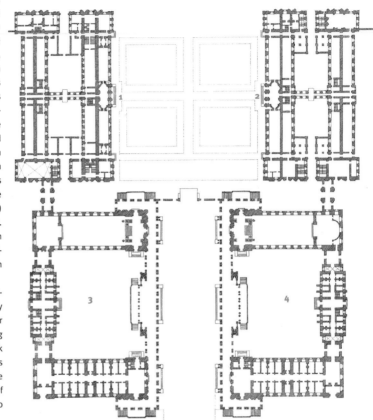

3.68c @ 1:2000

3.68d

3.68e

3.69a

3.68f

tial style: with neither the relief nor the élan derived by Le Brun from Cortona's fusion of the arts, they honour Britannia and the Glorious Revolution rather than absolute monarchy but nevertheless offer grand compensation for May's lost work at Windsor (see page 401).

At Greenwich the eccentric strain of Wren's ingenuity was developed into the first manifestation of the style of

3.69b

3.69e

3.69c

the next generation, as much Mannerist as Baroque. The point of departure is marked by a proposal for rebuilding the Whitehall palace after its destruction by fire in 1698 which is most plausibly credited to Hawksmoor: assertively Baroque in the scale of its massing and ordonnance, in theatrical scenography if not in movement, it would have overwhelmed the Banqueting House with a colossal Order and ancillary semi-peripteral 'temples'. At Greenwich the west wing of the King William Block was initiated well after Hawksmoor first appears independently, well before the advent of Vanbrugh: the dramatic intervention of the frontispieces, their weight and giant scale and especially the encapsulation of a colossal aedicule on the court side, is unprecedented in Wren's earlier work but not uncharacteristic of the independent product of either of the younger men.**3.69**

A dramatist, Vanbrugh would think in terms of dramatic mass and there would be much of the theatrical stage set in his perspective. A Whig, he naturally enjoyed Whig patronage. He began his career at the start of the 18th century with his own peculiar London house: rusticated arcaded loggias on two levels were flanked by truncated towers – but all is lost. He went straight on from this modest building to one of the grandest mansions ever built in England: Castle Howard for the Whig politician Charles Howard, Earl of Carlisle, First Lord of the Treasury from 1701 (when he began his palace). On Howard's recommendation he replaced William Talman as Comptroller in 1702 but was central to the diversion in the mainstream of patronage from Crown to magnate.

At the opening of the new century and the inception of Castle Howard, Hawksmoor was called into collaboration

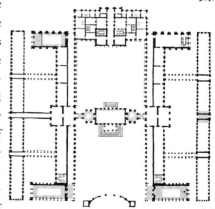

3.69d

›3.69 WORKS OF WREN'S OFFICE PRIMARILY ASSOCIATED WITH HAWKSMOOR: (a, b) Greenwich, Royal Naval Hospital, east and west fronts of western dormitory range of King William complex (from 1699); (c, d) Whitehall Palace, project for rebuilding (after 1698); (e) Temple of Baalbek (Bacchus) from *Le Grand Marot* (1670).

Jones's Banqueting House is in the centre of the Whitehall scheme but with cylindrical towers and a colossal Corinthian portico between the colossal colonnaded fronts of the side pavilions. These are derived from the reconstructions of the most Baroque of imperial Roman sites, Baalbek (AIC1, page 600), which were curiously inserted into *Le Grand Marot* (the alternative project repeats the Banqueting House beyond a giant portico). Scholarly, Hawksmoor drew on that source for illustrations to Henry Maundrell's *Journey from Aleppo to Jerusalem* (1714). Characteristically, he supplemented it with his own imaginative reconstructions of more-or-less fantastic antique exercises in his designs for building: as he explained in reference to his mausoleum at Castle Howard (which we are about to visit): 'I don't mean that one need to Coppy ... but to be on ye Same principalls [sic]'. Montano will be recalled (see pages 68f).

Hawksmoor was Surveyor's Clerk at Greenwich from 1698 and Deputy Secretary of Works from 1705. From 1715 he held a similar position for the royal palaces of Whitehall, Saint James's and Westminster. He lost the last post in 1718 but was Deputy Comptroller of Works to Vanbrugh in 1721 and Chief Surveyor to Westminster Abbey in 1723. Vanbrugh is sometimes associated with Hawksmoor at Greenwich in an undefined capacity even before his appointment as Commissioner there in 1703 – when the King William complex was far advanced. He had been projected to stardom by the Earl of Carlisle in 1701, as we are about to see, and was promoted by his political connections as a gentleman to several of the posts which Hawksmoor might have expected for himself: these included Comptroller of Royal Works in 1702 (in place of Talman) which ranked him next to Wren. He succeeded the old master as Surveyor at Greenwich in 1716 but not, two years later, as Surveyor-General of the King's Works: that post, from which the aged Wren was dismissed by Whig political jobbery, went to the undistinguished William Benson whose brother replaced Hawksmoor in his capacity as Secretary of Works.

3.70a

›3.70 THE PECULIAR ŒUVRE OF VANBRUGH AND HAWKSMOOR: (a) Kensington Palace, London, Queen Anne's Orangery (1704), entrance front; (b–i) Castle Howard, Yorkshire, (from c. 1701, not completed to the architect's original design) plan and ideal perspective view with bosquets beyond an apparently plain terrace (*VB*, 1725, before insertion of the western gallery range), detail of entrance front, great hall, general view of garden front, Temple of the Four Winds, mausoleum (page 455);

with Vanbrugh in place of rejected Talman. As a soldier, Vanbrugh knew France: prisoner-of-war at Vincennes and in the Bastille, he obviously studied architecture there. Hawksmoor knew how to build and to design palaces with Wren. Beyond his mentor's refined sense of surface articulation, however, he also brought a bold conception of the plasticity of masonry mass, charged with elemental rhythm in projection and recession, which appealed to the younger man's ebullient personality. An early manifestation of cooperative achievement in this mode (c. 1704) is the vigorously rusticated front of Queen Anne's Orangery at Kensington Palace – which, with Whitehall in ruins, was the suburban resort of the last of the Stuarts. As elsewhere, shared proclivities make it hard to disentangle the respective contributions of this eccentric pair.

The impact of the Castle Howard vision – and political connections – won Vanbrugh the huge state commission to design a palace for the Duke of Marlborough, hero of the War of the Spanish Succession: it was to be named in honour of the general's decisive victory over the forces of Louis XIV at Blenheim. With work underway there, from 1705 – and continuing at Castle Howard – Vanbrugh's career as a builder of massive houses extended in the main to remodelling the medieval fortress of Kimbolton (from 1708) for Sir Henry Montagu, 1st Earl of Manchester, to King's Weston (from 1710) for Sir Edward Southwell, to Cleremont House (from 1711, lost) for the Duke of Newcastle, to Grimsthorp (from 1715) for the Duke of Ancaster, to Eastbury Manor (from 1716, mainly lost) for George Dodington, to Seaton Delaval (from 1718, gutted) for the eponymous admiral George Deleval, and to Stowe for Sir Richard Temple, Viscount Cobham (from c. 1720). None of this survives complete with the gardens which complemented it in the French mode introduced by the restored king in the 1660s.**3.70, 3.71**

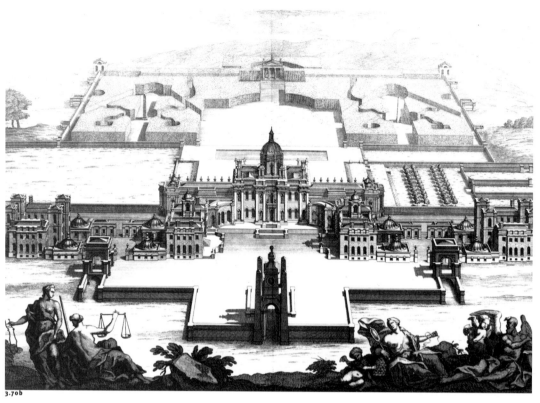

3.70b

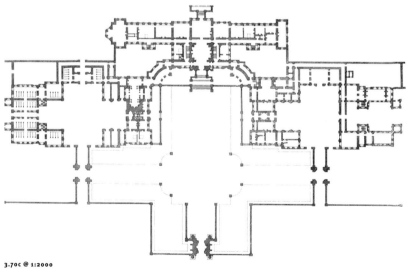

3.70c @ 1:2000

The apogee of the country house

'Lie heavy on, Earth! For he
Laid many heavy loads on thee!' (Abel Evans, cleric and Oxford don)

In Vanbrugh's astonishing first project, even to a greater extent at Blenheim Palace, the disposition of the masses about receding open courts with inner quadrants linking central and service blocks follows the Wren/Hawksmoor schemes for Winchester and Greenwich. As for many other palace builders across Europe, the ultimate model for the distribution overall was Le Vau's stepped forecourt development at Versailles and its subsequent lateral extension (see pages 253f): beyond that, the forecourt is closed with a screen and triumphal entrance pavilion in the manner of the du Cerceaux or de Brosse (AIC5, pages 368f, 390ff). Within, Le Vau's agency is apparent especially in felicitous planning which ran to the insertion of the novel corridor backing the main enfilades. These were not doubled at Castle Howard, where the apartments were exaggerated in extension way beyond the entrance block with its hall flanked by unassertive stairs. Sprawl is corrected at Blenheim Palace with clearer reference to the bifocal development of Versailles within Le Vau's 'envelope'.

3.70g

The dome at Castle Howard – replacing the familiar lantern cupola to a scale unprecedented in an English country house – may not be seen to preside as authoritatively as it would have done on the unrealized central range at Winchester or Greenwich but at least it echoes the fenestration of the upper storey of the block below. Vanbrugh was aware of the west front of Chatsworth in designing his garden front but his entrance front's juxtaposition of a colossal Doric Order and rusticated walls recalls the fantasies of Le Pautre and the frontispieces of Le Vau's Vincennes (see page 229). In contrast to the latter, Blenheim's portico is adapted from the south front of Le Vau's Louvre and its complement, the scheme in antis of the Collège des Quatre-Nations on the other side of the Seine (see pages 238f). The incoherence of the latter's general ordonnance is obviated by the wayward consistency of Vanbrugh's minor Order as it emerges from the central portico to sweep along the median quadrants and pass through the great rusticated corner blocks to achieve full plasticity in the galleries which frame the court.

3.70h

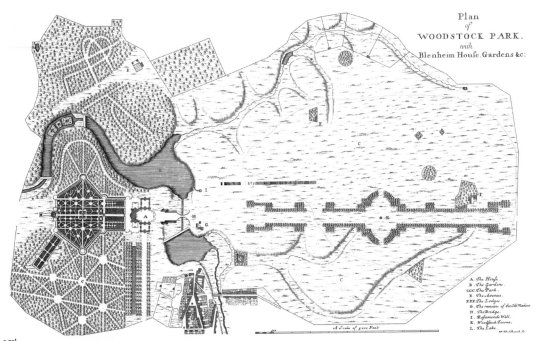

Plan
of
WOODSTOCK PARK,
with
Blenheim House, Gardens &c:

A. The House.
B. The Gardens.
C.C.C. The Park.
K. The Avenue.
ZZZ. The Lodges.
G. The remains of the Old Manor.
H. The Bridge.
I. Rosamonds Well.
K. Woodstock Towne.
L. The Lake.

A Scale of 4000 Feet

3.70j

3.70k

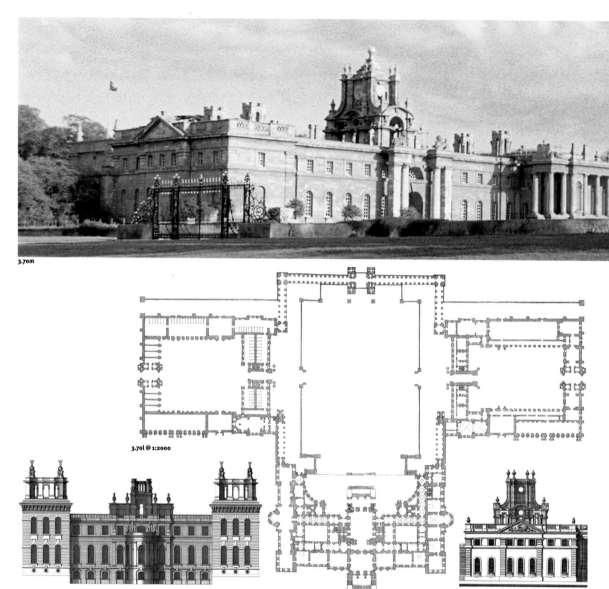

3.70m

3.70l @ 1:2000

3.70q

3.70p

The astylar treatment of those corner blocks derives from the elevations of the pavilions flanking the service wings at Castle Howard. Instead of a dome, a weighty, deeply recessed, pedimented attic gives presence back to the centre of Blenheim in opposition to the outer corners of the complex, where

(j–t) Blenheim Palace (Woodstock, Oxfordshire), site plan with Vanbrugh's bridge to north and formal garden (*VB*, c. 1725), aerial view, plan (*VB*), view from north-west, entrance front, park front, west garden front and north-east pavilion elevations (*VB*), hall, saloon, library.

3.70n

3.70o

›ARCHITECTURE IN CONTEXT »NORTHERN PROTESTANTS

3.70r

3.70s

3.70t

the pavilions are crowned with extraordinary open arcading bearing coroneted cannonball finials – towers which seem to paraphrase Elizabethan work in gargantuan terms. The attic does not reach through to the garden front: there a rectangular parapet supports a trophy sculpture of Louis XIV.

There are several significant Palladian references in the amazing corpus of works here associated with Vanbrugh, notably the north portico at Stoe and the southern one projected for Grimsthorp, the plan and Serlian windows of Seaton Delaval, even the rusticated columns borrowed for the latter, for Grimsthorpe and for Eastbury from the Villa Sarego near Verona (AIC5, page 248). The first permutation of that motif, for the Orangery at Kensington and the entrances to the Blenheim service courts, may have been inspired by the rusticated Doric of de Brosse's Luxembourg in Paris. But Classicism is overwhelmed. In fantasy and scale Blenheim and all these later works may be classified as Baroque but they are Mannerist in important respects: in particular in the peculiar castellation of Blenheim or the linking of chimneys into a crenellated miniature Roman viaduct describing a square over the severities of King's Weston for instance; in general in the contrary imperatives to unify and diversify, to conjure harmony over the willful clash of starkly contrasted elements which often seem meant to be jarring rather than to elide in progressive development or sinuous curve.

3.71a @ 1:1000

›3.71 VANBRUGH'S INDIVIDUAL HOUSES: (a–c) King's Weston House, Somerset (from 1710), plan (with staircase moved from lateral canyons to the centre where it climbs around three sides of its square cage to serve twin apartments), south front and detail of north front with portal;

3.71c

3.71b

(e–h) Kimbolton Castle, Cambridgeshire (from 1708), general views from the south-west and south-east (like the west and south, the east front was refaced in the faux-medieval style of May's Windsor c. 1710 but the inconsistent eastern portico seems to have resulted from correspondence in 1719 between the patron, Lord Manchester, and the Florentine architect Alessandro Galilei who had been in England since 1714), staircase (extracted from Vanbrugh's usual canyon beside the hall, there is no room for an imposing architectural envelope but only a lightly relieved screen and the murals of the Venetian Giovanni Pellegrini, 1710), saloon; (i–l) Seaton Delaval Hall, Northumber-

3.71d

Beyond reforming the articulation of Le Vau, schooled no doubt by the rigours of Wren, Vanbrugh and Hawksmoor emulate Le Pautre in their conception of building primarily in terms of mass to be manipulated, in their use of rustication, in the tendency towards the fantastic, and above all in the gargantuan scale promoted throughout their collaboration. At Blenheim that ended in 1716 when Vanbrugh fell out with the patron's wife and resigned: completion (from 1722) was left to Hawksmoor whose masterly contribution culminated in the library. At Castle Howard, Hawksmoor com-

3.71f

3.71e

3.71g

3.71j

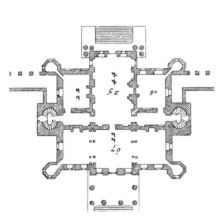

3.71h @ 1:1000

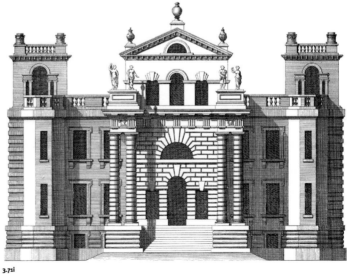

3.71i

land (from 1720), plan, north elevation (*VB*), south front; (m–p) Grimsthorp, Lincolnshire, entrance front

3.71k

3.71l

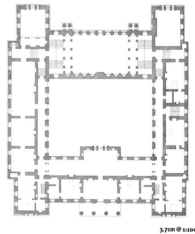

3.71m @ 1:1000

3.71n

and hall (from 1722), south front with Palladian portico (*VB*; the fenestration, derived from the towers but out of accord with the hall front, was probably revised by Vanbrugh after construction had begun); (q, r) Eastbury, Berkshire (from 1724, destroyed, the plan was at first to be a contraction of Blenheim without corridors and with twin staircases of the King's Weston type to either side of the longitudinal hall), Vanbrugh's west elevation and Bridgeman's paraphrase of Marly for the garden (*VB*);

pleted the late Vanbrugh's Belvedere Temple in 1726 and three years later he embarked on his brooding essay in the reinvention of Roman mortuary building for the Howard mausoleum – ultimately opting for a monumental Doric revision of a Vesta temple with reference to Bramante's Tempietto.

3.71o

3.70i

The English formal garden

In 1718, when work was well under way again at Blenheim, Stephen Switzer praised Louis XIV for taking gardening to 'the most magnificent height and splendour imaginable'. The author was a garden designer trained under England's principal practitioners, George London and Henry Wise. They took their departure from gardens designed 'in the Italian manner' - like Wilton (AIC5, page 637). Restored at several sites between Pitmedden in Aberdeenshire and Ham House in Surrey, that mode had its equivalents in Holland: there water was plentiful for canals but land shortage enforced the reduction of the expansive French style, with its terraced *parterres*, *bosquets* and vast network of forest rides, which was envied even by anti-absolutist rulers like the Stadtholder.**3.8c** The future William III's cousin, Charles II brought greater pretension with him on return from exile in both Holland and France. Failing to borrow Le Nôtre, as we have noted, he was compensated with André Mollet: he had worked at Wilton and for the court before the revolution and his *Le Jardin de plaisir* (1651) was the textbook of the French style which he adapted for the restored king at the Court of Saint James. **3.50a** Nevertheless, the acute-angled divergence of canal and avenue there, foreign to French rationalism, seems to be due to English pragmatism – and the latter would ultimately prevail.

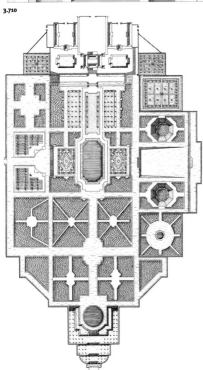

3.71p

Mollet was joined by several members of his clan and they promoted the native John Rose (1629–77) to assume their responsibilities. Rose had trained under Le Nôtre and was appointed Keeper at Saint James's Park in 1666. He trained George London (c. 1640–1714) who in turn trained Henry Wise (1653–1738). They employed Charles Bridgeman (1690–1738) and Switzer. London was Superintendent of the Royal Gardens but Switzer identifies him as director-general of most of the great gardens of England: his masterpieces were at Longleat and Chatsworth.**3.62f** At the latter site *parterres* lead to an extensive canal on axis with the south front but to the east the residual legacy of the old chequerboard tradition still displays a patchwork of planting, including a maze.

London and Wise are credited with assisting Vanbrugh at Castle Howard: Wise, Royal Gardener to Queen Anne and George I, is credited with the Blenheim scheme. Devoid of *parterres de broderie*, the southern aspect of both these houses was apparently dominated by *bosquets* cut into 'rooms' served by diagonal and serpentine paths; twin blocks joined, those at the earlier work derive from the Anglo-Dutch tradition of the maze in its chequerboard square; Blenheim's zones are multiplied on a grid in the French manner but within a hexagon defined by avenues leading to a vast network of 'rides'.**3.70b,j** In marked contrast is the great radial scheme for Hampton Court which, uncompromised by a conservative grid, radiates in avenues through bosquets from a semi-circular *parterre de broderie* spanning the entire south front.**3.61k** London and Wise are credited with implementing that scheme of the French Huguenot Daniel Marot who had been imported from Het Loo by William III in 1689. Restored, the formal exercise at Hampton Court is the great survivor: little of formality remains in the fields of the magnates, beyond the bones of Melbourne and the occasional canal or cascade elsewhere. Copious in compensation, however, are the engraved records in *Vitruvius Britannicus* and, above all, in *Britannia Illustrata*.

London and Wise were devotees of Dezallier d'Argenville's treatise on the French mode (*La Théorie et la pratique du jardinage*, 1709). Published in English in 1712, its impact is marked on the work attributed to Wise at Blenheim later in the decade (plate 2c, figure 4, for instance): its principles prevail at Stowe where Bridgeman made his name. The former is based on

3.71s

(s–u) Stowe House, Buckinghamshire (from c. 1722), Vanbrugh's north portico and overview of Bridgeman's quirky formal garden c. 1720, the statue of George I (1723, John van Nost) at the north focal point of the extensive scheme.

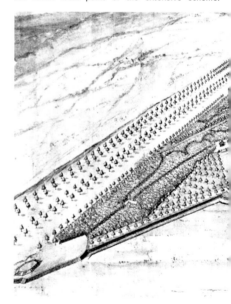

3.7u

a rigid grid: Bridgeman's scheme is more supple, indeed he is credited with initiating the move away from formality – presumably aware that Le Nôtre had flirted with wilderness (not least at Trianon; see page 256). Within the boundary of 'rides' pivoting on 'bastions' – and the concealed ditches (*ha-ha*, derived from Dezallier d'Argenville, *op.cit.*) protecting the parterres from grazing animals – room was left to the east for his young collaborator, William Kent, to introduce Arcadia: wilderness was to eventuate much later.

Delighting in his rural retreat of Moor Park in Surrey, which conformed to the Dutch formal mode, the retired statesman William Temple mused (in 1685): 'there may be other forms, wholly irregular that may ... have more beauty'. His words were prophetic. Inspired by the landscapes of Annibale Carracci and his followers, especially Poussin and Claude, Kent's exercise in Classical informality would revolutionize the approach to ordering the landscape, not only in erasing most of England's formality but throughout the western world. It is, naturally, the subject of a later volume.

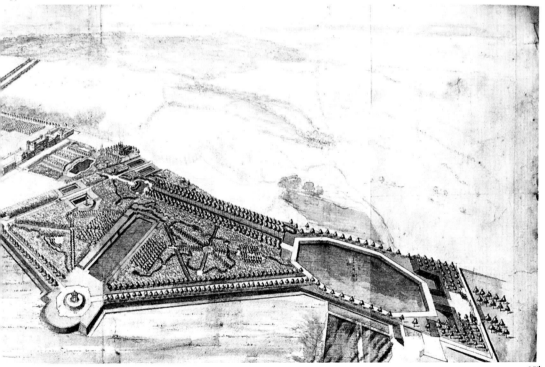
3.71t

NICHOLAS HAWKSMOOR, HIS CONTEMPORARIES AND THE CHURCH

Hawksmoor is not known to have crossed the Channel but he supplemented his passion for geometry with extensive study of the pattern-book literature. There is perhaps less of the French, more of the Italian Mannerists, about his virile conception of rustication – which characteristically ran to overscaled keystones surpassing even those of Giulio Romano. Ambiguity in the relationship between the active and passive agents of elevation had its counterpart in his planning. More than Vanbrugh, Hawksmoor loved to experiment with variations on hybrid plan forms after the example set by Wren but he exceeded his master in the willful confusion of the formal and the functional in church planning. His opportunity to demonstrate his peculiar native talent for this came in 1711 when the high church Anglican establishment embarked on an extensive campaign of parish church building at the behest of Queen Anne's Tory government. The Peace of Utrecht (1713) released funds for this and much private building besides.

Few churches were built outside London while the capital's parishes were completing their works to Wren's designs. There are notable exceptions: All Saint's in Oxford with its assertive Order of Corinthian pilasters progressing to paired twin columns for the portico and a spire rising through a tempietto; S. Philip's, Birmingham, built to the designs of Thomas Archer and distinguished by its architect's mannered interpretation of Roman Baroque curvature and counter-curvature.**3.72** The situation was to be redressed by the 1711 Act of Parliament which decreed the building of fifty new churches mainly to serve the expanding suburbs of London where, as we have noted, only fifty-one churches replaced the eighty-seven lost to the Great Fire. **3.73**

›3.72 BIRMINGHAM, S. PHILIP'S CHURCH, from 1710, refaced and extended in the 19th century, now the cathedral: (a) west front and its tower, (b) plan, (c) interior before alteration (record of c. 1825).

3.72a

3.72b @ 1:1000

3.72c

As we shall see in London, the new parish church was needed to cater for an expanding population: building lasted fifteen years until the tower was completed. Archer's basilican plan with western tower projection recalls Wren's S. James's, Piccadilly, except for the curvature at the east end, which recalls S. Clement Danes: unlike either of these, but as at S. Bride, the galleries are suspended from a colossal Order. The main storey of the tower has the curvature of S. Vedast's tetrapylon but that is not countered in the upper zone, as there.

›3.73 LONDON, THE CHURCH COMMISSION-ERS' CHURCHES.

1 ARCHER'S CONTRIBUTION: (a–d) S. Paul, Deptford (from 1712), plan, interior and exterior west and east; (e–g) S. John, Smith Square, Westminster (from 1714), plan and exterior north and west.

3.73.1d

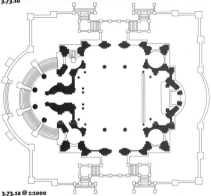

3.73.1a @ 1:1000

3.73.1c

3.73.1b

The Church Commissioner's churches

The Act of Parliament for the building of the new churches constituted a commission to further the project under the supervision of two principal surveyors: of these, Hawksmoor provided continuity over a quarter of a century during which his colleagues included Thomas Archer, James Gibbs and John James. Of the twelve churches realized in the second decade of the century, Hawksmoor achieved six, Archer two, Gibbs and James one each. Later anonymous architects are notable mainly for their attempts to supplant a spire with a colossal column or an obelisk (S. John, Horsleydown and S. Luke, Old Street respectively, c. 1730).

At Deptford Archer referred to the Greek-cross precedent set for S. Agnese in Piazza Navona, Rome, by Borromini and Rainaldi (see pages 82ff) but he avoided a dome over the octagonal crossing: to the fore, instead, is a tempietto tower with buttressed spire rising from an amplified version of Cortona's S. Maria della Pace porch; the colossal Doric Order is rusticated on the main body of the building but not on the portico. A precedent for the near-square arrangement of S. John, Smith Square, is elusive – though the ideal of a Greek cross with four corner towers may have come from Leonardo or Bramante, if not from its incomplete realization at Montepulciano by Antonio da Sangallo the Elder (AIC4, page 845). As there, the articulation is assertively Doric and runs to columns in antis but the pediment motif is a Mannerist confection derived from Giacomo della Porta's Villa Aldobran-

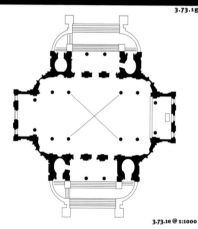

2 HAWKSMOOR'S CONTRIBUTION: (a–c) Christ Church, Spitalfields (from 1714), plan, west front and interior; (d–f) S. Alfege, Green-

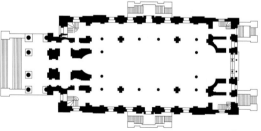

3.73.2b

3.73.2c

dini at Frascati (also recalled in Archer's London town houses, as we have seen): the tower form is like the one at Deptford but open and without spire. In contrast to all this, James Gibbs's contribution, S. Mary-le-Strand on its island site, has the volume of a Roman temple cella with apse and a circular portico emerging from a Palladian external ordonnance of superimposed columns: the ordonnance of Inigo Jones's Banqueting House is revised for extra relief and the insertion of serlianas.

Hawksmoor's response admirably demonstrates his ingenuity in developing major and minor cross-axes in the longitudinal spaces of the ancient basilica – or actually imposing centralizing geometry on it. The colonnades screening entrance and sanctuary in Christ Church, Spital-fields, for instance, at once define a square nave and assert the main axis from portal to altar as in a basilica but with contrary lateral tunnel vaulting to the side bay triads. The approach is varied with less precise geometry and no lateral vaulting for S. Anne's, Limehouse. There galleries span between high pedestals as defining agents: free of colonnades, they play a similar role in S. Alfege, Greenwich; they counter the logic of S. George in the East's Greek-cross plan; they define a square for the main volume within S. George, Bloomsbury. Without galleries, squares are telescoped within S. Mary Woolnoth.

Like Wren, Hawksmoor coped admirably with the Anglican will to Clas-sicize medieval forms in elevation, especially of steeples, but in doing so he relished a more Mannerist complexity and contradiction of expectation: his eclectic approach preserved much that was Gothic in profile but the sub-stance was transformed in accordance with more-or-less ingenious recon-structions of the antique. The earliest, S. Alfege, is the nearest to Wren in its superimposition of a tempietto over a tetrapylon but a crenellated tower was Hawksmoor's intention: the east end incorporates the antique imperial fastigium motif of apotheosis which Wren had recalled for the transepts of both S. Paul's Great Model and the executed building (see pages 409ff).

The departure to new directions is marked by the setting of a rectangular tower across the main axis. At Spitalfields the central bays of the west front are raised high above the freestanding portico, varying the triumphal-arch motif, extending it beyond the confines of a conventional tower, doubling it and gouging out niches to differentiate the sides, then perching an obelisk-

3.73.2e

3.73.2f

like spire on the top. Variants of the approach were crowned with quasi-medieval turrets at S. Anne, Limehouse, and S. George-in-the-East. Related to the unrealized S. Alfege project, the latter has Roman altars instead of crenellations and the motif is reiterated to a smaller scale with domes – perhaps in emulation of King's College Chapel, Cambridge – over lateral extensions to the main body of the building where keystones of exaggerated scale menace the crushing of doors. At S. Mary Woolnoth a boldly rusti-

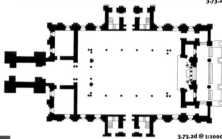

3.73.2d @ 1:1000

wich (from 1712), plan, exterior and interior; (g–i) S. George-in-the-East (from 1714), plan, exterior from south-east and pre-War interior;

3.73.2g @ 1:1000

3.73.2h

3.73.2i

3.73.2j

(j–n) S. Anne, Limehouse (from 1714), exterior from
west, detail of east end, plan, interiors to east and west;

3.73.2m

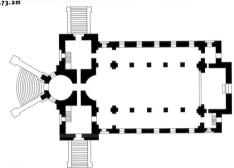

3.73.2l @ 1:1000

3.73.2k

3.73.2n

3.73.2p

3.73..2s

3.73.2q

3.73.2t

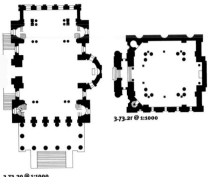

3.73.2r @ 1:1000

3.73.2o @ 1:1000

(o–q) S. George, Bloomsbury (from 1716), plan, exterior from south-west and interior; (r–t) S. Mary Woolnoth (from 1716), plan, exterior from west and interior.

3 JAMES GIBBS'S CONTRIBUTION: (a–d) S. Mary-le-Strand (from 1714), west front, interior, floor and vault plans (from Gibbs's *Book of Architecture*, 1728), model.

cated arch, echoed above a stringcourse and flanked by attenuated rusticated columns, supports the flank of a peristyle – and twin turrets. Even more startling is the re-evocation of the Mausoleum of Halicarnassus for the offset tower of S. George's, Bloomsbury: George I rises from a stepped pyramid supported by lions and unicorns over a tempietto with four pedimented porticoes and a tetrapylon; the whole is offset to the side beyond a hexastyle portico of Baalbek provenance which shelters access perpendicular to the axis of orientation. That form of portico was introduced to the series by John James for S. George, Hanover Square.

Plan of the Upper Order

Plan of the Under Order

3.73.3c

3.73.3d

3.73.3a

3.73.3b

GOTHIC REVISION

Vanbrugh and Hawksmoor are significant in the European context as a whole, not for their idiosyncratic Baroque mannerism, but because they were the first to revive and consciously work within the Gothic tradition – except for Wren's occasional excursions into it when in a Gothic

3·74a

›**3.74 HAWKSMOOR AT OXFORD:** (a) Clarendon Building (1710); (b) All Souls College (from 1715).

Oxford University retained Hawksmoor as its principal consultant on architecture: he left the construction to the local master-mason William Townesend. Apart from advising on the design of Queen's College, with Townesend as builder, Hawksmoor's main legacy to the city consists of two sharply contrasted works: the single-volume Clarendon printing house building, with its grand Doric portico emerging from an astylar ordonnance except for the continuation of the Doric frieze; and the largely neo-Gothic complex of All Souls College. The latter was founded in 1438 by Archbishop Chichele under the auspices of King Henry VI: the chapel survived in the southern wing of the quadrangle entered from Radcliff Square. Flanked by Gothic pinnacles, his eclectic domed gatehouse is in stark contrast to Queen's Classical tempietto (of distant Baalbek derivation). At the head of the court, the twin towers of the central block are a permutation of a Gothic cathedral front: that was deemed to accord with the style of the surviving chapel and adjacent hall in the southern wing which was matched by the northern wing containing the Codrington Library (begun

1715). The Gothic style does not extend to the major 18th-century interiors.

›3.75 LONDON, WESTMINSTER ABBEY: west front (1735).

Having evoked a twin-towered cathedral front out of context and with Classical symmetry for All Souls College, Oxford, Hawksmoor had a late chance – at the very end of his career – to attempt the real thing in completing the twin towers of Westminster. The impressive result avoids the complex profile of the earlier work in continuation of the existing pier buttresses which define the rectangularity. The example was set by Wren at Christ Church, Oxford (see above).

›3.76 GREENWICH, VANBRUGH CASTLE, 1717: general view from the south of the original square 'keep', with its central cylindrical staircase tower, and (right) the east wing added after the architect's marriage in 1719 (and further extended from the late-19th century).

The original conception was symmetrical, indeed Classical in its ordered geometry but not in the pseudo-medieval brick style. That probably derived from regular 15th-century works like Herstmonceux in Sussex or Tattershall in Lincolnshire (AIC4, pages 540, 558): it ran not only to turrets with arrow-slit fenestration but to arcaded false machicolations which are also to be found at 'castellated' Kings Weston. The additional wing transformed the complex with willful asymmetry which might well be seen as inspiring the English after a lapse of some thirty years – as may be seen in another volume.

3·75

3·76

context. Apart from the towers of Westminster Abbey, which clearly come into the latter category, Hawksmoor executed the commission to complete the college of All Souls, Oxford, entirely in his interpretation of the English Perpendicular style.**3·75, 3·74b** This might be seen as a complement to Oxford's medieval inheritance, though in the nearby Clarendon Building the same architect had followed the precedent set by Wren – among others – of building in the contemporary Neoclassical mode.**3·74a** Quite unconstrained, Vanbrugh went even further in building his own house at Greenwich (1717).**3·76** Vanbrugh Castle, inspired by a building type evolved in response to the exigencies of military engineering rather than to a conception of architectural order, is a pioneering exercise in asymmetrical composition the importance of which it would be difficult to exaggerate. This approach to design, capturing the qualities of a picture – unlike the mannered post-Renaissance castellation of Blenheim Palace – came to be identified as 'Picturesque' and it was to be England's greatest contribution to European culture: in building and in landscaping.

POSTLUDE AND PRELUDE

The eccentric duo, Hawksmoor and Vanbrugh, naturally had their followers in the Mannerist-Baroque mode. Prominent examples include William Wakefield's Duncombe Park, Yorkshire, anonymous Powis House in London, and William Adam's variation for Duff House in Banffshire. Rustication is largely dispensed with in these works. That trend is countered by Sir James Thornhill's Moor Park, by the town and country houses of the Duke of Chandos, attributed variously to James Gibbs and John Price, and by Francis Smith at Sutton Scarsdale.**3.77–3.81**

›3.77 LONDON, POWIS HOUSE, c. 1712, unattributed: engraved street front (*VB*).

The patron was the eponymous nobleman. The elevation is an enrichment of the Buckingham House scheme but also adapts the ordinance of Castle Howard's entrance front, apparently without quadrant colonnades.

›3.78 CANONS, MIDDLESEX: entrance front (attributed to James Gibbs c. 1719 and engraved by John Price).

James Brydges (1673–1744, Earl of Carnarvon in 1714 and Duke of Chandos in 1719) amassed a fortune as Paymaster General of the army during the War of the Spanish Succession. He resigned in 1713 and began projecting the replacement of the Jacobean house at Canons with Talman as architect. The latter ceded to John James late in 1714 but Gibbs took over within six months and he is credited with the elevations published in *Vitruvius Britannicus*. Engraved by Price, they match the same engraver's record of the London house.

›3.79 SUTTON SCARSDALE HALL, from 1724, deroofed and pillaged after 1919: east front.

The patron was Nicholas Leke, Earl of Scarsdale: Smith, the architect classified as a gentleman, referred to Castle Howard but based his colossal Order and rusticated wall directly on the ground. Ten years earlier at Stonleigh the colossal Ionic Order is confined to the corners of the central and lateral projections and rustication is avoided.

›3.80 DUNCOMBE PARK, YORKSHIRE, from c. 1713, remodelled by Charles Barry from 1843, gutted by fire in 1879, rebuilt internally from 1895: west front.

The patron was Thomas Browne, nephew by marriage and business partner of Sir Charles Duncombe, Receiver General of Excise (died 1711). The style is developed with some knowledge of Vanbrugh and the plan recalls Eastbury.

›3.81 DUFF HOUSE, BANFFSHIRE, SCOTLAND, c. 1735: south front.

The patron was the Earl of Fife. William Adam (1689–1748, active from 1721) was the progenitor of Scotland's foremost architectural dynasty – about which there will be a great deal more in a later volume.

3.80

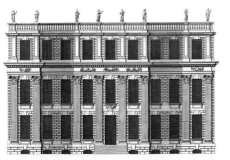
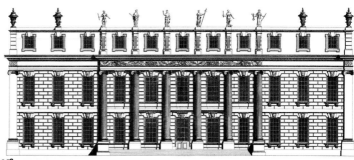

3·77   3·78

3·79

3·81

Conceived to celebrate national triumph, the Blenheim project was beset with escalating problems of resolution and cost when the Duke of Marlborough died in 1722: the pretentions of the widowed duchess apart, the absolutist ethos of the vast pile was anathema to the Whigs then ascendant. The manifesto of opposition had already been published in 1715, as we have noted: in that same year – seven years before Hawksmoor resumed work at Woodstock and Vanbrugh embarked on his last protean project at Grimsthorp – Campbell began realizing the Palladian ideal of the *Vitruvius Britannicus* at Wanstead for the East India plutocrat Sir Richard Child, and projected it at Houghton for the 'prime minister' Sir Robert Walpole (from 1713 and 1722 respectively). He went on to emulate the Italian master's Vicentine Villa Rotonda for the retreat of John Fane, later Earl of Westmorland, at Mereworth and inspired Lord Burlington and his protégé William Kent to follow Scamozzi at Chiswick (in 1723 and 1725). Hawksmoor, often Palladian in motifs such as the serliana, charted a similar course in his late works: the Oxford Clarendon Building in particular.

The Palladian – or Jonesian – example was not ignored by Vanbrugh, who is known to have owned no other treatise than *I quattro libri dell'architettura*. We have detected numerous Palladian details in his works, such as at Stowe where he set a Palladian portico between quadrant wings inspired by the Villa Badoer at Fratte Polesine (AIC5, pages

248f), and at Seaton Delaval where he varied the portico motif in the context of mannered rustication. As we have seen with the French, noble simplicity was the Palladian ideal of confining relief to the agents of load and support, like an antique temple: a clear manifestation of this is the application of the temple-front motif to a wall articulated only with the frames of the doors and windows. Vanbrugh's late works, King's Weston, even Stowe, show this trend away from the complexity of his earlier elevations.

Beyond the great eclectics turned Palladian is Dean Aldrich (1647-1710), Dean of Christ Church, Oxford, Vice-Chancellor of the University, who is credited with the design of two notable buildings there: the church of All Saints and the Peckwater quadrangle of Christ Church. His church style may be seen to derive from re-ordering Wren. On the other hand, his 'neo-Palladian' secular style derives

3.82a

3.82b

›3.82 OXFORD OF DEAN ALDRICH: (a) Church of All Saints (directed by Hawksmoor to completion in 1720 but designed after the medieval original was severly damaged by the collapse of its tower in 1700); (b) Christ Church Peckwater Quadrangle (from 1707).

Dean Aldrich, trustee of the parish of All Saints, was responsible for the design of several university works: his sole excursion into the specifically ecclesiastical field was for his church. The precedent for the hall-church volume was provided by Wren's S. Lawrence Jewry but there is no one-sided lateral extension here and the comprehensive ordonnance is more regular. Two zones of S. Mary-le-Bow's tower, simplified, satisfied Aldrich's revision.

›3.83 WENTWORTH WOODHOUSE, YORK-SHIRE: west range (from c. 1720).

not directly from Palladio – who he called his master – but from the author of London works like Lindsey House in Lincoln's Inn Fields (AIC5, page 629).**3.82**

Thus, inevitably in a complex period of flux, Jonesian revivalism preceded Campbell's missive. And, of course, there was Baroque convolution afterwards: the detail of Wentworth Woodhouse's west front is an important example (c. 1720).**3.83** The east front there followed Wanstead which, with Houghton, Mereworth and Chiswick, were seminal to English Palladianism as it emerged c. 1730: they would inform practice at home and in the expanding empire until well into the second half of the century. Though we shall encounter their like elsewhere in this volume, as an early manifestation of Enlightenment, they, their progeny and their Arcadian context are best left to open a new volume on a new age.

3.83

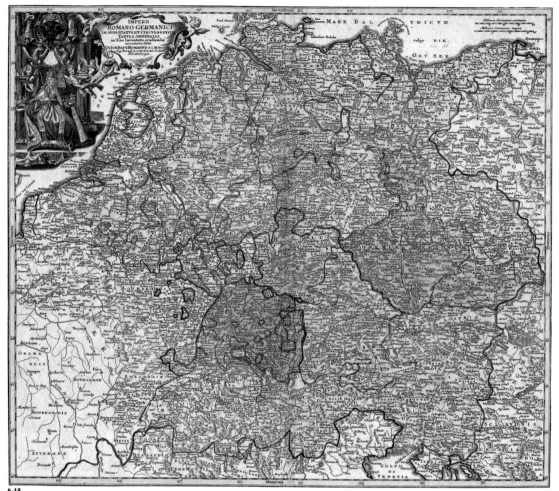

4.1a

PART 4 DIVIDED CENTRE AND ORTHODOX EAST

4.1c

4.1b

>4.1 THE WESTERN AND EASTERN EMPIRES:

(a, b) maps by Johann Baptist Homann (c. 1740 and
1730 respectively); (c, d) their insignias.

4.1d

INTRODUCTION

Devised for the Church Triumphant, Baroque techniques were pressed with hardly less theatricality into the services of the State Triumphant by Louis XIV, as we have seen. Versailles – or Trianon or Marly – set the model for princes all over Europe, vying to impress one another with their richness and glory. In so far as secular glory was thus to the fore in the 18th century, the French capital eclipsed Rome as the cultural centre of the western world: Italians remained unsurpassed at producing the desired spectacle, but wide was the diffusion of French academicism and its complementary decorative style.

After Versailles, essential to the palace were twin suites of *grands appartements* for the prince and his consort. Extended through multiple antechambers in accordance with the rank of the patron, they were no longer simply *en enfilade* but backed by *petits appartements*, informal in embellishment. Aligned on the central cross-axis between these were the core state rooms: a monumental staircase, usually a variant of the imperial type in a galleried cage, served a grand vestibule which opened into a ceremonial hall over a sala terrena that projected into the upper parterre of extensive formal gardens.

Vast scale was typical of imperial, royal and princely building, of course, not only in the superficial area covered by complex centralized massing but in articulation: their colossal Orders rose either from the ground or from a rusticated base in either manner established by Michelangelo on the Campidoglio and introduced to France by Bernini in his projects for the Louvre. Equally essential were exuberance and colour, in the vast formal gardens laid out – with varying degrees of comprehension – to the formula of André Le Nôtre and in the buildings themselves: in the dazzling apartments decorated after the example of Charles Le Brun, or on the original model

›4.2 PAUL DECKER AND THE SECULAR PARADIGM: (a–c) allegory of princely architecture, the ideal royal palace and throne room detail (*Fürstlicher Baumeister*, frontispiece to first part, 1711, overview and throne room plates from second part, 1716).

Decker (1677–1713) was a pupil of Andreas Schlüter, whom we shall encounter as principal architect to the elector of Brandenburg, Fredrich III (later King Fredrich I of Prussia). *Fürstlicher Baumeister* was meant to open a full typology: the first two parts (the second published incomplete after the author's death) constitute the most lavish of early 18th-century folios of large-scale palace design – at least in Germany. There are descriptions but no evolved theory: however, the exhaustive nature of each individual exercise – cover-

ing structure, articulation, interior decoration and furnishing – demonstrates the unity of all three arts. And that is the theme of the allegorical frontispiece: architecture, divinely inspired and guided by the Ancients, is served by painting and sculpture. As we shall see, the ideal of the fusion of the arts in a *Gesamtkunstwerk* was to be a very real achievement in the southern orbit of empire – especially for the church.

provided by Pietro da Cortona at the Palazzo Pitti – and, later, in the Rococo style of Hardouin-Mansart's heirs. And the prolixity of all this was at its most astonishing in the states of the fragmented empire, its neighbours and rivals.**4.1, 4.2**

The Catholic empire had spent much of the 17th century in turmoil. Until 1648 it was ravaged by the Thirty Years' War with Protestants, inside and out. Recovery and rebuilding had hardly begun under Leopold I (1658–1705) when the seat of imperial power itself was confronted by a resurgence of the Turkish menace. When the Ottoman forces were finally repelled from the gates of Vienna in 1683 and pushed back down the Danube to their Balkan strongholds, Austria, Bohemia and the numerous principalities into which Germany was divided could rebuild. And rarely has more magnificent building, secular and religious, been undertaken at any one time.

4.2c   4.2b

4.3a, b

PATRONS AND BUILDERS

Apart from the emperor as archduke of Austria and king of Bohemia and Hungary, the main patrons in the fragmented empire were the electors of Brandenburg, Saxony, Bavaria and the Palatinate; then there were the hundreds of dukes and margraves and their collaterals. Whether or not their medieval or Renaissance seats emerged unscathed from the war, rulers from the emperor down – princes of church and state – wished to conform to modern conceptions of comfort and convenience. They also needed to cater for the strictures of etiquette imposed on the Spanish Habsburg court by the king-emperor Charles V on the Burgundian model, developed under his three Philippine successors – to a stultifying degree – and transmitted to the France of Louis XIV with his Spanish marriage.**4.3**

Even before the French king reformed the context of his court – but after the transformation of the Madrid Alcázar for Philip IV (AIC5, pages 693, 757) – Emperor Leopold led with a new wing to the inconveniently organic Hofburg in the imperial capital of Vienna: grandiose plans for an equivalent to Versailles outside the walls awaited his son but were never to be fully realized, as we shall see. Lesser rulers, more seriously inconvenienced in burgs perched on barely accessible eminences, descended to expansive sites on the plains below. For

>4.3 IMPERIAL PATRONS AT THE APOGEE OF PALATINE BUILDING IN THE ORBIT OF EMPIRE: (a, b) Emperor Joseph I (1705–11) and his brother, Emperor Charles VI (1711–40); (c, d) elector Maximilian II Emanuel of Bavaria (1662–1726) and his brother, archbishop-elector Joseph Clemens of Cologne (1671–1723); (e, f) archbishop-elector Lothar Franz von Schönborn of Mainz (1655–1729) and his nephew Friedrich Karl, prince-bishop of Würzburg (1674–1746).

Oldest son of Emperor Leopold I and Eleonore Magdalene of Neuburg, Archduke Joseph acceded to the crown of Hungary in 1687, was king of the Romans from 1690 and was elected to succeed his father as emperor in 1705. On his untimely death in 1711, his brother Charles was elected to replace him: having claimed Spain on the death of Charles II and asserted himself in the Peninsula for five years, Charles lost the support of Britain in that endeavour after his return to Vienna as emperor (see pages 21ff).

Oldest son of the Wittelsbach elector Ferdinand Maria of Bavaria and his wife Henriette Adelaide of Savoy, Maximilian II Emanuel succeeded his father in 1679. He was successful in the imperial cause against the Ottomans in the Balkans, married the daughter of Emperor Leopold I and Margarita Teresa of Spain and was posted to the Spanish Netherlands as governor in 1691. His espousal of the French cause in the War of the Spanish Succession, against his erstwhile Habsburg allies whom he sought to supplant, led to his exile in the Netherlands from 1704 and in France two years later. He regained his electorate as part of the peace settlement in 1714. His brother Joseph Clemens, Archbishop-elector of Cologne from 1688, also supported the French cause, was exiled in France from 1702 and was restored to his ecclesiastical dominion in 1714: on his death in 1723 he was succeeded by his brother's son, Clemens August.

Nephew of Johann Philipp von Schönborn (1605–73), bishop of Würzburg and archbishop-elector of Mainz (from 1642 and 1647 respectively), Lothar Franz was bishop of Bamberg from 1693 and succeeded to his uncle's Mainz electorate in 1695: in that capacity he was honorary chancellor of the empire. His nephew Friedrich Karl, vice-chancellor of the empire (from 1705), was bishop of Würzburg from 1729 in place of his brother Johann Philipp Franz who was appointed to that post in 1719.

4.3c,d

4.3e

4.3f
The dimension of royal patronage – hitherto the preserve of the emperor as king of Bohemia and Hungary – was expanded about the turn of the century when the electors of Saxony and Brandenburg acquired, respectively, the crowns of Poland and Prussia. The elector of Bavaria had to wait another century for promotion to royalty.

them Trianon or Marly provided more practicable inspiration than the vast complex of town, palace and garden at Versailles itself – though they plotted as many degrees of mean between these extremes as the facets of their lives in representation and retreat. The obvious alternative was the Louvre, not least the Roman contributions to the evolution of its east front (see pages 246ff).

The princely patrons included electoral and quasi-sovereign prelates, princes of the empire, whose pretensions were bathed in the glory of the post-Tridentine Church Triumphant and backed by the prestige of their venerable offices: great land holdings made them rich; pilgrimage made them even richer. Episcopal palaces in town and country apart, their seats were usually imperial abbeys, free of feudal obligation under the emperor, which needed comprehensive reordering, even reconstruction, to cater for that exalted visitor – together with, or apart from, lesser mortals. And, of course, there was the accommodation of the abbot in appropriate splendour and of the monks in a considerable measure of privacy complemented by common rooms. The ideal model was the Escorial but even the most determined ambition to override medieval organicism with a grid of courts flanking a grand central basilica had to compromise with prestigious inherited hilltop sites.

Abbeys apart, grand ecclesiastical patronage extended to urban parish facilities and particularly to pilgrimage churches which proliferated anew at miraculous rural locations in the post-Counter-Reformation age of popular piety. Both were usually – if not always – of the aisleless wall-pillar type widely popular in late-Gothic Germany, with internal spur walls as pier buttresses framing chapels and rising through a clerestory to support tunnel or groin vaulting (AIC4, pages 436ff, and AIC5, pages 517ff). The great abbey churches often inherited the venerable basilican form, with aisles flanking a high nave: it was far from uncommon, however, for their modern rebuilders to prefer variations on the wall-pillar scheme if they did not conform to the Counter-Reformation prototype provided by Vignola in the Roman Gesù – both of which could have interconnected chapels instead of aisles.

Furthering the architectural literacy traditionally gleaned from treatises or acquired from experience on campaign, many in the new generation of princely patrons – secular and ecclesiastical – had travelled widely in war or peace. Many felt themselves thus equipped to participate in designing the complex context of their lives, ideally with architects familiar with modern developments abroad: foreign or native, these usually began as military engineers, widely deployed on campaign. Others emerged from the studios of the greatest masters, particularly Bernini and Carlo Fontana in Rome, until the Peace of Rastatt (1714) finally cleared the way to regular concourse with members of the Académie Royale in Paris. Then French architects were particularly active in the north and west and French interior designers and gardeners ranged widely.

Before the promotion of the French to predominance, the Netherlanders had prevailed in the northern orbit of empire – though there had been a stratum of French influence at least since the early 1560s (AIC5, pages 480f). As the 18th century progressed, native Germans came to the fore: the most prominent examples, in the greatest powers, are Matthäus Daniel Pöppelmann in Saxony, and Andreas Schlüter and Georg Wenzeslaus von Knobelsdorff in Prussia.

In Austria, Bohemia and southern Germany, an initial shortage of native architects and craftsmen led to the post-war augmentation of the bands of north Italians and Italian-speaking Swiss – in particular extended Comesque

›**4.4 SOUTH-EAST SWISS CANTONS AND THE NORTHERN ITALIAN LAKE REGION:** (a, b) early 18th-century map and modern Swiss key. The area was home to the Graubündners and the Ticinese, north of the Luganese and the Comasques, who dominated the building industry in the orbit of empire for several generations after the Thirty Years' War.

Senior by birth, the Graubündner Domenico Sciassia (c. 1600–79) worked at the great Austrian Benedictine abbey of Göttweig under the Lombard Cipriano Biasino (1580–1636), at Mariazell and at Sankt Lambrecht (1639): his son or nephew Lorenzo was active in Bavaria on relatively minor works. Next the Ticinese Filiberto Lucchese (1606–66, descended from Giovanni and Alberto who served Archduke Ferdinand, Regent of Tyrol from 1563), was principal architect to Emperor Leopold I in Vienna (from 1660), built the Servite church there, worked for the Abensberg-Traun family in and beyond the capital, for the abbey of Lambach, for the Esterházys at Eisenstadt, for the Czernins in Prague and for the bishop of Olomouc at Kroměříž (1665): his clan mantle was inherited by the brothers Domenico and Bartolomeo (stuccador and painter respectively) but he was succeeded in Vienna, Kroměříž and elsewhere by his Ticinese assistant Giovanni Pietro Tencalla (1629–1702) who also worked for several religious orders in Moravia, most notably the Premonstratensians of Hradisko near Olomouc. Meanwhile the Comesque Carlo Lurago (1615–84), who was responsible principally for the Clementinum in Prague (from 1638), was mainly active in Bohemia but was called to Passau to build the cathedral (from 1668). His younger Trentine contemporary Antonio Petrini (1621–1701) worked mainly for archiepiscopal and electoral princes between Mainz and Bamberg. Next the Graubündner Enrico Zuccalli (c. 1642–1724) supplanted the Bolognese Agostino Barelli (from 1674) as principal architect to the elector of Bavaria and worked on the Nymphenburg palace, at Schleissheim (from 1684) and at Ettal (from 1709): his nephew Giovanni Gaspare Zuccalli (1667–1717) was active in Salzburg from c. 1685, principally on the Theatiner and S. Erhard churches. Next comes the Graubündner Giovanni Antonio Viscardi (1645–1713), bitter rival and ultimate successor to Zuccalli in Munich where he worked on the Nymphenburg palace, the Bürgersaalkirche and Dreifaltigkeitskirche (1709, 1711) as well as Schäftlarn,

4.4a
Benediktbeuern and Fürstenfeld abbeys (from 1701).

Finally are the members of the Comesque Canevale and Carlone dynasties. The former first appear with Antonio on the Dominican site in Vienna: in the next generation Carlo (1625–90) worked at Waldhausen and in Vienna. The Carlone first appear at Graz during the regency of Archduke Ferdinand of Styria (before 1620): the principals active in the era of transition from Mannerism to Baroque include Pietro Francesco (c. 1600–c. 1681) who worked extensively for the Jesuits in their early post-war building campaigns, the brothers Domenico (1615–79) and Carlo Martino (1616–67) who worked as master-builders for Lucchese in Vienna and Eisenstadt, and above all the architect/master-builder Carlo Antonio (1635–1708) and his stuccador brothers Bartolomeo (died 1717) and Giovanni Battista (died c. 1720) – sons of Pietro Francesco – who worked with Carlo Lurago at Passau, and variously at Waldsassen, in Vienna, at Eisenstadt, Garsten, Kremsmünster, Admont, Schlierbach and Sankt Florian – among many other sites.

4.4b

and Graubündner clans respectively – who had played a leading role in all aspects of the building industry at least since the first phase of the Renaissance: their stars were waning early in the new century. Largely conservative of pre-war styles – usually unmoved by developments in Baroque Rome, anyway – they were supplanted in the service of the greatest powers by adventurous native talents: particularly Johann Bernhard Fischer von Erlach and Johann Lukas von Hildebrandt, who had studied in Italy, and the more lowly Tyrolean craft-trained Jakob Prandtauer. The several innovative Bohemian members of the Dientzenhofer family were followed by Johann Balthasar Neumann, especially in Franconia. However, favoured by the proliferation of minor powers which could not afford to sustain a permanent architectural establishment, the Italian speakers were long to avoid total eclipse.

From the eastern canton of Switzerland, Graubündners had dominated the building industry in Renaissance Bavaria but soon after the Thirty Years' War they were challenged by German-speaking teams from the neighbouring western Austrian province of Vorarlberg. The latter had developed a fruitful working relationship with a school of decorators, particularly stuccadors, from Weilheim just across the border in Bavaria, where they flourished under the patronage of the Benedictine abbots of Wessobrunn. Family connections were important to the Comasques and Graubündners: they were hardly less so to the Vorarlbergers and to Wessobrunners – to the Beer and Thumb clans of Au in Vorarlberg, in particular, to the Zimmermanns and Feichtmayrs who emerged from Wessobrunn.**4.4**

The Vorarlbergers ceded to local talent in the 1720s but the Wessobrunners sustained their influence to great creative effect in their susceptibility to the French *style moderne* which flourished at the Munich court after the post-war restoration of Wittelsbach fortunes. Crucially, they transformed it for deployment on the large scale of the church interior – contrary to the norm in France. Much credit is due to collaborators with the Asam brothers, who emerged from Weilheim's fraternal foundation at nearby Benediktbeuren in the second decade of the century.**4.5** Much too is due to Johann Michael Fischer, who took Bavarian Baroque to its apogee at mid-century.

ADVENT OF ROCOCO: DEFINITION

Exiled in France until the Peace of Rastatt in 1714, the Wittelsbach electors of Bavaria and Cologne – Maximilian II Emanuel and Joseph Clemens – returned to their seats with fashionable French tastes. As we shall see, the latter called on Robert de Cotte for the design of his new Bonn palace in the restrained mode of academic Classicism. As we shall also see, his brother returned to Munich with French-trained protégés, the German Joseph Effner and the Fleming François Cuvilliés: they introduced the Rococo, ultimately the *genre pittoresque*, to Bavaria with great effect.

As we have seen, critics from the French Académie Royale d'Architecture tolerated the style invented by their compatriots for the informal decoration of interiors, indeed they welcomed it for private rooms – until they saw the fundamental principles of Classical art threatened by the 'licentiousness' of the *genre pittoresque*. Thus, that ultimate permutation of Rococo found its future abroad: in Romanov Russia, in Habsburg domains and especially in Wittelsbach Bavaria and in Swabia. There the appeal of the style beyond court circles was exploited by the engravers of Augsburg. Their plates informed developments in decorative stucco work led by the artisans of Wessobrunn, contributing the anti-architectonic ingredient which transmogrified a hitherto purely Baroque architectural mode into a peculiarly seductive hybrid confection.**4.6**

4.5

›**4.5 COSMOS DAMIAN ASAM:** at the Benedictine abbey church of Weltenburg.

›**4.6 CARTOUCHE DESIGNS OF THE 1730S:** (a) François Cuvilliés; (b) Gottfried Bernhard Götz.

Like those of Jean Mondon and Lajou (see page 331), these designs develop the inventions pirated by the engravers of Augsburg which influenced interior decorative stuccowork.

Moravian in origin, Götz (1708–74) was a pupil of the painter Johann Georg Bergmüller in Augsburg where he graduated as master and became a citizen in 1733. He was court painter and engraver to the Wittelsbach imperial pretender, Charles VII (1742–45), who was short-lived in rivalry with the Habsburgs.

4.6a

4.6b

The definition of the syncretic style which flourished in the second quarter of the 18th century throughout central and eastern Europe – but most ingratiatingly in southern Germany – is attended with confusion. In my view, the contention that 'Rococo architecture' is a contradiction in terms, that Rococo is an anti-architectonic decorative style which may not logically be applied to the essentially tectonic science of building, is not convincingly denied even by this most radical of movements.

Transformative indeed, the anti-architectural imperative in German design usually operates at vault level where stone often gave way to wood and plaster, as we shall see: below, the buildings are Baroque in their authors' bold manipulation of structuralist conventions. These ultimately derive from Rome: so too do the techniques of illusionist fresco which, within a rocaille framework, deny structural significance to vaulting in the service of transcendental purpose. Not dismissable as icing on a Baroque cake, the stuccowork of those transitory frames is essential to the fulfilment of that purpose in the complete fusion of the arts – in *Gesamtkunstwerk*. However, though Rococo motifs may well stray into the structurally crucial zone of transition from support to load, rarely do palmiers or other willowy vegetal motifs displace columns or even pilasters as the principal representatives of support – even in transforming a medieval church, which was a major German Rococo exercise. The main exceptions are to be found in private apartments, in the occasional banker's Festsaal, in the theatre and in wilfully exotic garden follies. Long before we encounter these, we must review developments – in all the orbit of empire – across the three generations that followed the Thirty Years' War.

1 ADVANCE OF BAROQUE BETWEEN TWO WARS

In the half-century or more after the Peace of Westphalia, before the War of the Spanish Succession, reconstruction was unsurprisingly conservative – even when expanded to meet modern needs. As we have seen, the practitioners were mainly cliquish clansmen usually trained by their fathers or uncles who comprehended little of dynamic developments abroad, even in Italy, though they were north Italian or Italian-speaking Swiss in origin.

AUSTRIAN PRIMACY

The rectangular block-like masses of many post-war castles and palaces are strictly regular in their repetitive fenestration, abstract in articulation if not with a thin Order of regularly repeated colossal pilasters. Sixty years after austere works like Rudolf II's Linzer Schloss or Giovanni Maria Filippi's marginally more articulate

›**4.7 VIENNA, HOFBURG, LEOPOLDINISCHER TRAKT,** from 1660: exterior from south.

The Leopoldinischer Trakt connected the Schweizertrakt of Ferdinand I with the Amalienburg of Maximilian II and his son Rudolf II (AIC5, pages 98f, 436). It contained the suite of state rooms required by the strictures of court etiquette imposed on themselves by the Spanish and Austrian Habsburgs – after the Burgundian model, to varying degrees (AIC5, pages 692ff). The emperor's accommodation in his principal seat had hitherto been surpassed by the pre-war Kaiserhof in the Residenz at Munich and Hans Krumper's articulation of that quadrangular building provided something of a precedent for Filiberto Lucchese's attempt to elude monotony with a giant, if insubstantial, order of panelled pilasters.

The wing was renovated and extended by Lucchese's assistant Giovanni Pietro Tencalla from 1685 after a fire in 1672 and damage inflicted by the Turkish siege in 1683.

4·7

‹**4.8 EISENSTADT, ESTERHÁZY PALACE,** from 1663: (a) entrance front, (b) Great Hall (now known as the Haydn Hall because of the great composer's long service to the family there).

After the repulse of the Turks Prince Paul Esterházy earned promotion to the top rank of nobility by his support for the emperor's claim to the Hungarian throne against the largely Protestant secessionist opposition. The attribution of his provincial town palace to Lucchese depends on style rather than documents: the executive architect was Carlo Martino Carlone. The building rose over the base of a medieval castle, hence the corner towers. The unadventurous repetitive ordonnance is typical of Lucchese elsewhere but the opening of the façade with generous fenestration above a loggia is novel for a seat established in the context of former fortification in hitherto exposed terrain. The interior is much changed but the Great Hall preserves the frescoes of Carpoforo Tencalla (from c. 1665): 'The Wedding of Cupid and Psyche' and 'The Garden of the Hesperides' are important markers of his introduction to the imperial domain of mythological imagery in illusionist painting.

4.8b

building for the same emperor in Prague Castle (AIC5, page 509), Filiberto Lucchese perpetuated the block-like form but had progressed to an ordonnance which subjects obsessively repetitive bays to the overt discipline of definition. The occasion, just over a decade after the end of the Thirty Years' War, was the commissioning by Emperor Leopold I of extensive new building in the Viennese Hofburg (from 1660).**4·7** Three years later the imperial architect provided the designs for the palace of the great Hungarian magnate Paul Esterházy (1635–1713) at Eisenstadt.**4·8** And Lucchese was similarly active at Moravian Kroměříž, the principal seat of the archbishop of Olomouc, which had been devastated during the war. Some advance towards diversification of mass, if not rhythmic ordonnance, is credited to Giovanni Pietro Tencalla at the great Premonstratensian monastery of Hradisko on the outskirts of Olomouc.**4·9**

4.9a

4.9c

›4.9 GIOVANNI PIETRO TENCALLA IN MORA-VIA: (a–c) Kroměříž, archiepiscopal palace (from c. 1665), garden front, court and pavilion vault detail; (d) Olomouc, Kloster Hradisko, court detail.

The first residence on the Kroměříž site was founded by Bishop Stanislas Thurzo in 1497: it was sacked by the Swedish army in 1643 but provided the basis for reconstruction. Archbishop from 1664 to 1695, Karl von Liechtenstein-Castlekorn called for the comprehensive reconstruction of the palace by Lucchese but the latter's death in Vienna in 1666 left the project to be achieved by Tencalla (from 1684 to revisions of 1679). Conservative of the pre-war norm in its quadrangular form, the great bulk of the complex projects at the corner facing the town square, beneath a tower built on the medieval foundations. However it is barely relieved with a giant panelled Doric Order which recalls the system of articulation adopted by the chief imperial court architect in Vienna – though variation is provided by the rusticated basement of the entrance front and blind arcades to the court elevations. Much of the interior was redecorated after a fire in 1752.

4.9b

4.9d

**›4.10 LATE-17TH-CENTURY VIENNESE PAL-
ACES:** (a) Abensperg-Traun (from c. 1651 and again
from 1700, demolished 1855), façade (late-17th-cen-
tury engraving by Salomon Kleiner); (b) Dietrichstein
(or Lobkowicz), view of street front (1671, Bernardo Bellotto; Vienna, Kunsthistorisches Museum).

Count Ernst Abensperg-Traun acquired his site in
1651 and initiated development embracing its neighbour: attribution to Lucchese is likely but not securely
documented. Severely damaged during the Turkish
siege, the complex was rebuilt in 1700.

The Dietrichstein site was acquired in 1685 and Tencalla was commissioned forthwith to begin work on the
palace – the first after the relief of Vienna in 1683, its
façade survives largely in its original state. Rusticated
pier-pilasters distinguish the higher seven-bay central
block from the five-bay wings in the manner – if not the
style – of Bernini's Palazzo Chigi. The portal was redesigned in 1709 by Johann Bernhard Fischer von Erlach.

4.10b

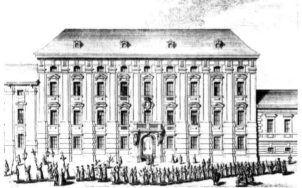

4.10a

Viennese town-house building soon revived too: it was
boosted after the final expulsion of the Turks and the
release of aristocratic funds from military subvention. In
his design for the palace of the Abensperg-Traun (after
1651) Lucchese reiterated the repetitive system of ordonnance in terms of colossal pilasters in light relief which
he had applied to the Hofburg's Leopold wing. Tencalla
offered advance on this in his designs for the Dietrichstein
palace (from 1685): regular repetition cedes to more vigorous centralization.**4.10**

Ecclesiastical activity in Austria was limited in the decade following the Peace of Westphalia (1648). Three years
into the post-war era Lucchese began the Servite church
in Vienna: the longitudinal elliptical plan, with transept
and twin-towered façade, was to prove highly influential
in the city when major building was resumed after the
repulsion of the Ottomans in 1683.**4.11** He is also associated with work of the early 1660s on the Church of the
Nine Choirs of Angels (Kirche am Hof) which was to
be completed by Carlo Antonio Carlone with a revised

façade, as we shall see. In Innsbruck, meanwhile, Christoph Gumpp (1600–72) had begun post-war activity with the Mariahilferkirche (from 1647) and the Premonstratensian abbey church of Wilten (from 1651): the former is a domed rotunda, distantly Palladian; the latter was built in wall-pillar form in place of a Gothic basilica destroyed by the collapsing tower.**4.12**

Gumpp began his career in his twenties, working ostensibly under Father Karl Fontaner on the Innsbruck Jesuit church (AIC5, page 529). Still active in the early years of the war, as there, the Jesuits played a principal role in the revival of church building after it. Pietro Francesco Carlone served them widely, notably at Loeben and Linz

>4.11 VIENNA, SERVITE CHURCH, from 1651: (a) exterior, (b) interior.

The order, licensed in Vienna by Ferdinand III in 1638, founded their church at the end of the war. The identity of the architect is disputed between Carlo Canevale and Carlo Martino Carlone, with the latter more recently favoured: Filiberto Lucchese may also have been involved during the twenty years of construction.

4.12

4.13

(from c. 1660 and c. 1669 respectively). There he perpetuated the wall-pillar tradition.[4.13]

While Pietro Francesco Carlone was active in Linz, his son Carlo Antonio was working as foreman for Carlo Lurago on the construction of the cathedral upstream at Passau (from 1668). The scheme followed that of Salzburg cathedral in its twin-towered front to a post-Vignolan volume: as in the prototype, there is a dome over the crossing but, instead of tunnel vaulting, Lurago introduced a succession of domical vaults to the nave bays for the first time in the orbit of the empire.[4.14] The older Carlone followed this for the Cistercian abbey church of Schlierbach in Upper Austria – where the stucco embellishment of the wall-pillar structure best represents the ripe style of his last years.[4.15] Their work was completed by his son who was to take the work of his clan to its apogee, as we shall see in due course.

›**4.12 INNSBRUCK, WILTEN, COLLEGIATE ABBEY CHURCH,** from 1651: interior.

The Romanesque basilica, with triapsidal sanctuary over a burial crypt, was rebuilt in 1300 but severely damaged by the collapse of the tower in the 1640s. Rebuilding to Gumpp's plans was undertaken by Abbot Dominic Loehr (1651–1687): consecration eventuated in 1665, the north tower followed two years later; the south tower remained incomplete after Gumpp's death in 1672.

›**4.13 LINZ, ALTER DOM** (former Jesuit church of S. Ignatius), from 1669: interior.

Consecrated in 1678, Pietro Francesco Carlone's variant of the traditional wall-pillar form follows precedents set for the order, *inter alia*, at Dillingen (from 1610 by the Graubündner Hans Alberthal; see AIC5, page 520) and at Steyr for both the Jesuits and Dominicans (from 1631 and 1642 respectively, probably by a Comesque architect from the Carlone or Canevale families). Furthered at Waldhausen (from 1650) by Carlo Canevale, the wall-pillar tradition was widely favoured for lesser ecclesiastical works – at parish or pilgrimage level – not least by the Graubündners.

4.14b

4.14a

›4.14 PASSAU, CATHEDRAL OF S. STEPHAN,
from 1668: (a, b) exterior and interior.

Founded in 1221, the early Gothic church was enlarged at various reprises in the 15th and 16th centuries. Part of the east end was retained in the otherwise comprehensive rebuilding initiated after a fire in 1662. Carlo Lurago was assisted by the masons Francesco della Torre and Giovanni Battista Passerini as well as Carlo Antonio Carlone.

The basilican scheme is conventionally cruciform, with domed crossing, but the novel succession of sail vaults over the nave reasserts the discretion of the bays in reverse of the Gothic trend towards horizontal unity reiterated by Neoclassical tunnel vaulting. The boldly sculpted stucco relief, designed by the architect who had trained as a stuccador but executed by Giovanni Battista Carlone, is characteristic of Comesque artisans; the frescoes are due to Carpoforo Tencalla who was also Comesque.

›4.15 SCHLIERBACH, CISTERCIAN ABBEY CHURCH, from 1680: sanctuary.

Converted to Protestantism, Schlierbach reverted to the Cistercians of Kremsmünster under the Counter-Reformation regime of Emperor Ferdinand II: Abbot Gülger Mattias recruited a colony of monks from Graz in 1620. Local discontent delayed rebuilding of the dilapidated monastic complex until Abbot Geyregger (1660–79). Abbot Rieger Benedict (1679–95) commissioned the reconstruction of the church.

4.15

4.16b

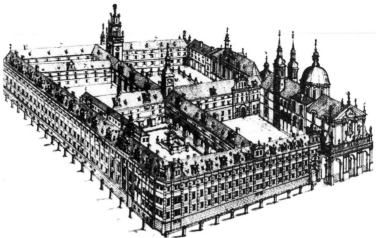

4.16a

>**4.16 CARLO LURAGO AND FRANCESCO CAR-
ATTI IN PRAGUE:** (a–c) Clementinum, overview,
detail of street front, interior of S. Saviour; (d) Czernin
Palace (from 1669), exterior.

The Clementinum site was developed by the Dominicans from 1232 after they acquired its 11th-century
chapel of S. Clement. It was ceded to the Jesuits in 1556
under imperial auspices to promote Counter-Reformation
dogma. Absorbing Charles University after the defence
of the imperial Catholic cause in Bohemia in the Thirty
Years' War (formal merger 1654), most of the collegiate
complex on the expanded site was developed in the late-
17th and early 18th century: the early work was overseen
by Francesco Caratti (died 1677) and Carlo Lurago (died
1684) with the principal assistance of Giovanni Domenico Orsi (born in Vienna c. 1634, died in Prague 1679); the
later phase, including the embellishment of the great
library and much other interior decoration, was led by
František Kanka (died 1766). S. Saviour (built from 1593)
was redecorated over an extended period beginning
with Caratti's introduction of the domed crossing (1648):
the Roman High Renaissance façade survives behind
Caratti's triumphal arch (mid-1650s) which forms its
portico in variance of the model as transmitted by Serlio
(AIC5, page 157, and right in the overview).

4.16c

INTO BOHEMIA AND ON TO
FRANCONIA

Carlo Lurago had been called to Passau from Prague where
his major work was for the Jesuit college known as the
Clementinum (begun in 1653). As Vienna was under siege
until 1683, Prague was the first Habsburg seat to embark
on grand new building projects beyond the imperial-royal
court. Comasques had been dominant in Bohemia's building industry from the outset of the Renaissance in Prague
(AIC5, pages 437ff) and the Comesque Lurago was first in
the post-war era: he had an extensive practice throughout
Bohemia in both the religious and secular fields. In Prague
he collaborated with the Ticinese Francesco Caratti who
also had a busy ecclesiastical and secular career: beyond
the Clementinum, his major building in Prague is the
Czernin Palace (from 1669), ostensibly based on a sketch
by Bernini. In the previous decade he was involved with
work at Roudnice nad Labem on the quasi-monastic Lobkowicz Palace: the plans were provided by the Luganese
architect Antonio della Porta (1631–1702) who also worked
for the Lobkowicz at Neustadt an der Waldnaab in north-
west Bavaria.**4.16, 4.17**

Count Humprecht Jan Czernin commissioned the palace on the prominent site at the western end of the spur crowned by the Hradčany to the east: Caratti's response was certainly Baroque in scale but the specific precedent for his colossal Order of engaged columns rising over a rusticated basement may be found in late Palladian works like the Palazzo Porto in Piazza Castello in Vicenza (AIC5, page 246), rather than the work of a Roman High Baroque master.

›4.17 ROUDNICE NAD LABEM, LOBKOWICZ PALACE, from 1652: exterior.

The medieval complex, the favoured summer residence of the archbishops of Prague, had passed to the Lobkowicz in 1603. Rebuilding for the second prince incorporated the church and parts of the monastery.

The basic quadrangular form has its Bohemian precedent in the Lobkowicz Palace at Nelahozeves (AIC5, page 454) but the entrance screen with tower may be seen as a substantial variant of the du Cerceau/de Brosse formula or – more likely, perhaps – of Amedeo di Castellamonte's designs for the Savoy palaces in Turin and La Venaria Reale (see pages 151f).

4.16d

4.17

4.18c

4.18b

›4.18 JEAN-BAPTISTE MATHEY IN PRAGUE,
from 1679: (a–c) S. Francis Seraphicus, plan, exterior,
interior; (d–f) Troja Palace, plan, exterior, great hall; (g)
Archbishop's Palace, façade on Hradčany Square.

The cubical mass of S. Francis Seraphicus, the church
of the Knights of the Cross with the Red Star, rises on a
Greek cross to an elliptical dome over the crossing in
variation on the centralized norm most pertinently represented by Borromini's S. Agnese in Piazza Navona,
Rome: the brotherhood was founded in 1233 by S. Agnes
of Bohemia. With its colossal Order of Doric pilasters

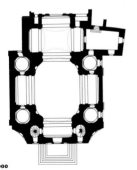

4.18a @ 1:1000

Prague's last great pre-war palace was built by the
Comesque Andrea Spezza for the imperial commander-in-
chief Albrecht von Wallenstein (or Waldstein), victor of the
Battle of the White Mountain (1620, AIC5, pages 510f). In
the second decade of post-war construction, Johann Friedrich von Waldstein (1642–94) – from a collateral branch of
the clan – changed the pattern of patronage to the limited
disadvantage of the Comasques and Graubündners after he
was elected archbishop of Prague in 1675. He imported the
Burgundian Jean-Baptiste Mathey (1630–96) – whom he
had found studying in Rome – as court painter but before the
decade was out he had entrusted him with the design of the
archiepiscopal palace and the church of S. Francis Seraphicus
for the Knights of the Cross with the Red Star – the hospi-
taler brotherhood of which he was grand master.**4.18** At the
end of the decade, Count Wenzel Adalbert von Sternberg
followed with the commission for his suburban Troja

4.18e

4.18f

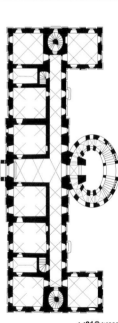

4.18d @ 1:1000

4.18g

applied to the rusticated wall, the exterior is rather more reminiscent of a pavilion by Antoine Le Pautre or even Louis Le Vau than anything Italian – unlike the dome (see pages 223 and 228ff).

The new Archbishop's Palace echoes French practice in its projecting bays but is distantly aware of the intervention of Italians in the project to complete the Louvre (page 246). On the other hand, the central block of the Troja palace is rather more Italian than French – indeed, even the juxtaposition of the wings may be seen as recalling Bernini's Palazzo Chigi (page 107). The staircase has precedents in both those seminal traditions: the atlante supporting the central landing may be Milanese in origin or they may well derive from the first or second of Le Pautre's *Dessins de plusieurs palais* (published c. 1652) though an earlier generation of their Germanic relatives had been extensively enslaved by Wendel Dietterlin (AIC5, pages 490f).

Palace. All three may be seen as hybrid Franco-Italian novelties but, significantly, their execution was directed by members of the old guard – Francesco Lurago, Giovanni Domenico Canevale and Silvestro Carlone.

The challenge to the Italians and their Swiss relatives was also furthered in Prague by Abraham Leuthner (1639–1701), a Bohemian of German descent who claimed to have been to Rome: certainly trained under Comesque masons in Prague, he first appears as an assistant master on the Czernin palace project. He led his co-linguists as a compiler of a treatise/pattern book (published 1677), notable for its promotion of the wall-pillar form of church along with variations on central planning. His major building exercise, for the Cistercians of Waldsassen (from 1681), was influenced by Carlo Lurago at Passau: Comesque stuccadors, led by Giovanni Battista Carlone, embellished the interior in their current mode of chunky relief.**4.19a–c**

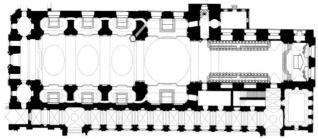

4.19a @ 1:1000

4.19b

4.19c

›4.19 WALDSASSEN: (a–c) abbey church (from 1681), plan, exterior, nave to sanctuary; (d, e) Dreifaltigkeitskirche (from 1685), exterior and plan.

The medieval foundation was sacked during the internecine strife of early 16th-century Bavaria. After reconstruction it was secularized in 1543 and passed to the Lutherans in 1555. Assigned to the Jesuits after the Wittelsbachs regained the Upper Palatinate in 1626 in promotion of the Counter Reformation, it was reassigned to the Cistercians in 1661: they had retrieved all its property by 1690 when their establishment was raised from priory to abbey status. Badly damaged by Swedes in the closing stages of the Thirty Years' War, its reconstruction was commissioned from Abraham Leuthner in 1681. The church was refounded in 1685, reconstruction began in 1689 and lasted until 1701; interior decoration was completed after consecration in 1704.

Fürstenfeld – the priory's mother abbey which was later to be rebuilt in variant wall-pillar form – provided

Waldsassen's first project architect, Kaspar Feichtmayr, who was assisted by his fellow Wessobrunner Benedikt Schaidhauf. Unable to cope on the required scale, they were supplanted by Leuthner's team in which Georg Dientzenhofer was principal executant. The stuccadors worked under Giovanni Battista Carlone. The frescoes are due to the Prague artist Johann Jakob Stevens von Steinfels (1651–1730).

The wall-pillar format is preferred to the standard basilica: the nave follows Carlo Lurago at Passau with a succession of domical vaults; the crossing of the limited transepts is covered with a saucer dome. The chapels between the internal buttresses are lit through pierced vaults at gallery level. The twin-towered façade – not the Cistercian norm – was begun in 1697 to the design of Bernhard Schiesser who was promoted to prime responsibility on Georg Dientzenhofer's death in 1689 (and married his widow): apart from typological relationship to the front of Salzburg cathedral, the specific influence of Dientzenhofer's work for the Jesuits of S. Martin in Bamberg is apparent in the lower zone with its bold segmental arch (see below).

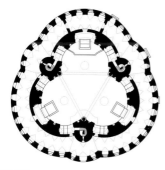

4.19e @ 1:1000

On the slopes of the Glasberg near Waldsassen, the Trinity pilgrimage church is resolutely Trinitarian in its equilateral triangular geometry which expands into three semi-circular apses.

›4.20 ERFURT, PETERSBERG CITADEL: Peterstor (from 1668).

Linked to the diocese of Mainz since the mid-8th century, the city was protected by a Carolingian hilltop fort. In 1060 the archbishop founded a Benedictine monastery in the protected area of the Petersberg and

At Waldsassen Leuthner was assisted by four important members of the Bavarian Dientzenhofer family – Georg (1643–89), Wolfgang (1648–1706), Christoph (1655–1722) and Leonhard (1660–1707), whose sister he married. Georg, who had been translated from Prague as foreman from 1682, contributed the symbolic triangular, triapsidal Dreifaltigkeitskirche within the abbey's purview (from 1685).**4.19d, e**

4.19d

Georg Dientzenhofer progressed to major work for the Jesuits in Bamberg in 1686. When he arrived there the prince-bishop was Marquard Sebastian Schenk von Stauffenberg (1644–93, canon of Würzburg and Augsburg) who employed the Trentine Antonio Petrini (c. 1621–1701). The latter was first active from c. 1660 at the command of Johann Philipp von Schönborn (bishop of Würzburg from 1642, archbishop-elector of Mainz from 1647; see pages 476f) in improving the citadels at Mainz, Würzburg and Erfurt: most notable is the Erfurt Peterstor of 1668.**4.20**

4.20

dedicated it to S. Peter and S. Paul. Rebuilt after a fire early in the following century in association with a palace, it occasionally accommodated the entourage of emperors and German kings. Of considerable strategic importance, the complex was occupied by the invading Swedes in the last decade of the Thirty Years' War: thereafter the citadel was strengthened by the electoral regime, as much against Protestant opposition to restored Catholic rule as against external threat.

Petrini had several ecclesiastical commissions in the later 1660s and many thereafter. His first secure attribution is the Wurzburg Stift Haug (from 1670): the first major post-war exercise of its kind in Franconia, the church was a wall-pillar variant of the twin-towered Salzburg cathedral type. From 1678 he was working in Bamberg on the collegiate church of S. Stephen.

›**4.21 SEEHOF,** from 1687: from the south-west.

Petrini's quadrangular building replaced a 15th-century hunting lodge for Bishop Marquard von Stauffen-

4.21

berg: it was completed in 1696 for his successor Lothar Franz von Schönborn who furthered the interior decoration and added the garden. The latter was elaborated and the interiors modernized under Bishop Adam Friedrich von Seinsheim (1757–79). Downgraded thereafter, the house found little favour with the Wittelsbach kings after the dissolution of the prince-bishopric and the accretion of their domain to the Crown in 1806.

›4.22 GEORG DIENTZENHOFER IN BAMBERG:
(a, b) Jesuit church of S. Martin (from 1686), façade and interior towards sanctuary.

Somewhat confused in its Mannerist complexity, S. Martin's façade begins with the conventional Roman basilican system at base level and expands it beyond the extraordinary segmental arc which oversails the portal niche with its superimposed aedicules. Transition from nave to sanctuary is assisted with pediments broken around corners: fragmentation here echoes a Fontana Mannerist fantasy (see page 116).

4.22b

4.22a

Involved in ecclesiastical work at Bamberg until 1681, Petrini then attracted the patronage of prince-bishop Marquard von Stauffenberg and was commissioned to build the Seehof (Marquardsburg) country retreat. Typically of his conservative compatriots, that is a retrospective exercise: a variant to a reduced scale of the early 17th-century Aschaffenburg Palace of the archiepiscopal electors of Mainz (AIC5, pages 483f).**4.21** Before completing the Seehof (c. 1696), Petrini had returned to Wurzburg for commissions by the Teutonic Knights and the Jesuits. Meanwhile Georg Dientzenhofer's great work for that order, their Bamberg collegiate church now dedicated to S. Martin, was furthered after his death in 1689 by his brothers Christoph, Leonhard and Johann: the domical vaulting of the quasi-wall-pillar nave clearly follows developments at Waldsassen; the complex façade precedes the latter.**4.22**

Wolfgang Dientzenhofer worked for the Jesuits at Amberg in the Upper Palatinate before being taken up by the Benedictines at Ensdorf and the Premonstratensians of Speinshart. At the latter site, his conventional wall-pillar

4.23a

›**4.23 WOLFGANG DIENTZENHOFER AND THE LUCCHESE BROTHERS:**
(a) Speinshart abbey church (from 1691), interior; (b) Coburg, Schloss Ehrenburg (from 1690), Hall of Giants.

Converted to Protestantism and then secularized, Speinshart reverted to Catholicism under the Wittelsbach elector Ferdinand Maria in 1661 and was assigned to the Premonstratensians. Interim repairs to the abbey church gave way to reconstruction from 1691 to Dientzenhofer's plans: the work was completed, with the internal embellishments of the Lucchese brothers, by 1696.

The Coburg town residence of Johann Ernst, Duke of Saxony, was built in place of a dissolved Franciscan monastery from 1543: it consisted of three wings around a court, with the main accommodation in the central range to the north. An outer entrance court was added to the south in 1623 by Giovanni Bonalino for Duke Johann Casimir and the eastern side of the original court was closed in 1680 for Duke Albrecht III. Ten years later the northern range was badly damaged by fire: reconstruction and redecoration of the main state rooms was complete by 1699.

4.23b

›4.24 BAMBERG, NEUE RESIDENZ, from 1697, (a) exterior, (b) reception room detail, (c, d) Kaisersaal.

The Ottonian seat of the bishop was replaced from 1489 by the building now known as the Alte Hofhaltung. The Neue Residenz was begun in 1602 to the order of the prince-bishop Johann Philipp von Gebsattel. Much damage was wreaked by the Swedes in the last decade of the Thirty Years' War: restoration turned to vast extension by Leonhard Dientzenhofer to the order of Lothar Franz von Schönborn in the last decade of the century. The scheme provided a new south-eastern face to von Gebsattel's court and a perpendicular three-storey range extending well out towards the cathedral and terminating in a four-storey tower block – a parallel range framing the court was not to be realized: the articulation with superimposed Orders is disciplined by a regular grid throughout.

There is a genetic relationship between the work of Carlo Domenico Lucchese at Speinshart and the high-relief stucco embellishment of the chimneypiece in the Kaisersaal: the frescoes are by Melchior Steidl. Antonio Bossi was the principal stuccador for the delicate Rococo work executed for Friedrich Karl von Schönborn elsewhere in the palace.

4.24a

4.24b

church was transformed by Carlo Domenico Lucchese's bold figural stuccowork supporting the frames of his brother Bartolomeo's illusionist vault frescoes. Similarly assertive in high relief, the Luccheses' most prominent secular work is the Hall of Giants in Schloss Ehrenburg, Coburg.**4.23**

Elaborate stuccowork in high relief also distinguishes the principal rooms of the Neue Residenz in Bamberg.**4.24**

4.24d

4.24c

4.25b

4.25c

4.25d

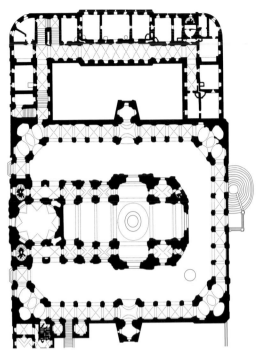

4.25a @ 1:1000

›4.25 CHLUM, S. MÁRÍ PILGRIMAGE CHURCH, from 1664 and 1690: (a) plan, (b) west front, (c) elliptical shrine of the sacred image, (d) nave to sanctuary.

Chlum was the destination of pilgrimage to the shrine of a miraculous image of the Virgin from the 13th century. The primitive wooden chapel was replaced by stone after sack by the Hussites in 1429. A settlement was established by the Knights of the Cross with the Red Star: established as a Bohemian brotherhood of hospitalers in 1233, as noted above, they tended the Marian pilgrims. To cater for the great increase in the files of the latter after the Thirty Years' War, a new church was commissioned by the archbishop of Prague, grand-master of the order, Count Johann Freidrich von Waldstein: incorporating a new elliptical shrine built for the sacred image in 1664, it was begun in 1690. Waldstein's patronage links Mathey to the project for which Dientzenhofer seems to have been executive architect. The frescoes are due to Elias Dollhopf, the high altar to Karl Stilp (1730). The precinct arcade (begun 1708) is credited to Jan Santini Aichel.

For that building Prince-bishop Marquard's successor, Johann Philipp von Schönborn's nephew Lothar Franz (1655– 1729, acceded at Bamberg 1693, archbishop-elector of Mainz from 1694) called on Leonhard and Johann Dientzenhofer. Work began on Leonhard's somewhat monotonous scheme in 1697. Johann went on to greater things, most notably the Benedictine abbey at Banz and the Schönborn palace at Pommersfelden – both of which will be visited after their context has been established.

After completing his brother's Waldsassen Trinity chapel in 1689, Christoph Dientzenhofer appears in the vicinity of nearby Cheb, where he is credited with building the pilgrimage church of Chlum, S. Márí (from 1690), to the domed basilican design associated with Jean-Baptiste Mathey.**4.25** Before the year was out he was in Italy, particularly to see Guarino Guarini's work in Turin. On the basis of that experience he went on to important achievements in Bohemia – in and beyond Prague where he was inspired by Guarini's unexecuted (but published) plans for the Theatine Church of the Blessed Virgin of Altötting (see pages 143f). We shall view the results in opening the chapter on Bohemia and Franconia.

It must be reiterated at this point that although Germans and Czechs were seizing the initiative in their native lands, Italians had not lost it altogether. We shall find plenty of Comasques and Graubündners still active in Bavaria and Austria when we return there shortly but in Bohemia in the first decade of the new century the Italian names often attach to families domesticated there for several generations. Foremost in the north-west was Ottavio Broggio (1668–1742) whose masterpiece is the church of the Cistercian abbey at Osek (1712): a conventional basilica in the main, it is distinguished by an undulating façade expanding across an open narthex to the west and a concave façade squeezed between twin towers to the east.**4.26**

4.26a

4.26b

4.26c

›**4.26 OSEK, CISTERCIAN ABBEY CHURCH,**
from 1712: (a) general view from the north-east, (b)
west front, (c) interior.

The monastery was founded in 1191 by Cistercian
monks from Waldsassen. Plundered by Brandenburg-
ers in 1278 and burned by Hussites in 1421, it was
abandoned by the monks for Altzella near Meissen.
After the Battle of the White Mountain of 1620 it was
revived at the instigation of the archbishop of Prague
and the property returned to the Cistercians in 1626.
By the end of the century Abbot Benedikt Litwerich
was restoring his community's finances on the basis of
cloth weaving and could conceive rebuilding, first the
monastic quarters (from 1705) and then the church on
the grand scale of Ottavio Broggio's basilican project.
Outside and in the sculpture is mainly by Franz Anton
Kuen (from 1714).

›**4.27 ECCENTRICITIES OF JAN SANTINI
AICHEL:** (a–c) Kladruby, plan, exterior from north-
west, detail of vaulting; (d) Sedlec abbey church (from
1702), west end; (e–h) Zelená Hora (Zd'ár), pilgrimage
church of S. Jan Nepomucky (from 1720), overview,
exterior, detail of interior and plan.

4.27c

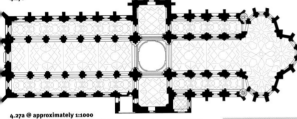
4.27a @ approximately 1:1000

Broggio's Osek takes us too far forward: we shall see work associated with Johann Lukas von Hildebrandt a decade earlier as providing a possible precedent. But it is convenient to press on and encounter here another Bohemian of Italian extraction whose most celebrated ecclesiastical work is so idiosyncratic that it may be fitted anywhere – or nowhere – in an account of proto-Baroque architecture. This is Jan Santini Aichel (1677–1723) who enclosed the church of S. Mári, Chlum, with a High Renaissance arcaded gallery, unexceptional except for the tiny elliptical cupolas of its intermediate pavilions: he went on to indulge an altogether different mode. That has been described as 'Baroque Gothic' but is rather more engaging for its rooting in the latter than its departure for the former. The outstanding examples are his Cistercian and Benedictine abbey churches at Sedlec (from 1702) and

Basilican, the Benedictine Kladruby church's tunnel-vaulted nave and choir are separated by a domed crossing and the aisle arcades are semi-circular: however, the elongated pilasters support varied webs of decorative ribbing in furtherance of Benedikt Ried's late-Gothic manner (AIC4, pages 444f) and the dome is a fantasia on themes never developed by Gothic architects. At Cistercian Sedlec, tall slender shafts rise from pointed arches to another spaghetti of decorative ribs in the pointed tunnel vault.

4.27d

4.27b

4.27e
4.27f

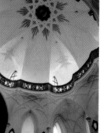

4.27g
4.27h @ 1:500

Kladruby (from 1712). Even more extraordinary, to give but one other example, is the multi-pentagonal votive church of S. Jan Nepomucky at Zd'ár which seems to penetrate east into Orthodox land for its highly unorthodox anti-quarianism.**4.27** On the other hand, in his extensive secular practice Santini Aichel usually conformed more closely to prevalent modes – but could surprise even in that context, as we shall see when it is relevant.

TO BAVARIA

As we have noted, the first challenge to the dominance of the Graubündners in Bavaria came from Vorarlberg-ers. The first figure of individual importance to emerge from their ranks was Michael Beer (c. 1605–66), who founded the confraternity of Vorarlberger building workers (Auer Zunft) in 1657. Initially responsible for S. Lorenz at Benedictine Kempten (from 1652), Beer suc-cumbed to the opposition of the Graubündner Giovanni Serro in the execution of that hybrid centralized/longitu-dinal project but the reverse did not go unredressed.**4.28**

Working with Wessobrunn stuccadors, Vorarlbergers retrieved ascendancy against the Graubündners in west-ern Bavaria with Beer's protégé Michael Thumb (1640–90) and son Franz Beer (1660–1726). Together with their

On the Zelená Hora (Green Hill) at Zd'ár the chapel was commissioned ex voto for the discovery of the intact tongue of S. Jan Nepomucky exactly five cen-turies after the foundation of the abbey: five unequal tongue-shaped projections, mainly for stairs, sepa-rate five oval vestibules with tongue-shaped attics opening off a circular 'nave'; into the latter's dome five pointed elliptical clerestory vaults – tongue-shaped at both ends – intrude over the radial tongues, leaving five broad domical membranes crossing over the cen-tre where the saint's tongue is glorified.

›4.28 KEMPTEN, BASILICA OF S. LORENZ, from 1652: (a) plan, (b) interior to sanctuary.

The first important abbey church to be rebuilt in Bavaria after the Thirty Years' War, the extruded cen-tralized scheme with its twin-towered front was clearly inspired by Salzburg cathedral, the last great pre-war church in trans-Alpine domains. However, the crossing, with its octagonal dome, is expanded into a distinct centralized space without specific votive purpose.

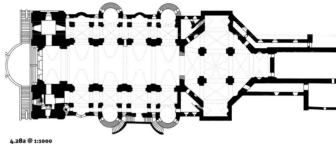

4.28a @ 1:1000

brothers and sons – notably Peter Thumb (1681–1766), who married Franz's daughter – they played a leading role from the mid-1680s working on the main types of ecclesiastical commission: the abbey church, the pilgrimage church and the rare combination of the two. Succeeding to his mas-

4.28b

4.29a

4.29b

4.29c

›4.29 THUMB AND THE WALL-PILLAR CHURCH:
(a, b) Ellwangen, Schönenberg (from 1682), exteriors from east and west; (c) Obermarchtal (from 1686 to plans of two years earlier), interior to sanctuary.

Development of the form by Michael Thumb and his relatives runs to the separation of the buttress pillars from the spur walls as pier pilasters, by increasing the height of the communication passage between the chapels, and the corresponding assertion of nave bay autonomy with groin or canopy vaults instead of the traditional continuous tunnel. Peter Thumb continued the process for the Benedictines of Ebermünster and S. Peter in the Black Forest (from 1719 and 1724).

ter's practice – via several incomplete projects – Michael Thumb displaced a Graubündner at the Premonstratensian abbey of Obermarchtal. Completed by Franz Beer, that work initiated a monumental series of wall-pillar churches (from 1686). As we have already seen, the form had appealed widely to the Jesuits before the war as a local variant on the Roman Gesù type (AIC5, pages 184f): at their instigation Thumb reiterated it on the small scale of the pilgrimage church at Schönenberg on its isolated mountain site by Ellwangen (from 1682).**4.29**

In Munich, Italians were entrenched in the service of the elector of Bavaria, Ferdinand Maria, and his Savoyard wife, Henriette Adelaide. They had tried to attract the Theatiner Guarino Guarini, active in the electress's dynastic seat but on his way between Prague and Paris in the service of his order. They wanted him for the Munich church of S. Kajetan or Theatinerkirche – their seat's first great post-war ecclesiastical project – conceived ex voto for the birth of their son (the future Maximilian II Emanuel) in 1662. Unsuccessful in this, they made do with the undistinguished Bolognese Agostino Barelli (1627–79)

›4.30 MUNICH, THEATINERKIRCHE, from 1663: (a) west front, (b) interior to sanctuary.

Agostino Barelli was awarded the Theatine commission on plans of April 1663 derived from the order's Roman mother church. Facing the Residenz, it was to be a ceremonial hall for the court and burial church as well as the principal Theatine facility. Revision was necessary in 1667, after it was realized – by the Theatine brother Antonio Spinelli – that Barelli had miscalculated the width of the nave when converting the proportions of S. Andrea in accordance with the scale of measurements used in Munich. That was corrected but the Roman model was varied for the internal articulation: half-columns frame the bays, of which there is one for the apsidal sanctuary, three major ones for the nave and minor ones within the entrance and before the crossing. The last is crowned with a dome closely related to Carlo Maderno's design for S. Andrea. The west front is genetically Roman, but Barelli projected flanking towers in conformity with Bavarian and Austrian practice asserted most prestigiously in Salzburg by Santino Solari. Dome, towers and façade were not to be realized under Barelli: he returned to Bologna apparently worsted by Spinelli who had been appointed master of works after discovering the mistake in proportioning the nave. Spinelli worked under the direction of Enrico Zuccalli: the dome was finished in 1688 but the façade, redesigned by Cuvilliés, was not realized until 1768.

who had worked for the Theatines in his home town. In response, he was instructed to follow the obvious course of modelling his work on the church of the order's Roman headquarters, S. Andrea della Valle (AIC5, page 291). After a protracted dispute with the Theatine brother Antonio Spinelli, master of the works, Barelli returned to Bologna in 1674, leaving his great work incomplete. Except for the façade, that was effected by his successor as court architect, the Graubündner Enrico Zuccalli (c. 1642–1724) who had experienced the work of Bernini – probably in Rome, possibly in Paris in the late-1660s.**4.30**

4.30b

4.31

Barelli is also credited with – or blamed for – the original block-like pavilion of the Nymphenburg palace in the western suburbs of Munich, though he may have been commissioned to revise an anonymous German design. In any case, the original work may be seen as an overgrown Marly – in purpose if not in scale or style and devoid even of *sgraffito*. Barelli ceded to Zuccalli here too in 1674 but work ceased after the electress's death two years later.**4.31**

Henriette Adelaide's son Maximilian II Emanuel, who had succeeded to the electorate in 1679, focused his attention on Schleissheim where a hermitage built for Duke

In gratitude for the birth of his heir, the elector Ferdinand Maria gave his wife a tract of land west of his seat for development as a garden retreat with a substantial villa. According to this engraving of 1701, before Zuccalli's major campaign of alterations, Barelli's main block had five storeys of some thirteen bays' width and ten in depth: the only relieving feature was the portal at the head of the twin-flight external staircase. Though it is not apparent, these led to a double-height hall which penetrated the centre to superimposed rooms linking the electoral apartments on the garden side. Surviving in plan and section, this prompted Zuccalli's revision of the unprogressive exterior elevations with their mechanically repetitive rectilinear fenestration (as we shall see in due course).

4.32a

›**4.32 ENRICO ZUCCALLI AT SCHLEISSHEIM:**
(a–c) Altes Schloss (from 1598), reconstructed after World War II), overview (engraved illustration to the

4.32c

4.32b

electoral atlas of Anton Wilhelm Ertl, 1687), east front and court tower; (d) Lustheim (from 1684), west front.

Duke Wilhelm V founded a hermitage and retreat at the site near Dachau in 1598. Maximilian I commissioned a second courtyard from Hans Krumper (1617): the original cross-wing and clock tower were preserved between the two courts. Maximilian II Emanuel had Zuccalli build the Lustheim banqueting house (from 1684) in preparation for his marriage to the emperor's daughter, Archduchess Maria Antonia: it projects from the garden side in the French manner but the entrance front, articulated with a colossal Order rising from the ground, is recessed between short wings fenestrated at base level in the Italian High Renaissance manner. The hall and the chapel (in the left wing) are due to Johann Anton Gumpp, Francesco Rosa and Giovanni Trubillio.

The palace was conceived as a new seat and was greatly to be augmented when the Wittelsbach elector was ambitious for the imperial crown: though that cause was lost and exile ensued during the War of the Spanish Succession, the patron sustained the project on his return to power – as we shall see.

4.32d

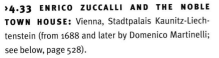

›4.33 ENRICO ZUCCALLI AND THE NOBLE TOWN HOUSE: Vienna, Stadtpalais Kaunitz-Liechtenstein (from 1688 and later by Domenico Martinelli; see below, page 528).

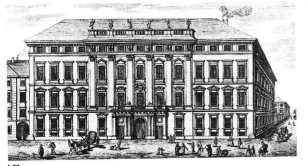

4.33

William V had been extended into a more substantial residence (from 1617; subsequently known as the Altes Schloss). In 1684 Zuccalli was commissioned to build a banqueting house with ancillary accommodation (which was subsequently known as Lustheim).**4.32**

Viceroy of the Netherlands from 1691 to 1701, the elector resumed the suspended work at Nymphenburg on his return to Munich: simultaneously, he charged Zuccalli with executing a grand project for a new palace at Schleissheim. Work lapsed with the elector's exile during the War of the Spanish Succession. That history repeated itself at Bonn where Maximilian Emanuel's brother Joseph Clemens, the archbishop-elector of Cologne, called on Zuccalli for a new residence. Both will be reviewed as they developed.

Zuccalli introduced the Roman form of Baroque palace façade, specifically that of Bernini's Palazzo Chigi, to Vienna for Count Dominik Andreas von Kaunitz (from 1688) and to Munich for Count Fugger (from 1693).**4.33** And it was to his Roman sources that Zuccalli returned for his last great ecclesiastical commission, undertaken when out of work at court with the exile of his patron during the War of the Spanish Succession: the transfor-

4.34b

4.34c

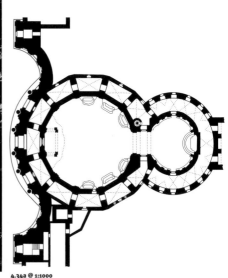

4.34a @ 1:1000

›4.34 ENRICO ZUCCALLI AT THE BENEDIC-
TINE ABBEY OF ETTAL (from 1709): (a) plan, (b)
general view, (c) church from west.

The rotunda pushes out into a façade articulated
with a colossal Order of columns marching with the
curve but stops short of generating movement in Borromini's serpentine manner. It was later severely damaged by fire and redecorated inside.

›4.35 FÜRSTENFELDBRUCKE, CISTERCIAN
ABBEY CHURCH: (a) plan, (b) interior to sanctuary,
(c) west front.

The monastery was founded c. 1258 by Duke Ludwig II of Bavaria (1253–94) in penance for the execution
of his wife: it moved to its present site in 1263. It was
granted princely status by the anti-pope Nicholas V c.
1329 and served as a Wittelsbach necropolis in the 14th
century. Badly damaged by the Swedes in the Thirty
Years' War, the monastic quarters were rebuilt from
1691 at the instigation of the abbots Martin Dallmayr
(1640–90) and Baldwin Helm (1690–1705): in 1700 the
latter also began the replacement of the Gothic church
to Viscardi's conservative but exceptionally grand
wall-pillar scheme which recalls the order's recent
work at Waldsassen. Progress lapsed during the War
of the Spanish Succession: when work began again in
1714 Viscardi was dead but his plans were ostensibly
honoured by his less-celebrated successors – except,
no doubt, for the unusually elevated west front. The
interior decoration was still incomplete at mid-century:
Pietro and Jacopo Appiani were responsible for most
of the stuccowork; Cosmas Damian Asam for the vault
frescoes in the nave and choir.

mation of the unusually centralized volume of the Gothic
abbey of Ettal into a Baroque rotunda (from 1709).**4·34**

During his elevated patron's exile, Zuccalli was eclipsed
by his bitter rival Giovanni Antonio Viscardi (1645–1713),
even in ecclesiastical commissions. Of these, the Cistercian monastery of Fürstenfeld was begun to Viscardi's
plans in 1691 but after his death and the end of the War
of the Spanish Succession the building was furthered by
local master-masons and then to revised plans attributed
to Johann George Ettenhofer: decorated in part by the
Asam brothers (as we shall see), it was ready for consecration only in 1747.**4·35** In Munich, Viscardi's undistin-

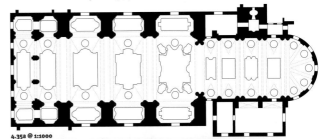

4.35a @ 1:1000

4.35c

4.35b

4.36a

4.36b

The Burgersaalkirche is a simple cuboid structure relieved only with thin pilasters to the street front. in contrast, the Dreifaltigkeitskirche is a Greek-cross exercise which takes its departure from the Milanese work of Francesco Maria Ricchino, particularly S. Giuseppe, but projects the octagonal form of the dome's drum on to the façade (see page 59).

>4.37 GIOVANNI GASPARE ZUCCALLI'S SALZBURG CHURCHES, from 1685: (a, b) Erhardkirche, entrance front, interior; (c, d) Theatinerkirche, overview, interior.

Zuccalli's two churches have eminent Roman centralized precedents: the Erhardskirche is derived from Pietro da Cortona's church of Ss. Luca e Martina in plan and in its elevation to a circular drum carrying the cupola; with its elliptical domical volume set with the main axis perpendicular to the entrance, the Theatinerkirche derives from Bernini's S. Andrea al Quirinale. As we shall see, Fischer von Erlach was not immune to their influence.

guished rectangular Burgersaal prayer hall (from 1711) is entirely eclipsed by his centralized Dreifaltigkeitskirche with its boldly faceted façade (from 1709).**4.36**

BACK TO AUSTRIA

Enrico Zuccalli trained his nephew Giovanni Gaspare (c. 1654–1717), whose career centred on Salzburg. There he followed his uncle's example in reference to Rome but not in introducing Berninesque elliptical planning for the Theatinerkirche and Cortonesque Greek-cross planning for the Erhardkirche (both from c. 1685).**4.37**

In the 1680s, while the Theatines were furthering their Munich and Salzburg works to the direction of the Zuccallis, other orders were busy building churches in southern Germany and Austria. Tyrolean talent still made its mark, not least in sculptural form: Jakob Auer (1645–1706), for exceptional example, provided the High Baroque portal of Lambach (c. 1690).**4.38** However, much

4.38

>4.38 LAMBACH, BENEDICTINE ABBEY CHURCH: portal (c. 1707) attributed to Jakob Auer.

>4.39 VIENNA, CHURCH OF THE NINE CHOIRS OF ANGELS (Kirche am Hof): façade (from 1662).

4·37a

4·37b

4·37c

4·37d

4·39

of the work went to members of the Carlone dynasty –
above all to Carlo Antonio who we met when engaged
on the realization of Carlo Lurago's project for Passau
cathedral in the 1660s. Thereafter he worked mainly
in Austria in varying capacities on various projects for
several of the major orders. *Inter alia* these included:
the Jesuits of Vienna, masking the Church of the Nine
Choirs of Angels with a semi-collegiate façade (from
1662); the Cistercians at Schlierbach (with his father
from 1680, as noted above) and Baumgartenberg (from
1697); the Augustinians at Sankt Florian and Reichers-
berg (from 1686 and 1691 respectively); the Benedictines
of Kremsmünster and Garsten (both from 1680), most
notably under the latter's auspices on the Christkindl
pilgrimage church in Steyr (from 1702). Of all these, his
most substantial legacy is the general distribution and
the twin-towered basilican church of Sankt Florian, his
most seductive is the Christkindl sanctuary.**4·39–4·41**

4.40b

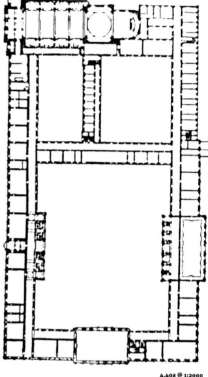

4.40a @ 1:2000

On the much-reduced scale of the pilgrimage church, Carlo Antonio favoured varying the traditional German wall-pillar form – at Frauenberg bei Admont, for example. For that genre as for the smaller of his parish churches, however, he experimented with centralized planning which echoes Roman Baroque prototypes. The rotunda of the Christkindl sanctuary may be seen as homage to Bernini at Ariccia, ultimately to the Pantheon: intimate in scale appropriate to its dedication, its façade is squeezed between twin towers without giving way to canting, convexity or concavity in the manner which we shall see in the contemporary works of the younger generation in Austria and Bohemia – notably Prandtauer who brought the project to conclusion.

›4.40 SANKT FLORIAN, AUGUSTINIAN PRIORY: (a, b) plan and exterior of outer prelatial quadrangle, exterior, (c, d) church exterior and interior.

Carlo Antonio Carlone's last great work was for the Augustinian friars of Sankt Florian at the instigation of the provost Philipp David Fuhrmann (1667–89) in celebration of the repulsion of the Ottomans from the imperial heartland in 1683. The monastic buildings surround two courtyards behind the extended entrance front with its repetitive ordonnance of colossal pilasters typical of Carlone's Italianate contemporaries. At the northern end, the church was rebuilt over early medieval foundations (from 1686): the twin-towered basilican form acknowledges the influence of Salzburg cathedral but the tunnel vault is replaced with a succession of sail vaults after the precedent set at Passau by Lurago. Carlo Antonio's brother Bartolomeo contributed the bold stuccowork to the level of the assertive cornice (by 1690) but was restrained from invading the vaults by Fuhrmann's

4.40c

4.40d

successor: he favoured frescoes by the Tyrolean team of Johann Anton Gumpp and Michael Steidl.

In accordance with venerable tradition, the monastic cloisters were to the south of the church. However, Carlone proposed punctuating the framing ranges of the outer court with pavilions containing the staircase, the great hall and the library: of these only the cupola-crowned ceremonial staircase, to the inner side of the western entrance wing, was begun in his lifetime. The accenting of major reception facilities in this way derives from the secular field – recent examples range from Jean-Baptiste Mathey's Troja Palace to Enrico Zuccalli's Lustheim – ultimately from the traditional French distinction of pavillons from corps de logis if not from Bernini's Palazzo Chigi in Rome.

›4.41 STEYR, CHRISTKINDL PILGRIMAGE CHURCH: (a, b) sanctuary entrance front and interior (Jakob Prandtauer to the plans of Carlone, from 1702).

4.41a

4.41b

2 IMPERIAL BAROQUE AND ITS AUSTRIAN MONASTIC DERIVATIVE

Predictably, the greatest adversary of the king of France, the Holy Roman Emperor, embarked on one of the earliest and most grandiose projects of architectural rivalry with Versailles. Like Versailles, it was to be beyond the capital – beyond the defences where it was safe to build after the repulsion of the Turks in 1683.**4.42** The great imperial palace concept was defined by the emperor's new first architect who had, for once, a talent worthy of the occasion.

FISCHER VON ERLACH

The son of a sculptor, Johann Bernhard Fischer von Erlach (1656–1723) returned to his homeland in 1687 from a decade and a half of study in the Rome of the late Bernini and Carlo Fontana. Little of an incipient career in sculpture materialized. However, his association with the school of the master lauded as the premier architect of the age –

4.44a

4.43a

4.43b

›4.43 VRANOV (FRAIN), SCHLOSS, 1688: (a) general view of clifftop complex, (b) interior of the Hall of Ancestors (Ahnensaal, from 1688).

The patron was chamberlane and imperial privy councilor. His freestanding domed elliptical hall has no precise secular precedent but is obviously more closely related to the central element of Le Vau's Château du Raincy than to the ecclesiastical exercises with which Fischer would have been familiar in High Baroque Rome. Of the other hand, the illusionist vault fresco is more readily associated with Italian practice: it is due to Johann Michael Rottmayr (from 1696).

especially by the anti-French – prompted Count Johann Michael von Althann to call on him to design the great elliptical Hall of Ancestors in his clifftop castle at Vranov (Frain) in Moravia (1688).**4.43**

With Althann's bold project hardly out of gestation, its young Austrian author was promoted to championship of indigenous talents against the entrenched Italians with his appointment as architectural tutor to Crown Prince Joseph in 1689. Practice in Vienna was then dominated by Giovanni Pietro Tencalla, as we have seen. Beyond the court, he and his co-linguists were increasingly active for the great nobility who responded to the expulsion of the Turks by diverting funds from military obligations to palace building. Domenico Egidio Rossi (died 1715), a painter from Fano, was designing a summer palace for Prince Johann Adam von Liechtenstein in 1790. In that same year Domenico Martinelli (1650–1718), the Lucchese associate of Carlo Fontana in Rome, arrived in Vienna at the invitation of counts Ferdinand Bonaventura von Harrach and Dominik Andreas von Kaunitz. Busy for the latter in particular, three years later he was also serving Liechtenstein in place of Rossi. On Tencalla's demise in 1702 he was a pretender to the succession against the native claims of Fischer, who had made his name at court and among Althann's peers but was busy in Salzburg.

On Archduke Joseph's acclamation as King of the Romans and ceremonial entry into Vienna in 1690, Fischer was directed to apply his experience of the Eternal City's antique and High Baroque heritage to the design of triumphal arches. In competition with representatives of the traditional practitioners led by the Tyrolean Peter Strudel, he won two places: the éclat of his response entirely eclipsed the provincial efforts of his colleagues who remained uninvigorated from the resource of the Baroque fountainhead.**4.44a** In the same year he was com-

4.44b

missioned to project the imperial response to Versailles, a vast terraced palace on the eminence of the Schönbrunn to the south-west of the capital. Prepared to make do with his eponymous wing at the old organic Hofburg palace, Emperor Leopold ostensibly conceived the projected complex as the summer seat of his heirs' future but such expensive ambitions were unaffordable. By 1696 Fischer had produced a revised palace project which, though no

›4.44 THE INCEPTION OF IMPERIAL ARCHITECTURE: (a) Arch of the Citizens of Vienna (c. 1690); (b, c) Schönbrunn, initial and revised projects for the imperial palace (c. 1690 and after 1696 respectively); (d, e) plates from *Entwurf einer historischen Architektur*, reconstruction of Nero's Domus Aurea and Trajan's Forum (1721).

The triumphal arches of 1690, three-dimensional and sculptural intrinsically as well as in embellishment emphasizing plasticity, admirably mark their author's

4.44c

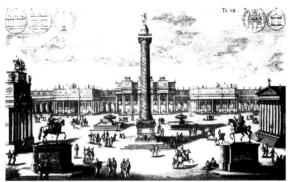

4.44e

transition from training as a sculptor into architecture –
though the Hall of Ancestors at Vranov had already demonstrated native capacity to think in terms of bold shape.

The first grandiose project for the imperial summer
residence at Schönbrunn, on the outskirts of Vienna,
was produced within a decade of the final repulse of
the Turks. The project went through several permutations of reduced scale after it was moved down from the
hilltop site where it began as a hunting lodge for Archduke Joseph. By 1696 the emperor had called for contraction of the sprawling wings into twin lateral blocks,
each enclosing courtyards. In the original scheme, the
articulation in terms of a regular Order and attic over an
arcaded basement derives from Le Vau's garden front
of Versailles as extended by Jules Hardouin-Mansart
– though the arcading is projected to a forward plane:
still further forward it recalls the Versailles Orangerie. The revised scheme follows the Roman Baroque
format of a colossal Order on a rusticated basement
which was translated into French by the commission
established to complete the Louvre – and adapted by
Hardouin-Mansart to his urban schemes. The eagle-
topped commemorative columns of the first scheme
become obelisks in execution.

The central block was complete by the end of the
century and most of the rest of the revised project had
been realized by the end of Joseph's reign as emperor
just over a decade later. The residence of his widow,
after her retirement to a convent in 1722, it was bought
by her brother-in-law, Emperor Charles VI: renovation
and much of the interior decoration was delayed until
the War of the Austrian Succession had been satisfac-
torily concluded in the mid-1740s.

longer utopian, was still meant to rival Versailles in scale
and style.**4.44b, c**

The ceremonial structures of 1690 were ephemeral, the
first palace project unrealizable, but the Roman imperial
motifs borrowed for their symbolism were to be essential
to Fischer's eclectic imperial style: the triumphal arch
itself, of course, the temple-front portico, even the Prae-
nestian arcaded terrace, the *quadriga* and chariot of the
sun, the obelisk, especially the commemorative column
of the Trajanic type. And like the syncretic exercise at
Schönbrunn, the scope of his imperial ambition is forever
commemorated in print: his quasi-theoretical *Entwurf
einer historischen Architektur* is a wide-ranging suite of
imaginative reconstructions of the great religious and
secular complexes of the past which was published in 1721
but conceived during the century's first decade.**4.44d, e**

Fischer would draw upon the repertory of imperial
antique symbolic motifs for idiosyncratic incorporation in
his last great syncretic masterpiece, the votive Karlskirche.
That work marks the culmination of his lifelong interest in
great oval salons with dependent wings – developed from
his High Baroque experience throughout his career in suburban villas and churches. His ecclesiastical career began in
Salzburg while progress at Schönbrunn stalled.

4.44d

4.45b

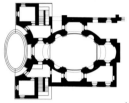

4.45c

4.45a @ 1:1000

DIGRESSION TO SALZBURG

Antipathetic to the Italian architectural establishment, Prince-archbishop Johann Ernst von Thun-Hohenstein (1687– 1709) had not been long in power at Salzburg when he called Fischer to assume the role of principal court architect instead of Giovanni Gaspare Zuccalli. As we have seen, the latter had built the Theatinerkirche on the recommendation of his uncle Enrico – who completed the Theatinerkirche in Munich – but the new regime stopped work on its decoration and withheld payment to the Italians involved. Busy in Vienna, Fischer was unable to accept the archbishop's invitation until 1694. He was immediately commissioned to design the court stables and the Dreifaltigkeitskirche. He responded to the former with characteristically sculptural élan, at least in the portal with its three-dimensional arch. The church is a domed ellipse with a concave façade between twin towers. A second commission, for the Benedictine Kollegienkirche, is a more complex exercise in cruciform and elliptical geometry, with a novel convex façade: it was not to be without influence on Fischer's followers in the orbit of empire.**4.45**

>**4.45 FISCHER AND THE SALZBURG CHURCH:** (a–c) Dreifaltigkeitskirche (from 1694), plan, exterior (as recorded by an early 18th-century engraver), interior; (d–g) Kollegienkirche (from 1696), plan, exterior, interior to sanctuary and to entrance.

The earlier work is orientated conventionally with the long axis culminating in the sanctuary and the short one terminating in chapels – as in Vignola's Roman Gesù prototype (AIC5, page 183) – but its dynamic is countered by the façade bent into concavity between the twin towers. Giovanni Gaspare Zuccalli had also deployed the ellipse for the Theatinerkirche, naturally enjoying the convexity of the dome, but had not staged the drama of confronting it with semi-elliptical concavity after the example of Borromini's S. Agnese in Rome (see page 91).

Fischer responded to the commission for the Kollegienkirche with an essay informed by Rosato Rosati's S. Carlo ai Catinari, which we have related to the chapel of the Sorbonne in Paris (see pages 57 and 186): unlike the model, however, the dome is an ellipse set with its dominant axis reinforcing the short line of the centrally placed transept; on the dominant axis opposite the semi-elliptical sanctuary apse, on the other hand, an oval vestibule pushes the clerestory-crowned façade out into bold convexity between the twin towers.

4.45f

4.45e

4.45g

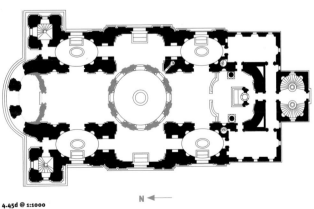

4.45d @ 1:1000

N ◄—

›ARCHITECTURE IN CONTEXT »DIVIDED CENTRE AND ORTHODOX EAST

BACK TO THE CENTRE

In virtue of his work for Althann at Vranov, Fischer received several commissions for retreats (*Lustgebäude*) in the capital's new suburbs beyond the walls and therefore open to experimentation in massing – like the French maison de plaisance. Count Theodor von Straatmann was first in the field in 1692. After that a flood of invention produced influential variations on themes drawn from Le Vau's schemes with projecting salons, from Bernini's first project for the Louvre and from Guarino Guarini's Palazzo Carignano in Turin. Alternative approaches, recalled by Juvarra's Stupinigi and Turinese Palazzo Madama, were adopted respectively for Althann at Rossau and for Archbishop Thun at Klessheim. The latter was in 1700: thereafter, Fischer was rarely to be distracted from the centre of imperial architectural gravity.**4.46**

›4.46 FISCHER AND THE LUSTGEBÄUDE: (a) for Count Ernst Rüdiger von Starhemberg at Engelhartstetten (1693), entrance front; (b–d) for Prince von Liechtenstein at Rossau (1688) and its ideal development, plan and elevations (from *Entwurf einer historischen Architektur*); (e, f) for Count von Althann at Rossau (1693), plan and elevation; (g–i) for Archbishop Thun-Hohenstein at Klessheim in the suburbs of Salzburg (from 1700), main house elevation and garden pavilion, alternative plans and elevations.

4.46a

Fischer's Lustgebäude

If the elliptical Hall of Ancestors at Vranov distantly recalled Le Vau's Château du Raincy, the projection of the oval salon of Count Straatmann's villa at Neuwaldegg is reminiscent of Vaux-le-Vicomte: a variant was produced for Count Ernst Rüdiger von Starhemberg's hunting lodge at

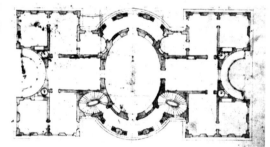

4.46b

4.46c

4.46d

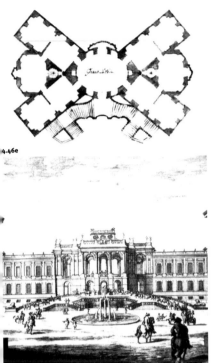

4.46e

4.46f

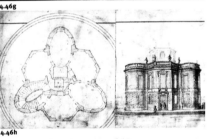

4.46g

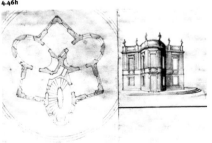

4.46h

4.46i

Engelhartstetten.**4·46a** These schemes are devoid of the airy arcading of Bernini's first project for the Louvre. However, Fischer had ended the 1680s and begun the next decade with reference to that work in his competition project for Prince Johann Adam von Liechtenstein at Rossau (rejected in favour of Domenico Egidio Rossi's scheme).**4·46b, c** He retained it for Count Schlick's Villa Eckhard and in the ideal scheme published in the last volume of his *Entwurf einer historischen Architektur*.**4·46d** The recession in these is shallower than Bernini's great concavity – like Guarino Guarini's Palazzo Carignano without the undulating curves – but the flat planes of Bernini's terrace roof were singularly inappropriate for anything other than formal idealism in the Central European climate.

In the ideal variant on the Liechtenstein scheme the ellipse is expressed on both fronts; in the Starhemberg project the entrance front is concave in contrast to the convex garden front; Schlick's entrance front was recessed with re-entrant corners. At the beginning of the new century that situation is reversed for the *Lustgebäude* of the Salzburg archbishop at Klessheim: the elliptical profile of the arcaded front cedes to the orthogonal but the concave quadrants are redeployed to break the three central bays forward.**4·46g**

In the garden at Klessheim, Fischer built a hexagonal retreat with three ovals projecting on their long axes and three squares projecting on their diagonals.**4·46h, i** Seven years earlier, moreover, he had produced a variation on the elliptical theme at the crux of diagonally disposed wings for Count von Althann at Rossau (1693).**4·46e, f** The device may derive from Carlo Fontana's Montecitorio project which Fischer could have seen in the master's Roman studio (see page 116). Already in this Althann project, the absence of open arcades indicates the triumph of pragmatism over idealism – at least insofar as coping with the Austrian climate was concerned.

4.47a

FISCHER VON ERLACH'S ITALIAN CONTEMPORARIES AT LARGE

Several well-preserved country houses from the beginning of the 18th century, when Fischer's Franco-Italian invention was in full flight, are well represented in central Bohemia and in Moravia. Due to the Comesque Giovanni Battista Alliprandi (1665–1720), whose career was largely Bohemian, Zámek Liblice (from 1699) – north-east of Prague – clearly derives from Fischer's Liechtenstein scheme.**4.47ª** Alliprandi provided another variant for Count František Karel Přehořovský (from 1702), below Prague's Hradčany.**4.47b, c**

4.47c

›**4.47 GIOVANNI BATTISTA ALLIPRANDI AND THE FRANCO-ITALIAN PALACE:** (a) Liblice (from 1699, extended in the later 18th century, interiors renovated mid-19th century), garden front; (b, c) Prague, Přehořovský (from 1702, later Lobkowicz, now German Embassy), plan and garden front; (d–f) Veltrusy (from c. 1711, revised from 1764 and again in the 19th century), plan, mid-18th-century engraved record and general view of garden front.

The palace at Liblice was built for Count Arnost Josef Pachta of Rájov, scion of a recently ennobled bourgeois family, royal governor of the district, who acquired the estate in 1669 from the heiress of the old Liblice dynasty (first mentioned in 1254). The palace in Prague's 'Lesser Town' (Malá Strana) now occupied by the German Embassy was built for Count Přehořovský, governor of the royal mint, whose debts forced him to sell to the Lobkowicz in 1714. Both these buildings vary Fischer's Liechtenstein scheme with greater enclosure: both were altered later in the 18th century.

The patron of Veltrusy was Count Václav Antonín Chotek (died 1754). The original plan and the open staircase echo Fischer's works for Althann to a contracted scale: it was due to Alliprandi. Completed in the mid-1740s, the building was damaged by a flood in 1764: the restoration extended to doubling the length of the wings and the redecoration of the central rotunda in Rococo style but the sala terrena retained its original decoration. The garden, originally laid out along formal French lines and unfashionable in the mid-1760s, was transformed into a park in the English informal style and ultimately endowed with an eclectic range of pavilions. The dome replaced the conical roof of the central rotunda in the 19th century and the wings were heightened.

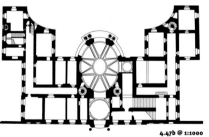

4.47b @ 1:1000

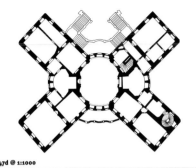

4.47d @ 1:1000

4.47e

4.47f

4.48 JAN SANTINI AICHEL AT KARLSKRONE:
(a) plan, (b) exterior.

Santini Aichel had a very extensive secular and monastic practice in which he rarely subjected his clients to the eccentricities of his imagination, as here. Even here, however, the articulation of the three rectangular blocks is unexceptionally astylar: reasonably, aedicules and broken pediments are reserved for the exposed faces of the core rotunda. The extruded hexagon has its precedent in the unexecuted pavilion project of Carlo Fontana (see page 116).

First in a distinguished line of X-shaped projects, Fischer's work for Althann at Rossau anticipated Boffrand's first scheme for the château of La Malgrange (1712) and the most splendid surviving example, the hunting lodge at Stupinigi built by Juvarra for the king of Savoy after 1729 (see pages 298, 167f). However, its closest and its most eccentric followers are to be found in Bohemia, respectively at Veltrusy (from c. 1711) and Karlskrone (from 1721). Alliprandi is credited with the former.**4.47d–f** The triangular disposition of Karlskrone is due to Santini Aichel, who may also have been inspired by Fischer's Klessheim garden pavilion in his extraordinary work at Zd'ár.**4.48, 4.27d–g**

4.48a @ 1:1000

4.48b

4.4c

4.49b

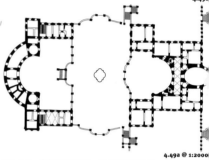

4.49a @ 1:2000

4.49d

›4.49 DOMENICO MARTINELLI AND THE FRANCO-ITALIAN PALACE: (a–d) Buchlovice (former Petřwald Palace, from 1702), plan, fronts to service wing and residential block, garden front; (e–g) Slavkov (Austerlitz), Schloss Kaunitz, (from c. 1695), plan, forecourt and entrance front, garden front.

His medieval castle no longer meeting modern needs, Jan Dětřich Petřwald called on Martinelli ostensibly for an Italianate villa at Buchlovice: completed by 1728, its semicircular court recalls Serlian and Palladian schemes informed by Raphael's Villa Madama in Rome (AIC5, pages 112f) but the oval salon (the music room) projects into the garden in the French manner. The stucco embellishment of the interior is due to Baltazar Fontana (1658–1736).

For Count von Kaunitz at Slavkov, Martinelli redesigned the palace along quadrangular lines: from 1695 work was in train on the west wing with its projecting central ellipse but progressed no further after 1705. In 1731 the scheme was comprehensively revised by Ignazio Valmaggini and Václav Petruzzi under the technical supervision of Johann Bernhard Fischer's son Joseph Emanuel. The east wing of Martinelli's quadrangle survives only as a pair of pavilions with semi-elliptical concave sides leading into an elongated court at the

4.49f

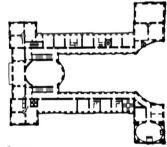

4.49e @ 1:2000

4.49g

head of which is the convex façade of the great hall: no longer a true ellipse, and set longitudinally, it is oblong with curved ends. The external articulation is inconsistent: over an arcaded basement, the hall has a colossal Order of paired Corinthian pilasters inherited from Martinelli, the side wings have an abstract Order of pier pilasters also rising from the basement, the end pavilions have colossal Corinthian pilasters rising from the ground. Unfinished until 1767, the interiors were decorated largely in the so-called Neoclassical style.

Due to Domenico Martinelli, the Petřwald retreat at Buchlovice is a maison de plaisance – if not a suburban villa – which recalls Fischer's Schloss Starhemberg with its concavity and convexity of fronts. Martinelli attempted another Franco-Italian synthesis on a grander scale at Slavkov (Austerlitz) for Count von Kaunitz: quadrangular, the west wing with its elliptical central volume was realized (by 1705) but the scheme was subsequently revised to frame an open *cour d'honneur*.**4·49**

4.50a

TOWN PALACES

Within stellar defences which might well need to withstand a reprise of the recently repulsed Ottoman onslaught, the confines of Vienna promoted height in compensation for the limits to lateral expansion: the Italian palazzo was the

›4.50 DOMENICO MARTINELLI AND THE VIENNESE PALACE, c. 1690: (a) Harrach (begun 1696), street front; (b, c) Liechtenstein (from 1692), street front and staircase.

Articulated with a colossal Order of pilasters throughout, Count Ferdinand Bonaventura von Harrach's palace was innovative in the slight projection of side 'pavillons'. In the revision of Enrico Zuccalli's scheme for Count Kaunitz (see page 509), in contrast, Prince Johann Adam von Liechtenstein was provided with an Italianate block, though the central bays of the entrance front are distinguished by an Order of colossal pilasters supporting an attic balustrade. That distinction was developed in Martinelli's revision. The staircase is of momentous scale but, with one long flight between two short returns skirting the walls of a rectangular hall, the form was relatively conventional. It was completed in Martinelli's absence (from 1705), probably by the Graubündner master-mason Gabriel de Gabrieli, perhaps with the intervention of Fischer.

4.50b

4.50c

practicable model, not the grand Parisian form of *hôtel particulier* with court, porte cochère and garden. However, the impact of an oblique view along narrow streets was seen to depend on as much recession and projection as the site could afford, not on the regular repetition of ordonnance in a single plane – like Tencalla's Dietrichstein Palace.**4.10** In contrast to that, Martinelli opted for selectivity in the context of slight changes of plane in the centre or even the sides of his most influential works – for Liechtenstein and Harrach respectively.**4.50** Fischer's earliest palace marks a distinct advance over the efforts of the Italian opposition – even of the innovative Martinelli.**4.51**

4.51a

The diversification of the Viennese palace

Preferring radical diversity to conventional consistency in his Straatmann essay (from 1692), Fischer sandwiched a minor Order on the corps de logis between a major one on the slightly projecting side pavillons – as Louis Le Vau was wont to do on more generous sites. Contrary to the latter, incoherence is obviated by relatively congruent rectilinear composition over the continuous rustication of the base: eye-catching relief is provided, as usual, by the stepped Order of the projecting portal and, more originally, by herms defining the central bays of the attic. These herms are related to those of Pierre Puget in Toulon but, as we have seen, they emigrated from the circle of Galeazzo Alessi and his followers in Genoa and Milan, where Fischer is unlikely to have missed them in passing (AIC5, pages 266f, and see above, page 222).

›**4.51 FISCHER AND THE TOWN PALACE IN VIENNA AND PRAGUE:** (a) Straatmann (from 1692), 18th-century record of street front (this and subsequent engravings after Salomon Kleiner, *Wahrhafte und eigentliche Abbildung*, 1737 – SK); (b–e) Prince Eugene (from c. 1695), engraved street front, general view and staircase details; (f) Batthyány (before 1700, later Schönborn), engraved street front; (g–i) Bohemian Chancellery (from 1708), engraved street front, portal detail and staircase; (j–m) Trautson (1710), engraved entrance front, general view, staircase and undercoft; (n) Liechenstein, side entrance (here associated with Fischer); (o, p) Prague, Clam-Gallas (1713), engraved street front and portal detail.

4.51b

Two years after beginning work for Straatmann, Fischer reverted to the Italian ordonnance of repetitive colossal pilasters in a scheme for Prince Eugene of Savoy which anticipated lateral expansion and complemented it with lavish sculpture. At the end of the decade he developed the mode for Count Ádám Batthyány: flanked by unarticulated rusticated wings, the scheme clearly follows Bernini's Palazzo Chigi but the colossal Corinthian Order of the central block cedes to tapered pilasters of Borrominian derivation. In several later works, notably the Bohemian Chancellery (from 1708) and the Trautson Palace in Vienna (from 1710), as also for the Clam-Gallas Palace in Prague (from

4.51c

4.51d

4.51e

4.51h

4.51f

1713), the centre is asserted with a pedimented pavillon from which the colossal Order is variously devolved to the side bays. In the later work pavillons project beyond the corps de logis, abstract in their ordonnance: contrary to the impetus of the Order, the frames of the piano-nobile windows increase in elaboration from the centre to the sides where rich serliana issue from the tripartite voids which rise through the two main storeys from twin portals. We shall see something similar in Andreas Schlüter's compositions on the Lustgarten side of the royal palace in Berlin (page 691). The latter incorporate herms but Fischer – or his follower Mathias Bernhard Braun – assigns support of the porticoes to atlante as he did elsewhere, probably including the revision of Martinelli's Liechtenstein portals.

4.51i

4.51g

4.51j

4.51l

4.51m

4.51k

Clearly endorsed by Hardouin-Mansart's colleagues in the French Académie Royale, justification for applying a pedimented portico to domestic building is Palladian – as Fischer would have known (AIC5, pages 229, 247, etc.). However, only Palladio's earlier English followers had hitherto elevated a temple-front motif to crown the central projection of a great house – as Fischer is less likely to have known (AIC5, page 634). Novel synthesis of French and Italian modes certainly distinguishes his late palaces: his staircases were outstanding from the outset.

4.51n

4.51o

4.51p

4.52
›4.52 PRAGUE, THUN-HOHENSTEIN PALACE:
detail of portal by Jon Santini Aichel (c. 1725).

By the last decades of the 17th century, Vienna was familiar with variations on the Spanish imperial type of staircase, with a single central base flight dividing in opposite
directions from an intermediate landing and returning in
parallel flights to reach the cross-landing of the main floor.
Martinelli had followed it closely in his work for Harrach
c. 1696. For Liechtenstein four years earlier, he had adopted
parallel flights like those of Le Vau's Hôtel Lambert: Fischer
would complete the exercise. Meanwhile, he combined the
two approaches for Prince Eugene of Savoy: he expanded
the 'imperial' formula by returning the intermediate flights
back upon themselves as a zone of transition between the
overshadowed, overbearing beginning and the liberation
of the luminous culmination. At the outset the usual serried stands of balusters cede to waves and whorls which
break with the momentum of surf to the encouragement
of ascent – perhaps inspired by Mansart at Maisons – and
atlante strain under elevating effort in place of columns, as
at Mathey's Troja Palace (AIC5, page 292).[4.51d, e] Inside and
out, supporting flights of stairs and the canopies of porticoes,
atlante played the lead part in providing vigour to the palatial
Baroque of Vienna and Prague.[4.51n–o] In Prague, Santini
Aichel was characteristically heterodox in this respect.[4.52]

After the accession of Emperor Joseph in 1705, Fischer was commissioned to extend and upgrade the old Hofburg in Vienna as the winter palace: the more agreeable seasons, extending to hunting, were still ideally to be spent at Schönbrunn. Joseph died before peace enabled his fraternal successor, Charles VI (1711–40), to contemplate large-scale works. The first of these, a court library and a great church, were commissioned from Fischer c. 1715. Planning was delayed on the former until 1723, the last year of its author's life – as we shall see. The Karlskirche, dedicated to S. Charles Borromeo ex voto for Vienna's relief from the Turks and plague, would soon eventuate to Fischer's design. That was chosen by the patron from a competition: highly eclectic endeavour was taken to its apotheosis, with wide-ranging reference to ancient and modern achievement, in the principal imperial architect's late ecclesiastical masterpiece.**4·53**

Karlskirche

The main volume of the great church dedicated to the emperor's namesake is elliptical from floor plan to dome, like that of the Salzburg Dreifaltigkeitskirche, but it expands laterally into generous chapels and longitudinally into a scenography extending from portico and vestibule to sanctuary and choir: the former recalls Roman works like Francesco da Voltera's S. Giacomo degli Incurabili (AIC5, page 292), the latter is worthy of an imperial Roman thermal architect – or his post-Palladian Venetian admirers (AIC5, page 228, 239f, and see above, pages 126ff). Scenographic outside too, Fischer is at his most original in incorporating freestanding columns appropriately modelled on the Roman prototype commemorating Trajan's victory over the barbarians on the Danube. They also recall the freestanding columns of Jachin and Boaz which framed the entrance to Solomon's Temple in Jerusalem as emblems of fortitude and constancy: these were the virtues espoused by the emperor on his election and associated with the church's dedicatee whose mission is depicted in the spiral reliefs. It is hardly insignificant, too, that paired columns were incorporated into the arms of Spain

›4.53 THE FISCHERS AND THE VIENNESE KARLSKIRCHE, from 1715: (a) plan, (b, c) west front original project (SK) and general view, (d) elevation to north, (e) section through original scheme, (f–i) interior details.

The foundation stone was laid early in 1716. The structure was completed in late 1725 under Johann Bernhard's son Joseph Emanuel who had assumed charge three years earlier in place of his dying father. The changes to the scheme as engraved for the *Entwurf* are significant but seem to have been made before the old master's demise: an attic was interpolated between the portico and the drum of the dome, the articulation of the drum with paired columns was revised from regular repetition to selective emphasis on the diagonals and the outer shell of the dome was heightened along parabolic lines exceeding a hemisphere – rather as Giacomo della Porta reformed Michelangelo's design for S. Pietro's dome. The interior was decorated between 1725 and 1738 – the exercise culminating in the substitution for coffering of an illusionist fresco on the dome's inner shell.

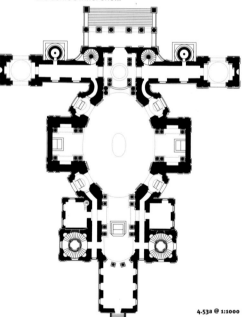

4.53a @ 1:1000

4.53b

4.53d

4.53c

by the emperor's great namesake as representative of the 'Pillars of Hercules' (Gibraltar) and hence of the unbridled dominion to which the Habsburgs laid claim as the rightful rulers of Spain – unrequited though that remained after the War of the Spanish Succession.

Redeployed from the original Schönbrunn scheme, the two interpolated symbolic verticals are embraced by the semi-elliptical arms which reach out to the lateral towers. That purpose was promoted by Borromini at S. Agnese but the concave profile is broken into two reversed segments by the counter-thrust of Fischer's ellipse: asserting that dynamic, the dome recalls Hardouin-Mansart's Invalides in its projecting piers with paired columns set more widely apart to the front than to the sides (though here that was required by the elliptical plan); on the other hand, the squat towers are reminiscent of François Mansart's church of the Minimes (see pages 219 and 281). The projecting central zone is orthogonal and endowed with a temple front, like the Roman Pantheon, rather than the triumphal-arch motif more usually adopted by Christians to symbolize the threshold of heaven. Idiosyncratic, this astonishing composition was not to be without influence: most notably, the internal scenography and the relationship between portico, dome and towers impressed Filippo Juvarra – as we have already seen.

4.53f

4.53g

4.53e

4.53h

4·53ⁱ

THE ADVENT OF JOHANN LUKAS VON HILDEBRANDT

The Karlskirche composition may be seen as pressing frontally rather than compressed laterally: assertive in complexity though they may be, the towers stand to the sides as adjuncts. In the Salzburg Kollegienkirche, how-

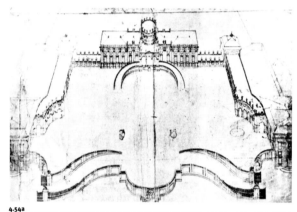

4.54a

›4.54 **VIENNA, LUSTGEBÄUDE OF THE MANS-FELD-FONDI VILLA** (later Schwarzenberg), from c. 1698: (a) Hildebrandt's initial scheme of c. 1697, (b) garden front as completed by Fischer (from 1720).

After the death of the original patron in 1715, the villa was bought by Prince Schwarzenberg and Hildebrandt was dismissed in favour of Fischer who was working on the new patron's city palace. Renewed activity awaited completion of the latter in 1720. Meanwhile, with the completed right wing obviously dictating the form of its pendant, Fischer revised the centre: instead of the garden front's repetitive aedicular fenestration – derived from the Althann scheme where it effectively integrated the canted wings – great arched windows of the Salzburg Kollegienkirche's type would enhance definition of the distinct elliptical element and improve lighting; instead of a cylindrical superstructure, the clerestory zone of the oculii would swell in response to the substitution of an internal saucer dome for a flat roof with lantern. The forecourt and undulating outer access ramps would not materialize but Hildebrandt's semicircular inner ramps would serve his arcaded porte cochère.

4.54b

›**4.55** VIENNA, JESUIT CHURCH, from 1623,
redecorated from 1703: (a–c) interior towards sanctuary,
details of transeptual chapel.

Founded during the Thirty Years' War, the church was
completed and embellished with the return to security
towards the end of the century: Fra Andrea Pozzo was
imported from his triumph in the Roman Jesuit church of
S. Ignazio.

4.55b   4.55c

4.55a

ever, greater constraint compounds force as elliptical volume pushes corresponding convex fabric forward through
the relatively close-set towers. The impact was soon felt
by Fischer's younger contemporary, Johann Lukas von
Hildebrandt (1668–1745). And he began his career with
a paraphrase of Fischer's early civil work in the French
château form with a central elliptical volume asserting its
dominance over its rectangular context.

Born to a German officer in the Genoese army, Hildebrandt gravitated to Rome where he extended study of
military engineering to architecture in the school of Carlo
Fontana. He was first employed on fortifications in Piedmont from 1695, towards the end of Prince Eugene of
Savoy's campaign there: with peace he graduated to Vienna
where the plethora of post-siege domestic building gave
him the opportunity of presenting the architectural cre-
dentials he had gained in Fontana's Rome. Heinrich Franz
von Mansfeld-Fondi responded with the commission for a
villa: work began in 1697 but it was not until after 1720 that
the initial project, derived from an orthogonal regulation
of Fischer's diagonal scheme for Althann at Rossau, was
revised for a new patron by Fischer himself.**4·54**

With progress on Mansfeld's commission disrupted by
controversy over its siting on Vienna's protective glacis,
Hildebrandt's career was furthered in the ecclesiastical field.
That was most prominently occupied for the Jesuits by Fra
Andrea Pozzo with his characteristic opulence and brilliant
trompe-l'oeil technique which would not have escaped the
attention of the young Austrian in Rome (see page 73).**4·55**

Hildebrandt's sole secure ecclesiastical claim is to S.
Laurentius in the northern Bohemian town of Jablonné v
Podještědí. Flanked by elliptical vestibule and sanctuary, the
plan follows Guarino Guarini's Turinese church of S. Lorenzo in the main: the central volume is modified in internal
elevation but the ellipse of the sanctuary is repeated for the

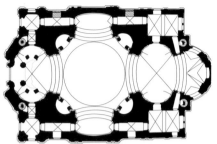

4.56b

4.56c

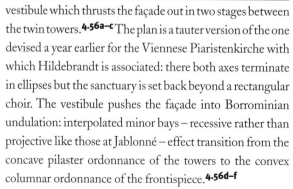

4.56c

›**4.56 CHURCHES ASSOCIATED WITH HILDE-BRANDT:** (a–c) Jablonné v Podještědí (Gabel), S. Laurentius (from 1699), plan, west front, interior; (d–f) Vienna, Piaristenkirche (from 1698, construction from 1716, consecration 1734), plan, east front, interior; (g–i) Vienna, Peterskirche (from 1701), plan, exterior, interior.

The church at Jablonné was commissioned by Count František Antonín Berka, governor of Bohemia, in 1699. Hildebrandt was largely absent from the site after providing the plans: the master-mason Pietro Bianco was replaced by Domenico Petrini in 1706. By then the structure had risen to the main cornice, the vaulting and dome were changed in completion by 1712 – to Hilderbrandt's disgust. Like Guarini's great Turinese work, Hildebrandt's essay defines a central octagon with convex colonnaded screens but, unlike the model, it has side passages through miniature transepts and an elliptical vestibule as well as the elliptical sanctuary.

Founded in 1597 by S. Joseph Calasanz, the Piarist order provided schooling for poor children. Lack of funds delayed work for nearly two decades after Hildebrandt's

vestibule which thrusts the façade out in two stages between the twin towers. **4.56a–c** The plan is a tauter version of the one devised a year earlier for the Viennese Piaristenkirche with which Hildebrandt is associated: there both axes terminate in ellipses but the sanctuary is set back beyond a rectangular choir. The vestibule pushes the façade into Borrominian undulation: interpolated minor bays – recessive rather than projective like those at Jablonné – effect transition from the concave pilaster ordonnance of the towers to the convex columnar ordonnance of the frontispiece. **4.56d–f**

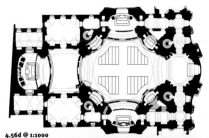

4.56d @ 1:1000

4.56e

plans were presented (c. 1698): much of the structure was complete by 1720. Financial difficulties again stopped progress: Hildebrandt resigned in frustration in the early 1730s. The façade was completed c. 1750.

The construction of the Peterskirche was begun around 1701 under Gabriele Montani: Hildebrandt's involvement does not appear to predate 1703. The dome was mainly designed by Matthias Steinl who was also responsible for overseeing the interior decoration. Andrea Pozzo was commissioned to fresco the domical vault but the work was incomplete on his death in 1709: he was replaced by Johann Michael Rottmayr. The high altar was designed by Antonio Galli Bibiena to frame Martino Altomonte's 'The Healing of the Lame by S. Peter and S. John in Jerusalem'.

4.56f

If the façade of S. Laurentius seems to burst forth from compression and the Piaristenkirche turns to the mellifluous, the opposite to either is the case in the first ecclesiastical exercise with which Hildebrandt was associated in the early years of the new century: the Peterskirche in Vienna. The elliptical plan is orientated with the sanctuary at the culmination of the long axis; the short axis terminates in chapels larger than those in the quadrants – as in Francesco da Volterra's S. Giacomo degli Incurabili in Rome or, nearer to home, Ascanio Vitozzi's pilgrimage

4.56h

4.56i

church at Vicoforte di Mondovì (AIC5, page 292). But the tight site enforced contraction, the squeezed frontispiece buckling under pressure from the canted towers in dramatic counterpoint to the swelling of the ellipse asserted by the dome.**4.56g–i** The orchestration of this spectacle is not unworthy of Hildebrandt though, as at Jablonné, the crowning element is less than inspired. Be that as it may, the plan was widely influential as an alternative to the single-volume rectilinear hall with or without transepts or side chapels in the post-Vignolan Roman manner, not least in Buda towards mid-century.**4.57**

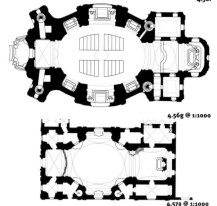

4.56g @ 1:1000

4.57a @ 1:1000

›**4.57 BUDAPEST** (Buda-Vízivaros): S. Anna (from 1740), (a) plan, (b, c) exterior and interior.

The initial architect of S. Anna was Kristóf Hamon (c. 1693–1748); the building was completed in 1762 by Matyas Nepauer (active 1759–67). Not squeezed by the site, the orthogonal twin-towered façade is resistant to movement generated by the elongated elliptical plan.

In contrast to S. Anna, the Franciscan church (S. Ferenc, consecrated 1745 after nearly twenty years of building works) is conventional in its single-volume nave with arcaded chapels. The University Chapel has traditionally been attributed to András Mayerhoffer but recent scholarship questions whether a master-mason could have produced Pest's most sumptuous Baroque interior – to date – without the assistance of a metropolitan master architect.

4.57c

No less than in his churches, Hildebrandt mastered Baroque techniques in his domestic work. His Viennese career began with the Prince of Mansfeld-Fondi's unfulfilled commission but progress was assured after he attracted the patronage of Prince Eugene – his erstwhile army commander in Piedmont – away from Fischer (1702). It was boosted by winning the patronage of two important ecclesiastical princes. The most assiduous was Friedrich Karl von Schönborn, vice-chancellor of the empire, who we encountered at Bamberg (see pages 476f). The other was Franz Anton von Harrach, Johann Ernst von Thun-Hohenstein's successor as prince-archbishop of Salzburg (1709).

Harrach engaged Hildebrandt to renovate Salzburg's Mirabell palace after ceasing work on his predecessor's

4.58a

Klessheim and dismissing Fischer. However, the new staircase – the main survivor of fire which destroyed much of the building in 1818 – deploys the volute type of balustrade which Fischer had invented for Prince Eugene's town palace and possibly extended for Liechtenstein. Hildebrandt further varied the type to fill a vast triple-height hall in the Viennese palace built for Count Wirich Philipp von Daun (from 1713): slightly later than the Salzburg work, whose articulation and fenestration he had modernized freely, the eclectic façade incorporates tapered pilasters and window frames with alternating convex and concave pediments all of which derive from Borromini – mostly via Fischer (see pages 108f). **4.58**

›4.58 HILDEBRANDT AND THE PALATIAL STAIRCASE: (a) Salzburg, Mirabell, detail of ascent (1709); (b, c) Vienne for Daun-Kinsky (1713), interior vertical perspective, entrance front.

Daun was a field marshal in the War of the Spanish Succession, viceroy of Naples from 1713 and thus absent from Vienna when his palace was being built. The portal – with female figures reclining on the detached segments of a broken pediment in the Michelangelesque manner – derives from Carlo Fontana's Roman church of S. Marcello al Corso (see page 116): it incorporates herms like the side portal of the Liechtenstein Palace which is most plausibly credited to Fischer and the latter's Batthyány Palace is recalled in the Order of tapered pilasters (see page 529). As the site was restricted, the main rooms were stacked on two floors. As in many Turinese examples, a vaulted elliptical porte cochère served the staircase of which all the flights were hung on a blind inner wall and the corridor returns were lit through the courtyard wall: as at the Schloss Mirabell, ascent through closed and partially open tunnels was drawn into openness and light at the top but that was further dramatized by a clerestory gallery framing an illusionist ceiling.

4.58c

4.58b

**›4.59 GÖLLERSDORF, SCHLOSS SCHÖN-
BORN,** from c. 1713: garden front.

Distinct from the official residence of the patron as imperial vice-chancellor, the project was for a modern retreat on the foundations of the Mühlburg castle. The quadrangle became the nearly square court framed by three two-storey ranges. The Bérainesque stucco embellishment of the interiors is due either the Comesque Santino Bussi or to Daniel Schenk, who would shortly serve Friedrich Karl's uncle Lothar Franz at Pommersfelden.

**›4.60 POMMERSFELDEN, SCHLOSS WEIS-
SENSTEIN,** from 1711: (a) engraved overview (SK),

HILDEBRANDT AND THE SCHÖNBORN

Friedrich Karl von Schönborn's promotion of Hildebrandt was to be extensive, especially in Franconia. He first called for the enlargement of an existing Viennese suburban villa into a quadrangular *Lustgebäude*: before it neared completion (c. 1713) he moved his architect on to Göllersdorf where he was commissioned to transform the remains of a medieval castle into a maison de plaisance of the French type most relevantly represented by Jules Hardouin-Mansart's Château de Clagny – at least in its interior distribution (see page 267).**4·59** Here Hildebrandt directed the stuccador in the embellishment of the major interiors with variations on French Régence arabesque ribbonwork inspired by engravings after Jean Bérain (see page 291). He furthered the mode in the *Lustgebäude* he was currently building for Prince Eugene, as we shall see, and in the great Schönborn palace at Pommersfelden.

Well pleased with his project at Göllersdorf, Friedrich Karl urged his uncle Lothar Franz to entrust Hildebrandt with the project he was conceiving for the reconstruction of the castle at Pommersfelden in his Franconian domain. The commission had been let in 1711 to Johann Dientzenhofer, who had succeeded his brother as principal architect at the Bamberg court. The plans for a great E-shaped building of three storeys under double mansards were partly the prelate's own and work had begun on one wing in 1712: nevertheless, they were dispatched with Dientzenhofer for review by the Viennese master.**4.60**

4.60e

4.60c

4.60d

Pommersfelden

Originally intending to rebuild the medieval castle which provided him with a country seat, Lothar Franz von Schönborn, archbishop-elector of Mainz, was directed by practical difficulties to commission the projection of an entirely new building on a new site. The plan was an expansion of the three-winged French château type but the articulation of the central pavilion is more in keeping with Austro-German taste: the clustering of pilasters, the doubling of engaged columns and the projection of the entablature out over the Order was not to be characteristic of French academic Classicism.

As usual the central axis embraces the core of representational spaces – vestibule and salon over hall and sala terrena – but unusually it opened with the spectacular staircase. The central projection of the E was a distinct pavilion devised to accommodate bifurcated flights which, rising through the

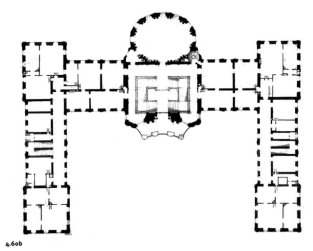

4.60b

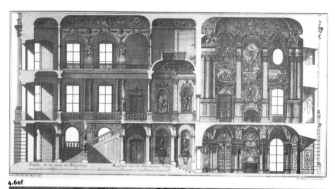

4.60k
(b) plan, (c, d) entrance front and detail, (e) garden front, (f) axial section through staircase and Marmorsaal, (g, h) staircase and piano nobile vestibule vault, (i, j) ground-floor vestibule and sala terrena, (k) Spiegelkabinett.

4.60j

base storey to the piano nobile landing over the arcaded passage to the sala terrena, would be free of dependence on the sides of the cage. This Hildebrandt was able to revise: to limit the extraordinary span of the vault, superimposed galleries were inserted between the initial flights and the wall. The form of staircase, usually applied externally, was probably derived by the patron from Fischer's revised design for Schönbrunn but a precedent for the revision with superimposed colonnaded galleries may be found among Claude Perrault's designs for the Louvre. The upper arcades support a coved vault frescoed by the Swiss painter Johann Rudolf Byss with the assistance of Giovanni Francesco Marchini – the scale was unpre-cedented north of the Alps, though Hildebrandt had anticipated it in Vienna.

At base level Bérainesque patterning extended to the sala terrena into whose elliptical vaulting Johann Dientzenhofer had introduced the three-dimensional tangential arches which he was simultaneously deploying to even greater effect at the abbey at Banz – as we shall see when we review ecclesiastical architecture in Bohemia and Franconia (below, page 621). Hildebrandt imposed the Viennese permutation of Parisian Régence arabesque patterning, currently being elaborated in his Viennese works, on the stuccadors responsible for embellishing the main spaces. On axis with the staircase hall, the double-height vestibule has a galleried oculus in a vault within which vigorous figural sculpture oversails the Bérainesque stuccowork of Daniel Schenk, who had visited Vienna – and Göllersdorf – in the previous year. Beyond that, the Marmorsaal is articulated with an Order of engaged columns in Hildebrandt's Italianate manner and the vault is covered with an illusionist fresco by Johann Michael Rottmayr, an Austrian trained in Venice: in the zone of transition between Order and fantasy, Schenk again wove his Bérainesque stuccowork and, beyond that, he varied the mode for the cabinet in which mirrors predominate.

Over walls destined to be hung with paintings – and therefore not articulated – the vault of the Grosse Galerie is divided into three frescoed zones framed again by Schenk's stuccowork to designs produced in Vienna, presumably under Hildebrandt's direction. Here, however, the framework departs from regular geometry to free undulation: the fresco in the chapel vault had already been framed in this scalloped mode (from 1714) which was to be of spectacular significance.

4.61a

4.61b

HILDEBRANDT AND PRINCE EUGENE: FROM RÁCKEVE TO VIENNA

A decade before his digression to Salzburg, Hildebrandt began to work for Prince Eugene far off in the other direction, at Ráckeve on the Danube beyond Buda: he referred to Fischer's Engelhartstetten hunting lodge and provided a single-storey entrance portico to a central pavilion with clerestory but reformed its garden front on orthogonal lines beyond concave quadrants. As with the churches attributed to him, his influence in this genre was widespread in the orbit of empire, not least on his Austrian follower Andreas Mayerhoffer (1690–1771). He had settled in Budapest in 1724 where he had a considerable practice, at least as a mason: among his most notable attributions are the Péterffy Palace in Pest and the Grassalkovich country house at Gödöllő to the east of the city.**4.61**

›4.61 HILDEBRANDT AND HUNGARIAN SECULAR BUILDING: (a, b) Ráckeve Castle (1702–22), garden front and overview; (c, d) Gödöllö, Grassalkovich Palace (from 1744), court front and overview.

Born in Salzburg, Andreas Mayerhoffer was trained as a mason and rose to be master of the guild of masons and carpenters in Pest: his responsibility for the palace of Baron Péterffy there is undisputed. With herms supporting its balcony in the Viennese manner, it is a rare survivor of its period and place but was typically much smaller than the norm in Vienna or Prague.

At Gödöllö the patron was Antal Grassalkovich (1694–1771), a confidant of Empress Maria Theresa. His architect was possibly drawn from the circle of Joseph Emanuel Fischer, if not from that of Hildebrandt. Mayerhoffer may have had only a technical role in association with his sons János and András (born 1721 and 1725 respectively). The form, with a central corps de logis addressing a *cour d'honneur* and a wider outer court, is an advance over the single broad court of Ráckeve but – with the courts open to the formerly formal French-style garden – it is in reverse of the norm well represented elsewhere in Hungary, notably at Fertod (see below).

4.61c

4.61d

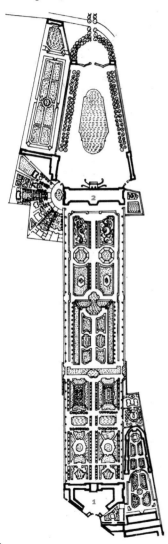

›**4.62 VIENNA, PRINCE EUGENE'S BELVE-
DERE,** 1721: (a, b) overview and site plan with Lower
and Upper Belvedere at 1 and 2 (18th-century engravings), (c–g) Lower Belvedere, garden front, Marmorsaal, Marmorgalerie, Goldkabinett, Groteskensaal,

Hildebrandt won the Ráckeve commission in the year
he displaced Fischer in effecting the anticipated extension
of the prince's town palace (from 1702). The original architect defined the terms there, of course, but Hildebrandt's
major work for the great soldier was an entirely new venture to which he brought his highly colourful eclecticism.
A summer palace beyond the glacis to the south-east –
beyond Mansfeld-Fondi's site – the scale of the project
was to escalate between 1714 and 1720, when work began
respectively on buildings later known as the Lower and
Upper Belvedere: between them, the terraced garden was
not the least impressive aspect of the complex.**4.62**

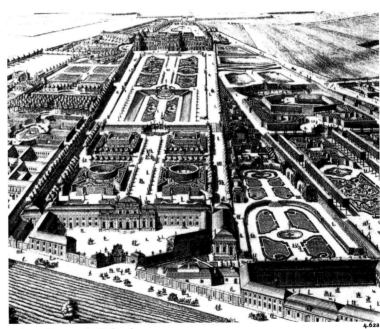

4.62a

Prince Eugene's Belvedere

The sloping terrain was acquired by Prince Eugene in stages from 1702 but
building work on it awaited the end of the War of the Spanish Succession
in 1714. The initial commission for the *Lustgebäude* first ran to the building
at the base of the hill, nearest the city, now known as the Lower Belvedere.

4.62b

4.62c

4.62d

4.62e

4.62f

Like the villa at Ráckeve, this was a straightforward variation of Fischer's early formula for a single-storey range centred on a double-height salon and articulated with a regular Order of pilasters: unlike either, the perimeter is rectilinear and the central pavilion is basically integral – projecting with adjacent bays more prominently on the entrance front than towards the garden. Relative simplicity outside is countered by the lavishly stuccoed and frescoed interiors – most notably the Goldkabinett, the Marmorgalerie and the Bérainesque scheme of the Groteskensaal (1714–16) attributed to Jonas Drentwett.

At the outset a belvedere was provided at the top of the site in the form of a gazebo. By 1720 the prince had much grander ideas. Hildebrandt was commissioned to build a palace larger even than the revised project for imperial Schönbrunn – and in the equivalent to the elevated position which had been abandoned there. Differentiation of mass is most vigorous on the south-east entrance front where the porte cochère stands forth on the axis of the salon, as in the neighbouring work originally devised for Mansfeld-Fondi and currently being completed by Fischer. To either side, the main blocks have two storeys with mansards and low basements: the piano nobile extends to octagonal pavilions. The fall of the ground led to the elevation of the basement on the garden side: here the differentiation of mass is concentrated on the central pavilion in the French manner but effective closure is provided by side pavilions which naturally double those of the front to provide incidence to the short sides. Extending into these, the state and private apartments exceed even the main room of the

4.62g

Lower Belvedere in the sumptuousness of embellishment: the dominant stuccowork is due to the Comesque Santino Bussi.

For exuberance and colouristic effect, few Baroque palaces outside Turin surpass the Upper Belvedere. Little was taken directly from the French for this extensive complex, other than the formula for formal garden design and the projection of the salon into it in the manner familiar to the Viennese since Fischer's first excursions into the field of the *Lustgebäude*. Little is distinctly Italian either, though the double-curved portico pediment and much in the articulation is Borrominian – the former already varied by Hildebrandt at Göllersdorf, the latter following on precedents provided by Fischer.

The French flirted with anthropomorphic Orders on rare occasions, the Italians more often, as we have seen (see pages 59, 222). Fischer doubtless knew the Milanese herms but almost certainly introduced the atlante to Vienna from Prague, as we speculated above. His work for Straattmann provided the precedent for the herms of Hildebrandt's portico: their brothers support the vault of the great staircase within; their exceptionally pow-

4.62i

(h–n) plan of Upper Palace, garden front, Turkish tent, entrance front, staircase and lower vestibule, Marmorsaal.

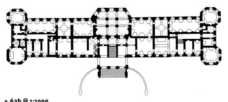
4.62h @ 1:1000

4.62j

4.62k

erful, fully developed relatives supporting the vaults of the vestibule – or sala terrena – on the lower level are clearly affiliated to those pressed by Fischer into a similar protean role in Prince Eugene's winter palace. Fusing sculpture and architecture, they set a standard often to be emulated in 18th-century Central Europe.

The French contributed the mansards – but not the skyline. The Turks reluctantly submitted the exotic motif of the campaign tent for the roof of the great central pavilion. As we have seen, exoticism was essential to the French Rococo. There, of course, it was opposed to the Classical tradition. Here it is grafted on to a Baroque permutation of that tradition, anticipating the pluralism with which architectural inspiration was to enrich itself in the later decades of the century.

4.62l

4.62n

4.62m

›ARCHITECTURE IN CONTEXT »DIVIDED CENTRE AND ORTHODOX EAST

THE EMPEROR'S WORKS

Having displaced Fischer in the patronage of Prince Eugene at the outset of his career, Hildebrandt lost to the ageing master and his son in imperial patronage while preoccupied with the Belvedere project. Emperor Charles VI finally decided on the upgrading of the Hofburg in the early 1720s. As we have seen, the most important issue then was the imperial library which had been commissioned from Johann Bernhard in 1716: funds were at last avail-

>**4.63** THE FISCHERS AT THE VIENNESE **HOFBURG:** (a) imperial stable (from 1719), overview; (b–g) imperial library (Hofbibliothek), Josefsplatz façade and record of Fischer's scheme, plan, section and detail of antiquarian antechamber, interior; (h) Joseph Emanuel's scheme for the comprehensive reordering of the Hofburg; (i) Burgplatz façade; (j, k) Michaelerplatz façade and extent of 18th-century construction (anon.); (l) Winter Riding School interior.

The stable complex was truly imperial in scale and also in derivation: the culmination of Fischer's suprapractical application of his antiquarian theorizing, it

4.63b

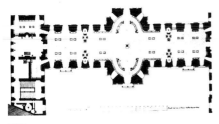

4.63c

4.63d

4.63e

was modelled on his reconstruction of Nero's Domus Aurea (see page 519). The library building may also be seen as imperial Roman in inspiration, at least in its scenography through tunnel-vaulted and domed elliptical space: intermediacy was effected by the near-contemporary Roman Palazzo Colonna, with its colonnaded screens and illusionist vault paintings – here emulated to the glory of the emperor and learning.

Unexcelled in its genre, the library building also wholly assimilated the influence of France on its massing about a great central 'salon': striding forth from it is the *quadriga* of Minerva bent on banishing envy and ignorance. Hardly had work begun in 1723 when the old master's death left the project's realization to his son, ostensibly with due respect for the original magnificent conception – but the wings were executed by Empress Maria Theresa's architect Niccolò Pacassi to his own designs in the late-1740s. At that time the 'antiquarian' antechamber – an extraordinary collage of pseudo-antique architectural fragments not incompatible with

4.63f

4.63g

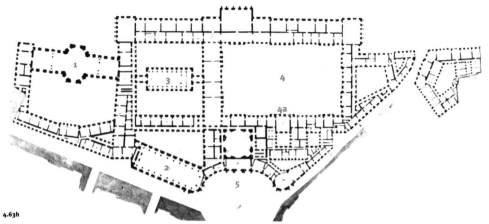

4.63h

able for work to begin in 1722. The year before, the ailing master was called on for a new stable block. In that year too, a comprehensive plan was produced by Hildebrandt to Chancellor Schönborn's direction and work began on the Reichskanzleitrakt (chancellery wing) which lined the northern side of the Burgplatz in parallel to the Leopoldinischertrakt. With the Fischer genius prominently

Johann Bernhard's œuvre – was lost to the relocated staircase (engravings SK).

Joseph Emanuel's scheme for rebuilding most of the Hofburg naturally developed with various alternatives: the plan reproduced here is reconstructed from the partially executed, rather more empirical version (from 1726) with the Hofbibliothek (1), Winter Riding School (Winterreitschule, 2), Chapel Court (with Hofkapelle 3), Great Court (Burgplatz, 4) with Imperial

4.63i

Chancellery (Reichkanzlei, 4a), Michaelerplatz (5). The Burgplatz façade, articulated with colossal pilasters like the library, survives before imperial apartments developed in the 19th century from the rooms of the chancellery. To the north-east Fischer was further commissioned to build the Winter Riding School: his design may be seen as a semi-basilican variant of the Vitruvian Egyptian hall with herms at clerestory level in place of an attic Order. Departing from the curved corners of the latter – in an early exercise of contextualism – the concave range extending westwards from it provides supple formality to the Michaelerplatz possibly with reference to Cortona's Roman Colonna scheme (see page 107): beyond the central portal, it was completed largely to the original scheme only in 1889 – with the addition of a dome over the grand central vestibule.

4.63l

4.63j

on display to the east of the Burgplatz, Hildebrandt was superseded there and his work demolished by Johann Bernhard's son Joseph Emanuel.**4.63**

Joseph Emanuel had studied in Rome (from 1713) and under Robert de Cotte in Paris (from 1717). The Michaelerplatz façades may well be seen as a free reworking of the formula varied for the south and east fronts of the Louvre: the rhythm of the Versailles chapel colonnade distantly echoes through the Winter Riding School. His studies ultimately took him to the Netherlands and London

4.63k

4.64a

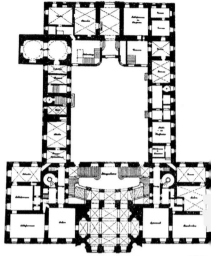

4.64c

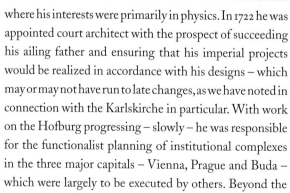

4.64b

4.64d

where his interests were primarily in physics. In 1722 he was appointed court architect with the prospect of succeeding his ailing father and ensuring that his imperial projects would be realized in accordance with his designs – which may or may not have run to late changes, as we have noted in connection with the Karlskirche in particular. With work on the Hofburg progressing – slowly – he was responsible for the functionalist planning of institutional complexes in the three major capitals – Vienna, Prague and Buda – which were largely to be executed by others. Beyond the

›**4.64** SELECT PRIVATE WORKS ATTRIBUTED TO JOSEPH EMANUEL FISCHER, c. 1730: (a–d) Jagdschloss Eckartsau (conversion of a moated castle into a hunting lodge for Count Franz Ferdinand Kinsky), park front, court, plan and great hall; (e) Vienna, Palais Rauchmiller, street front (attributed adaptation in alteration of c. 1735 to Palais Ursenbeck of 1655); (f–h) Gartenpalais Althann, plan and elevations of main pavilions (e–h after SK).

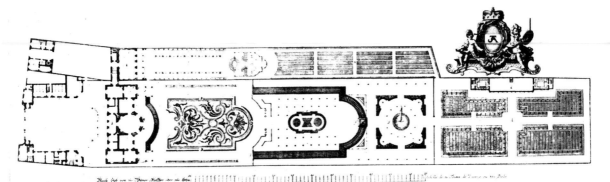

4.64f

4.64g

4.64h

4.64e

court, he was involved in altering several country houses or their plans – Slavkov, for example – but in no substantiated entirely new work in the genre: clearly indebted to the school of de Cotte, the central block at Eckartsau is perhaps the most complete of the secure attributions.**4.64a–d**

Like his father, Joseph Emanuel seems to have produced numerous schemes for town houses and *Lustegebäude*. Of the former – inadequately documented – the sole survivor is the Palais Rauchmiller on the Vienna Neuer Markt (c. 1735).**4.64e** Of the garden retreats, the most admirable was built for his ministerial superior, the Surveyor of Imperial Works, Count Ludwig Josef von Althann (from 1730): a variant on the theme of the French maison de plaisance, it is articulated in reduction of the Trianon system as developed for the Palais Bourbon (see page 323).**4.64f–h**

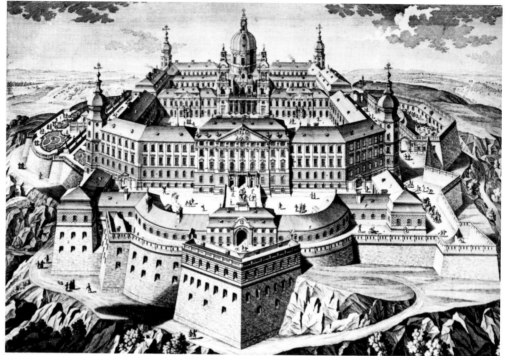

THE GREAT ABBEY

Apart from the great palace, the dominant building type in
Central Europe in the age of Baroque reconstruction was
the great monastery – especially the foundations accorded
imperial freedom under the abbacy of a prince of the
empire who was prepared to spend lavishly in assertion of
his politico-ecclesiastical status. Recommended to Abbot
Gottfried Bessel by his former superior, the archbishop-
elector Lothar Franz von Schönborn of Mainz, Hildebrandt supplied projects for the most ambitious of these:
the ideal reconstruction of Benedictine Göttweig after its
destruction by fire in 1718, drawn up in consultation with
the imperial vice-chancellor Friedrich Karl von Schönborn.

Hildebrandt's origins as a military engineer are nowhere
better recalled than in the engravings of Göttweig on its
massive fortified platform with its arrow-head bastions.

>**4.65 GÖTTWEIG, BENEDICTINE ABBEY:**
record of Hildebrandt's scheme for reconstruction
(after 1718; SK).

The scheme was too ambitious: progress slowed
after a decade or so and stalled on the death of the
assertive Abbot Gottfried Bessel in 1749 with the
church and one staircase partly realized.

4.66a

›4.66 KLOSTERNEUBURG, BENEDICTINE ABBEY: (a, b) overviews of project and its partial realization.

The patron was the emperor. The author was the Comesque master-mason Donato Felice d'Allio (from 1730): he was chosen against native opposition which included Jakob Prandtauer whose great work at Melk we are about to visit. The vast project was conceived in emulation of El Escorial but in the Franco-Italian style of Domenico Martinelli and his followers. In 1730 it was decreed that the project be augmented to include an imperial residence: Joseph Emanuel Fischer was entrusted with the modifications which ran to the introduction of a grander imperial style: d'Allio conformed. Work ceased with the death of Charles VI in 1740 with little more than a quarter completed. Joseph Kornhäusel was commissioned to further the project a century later but little more eventuated.

4.66b

The scheme emulates El Escorial in its grid of courts dominated by the centrally placed domed basilica (AIC5, pages 730f). It also follows the priory of Sankt Florian in distinguishing the main representational elements – the staircase, the imperial hall and the library – in mansard-roofed blocks (see pages 514f). Another Escorial emulation, Klosterneuburg came closer to realization than grandiose Göttweig – before imperial resources were drained into war.**4.65, 4.66**

The supreme achievement in the abbatical genre is unquestionably Melk where all the elements of a venerable Benedictine complex were rebuilt to the one opulent masterplan of Jakob Prandtauer (1660–1726). Begun to the order of the assertive young abbot, Berthold Dietmayr, who was elected in 1700, it was well advanced before the fire at Göttweig gave Hildebrandt and his savant aristocratic backers their chance to challenge it in magnificence. The challenge was not merely architectural but of architectural pride: as noted above, Prandtauer was not a metropolitan architect of international experience, like the two major imperial servants we have so far encountered, but a guild-trained Tyrolean sculptor who emerged from the Comesque circle. Unsurprisingly, however, he was not unschooled there in standard Vitruvian theory – probably through the agency of Palladio and Vincenzo Scamozzi. And he was to triumph – given the fortune of perseverant patronage.

Prandtauer first emerged as an architect in the mid-1690s and assumed the mantle of the erstwhile leading Comesque practitioner, Carlo Antonio Carlone, on the latter's death in 1708 – most notably at Sankt Florian where he was responsible for the definitive form of the staircase and the Marmorsaal.**4.40, 4.67** Meanwhile, he was making his mark at Melk where he was to work for a quarter of a century, until he died and was succeeded in his provincial ecclesiastical practice by his nephew Josef Munggenast (1680–1741) who had been an independent builder since 1717.**4.68**

4.67a

4.67b

4.67f

4.67c

(a) Prunkportal (from 1709), (b, c) exterior and interior
of the staircase in the west wing (begun by Carlone
after 1686, revised by Prandtauer after 1708), (d, e)
exterior and interior of the Marmorsaal in the south
wing (begun by Prandtauer in 1717), (f) library (Hayberger after Prandtauer, from 1744).

As we have seen, Carlone provided distinct pavilions
for the grand staircase serving the monastic quarters,
for the library and for the great hall: Prandtauer transformed the first and the last of these and redesigned
the main entrance portal in the High Baroque sculptural mode developed from the anthropomorphic
compositions of Fischer and his followers (from 1709).
Carlone's staircase, opening into the large outer prelatial court from the inner side of the west wing (begun
1695), consisted of two opposing flights rising to an
arcaded gallery: Prandtauer removed the arcade, substituting a balustrade beneath a continuous vault, and
enhanced the lighting by opening the central bay of the
façade with a great serliana echoed in minor mode on
both levels between a colossal Order of pier-pilasters.
Prandtauer's south wing (begun in 1717) is centred on
an expansive pavilion roofed in the French style within
which is the Marmorsaal, a High Baroque interpretation of a Vitruvian Corinthian hall lit through scalloped
clerestory oculii over bays flanked by paired pilasters
progressing to columns in the central recessions of the
long sides. The theme of Bartolomeo Altomonte's great
vault fresco (from 1722) is the triumph of Prince Eugene
of Savoy and his imperial sovereign over the Turks.

After Prandtauer's death in 1726 work continued
under the direction of his foreman Jakob Steinhueber
but the Steyr master Johann Gotthard Hayberger was
brought in to build the library (from 1744 ostensibly
to Prandtauer's plans, at least insofar as its external
massing is concerned): the interior is a masterly exercise in the mode developed after Prandtauer's initial
achievement at Melk – which we shall now see.

4.67d

4.67e

4.68a

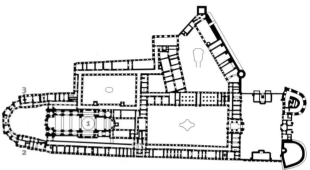

4.68c @ 1:4000

4.68b

Melk

Committed to spectacle, equipped with the unpedantic ingenuity needed to further it, possessed of a site with exceptional possibilities for dramatic staging, Berthold Dietmayr (abbot 1700–39) held a competition among various practitioners – mainly masons – for the elevation of the twin-towered, domed basilican scheme of Sankt Florian to greater eminence. Jakob Prandtauer was called on for a synthesis of the competitors' ideas in the light of his work at the latter site. A comprehensive plan for rebuilding the abbatical complex was being developed a decade later but the circumspection of the inmates – financial as well as architectural – had to be overcome in gradual stages.

4.68d

4.68e

4.68f

4.68l

4.68j

4.68k

The result of the abbot's perseverance is a vast complex of courts culminating in a terrace overlooking the river and dominated by a huge church. Built on medieval foundations, the massing perpetuates the great tradition of the feudal fortified monastery – like Hradčany in Prague, itself magnificently transformed in the Baroque age. The profile of the arcaded terrace which launches the prospect of the complex forward upriver reveals the original métier of its author: three-dimensional, the great arch of the serliana also marks the architect's graduation from provincial sculptor to metropolitan architect – at least in his awareness of one of the devices favoured by Fischer upcountry at Salzburg and downriver in Vienna. At the other end of the site, moreover, the entrance front recalls Fischer's Trautson Palace façade. Between the two, the church is international in derivation.

The sinuous moulding of the church's cornices, belfries and cupola is the hallmark of the erstwhile sculptor's endeavour. If he thus transformed Comesque conventions in the mass, he also adopted the Comesque mode of sail vaulting over the square compartments of the nave – as in Sankt Florian's church. Beyond that, however, the resplendent interiors emulate all three masters of the Roman Baroque – Bernini in richness of materials, Borromini in undulating forms, Cortona in dazzling illusionism.

The church rises between the pincers of immense wings which, uncompetitive with its complexity, are barely relieved in their repetitive fenestration before termination in twin pavilions containing the hall for the reception of the emperor and the library. This distribution exploits the drama of the site brilliantly in countering Carlone's centralized directive for Sankt Florian's very different situation. Not unnaturally, however, Prandtauer reiterated the colossal Order he himself had applied to the interior of the great hall there after the mode defined by Vitruvius – and illustrated by Palladio – as Corinthian: between the columns the bays are void, three levels of fenestration eliminating enclosing fabric. The library, with its regular Order defining blind bays filled with bookshelves and supporting a bracketed gallery, may be seen as varying Vitruvius's Egyptian mode: contrary to the great hall, the incentive was naturally introverted. Both of these great rooms, with their illusionistic ceilings proclaiming the virtues of Charles VI and virtue and knowledge as the roads to God, were completed after their author's death by his nephew Josef Munggenast – to the sustained direction of Dietmayr.

4.69

›4.69 ZWETTL, CISTERCIAN ABBEY, founded 1138, rebuilt from 1490: church front (from 1722).

Celebration of the Church Triumphant over Protestantism – in Austria, at least – ran to the Baroque single-tower façade but here left the late-Gothic church intact.

4.70 DÜRNSTEIN, AUGUSTINIAN PRIORY, founded 1410, rebuilt from 1710: (a) general view from the river, (b, c) portals, (d) church interior.

The patron of renovation was Provost Hieronymus Überbacher (1710–40): he had meagre resources but grand connections – including his neighbour, the abbot of Melk. Economy obviated departure to axial order from the irregular medieval foundations. Matthias Steinl was responsible for the altar-like portal: he was a sculptor who graduated from ivory carving to collaboration with Carlo Antonio Carlone on church building in Vienna. The church is attributed to Josef Munggenast: the undulating internal elevations echo Jakob Prandtauer's Melk without the lavish scagliola and gilding.

4.70b   4.70c   4.70a

4.69d

The abbey church form with one central western tower – as venerable as the more usual twin-towered type especially in Austria and southern Germany – was adopted by Prandtauer for the Augustinians of Dürnstein where Munggenast was the executant. Spectacularly sited on a promontory at a bend in the Danube downstream from Melk, the monastery was rebuilt after 1710 over the organically disposed medieval foundations: projected by Prandtauer, the tower was probably moulded to the design of Matthias Steinl (c. 1644–1727) who began his career as an ivory carver. Munggenast worked to designs of Steinl again at Zwettl where, even more forcefully than at Dürnstein (from 1733), the tower of the Cistercian abbey rises dramatically through attenuated pilasters and sculptural volutes. **4.69, 4.70**

4.71a

4.71b

›**4.71 ALTENBURG, BENEDICTINE ABBEY:** (a) church interior (from 1730), (b) library (from 1740).

Founded in 1144, the abbey was ravaged by the Swedes in the 1640s and by the Turks in 1681: nearly half a century elapsed before adequate funds were available for extensive rebuilding in celebration of the Church and Empire Triumphant. The elliptical volume of the church was vaulted with a drumless saucer dome to enhance the immanence – or intermediacy – of apocalyptic scenes from the Book of Revelations (Paul Troger, from 1733). Rivalling the church in the sumptuous articulation of its three domed spaces and their tunnel-vaulted links, the library is surpassed in Austria in the scale of its scenographic conception only by the Fischers' imperial masterpiece at the Hofburg.

The single-towered church front at Altenburg is the legacy of Munggenast working alone on rebuilding the Benedictine abbey in compromise with the medieval organism (from 1730). Beyond the tower, ingeniously, he inserted an elliptical nave into the existing rectangular perimeter: that recalls Vignola's S. Anna dei Palafrenieri

›4.72 ADMONT, BENEDICTINE ABBEY: library interior (completed c. 1780).

Founded in 1074 and much rebuilt after the Thirty Years' War and the expulsion of the Turks, the abbey was largely destroyed by fire in 1868: only the library survived. The largest of its monastic kind, it contrasts in its scenography with its counterpart at Altenburg: there the domical vaults of the central and end compartments are carried on transverse arches which spring from columns in consistent alignment; here the central saucer dome is carried on wall pillars which intrude into a broad hall with depressed tunnel vaulting. Responsibility is undocumented but generally attributed to Josef Hueber (died 1787) who graduated from masonry in Vienna to architecture in Graz, where he assumed the practice of the last of the Comesques, and is notable for his inventive combination of traditional wall-pillar structure and domical vaulting elsewhere (in the Weizberg pilgrimage church near Graz, for example).

›4.73 LAMBACH, STADL-PAURA, HEILIGE DREIFALTIGKEIT PILGRIMAGE CHURCH, from 1714: (a) plan, (b) exterior, (c) interior.

Abbot Maximilian Pagle of Lambach let the commission ex voto for relief from the plague of 1713 – as the emperor did with his Karleskirche. Johann Michael Prunner (from Linz) was clearly aware of the churches associated with Hildebrandt in Vienna: over a Trinitarian base, he projected a rotunda with three undulating frontispieces of the Piaristenkirche type between towers canted like those of the Peterskirche – also dedicated to the Holy Trinity.

4.72

4.73a

4.73b   4.73c

in Rome via the Peterskirche in Vienna. Vienna too provided the inspiration for the library in its semi-detached wing: its author's greatest single achievement, it emulates the Fischers' imperial masterpiece in its scale, its scenographic diversification of space, its sumptuous materials and in Paul Troger's illusionist vault frescoes glorifying learning.[4.71] In the monastic context, only the abbey of Admont attempted to challenge Altenburg in the scale of its library – and in an efflorescence of Baroque splendour well into its eve by c. 1770 when it was begun.[4.72]

As elsewhere in the orbit of Catholic empire, in Austria the extensive ecclesiastical building activity of the first half of the 18th century, and beyond, ranged from the large scale of the monastic complex to the opposite extreme of the pilgrimage church. Significantly symbolic, examples of the latter are well represented by the Heilige Dreifaltigkeit pilgrimage church at Stadl-Paura near Lambach, by Johann Michael Prunner (1669–1739).[4.73]

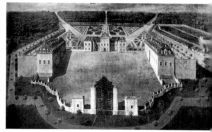

›4.74 FERTŐD, ESTERHÁZY PALACE, from 1721, revised from 1764: (a, b) overviews, 1721 and c. 2000, (c) garden front.

The original patrons were the brothers Michael and Joseph Esterházy (1671–1721 and 1688–1721). The original architect was Anton Erhard Martinelli (1684–1747) whose Comesque father Franz had rebuilt the Esterházy family palace in Vienna (from 1685, restyled in the early 19th century). The original hunting lodge of 1721 consisted of a corps de logis with a three-storey central pavilion addressing a forecourt flanked by detached wings. All three buildings provided the basis for expansion: the central pavilion (still in recognizable form) relates to works like Fischer's palace designs for the Trautson in Vienna or the Clam-Gallas in Prague.

The complex achieved its expanded form for Prince Nicholas (1714–90, acceded 1762). The enlarged wings were linked to the main block with quadrant ranges (from 1764) by Melchior Hefele and Nikolaus Jacoby ostensibly to the patron's own plans: though of three storeys like the central block, they coordinate with the latter neither in height nor detail of articulation but relate more closely to the style of the garden front. The scheme was completed with the semicircular single-storey outer enclosure ascribed to Johann Ferdinand Mödlhammer.

Inspired by developments at Schönbrunn from the outset – not least the expansion of a hunting lodge into a great palace – the central block is articulated in the style of Fischer's Schönbrunn scheme as begun for Joseph I. Further, it acquired an open staircase to the entrance front which is clearly modelled on Niccolò Pacassi's new one at Schönbrunn. The interiors include much ephemeral Rococo – even in the main hall – and several Chinoiserie cabinets inspired by those installed for Empress Maria Theresa at Schönbrunn.

4.74b

4.74c

THE GREAT PALACE AT MID-CENTURY

By the time Melk was being decorated in the third decade of the 18th century, the Rococo was ramping over central Europe: indeed extremely refined Rococo detail relieves the Baroque grandeur of his great abbey church itself. By the median decade it had reached Fertőd in Hungary, where

›**4.75 BUDA, ROYAL PALACE:** court front of central block (from c. 1749).

A small rectangular building was begun over medieval foundations in 1715 but was destroyed by fire in 1723 – before the completion of the interiors. Public subscription was invited in 1748 for the raising of funds to replace the ruin: popular response after the successful outcome of the War of the Austrian Succession, confirming the position of Empress Maria Theresa, led to the commissioning of Jean-Nicolas Jadot (1710–61), the court architect of Emperor Francis I (ex-duke of Lorraine). It is hardly surprising, therefore, that the scheme echoes the Louvre ordonnance transmitted via Boffrand at Nancy – or Joseph Emanuel Fischer's Hofburg Michaelerplatz project on which Jadot was working at the outset of his Viennese career. On his departure for Brussels on imperial service in 1753, his scheme for three blocks framing a cour d'honneur was modified in elevation by Pacassi and again by Franz Anton Hillebrandt who brought the first phase of the project to completion in 1769. The attic storey was added from 1850, at the beginning of the extensive third phase of expansion which achieved the vast complex – sprawling over and beyond its clifftop site – by 1912.

4.75

the several generations of Esterházy princes – the emperor's greatest subjects in Hungary – were bent on emulating Schönbrunn.**4.74** There Fischer's original scheme was being revised by Niccolò Pacassi (1716–90) who we met altering the Hofburg library and who was also working on the royal palace in Buda at the time.**4.75** That has been much altered

4.76a

4.76b

4.76c

›4.76 VIENNA, SCHÖNBRUNN PALACE: (a) exterior from garden, (b) Grosse Galerie, (c) Vieux-Laque-Zimmer, (d) Millionenzimmer, (e) entrance court (1759, Bernardo Bellotto; Vienna, Kunsthistorische Museum).

Bought by Charles VI from his widowed sister-in-law, as we have seen, the Schönbrunn palace was remodelled and modernized by his daughter, Empress Maria Theresa, after the first phase of the War of the Austrian Succession had ended with peace between Austria and Prussia in mid-1742. The commission was let to Niccolò Pacassi: the upper storey was increased in height and a mezzanine inserted in the side blocks; a high pitched roof, added to Johann Bernhard Fischer's complex by Joseph Emanuel, was lowered and the central pediments replaced with an attic to both sides – the front one a reduced version of the original arcaded belvedere; the entrance court was reformed and Fischer's elliptical external staircase was replaced with twin ramps ascending through curves to a first-floor terrace over a new porte cochère.

Inside, the most dramatic change was the suppression of Fischer's double-height hall, which ran through the central pavilion on axis with the entrance, in favour of a great gallery extending laterally throughout the central block: this Grosse Galerie (with frescoes glorifying the House of Habsburg by Gregorio Guglielmi) is lit from the entrance court façade to the north where the mezzanine was eliminated by its coved vault; it is backed on the garden side by Pacassi's Kleine Galerie and its terminal cabinets. These and the two orientalist cabinets, the Vieux-Laque-Zimmer and the Millionenzimmer, mark the high point of Austrian Rococo development.

4.76d

and expanded but, like Schönbrunn, was virtually complete by mid-century when Empress Maria Theresa was undertaking the decoration of the main rooms. Most of the originals at Buda have been lost to whim or war. At Schönbrunn a synthesis between Rococo and Baroque had been effected for the great hall and the *genre pittoresque* was at home in the cabinets – especially to frame Mughal miniatures in the so-called Millionenzimmer. To trace the origin of this development we must return to Bavaria where a Francophile elector had promoted French fashion in marked contrast to the mode of the previous generation.**4.76**

4.76e

3 ADVANCED BAROQUE AND THE ADVENT OF ROCOCO

Architectural activity in Bavaria was inhibited by the War of the Spanish Succession (1701–14). As we have seen, court patronage had been suspended with the exile of the elector Maximilian II Emanuel in 1704 for pursuing his imperial pretensions in alliance with the Bourbons against the Habsburgs. Not lacking in architectural ambitions, matching sovereign will to celebrate the Church Triumphant from the perspective of their orders, Bavarian monastic patrons also found it difficult to make a start on realizing them until peace returned. Building activity was retarded even in neighbouring Swabia, where political fragmentation ran to numerous imperial free towns and monasteries.

While the Graubündner rivals, Zuccalli and Viscardi, were jostling for preference when prosperity returned to Munich, Vorarlbergers were prominent in Swabia: their activities even penetrated into the north-eastern cantons of Switzerland which marched with their Austrian provincial homeland. Well before Hildebrandt was evolving his plans

4.77 a

4.77 b

4.77 c

4.77 d

>**4.77 WEINGARTEN, BENEDICTINE ABBEY OF S. MARTIN** (from 1715): (a) ideal project for reconstruction (engraved after Stadtmüller, 1723), (b) overview, (c, d) church exterior and interior.

The monastery was founded in 1056. In 1096 the wife of Duke Welf I of Bavaria endowed it with a phial of the soil of Calvary soaked in the Holy Blood: thereafter the monastic church, the Bavarian Welf necropolis, was also a focus of pilgrimage. The church was rebuilt from 1274 when the monastery was accorded imperial status. Exceptionally rich again (from its forests and vineyards) sixty years after the devastation of the Thirty Years' War, the Romanesque abbey was comprehensively rebuilt to the order of Abbot Sebastian Hyller who sought to emulate S. Pietro in Rome in scale. From a competition he chose the scheme of Franz Beer but subjected it to the scrutiny of the Vorarlberger lay brother Andreas Schreck and the Württemberg ducal stuccador turned architect, the Comesque Donato Giuseppe Frisoni (1683–1735): disenchanted, Beer resigned. The result is an enormous domed basilica of wall-pillar type with concave galleries to each bay: the passages through the spur walls separate the pillars as pier-pilasters supporting saucer domes instead of tunnel vaulting; the raising of the dome over a drum at the crossing is rare among the works of the Vorarlbergers. The stuccowork – markedly less chunky than that of the late Comesques – is due to Franz Schmutzer.

for the abbey of Göttweig in emulation of the El Escorial, the Vorarlbergers were referring to the same model in several projects first conceived before the war but delayed in execution. Most notable among these are Swabian Weingarten (from 1715) and Swiss Einsiedeln (from 1719). The basic plan of the former is credited to Franz Beer (1660–1726), son of Michael, apprentice to Michael Thumb whose work at Obermachtal he completed. Einsiedeln is due to Kaspar Moosbrugger (1656–1723). If the intermediacy of Hildebrandt may be discounted in the evolution of the definitive grid of both monastic complexes, it is harder to deny Fischer credit for the convex façade type adopted for their churches.**4.77, 4.78**

Moosbrugger was born in Au and served his apprenticeship under Christian Thumb in the circle of Michael Beer's Auer Zunft: rather than the latter, he entered the Benedictine order at Einsiedeln and assumed responsibility for many Benedictine projects in southern Germany and

4.78a

4.78d

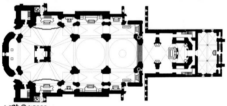

4.78b @ 1:2000

4.78c

> **4.78 EINSIEDELN, BENEDICTINE ABBEY AND PILGRIMAGE CHURCH,** from 1719: (a) west front, (b) plan, (c, d) interior to east and shrine rotunda.

The monastery was established around the site of a hermitage by Emperor Otto I in 947. The great Romanesque basilican church built from 1131, after a fire had devastated its predecessor, was augmented at a lower level from 1230 for the reception of pilgrims on the way to Santiago and, specifically, to the hermitage shrine which housed the miraculous image of the Black Madonna (a soot-blackened late-Gothic statue which replaced the Romanesque original destroyed by fire in 1465). Several more fires and war damage prompted rebuilding which began with the choir of Hans Georg Kuen in 1674. After several changes of strategy, Kaspar Moosbrugger was commissioned to rebuild the entire complex in 1704 but the design process was protracted: in the event, his brother Johann was the executive architect (from 1719). The lower church was reformed with an octagonal ambulatory which pushed the façade into convexity: the central space was vaulted over arches radiating from a great central aedicule, around the hermit's shrine before two domically-vaulted nave bays. Kuen's work was incorporated in the narrower groin-vaulted sanctuary which culminated in the domical choir. The stuccowork and frescoes are due to the Asam brothers.

> **4.79 RASTATT, SCHLOSS,** from 1700: (a) pre-War view showing radial avenues, (b) sketch for a courtyard scheme (Domenico Egidio Rossi, c. 1697), (c) court front.

The seat of his ancestors having been destroyed in the French wars, the margrave Ludwig Wilhelm of Baden-Baden inaugurated the new town of Rastatt, his principal seat from 1700. Uniform in its domestic style within the grid of streets, three avenues radiate from the palace, as at Versailles.

4.79a

After his marriage in 1690, Ludwig Wilhelm called Domenico Egidio Rossi from Vienna to design a palace modern in its standards of dignity and commodity. A preliminary sketch combines Roman High Baroque church and palace façades and the pavillons introduced by Bernini to his schemes for the Louvre in attempted conformity with French tradition. The executed project was French in its distribution about an open cour d'honneur but the articulation of the three-storey central block, with Orders for the arcaded basement and *bel étage* under an attic, may even be seen to look back to Lescot's Louvre – though the superstructure counters that association in reference to the Netherlands. As in several Viennese works and the Italian norm, moreover, the saloon is disposed laterally rather than longitudinally on the main axis.

Ludwig Wilhelm's widow Sibylla Augusta of Sachsen-Lauenburg replaced Rossi with Johann Michael Ludwig Rohrer, the master-mason son of the court hydraulics engineer. He built the court church (from 1720) and provided his patroness with the suburban Schloss Favorit (from 1710) in a highly colourful fantasy style which has nothing to do with its supposed typological model, the French maison de plaisance.

north-east Switzerland. Meanwhile, Beer's heirs were busy for other orders. Of these Christian Thumb, primarily a technician, went on from completing his brother Michael's work at various sites to build service wings at Weingarten and – as master of the Auer Zunft from 1708 – assisting in the construction of the great church there. Most important in the next generation was Peter Thumb (1681–1767), Franz Beer's son-in-law. His activities range from the abbey churches of Alsatian Ebermünster and S. Peter in the Black Forest (from 1724) to the pilgrimage church of Neu-Birnau (from 1746; see below, page 614). His career culminated in the complex gestation of the plans for rebuilding the great church and library of Sankt Gallen (from 1755; see below).

Thumb, Moosbrugger and their Vorarlberger contemporaries were rarely detached from ecclesiastical work: the modern palace was a foreign concept, after all. In south-west Germany – as elsewhere, indeed – Italians (or Italian speakers) were still active in the secular field but were challenged by the French and even by natives. Of the several works begun about the turn of the new century, primacy among new developments embracing planned new towns is claimed by Rastatt, the seat of the margrave Ludwig Wilhelm of Baden-Baden (1655–1707) in the north-western reaches of Swabia (from 1700): its authorship was polyglot.**4.79** Also in Swabia, German

4.79b

4.79c

4.80a

›4.80 LUDWIGSBURG, SCHLOSS, from 1704: (a) aerial view with Furstenbau to the rear, (b, c) inner and outer fronts of garden range, (d–f) gallery, mirror cabinet and Ordennsaal, (g) Favorita, (h) Monrepos.

The residence of the dukes of Württemberg from 1717, Ludwigsburg was conceived as a Versailles on an expansive site close to the ancestral seat of Stuttgart: beside the palace rather than on axis with it, the planned town was founded in 1709. The patron had visited Versailles in 1700.

The commission for a palace in place of a hunting lodge was let by Duke Eberhard Ludwig of Württemberg, first to the obscure Philipp Joseph Jenisch, who began a rectangular block on the top of the sloping site in 1704. Soon Jenisch was replaced by the military engineer Johann Frederick Nette (1672–1714): over his predecessor's base, he erected the three-storey, eleven-bay Fürstenbau, fenestrated like a typical Italian palazzo, and extended it with lower wings terminating in square pavilions. He had called in a Comesque team of executive builders and decorators from Prague: their leader, the stuccador Donato Giuseppe Frisoni (whom we encountered at Weingarten), replaced him on his death in 1714 when the main concern was interior decoration. Like many of his compatriots, the stuccador soon graduated to architecture and began by raising an attic with a hipped mansard over the central bays of the Fürstenbau's central block.

speakers were responsible for the most extensive contemporary development from hunting lodge to palace and new town: a veritable Versailles indeed, it was initiated by Duke Eberhard Ludwig of Württemberg for his new seat of Ludwigsburg (from 1704).**4.80** Further north,

4.80b

4.8od

4.8oe

4.8of

The site was on a slight eminence more easily approached from either side of the forecourt than from its front. Frisoni was instructed to enclose it and responded, in contrast to the original Italianate range, with a garden range of two storeys and an attic in mansard roofs: in the current Franco-Viennese manner, it was centred on an elliptical marble hall projecting into a formal garden in the French mode. On a further eminence beyond the garden, Frisoni provided the duke with his Trianon (from 1713): the Favorita was a *Lustgebäude* of the type copiously illustrated by Fischer. Frisoni's work was finished in 1733. Philippe de La Guêpière added the 'Marly' of Monrepos (from 1764).

4.8og

4.8oc

4.8oh

4.81b

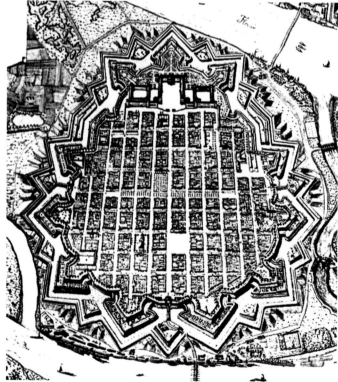

4.81a

4.81c

>**4.81 MANNHEIM, TOWN AND SCHLOSS** (from 1720): (a) overview (by Josef Anton Baertels, *Plan der Residenzstadt Mannheim*, 1758), (b, c) cour d'honneur and chapel.

The town was founded in 1606 on a regular grid and fortified as a secondary residence of the elector palatine – of the Lower Palatinate after 1648 when Bavaria retained the rest. The Friedrichsburg, on which the defences were dependent, was replaced with a modern palace by the elector Karl III Philipp (1661–1742) who made Mannheim his capital instead of Heidelberg where his Catholicism offended his Protestant subjects. Construction began in 1720, the court took possession in 1731 but work continued under Karl Philipp's successor, Karl Theodor (1724–99), until 1760.

The initial plan is credited to Louis Rémy de la Fosse, court architect of Hesse-Darmstadt: beyond the general distribution around a cour d'honneur, however, there is little French in the central building – the Mittelbau – begun by the Mainz master-builder Johann Kaspar Herwarthel (1675–1720) who must be presumed to have comprehensively revised the massing and the style of articulation in advance as he died within the year. His successor was the master-builder Johann Clemens Froimon ('Froimont') of Speyer. The eclectic style of the Mittelbau seems to derive in part from Serlio – perhaps via Rubens's *Palazzi di Genova* – in part from Schönbrunn, that of the chapel and library blocks from the provincial interpretation of Italian Baroque palace ordonnance. Quite different, the wings flanking the cour d'honneur may be defined in terms of French academic Classicism at its simplest: they are doubtless due to Guillaume d'Hauberat (died 1749) who had been sent by Robert de Cotte to Bonn in 1716 to serve the elector Joseph Clemens and was called to Mannheim to replace Froimon on his death in 1726.

›**4.82 KARLSRUHE:** ideal plan (1715).

The margrave Karl III Wilhelm's ancestral seat, Durlach, was plundered by the French c. 1690. In dispute with the citizens over the means to economic recovery, he emulated his Baden-Baden relative – whose forces he supported with his own in the War of the Spanish Succession – and settled on an entirely new site. The military engineer Friedrich von Batzendorf was commissioned to produce the design: a complete circle defined by a ring road, this was centred on a tower before which the palace was to be built with canted wings on radii defining a quadrant of the circle filled with formal gardens; other radial routes led out into the surrounding hunting forest. The original buildings – even the palace – were half-timbered but were rebuilt in stone by the margrave Karl Friedrich (1728–1811, succeeded his grandfather in 1738, inherited Baden-Baden in 1771, raised to Grand-Duke of Baden in 1806).

at the somewhat later new town of Mannheim, another Versailles was projected for the elector palatine Karl III Philipp (from 1720): Louis Rémy de la Fosse is credited with the plans which, naturally, were developed around a cour d'honneur but the German builder initially had his own way.**4.81** Meanwhile, in 1715 the margrave Karl III Wilhelm of Baden-Durlach (1679–1738) responded to the Rastatt of his distant cousin of Baden-Baden with the most expansive, most absolutist of such urban schemes for his new seat of Karlsruhe (from 1715) – but the palace at the apex belongs to a later era.**4.82**

4.82

4.83a

4.83c

4.83d

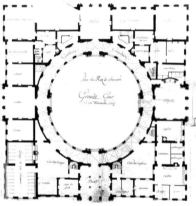

4.83b

>4.83 POPPELSDORF, SCHLOSS CLEMENS-
RUHE, from 1718: (a) entrance front, (b, c) plan and garden elevation project, (d) garden front.

De Cotte's project for the Bonn residence naturally included the main interiors but these have survived only in the drawings. The scheme for Poppelsdorf was drawn in 1715: Marly was the inspiration in function and form but the more expansive programme was centred on a circular court instead of a salon. It was executed by the master's nominee Guillaume d'Hauberat but the interior decoration was not carried out until 1744 when the building had been inherited by Joseph Clemens's nephew Clemens August.

Hauberat went on to Mannheim in 1726, as we have seen, and then in 1732 to execute de Cotte's design of 1727 for the Frankfurt palace of Thurn und Taxis (destroyed in World War II).

ELECTORAL INITIATIVE: JOSEPH EFFNER ASCENDANT

As noted, the Wittelsbach courts were two: Munich and Cologne were the respective seats of the electoral brothers Maximilian II Emanuel and Joseph Clemens. As also noted, both were exiled for injudicious support of the French in the War of the Spanish Succession and both returned from France in 1714 with sophisticated French taste. Maximilian Emanuel had employed Boffrand to build a hunting

4.84a

4.84b

4.84c

4.84d

**›4.84 JOSEPH EFFNER AFTER ENRICO ZUCCA-
LLI AT NYMPHENBURG,** from 1714: (a–d) Baden-
burg (bath house), exterior, Pagodenburg, exterior
and interior details (from 1716), (e) Zuccalli's scheme,
extended entrance elevation, (f, g) plan after Effner and
general view of revised entrance front, (h) north antechamber detail (from 1720), (i) state bedroom.

The Pagodenburg – a miniature essay inspired by Le
Vau's Trianon de Porcelaine which disappeared from
Louis XIV's garden under Jules Hardouin-Mansart, as
we have seen (page 257) – preserves the earliest surviving Rococo rooms in Germany: not for Chinoiserie
styling, the latter is outstanding for the tiling of the
ground-floor salon in Wittelsbach blue and silvery-
white below an Audranesque ceiling (by the Austrian
Johann Anton Gumpp) and for the Bérainesque panelling of the upper-floor withdrawing room. The latter follows the mode as developed in Hildebrandt's Viennese
school – though engravings after Bérain were presumably as readily available in Munich as in Vienna. Effner's
Palais Preysing, built (from 1723) near the Munich
Residenz, also follows Hildebrandt in the style of its
façade.

lodge in the Flemish forest of Soignies (1705) and to work
on his residence in exile at Saint-Cloud: in 1706 he had
engaged him to train his protégé, the Saxon Joseph Effner
(1687–1745). Joseph Clemens favoured Robert de Cotte.

Enrico Zuccalli's conservative quadrangular schemes
for both Maximilian Emanuel's Schleissheim and for his
brother's Bonn palace had been left incompletely realized
on their patrons' exile. Both commissioned comprehensive new plans from de Cotte. Maximilian Emanuel was to
look elsewhere, first to Effner as we shall see. Joseph Clemens, calling for grandeur at the outset, ultimately made
do with modified implementation of Zucall's designs for
his Bonn palace. On axis with the palace, however, Schloss
Clemensruhe at Poppelsdorf was designed by de Cotte
*ab initio.***4.83**

With Vorarlbergers in the ascendant in western Bavaria,
Graubündners were in terminal decline at the Munich
court when Maximilian Emanuel returned from exile: Viscardi had died the year before; Zuccalli lived on for another
ten years, nominally as chief architect but actually sidelined
by his patron's new protégés. Effner was appointed Hof-
baumeister in 1715. Meanwhile work had resumed on Zuccalli's projects for both Nymphenburg and Schleissheim.

The Neues Schloss at Schleissheim was conceived as
a new seat and was greatly to be augmented when Wittelsbach was ambitious for the imperial crown: that cause
was lost but the grandeur of the project was sustained. In
it French influence may be detected as dominant: Zuccalli had experienced current French practice, particularly
developments in and around Versailles associated with Jules
Hardouin-Mansart and his circle, in 1684. On the other
hand, his extensions to Nymphenburg follow the example
of the Dutch stadtholder's seat at Het Loo (from 1684): he
was in the Netherlands when Maximilian Emanuel was
viceroy there in the 1690s.**4.84**

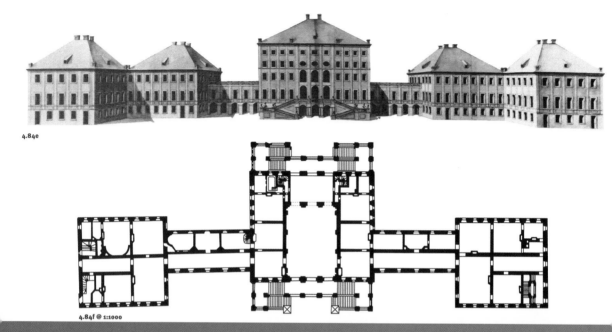

4.84e

4.84f @ 1:1000

4.84g

›ARCHITECTURE IN CONTEXT »DIVIDED CENTRE AND ORTHODOX EAST

As noted above, Agostino Barelli's double-height core ceremonial space prompted Zuccalli's revision of the main residence: the five windows in the centre of each front were reformed into larger triads and arcaded on the levels embraced by the double-height hall. In response, new internal arcading opened the hall to lighting borrowed from the central rooms addressing the garden. Further, wings and doubled side pavilions were added to relieve the monotonous self-assertion of Barelli's lugubrious block (page 508). When work was resumed after the war, Effner reduced the number of the latter's side bays from four to three, reforming the windows, and added pilasters to distinguish the arcaded bays of the garden front. Inside the palace itself, he introduced Régence embellishment to the more formal geometrical style of the north antechamber but the electoral bedroom retains its allegiance to the essentially tectonic style of Louis XIV's lesser apartments (see page 190).

4.84h

Effner was entrusted with the completion of Nymphenburg, particularly with improvements to the fenestration. In the park he built a hermitage, a bath house and the Pagodenburg reception pavilion (from 1717): in the last of these he introduced Rococo to Bavaria in the Régence terms of filigree strapwork enmeshing grotesque motifs. He was then

4.84i

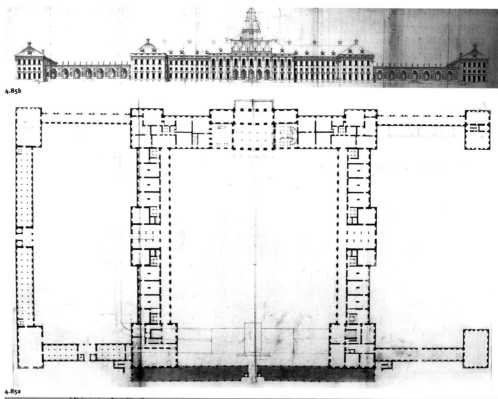

4.85b

4.85a

4.85f

>4.85 EFFNER AFTER ZUCCALLI AT SCHLEIS-
SHEIM: (a–c) Zuccalli's project of c. 1701, plan,
garden-front and court elevations, (d) idealized view
of Effner's revised complex over the reformed Altes
Schloss (c. 1730, Maximilian de Geer, Munich Residenz), (e) plan after Effner with (1) staircase hall, (2)
Great Hall, (3) Victory Hall, (4) Great Gallery, (5) first
room of the elector's apartments in the north wing, (6)
first room of the electoress's apartments in the south
wing, (f) general view from park, (g, h) colonnaded
undercroft and staircase, (i) Great Hall, (j) Great Gallery, (k) elector's bedroom, (l–n) Red Cabinet and Dutch
Cabinet ceiling detail.

Zuccalli's original project was drawn in 1693 but work
began on the main east range only in 1701, after the
patron returned from his vice royalty of the Netherlands,
and ended in 1704 with his exile. The conservative quadrangular scheme initially emulated Bernini's Louvre
projects but with an entrance screen closing the court to
the west in the standard French manner. That work was
incorporated in Effner's revisions (from 1719) which did
not extend to the wings but concentrated on the centre
and its internal distribution. His scheme is a Franco-Italian hybrid with three pavillons, the central one as extensive as an entire palazzo. The thirty-seven-bay façade
is articulated in expansion of Zuccalli's Lustheim style
with a colossal Order rising from the ground in the centre
(page 509): there is a full attic over the central block, and

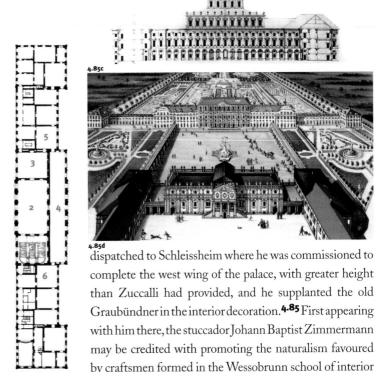

4.85c

4.85d

4.85e @ 1:2000

dispatched to Schleissheim where he was commissioned to
complete the west wing of the palace, with greater height
than Zuccalli had provided, and he supplanted the old
Graubündner in the interior decoration.**4.85** First appearing
with him there, the stuccador Johann Baptist Zimmermann
may be credited with promoting the naturalism favoured
by craftsmen formed in the Wessobrunn school of interior

an Italianate mezzanine in the wings. Zuccalli's core of state reception rooms embraced the colonnaded vestibule with a staircase to one side leading to the Great Hall (much varied in the planning process before 1701) and its adjunct dedicated to victory against the Turks in 1683. These survive but Effner's alterations ran to a grand gallery: derived from the scheme provided by de Cotte, that extends through the full length of the central block, like its model at Versailles.

Effner had brought the main rooms of the twin electoral apartment largely to completion by his patron's death in 1726. Supplemented by Johann Adam Pichler, he introduced French Rococo elegance of the fretted Régence type to the Victory Hall, the state bedroom and elsewhere in the twin electoral apartments. For the great staircase and core parade rooms and for the grand gallery he presided over a collaborative synthesis of French – Bérainesque – stylization, Italian exuberance and native naturalism: Cosmas Damian Asam frescoed the staircase cupola and the chapel but the Venetian Jacopo Amigoni was responsible for the greatest of the illusionist frescoes; bolder than the Parisian norm, the relief is due to the French stuccador Charles Dubut working with the fluent Johann Baptist Zimmermann.

4.85h

4.85g

4.85j

4.85i

4.85m

4.85l

4.85n

4.85k

decoration – as elsewhere in the era of high Rococo, in Flanders, for example.**4.86**

To broaden his views, Effner had been sent to Rome for further experience in 1717. He was preceded there in 1711 by the brothers Cosmas Damian and Egid Quirin Asam (1686–1739 and 1692–1750): sons of a painter working for the Benedictine monastery of Tegernsee, they went as protégés of the abbot. Experienced in one or other or both the cultural capitals of Europe, employed by ruler or prelate, these scions of the new generation – Effner, Asam and Zimmermann – led in the transformation of Bavarian architecture and decoration.

4.86

›**4.86 GHENT, CATHEDRAL OF S. BAVO (SINT-BAAFSKATHEDRAAL):** pulpit by Laurent Delvaux (1741).

The Wessobrunn school

Just to the north of the Vorarlberg–Bavarian border, south of Munich, the area around Weilheim had produced building workers for the electoral seat – and many monasteries – for well over a century. Within the area (as noted above, page 479) the Benedictine monastery of Wessobrunn fostered a school specializing in stuccowork whose chosen graduates went on to stylistic training with Italian masters at court. Working largely for monastic clients, not least the Benedictines, the Vorarlberger masons in south-western Bavaria and Swabia naturally formed a close relationship with the Wessobrunner stuccadors which would be of far-reaching consequence when the Italian mode ceded to the French at court. The occasion was prepared by Johann Baptist Zimmermann (1680–1758): as we shall see, after pioneering work with the Asam brothers – and working for Effner at Schleissheim – he went on to Munich as court stuccador under the principal agent of Rococo reform, François Cuvilliés. Thereafter, however, he developed primarily as a fresco painter and left the furthering of rocaille fantasy to his dedicated stuccador brother Dominikus (1685–1766): his would be the foam of rocaille which dissolved the boundary between physics and fantasy.

The court lead was followed, of course, and the engravers of Augsburg – the centre of the Bavarian printing industry – traded lucratively without licence in prints regurgitating fashionable French cartouche designs (see pages 480f). These extended to less-defined decorative confections

>4.87 BRÜHL (NEAR COLOGNE), SCHLOSS AUGUSTUSBURG, from 1725: (a, b) garden and entrance fronts.

Working on the basis of the moated quadrangular castle (from 1723), Johann Conrad Schlaun incorporated two round towers – one of them original – as terminal pavilions to the west front but remodelled the ranges between and dependent on them as the U-shaped enclosure of a cour d'honneur open to the east: the formula of two storeys and a mansard attic over an arcaded basement is French but French academic Classical discretion lapses in the articulation of the central and end pavilions with broken pediments supported by colossal pilasters in two planes on the latter. This echoes the style of works like Pommersfelden and the sculptural pediment of the south wing's central pavilion, at least, is comparable with Fischer von Erlach's contemporary additions to the Hofburg in Vienna.

While construction was nearing its conclusion in 1728, Cuvilliés was imported to embellish the interiors. Meanwhile, André Le Nôtre's pupil Dominique Girard had been retained for the landscaping: he eliminated the moat and replaced it with a terrace to the south from which a double staircase provided access to his formal garden. In response (from 1735), Cuvilliés removed the other medieval relics, the round towers, and reorientated the electoral apartments to face south over the garden.

which strayed from arabesque strapwork – or ribbonwork as it may be called more effectively – to the flexibility of plant life and beyond to the motifs of a shelly, watery world. Ultimately from Wessobrunn, the brilliant pair of brothers Feuchtmayr and Finsterwalder found employment and stylistic inspiration as decorators in sculpture and paint in Augsburg. There, moreover, they were joined by Johann Georg Übelhör, a fellow Wessobrunner, who had worked with Zimmermann at Munich where he had first-hand familiarity with current practice in the French mode. The second-hand familiarity acquired through working extensively in the vicinity of Augsburg, at first, informed the Wessobrunner stuccador-architect Joseph Schmuzer who progressed to maturity in the rocaille mode. In the previous generation, on the other hand, Franz Schmuzer – who worked for Kaspar Moosbrugger at Weingarten in continuation of his family's close connection with the circle of Franz Beer – drew his inspiration from current Viennese development of the Régence style of Bérain. The careers of many of these are ahead of us but from the outset they were the sculptors and painters with whom native architects effected the *Gesamtkunstwerk*: the indissoluble synthesis of all three arts unique to 18th-century southern Germany, which eludes precise definition in terms of architecture or decoration, Baroque or Rococo – as we have seen.

RENEWED ELECTORAL INITIATIVE: CUVILLIÉS ASCENDANT

Secondary to Effner, at first, was the Fleming François Cuvilliés (1695–1768): with Maximilian Emanuel in Soignies and brought to Munich in 1714, he was trained in mathematics and military engineering while employed as Effner's draughtsman. He was sent to Paris in 1720 to study in the circle of the Académie Royale – where he was a contemporary of Jacques-François Blondel. There, of course, he witnessed the development of Rococo which had yet to turn asymmetrical: the seminal contributions of Pineau and Meissonnier in launching the *genre pittoresque* were still a decade away. On his return to Munich in 1724 he was still officially Effner's draughtsman for the projects of Maxi-

4.87a

milian Emanuel – designing ceilings for Schleissheim in particular – but his career advanced after the accession of Karl Albrecht in 1726. Meanwhile, he was called to Bonn by his patron's brother Clemens August who had recently been installed as archbishop-elector of Cologne on the demise of his uncle, Joseph Clemens.

Towards the end of his life Joseph Clemens had commissioned Robert de Cotte to plan the rebuilding of the electoral castle at Brühl, which had been virtually destroyed by French troops in 1689.**4.87** Clemens August determined to realize the project but employed Johann Conrad Schlaun

›4.88 MÜNSTER, ERBDROSTENHOF, from 1755: (a, b) plan and entrance elevation.

Erbdrostenhof's triangular site promoted ingenious symmetry, worthy of a French master, but the elevation with its concave frontispiece is as much Austrian as French: beyond knowledge of Joseph Emanuel Fischer von Erlach, the influence of Hildebrandt and his Italian mentors is not to be discounted. Pommersfelden is recalled for the prince-bishop's palace – with fading elan except for the convex frontispiece.

4.88b

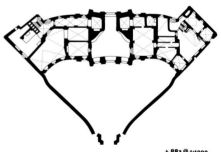

4.88a @ 1:1000

4.89a

**›4.89 CUVILLIÉS AND THE PRIVATE RESI-
DENCE IN MUNICH:** (a) Palais Porcia (by Zuccalli
from 1693, remodelled from 1731); (b) Palais Holnstein
(from 1733; now the archbishop's palace).

Apart from his work for the elector and his court,
Cuvilliés had a limited private practice. Following in
general the constrained quadrangular form of Joseph
Effner's Palais Preysing, itself not unindebted to Fischer's developments in Vienna, his most notable works
in the genre of the town house are the Holnstein and
Porcia palaces, both built – or modernized – at the instigation of the elector Karl Albrecht for his mistresses,
Countess Morawitzka (later Princess Porcia) and Countess Holnstein respectively.

4.89b

– the architect from his Münster see – instead of de Cotte.
But Schlaun went on to serve his ecclesiastical patron and
other clients in Münster where the Clemenshospital, the
Erbdrostenhof and the prince-bishop's palace are his major
legacies.[4.88] Not equipped to satisfy the elector's taste for
French design, he was superseded in Bonn by Cuvilliés.

The suites of the Bonn palace decorated by Cuvilliés
from 1728 were the most modern in Germany, the equal
of the current generation in France – or the latest Parisian
designs published in that same year by Jean Mariette in
his *L'architecture françoise* (see pages 312f). On the Bavarian
elector's behalf, he returned to Munich where he was to have
a limited domestic practice but primarily served at court
with great panache – not least due to the executive services
of Johann Baptist Zimmermann.[4.89]

Ambitious to succeed Emperor Charles VI who had
no son, Karl Albrecht commissioned a new suite of state
rooms embracing a didactic gallery of ancestors: imperial
in magnificence, the constituents were to be known as
Reiche Zimmer and embraced a picture gallery hung with
green silk damask, audience rooms and antechambers, the
state bedroom and cabinets (all reconstructed post-World
War II). Beyond that, Cuvilliés's greatest contribution to
the elector's delight was the Amalienburg pavilion in the
Nymphenburg park. Finally, back at the centre, he devised
the court theatre which now bears his name.[4.90, 4.91]

The apogee of Rococo in Munich

Work began on the Residenz's Reiche Zimmer before Cuvilliés went to Cologne
and continued for several years thereafter. Effner was initially responsible
and would have had ready access to the latest printed French publications,
primarily Mariette's *L' architecture françoise*. Able to review such sources in
the light of practical experience, Cuvilliés modified the designs in the drafting
and effectively supplanted his superior after a fire in 1729 occasioned a new
start – and even a new façade for the Grottenhof.

4.90a

4.90b

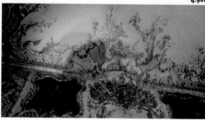

4.90d

4.90c

4.90e

4.90h

›4.90 CUVILLIÉS AND ZIMMERMANN AT THE MUNICH RESIDENCE AFTER EFFNER: (a) Ancestors' Gallery (by Effner from 1726, revised from 1728), (b) Treasury (from 1730, now Porcelain Cabinet), (c, d) elector's bedroom (from 1730), general view and ceiling detail, (e, f) Mirror Cabinet (from 1731), (g, h) Green Gallery and annexe (from 1731), general view and ceiling detail; (i, j) Cuvilliés's theatre, auditorium (from 1751).

4.90g

4.90f

Effner's serried superimposition of electoral portraits in opulent frames survives in the Ancestors' Gallery (Ahnengalerie) but the much freer treatment of its coved ceiling is due to Cuvilliés and Zimmermann: there symmetry is respected in the general disposition but playful parts are allotted to naturally asymmetrical flora and fauna. That approach was further developed – with watery motifs and dragons – from the cove into the ceiling of the Schatzkammer treasury in which the hall terminates. And that in turn was the starting point for Cuvilliés's transformation of the Reiche Zimmer. These included the Mirror Cabinet (Spiegelkabinett), Red Cabinet (Rotes Kabinett) and Green Gallery (Grüne Galerie) by 1733 and asymmetrical informality advanced with them towards the rocaillerie with which Meissonnier was currently experimenting.

Cuvilliés's development as a designer of stucco embellishment took the medium from framing painting to supplanting it in representation – allegorical or naturalistic. The culmination was reached in the second half of the decade in the Amalienburg pavilion which Karl Albrecht called on Cuvilliés to produce for him as a base for pheasant shooting at Nymphenburg. The idea may derive from the vanished Trianon de Porcelaine at Versailles but the form is expanded from the Pavillon de l'Aurore at Sceaux: instead of a semi-octagonal frontispiece to the rotunda, curve counters curve in Cuvilliés's design and instead of strict sobriety there is restrained sculptural relief in the screen façade. Inside enfilades through cabinets with rounded corners flank the central mirror salon (Spiegelsaal). Naturalism in asymmetry, indeed the delightful intrusion of wildlife (especially game), is nowhere better demonstrated than in that ravishing room.

4.90j

4.91a

4.91b

4.91c

4.90d

›ARCHITECTURE IN CONTEXT »DIVIDED CENTRE AND ORTHODOX EAST

Cuvilliés and his Flemish compatriots were no strangers to naturalism: it we have seen its extreme in Flemish pulpits.[4.86] An unsurpassed manifestation of the *genre pittoresque* not essentially derivative from Meissonnier, the design of the Amalienburg salon is based on the syncopated undulation of continuous door, window and mirror frame mouldings. The result suggests knowledge of Boffrand in Lunéville and Paris: unlike the Salon de la Princesse de Soubise, however, equal sides have equal voids which leave no spandrels for painting. Picked out in silver over blue – the Wittelsbach colours – all is sculpted and the motifs range from the panoplies of power and the instruments of art to ramping plants and flying birds.

›4.91 CUVILLIÉS AND ZIMMERMANN AT NYMPHENBURG AFTER EFFNER: (a–d) Great Hall, interior (Enrico Zuccalli after 1702, adapted by Effner from c. 1716, Rococo embellishment from 1755), general view and details of cartouches, (e–i) Amalienburg pavilion (from 1734), plan, exterior, antechamber and mirror salon, general view and ceiling detail.

4.91e @ 1:1000

4.91f

4.91i

4.91g

4.91h

4.92

›4.92 AUGSBURG, SCHAEZLERPALAIS: Festsaal (1765–70).

The patron was the banker Benedikt Adam Freiherr von Liebert (1731–1810) whose father (Johann Adam, 1697–1766), a principal in the silver trade in Augsburg from 1733, was ennobled in 1763. To suit the family's new status, the prestigious site was acquired in the following year and work on the new house projected forthwith: the architect was Karl Albrecht von Lespilliez, a follower of Cuvilliés; the stuccador was a nephew of J.M. Feichtmayr.

As in the Reiche Zimmer, the execution of the Amalienburg stuccowork was entrusted to Zimmermann. His Wessobrunn origins would have equipped him to exercise a formative influence on the evolution of Cuvilliés's organic style – which reached its final phase in the Residenztheater at mid-century. It was perpetuated in the next decade – its last – by the *haute-bourgeoisie*. A major manifestation of patronage from this wealthy class is the Festsaal of the Schaezlerpalais in Augsburg.**4.92**

›4.93

›4.93 ROHR, AUGUSTINIAN PRIORY CHURCH
OF THE ASSUMPTION: retable altarpiece recreating the dedication (from 1722).

The high altar installed by Egid Quirin Asam is unequivocally Baroque. It vies with Bernini in the fusion of the arts to mount a theatrical extension of the dedication theme: its stage extended vertically, the drama is seen through a proscenium arch supported by a complete Order (see page 75).

›4.94 WELTENBURG, BENEDICTINE ABBEY
CHURCH OF S. GEORG, from 1716: (a, b) plan and section, (c–e) interior, details of dome and proscenium, (f) overview.

The patron was Abbot Maurus Bachl. His reason for commissioning an untried young architect is obscure: his faith was rewarded spectacularly. The elliptical plan, extended longitudinally for the monks' choir over the vestibule and the sanctuary, is unusually compact for the Benedictines – but the site, though exposed, was constrained on the bend of the Danube. Surrounded by chapels in niches and the truncated transepts, the auditorium of richly coloured scagliola was the foil for dramatic stage lighting both beyond the proscenium and overhead in the cut-away vault: S. George project-

4·94e

ASAM GESAMTKUNSTWERK

Cuvilliés's court theatre takes us well beyond developments in the Theatre of Grace. As far as we are concerned here, these begin soon after the Asam brothers returned from Rome. Most theatrically in the Augustinian priory Church of the Assumption at Rohr (in 1717), Egid Quirin Asam set the stage for the Berninesque realization of the Assumption in dramatic sculpture.**4·93**

The Asam brothers rank first among the native architects who forged the new syncretic style in the second and third decades of the century – though Cosmas Damian returned home as a specialist in fresco, Egid Quirin as a sculptor, and their works of architecture are few. They

4.94d

4.94c

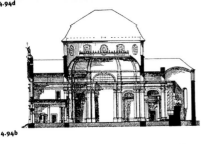

4.94b

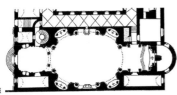

4.94a @ 1:1000

ing his coup de théâtre against the glow illuminating the painted backdrop of the former, the Coronation of the Virgin in the unrevealed source of the empyrean's radiance. The Régence patterning in the cove of the vault, ultimately Bérainesque, was probably informed by Effner's Pagodenburg pavilion in the Nymphenburg park but there is nothing French about the frescoes.

first tendered together to build and decorate the abbey of Fürstenfeldbruck but were unsuccessful (1716). Two years later, while his brother was busy at Rohr, Cosmas Damian staged a resoundingly successful Berninesque fusion of architecture, painting and sculpture for the Benedictines of Weltenburg (from 1716).**4·94**

4.94f

4.95

›4.95 ALDERSBACH, CISTERCIAN ABBEY
CHURCH: interior (redecorated from 1720).

Founded by the Augustinians c. 1120, the establishment was ceded to the Cistercians from Ebrach in 1146.
The early 13th-century church was restored several
times after fire damage: the choir was rebuilt in 1612 but
the building was badly damaged again by the Swedes
during the Thirty Years' War. Successive renovations culminated in rebuilding in wall-pillar form from 1718 under
Abbot Theobald I: the master-builder engaged for the
nave and tower is identified as Domenico Magazin. Commissioned to decorate the vault in 1720, the Asams introduced cartouches to the pendentives and a curvilinear
frame to a continuous fresco, perhaps under the inspiration of the Kaisersaal of the Cistercian abbey of Ebrach.
There the great elliptical vault was painted by Anton Clemens Lunenschloss (c. 1685–1762) within a scalloped
stucco frame provided by Daniel Schenk, fresh from
Pommersfelden: that may be related to developments in
the Viennese circle of Hildebrandt – though there cornice
lines and fresco framework were as yet to be as convoluted as those of the Pommersfelden chapel.

›4.96 FREISING, CATHEDRAL OF S. MARIA
AND S. KORBINIAN: (a) interior, (b) detail of gallery (from 1723).

Incorporating a shrine of 715, the foundation of the
episcopal and monastery church is traditionally dated
to the early 720s and credited to S. Korbinian (c. 675–c.
725), who was sent by Pope Gregory II to minister to
Duke Grimoald of Bavaria. A Romanesque church was
built over a 9th-century basilica destroyed by fire in
1159 and vaulted over Gothic arches from 1481. The
Asams' transformation of the hybrid medieval building was commissioned for the foundation millennium.
The arcaded bays of the nave are defined by colossal
pilasters supporting projections in the continuous
cornice: above that all is paint. The Gothic ribs having
been removed in a first attempt at redecoration in 1619,
Cosmas Damian re-evoked them selectively as feigned
coffered arches to divide the vault into twin double-bay
compartments flanking the tripled central zone; all
three are open to the illusion of the empyrean as the
context for the glorification of the church's co-dedica-
tee, S. Korbinian. As in Fra Andrea Pozzo's masterworks
for the Jesuits in Rome, figures spill out of the frame and
over the arches towards the world of the worshipper.

After Weltenburg, the Asam brothers were mainly commissioned to transform existing interiors, Gothic or post-
Reformation or new, with modern stuccowork, sculpture
and fresco. Of these, the great Gothic legacy provided special challenges in reversing dilapidation. Obviously existing structure invited rearticulation with applied Orders
in the Baroque mode – incongruous in a wholly pointed
context – or obliteration. The latter may be seen as a test
for the proposition that Rococo architecture is a 'contradiction in terms' even when applied to a comprehensive
interior scheme: 'obliteration' being the operative word in

4.96a

4.96b

effecting transition from physics to fantasy. Be that as it may, the release from the Baroque armature of church interiors had advanced the development of the Rococo style away from its Régence beginnings – indeed away from current French practice which rarely abandoned Classical rule in ecclesiastical building. This was in the light of Cuvilliés's secular achievement and largely at the hands of the Wessobrunner stuccadors with whom the Asams sometimes collaborated.

Cosmas Damian's earliest works on a grand scale are the frescoes in the nave bays of Weingarten abbey church (from 1718): his experience in the Rome of Andrea Pozzo is clearly apparent. His collaboration with his brother on such projects began in 1720, notably in the Cistercian abbey church of Aldersbach and continued spectacularly in the medieval cathedral of Freising where they were assisted by Zimmermann (from 1723). Novel in the latter was the lavish colour brought down to the scagliola pilaster shafts from the simulated framework of the illusionist revelations in the vault. That partially perpetuated bay divisions with transverse arches but novel at Aldersbach was the obliteration of vault compartments with a continuous illusionist fresco in an undulating frame supported by – or, rather, rising from – great cartouches: Cosmas Damian evoked the vision of the miraculous in paint and the stucco framework; the monumental iconic sculpture was produced by his brother.**4.95, 4.96** That formula, developed by the Asams in collaboration with Kaspar Moosbrugger at Einsiedeln (from 1726; see page 580), was to evolve over the next two decades, as we shall see when we review the work of the era's main architects.

The difference between the Asam brothers' transformative interventions in spaces devised by others and their own original buildings is stunningly illustrated on one other occasion, fifteen years after work began at Welten-

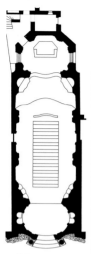

4.97b @ 1:1000

4.97c

4.97a

›4.97 MUNICH, S. JOHANN NEPOMUK, from 1733: (a) exterior, (b) plan, (c) interior.

burg: the public-private church of S. Johann Nepomuk in Munich. To this Egid Quirin devoted most of his efforts (from 1733) with the assistance of his brother as painter – and to it the family name is generally applied. Undulating to climax in three tiers of complex pediments, richly sculpted, its narrow street front is far more assertive than isolation required at Weltenburg. The interior is no less rich in its simulated marble revetment below illusionist fresco and equally theatrical in its staging of the dedicatee: sculptural in form as in detail, it is highly uncanonical in architectural motifs which seem to deny, rather than to constitute, a coherent tectonic frame – yet there is little of the Rococo in the ornament.**4·97**

The Bohemian martyr from Nepomuk (1345–93) – believed to have been drowned for refusing to breach the secrecy of the confessional – was canonized in 1729: the cult appealed to Egid Quirin, as, naturally, to many of his Bohemian contemporaries. The complex attributed to him in response to the promise of relics included houses for himself and for the priest beside the church. The latter's vigorous façade, rising from a rocky base to a Borrominian pediment via increasingly freeform aedicular caps, admirably compensates for its straitened scale. The elongated, undulating octagonal 'nave' is preceded and succeeded by the elliptical vestibule and sanctuary. Canopied by a cove – behind which Cosmas Damian's fresco rises from the source of concealed lighting – the interior's two levels are divided by a canted gallery supported by angelic herms and supporting Solomonic columns: these intrude into the zone of the cove to provide a proscenium for the presentation of the saint in backlit glory (Egid Quirin's relief of the dedicatee was removed in the 19th century in favour of a painting of the Assumption which in turn has ceded to a sculpture of the same subject). At that level and below it, two altars cater for the public and for the private worship of the patron/architect in the manner of the typical palatine chapel: thus far had a brilliant artist elevated himself – clearly not without approbation.

4.98
›4.98 FÜRSTENFELDBRUCK CISTERCIAN ABBEY: frescoes over the first bay of the choir by Cosmos Damian Asam (from 172), Régence decorative detail by assistants.

Here the Asams had been unsuccesful in conternding for the decoration of the whole but ultimately won an important part.

The comprehensive fusion of the arts in the manner of the Asams at Weltenburg or Munich – their type of *Gesamtkunstwerk* – found few emulators in Bavaria, except in the confection of scenographic altar retables. However, Cosmas Damian's expansive combination of *quadratura* and *quadrata riportata* in fresco was to be of lasting influence on the development of the non-compartmentalized nave vault and Egid Quirin's extension of its stucco frame mouldings down into colourful cartouches set the theme for much inventive variation.**4.98**

THE ZIMMERMANNS AND OTHER WESSOBRUNNERS

The Asams had pupils to develop their métiers. Naturally the credit to be won from furthering their permutations of traditional Vorarlberger media also appealed to the most innovative craftsmen of the Wessobrunner school who, closed to foreign experience, were open to the possibilities of native modes of decoration. These were led by Johann Baptist Zimmermann, whom we have already encountered as court stuccador but who went on to master illusionism in fresco, and his brother Dominikus (1685–1766) who began as a stuccador and a scagliola specialist but extended his range to fresco painting and ultimately to architecture.

The poles between which architecture and decoration contended are established by the early works of the Asam brothers - unequivocally High Baroque despite the application of Régence ornament at Weltenburg, as we have seen – and the prime works of collaboration by the brothers Zimmermann. Outstanding from these, the pilgrimage churches of Steinhausen (from 1730) and Wies (from 1746) span Dominikus's career of bringing his facility as a stuccador to bear on his conception of architecture.**4.99, 4.100**

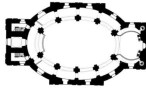

›4.99 STEINHAUSEN, PARISH AND PILGRIM-
AGE CHURCH OF UNSERE LIEBEN FRAU AND
SS. PETER AND PAUL, from 1728: (a) plan, (b) exte-
rior, (c, d) interior to sanctuary and vault detail.

The parish church dedicated to the Virgin Mary
was acquired by the Premonstratensians of Schussenried's imperial abbey in 1363 and developed as
a Marian way-station on the Upper Swabian route
to Santiago de Compostela. The Gothic pilgrimage
church was renovated in 1652 after devastation in the
Thirty Years' War. As elsewhere, the swelling influx of
pilgrims prompted its replacement in the third decade
of the 18th century: it has served the parish again since
1865. Zimmermann was chosen on the strength of his
designs for the chapel of the Dominican convent of
Siessen (from 1725). That was a rectangular wall-pillar

4.99d

Zimmermann Gesamtkunstwerk

As elsewhere in the œuvre of these two Wessobrunners who had not ven-
tured abroad, both the Steinhausen and Wies churches are of the traditional
German wall-pillar type but they are exceptional elliptical cages of light
with ambulatories around naves and, in the later example, an extended galleried choir. In both cases too, nave walls and pillars are all pure white in
contrast with the assertively colourful mouldings of the uncanonical capi-

4.99c

4.99b

structure with a succession of domical bays lit through hybrid thermal/serlianas and trilobed ellipses. Variations on these window forms light the elliptical volume of Steinhausen through the ambulatory won from the wall-pillar format: the ellipse may have been inspired by Serlio through plans of Kaspar Moosbrugger held in the Schussenried abbey library; the rectangular extension west, the base of the tower, accommodates the tiny square vestibule between stairs; the matching western projection encloses the elliptical sanctuary with its double-height altar, the upper zone enshrining the Marian icon which was the focus of the pilgrimage.

›4.100 WIES, PILGRIMAGE CHURCH ZUM GEGEISSELTEN HEILAND AUF DER WIES, from 1746: (a) plan, (b) exterior, (c) sanctuary, (d, e) interior towards entrance and towards sanctuary.

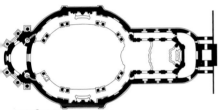

4.100a @ 1:1000

4.100c

tals and cornices and any semblance of structure is banished from the lath and plaster vaults: the distinction between frame and framed is denied in the undulating zone of transition by the brothers' collaborative free-form representation of a balustrade which transmutes into a scalloped valance.

At Steinhausen, garlanded putti wing their stuccoed way from the upturned valance into the realm of fresco. Behind statues of the Apostles in the residual pendentive zones, on the other hand, the valance dips to reveal palmettes supporting pedestals supporting urns – the simulated structural elements establishing the *quadratura* lines – marking entrance to the garden in which Johann Baptist revived medieval imagery in his frescoed glorification of the Marian dedicatee.

In advanced development, the vaults over the elevated ambulatory bays at Wies are penetrated with real and feigned fimbriated voids to admit varied light through characteristically playful variations on the motif of the thermal window: they have the strength-denying delicacy of porcelain. In the choir, moreover, a riot of gorgeous rocaille mouldings overwhelms any semblance of a loadbearing cornice above the confectionery columns and even the capitals have ceded their Classical identity. Brilliant white and flagrantly uncanonical though they may be, the columnar piers reign in the nave but if the paradox of an anti-architectonic architecture has ever been realized outside the realm of folly, it is in Wies's seductively subversive choir.

4.100b

4.100d

4.100e

Between the two Zimmermann masterpieces, between the beginning of the century's third decade and the middle of its fourth, important contributions were made to the repertory of decorative motifs by other artisans from Wessobrunn – in particular the Schmuzers, the Feichtmayr brothers Franz Xaver and Johann Michael II (1696–1764, 1709–72) and their cousin Joseph Anton Feuchtmayer (1698–1770). Joseph Schmuzer (1683–1752), primarily a stuccador, worked in southern Bavaria as an architect for parishes, pilgrims and priories in collaboration with a fellow Wessobrunner, the painter Matthäus Günther – most notably, perhaps, in the transformation of the interiors of the Augustinian priory church at Rottenbuch (from 1737) and the Benedictine abbey church of Ettal.**4.101**

The Wies pilgrimage was to an image of the Scourged Christ, carved and consecrated in 1730 by Premonstratensian monks of Steingaden for use in processions, which was seen to weep by a peasant woman as it was carried through a field. Within a decade the flood of pilgrims overwhelmed the chapel built at the scene of the miracle and replacement was projected. For that Dominikus reverted to the 'nave' of Steinhausen but paired the wall pillars and added an extended choir with a straitened continuation of the ambulatory: this was stipulated by the commissioning authority so that it would suffice in case the cult withered – which it did not. In contrast with the pure white pier pilasters rising through the full height of the nave, the choir is flanked by arcades supporting columns at gallery level: predominantly blue in reference to the Virgin, these contrast with the red of the columns flanking the high altar which stand for the pillar of Christ's scourging. That and the other instruments of the Passion, the prelude to Salvation, are displayed in Johann Baptist's fresco above; the prelude to the Last Judgment is represented in the fresco over the nave. There the empty throne of Grace provides the *quadratura* lines and the coved valance rises from an undulating cornice which had not played such a role at Steinhausen: the pendentive zones are treated to cartouches in the manner which was now widely deployed by Zimmermann's contemporaries.

>4.101 TRANSFORMATIONS IN DECOR: (a) Ettal, Benedictine abbey church, detail of rotunda (from 1745); (b) Rottenbuch, Augustine priory church of Ss. Peter und Paul, interior (from 1737).

The Rottenbuch basilican church dates from 1073 but the Romanesque form ultimately ceded to Gothic vaulting in the 1470s, shortly after the construction of a new choir and transept. Wealth recouped after the devastation of 17th-century warfare funded modernization – in style at least – by Joseph Schmuzer and Matthäus Günther: unlike other comparable exercises – at near-contemporary Steingaden, for example, or Ettal, and as earlier at Freising or Regensburg's S. Emmeram – any semblance of an Order is annihilated by florid growth in a rampantly rocaille context. At Ettal Schmuzer was called on for redecoration after Zuccalli's work was gutted by fire in 1745.

Joseph Anton Feuchtmayr collaborated with the Vorarlberger Peter Thumb, whose career extended beyond mid-century when his team completed the pilgrimage church at Neu-Birnau (1746–51) and embarked on the huge project of transforming the extremely important Benedictine monastery of Sankt Gallen (from 1749).**4.102, 4.103** Franz Xaver and Johann Michael Feichtmayr, who graduated from Wessobrunn to Augsburg, worked first at Diessen in collaboration with the foremost architect of the era in south Germany, Johann Michael Fischer – who is the subject of a new chapter.

4.101a

4.101b

4.102b

4.102c

4.102a @ 1:1000

›4.102 NEU-BIRNAU, from 1746: (a) plan, (b) exterior, (c) interior.

The pilgrimage to a miraculous image of the Madonna, overseen by the Cistercians of Salem abbey, dates from the 15th century: the original chapel was rebuilt after the Thirty Years' War but – as usual in the aftermath of the Counter Reformation – it proved too small for the influx of pilgrims as the 18th century progressed. The old site was deemed too near town for the requisite expansion and a new one was chosen above the shore of Lake Constance. Crowning the eminence, the tower marks the entrance to the church in the centre of the limited quarters provided for the summer retreat of the abbot and his entourage: newly appointed in 1745, that abbot was Stephen Euroth who knew of Peter Thumb's extensive work for other Cistercians. The plan (from 1746) extends a square sanctuary from a simple rectangular nave without aisles or wall pillars: apart from semi-elliptical miniature transepts, movement is introduced somewhat inorganically with the projection and recession of the discontinuous galleries – in sharp contrast to the works of the Asams or Zimmermanns which we have so far encountered and despite the efforts of Feuchtmayr. The ceiling frescoes in their jagged frame over the nave, in a clearly circular one before the sanctuary, are due to Gottfried Bernhard Göz (1708–60).

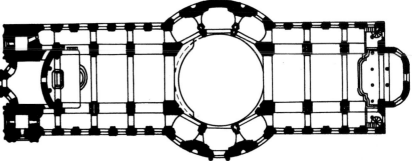

4.103b

4.103a @ 1:1000

›4.103 SANKT GALLEN, BENEDICTINE ABBEY CHURCH, from c. 1755: (a) plan, (b) Peter Thumb's central pavilion, (c) detail of central rotunda, (d) library.

In 1720 Kaspar Moosbrugger projected the reconstruction of the dilapidated church. A decade later the Vorarlberger Johann Michael Beer of Bleichten (1700–67) was commissioned to survey the fabric. Repeating this in 1749, Thumb offered an alternative project for reconstruction – as did several others. Still prevaricating, the monastic chapter decided to retain the old choir. The nave was demolished from 1755 and Thumb was commissioned to build a new one: his project incorporated a central domed space which had been proposed to varying degrees by other contenders for the project. Work had begun on the wall-pillar structure of Thumb's synthesis before the end of 1755 and was complete when the old master retired in 1758. Decoration by Christian Wenzinger (1710–97) took at least another two years but the church was consecrated in 1760. In that year Thumb's fellow Vorarlberger Johann Michael Beer of Bildstein (1696–1780, unrelated to the other J.M. Beer of Bleichten) was commissioned to rebuild the choir: asserting the axial symmetry through the rotunda which Thumb seems to have desired from the outset (with no precisely identifiable precedent but various contemporary essays), this was largely ready for Wenzinger to stucco in 1764 (the frescoes are later).

Essentially architectonic – except for the displacement of pendentives by applied cartouches – the church interior is in marked contrast to the exuberance of the library. That late-Rococo masterpiece was begun by Thumb in the year before his retirement: it was completed under the supervision of his son Michael Peter (1725–69) with stuccowork by Johann Georg and Mathias Gigl and paintings by Joseph Wannenmacher.

4.103c

4.103d

4 EXCEPTIONAL TALENT IN BOHEMIA AND BAVARIA

As we have seen (page 539), Guarino Guarini exerted a formative influence on the design of the three important churches associated with Lukas von Hildebrandt: S. Lorenzo in Turin was the main model. Much that was crucial in the last phase of Baroque-Rococo development in the orbit of empire is also predicated on knowledge of Guarini's work in Turin but also, especially, of his projects for the church of S. Maria della Divina Providência in Lisbon and S. Maria Altötting in Prague: not executed but published, the latter is unsurprisingly significant as these later developments were initiated in Bohemia.

JOHANN, CHRISTOPH AND KILIAN IGNAZ DIENTZENHOFER

The influence of Guarini is apparent on all the major works credited to Christoph Dientzenhofer in the first decade of the new century, after his departure from Chlum and return from his Italian journey: the Sternberg palace chapel at Smiřice (begun 1699), the Pauline friary church at Obořiště (begun 1702), the great Jesuit church of S. Mikuláš on Prague's Malá Strana (begun 1703), the church of S. Kláry in Cheb (begun 1707) and the Benedictine abbey church of S. Markéty, in the Prague suburb of Břevnov (from 1708). Variations on the ellipse, single or interlocking in duality, were the basis for taking the wall pillar tradition to a new age.**4.104**

›**4.104** CHRISTOPH DIENTZENHOFER'S ELLIPTICAL EXPERIMENTS: (a–c) Smiřice, Sternberg Palace, Chapel of the Epiphany (from 1699), plan, exterior, interior detail; (d, e) Obořiště, Pauline friary church of S. Josefa (from 1702), plan and vault detail; (f–h) Cheb, S. Kláry (from 1707), plan, exterior and vault detail; (i–m) Prague, former Jesuit church of S. Mikuláš Malá Strana (1703), plan, nave elevation, details of organ and side galleries, façade detail; (n–q) Břevnov,

4.104b

4.104c

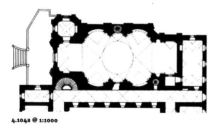

4.104a @ 1:1000

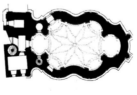

4.104d @ 1:1000

4.104e
S. Markéty (from 1708), plan, exterior, sanctuary and nave vault detail.

The star vault of the Sternberg chapel refers to the patron's title and the sign of the Epiphany to which it is dedicated. It covers an octagon, like Hildebrandt's near-contemporary S. Laurentius at Jablonné but with greater length: both are preceded by an elliptical vestibule and succeeded by a similar sanctuary. Crucially, Hildebrandt's work has miniature transepts – or transeptal chapels – in amplification of Guarini's Turinese masterpiece of the same dedication: instead, Dientzenhofer incurves his perimeter in the centre – as in the nave elevation of Guarini's Lisbon church of Divina Providência but in response to the sustained undulation of the exterior.

4.104h

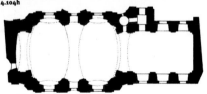

4.104f @ 1:1000

The Obořiště plan also follows the nave of Guarini's Lisbon exercise but it is composed of three interlocking ellipses, the smaller central one imposing concavity on the central piers: only the entrance front is concave. At Cheb – the simplest of these exercises as

Wall-pillar transformations

Composed of interlocking ovals, like the nave of Guarini's Lisbon church of S. Maria della Divina Providência, all Christoph Dientzenhofer's smaller works undulate in their perimeters through colossal pilaster Orders with continuous entablatures: inside, the pier pilasters – retracted wall pillars framing altars – are isolated from one another by unarticulated walls like a skeleton distinct from the skin – or an enshrouded baldacchino. Over each of the two lobes at Smiřice, the piers carry canopy-like star vaults which derive from the local late-Gothic tradition rather than from Guarini. The latter, however, seems to have inspired the diagonal cross-vaulting at Obořiště in motif if not in motive: ribs cede to broad arches which, leaving no domical void, cross over the main space to meet in the intermediate zone – or might have done before

4.104g

the scheme was obscured by unfortunate later frescoes. At Břevnov, as in the Cheb work, ribs fly off from the canted piers towards one another across each bay: they squeeze the vault membrane over the intermediate bay at Cheb but meet over the main spaces at Břevnov to the advantage of the intermediate zones. This was probably intended for the Prague church of S. Mikuláš too but it is denied by the continuous vault over the wall pillar nave: the piers are again isolated but the outward curvature of their fragmentary entablatures implies undulation; developed in the façade, that is echoed – indeed realized on a lower level – by the balconies carried on three-dimensional arches over the chapels.

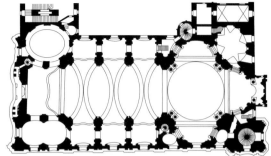

4.104i @ 1:1000

4.104k

4.104j

Christoph Dientzenhofer's inventive approach to the articulation of vaults was to be developed by the greatest architect of the era, Johann Balthasar Neumann (1687–1753), as a radical architectonic means of assisting transition from the rational to the supernatural: the intermediary was Christoph's younger brother, Johann. He had worked as foreman for his elder brother Leonhard, principal architect

4.104l

4.104m

4.104o

the order of the Poor Clares required – there are two non-tangential ellipses at ground level and these are allowed free rein at vault level: contrary to the articulation at Oboříště, discontinuous cornices reassert the idea of the baldacchino.

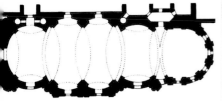

4.104n @ approximately 1:1000

Like the church at Oboříště, S. Mikulás in Prague's 'Lesser Town' is composed of three transverse ellipses but they are equal in longitudinal extent and impose concavity only on the balconies between the canted pairs of isolated wall pillar pilasters.

This and two transverse ellipses recur at Břevnov but now the latter intersect at the centre and encroach on two more rotund ellipses at either end: none of the four is allowed expression at vault level.

4.104p

4.104q

to the prince-bishop Lothar Franz von Schönborn who sent the young man to Rome in 1699. With no chance of advancement on his return to Bamberg, he found favour at Fulda where the Benedictine prince-abbot charged him with rebuilding the abbey church: conservatism dictated the retention of the basilican plan and twin western towers but Johann dressed them in modern Roman garb. And the lingering impact of his Roman experience is displayed in the façade of Würzburg's Neumünster (from 1712): Carlo Fontana's S. Marcello al Corso is the obvious source but is varied and revivified with sculptural exuberance characteristic of its author's context. **4.105, 4.106, 1.40e**

4.105a

4.105b

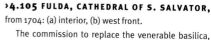

›4.105 FULDA, CATHEDRAL OF S. SALVATOR, from 1704: (a) interior, (b) west front.

The commission to replace the venerable basilica, Carolingian in origin and enshrining the remains of Germany's apostle S. Bonifatius, was let to Dientzenhofer by the prince-abbot Adalbert von Schleifras in 1700 to mark the opening of the foundation's millennial century. The old cathedral, the largest north of the Alps, was modelled on the Constantinian basilica of S. Pietro in Rome: the latter's successor was to be emulated by Fulda's successor. Demolition began early in 1704: the new building was roofed in 1708, consecrated in 1712. The structure is a domed basilica with lean-to aisle roofs below the clerestory: twin western towers were retained on demand as commemorative of the past. There is a progression from pilaster to column in the façade – but not in the graduated stages which characterize Maderno's great work in Rome.

›4.106 WÜRZBURG, NEUMÜNSTER, from 1712: façade.

Authorship is traditionally credited to Johann Dientzenhofer: the master-builder of the church was the Vorarlberger Joseph Greissing (1664–1721).

4.106

On Leonhard's death in 1707 his brother Johann had returned to succeed him at Bamberg and further work on the palace there. However, as we have seen, his major secular commission from his Schönborn patron was to develop the project for the palace at Pommersfelden before and after the involvement of Hildebrandt in 1712 (pages 545ff). That would recommend him for collaboration with the master on even greater work at Würzburg – as we shall see.

The prestige of Leonhard's position led to his engagement by the abbot of Benedictine Banz for the comprehensive rebuilding of his great monastery (from 1698).**4.107** The church awaited Johann's advent: the enlightened client approved the High Baroque plan drawn from contiguous ellipses. Variation on the wall pillar format runs to detaching the piers from the enclosing fabric, approximating a double-shell with contrasting active and passive structural systems. And in the vaulting Johann realized the logical – or illogical – conclusion of the syncopated premises his brother Christoph

›**4.107 BANZ, BENEDICTINE ABBEY CHURCH,** from 1710: (a) general view from south, (b) east entrance front, (c) interior, (d) plan.

4.107a

4.107b

4.107c

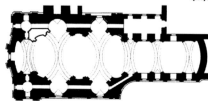

had recently posed at Břevnov. In counterpoint to the plan, with its two ovals touching in the centre, three-dimensional vault ribs billow out from the canted pilasters of the piers to sail away into the centre of the main bays, closing them to open the zone of their original contiguity, reversing the order of intermediacy – reversing the norm, indeed.

Embarking on the construction of a new residence at Würzburg in 1720, the prince-bishop Johann Philipp von Schönborn – Lothar Franz's nephew – borrowed Dientzenhofer to collaborate with the brilliant young engineer Johann Balthasar Neumann: the latter learned much from his older colleague – not least syncopated vaulting with three-dimensional arches – as we shall see in due course.

The nave's outer ellipse generates the convex façade at one remove, across the semi-elliptical vestibule. The wall pillar nave gives way to a deep choir which shares a brilliantly bifocal altar with the semi-elliptical sanctuary: that follows from the truncated ellipses defined by canted pilasters attached to the perimeter piers from which the three-dimensional vaulting ribs spring in the opposite direction – as in the nave but less dramatically due to the confined context.

4.108a

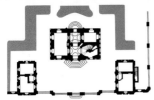

4.108b @ 1:1000

›**4.108** VILLA FOR COUNT MICHNA (NOW 'VILLA AMERIKA' AS THE ANTONÍN DVOŘÁK MUSEUM),** from 1717: (a) entrance front, (b) plan.

The façade departs from the academic towards the Hildebrantian in its articulation – in the pediments of the piano nobile windows and the uncanonical pilaster capitals – but it is characteristic of its locality in the aedicular attic motif which crowns the gratuitously out-curved central bay and idiosyncratic in the bizarre banding of the basement piers.

4.109a

Meanwhile we shall digress to Prague and the relationship between Christoph Dientzenhofer and his son Kilian Ignaz (1689–1751), Neumann's almost exact contemporary.

In 1717, on his return to Prague from a decade of formal training in Vienna, Kilian Ignaz was commissioned to build a suburban villa for Count Michna and produced a charming little cube whose eclectic articulation naturally ran to Viennese motifs: it is his single most celebrated secular work.**4.108** Father and son on several projects, notably the façade of the Loreto convent above Malá Strana, but the son was responsible for the church whose elliptical plan owes more to the Viennese masters than to the complex visions of the father. Not necessarily elliptical, central planning would be Kilian Ignaz's norm but his extensive career offered many opportunities for variation: squares with canted corners and predominantly longitudinal extensions, broader octagons also extended longitudinally, ellipses and double ellipses.**4.109**

Kilian Ignaz Dientzenhofer and centralized church planning

Kilian Ignaz was responsible for two Prague churches dedicated to S. Jan Nepomuky, the first on Hradčany (from 1720), the second S. Jana na Skalce ('on the Rock', from 1730). For the former, as for the contemporary pilgrimage church of the Narození Panny Marie at Nicov, he varied the octagonal format of Guarini via Hildebrandt's S. Laurentius at Jablonné in replacing the elliptical vestibule and sanctuary with rectilinear spaces. For S. Jana na Skalce, as in the parish church of S. Vojtecha at Počaply (1724), he extruded the octagon, incurved its sides and restored elliptical geometry to the ancillary spaces. Finally, for S. Klimenta at Odolena Voda (1733), the octagon becomes a square with rounded corners conjoined mellifluously with the preceding and succeeding ellipses. The rigid perimeter of the earliest work in this series cedes to undulation at Počaply and S. Jana na Scalce but at Odolena Voda mural curvature responds only to the treatment of the central space: the latter, like Počaply, has a single tower and side entrance; the

4.109c

4.109b @ 1:1000

4.109d @ 1:1000

4.109f @ 1:1000

4.109i @ 1:1000

4.109e

›**4.109 KILIAN IGNAZ DIENTZENHOFER'S
ELLIPTICAL EXPERIMENTS:** (a–e) Prague, Loreto,
monastic exterior (1721, probably with Christoph), S.
Jan Nepomucky on Hradčany (from 1720), plan and
interior, S. Jana na Skalce ('on the Rock,' from 1730),
plan and exterior; (f–h) Odolena Voda, S. Klimenta
(from 1733), plan, exterior and interior; (i) Opařany, the
Jesuit church of S. František Xaverský (from 1732), plan;

4.109g

4.109h

(j, k) Počaply, S. Vojtecha (from 1724), exterior and interior; (l–n) Legnickie Pole (Wahlstadt), the Benedictine monastery church of S. Jadwiga (1732), plan, exterior, interior; (o–r) Karlovy Vary, the parish church of S. Márí Magdalény (from 1733), plan, exterior, interior and detail of vault; (s–u) Prague, Benedictine monastery church of S. Mikulás in the Old Town (from 1732), plan, exterior and interior; (v–x) former Jesuit church of S. Mikulás Malá Strana, tower and dome, interior to crossing and dome detail.

4.109j

4.109k

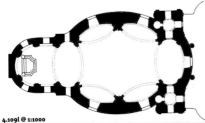

4.109l @ 1:1000

convex façade of the church 'on the Rock' is squeezed between canted twin towers. Inside, all these vary the baldachin formula derived by Christoph from the wall pillar tradition. In all of them the pilasters carry entablatures across the blind planes of the canted corners, between the great arches which penetrate the canopy domes: at S. Jana na Skalce the architrave curves out over the infill of the side bays under a peaked cornice; at Odolena Voda, a three-dimensional incurved pediment is extended across minor arches in the corners.

4.109m

4.109n

4.109q

4.109r

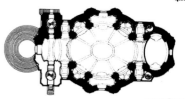

4.109o @ 1:1000

Apart from the Loreto chapel, several variations on the elliptical theme may here be represented by the Benedictine abbey church of S. Jadwige at Legnickie Pole in Silesia (1732), the Jesuit church at Opařany (1732) and the church of S. Márí Magdalény at Karlovy Vary (1733). Extraordinary, the first of these is based on an extruded hexagon within an elliptical perimeter and with elliptical ancillary spaces: here the baldachin formula is most clearly articulated with pilasters and engaged columns carrying convex entablatures around isolated wall pillars. Like S. Kláry at Cheb, the Opařany exercise deploys a pair of tangential ellipses defined by pilasters applied to canted piers – wall pillar residues of a baldacchin system – from which three-dimensional ribs do not swell out in counter-opposition to the logic of the plan but collide in the intermediate zone. Finally in this group, S. Márí Magdalény at Karlovy Vary offers scenographic progression through a great elliptical volume with the long axis stretching from a transverse oval vestibule to a larger transverse oval sanctuary and the short axis terminating in semi-elliptical chapels. The procedure is reminiscent of Fischer's Viennese Karlskirche but the doubling of passive with active structural elements – of the trabeated and the mural – is effected on the basis

4.109p

4.109u

4.109t

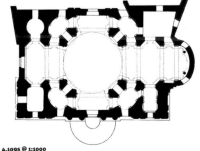
4.109s @ 1:1000

of the traditional wall pillar. The great axial arches of the main space and the radial ribs of the dome span from colossal columns attached to paired spurs: under curved pediments, these are connected by balconies carried on subsidiary arches which are expanded to bridge the shallow transepts. The clerestory lighting of their galleries asserts the distinction between the outer and inner – passive and active – structural systems.

The prime example of elongated planning centred on a square with canted corners is the great church of S. Mikuláš in Prague's Old Town: this responded to the cramped site entered from the south which also prompted the elevation of the central zone. Isolated from the perimeter wall by a semi-transept opposite the entrance, the colossal columns of the great piers carry curved pediments over which herms support projections to the entablature above the spandrel zone of the high arches: over these a third Order frames the canted corners of the high square dome. The nave extends west, the sanctuary east, behind the pair of towers flanking the dome and the colossal Order of the frontispiece with its fragments of curved and triangular pediment: it may be noted that the extraordinary upper entablatures of the towers repeat the plan of the main volume in miniature.

4.109x

4.109w

4.109v

Kilian Ignaz's last work was circular in its geometry: a trilobed composition of axial sanctuary and transept with a domed crossing which he was commissioned to add to his father's great church of S. Mikuláš Malá Strana (see page 618). The undulations of the nave have no impact on the relatively conventional new crossing; indeed it is curtailed by the sets of twin columns which support the pendentives – visually if not physically. Outside the superb dome is rich in relief and its curvature is complemented by the concave complexity of the close-set corner tower.

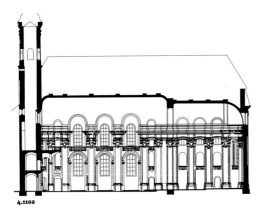

4.110a

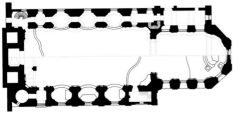

4.110b @ 1:1000

4.110c

›4.110 JOHANN MICHAEL FISCHER AND THE WALL PILLAR: (a–c) Osterhofen, Premonstratensian abbey church (from 1726), section, plan and interior; (d–g) Diessen, Augustinian priory of Marienmünster (from 1720, revised from 1729, completed c. 1739), plan, exterior, interior and vault; (h–j) Munich, Hieronymite priory church of S. Anna im Lehel (from 1727), plan, interior to sanctuary, vault detail.

JOHANN MICHAEL FISCHER

Born to a mason and trained in the craft, Fischer (1692–1766) was almost the exact contemporary of both Balthasar Neumann and Kilian Ignaz Dientzenhofer. He is not known to have had experience in Italy or France but did travel to Moravia through Bohemia (c. 1715): there he would certainly have seen the works of Christoph Dientzenhofer with their undulating perimeters generated by complex elliptical planning – and was probably shown Guarini's seminal exercise of the kind for the Theatines of S. Maria Altötting in Prague (see page 143). The core octagonal planning of a series of works stretching into the 1730s suggests that he kept abreast of Kilian Ignaz's achievements as well – as we shall soon see.

Settled in Munich in 1718 as an assistant master-mason, Fischer married the daughter of the city's principal mason, Johann Mayr – and thus into the upper echelons of the building hierarchy then presided over by Effner. Collaborating with Mayr, he soon established himself as an architect: first for the Benedictines of Niederaltaich and Rinchnach, then for the Hieronymites in Munich. His long career (1718–66) would be exclusively ecclesiastical: like his great contemporary Neumann, who also knew Bohemia, his genius found in church planning the spur to brilliance in the forging of complex spaces from centralized geometry.

Coming to architecture from masonry, unlike the Asams and the Wessobrunner brothers, Fischer provided the building fabric for others to transform with stucco and paint: the unique symbiosis of fraternal collaboration on all aspects of an exercise cedes to collaboration between a highly inventive structuralist and individual craftsmen acute to the possibilities of celebrating – or denying – the physics of tension and compression. And that had been a recurrent objective of church builders and their embellishers since the evocation of the threshold to the supernatural world of divinity was first illuminated in the dawn of Byzantium.

4.110e

4.110d @ 1:1000

Commissioned by Abbot Joseph Mari in the light of assessment that repairs to his monastery's Romanesque church were impracticable, Fischer's Osterhofen plan is of the rectilinear type usually deployed by Vorarlbergers. Within, however, the corners are in-curved – perhaps after Effner's secular work – in response to the shallow concavity of the pillars: these frame the convex balconies on three-dimensional arches along the nave, but not the choir. The undulations, at least, recall Christoph Dientzenhofer's S. Mikulás Malá Strana – with less fluidity but enough momentum to generate the undulating framework of the central frescoed zone of the Asam brothers' luxurious nave vault. The minor zones are defined by improbably swollen transverse arches.

The church at Diessen was begun in 1720 by a Weilheim master-builder – perhaps of the Feichtmayr line – but work proceeded slowly until a new abbot (Herkulan Karg) called on Fischer in 1729. The foundations – hence the plan – were retained but a new start was made on the wall pillar structure in 1732: undulating

4.110cg

4.110f

movement was introduced only to the façade. Johann Georg Übelhör assisted the brothers Franz Xaver and Johann Michael Feichtmayr, whose stuccowork ranges from the figurative to Bérainesque grotesques and on to the asymmetrical rocaille. Fischer's other transformative collaborators included Cuvilliés for the high altar, Johann Georg Bergmüller for the vault frescoes (depicting the refounding of the monastery and the glorification of its patrons) and the Venetian masters Pittoni and Tiepolo for the altarpieces.

The Hieronymites entered Munich in 1725 and turned to Fischer as an increasingly favoured member of the city's building service for their new church of S. Anna on the river Lech: work began in 1727 and took ten years to complete. The Asam brothers' transformative intervention at vault level (from 1729) was largely destroyed in 1944 but has been reinvoked.

The first of the craftsmen to collaborate with Fischer were the Asam brothers at Osterhofen (from 1726): *Gesamt-kunstwerk* is scarcely the result. The traditional wall pillar structure is asserted below, countered above. The system was sustained at base in Fischer's next major work, again with the Asams for the Hieronymites of S. Anna im Lehel in Munich. Here, however, he bent it around a central ellipse. He returned to the rectilinear norm for the Augustinian priory church of Diessen (from 1731). There he was constrained by the patron to avoid the Asams in favour of the Wessobrunner brothers Franz Xaver and Johann Michael Feichtmayr. They were known to the prior at Augsburg where, as we have noted, native sensitivity to the asymmetry of plant life had been sophisticated through exposure to suites of engravings copied from the French – and contorted under the impact of Meissonnier's rocaillerie. In Diessen, moreover, they were joined by Johann Georg Übelhör after the short journey south from Munich where he had assisted Cuvilliés and Zimmermann in the achievement of the Reiche Zimmer. **4.110**

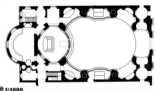

4.110h @ 1:1000

4.110j

4.110i

Maturing in the mid-1730s, Fischer turned his attention to octagonal centralized planning with and without recollection of the wall pillar tradition but in the light of Guarino Guarini's Turinese Laurentian masterpiece most probably reflected through the Dientzenhofer lens. The major works were for the Confraternity of S. Michael in the Munich suburb of Berg am Laim, for Augustinian friars at Ingolstadt and for the Oratorians at Aufhausen. And in these it was with Zimmermann, rather than the Feichtmayrs, that he collaborated: the original patron of the Munich work was Clemens August of Cologne, brother of the Bavarian elector for whom Zimmermann had recently completed work on the Reiche Zimmer.[4.111]

The trajectory of Johann Michael Fischer

The debut at Osterhofen (from 1726) perpetuated the wall-pillar system: here, however, the pillars are concave. Their canted outer edges support three-dimensional arches which carry convex balconies and naturally rise to the greater three-dimensional arches profiling the lateral vaulting in the clerestory zone. The residual pilasters of their central zones 'support' transverse arches but their careers are cut short by the undulating frames of semi-illusionist frescoes.

Next, dichotomy between structural purpose and decorative pretension is complete in S. Anna im Lehel (1727). The Guarian plan is related to Christoph Dientzenhofer's elliptical exercise at Obořiště: the logic of the radial wall pillar structure and the elliptical series of arches which spring from it is acknowledged only insofar as multi-curved panels rise from the cross-axial arches to engage the stuccoed frame of the illusionist vault. That swells out in extensions to the pendentives but their sole purpose is to support the frame which forms them.

Articulated with pilasters, the Diessen nave is a relatively traditional wall pillar structure up to the entablature: there are no galleries except for the organ at the west end and in the lateral extensions of the ante-sanctuary zone. Semi-elliptical arches span the vault from the first and fourth spur walls, between which no semblance of structure inhibits the field for illu-

4.111b

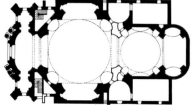

4.111a @ 1:1000

›4.111 FISCHER AND THE OCTAGON: (a–e) Munich, confraternity church of S. Michael Berg am Laim (from 1735, revised 1739), plan, exterior, interior, main and sanctuary vault details; (f) Ingolstadt, Augustinian (later Franciscan) priory church of Unsere Lieben Frau ob der Schutter (Our Lady of the Rubble, from 1736, destroyed 1944), plan; (g, h) Aufhausen, Oratorian pilgrimage church of Maria Schnee (Our Lady of the Snows, from 1736), plan and interior.

The starting point for these experiments was prob-

4.111d

4.111c

4.111e

ably the parish church of Murnau (near the abbey of Schlehdorf where Fischer was involved with his future father-in-law in the construction of the monastic buildings): its octagonal nave is preceded by a shallow narthex and succeeded (later) by a trilobed sanctuary. That had previously been varied along rectilinear lines for the choir at Niederaltaich, with the curvature of the square central space's corners leading to the arms, and the octagon had been doubled for the nave of Rinchnach. Thereafter, at the outset of the 1730s, Fischer returned to the plan of Schlehdorf for the parish church of Unering – even encapsulating a trilobed sanctuary into a rectangular extension. The trilobed sanctuary survives only in its reduced Greek-cross – or octagonal – nucleus in all three of the churches listed here. The narthex reappears in the Munich work within its convex façade: that was begun before Fischer's decisive intervention but he was responsible for the Aufhausen variation on the Diessen formula.

sion. The clerestory arches sway through three dimensions at the irritation of fantastic ornament – definable as neither flora nor fauna nor even the crustaceous – which seems to tickle them into touch with the fresco's equally elusive frame, while any connection between the latter and the transverse arches is masked by applied cartouches: the architecture severely divides, the ornament teasingly unites. The sanctuary zone is defined by engaged columns supporting semi-circular arches narrower than the semi-elliptical ones spanning the nave. Before the apse, the square crossing is even more assertively structured but huge cartouches are again used anti-architecturally: applied to the near-obliteration of the pendentives, they interrupt the clearly defined rim of the saucer dome – ironically enough, as such cartouches were originally deployed somewhat more supportively by the Asams at Aldersbach not long before they toyed with the inflation of the pendentive in their latest work for Fischer.

The confraternity church at Berg am Laim, Munich, the Augustinian priory church at Ingolstadt and the pilgrimage church of Aufhausen, all initially planned in 1735, are basically octagonal. All are firmly articulated with pier-pilasters – uncanonical in their free variation of the Composite capital – but the three-dimensional clerestory arches of the Munich work cede to the orthogonal in the definition of the octagon and its ancillary spaces in the others – and, hence, a much firmer expression of structure though the four elliptical greater arches are coved in support of the domical vault fresco's frame.

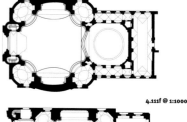

4.111f @ 1:1000

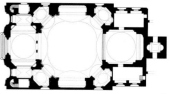

4.111g @ 1:1000

4.111h

All three octagonal variants are extended laterally into truncated transepts, all are extended longitudinally into a square sanctuary with canted corners but all three differ in their entrance arrangements and their diagonal chapels: S. Michael Berg am Laim is accorded a narthex centred on an ellipse which pushes the façade out into convexity and has minor concave corner chapels; Ingolstadt made do with entrance through the truncated fore arm of the cross implied by the transepts, without their curvature, but had generous elliptical corner chapels; at Aufhausen the sanctuary is prefigured to a smaller scale within a vestibule and the corner chapels are semi-hexagonal. The scenographic approach was finally to be perfected for the Benedictines at Rott am Inn where equal spaces precede and succeed the circular-domed octagonal centre.

At Aufhausen, where the wall pillar system is deployed to octagonal purpose, the large and small (elliptical and semi-circular) arches support the frescoed vault's undulating framework which extends to pendentive cartouches only in the sanctuary. Rising from octagon to circle, S. Michael's nave is also stoutly articulated with pilasters: rising over them, however, the three-dimensional arches of the clerestory support the clearly defined rim of the saucer dome, unambiguously delineating the zone of Zimmermann's pastoral illusionism. Only on the main axis are there cartouches but they have no pretension either to reinforce or subvert support: otherwise embellishment is virtually confined to the furniture – especially the altarpieces.

A chapel (of 1692) had been provided by the Cologne elector for his new confraternity at Berg am Laim: Fischer seems to have been commissioned to replace it to cater for swelling numbers c. 1735 but was confirmed in charge in 1739 and completed construction three years later: Zimmermann began decorating early in 1743. The design processes of both the Ingolstadt and Aufhausen churches were also initiated in 1735: both seem to have been built by 1739. The stuccowork and frescoes at Aufhausen are unattributed. Ingolstadt is lost.

›4.112 NEUMANN AND HIS EARLY CHURCH DESIGNS: (a, b) Würzburg cathedral, Schönborn mortuary chapel: half section and elevation, plan (1721); (c) Holzkirche, plan (1726); (d) Gössweinstein, plan (1729).

The Crispinus chapel of Würzburg cathedral in a ruinous state, Johann Philipp Franz decided in 1718 to demolish it and replace it with a domed mortuary chapel for his family: he received the approval of the chapter when he was elected prince-bishop in the following year. The commission was first let to Maximilian von Welsch, the Mainz architect of the patron's uncle Lothar Franz. Called to Würzburg to work on the new palace, his scheme survives on the exterior but Neumann displayed his facility for spatial conception by proposing the revisions after construction had begun in 1721.

4.112c @ 1:1000

4.112a

4.112b

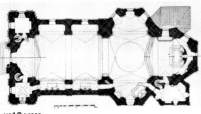

4.112d @ 1:1000

JOHANN BALTHASAR NEUMANN

Born in Cheb (Eger) to a cloth weaver, Johann Balthasar Neumann (1687–1753) completed an apprenticeship in a cannon foundry in 1712 and entered the army as an artillery engineer: commissioned in 1714, his abilities recommended him for the study of civil and military engineering. Advancing in his army career in the Würzburg episcopal force, he served in Hungary, the Balkans and northern Italy in the course of which he gained first-hand experience of recent practice in Vienna, Milan and Turin – of Guarino Guarini, Fischer von Erlach and Lukas von Hildebrandt. After the election of Johann Philipp Franz von Schönborn as bishop of Würzburg (1719), he was appointed to the episcopal architectural service as chief engineer in association with Johann Dientzenhofer who had been imported from Bamberg to further the new bishop's project for a residence.

Neumann would develop to the theme of centralized planning about an octagon in the early 1740s, when Fischer's Berg am Laim exercise in that genre had recently been completed and the ones at Ingolstadt and Aufhausen were still under construction. At the outset of his career, on the other hand, he was bent on transforming an octagon with lateral extensions into a series of mellifluous curves for the Schönborn's mortuary chapel attached to Würzburg cathedral (1721): due to Maximilian von Welsch, the original project (of c. 1720) was similar to Dientzenhofer's S. Jan Nepomucky on the Hradčany but extended laterally rather than longitudinally; Neumann's revision may be seen to take its departure from works of both the brothers Johann and Christoph Dientzenhofer – the nave of Banz and even the Sternberg chapel at Smiřice.[4.112a,b]

In his first independent ecclesiastcal exercise, Holzkirche inherited from Johann Dientzenhofer, Neumann rejected elliptical geometry in favour of a simple rectangle with engaged columns distinguishing the entrance and the cardinal chapels.**4.112c** Conservative there, he was not unconventional in the twin-towered, wall pillar basilican form of his first large-scale churches: for the Benedictines of Münsterschwarzach (1727, destroyed in the early 19th century) and for the pilgrims of Gössweinstein (from 1729). Dedicated to the Holy Trinity, the latter's concession to Trinitarian symbolism was a faceted trilobed crossing in distant homage to Salzburg cathedral.**4.112d** From the outset he was more adventurous in his work for the Schönborns, rising to the chal-

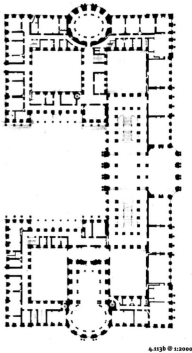

4.113b @ 1:2000

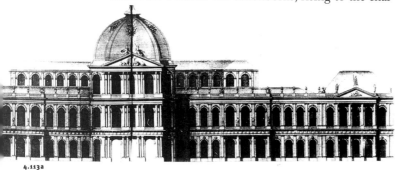

4.113a

lenge of realizing his patron's ideas for the new Residenz in collaboration with his Dientzenhofer mentor.

Impressed with the first draft revisions of the Residenz plans initially provided by Welsch, Johann Philipp Franz sent them to his uncle Lothar Franz and his brother Friedrich Karl. With their encouragement, Neumann was sent to Paris in 1723 to submit the scheme to the scrutiny of Robert de Cotte and Germain Boffrand – and to supplement his experience of advanced current practice at the centre of modern developments. Within a year his patron had died and work was suspended until 1729. In that year Friedrich Karl was elected to the sees of his uncle and brother at Bamberg and Würzburg respectively: Neumann was forthwith adopted as his principal architect and thus oversaw most of the construction work which realized his patron's brother's conception.**4.113**

›**4.113 WÜRZBURG RESIDENZ,** from 1720: (a, b) Boffrand's garden front and ground-floor plan, (c) first-floor plan of executed scheme, (d) entrance front, (e–g) staircase and detail of undercroft, (h, i) Weisser Saal, general view and detail of stuccowork, (j) antechamber, (k, l) Kaisersaal, interior and detail of Giovanni Battista Tiepolo's vault fresco, (m, n) east and south garden fronts, (o–r) chapel, plan, section and interiors.

Work began in 1720 on the north wing, which was to contain the prince-bishop's apartments: it was well advanced in 1723 when Neumann left for France but lay dormant during the (happily) short reign of the austere prince-bishop Christoph Franz von Hutten (1724–29). From his succession to his uncle at both Würzburg and Bamberg until his death in 1746, Friedrich Karl saw the project to near completion with Neumann as his preferred architect.

The conception of the great spaces, the staircase and the Kaisersaal, dates from 1735: work began on the former in 1737 and the latter's projection into the garden was complete in 1741; both had been vaulted

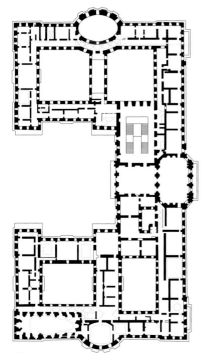

4.113c @ 1:2000

The Würzburg Residenz

The Schönborn family of the prince-bishops of Würzburg were among the most prolific patrons of the early 18th century in Germany and the palace at Würzburg was their principal work: it began with the perceived need for a modern town residence, developing an existing mansion near the cathedral in place of the medieval hilltop Marienberg. When the existing structure proved inadequate, Johann Philip Franz was pressed by his brother Friedrich Karl to consult Hildebrandt for a much grander scheme (1719) and by his uncle Lothar Franz to use his architect, Maximilian von Welsch. Two schemes were thus evolved. Welsch largely prevailed for the general distribution in the manner of a French château: an open forecourt and a great semi-elliptical salon projected into the garden over a sala terrena – as at Pommersfelden – but with doubled staircases to either side of the central vestibule and doubled side wings enclosing inner courts like Fischer von Erlach's revised scheme for Schönbrunn (see above page 518). Hildebrandt provided the basis for the ordonnance, including the insertion of a mezzanine between the ground and first floors, which was subsequently deleted from the central block.

In collaboration with Johann Dientzenhofer, Neumann was the executive architect from 1720, when work began on the north wing which was to contain the prince-bishop's apartments. That was well advanced when it was decided that the inexperienced military engineer from Cheb would go to Paris to submit the scheme to the scrutiny of de Cotte and Boffrand. Hildebrandt's

within a year and were ready for decoration. Neumann indicates the scope admissible for Rococo stuccowork in the Weisser Saal – and, thus, his espousal of the style of the era. Antonio Bossi's exceptionally fine

4.113d

4.113e

4.113f

ordonnance did not cede to their academic corrections – indeed Neumann subsequently enriched it. Though still present in Boffrand's published scheme, which its author brought to the site, Welsch's idea of paired staircases was dropped in favour of a single enormous exercise of the imperial type to the north of the vestibule.

Promoted to prime responsibility in place of Welsch when Friedrich Karl acceded in 1729, Neumann opted to retain the imperial form of staircase recommended by the French though he would soon prove himself at Schloss Bruchsal to be a consummate master of the art of staircase design. Constructed in timber and plaster from the outer walls rather than a colonnaded gallery, its vast ceiling was frescoed by Giovanni Battista Tiepolo: at the peak of his brilliant career, he progressed to the great hall.

Neumann also opted to retain the French core of ceremonial spaces culminating in the Kaisersaal which projects from the central pavilion. However, in 1730 he ceded to Hildebrandt for the detailed design of both main fronts, the undulating curve of the pediments being characteristic of the Viennese master's style – as we have seen. With no pretensions to mastery as an interior decorator, Neumann worked with a team of painters and

extension of it in the *genre pittoresque* mode across the wall planes and ceiling of the room was complete by 1744: thereafter he was preparing the scene in the Kaisersaal for Tiepolo. The latter finished his stupendous fresco over the staircase (1750–51) and in the Kaisersaal (1752–53) under Karl Philipp von Greiffenclau (who reigned from 1749 to 1754 in succession to Anselm Franz von Ingelheim).

Neumann's main change of plan was to move the chapel to the end of the south wing from a spur

4.113g

4.113i

4.113h

4.113j

sculptors led by the brilliant Luganesque stuccador Antonio Bossi (died 1764). Doubtless under Dientzenhofer's inspiration, he introduced the baldacchino system – of freestanding Doric columns supporting a canopy vault – to the sala terrena. Bossi's role was marginal to Johannes Zick's fresco there but his extraordinary skill is well demonstrated by the scintillating interpretation of the Franco-German *genre pittoresque* with which the Weisser Saal is entirely revetted. A rectangle with canted corners, the Kaisersaal is unparalleled in its uncanonically convoluted detail except by the most sumptuous of the era's churches. Over the colossal scagliola columns and sustained cornice, exquisite Rococo ornament dissolves the fabric of the vault: indeed it fringes the fabric of curtains drawn back to reveal Tiepolo's celebration of Emperor Frederick II appointing the bishop of Würzburg as duke of Franconia and an earlier incumbent marrying Beatrice of Burgundy to Frederick I Barbarossa.

between two courts (as represented in Boffrand's scheme). Elevating it to the full height of the building, he suppressed a domical scheme approved under the auspices of Hildebrandt in 1730 in favour of an ellipse with longitudinal extensions from which he developed one of his supreme masterpieces of ecclesiastical architecture.

Turning to the chapel in the early 1730s, Neumann progressed to one of his supreme masterpieces of ecclesiastical architecture against the constraints of existing work: in 1730 he devised an elliptical scheme as an alternative to the plans of both Boffrand and Hildebrandt; by mid-1734 that had

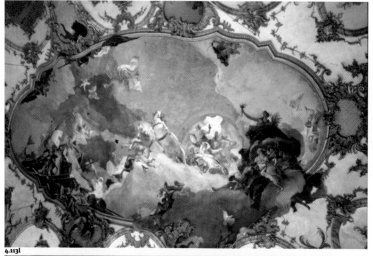

4.113l

4.113k

4.113m

4.113n

been reformed into the masterly intersection of five ellipses, the central one longitudinal, the outer ones lateral. At ground level the vestibule is invaded by a colonnaded screen describing the elliptical perimeter of the first intermediate zone and freestanding columns begin the same process on the inner side but at the sanctuary end the screen is diverted into a semi-circle to frame the high altar. The colonnades, advanced in the final stage of the planning process, support galleries between the public base level and the zone of heavenly illusion: thus the musicians were accommodated opposite the prince-bishop at worship before his exclusive upper altar in his tribune gained from his private apartment – as in most court chapels. Contrary to

4.113p

4.113o @ 1:1000

4.113q

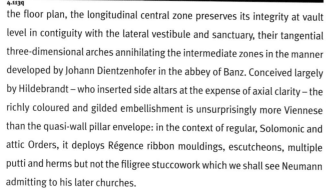

4.113r

the floor plan, the longitudinal central zone preserves its integrity at vault level in contiguity with the lateral vestibule and sanctuary, their tangential three-dimensional arches annihilating the intermediate zones in the manner developed by Johann Dientzenhofer in the abbey of Banz. Conceived largely by Hildebrandt – who inserted side altars at the expense of axial clarity – the richly coloured and gilded embellishment is unsurprisingly more Viennese than the quasi-wall pillar envelope: in the context of regular, Solomonic and attic Orders, it deploys Régence ribbon mouldings, escutcheons, multiple putti and herms but not the filigree stuccowork which we shall see Neumann admitting to his later churches.

from c. 1730:
(a) plan, (b) court front, (c, d) staircase.

The town residence of the prince-bishops of Speyer
had been destroyed by the French in 1689: the burghers were antipathetic to its reconstruction as the seat of
their ecclesiastical overlord. Damian Hugo relocated to
the entirely new site at Bruchsal to the south and commissioned his uncle's architect, Maximilian von Welsch,
to collaborate with him – in the usual Schönborn manner – on palatial planning. The main block addresses
an open court flanked by wings in the manner of
Hardouin-Mansart's Château de Clagny and its followers: the semi-detachment of the three buildings was
proposed by the patron to limit any damage from fire.

4.114b

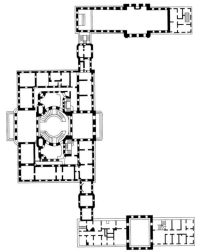

4.114a @ 1:2000

4.114c

4.114d

The extraordinary circular staircase well also seems to
have originated with the patron: the insertion of a mezzanine for extra accommodation between the ground
and first floors, obviously enhancing the height of the
staircase cage, obviated the initial plans for developing
twin flights around the curved perimeter and Neumann
was called in to solve the problem. Instead of a bridge
over an open well between the two flights, linking the
reception rooms facing the court and the garden, the
flights were walled to both sides: through the resulting
cylinder a passage simulating a grotto led to the sala
terrena; around the cylinder the curved flights ascend
from dimness to the light of the curved platform in the
upper vestibule.

During the first hiatus in the great work in Würzburg
following the death of Johann Philip Franz, Neumann
readily found employment elsewhere, notably at Bruchsal
for Cardinal Damian Hugo von Schönborn – nephew of
Lothar Franz, brother of Philip Franz and Friedrich Karl
– who was elected prince-bishop of Speyer in 1719. The
stunning success of the staircase there led to its author's
engagement as advisory architect by many other German
princely builders, particularly for staircases. Outstanding
in this context is his intervention at Bruhl: he was commissioned to reform the circulation after Cuvilliés had
reorientated the palace.**4.114, 4.115**

4.115

4.116a

4.116b

›4.115 BRUHL, ARCHIEPISCOPAL-ELECTORAL
PALACE: ceremonial staircase (from 1743).

In charge of alterations commissioned by the elector Clemens August, Cuvilliés presented the main face
to the south instead of to the eastern entrance court
(see page 595). Neumann was commissioned to provide a new staircase in the south range and responded
with a variation on the imperial type: flanked by the
pair of passages leading to the north wing, the initial
flight in the centre rises to a landing dominated by a
monument to the patron. Twin return flights, borne by
caryatids over the ground-floor passages, serve the
principal apartment on the piano nobile of the south
range; overall, a circular gallery reveals the frescoed
dome. Neumann was supplemented by Michael Lev-
eilly who worked with Luganese and Comasque teams
of stuccadors and painters including Carlo Pietro
Morsegno, Giuseppe Antonio Brilli, Giuseppe Artari
and Carlo Carlone.

›4.116 WERNECK, SCHLOSS, from 1733: (a) garden front, (b) chapel interior detail.

A medieval castle which had passed to the bishops
of Würzburg was destroyed in 1553 but not completely
rebuilt for half a century. Its replacement succumbed
to fire in 1723, was patched up then replaced for the
prince-bishop Friedrich Karl by Neumann from 1733
to 1745: involvement in the initial stages of the design
process with Hildebrandt – the plans were submitted
to him at a meeting with the patron in Vienna in 1733 –
produced a reduced variant on the theme of Pommersfelden, even running to a semi-circular range of service

buildings enclosing the forecourt. However, the conception of the central pavilion – especially at pediment and bulbous roof level which follow the Würzburg form – is due to Neumann. So too are the main interiors. The chapel is elliptical with a complete ring of semi-circular exedrae: an uncanonical Order of tapered pilasters, impressed with the curvature of the plan, supports a canopy vault; rocaille flourishes relieve the convex organ gallery parapets, the main entablature and the otherwise undifferentiated pendentive zone.

With Veitshöchheim (also developed by Neumann), Werneck was the summer residence of the prince-bishops of Würzburg until 1802 when the last incumbent, Georg Karl von Fechenbach, ceded to the new regional overlord, Maximilian, prince-elector of Bavaria. Thereafter the interiors were considerably altered.

›4.117 VIENNA, HOFBURG: (a) 'medium' project, staircase, half plan and section, (b) 'large' project, plan, (c) chapel plan and section.

Friedrich Karl von Schönborn, the former imperial vice-chancellor who had engaged Hildebrandt to rebuild the Reichskanzleitrakt (see page 558), may have prompted the exercise of imposing formality on the organic complex. However, the drawings are usually dated to the year after his death – when Neumann was underemployed in the service of the new prince-bishop at Würzburg. Differing in the scale of proposed intervention into the existing situation, three groups of drawings vary the Würzburg formula with its side wings doubled to frame divided courts. The most comprehensive completes Joseph Emanuel Fischer von Erlach's Michaelerplatz front with a deeper central recession and otherwise replaces everything except the great library and the riding school. Elaborated from a more limited scheme, the chapel and staircase are represented in plan and section: the former was to be an elliptical rotunda with lateral extensions in the general manner of Fischer's Hofburg library but with an ambulatory at two levels throughout. The plan was soon to be varied for the Benedictine abbey church of Neresheim (and had been pre-echoed in miniature in the evolution of the Schönborn mortuary chapel project at Würzburg). In a huge cage, the staircase plan doubled the imperial form to serve major reception rooms in the pavilions facing the revised Burgplatz and a new garden.

Neumann was busily employed by the Schönborn throughout the 1740s: as bishop of Würzburg, Friedrich Karl commissioned him to enlarge the late-17th-century retreat at Veitschöchheim and build him a new summer residence at Werneck.**4.116** Bent on surpassing Lothar Franz at Pommersfelden, the patron called in Hildebrandt for advice here as his uncle had done there: chancellor of the empire, it will be recalled, Friedrich Karl had retained Hildebrandt for his Austrian houses and to produce designs for reconstructing the Hofburg Reichskanzleitrakt.

Such was Neumann's prestige even in Vienna in the year of Friedrich Karl's passing that he was invited to produce schemes for the comprehensive rebuilding of the Hofburg: the section through the centre with a double

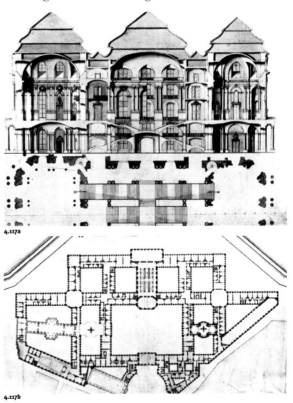

4.117a

4.117b

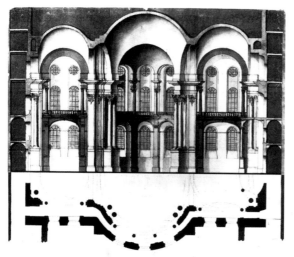

4.118b

4.117c

4.118a @ 1:1000

imperial staircase and the chapel were most fully developed, but nothing came of them. At the same time he was working on similarly grandiose schemes for Stuttgart (from 1747) and Karlsruhe from 1750, and for the Schönborn archbishop-elector of Trier (from 1748).**4.117**

Under Friedrich Karl, Neumann's extensive ecclesiastical practice ranged from the parish and pilgrimage to the monastic. Begun a little earlier, the first of the last was the lost Benedictine Latin-cross basilican abbey church of Münsterschwarzach (from 1727); the first of the smaller exercises was for the pilgrims to the Holy Trinity church at Gössweinstein. The Heiligste Dreifaltigkeitskirche at Gaibach, with its trilobed crossing based entirely on elliptical geometry (from 1740), opens a median phase which extended to the complex design of the Würzburg Käppele – a pilgrimage church dedicated to the Visitation.**4.118** The court chapel apart, the last and greatest essays in the genre were begun just before and just after the end of the Schönborn era: the Franconian pilgrimage church of Vierzehnheiligen (begun 1743) and the Swabian Benedictine abbey church of Neresheim (from 1747).**4.119, 4.120**

›4.118 NEUMANN'S ELLIPTICAL VARIANTS IN CHURCH DESIGN: (a, b) Gaibach, Heiligste Dreifaltigkeitskirche (Holy Trinity), plan and section; (c) Würzburg, Käppele, plan.

The Gössweinstein scheme, with its trilobed elliptical crossing beyond a two-bay nave, was revised on several occasions (page 635): preserving the Latin cross at Gaibach but redrawing the crossing on elliptical lines; promoting centralization at Etwashausen (from 1741) and for the Würzburg pilgrimage chapel (from 1747). The trilobed crossing remains in the latter but the circular nucleus is defined by pairs of freestanding columns and the nave is reduced to a northern entrance vestibule: in compensation, the executed scheme extended into an elliptical volume to the east. At Etwashausen a two-bay nave is retained but the circular crossing is again defined by pairs of freestanding columns supporting a canopy vault cut into by the three-dimensional arches of the rectangular transepts and the apsidal sanctuary.

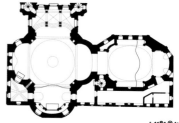

4.118c @ 1:1000

from 1742: (a) model, (b, c) plan and section, (d) west front, (e, f) interior and detail of crossing vault.

The site was deemed sacred in virtue of a shepherd's miraculous vision (in 1445) of the Christ child surrounded by fourteen other children, identified with the 'Fourteen Saints in Time of Need'. The pilgrimage facilities, in the purview of Cistercian Langheim under the authority of the bishop of Bamberg, were overstretched by swollen influx in the post-Counter-Reformation era: Abbot Stephan Mösinger decided on rebuilding in 1735 but needed the approbation of Bishop Freidrich Karl von Schönborn. The latter rejected the plans of the former. Neumann responded with a twin-towered

4.119a

4.119c

4.119d

4.119b @ 1:1000

4.119e

Neumann and select churches

At Vierzehnheiligen, a basilican plan with apsidal transepts and sanctuary is transformed into a stunning cage of celestial imagery by the insertion into the nave of a skeleton of piers with engaged colossal columns. These define interlocking ovals within galleried circulation space: curvature is introduced to the inner surface of the unarticulated, largely fenestrated outer walls only for chapels on the minor cross-axis of the nave and to the outer surface of the façade. Movement in the latter is generated by the elliptical vestibule which precedes the generous elliptical cage enshrining the principal object of veneration, the altar dedicated to the miraculous appearance at the site of the Christ child attended by fourteen juvenile saintly 'helpers' (*Gnadenaltar*). Over this central space, disposed longitudinally, the elliptical vault is aligned with the longitudinal ellipses of the sanctuary and vestibule vaults and their tangential three-dimensional

basilican revision derived from his earlier pilgrimage exercise at Gössweinstein but with an expanded elliptical crossing as the context for the altar and its multiple dedicatees (July 1742): an alternative version introduced an elliptical vault over columns disposed to deny the rectiliniarity of the nave.

The abbot retained the original architect (Gottfried Heinrich Krohne) as executive of Neumann's conventional basilican scheme (from April 1743): he departed from it in the initial building phase and was dismissed at the bishop's insistence but his substantial work, predisposing the altar at the head of the nave rather than under the crossing dome, had to be accommodated in a revised plan. In evolving this (before March 1744) Neumann reformed choir, transept, vestibule and façade along elliptical lines. In the inner zone of what had been his basilican nave, he returned to his preferred variation of 1742 and conjured an elliptical rotunda:

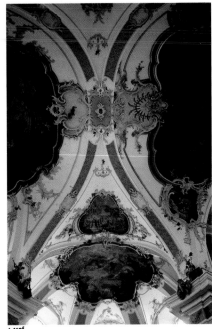

4.119f

now, however, it is within an ambulatory defined by freestanding piers carrying three-dimensional vaulting arches, the inner one tangential with the outer member of the choir vault to the annihilation of the crossing – and the process was seconded in reverse over a secondary crossing engaged with the vestibule.

arches meet over the two cross-axes of the main and secondary transept zones: the resulting elimination of domical vaults in those biaxial zones, where they were traditionally crucial, is in line with Johann Dientzenhofer's Banz abbey system. Giovanni Appiani was retained for the vault frescoes. Effecting transition to their illusion of heaven in the exquisite way which we shall see them perfecting at Zwiefalten, the Feichtmayrs and Johann Georg Übelhör contrived the stuccowork.

For Neresheim, Neumann referred back to his plan for the pilgrimage church of Gaibach (1742) and revised it (from 1747). Beyond the two-bay nave there, with its flattened recessions, the elliptical crossing was defined by pairs of columns before the semi-elliptical transepts and sanctuary: beyond the two-bay nave here, with its concave recessions, an ellipse was disposed longitudinally at the crossing and again defined by pairs of columns before the semi-elliptical transepts and double circular sanctuary. In the earlier work, ribs following the line of the great ellipse meet ribs describing the opposite curve over the transepts, the sanctuary and the transition to the second bay of the nave – in rather more distant homage to Dientzenhofer's Banz than Neumann's own Würzburg Residenz chapel.

An alignment of non-interpenetrating ellipses and circles across a bulging centre, the executed scheme at Neresheim may be seen to celebrate the release of Vierzehnheiligen's scenographic core from its captivity in its inherited straitjacket. Except in the varied geometry of the elongation, the result follows the recent final scheme for the Viennese Hofburg chapel which, in general disposition, relates to Fischer's imperial library. Way back beyond that, the conjunction of curves recalls Neumann's advent to architecture in the Schönborn Würzburg mortuary chapel. The active agents of structure again, the piers (no longer wall pillars) stand as the bones of a skeleton before the passive, unarticulated enclosing fabric breached by the generous fenestration. Springing from those piers, virile three-dimensional arches carry the elliptical or circular vaults but they swell into touch over the intermediate zones rather than to the obliteration of the main membranes in the syncopated Dientzenhofer manner. The later-18th-century stucco embellishment is minimal and generally refrains from breaking tectonic lines. The Tyroler Martin Knoller's frescoes are proto-Neoclassical': Neumann's richer vision succumbed to his demise.

4.120a

4.120b @ 1:1000

4.120c

›**4.120 NERESHEIM, HEILIG-KREUZ (BEN-EDICTINE ABBEY CHURCH OF THE HOLY CROSS),** construction from 1748: (a) section, (b) plan, (c) interior towards sanctuary.

Neumann began the planning process by projecting a basilican nave before a domed crossing and an extended choir in the conventional manner he had adopted on several previous occasions, most recently for the Cistercians of Langheim (from 1742): in accordance with the patron's requirement, the initial scheme incorporated the tower surviving from the Romanesque foundation and twin passages from the monastic quarters. In the second phase the crossing became elliptical (on the long axis), the arms of the cross were defined elliptically and an elliptical façade was generated by an elliptical vestibule. Over several revisions the crossing was expanded into a rotunda, moved to the median position (between the two passages to the monastery), where it is defined by freestanding columns forward of the ambulatory, and flanked by smaller ellipses which become the transept arms.

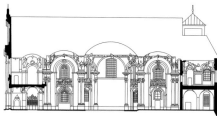

4.121b

4.121a @ 1:1000

›**4.121 ROTT AM INN, BENEDICTINE ABBEY CHURCH OF SS. MARINUS AND ANIANUS**, from 1759: (a, b) plan and section, (c) interior to sanctuary.

The last great work of Fischer's career, the church at Rott am Inn was begun in 1759 and finished six years later, just before the master's death. The symmetry of the plan extends to – rather begins with – the vestibule below the organ gallery which is similar in extent to the

4.121C

FISCHER REPRIEVED

Like Neumann's, Fischer's long career culminated in experiments with the scenographic extension of a core centralized space symmetrically: the clients were the Brigittine sisters of Altomünster (from 1763) and the Benedictine brothers of Ss. Marinus and Anianus at Rott am Inn (1759).**4.121** The largely rectilinear scheme of the latter may effectively be contrasted with the largely curvilinear format of Neumann's earlier work at Neresheim – also his last. Over the previous two decades Fischer effected basilican grandeur – unexcelled in 18th-century Bavaria, at least – under the constraint of existing work for the Cistercians of Fürstenzell, for the Benedictines of Ottobeuren who enjoyed imperial freedom (*Reichsfreiheit*), and for the Benedictines of Swabian Zwiefalten who aspired to that dispensation. In these great works he again collaborated with Feichtmayr to extraordinary effect.**4.122, 4.123**

sanctuary at the far end. As at Aufhausen, the structure is boldly articulated in support of the great and small arches but above all is an assertively circular frame to the frescoed saucer dome which tolerates no florid, fimbriated flux into fantasy – except in the topknots of the cartouches produced by the Feichtmayr son-in-law, Jakob Rauch.

›**4.122 FISCHER AND WALL PILLAR REVISIONS:** (a) Fürstenzell, Cistercian abbey church (from 1738, revised from 1740), interior towards sanctuary; (b–f) Zwiefalten, Benedictine abbey church (from 1738, revised from 1741), plan, west front, interior towards sanctuary, nave vault fresco and detail of pulpit.

In accordance with his ambitions, the abbot of Zwiefalten projected rebuilding of his medieval church on a monumental scale in 1738: so too in that year did the abbot of Fürstenzell. Each of these projects called for an architect of metropolitan experience but the commissions were let to local master-masons: each abbot regretted his first choice and called on Fischer after some two years of unsatisfactory construction of traditional wall pillar schemes. At Fürstenzell, near the eastern border of Bavaria, little more was admissible than change to the articulation and decoration of the interior: work was largely accomplished by the end of

4.122A

Fischer's late masterpieces: constraint unconstrained

As at Diessen, Fischer introduced an undulating dynamic to the façade of Zwiefalten. As at Osterhofen he introduced vitality – if not undulation – to the nave elevation, with convex balconies over chapels between the pillars and

4.122d

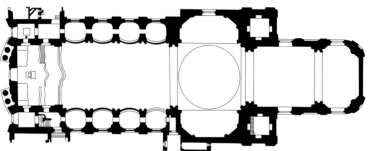

4.122b @ 1:1000

three-dimensional clerestory arches which cut into the tunnel vault. That is nearly matched in extent by the vault springing from the walls of the elongated choir: between them a saucer dome covers the square crossing which, unlike Diessen, is the only bay defined by transverse arches. The frescoes covering all three zones are due to Franz Joseph Spiegler (1691–1757): Johann Michael

4.122C

4.122f

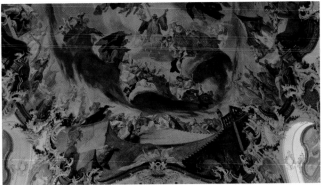

4.122e

Feichtmayr excelled himself for the stucco. At the crossing, cartouches are applied to the pendentives and interrupt the clearly defined rim of the dome, as at Diessen. Over the nave, however, cartouches rise free only from the intermediate piers. Here at Zwiefalten Fischer allowed Feichtmayr to avoid any sense of definition between realms of structure and fantasy, between the kaleidoscopic presence of the Order and the illusionism of the continuous fresco, where some semblance of a frame was usual: instead even the cartouches dissolve into brittle fragments of exquisite rocaille and floral mouldings tossed up like the spume of breaking waves.

1745. There was more scope for change to the contemporary project far to the west in Swabia.

Starting on a new crossing at Zwiefalten, with twin towers between projecting transepts and extended choir sanctuary, the original builders intended to proceed with replacing the nave in conservative accordance with the prevalent wall pillar tradition – all probably on the old foundations and apparently in accordance with the original relatively squat proportions. Fischer was called in only after that work was also in train and the abbot had lost confidence in his masons as architects. The revised work started in 1741. Six years later the east end had been vaulted and Feichtmayr was working on the stuccowork while Spiegler began his frescoes. Two years further on, the nave was being extended westward to include a generous organ gallery within the bold undulating façade: above the assertive Order of engaged columns – carried through to the façade – and the convex balconies of each bay, the nave was decorated by the same team from 1751, Spiegler's fresco extending throughout the whole length of the tunnel vault, above the cartouches which alone resolve the vertical lines of the structure.

The semi-basilican plan of Ottobeuren is cruciform but the apsidal transept arms project from a central square crossing with a domical vault: twin-bay extensions to the long axis terminate east in an apsidal sanctuary and west in a semi-elliptical narthex. Much in this is instructively to be compared with Neumann's more obsessively elliptical revisions of his initial project for contemporary Neresheim. The conservative elements here, especially the apsidal transept and interconnected side chapels, recall arch-conservative Salzburg cathedral but the bowed façade between the twin towers follows Fischer von Erlach's more modern Kollegienkirche in the same city – if not Weingarten, which was nearer to hand. Reforming the legacy of his conservative predecessors, Fischer responded to the logic of the plan with lateral and transverse arches defining each bay but he was able to heighten the architectonics of the inherited structure at the crossing, asserting its biaxiality with engaged columns. However, these flank convex piers which conflict with the concavity of the pendentives rising from them and that invites masking by cartouches.

At Ottobeuren Feichtmayr is less exuberant, more respectful of structure: indeed of the boundary between God's house on earth – glorious though that is – and the panoply of heaven. Ironically enough, thus, the three arts complement one another more completely in this work, where Fischer was most constrained, than at Zwiefalten. There however, where he allowed stucco and paint to overwhelm architecture, he clearly recog-

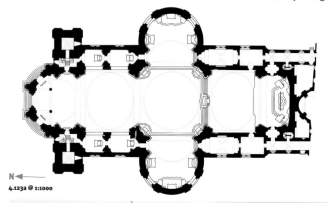

4.123a @ 1:1000

4.123d

4.123b

>**4.123 OTTOBEUREN, BENEDICTINE ABBEY CHURCH,** begun 1737, revised from 1748: (a) plan, (b) exterior from north-west, (c) interior to sanctuary, (d) crossing vault, (e) choir stalls.

The initial project for Ottobeuren, of c. 1710, was commissioned by the new abbot Rupert Ness who began rebuilding the monastic quarters to the plans of an inmate, Father Christoph Vogt. The latter's scheme for the church was revised by several outsiders, including Dominikus Zimmermann who proposed symmetry of plan on both axes, by making nave and choir square, and introduced the twin western towers. Work had began in 1737 to the compilation of the monastery's master-mason, Simpert Kramer, which retained the symmetries but extended each arm into an apse – producing the boldly convex façade.

As at Zwiefalten, the abbot had a crisis of confidence in his executive mason-architect: he called in outside assessors, including Effner, before opting for Fischer in 1748. Effner changed the proportions: so too did Fischer, contracting rather than expanding the nave and choir – and therefore, vaulting them over an ellipse rather than

4.123c

a circle. Effner engaged columns to the façade: Fischer introduced them to the interior. Feichtmayr was again responsible for the stuccowork but, most significantly, Fischer's surviving drawings for the executed scheme show that he predisposed the areas of Feichtmayr's rocaille embellishment. Martin Hörmann carved the furniture, especially the splendid choir stalls.

nized that what happens above his management of physics must further the innate purpose of the exercise as a whole: to elevate the spirit of the faithful from the constraints of this world to the infinite bliss of Salvation.

4.123e

Complemented by sculptors unsurpassed in Rococo refinement and collaborating with masters of illusionism in fresco, the work of Michael Fischer and Balthasar Neumann took the extraordinary genre of southern German Baroque architecture to its apogee. With the last of them all the delight begins with ovals ingeniously interlocked in plan. Playing round these, insubstantial arcades – emulating the miracles of medieval masonry – are pressed into undulation by the soaring Orders, admitting both light and colour. With colour and light rippling through the structure in counterpoint over a white ground, illuminating the wit of a putto or a rocaille fantasy, the *porta coeli* has never been more joyful to behold.

4.124a

AT THE SAXON COURT: (a) Green Vault Treasury, 'The Delhi court on the occasion of the Great
Mughal Aurangzeb's birthday' (gold and precious
stones; Johann Melchior Dinglinger and assistants,
1701–08); (b) Schloss Moritzburg chapel (1661); (c)
Dresden, Grosser Garten Summer Palace (from 1679).

Largely unscathed within its formidable defences
during the Thirty Years' War, Dresden began to expand
into garden suburbs early in the second half of the 17th
century. The most important survivor of this phase of
development, the Grosser Garten to the east of the
royal quarter was begun for the electoral heir c. 1675:
the initial radial plan of Martin Göttler was revised in
1683 along contemporary French cruciform lines by
the newly appointed head gardener Johann Friedrich
Karcher who extended it for Augustus I after peace prevailed in 1714.

Both the later phases of the garden design took
their departure from Johann Georg Starcke's palace.
This distantly recalls Salomon de Brosse's Rennes
Parlement de Bretagne and, beyond that, Primaticcio's Aile de la Belle Cheminée at Fontainebleau in both
registers (AIC5, pages 343, 397). The E becomes an H
in plan (ostensibly at the patron's instigation) and the

5 FROM AUGUSTAN DRESDEN TO WARSAW

Baroque Dresden was the creation of the Saxon elector
Frederick Augustus I (the Strong, 1694–1733), elected king
of the Polish-Lithuanian commonwealth on his conversion
to Catholicism in 1697 as Augustus II, and of his son Frederick Augustus II (1733–1763), king of Poland as Augustus
III. The father was the great builder but also an insatiable collector of bronze sculptures and works of applied art
in precious metals, ivory and gems.**4.124a** Completing his
father's building projects and devoted to the fine arts, the
son left government to his chief minister, Heinrich, Count
von Brühl. The opulence ended in the opening phase of the
War of the Austrian Succession, with the loss to Prussia of
Saxon influence in exploiting the mineral riches of western Silesia. Catastrophe attended Prussian invasion in the
opening phase of the Seven Years' War. A century earlier,
rehabilitation after the devastation of the Thirty Years' War
was advanced by the end of the reign of the elector Johann
Georg II (reigned 1656–80) and the golden age prepared.

4.124b

double external staircase tracks the walls of the great rectangular recession in both elevations. Over this, the composer then plays a range of galliard variations: a ground-floor Doric Order for the frontispiece in which the superimposition of the Ionic follows standard French precedent best represented by S.-Gervais-S.-Protais in Paris or – even more to the point – Lescot's Louvre where the ordonnance is more sumptuous (AIC5, pages 338, 398); an attic storey throughout, as at the Louvre, but here the frontispiece terminates before it in rather clumsy volutes; pseudo-serlianas for the wings which may also be seen as deriving from the rearrangement of elements found in the Louvre façade, again through the intermediacy of S.-Gervais-S.-Protais – if not, unexpectedly, the outer façade of Lemercier's Sorbonne chapel (see page 185) or, more probably, plates like 31 of *Palazzi di Genova* published by Rubens in 1622 (AIC5, page 541).

There was little advance over pre-war Mannerism in the Schloss Moritzburg chapel – as was appropriate to the late-16th-century context. Nor may the style of the Grosser Garten Summer Palace properly be defined as Baroque in modern Italian terms.

Primarily involved with restoring war-damaged castles from 1660, the Saxon military engineer Wolf Caspar von Klengel (1630–91) spent his formative years in the Netherlands and Italy. As an architect he was first engaged on the renovation of Schloss Moritzburg which extended to a new chapel.**4.124b** Thereafter, he was preoccupied with additions and modifications to the Dresden palace: most has been obliterated except the upper storeys of the tower (from 1674, restored; AIC5, pages 449ff).

Chief Inspector of Fortifications and Civil Building from 1672, Klengel's activities as town planner culminated in the projection of Dresden Neustadt in place of Altendresden which was destroyed by fire in 1684. Thus preoccupied, he delegated much design work to his successor as director of electoral building, Johann Georg Starcke (c. 1630–95), who had also studied in Italy, the Netherlands and France. His major surviving essay is the Summer Palace in Dresden's Grosser Garten, commissioned in 1678 by the future elector Johann Georg III (1680–91).**4.125**

4.125a

4.125c

›4.125 **BELLOTTO'S DRESDEN AND ITS FATE:**
(a) general view from the river towards the cathedral
(right) and of the Frauenkirche; (b) Neumarkt and Frauenkirche; (c–e) pre-War and post-War aerial views with
Frauenkirche centre; view from the ruins of the latter to
Neumarkt; (f) commercial district post-War.

Appallingly, Baroque Dresden was obliterated
by the Allies in the closing stages of World War II. Of
George Bähr's great domed Frauenkirche and the
organic complex of the royal palace, representing all
the main phases of German post-Renaissance architecture, only rubble and photographs remained – except
for the splendid topographical paintings of Bernardo
Bellotto. The extraordinary Zwinger garden palace, the
great 19th-century Opera House and the Hofkirche had
been resurrected by 1985: twenty years later, with the
royal palace well on the way to external restoration, the
Frauenkirche miraculously rose again to dominate the
skyline.

4.125b

4.125d

4.125e

4.124f

Starcke was succeeded by Marcus Conrad Dietze of Ulm (1658–1704) who was succeeded in turn by the Westphalian Matthäus Daniel Pöppelmann (1662–1736): by the end of the 1680s they had been followed by the Austrian sculptor Balthasar Permoser (1651–1732) who had spent fourteen years in Florence. Trained in the Office of Works from about 1680, Pöppelmann took Saxon Baroque to its apogee at the instigation of Frederick Augustus who unexpectedly succeeded his brother (Georg IV) to the electorate in 1694. Well travelled as a somewhat irresponsible prince, attuned to the theatrical, proud of his own capacity as a designer, he set about projecting a setting for his court of a dignity matching his new status as king of Poland from 1697.

First Dietze and Pöppelmann were called on for plans to reconstruct the late-medieval and early Renaissance Residenz: funds for such a massive project were to be absorbed by war. The same fate attended the equally ambitious plans for a new palace in Warsaw, as we shall

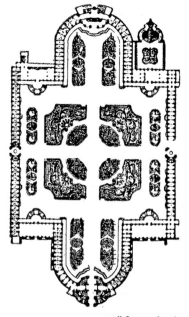

4.126b @ 1:approximately 1:2500

4.126a

4.126c

**›4.126 THE DRESDEN ZWINGER GARDEN
PALACE:** (a) overview from south, (b) plan with nymphaeum to north-east, (c) nymphaeum, (d) northern
pavilion, (e) Kronentor.

The name derives from the dry moat of the 'outer ward'
between the doubled walls of the city's north-western
defences. The orangery, first projected by Marcus Conrad Dietze late in his life, was associated with a staircase
between curved terraces for the display of the trees in
summer after Matthäus Daniel Pöppelmann revised the
plans (1709). Arcaded galleries with flat roofs were built
between the staircase and two display pavilions (from
1711), the southern one equipped with a sala terrena in
the form of a grotto. The long western side range of galleries (begun in 1714) is centred on the triumphal entrance
pavilion (Kronentor, named in virtue of its finial in the
form of the Polish crown).

The original pavilions and curved terraces were
repeated to the east; the northern one was extended
into a nymphaeum, and the staircases at both ends
were covered with their sculptural canopies (*Wallpa-
villons*, from 1718) – the linking of two accommodation
zones with a communication gallery may be seen as
reminiscent of the Grand Trianon in conception if not
in style. The highly assertive sculpture is due to Balthasar Permoser – that of the herm-supported festive
pavilions almost contradicting the thesis that 'Rococo
architecture' is a contradiction in terms.

The extensions were to be completed for the spectacles to be staged in celebration of the crown prince's
marriage to the emperor's daughter in 1719. The royal
library, print room, collection of technical objects and
cabinets of curiosities were moved into the corner pavilions from 1728. Pöppelmann planned a new palace for
the south side but it was not to be realized: a palatial picture gallery was built there instead in the 19th century.

see. However, funds were found for the extraordinary
adjunct to the palace known as the Zwinger (from
1709).**4.126** An enclosed garden arena, descended from
a jousting ground, the scheme began with an orangery
but developed into a series of exhibition buildings linked
by galleries with viewing terraces to the long sides and
festive staircase pavilions in the short sides: as is often
remarked, these stand as petrifications of the grand-
stands erected for the viewing of celebratory dynastic
spectacles. Pöppelmann was sent to Vienna and Rome
to study the architecture of palatial gardens: he returned
with an ideal reconstruction of the Roman Campus
Martius in mind. He also returned with the will to rival
his Austrian contemporaries in the Baroque spectacle
of sculptural architecture – Fischer and Hildebrandt as
masters of the *Lustgebäude*, of course, but also Prandtauer
whose great work at Melk he could hardly have missed
even if his route lay through Prague.

4.126d

4.126e

4.127a

4.127b

4.127c

>**4.127 PILNITZ, SCHLOSS,** from 1720: (a) Berg-palais, garden front, (b–d) Wasserpalais, river front, antechamber detail, and Chinoiserie andiron.

Elector Johann Georg IV acquired the Pillnitz estate and its late-Renaissance manor house in 1694: it soon passed to his brother and heir Frederick Augustus. The old house was assigned to the new patron's mistress and survived until 1818 when it was destroyed by fire. After the proprietress fell from favour, the elector-king began a modern palace on the adjacent riverside site in 1720: the Wasserpalais was then supplemented by the similar 'hillside' Bergpalais opposite it across an open garden court in 1723; they were designed pri-

4.127d

Assisted by the French master-builder Zacharias Longuelune (who arrived from Berlin c. 1717; see below, page 687), Pöppelmann's not-inextensive œuvre ran to the 'oriental' transformation of the Dresden Holländische Palais for the confection of a 'Japanese' palace to house the royal collection of oriental porcelain on the east bank of the Elbe opposite the Residenz (from 1727). The 'Chinese'

marily as reception pavilions but wings with suites of apartments were added to both buildings after 1765 when the complex became Frederick Augustus II's official summer residence.

The interiors of Pillnitz are much damaged and altered but some Chinoiserie stuccowork dates from the late years of Frederick Augustus II – well before official taste turned towards French academic Classicism. Orientalism survived on the exterior of the Neues Palais with which the east side of the garden court was closed after the fire of 1818: the interior is resolutely Classical.

›**4.128 MORITZBURG, SCHLOSS,** from 1542, enlarged from 1661 and again from 1723.

The original Moritzburg was a hunting lodge for Duke Moritz of Saxony: the elector Johann Georg II of Saxony had it extended and the chapel added from 1661 by Wolf Caspar von Klengel. Commissioned by Frederick Augustus I to remodel the building as a country seat, Pöppelmann was assisted by Zacharias Longuelune: the exterior was rebuilt, the round towers enlarged. The rectangular island site and formal park, developed with the renovation of the building, were supplemented in the informal 'English' style under Frederick Augustus II. The Fasanenschlösschen ('Little Pheasant Castle') was built between 1770 and 1776.

summer palace upriver at Pilnitz was an earlier exercise in the mode (from 1720). It is another 'arena' scheme with a garden originally enclosed by two reception pavilions with 'pagoda' roofs: the original concept was informed by the Trianon de Porcelaine, the exoticism – associated with oriental porcelain – supposedly derived from the Forbidden City in Beijing.**4.127**

When the second phase of the Pilnitz project was underway in 1723, its architect was also directed to rebuild the Renaissance palace of Moritzburg, retaining Klengel's chapel and complementing it with a new hall.**4.128** The park was developed from 1730 and the Fasanenschlösschen (*faisanderie*) added in a style which paid little concession to the 'noble simplicity' then governing taste elsewhere. Yet Pöppelmann's collaborator, the Huguenot Jean de Bodt (1670–1745) who followed Longuelune from Berlin in 1728, had introduced a note of academic Classical severity to the late style of the first Augustus at Moritzburg – certainly directing it away from the fluid, florid style of the Wessobrunners in the south.

4.129b

4.129d

4.129e

4.129a @ 1:1000

4.129c

After the accession of Frederick Augustus II in 1733, Pöppelmann was eclipsed by Jean de Bodt and, in accordance with a new set of building regulations, the day of excessive ornament was ended. As yet far from austere, the first work of the new regime was the Catholic Hofkirche commissioned from the Roman Gaetano Chiaveri (1689–1770): built between the Residenz and the river, it is biapsidal in plan but its interior elevation recalls the chapel at Versailles in the form, if not the proportions or detailing, of its colonnades. Oddly juxtaposed to the entrance end, the slender openwork

›4.129 RIVAL DRESDEN CHURCHES: (a–e) Hofkirche (from 1738), plan, exteriors and interiors to west and east; (f–k) Neumarkt and the Frauenkirche (from 1726, dedicated 1734), architect's plan, longitudinal section, lateral section (Willy Trede, 1946), interior details, exterior from south-west.

Gaetano Chiaveri had previously worked in Saint Petersburg, leaving as the fortunes of the young Francesco Bartolomeo Rastrelli were rising. Work on his main commission for Frederick Augustus II, the Hofkirche, began in 1738. Frustrated by slow progress and depleted funds, the architect resigned from the commission in 1748: he was replaced successively by Sebastian Wetzel, Johann Christoph Knöffel and Julius Heinrich Schwarze, all ostensibly faithful to the original conception. The church was consecrated to the Holy Trinity in 1751: the city's last great Baroque building, it is a synthesis of northern and southern modes with its single tower before its basilican body.

First projected in 1717, the replacement of the 11th-century church on the Frauenkirche site was the sub-

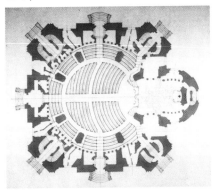

4.129f

ject of a competition in 1725 from which Georg Bähr emerged victorious after revising his first thoughts along lines drawn by his competitors: the inspiration seems to have come from the Protestant church at Carlsfeld (begun 1684) in Bähr's native Erz mountains. Over a square plan, the identical northern, southern and western sides have pilastered and pedimented frontispieces which, like the similarly articulated canted towers, rise over a low basement punctuated by entrances from the three cardinal and four diagonal directions: the sanctuary apse projects from the east side. Instead of the usual drum, the elongated dome and enormous lantern rise over a scalloped valance which rings a concave zone of transition from the outer rectangular perimeter: it was completed after Bähr's death. Sandstone was used throughout, even for the revetment of the dome.

Served by the corner towers, the five differently profiled tiered galleries which swirl around the north, south and west sides of the interior – glazed and unglazed, increasing seating capacity to c. 3500 – are carried on a ring of slender pier-pilasters: they break back to reveal the pulpit before the sanctuary with its high altar surmounted by the organ. Designed by Johann Christian Feige (1689–1753), the latter are

tower complemented the great dome of the Frauenkirche as the principal vertical accents in the stunning Dresden skyline from the mid-1740s until 1945 and does so again after the bold post-War reconstruction: they stand for the opposition between the Catholic court and the Protestant burghers. A decade before Chiaveri's Italianate essay in French Baroque-

4.129g

4.129i

4.129j

4.129h

the most elaborately embellished elements of the whole exercise though the carnival colour scheme of the restoration is somewhat startling. As in the great domed churches of the past half-century, the Dôme des Invalides in Paris and its Mansartian antecedents in particular, an inner domical vault (painted by Johann Baptist Grone, 1682–1748) is opened to a vertical perspective through an oculus to the much higher outer dome and its towering lantern (pages 243, 281).

Classicism, the local carpenter-architect Georg Bähr (1666–1738) embarked on the construction of the greatest of all Germany's Protestant temples. The scheme depended less on lavish ornament than on those other cardinal Baroque characteristics, colossal size and dynamic form outside and in: the unique scale and form were well calculated to assert the faith of the burghers, inherited from its founding fathers, in the face of their ruler's expedient Catholicism.**4.129**

4.129k

4.130a

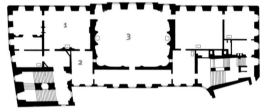

4.130b @ 1:1000

›4.130 RUDOLSTADT, SCHLOSS HEIDECKS-
BURG, 13th-century foundation, extensively rebuilt
from 1737: (a) court with west wing, centre, (b) plan
with (1) Rote Saal, (2) Weisse Zimmer, (3) Festsaal, (c)
Rote Saal, (d) Weisse Zimmer, (e) Festsaal.

His line raised to princely status in 1710, Friedrich
Anton von Schwarzburg-Rudolstadt decided to rebuild
his seat on a scale matching his new rank after a fire
destroyed most of the west wing in 1735. He first consulted Pöppelmann in Dresden but on the latter's death
in 1736 retained the principal Saxon architect's successor, Johann Christoph Knöffel: preoccupied by his work
on the Dresden Hofkirche, in 1743 he lost the project
to the Weimar court architect Gottfried Heinrich Krohne
who accelerated construction but work dragged on for
thirty years after his death in 1756.

The court façade of the replacement west wing has
clear affinity with the revisions to Moritzburg by Pöppelmann and his collaborators. Krohne revised the
planning of the twin apartments on the new building's
main floor – each with antechamber, bedroom and cabinets to either side of the great 'salon' – in accordance
with modern French conceptions of convenience. The
form and embellishment of the great hall, a Kaisersaal
in all but name, has more in common with Bavarian
or Franconian modes – even with the legacy of Hildebrandt – than anything French.

Johann Christoph Knöffel (1686–1752), who furthered
work on the Dresden Hofkirche, entered the Saxon
office of royal works about 1709 as a draughtsman and
was assisting Pöppelmann and Languelune on architectural projects by 1719. His independent works for private
patrons in Dresden, lost to war, were influenced rather
more by the latter than the former: his exteriors were
usually severe; his interiors enjoyed the incorporation of
Rococo elements. His most extensive private project, the
rebuilding of the west wing of Schloss Heidecksburg at
Rudolstadt, displays a wider range of interests in contemporary styles.**4.130**

4.130c

4.130d

4.130e

›ARCHITECTURE IN CONTEXT »DIVIDED CENTRE AND ORTHODOX EAST

4.131a

4.131b

›4.131 THE SILESIAN PROTESTANT CHURCH:
(a) Świdnica, church of the Holy Trinity, general view of exterior; (b) Jawor, church of the Holy Ghost, interior; (c) Jelenia Góra (Hirschberg), church of the Holy Cross (from 1708), exterior.

Assigned to Catholicism after the Thirty Years' War, 121 former Protestant churches were returned to the reformers under the terms conceded at Altranstädt. In addition, a 'grace church' was admitted – by imperial grace – in Jelenia Góra and six other major Silesian trading towns.

The church at Jawor, the grandest of the traditional half-timbered type, was completed in 1655 to the designs of the Wroclawmaster-builder Albrecht von Saebisch (1610–88). Unattributed, the one at Świdnica followed a year later. The third example, at Glogów, was destroyed by fire in 1758. The half-timbered tradition persisted at Cieszyn (Teschen), Milicz (Militsch), Kozuchów (Freystadt) and Zagan (Sagan).

The Stockholm model was followed in masonry at Kamienna Góra (Landeshut) and Jelenia Góra. Both the latter were built over centralized plans, derived from the church of S. Katarina in Stockholm, by Martin Frantz the Younger (1679–1742) who came from Reval (Tallinn) which then belonged to Sweden.

4.131c

SILESIA AND BEYOND

In Silesia, as elsewhere in the orbit of the Habsburgs, the old-established Cistercians were joined by the Counter-Reformation orders to lead the revival of architectural activity in a proto-Baroque style against the background of vernacular tradition. Unlike the former, the latter was usually modest in scale and relatively ephemeral in half-timbered structure. In scale at least, the great exceptions were the three so-called Churches of Peace which the Lutherans were allowed to build in Silesia under the terms of the 1648 Treaty of Westphalia.**4.131**

For an alternative to the vernacular, Polish Protestants would look to Sweden and its Dutch-derived tradition: the Altranstädt Convention on freedom of worship in Silesia (1707) had been exacted from Emperor Joseph I by Karl XII of Sweden, whose arms had carried him to the occupation of the province in the early phase of the Northern War.**4.132**

4.132a

4.132b

The design for the S. Elzbiety (or Hessen) Chapel is due to Giacomo Scianzi who returned to Bernin in the papal chapel of S. Tommaso at Castel Gandolfo – and the High Renaissance of Bramante – with superimposition of the hemispherical and the cylindrical over the cubical. Elsewhere others were bolder in their High Baroque borrowings – for the Vincentians of Krakow, for example.

Fischer's episcopal patron, Franz Ludwig von Pfalz Neuburg, was count palatine and elector of Trier from 1716: hence his Chapel of the Blessed Sacrament is usually called electoral. An elliptical dome rises from a semi-elliptical plan: rectangular geometry is imposed on the longitudinal axis but not to the sides.

Most active of the Catholic orders in Silesia at first were the Premonstratensians: attracting the particular antipathy of the Protestants, the Jesuits followed but by the beginning of the second decade of the 18th century they had made the transition from conservative twin-towered basilicas – such as the church of the Assumption at Nysa (from 1688) – to wall-pillar variants with undulating elevations inside and out, as in the Johanniskirche at Legnica (from 1714). That follows the example set by Christoph Dietzenhofer in S. Mikuláš in Prague's Malá Strana. The traditional Silesian Catholic focus was sustained on Prague – and on Vienna, ultimately on Rome. Thus Cardinal Friedrich von Hessen-Darmstadt looked to Rome for his memorial as bishop of Wrocław (Breslau) in the Silesian capital's cathedral. His successor, Franz Ludwig von Pfalz-Neuburg – whose long incumbency sustained patronage of formative importance – called on the office of Fischer von Erlach for the Chapel of the Blessed Sacrament added to the cathedral as his memorial. **4.132**

As usual elsewhere, Italians had dominated practice in the Polish capital for much of the 17th century: in the next century they were supplemented by Poles returning from Rome. However, the consequences of invasion from 1655 and recurrent conflict with Swedes, Russians and Turks

4.132c

The model was S. Andrea della Valle, except for the incorporation of the twin towers into the façade. The grand Roman style could well have been conceived in the light of Tylman von Gameren's own Roman experience but was certainly developed with the collaboration of Baldassare Fontana, ostensibly as sculptor.

The Vincentian congregation of secular priests was founded in 1625 by S. Vincent de Paul (c. 1580–1660) as a missionary body dedicated to extending salvation through religious understanding to the illiterate in countryside and town. For their church here, Kasper Bażanka (1680–1726), a Polish graduate of the Accademia di S. Luca, recalls Borromini's Propaganda Fide for the interior and Bernini at S. Andrea al Quirinale for the exterior.

4.133a

4.133b

4.133c

4.133d

thereafter left the Polish-Lithuanian establishment with sparse funds for building. Kraków, always outstanding as the royal seat until the turn of the 17th century (AIC5, pages 429f), was exceptional in High Baroque achievement during the lull in conflict prior to the outbreak of the Northern War in 1700: exceptional among the exceptions is the university church of S. Anny (from 1689); another, in Warsaw, is the church of the Benedictine Sisters of Perpetual Adoration of the Most Holy Sacrament (from 1688). Both these very different works are credited to the Dutch architect Tylman van Gameren (1632–1706) who came to Poland c. 1665 at the invitation of Prince Lubomirski, marshall of the Polish-Lithuanian commonwealth, for whom he built a palace at Puławy from 1671 and embarked on an eclectic career. **4.133, 4.134**

4.134a

4.134b

›**4.134 TYLMAN VAN GAMEREN AND THE CHURCH IN WARSAW:** (a, b) S. Anny, exterior as recorded in context by Bellotto in 1774 and interior; (c, d) S. Kazimierza (from 1690), exterior as recorded by Bellotto in 1778 and after post-War restoration.

The church of S. Anny was founded in the mid-15th century for the Franciscans. It was rebuilt to plans associated with Tylman after damage by the Swedes in the Thirty Years' War and the façade shown here was replaced in the late-18th century.

In 1688 Queen Maria Kazimiera Sobieska bought the Kotowski Palace for adaptation as the convent of the Benedictine Sisters of Perpetual Adoration of the Most Holy Sacrament, whom she had brought to Poland. Tylman followed the Dutch model in adopting centralized planning for the convent church: the severe articulation is also typical of his native land but its closest Catholic approximation is Mathey's church of the Knights of the Cross with the Red Star in Prague. In its centralized plan, as in its articulation, the chapel

4.134c

4.134d

stands in marked contrast to the same architect's work on the churches of S. Anny in both Kraków and Warsaw.

›4.135 TYLMAN AND THE KRASINSKI PALACE IN WARSAW: (a) in context as recorded by Bellotto and (b) as restored post-World War II.

The patron of Tylman's most important surviving secular work in Warsaw was the voivode of Plock, Jan Dobrogost Krasiński. The initial architect, Giuseppe Bellotti, was one of the many Itaian immigrants operating in Poland at the time: he conceded to the Polish tradition of prominent corner blocks. Working on the project from 1677–83, Tylman eliminated the corner pavilions and reformed the articulation on contemporary French lines.

From Utrecht, Tylman had spent much of the decade from 1650 in Italy after training in Amsterdam under Jacob van Campen during the construction of the great town hall on the Dam. Beyond memory of the latter, however, the articulation of his major secular building in Warsaw, the Krasinski Palace, is distantly indebted to the French academic Classical tradition stemming from the south front of the Louvre: Andreas Schlüter was employed to embellish it – transform it, indeed – as he was soon to do in the similar context of the Berlin Arsenal.**4.135**

4.135a

4.135b

4.136d

4.136a

4.136e

>**4.136 WILANÓW, PALACE,** from 1677: (a) general view from entrance court, (b, c) development drawings c. 1682 and 1696, (d, e) garden front after Bellotto, 1776, and after post-War restoration, (f, g) detail of side wings after Bellotto and after restoration.

The initial timber-framed manor house was built from 1677 over earlier foundations at the behest of Marek Matczyński, a confidant of King Jan III Sobieski: typical of its region, it was a rectangular block of one storey with four corner towers.**4.136b** The king commissioned a series of changes from early in the next decade. First the main block was transformed with an Order of pilasters rising through a new mezzanine to support a central pediment and galleries were extended from the outer pair of pavilions to two-storey towers. By 1696 the pediment had given way to a full second storey

4.136b

4.136c

Before departing for Berlin, Schlüter was employed in an undefined role at Wilanów (from 1692). There the great king Jan III Sobieski, whose role in repelling the Turks from Vienna in 1683 was crucial, had first employed Agostino Vincenzo Locci (c. 1650–1729) to transform a modest manor into a country retreat beyond the confines of the capital: after Schlüter, the palace reached its final form from 1720 under the direction of the Italians Giovanni Spazio and Giuseppe Giacomo Fontana.**4.136**

over the central three bays and the towers were given convoluted roofs.**4.136c** The later phases of the work, at least, were directed by Agostino Vincenzo Locci, the son of Agostino (1601–c. 1665), a minor nobleman from Narni who trained in Rome and was invited to Poland by King Vladislav IV Vasa (died 1648) as a theatre and stage-set designer: in a broader design capacity he continued to serve Jan II Kazimierz (reigned 1648–68) and trained his son as his successor. Giuseppe Bellotti led the Italian team responsible for the stuccowork and sculpture: the extent of Andreas Schlüter's role is unclear.

In 1720 the youngest of Sobieski's heirs, his son Konstanty, sold the property to Elżbieta Sieniawska, the wife of the commander-in-chief, who commissioned Giovanni Spazio and Giuseppe Giacomo Fontana to add wings flanking a cour d'honneur. Inside and out, new sculptural embellishment was provided by Francesco Fumo and Pietro Innocente Comparetti, frescoes by Giuseppe Rossi. In 1729 the Sieniawska heiress assigned the palace to Frederick Augustus I but on his death it reverted to her husband's Czartoryski family. It had passed to Stanisław Kostka Potocki by the end of the century: he established it as a museum open to the public – for which the wings were subsequently developed.

4.136f

4.136g

4.137b

4.137a

As the new century progressed the range of stylistic options still extended from late-Baroque Roman to Viennese imperial, to continued awareness of the Prague Dientzenhofers – not surprisingly – and to academic Classical French. The great Cistercian abbey church at Krzeszów (Grüssau) belongs to the sphere of influence of both Christoph and Kilian Ignaz Dientzenhofer (from 1728): at that time too Kilian Ignaz himself was employed by the Benedictines of Legnickie Pole, as we have seen. Disparate examples enrich Warsaw: the Salesian church expands on the post-Vignolan Roman basilican façade formula with remote variation on the organ fugue theme of Martino Longhi's Ss. Vincenzo e Anastasio in Trevi; the later Carmelite church opts for the formula promoted half a century earlier by Robert de Cotte and his school.**4.137, 4.138** The latter is attributed to the Polish architect Efraim Szreger

›4.137 KRZESZÓW, CISTERCIAN ABBEY CHURCH OF THE ASSUMPTION, from 1728: (a) exterior, (b) interior.

The abbey was founded in 1242 by Anna of Bohemia, wife of Duke Henryk the Pious of Silesia: the church (rebuilt from 1292) was destroyed by the Hussites in the 15th century and again in the Thirty Years' War. Restored, it needed replacement by the end of the second decade of the new century when funds were available for considerable celebration of Catholic triumph. The architect was Joseph Anton Jentsch, chief city mason of Jelenia Góra (Hirschberg) whose brother was a monk at Krzeszów and whose wife's uncle was abbot there from 1727. Behind obsessive articulation in a mode not foreign to Kilian Ignaz Dientzenhofer, the undulation of the façade amplifies soundings from S. Mikuláš Malá Strana in Prague: the canted pilasters of the wall-pillar system there are recalled but here they support transverse arches – rather than the diagonal or bowed ones which visual logic requires.

4.138a

4.138b

›4.138 WARSAW, CHURCH FAÇADES: (a) for the Carmelites (from 1777), as recorded by Bellotto; (b, c) for the Salesians (completed 1754), as recorded by Bellotto and as restored post-World War II.

The Salesian church (main volume roofed 1733, façade completed 1754), once credited to Carlo Bay (died c. 1740), is now attributed to Gaetano Chiaveri – on stylistic rather than documentary grounds: the transition from recession in antis to full-bodied projection of columns, without much concern for progressive development, relates to the articulation of the main storeys of the tower on the entrance front of the Dresden Hofkirche.

Wooden, the original church of the Discalced Carmelite was burned by the Swedes towards the end of the Thirty Years' War: it was rebuilt from 1692 to 1701 to the plans of Giuseppe Bellotti. Added from 1761, the façade is due to Efraim Szreger: the French-derived style is typical of the reign of King Stanisław Poniatowski (1764–95).

4.138c

›**4.139 LVIV, DOMINICAN CHURCH,** from 1749: (a, b) overview and entrance front detail, (c, d) interior towards sanctuary and detail of dome.

The vault threatening collapse, the Gothic church (of 1378 and 1407) was condemned to be replaced in 1745 to plans generally attributed to the military engineer Jan de Witte (1709–85), the son of a Dutch officer in the army of the Polish-Lithuanian commonwealth. Work began in 1749 and was completed in 1764: the disposition of the dome and the semi-detached towers distantly echoes the Viennese Karlskirche (only one tower survives).

4.139b

4.139d

(1727–83) and represents the threshold to a new age. Representing the late-Baroque generation, the Salesian work is now attributed to the Roman immigrant Gaetano Chiaveri. In contrast, again, Fischer's Karlskirche is recalled in splayed distribution – if little else – by Jan de Witte (from 1745) for the Dominicans of Lviv.**4.139**

Chiaveri had been invited to leave Saint Petersburg for Warsaw in 1727 to advise Augustus II the Strong on palace design: the Poles were yet to assert themselves against immigrants in the secular field where, in any case, private building was usually of limited scale and adventurousness. That was not entirely true of ecclesiastical work, as we have just seen, but Chiaveri was immediately involved in church building, notably for the Salesians (from 1728). His

4.139c

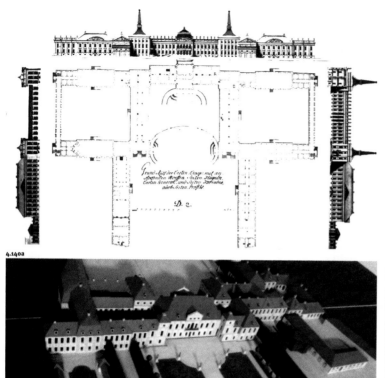

4.140a

4.140b

‹4.140 WARSAW, AUGUSTAN PROJECTS:
(a–c) Saxon Palace (destroyed), Pöppelmann's project
of c. 1730, models as completed by 1748 (to the revised
designs of Antonio Solari?) with Great Salon foreground;
(d, e) Royal Palace (restored), Chiaveri's project for the
river range of 1737 as altered in execution by Solari from
c. 1740 and recorded by Bellotto in 1770.

4.140c

first official achievement was the staging of the funerary ceremonial for his royal patron (in 1733). Finally, just prior to his departure for Dresden to undertake the Hofkirche commission in 1737, he presented Augustus II/III with his design for the extension to the royal palace (AIC5, pages 462f). Devised to provide a modern suite of apartments and mask the pentagonal Renaissance structure from the river, it was revised in execution by Antonio Solari (from 1740) and again in the 1760s.

The enlargement of the royal palace had been intended by Augustus I/II from the outset of his reign in Poland: Karcher, the architect of the Dresden Grosser Garten extension and collaborator with Pöppelmann on the initial stages of the Zwinger palace project, was sent to Warsaw to effect it after a visit to Paris in 1698 but progress was obviated by the outbreak of the Northern War in 1700. In

The 'Saxon' site, originally an extension of Warsaw's fortifications, was developed from c. 1665 by Tylman von Gameren for Jan Andrzej Morsztyn with a palace and a French formal garden. Augustus I/II bought the complex in 1713 and commissioned Joachim Heinrich Schultze to extend the garden to link the western outskirts of Warsaw with the Vistula River: the development was furthered by Gothard Paul Thörl from 1735. The reconstruction of the palace and the creation of the so-called Saxon Axis was begun by Pöppelmann in 1713, and continued under the direction of Pöppelmann's son, Carl Friedrich, and Joachim Daniel von Jauch in the 1730s and 1740s. The plan of the scheme as it had evolved by c. 1730 – with its place d'armes, its cour d'honneur and its twin side courts – is simplified from the Versailles model. The style is uncharacteristic of the older Pöppelmann's work in Dresden but its essence could hardly have been alien to his Huguenot collaborators: it follows current French practice in the regularity of the ordonnance of the central and side blocks, if not necessarily for their curved pediments

4.140d

4.140e

and certainly not for the terminal elevations of the wings or the spires.

The axis embraced the Potocki Palace which was bought by Augustus II for his illegitimate daughter Anna Karolina Orzelska and rebuilt from 1726 by Pöppelmann with the assistance of von Jauch: it is known as the Blue Palace from the colour of its roof tiles. The Ossolidnski Palace, begun by Tylman in 1681, was rebuilt by von Jauch for Count Brühl: it shared the forecourt of the projected royal residence. The Great Salon, situated on the axis in the centre of the Saxon Garden, was intended simply to provide a suitable end to the main garden axis. It was constructed after 1720 according to Pöppelmann's design: it was demolished in 1817.

1713, with peace and prosperity restored, the king's attention focused on the acquisition and development of a new site for his Warsaw seat: provisional work was undertaken over the following decade, including the purchase and conversion of neighbouring palaces and the construction of the 'Great Salon' at the head of the extended French garden axis, before Pöppelmann himself was dispatched to build an entirely new 'Saxon Palace' in 1728.**4.140a–c** Work was delayed by the outbreak of the War of the Polish Succession in 1733. Thereafter rebuilding to simplified designs was complete by 1748. Meanwhile, Augustus II/III had returned to the idea of extending the original royal palace.**4.140d, e**

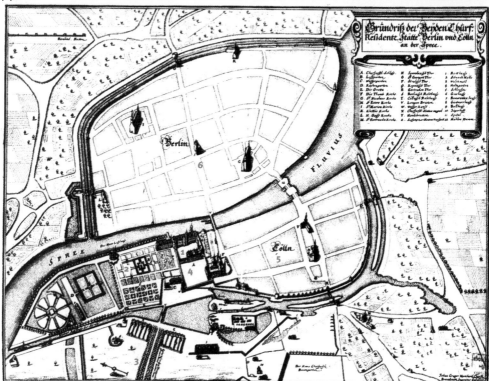

4.141b

6 FROM BERLIN TO BAYREUTH

The Brandenburg elector Friedrich Wilhelm I moved definitively to the Joachimsbau palace on the island of Cölln in the River Spree, opposite the bourgeois settlement of Berlin, in 1652 (AIC4, page 884).**4.141** There his military engineer was Johann Gregor Memhardt (1607–78) who had emigrated from Linz to the Netherlands as

>4.141 SEAT OF THE BRANDENBURG ELEC-TOR FRIEDRICH WILHELM I: (a) record of palace island (Johannes Ruischer, c. 1650) with Lustgarten and summerhouse of Johann Gregor Memhardt left, Joachimsbau centre and the cathedral (former Dominican church) right; (b) plan of the urban context with Joachimsbau (1), Lustgarten with the summerhouse on its north-east corner (2), Unter den Linden (3), Schlossplatz and cathedral (4), the walled town of Cölln (5) and Berlin with its Königstrasse artery (6), engraving after

Memhardt in Matthäus Merian's *Topographia*, 1652; (c) model of Joachimsbau; (d, e) antechamber of the electress's apartment (former oratory?) and gallery connecting the latter with the elector's private suite (from 1679, destroyed in World War II but recorded in early 20th-century photographs).

The Lustgarten was laid out on a conservative grid by Memhardt and Michael Hanf, who had worked for the patron at Königsberg: the main parterre, centred on the elector's statue, was on axis with the inner court of the Joachimsbau. The summerhouse, with basement grotto (sala terrena), was designed by Memhardt under the influence of Dutch works like Heemstede in Utrecht. To the west, beyond a bridge over the arm of the River Spree, a semi-diagonal arboreal artery – later Unter den Linden – was projected through extra-mural land which would soon be developed into suburban settlements.

Within the palace the doubling of the new state rooms with the ruler's private suite on the river side of the Joachimsbau was in advance of developments at Versailles where Louis XIV was still maintaining the essentially public life of his ancestors in contrast to more modern Spanish and Austrian – ultimately Burgundian – practice. On the opposite side of the palace, between the inner and outer courts, the assembly hall of the estates was enlarged in length and height as a suitable setting for asserting monarchical supremacy in the company of ancestral and imperial statuary.

4.141c

4.141d

4.141e

4.142a

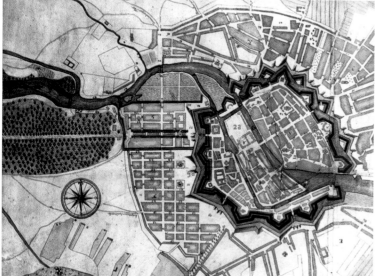

4.142b

(a) overview; (b) plan of nucleus and satellite towns with (1) Berlin, (2) Cölln and (2a) palace and Lustgarten site, (3) Friedrichswerder, (4) Dorotheenstadt, (5) Friedrichstadt with twin German and French churches on the future Gendarmenmarkt (5a) and (6) Unter den Linden leading west to Charlottenburg (engraved G.P. Busch, 1723); (c) pre-War overview up Unter den Linden to the Arsenal (Zeughaus, from 1695, centre left) and the royal palace (upper centre right); (d, e) Arsenal, façade on Unter den Linden and court.

The area between Cölln and the revised city defences to the west – extended by Memhardt from 1658 – was filled with Friedrichswerder (before 1670 when its district charter was granted): it was occupied largely by court officials and the new administrators. The area outside the new wall to the west was developed from 1674 in the name of the electress Sophie Dorothea: in accordance with the policy of religious tolerance, the development extended to the first church to be used in common by Calvinists and Lutherans. The area around the western artery was developed as Friedrichstadt from 1688, the year of accession of its namesake the elector Friedrich III: devised by Johann Arnold Nering in association with Michael Mathias Smids, it attracted numerous Huguenot refugees from France (after the revocation of the Edict of Nantes in 1685). All five of these urban entities were officially united into one polity called Berlin in 1709. The Lustgarten was destroyed by the militaristic elector Friedrich Wilhelm II and the site turned into a parade ground.

a young student. The engineer's prime responsibility was to refortify the electoral capital with a circuit of stellar defences. Within them to the west he left room for Friedrichswerder to be developed for the new administrative class and he projected the Lustgarten, with its 'new summerhouse', to the north of the Renaissance Joachimsbau's Spreeside range. Within the latter the elector commissioned new state and private apartments: the nondescript sobriety of the old building's exterior is in stark contrast to the mannered lavishness of its new interiors.

4.142C

The Brandenburg Elector Friedrich III (1688–1713, King Frederick I of Prussia from 1701) inherited a domain in which his father had managed to assert unity over religious and political disparity. The new ruler was bent on reordering his capital with grandeur matching regal pretensions and integrating its several distinct settlements. The process had begun in the previous reign with the development of the Königstrasse leading east from the south side of the palace across the river to Berlin and the axial artery leading in the opposite direction from the palace. This was flanked by the new extra-mural suburbs of Dorotheenstadt and Friedrichstadt (founded in 1674 and 1688 respectively): their union with the inter-mural Spree settlements of Berlin, Cölln and Friedrichswerder was decreed in 1709. **4.142a–c**

The first major project of the new era was the Arsenal (Zeughaus). **4.142d, e** Academic French in inspiration, the scheme was executed first under the direction of Johann Arnold Nering (1659–95) whose ancestry was probably Dutch: chief engineer since 1684, his principal responsibility hitherto was overseeing suburban developments – including a villa at Charlottenburg. The latter would be transformed by Nering's successors, as we shall see when we leave the centre. So too would the principal royal palace (the Stadtschloss) which Nering was commissioned to aggrandize. Neither that work – whose scope has not been conclusively determined – nor the Arsenal was well advanced when he died.

Andreas Schlüter (c. 1664–1714), the young sculptor from Warsaw, had been engaged to embellish the Arsenal with iconic images of warriors at the outset of the exercise in 1694: he assumed general executive duties there on Nering's death within a year. When structural faults demonstrated his limited ability in coping with the unstable conditions of the land reclaimed from swamp for the site,

4.142d

4.142e

The quadrangular Arsenal building on the prestigious site diagonally opposite the royal palace was designed on the advice of François Blondel whom we know as a military engineer, a founding member of the French Académie Royale d'Architecture and, as its principal professor, the author of the era's most influential *Cours d' architecture*. It is thus an outstanding example of French Baroque-Classicism – the style evolved for the great projects of Louis XIV's reign in the light of developments at the Louvre and Versailles.

he was displaced by the French Huguenot émigré Jean de Bodt and Zacharias Longuelune, whom we have met in Saxon service: they were invited to Berlin in 1699 – de Bodt, at least, primarily for military works.

In furtherance of Nering's plans, Schlüter was commissioned by Friedrich III to upgrade the architectural dignity of the palace, the hub of Berlin's quasi-radial development, in preparation for the elevation of the Brandenburg electorate to Prussian kingdom.**4.143b** Bernini's third scheme for the Louvre and Nicodemus Tessin's exercise in revising it for Stockholm recommended the development of the existing quadrangular form. Modern apartments were arranged in the reformed inner court (named after Schlüter), a grand staircase was provided to serve them and the exteriors were refaced: they were enlivened with sculpture on a suitably grand scale and articulated with a variety of regular and colossal Orders of pilasters or columns which betrayed a sculptor's feeling for relief rather than the will to coherence of an academic architect.**4.143c–i**

Structural faults threatened the collapse of the palace water tower which Schlüter was elevating with a belfry.**4.143a** Finally discredited as an engineer, he was again replaced by Jean de Bodt. His diversion from military works – and the condemned tower – extended to the delayed building of a tower for the Calvanist court and parish church which had been begun under Nering in 1695 and furthered to revised plans for consecration in 1703.

Meanwhile the French émigré's role in the last stages of work on the royal palace was doubled by the Swede Eosander von Göthe (1669–1728). Sent to study the Louvre and Versailles, he extended Schlüter's wings to frame an outer court and contributed the new western range with its great triumphal arch as grand entrance to the whole complex.**4.143j, k**

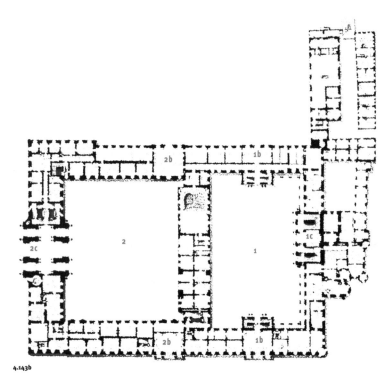

4.143b

4.143a

›4.143 BERLIN, STADTSCHLOSS (royal palace): (a) Andreas Schlüter's water-tower project; (b) plan with (1) Schlüter's court, entrance pavilions (1b) and staircase (1c), (2) Eosander von Göthe's court, entrance pavilions from forecourt and garden (2b) and new triumphal arch entrance from west (2c); (c–i) overview of Schlüter's court (engraved 1702), frontispieces to palace square and garden, north and east sides of court,

4.143c

4.143d

4.143f

4.143e

Stadtschloss Berlin

Renewed by the elector Friedrich II from 1443, the medieval seat of the Brandenburg Hohenzollerns on the bank of the Spree was transformed by Joachim II (from 1537; see AIC4, page 884). The riverine wing of the Joachimsbau contained the electoral apartments, its perpendicular adjunct faced the Lustgarten of Johann Georg (after 1571).

From 1679, Johann Arnold Nering was called on to augment the ceremonial facilities and was commissioned to project an entirely new and larger court to the west. That was furthered on his demise by Andreas Schlüter: his were the staircase in the inner range, the court fronts of the northern, southern and eastern ranges and the outer façades punctuated with the frontispieces facing the Lustgarten to the north and the palace square (Strechbahn) to the south. The frontispieces were differentiated according to their aspect: for the garden face, a variant of the court side had herms instead of a full lower Order; the town face had a colossal Corinthian Order in the rhythm of a triumphal arch over a rusticated base. That aspect bears a general affinity to

4.143g

4.143h

4.143j

4.143k

Bernini's third Louvre project and its several derivatives, most notably Tessin's designs for the south front of the royal palace in Stockholm (see pages 376f). The frontispiece there is more closely followed for the transformed eastern façade of the court.

The inner frontispiece to the Spreeside range of the old Joachimsbau introduced Schlüter's great new ceremonial staircase: twin flights (one of stairs, the other ramps) mounted to each side of a lobby in an open cage but returned round solid cores through two storeys. The base level was richly articulated with canonical Doric Orders, complemented with atlante in the outer vestibule; the Ionic of the upper level rises beside powerful recumbent nude figures. Secondary staircases within the northern and southern court frontispieces served major reception spaces in the side wings, notably the Throne Hall of the Knights of the Order of S. John which overlooked the garden from the centre of the king's new suite.

At the western end of the gallery which closed the forecourt to the Lustgarten, Schlüter was commissioned to replace the old Mint tower with a multi-storey structure supporting a water tank: construction began in 1704 but the marshy site soon rendered it unstable, revision failed to prevent

4.143i

further subsidence and Schlüter's fall. From 1706 his successor, Eosander von Göthe, was commissioned to extend the palace in the direction of the defunct tower in response to the king's determination to house the major offices of state beside a new forecourt. He doubled the completed court, inserted a great hall in the cross wing and closed the complex with the range centred on the western entrance: modelled on the Roman Arch of Septimius Severus, that was surmounted with a dome when the palace was comprehensively modernized in the middle of the 19th century.**4.142c**

Eosander may well have found it congenial to work on a project akin to the seat of his own king and to its main inspiration, Bernini's third Louvre project. However, his side-wing extensions can hardly be said to improve on Schlüter's proportions: a better alternative might have taken its departure from the articulation of his new western entrance arch, based on pedestals rather than basement projections like Schlüter's frontispieces.

›**4.144** BERLIN ECCLESIASTICAL DEVELOPMENTS: (a, b) Parochialkirche (from 1695), plan and elevation (as revised in execution); (c) Sophienkirche, west front with tower (1729).

Work began on the Calvinist parish church in August 1695 but funding was short: after Nering's death two months later the plans were revised to a reduced scale by the Prussian master builder Martin Grünberg (c. 1655–1706) and the body of the building was completed to them in 1703. The tower was completed in 1714 with simplifications demanded by the elector, Friedrich Wilhelm II, on his accession the previous year.

The Sophienkirche was founded in 1712 by Friedrich III's queen, Sophie Louise.

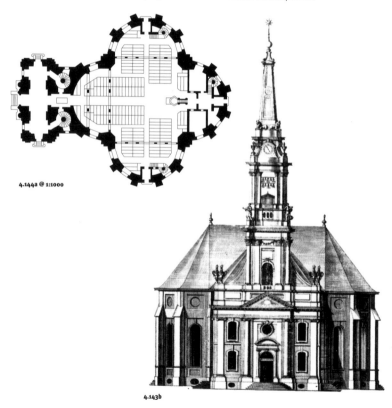

4.144a @ 1:1000

4.143b

4.144c

The inner open space of Friedrichstadt was endowed with a pair of centralized churches for the Lutherans and Huguenots respectively: centralized planning would be the Prussian ecclesiastical norm. Friedrich III, his family and a small community beyond it were Calvinists: commissioned in 1694 to design their church, Nering responded with a quatrelobe scheme focused on the pulpit in accordance with the sect's practice as exemplified in Amsterdam (AIC5, page 551). In 1713 Jean de Bodt was commissioned to revise the design for the unbuilt tower to accommodate bells which had been destined for Schlüter's ill-fated water tower. A variant, with superimposed cruciform tempietti supporting a convoluted spire, was built in 1729 by Johann Friedrich Grael (1707–40) over the west end of the Sophienkirche. Thus the Classicizing of the medieval steeple, begun in Holland a century earlier and developed with astonishing facility by Christopher Wren and his school in London, was to make its distinguished mark in the easternmost capital of Protestantism.**4.144**

PERIPHERAL PALACES

There were two important areas of electoral development beyond Berlin: Bötzow to the north, where Friedrich Wilhelm I's first wife, Luise Henrietta of Orange, developed an agricultural estate called 'New Holland' to the direction of Johann Gregor Memhardt (from 1651): at the centre was a small garden palace in the Dutch style called Oranienburg.**4.145a** In the other direction, south-west from the capital, the elector retook possession of the castle at the river crossing of Potsdam: formerly converted into a palace for the dowager electress Katharina (1549–1602) and the centre of a major hunting domain, but dilapidated in the war, it was rebuilt from 1664 in the elementary Dutch Classical style associated with Memhardt – who planned the development of a new town dependant on it (from 1672).**4.145b, c**

>**4.145** ELECTORAL COUNTRY ESTATES: (a) Oranienburg, overview of palace and garden (engraved by Memhardt, 1652); (b, c) Potsdam, original garden front and its enlargement with a third storey (engraved by Jean-Baptiste Broebes, *Vues des palais et maisons de plaisance de sa majesté le Roy de Prusse*, 1733).

On an embanked island in the River Havel, the original Oranienburg was a four-storey rectangular pavilion in a cloistered compound with smaller cubical pavilions to the sides and rear: an enclosed chequerboard garden was developed on the southern bank of the river, along diagonals off-axis with the house in the manner not uncommon in the Dutch Netherlands.

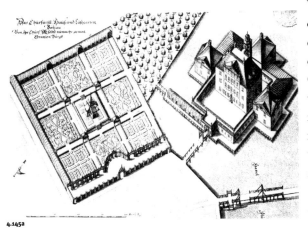

4.145a

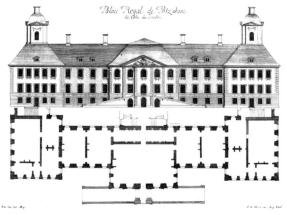

4.145b

4.145c

The attribution of the Potsdam palace to Memhardt depends on his production of the engraved records. It conformed to the French château type with its extended enfilade (novel in Germany) and its view out over a parterre de broderie to the countryside. However, its Dutch style is related to works like the Huis Honselaarsdijk, built by Jacob van Campen for the stadholder, Frederik Hendrik of Orange (and inherited by Frederick of Prussia). After the addition of a second storey and a lantern tower, it may even be related to the Amsterdam town hall – though the façade was rendered and whitewashed over a rusticated basement and the side pavilions were extended into wings flanking a forecourt closed with a semi-circular gallery (from 1679). Rides radiated out through the game park to smaller lodges, notably Caputh which was given to successive electresses.

›**4.146 PALACES OF FRIEDRICH III:** (a) Potsdam, enlarged scheme (from 1694; engraved by Jean-Baptiste Broebes, 1733); (b) Friedrichsfelde (from 1699), garden front; (c–f) Köpenick (from c. 1682), river front, armorial room, details of plasterwork; (g) Charlottenburg, the garden palace as originally conceived by Johann Arnold Nering (from 1695 as Lützelburg).

Back in possession of Potsdam in 1689 after the death of the electress Sophie Dorothea, Friedrich III called for extensions from Nering. After the latter's death, the pro-

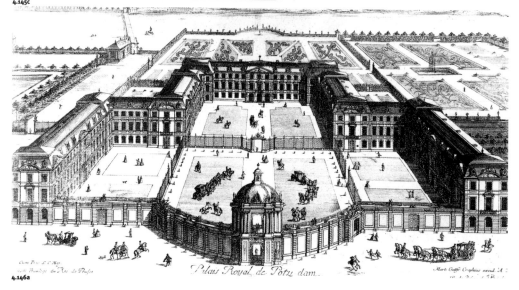

4.146a

4.146b

ject took shape in emulation of Versailles at the direction of Jean de Bodt (from 1700): the semi-circular gallery was demolished (probably under Nering) and recessed wings framed the new place d'armes before the original cour d'honneur; a new screen curves forward to a triumphal domed entrance pavilion on the main axis. The belvederes were removed, the fenestration reformed in the mode of Hardouin-Mansart and his school.

Köpenick, with three pavillons projecting from the corps de logis, conforms to the Franco-Dutch hybrid favoured by the Brandenburg rulers elsewhere: the mansards are French, except for the Dutch viewing gallery; the tall proportions and fenestration are not typically French but due to the Dutch painter-architect Rutger van Langerfeld. Nering seems to have been involved only with the detached chapel. Stuccadors working on the interiors in the 1690s include Giovanni Simonetti and Giovanni Carove: the latter was working at Gotha in the previous decade when the Lucchese brothers were doing not-dissimilar figurative work in bold relief at Coburg.

4.146c

4.146e

4.146d

On his accession, Friedrich III directed Nering to the expansion of Oranienburg and Potsdam with forecourts framed by extended wings: at Potsdam these were offset in the manner of Versailles to frame a place d'armes before the original cour d'honneur. As crown prince, he had employed Nering to build him a 'residence-in-waiting' at Köpenick at the confluence of the Dahme and Spree (from 1677): Franco-Dutch in style, it houses the reign's most sumptuous surviving Baroque interiors (completed c. 1690). Thereafter patron and architect turned their attention first to Schönhausen (from 1691), then via several smaller acquisitions to Friedrichsfelde (from 1699). By then Nering was dead: towards the end of his life, in 1695, he was called upon to provide the electress Sophie Charlotte with a palace at Lützelburg – later named Charlottenburg – in the western suburbs at the far end of the new axis of organization which was to be planted with linden trees.**4.146**

Eosander's over-extension of Schlüter's Berlin palace façades suggests he was uncomfortable working in that severest of Roman Baroque modes. Be that as it may, his style had little in common with the prime French exemplars, with Bernini, with Tessin or with Schlüter, when he

4.146f
At Oranienburg, the two main floors of the central pavilion were endowed with a colossal Order supporting an attic in place of the original pediment: on the other hand, extensive new wings were articulated with a regular Order over abstract pilasters applied to the basement. Both these systems were adopted for the other major suburban palace projects of Nering's latest years: the colossal Order – rising from the ground – for Friedrichsfelde (from 1695, for Admiral Benjamin Raule from whom it was confiscated in 1698); the regular ordonnance for Niederschönhausen (from 1691 in transformation of an earlier structure) and for the electress's retreat at Lietzenburg, where Nering's work follows modern French château development with its projecting salon. That survives in the centre of the complex which was greatly expanded early in the first decade of the new century, as we shall see.

4.146g

4.147b

4.147a

> **4.147 BERLIN, CHARLOTTENBURG PALACE,**
from 1695, revised with dome from 1704: (a, b) model
and view from entrance court, (c) chapel, (d, e) details
of antechambers, (f, g) Porcelain Cabinet, general view
and detail of vault.

To match the patron's new regal dignity, Nering's
eleven-bay Lietzenburg garden palace was extended
by Eosander with lower side wings of thirteen bays
each side on the garden front and, on the entrance
side, five returning in dependent ranges flanking a cour
d'honneur in the French manner (as at Potsdam): a central dome is not unprecedented in French palaces but
the high drum and sculptural detail are not common
to that domestic tradition. The palace was renamed
in memory of the electress Sophie Charlotte after she
died in 1705 with the new works far from complete. The
western orangery, but not its projected pendant, was
subsequently completed and the central core of rooms
decorated. The chapel and the Porcelain Cabinet are

was called upon to extend the Charlottenburg palace laterally and to add a central dome: certainly the Baroque élan
of the latter is in marked contrast to the relatively severe
Classicism of Nering's pedimented tetrastyle frontispiece
below it.**4.147**

4.147e

4.147g

4.147c

4.147d

4.147f

The second king of Prussia, Friedrich Wilhelm I (1713–40, the elector Friedrich Wilhelm II of Brandenburg), saw Eosander's work on the city palace to its completion. Otherwise grand works were suspended: Zacharias Longuelune was dismissed in 1717 and even Jean de Bodt found Saxon patronage preferable in 1728. The king's resources outstanding among the reformed state rooms, several with ceilings raised over deep coves and embellished in emulation of the variety which distinguishes their grander equivalents at Versailles. Work lapsed under the elector Friedrich Wilhelm II but was revived by Friedrich II, who completed the palace as his favoured residence with the east wing containing the Golden Gallery (1740–47, see below).

›4.148 POTSDAM, CIVIC EXPANSION: (a, b)

were strained by the schemes of his predecessor, not least the integration of the satellite towns and suburbs with the royal nucleus. That culminated in the destruction of part of the old city defences and the projection of a new artery (Wilhelmstrasse) to Dorotheenstadt (from 1736). In addition, Friedrichstadt was expanded into peripheral squares or, rather, a circus and an octagon as well as a square, modelled respectively on the Parisian Places des Victoires, Vendôme and Royale.

The new king was determined to concentrate on the creation of a formidable army. He built barracks between the German and French churches after which their broad place was known as Gendarmenmarkt (also from 1736). The Berlin Lustgarten was erased and turned into a parade ground. Potsdam was developed as a garrison town: extending it to house ever-increasing numbers of soldiers, the king looked to the Dutch who he had learnt to admire for their cleanliness, neatness and skill in building on marshy land – like the environment of Potsdam. Sobriety reigned until the opening of a new reign.**4.148**

›4.148 POTSDAM, CIVIC EXPANSION: (a, b) houses in the Dutch quarter (from 1737).

The first phase of Friedrich Wilhelm's expansion of Potsdam into a garrison town had been launched in 1722 under the direction of the military engineers Pierre de Gayette (c. 1688–1747) and Andreas Berger (1698–1748): concentrated around the Neuer Markt, the houses were timber-framed. That phase was continued further north from 1732. The third phase was inaugurated in 1737: a royal visit to Amsterdam prompted the importation from there of the civil architect Jan Bouman (1706–76) to project it in his native brick style. Dutch influence is not surprisingly apparent in the design of the Court and Garrison church, first built of timber but replaced in masonry from 1730.

4.148a   4.148b

FRIEDRICH II

Friedrich II (1740–80) was notorious in financial acumen but in reverse of his father's policy he embarked obsessively on a programme of expensive building: from the outset he guided his director-general of buildings, his mentor and protégé Georg Wenzeslaus von Knobelsdorff (1699–1753), in the design process and paid for the results with the riches of his conquests. France was often his enemy but the French monarchy set him the pre-eminent example to emulate in its expression of absolutism through its patronage of architecture and the fine arts. On the other hand, the French sought to learn from Prussia's military example – with somewhat delayed effect.

Knobelsdorff was an army officer who had served Friedrich when he was crown prince at his first married seats, Neuruppin and Rheinstadt, from 1732: on his patron's accession eight years later, he was sent to Paris for architectural enlightenment. On his return, his attention was immediately

>4.149 FRIEDERICH II AND BERLIN: (a–d) Charlottenburg, New Wing (from 1740), exterior, White Room, Golden Gallery general view and detail; (e, f) Unter den Linden, statue of the king, panoramic view with the Opera House left, Prince Heinrich's palace right (Karl Friedrich Fechhelm, c. 1760; Berlin, National-galerie; the palace is now part of Humboldt University); (g, h) Opera House (from 1741), elevation and section (Knobelsdorff, 1742); (i, j) Hedwigskirche (S. Hedwig's cathedral), Legeay's bizarre pseudo-structural section, exterior (from 1748); (k) Royal Library (Königliche Bibliothek, from 1774, now Staatsbibliothek zu Berlin), exterior.

4.149a

4.149b

4.149c

4.149d

Conceived to balance Eosander's western orangery wing, the main addition to the Charlottenburg palace was the great Golden Gallery extended to the east and centred on a pavilion containing a new audience chamber or dining room: the structure was complete within two years; the delicate Rococo decoration, credited to Johann Michael Hoppenhaupt the Elder, was finished in 1746. Knobelsdorff and his team were simultaneously directed to work on Monbijou, the residence of the queen mother, Sophie Dorothea, on the northern bank of the Spree opposite the tip of the palace island: badly damaged in World War II, it was destroyed in 1959.

Knobelsdorff credits the king with the conception of the Opera House (inaugurated in 1743): in view of later tension between patron and architect over the design of other aspects of the Forum, the claim is not generally dismissed as reflecting idle flattery. Credit is due to Francesco Algarotti's Palladian taste but Knobelsdorff had studied Palladio in Italy and had to hand the supreme master's *Quattro Libri* as well as Colen Campbell's *Vitruvius Britannicus*. It should be noted, moreover, that Knobelsdorff's first building for his patron as crown prince was a quasi-Palladian Doric rotunda – dedicated to Apollo – at Neuruppin. Apollo was also

focused on extending the Charlottenburg palace as the preferred royal residence and on developing the artery running west to it from the Berlin palace – Unter den Linden. To the south, the new king commissioned a square (the Forum Fridericianum). Addressed by a new palace on the opposite side of the avenue, this was to be flanked by an opera house (from 1741), a Catholic cathedral (from 1747) and a library (from 1774): the range of styles is striking. Knobelsdorff had been formed in the school of Andreas Schlüter's followers before learning from the French first hand but he was bidden to look elsewhere too. The king was eclectic in his tastes: he was equipped with wide-ranging libraries of architectural theories and compendia of Classical Roman, modern Italian, French, British and Austro-German imperial buildings. For the first fourteen years of his reign he retained Count Francesco Algarotti, a Venetian devotee of Palladio, to supplement the advice of Knobelsdorff.**4.149**

Entered through a portico facing the avenue from the north-east corner of the new square, the first of the Forum buildings is the Opera House: Knobelsdorff credits the design to the king but would certainly have endorsed Algarotti's promotion of Palladio. The director-general himself essayed conformity in the elevations of the palace opposite, which would be assigned to the king's brother Heinrich when the sovereign himself abandoned Berlin for Potsdam. Across the south-east corner, the cathedral was built by Jan Bouman to designs of Jean-Laurent Legeay inspired by the Roman Pantheon. In contrast to that forward-looking work of antique Classical revivalism, the Königliche Bibliothek was built along the Forum's western side to designs derived from the east front of the Louvre via Joseph Emanuel Fischer von Erlach's scheme for the Viennese Hofburg's Michaelerplatz (see page 559).

Prince Heinrich's palace occupied the site originally destined by the king for his own new palace associ-

4.149e

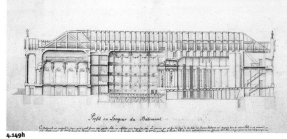

4.149h

4.149g

4.149j

4.149i

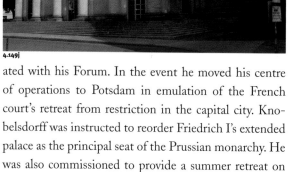

4.149j

ated with his Forum. In the event he moved his centre of operations to Potsdam in emulation of the French court's retreat from restriction in the capital city. Knobelsdorff was instructed to reorder Friedrich I's extended palace as the principal seat of the Prussian monarchy. He was also commissioned to provide a summer retreat on the outskirts of town: to be known as Sanssouci, it was

the dedicatee of the decorative programme for the Opera House's grand foyer. The Hedwigskirche, dedicated to the patron saint of newly conquered Silesia, was inserted into the south-east corner of the Forum scheme to accommodate the influx of Catholics from that province – the source of much of the wealth which funded the royal building projects. The Pantheon was chosen as the model to assert that the exercise exemplified the royal tolerance of all Christian communities, not only the Protestants dominant in Prussia. Legeay's scheme was altered in execution by Jan Bouman, working to the sketches of the king. The library was built by Georg Christian Unger to rehouse the collection begun by Friedrich Wilhelm I in 1661: the reference to Fischer's Michaelerplatz scheme – as engraved by Salomon

Kleiner (see page 559) – was somewhat whimsically willed by the king, contrary to the course of development away from the Baroque with the building of the Forum.

approached through a new Brandenburg Gate modelled (from 1770) on the Roman Arch of Septimius Severus as reinterpreted by Constantine. **4.150, 4.151**

4.150a

4.150e

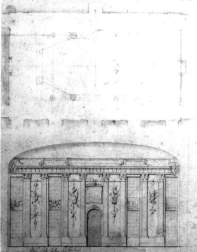

4.150f

4.150g

Friedrich II's palaces

The king's reason for abandoning the severity of the city palace is not far to seek in antipathy to the magniloquence of public display but the abandonment of more private, more relaxed Charlottenburg is harder to explain beyond preference for the riverine landscape of Potsdam. With extensive gardens beside a broad reach of the River Havel, the later palace was subjected to more than cosmetic alterations to the façade and the insertion of sumptuous new apartments (all lost to war and post-War vandalism). Knobelsdorff extended the wings either side of a single great court in place of the place d'armes, but kept most of the curved screen and its entrance pavilion of 1701 (the Fortuna Gate). The court façades were articulated consistently with a colossal Order of Ionic pilasters derived from the temple-front motifs of the pavilions which faced the town's Alter Markt.

In his Ionic staircase, Knobelsdroff pays homage to Schlüter by incorporating an anthropomorphic version of the Order. Corinthian, the style of the garden fronts was determined by the king's sketch of the central pavilion which was to be rebuilt around a new Marble Hall. That was itself Corinthian and retained the cornice produced c. 1705 by Schlüter: the expression of rigid structure cedes in the ceiling to Rococo palm trees for the support of the frame of Charles-Amédée-Philippe van Loo's 'Apotheosis of the Great Elector'. The conflation of entirely different modes of design is typical of Friedrich's eclectic patronage.

French cultural influence was strong at Friedrich's court, despite political rivalry with Louis XV. For Sanssouci, Knobelsdorff produced a Trianon

>**4.150 POTSDAM, STADTSCHLOSS:** (a–g) town and garden sides, staircase and Marble Hall (pre-War photographs), sketches attributed to the king and Knobelsdorff for exterior and interior of the Marble Hall, and to Johann August Nahl for the state bedroom.

4.150b

4.150c

4.150d

in gold sandstone and yellow plaster rather than pink marble, with herms instead of the Ionic Order, and with a great oval salon in the centre: thus, if similar in role to the Trianon, the form was a single-storey maison de plaisance more closely modelled on the Parisian Palais Bourbon – the hybrid urban villa built for Duchesse Louise Françoise in 1720 (see above page 323). The city and suburban projects were realized in tandem from 1744 but the summer's Arcadia was greatly to be augmented after the Seven Years' War.

Habitually resident in the city palace during winter, after the building works were finished in 1752 the king moved out to Sanssouci – which was built in the three years to 1747 on the site of the modest retreat erected by his father in the context of a sloping vineyard. The latter was ordered into a cascade of six concave terraces, for fruit trees as well as vines, on axis with the one-storey palace: rising from the vineyard, if set back beyond a broad parterre, the facade's anthropomorphic Order of Bacchic herms recalls the less specifically deified manifestation of the motif deployed by Schlüter on the garden front of the Berlin palace. To the north a grand Corinthian colonnade defined the entrance court – but left a gap in the middle for the prospect of the hill to the north with its artificial ruins: the

4.151b

›4.151 POTSDAM, SANSSOUCI: (a) north and south elevations and plan (studio of Knobelsdorff, c. 1745), (b–d) general views from below, south and north, main building, (e) detail of Bacchante, (f) Ruinenberg, (g) vestibule, (h) Marble Hall and vault detail, (i) gallery, (j) music room and ceiling detail, (k) antechamber, Bacchic cartouche, (l) library, (m) bedroom, (n) picture gallery and vault detail, (o) park plan with Sanssouci right and New Palace left, (p) Chinese pavilion and porch detail; (q–x) New Palace (from 1763), project plans and park front, general view from north-west, entrance screen and pavilion, Marble Hall, detail of Blue Room, gallery, sala terrena, Opera House interior.

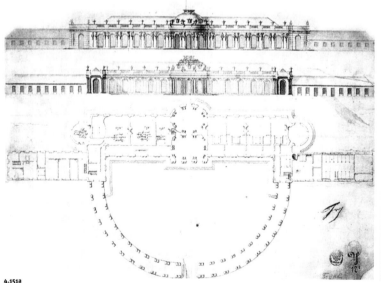

4.151a

4.151e

complex as a whole was viewed as Arcadia – 'et in Arcadia ego'. Recently enshrined in the English garden, hitherto the most celebrated evocation of that Ovidian idyll was in the paintings of Nicolas Poussin and French too was the distribution of the palace at its centre: the template was drawn from Jacques-François Blondel's *De la distribution des maisons de plaisance et de la décoration des édifices en général* (see pages 312ff). As always, however, the king revised it to suit himself in the east range and predispose his guest to the west. The entrance screen's Corinthian Order of doubled columns is carried into the vestibule and beyond, on axis, to

4.151d

4.151h2

4.151g

4.151h1

4.151i

4.151j2

4.151j1

the elliptical Marble Hall with its vault decorated *all' antica* – in marked contrast with its equivalent in the city palace. The suites were decorated with delightful variations on Rococo *genre pittoresque* themes (executed by Johann Michael Hoppenhaupt in collaboration with the designer Johann August Nahl). The apogee, clearly influenced by Lejoue (see page 331), was in the king's concert hall to which there was no stylistic transition from the central core of reception rooms. The antique style reigned unchallenged in the detached picture gallery – the first of its kind in the history of art exposition – which was extended to the east on a subsidiary terrace

4.151k

4.151l

4.151m1

4.151m2

4.151n1

(from 1755): Knobelsdorff having died two years earlier, it is due to the local master-builder Johann Gottfried Büring (1723–c. 1790). The gallery balanced Knobelsdorff's orangery (built to the west from 1747 and later converted to house additional guests).

Below the terraces an extended lateral axis leads from the eastern entrance to the estate, through formal gardens and a deer park straight on to the New Palace in the west. Diagonal alternatives are presented at the outset of the western promenade: the most rewarding leads south-west to a 'wilderness' – like the one tucked away in a corner of the Grand Trianon's

4.151n2

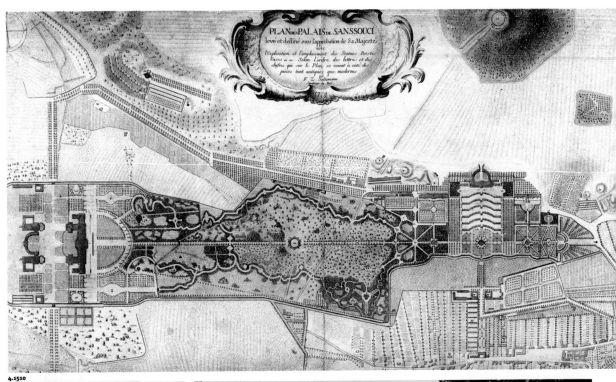

4.151o

4.151p2

4.151p1

4.151r

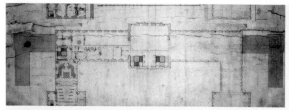

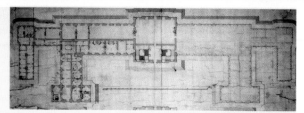

 4.151q

4.151s

compound – and the extraordinary Chinese folly realized by Büring from the whim of the king. The fantasy of that essay in Rococo 'architecture', with its palm trees instead of columns, is dispelled by the great bulk of Friedrich's last palatial structure. The successful outcome (for Prussia) of the Seven Years' War financed this huge work (from 1763): however, Baroque scale is meagrely served by the conventional articulation in terms of colossal Corinthian – like the garden fronts of the Potsdam city palace but without enlivening relief to the wings. Nor is it matched by the regurgitation of tired Rococo for much of the interior, beyond the dry variation on the quasi-architectonic scheme of the city palace's Marble Hall. For some of this Büring's initial responsibility had passed to the Mannheim architect Carl von Gontard (1731–91). Much more successful is his realization of Legeay's scenographic scheme for the twin service wings which close the palace forecourt (from 1766): linked by a curved colonnade – revised from Sanssouci – their bold reinterpretation of Palladianism was not surpassed even in contemporary England.

In France the Rococo was sustained long after the 'return to sound taste' – the restoration of architectural principles to interior design – which was dated to the return of Jean-Laurent Legeay from Berlin in 1752. In fact, as we shall see elsewhere, sound taste was never abandoned in French exteriors and Jacques-Ange Gabriel had returned to Classical Order in the most intimate interior of the

4.151t

Pavillon Français at Trianon in 1749. With its semi-anthropomorphic Order, Sanssouci is a special case: canonical Order had not been abandoned in the royal architecture of Berlin but the turn to a new permutation of 'sound taste' there may well be associated with Legeay's neo-Pantheon S. Hedwig's cathedral as well as Knobelsdorff's neo-Palladian Opera House.

Even at the height of their Rococo phase – sustained when aesthetic decorum required conformity with existing work – the French avoided indecorous contrast in their progress from the formal core of reception rooms through the parade rooms of the main apartments to the intimate cabinets beyond, as we have seen. Friedrich opted for Classical discipline in the central circular salon of Sanssouci, under the inspiration of Hardouin-Mansart's Salon Rond at Trianon, but preferred Rococo for the rooms to either side of it despite the shock of transition. The dichotomy persisted with less ameliorating charm in the New Palace. Towards the centre of the park meanwhile, the Chinese Pavilion – inside and out – fervently denies the impossibility of effecting a Rococo architecture.

4.151U

4.151V

4.151X

4.151W

4.152a

›4.152 BAYREUTH, COURT BUILDING: (a, b) Hermitage, Georg Wilhelm Pavilion (1715), exterior of Sonnentempel (1749); (c–f) Neues Schloss (from 1753), exterior, Chinese cabinet vault detail, great hall vault detail, dining room; (g–i) Opera House (from 1746), exterior and interiors.

The domain was a Hohenzollern dependency from the mid-13th century when a cadet branch of the dynasty built the Altes Schloss. It passed to Margrave Christian of Kulmbach-Bayreuth in 1603: he extended

4.152d

Stylistic dichotomy also characterizes the work of Friedrich II's sister Wilhelmine and her husband Margrave Friedrich of Bayreuth (reigned 1735–63) – a dependency passing through the cadet branch of the Hohenzollerns. French influence had been in the ascendant since Margrave Georg Wilhelm (reigned 1712–26) began the transformation of his palace in minor emulation of Versailles and added the suburban Hermitage with its cubicle adjuncts to stand for Marly: in the manner of the French maison de plaisance, the interiors are Rococo.**4.152a, b**

Dichotomy is pronounced in the next major building cycle at Bayreuth, when the margravine and her husband commissioned Joseph Saint-Pierre (c. 1708–54) to build them a court theatre and a new palace (from 1745 and 1753 respectively). Both follow French academic Classical formulae outside: without offending stylistic propriety, the latter's interiors range from the Classical core of reception rooms to cabinet Rococo and even to an original deployment of the *palmier* motif for the banquetting room. Marked, however, is the disparity between the Classical and Rococo elements within the palace – indeed, within the central hall.

4.152b

4.152c

4.152e

And the dichotomy between Saint-Pierre's design for the theatre's exterior and Giuseppe Galli Bibiena's conception of the auditorium could hardly be more striking: the most splendid of its type – instructively to be compared with the relatively meagre exercise installed in a wing of Friedrich II's New Palace at Potsdam less than a decade later – the latter is unsurpassed in its summation of the most spectacular characteristics of the most theatrical of styles.**4.152c–i**

4.152f

the Schloss and rebuilt the town after the second of two devastating fires in 1621. After further devastation in the Thirty Years' War recovery was desultory but the new century opened with vigour by the future Margrave Georg Wilhelm who laid out a new suburb on a formal plan, further extended the Schloss and built the Hermitage (from 1715). His architect was Johann David Räntz (1690–1735).

Margrave Friedrich turned to the Mannheim architect Joseph Saint-Pierre whose Francophile style, matching his name, was acquired in Paris where (c. 1740) he was a theatrical scene painter under Giovanni Servandoni (see page 333): that appealed to the Margravine Wilhelmine used to her brother's culturally Francophile court.

Following fire damage to the Altes Schloss, Saint-Pierre was commissioned to build the Neues Schloss (from 1753). The central hall has a canonical Order of Corinthian pilasters but they support an uncanonical heraldic cornice and a thoroughly anti-architectonic Rococo ceiling – where coffers might have been expected of a French Classicist, as in the slightly earlier Sonnentempel vault. Pervasive thereafter are novel permutations of the *genre pittoresque* – Chinoiserie in particular. The most original *palmier* room, almost Gothick in the pointed-arch profiles approximated by its arboreal 'structure', is now set up as a banqueting hall but seems to have been devised as the setting for the meetings of the margrave's Masonic lodge: the inspiration may have come from the description in the Bible of the sanctuary of the Temple of Solomon – the model of the just ruler. Beyond that, decoration ranges to cabinet Rococo in the Chinoiserie mode.

The first work of Wilhelmine's era was the further enlargement of the Hermitage and the replacement of the garden's axial formality with a freer arrangement of bosquets and a variety of pavilions (from 1735 for much of the reign): the most substantial intervention is the orangery whose semi-circular gallery is the setting for the Sonnentempel (from 1749).

Meanwhile, the court theatre (now the Opera House) was begun under the inspiration of Knobelsdorff's Berlin exercise but in a much more distinctly French academic Classical mode for the exterior (from 1745). The interior is due to the Bibiena usually rated as the most distinguished member of the celebrated Bolognese family of theatre and stage-set designers.

4.152g

4.152h

4.152i

4.153a

7 RUSSIA: FROM MOSCOW TO SAINT PETERSBURG

The other empire whose orbit is our focus here is the one burgeoning from Moscow – though it is rather the development of an axis than an orbit which we shall find ourselves observing in its capital architectural enterprises. Like the Holy Roman German emperors, the tsars of Russia maintained the double-headed eagle as their emblem which presumably represents the division of the Roman empire into western- and eastern-orientated polities under Diocletian and his successors: the Habsburgs were the heirs to the former, the Rurikids and the Romanovs – ultimately – to the latter.

›4.153 MOSCOW: (a) general view to the Kremlin with the cathedral of the Archangel Michael (Arkhangelski, left), bell-tower of Ivan the Great (centre left), Saviour Tower (Spasskaya, far right), and cathedral of the Intercession (Sobor Pokrova, 'S. Basil's', far right); (b) cathedral of the Dormition (Uspenski) from west; (c) the cathedral of the Archangel Michael; (d) cathedral of Christ the Saviour (Spasitelya, from 1839, destroyed 1931, rebuilt from 1994), west front.

The late-15th-century walls were repaired and the towers heightened with tapering superstructures (instead of wooden conical roofs) after the 'Time of Troubles' following the death of Tsar Boris (1605), which ended with the expulsion of the Polish invaders and the advent of the Romanovs (1613). The Frolov Tower of Antonio Solari (1491, later dedicated to an icon of the Saviour placed above the gate on the inner face) was transformed by Bazhen Ogurtsov in 1624.

THE THIRD ROME

The first centre of civilization in the domain of the Rus – the northerners who penetrated the river systems of eastern Europe for trade – was Kiev: it was challenged by less-vulnerable Novgorod, though the title of grand duke was claimed in turn by the rulers of Suzdal and Vladimir who emulated the old order. The latter was ultimately destroyed in 1240 by the Mongol forces unleashed across Asia by Genghiz Khan: the Tatar Golden Horde was to dominate Russia until the middle of the 16th century. A dozen or so rival dukedoms emerged as clients of the Tatar khans. Novgorod was potentially the most powerful but it was Moscow, where a citadel (*kremlin*) had been founded in the middle of the 12th century, which ultimately won.**4.153**

4.153b

The ruthless line of Muscovite dukes descended from a younger son of the northern Prince Alexander Nevski. Under the protection of the khans, they steadily absorbed their neighbours, including Suzdal and Vladimir – from whence the head of the Church moved to the Moscow Kremlin in 1325. In the championing of the nationalist cause against the khans, their success at Kulikovo in 1380 was followed by intermittent progress for nearly a century. However, with the absorption of Novgorod, Ivan III (the Great, 1462–1505) was powerful enough to refuse to pay the Tatars any longer and could truly claim to be ruler of 'all the Russias'.

Meanwhile Constantinople had fallen to the Turks and Ivan III, triumphant over the Muslim Tatars, presented himself as the defender of Orthodox Christianity, heir to Byzantium. To bolster his claim, he married the niece of the last emperor, Constantine XI Palaiologos. Importing Italian architects, he began the rebuilding of the Kremlin on an imperial scale worthy of his 'Third Rome', in particular emulating the cathedrals of Vladimir, Kiev and ultimately Constantinople to provide for the coronation, marriage and burial of his descendants (AIC4, pages 125ff).

THE CHURCH

Stone had replaced timber in the construction of churches at the centres of princely power, Kiev and its rivals, from the end of the 10th century (AIC4, pages 119ff). The formula for planning most commonly followed as the nucleus of the Russian church throughout history is the late-Byzantine quincunx: a square containing a domed Greek cross, defined by arches springing from relatively slender piers, with four subsidiary domed spaces in the corners and three apses projecting from the east end. Matching arches rising to full height within, outside the quasi-official type acquired a vertical articulation into

Inspired by the cathedral of the same dedication at Vladimir, the Dormition in the Kremlin restored the hallowed quincunx of cross-in-square with the crossing dome rising above those of the four corner bays. However, its Bolognese architect Aristotele Fioravanti extended the system into the three extra bays of an internal narthex (from 1475). Fioravanti's Venetian collegue Aleviz Novyi (Alevisio Lamberti) attempted a more thoroughgoing compromise between the inherited and the imported in his designs for the cathedral of the Archangel Michael (from c. 1505).

4.153c

The cathedral of Christ the Saviour was built at the instigation of Alexander I ex voto for victory over Emperor Napoleon in 1812. Rejecting the initial Neoclassical scheme, Nikolai I had Konstantin Thon produce an Orthodox essay elaborating on the traditional Byzantine quincunx: the design was approved in 1832, work began seven years later but was not finished until 1860. It was destroyed by Stalin's regime to make way for a Palace of the Soviets but that was not realized and the cathedral was rebuilt after the fall of Communism.

4.153d

largely blind arcaded bays: these traditionally terminated in semicircular pediments (*zakomari*), which moulded the eaves into undulation. As was usual throughout the Byzantine world in its latest centuries, all the domes had lanterns and the central one was naturally predominant. The type is represented by a string of impressive buildings stretching from Kiev to Vladimir to Suzdal and on to Moscow by 1475 – particularly to the Kremlin's Dormition (Uspenski).**4.153b** There Aristotele Fioravanti (born Bologna c. 1420) advanced not the Classicism of his early-Renaissance homeland but returned to early Russian Romanesque (AIC4, pages 892f).

Before and beyond its articulation in pseudo-Classical guise, the Russian quincunx was inevitably elaborated in every part at the seats of princes and in the monasteries which flourished under their patronage. The churches usually rise to greater height than their Greek antecedents, if not necessarily over correspondingly larger spaces. Galleries having been dispensed with within, the embracing square was wrapped in access corridors raised above ground level and served by a canopied staircase with portico. Inside, the impact of the many-tiered, richly framed iconostasis is stunning.**4.154**

4.154a

›4.154 SUZDAL: (a) Convent of the Intercession (Pokrova, founded 1264), cathedral (centre, from 1518), general view of complex (walled from the 16th century); (b, c) cathedral of the Nativity of the of Virgin (Theotokos, from 1222, rebuilt above base level from 1528), exterior from east, interior with iconostasis.

4.154c

Outside, typically, vertical aspiration was furthered by the superimposition of ogee diminutives of the zakomari (*kokoshniki*) in diminishing tiers to form a pyramid surmounted by a small cupola: a prime example is the Cathedral of the Transfiguration in Moscow's Andronikov Monastery but the mode was persistent, especially in small-scale works (AIC4, page 888). And, of course, vertical aspiration was essential to the bell-tower, usually placed over or beside the portico but occasionally freestanding: this might also be achieved with tiers of kokoshniki but more usual, ultimately, was a conical form of superstructure which may well descend from the tent of the Tatar tribes who occupied Russia after the invasion of the Golden Horde.

At the end of the reign of Ivan III the traditional indigenous and imported forms were overlaid with decorative motifs translated from the early Italian Renaissance by imported Italian journeymen – or their native followers. After Byzantium, the Venetian tradition was obviously most relevant to the Muscovite heirs of Byzantium but at first even the Serenissima's emigrés evinced little sophisticated comprehension of the essence of Classicism. If not the Kremlin's bell-tower (from 1505, completed from 1600), or the tsar's Faceted Palace (c. 1490), thus, the Arkhangelski (cathedral of the Archangel Michael, from c. 1505) best represents the introduction of provincial Venetian early Renaissance style to the centre of the realm: the architect was probably Alevisio Lamberti da Montagnana (Aleviz Novyi or Fryazin), who has been identified as one of Mauro Codussi's pupils in Venice (AIC4, page 894). However, there is little that is overtly Italian about the Kremlin's aggressively defensive walls as they were reformed with impressive regularity for Ivan III, nor with their many monastic and urban contemporaries: the star-shaped bastion was not imported for this largely urban exercise which had many followers.**4.153a, 4.155a**

4.154b

Church building was predominant in Russia throughout the 16th and 17th centuries. However, many monastic builders refused to compromise their hallowed tradition by succumbing to the latest mode of Western intrusion: their prime cathedral model – virtually the official prototype – was the Dormition, the most venerable of the Kremlin cathedrals. The Rostov Dormition is an early example (c. 1500). The cathedral of the Smolensk Mother of God in Moscow's Novodevichi Convent and the reconstruction of the Dormition at Suzdal followed a generation later (c. 1525 and 1528 respectively), the Divine Sophia of Vologda a generation after that (c. 1560). The Transfiguration at Bolshiye Vyazemski and the Trinity cathedral of Kostroma's Ipatevski Monastery carry the tradition beyond the end of the century. Unsurpassed is the Dormition of the Trinity of S. Sergius-Trinity Monastery at Sergiev Posad (begun 1559, completed 1585). In embracing the formula, such buildings acknowledge the supremacy of Moscow as the centre of Church and state – and, indeed, their dedication may have commemorated a significant development in the advance to empire. **4.154–4.156**

4.155b

›4.155 MOSCOW, NEW MAIDENS (NOVODE-VICHI) CONVENT, from 1524: (a) model of walls, (b) cathedral of the Smolensk Mother of God Icon (Smolenskoy Ikony Bogomateri, from 1525, extensively rebuilt from c. 1550).

The convent was founded by Grand Prince Basil III as a defensive establishment protecting the southern approach to the capital along the Moskva River. It was one of several such quasi-military monastic complexes but was favoured by ladies retreating – by choice or force – from the imperial or noble families. The cathedral was founded in commemoration of the incorporation of Smolensk into the grand duchy. The cathedral is raised over a burial crypt (*podklet*); unlike the Kremlin Uspenski model, the central zakomara of each front rises higher than those flanking it.

4.155a

4.156a

4.156b

›**4.156 SERGIEV POSAD (FORMERLY ZAGORSK), MONASTERY OF THE TRINITY OF S. SERGEI (TROITSE SERGEI):** (a, b) cathedral of the Dormition (from 1559), west front and east end.

The cathedral is larger than the Kremlin model, but follows the five-part apsidal east end and has a blind arcade band incorporating the main range of slit windows and uniform zakomari over equal bays. The original ogee-profiled domes (the 'helmet' type) were replaced with boldly incurved ('onion') ones.

The procedure attributed to Aleviz Noyvi was much followed with varying degrees of sophistication but nowhere is the synthesis of the oriental and occidental – Tatar, Byzantine, Roman and Renaissance – more bizarre or more seductive than in Moscow's cathedral of the Intercession (generally identified with its dedication to S. Basil): founded in 1555 ex voto for Ivan IV's early imperial triumphs over the Tatars, it remains the pre-eminent symbol of the 'Third Rome' to this day (AIC4, pages 889f, AIC5, page 86, and see below, page 730). Between that great work beyond the Kremlin's wall and the cathedral of the Archangel Michael within, there is little physical distance but, naturally, an extended line of experiments in furthering Moscow's peculiar architectural syncretism: exploiting the limitations of Russian masonry building technology, they typically promoted symbolic form over spatial purpose.

In consolidated centralized geometry and hierarchical massing, if not always in pseudo-Classical articulation, the main stages of 'progressive' development leading up to and beyond the tsar's commemorative masterpiece may be represented by works of varying size, form and purpose:

4.157a

4.15b

these range from the elementary church of the Metropolitan Peter in Moscow's Vysoko Petrovski Monastery to the highly complex Nativity church in Moscow's Putinki district (c. 1515 and c. 1650 respectively). Immediately relevant are two works in the vicinity of Moscow: the church of the Ascension at Kolomenskoe of c. 1530 and, a generation later, the more austere, bolder church of S. John the Baptist at Diakovo. In its complex form, as well as votive purpose, the earlier of these provided the major precedent for the stunning exercise popularly identified with S. Basil.**4.157**

›4.157 PRIME STAGES IN THE DEVELOPMENT OF THE MUSCOVITE TOWER CHURCH: (a) Moscow, Vysoko Petrovski Monastery, Church of the Metropolitan Pyotr (from c. 1515), restored exterior; (b–d) Kolomenskoe, bell-tower of S. Georgiya (c. 1535) and church of the Ascension (Vozneseniya, from c. 1530), cut-away axonometric and exterior; (e–h) Diakovo, church of S. John the Baptist (Predtechi, mid-century dating disputed but here assumed), elevation, section and plan of the entrance front (after J.G. Richter) and general view of exterior; (i–m) Moscow, Cathedral of the Intercession (and S. Basil, from c. 1555), plan, section, axial elevation of the entrance front (after Richter and general views from the south and west.

The small tower chapel dedicated to the memory of the Metropolitan Peter is credited to Aleviz Noyvi (the Venetian Alevisio Lamberti who worked for Ivan III on the Kremlin Arkangelski from 1505): its multilobed plan was to prove influential, most notably on the design of estate churches towards the end of the next century (see below, pages 746f).

Kolomenskoe church was commissioned by Basil III 1529 ex voto for the birth of the future Ivan IV. The Cathedral of the Intercession on Moscow's Red Square was commissioned by the latter in 1555 to commemorate victory over the Tatars of Kazan in 1552 and Astra-

4.15d

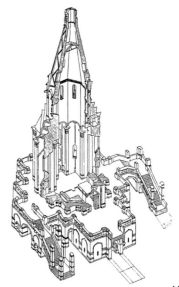

4.157c

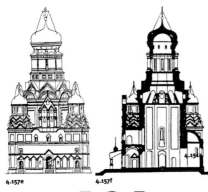

4.157e   4.157f

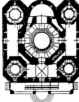

4.157g @ 1:1000

khan in 1554. The earlier event was commemorated in a church dedicated to the Trinity beside the Kremlin's moat at the Frolov Gate. The later victory prompted a grander project incorporating the Trinity shrine and centred on the cathedral of the Intercession of the

4.157h

Commemorative cathedrals

The centralized tower church with conical roof (*shatior*) is obscure in origin: reluctant to admit that it may have been the tent, some commentators recommend the throne baldachin, others the wooden tradition in general (AIC4, pages 120ff) or its special manifestation in the receding superstructure of the typical fortification tower. None of this precisely prepares for the Ascension at Kolomenskoe which, in form and articulation, stands in sharp contrast to the nearby, contemporary, Italianate bell-tower of S. Georgiya. Unprecedented in height – enhanced by its elevated site above the Moskva River – it is built over a contracted cross-on-square with minimal internal space, maximum mass: uniquely, it is endowed with the ruler's throne in place of an apse. Extending into the arms of the cross as buttresses, the construction exceeds the minimum needed to support the heavy load of the shatior and its drum which rises over three tiers of kokoshniki to a miniature dome. Outside and in, the walls are articulated with pier-pilasters supporting finely etched cushion capitals of no specific Order: more specific triglyph consoles support the window aedicules.

The Diakovo building's height is also enhanced by an elevated position overlooking the river. It is an elaborate variant of the regular tower type introduced for the Metropolitan Pyotr in Moscow's Petrovski Monastery: via tiers of semicircular and pointed kokoshniki, it progresses from an octagonal core on a square base (with chamfered corners and inset apse) to an octagonal drum ringed with semi-cylindrical pier buttresses; except for the latter, the form is reproduced to reduced scale for corner towers over chapels with individual dedications to relevant sacred births – S. John, of course, but also S. Anne. Beyond the Byzantine plan, the centralized massing with satellites is Italian in origin, as is the abstract ordonnance of panels below the architrave mouldings of the kokoshniki. A peculiar permutation of the traditional five-domed quincunx with the drums extruded into towers, it bears some resemblance to Leonardo da Vinci's sketch church projects. That may best be explained by reference to a common source, the Sforzinda of Filarete (Antonio Averlino; AIC4, pages 759ff): the treatise probably came to Moscow with Ivan III's architect Fioravanti who had worked for the Sforza.

Visible in the large open space (Red Square) to the north and from the Moskva River to the south, Ivan IV's votive church furthers Diakovo's mul-

4.157l

4.157j

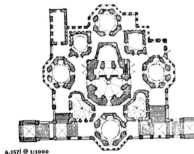

4.157i @ 1:1000

4.157k

tiplicilty of towers over an essentially rational plan but it incorporates the central tent-roofed core of Kolomenskoe. The quincunx survives as the basic plan formula but no longer as a coherent entity in an all-embracing square envelope: the nine spatial elements are distinguished in mass as independent churches, those on the cardinal axes transformed as octagons and projected beyond the orthogonal lines of their intermediate neighbours. A ring of eight domed towers rises around the octagonal central cathedral. Its multi-layered drum and multiple tiers of kokoshniki soaring over all, that is dedicated to the Intercession of the Virgin under whose protection the tsar placed his Orthodox realm. The axial churches and intermediate chapels on the northern and southern flanks are dedicated to saints and patriarchs whose feast days or missions were relevant to the achievement of Muscovite ambitions. Beyond the central cathedral, the Trinity Shrine is the ultimate eastern sanctum. The western one is dedicated to the Entry of Christ into Jerusalem: the focal point of the annual Palm Sunday procession in which the tsar led the patriarch mounted as Christ, it clearly equates the complex with the Holy City, its nucleus with Solomon's Temple. Thus, at the heart of the Third Rome, a manifestation of the New Jerusalem supercedes Byzantium as the vital dimension of the regime's theocratic identity.

Only the west aspect of the Intercession complex is symmetrical. In the view from the Kremlin's Frolov Gate opposite, overtly Trinitarian motive disposes three of the taller octagonal axial towers to frame two of the circular intermediate ones in front of the central mass: its disposition is complemented by the enclosure of the terrace with galleries ascending from tent-roofed porticoes in the 17th century. On the north and south flanks symmetry is disrupted by the extension of the central space eastwards into an apse. The order of the eastern aspect is compromised by the addition of the shrine of Basil the Blessed, the saint (deceased in the year of Kazan) with whom the entire complex is popularly identified.

Startling in its mannered – if not Mannerist – complexity, virtuoso in its heterodox juxtaposition of disparate forms, the network of decorative relief invented for Ivan IV's greatest work is essentially architectonic though the motifs range widely from the Byzantine and its Romanesque equivalent through the alien Gothic to the pseudo-Classical of the Russo-Italian Renaissance. Beyond reason, however, the hybrid confection is capped by the stunning variety of swirling, zig-zag and faceted mouldings of the domes with which the original 'helmets' were replaced after a fire of 1583: less appropriately likened to onions than to turbans, they may be seen as trophies of the tsar's victory over the Tatars under the auspices of the Orthodox Church. These are among the earliest manifestations of the type whose origin is much debated: it is perhaps most convincingly assumed to have derived from an imported reliquary model of the church of the Holy Sepulchre, or its central shrine, fashioned in the cultural context of Mamluk Palestine (see AIC3, pages 274ff, and AIC4, page 745).

Virgin whose feast coincided with the beginning of the end of the Kazan campaign. The architects recorded were Barma and Posnik – who may have been one person, probably from Pskov.

The date of the church of Diakovo is disputed: some would now place it at the beginning of the 1560s and deny it innovative significance. If it was built in commemoration of the coronation of Ivan IV in 1547 – the view derived from analysis of dedication inscriptions – it must be seen as a forerunner to the masterpiece of the age. Fully aware of the former view – but unenlightened by documentary evidence for it – I follow tradition here.

The tent form of Ivan IV's great complex on Red Square was retained for several other churches associated with the

4.157m

4.158

**›4.158 SUZDAL, MONASTERY OF THE SAV-
IOUR AND S. EUTHEMIUS (SPASSKAYA-
EVFIMI):** refectory church of the Dormition (late-16th
century) from the south-east.

›4.159 ALEKSANDROVA SLOBODA: (a) bell-
tower of the Crucifixion; (b, c) refectory church of the
Trinity (or Intercession, from 1570, bell-tower c. 1660),
north elevation (after N. Sibiriakov) and bell-tower.

The estate of Basil III was walled by Ivan IV as the
seat of the court from 1565: the Trinity refectory church
was commissioned in 1570 in hope of redemption for
the brutality visited on Tver and Novgorod in 1569–70.

regime but it seems that the tsar's enthusiasm for the commemorative type – indeed for commemoration – waned
with the onset of paranoia. Its prestige ensured the survival
of the form at large, particularly in bell-towers. More generally, however, decorative abundance would be characteristic of subsequent architecture: fashion favoured the
eclecticism displayed as the official style promoted by the
Imperial Department of Stonemasonry which was established at the end of the reign in 1584.

Decorative abundance persisted across the architecturally unproductive troubled decades which preceded
the establishment of a new order under the first of the
Romanovs, Tsar Mikhail (1613–45): it was sustained well
into the era which opened with the transfer of the capital
to the overtly Westernized foundation of Saint Petersburg by Peter the Great at the outset of the 18th century.
Over a long history it naturally went through several
permutations: the main stages may be represented by
churches ranging in size from the Trinity refectory and
the bell-tower of the Crucifixion in the walled compound
of Ivan IV at Aleksandrova Sloboda (1570s), the Dormition of the Saviour-Evfimi Monastery at Suzdal and the

4.159a

4.159b

4.159c

4.160

4.161

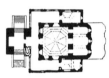

›4.160 UGLICH, MONASTERY OF S. ALEKSEI, REFECTORY CHURCH OF THE DORMITION, from 1628, from the south-east.

The church was rebuilt after destruction by the Poles, probably to commemorate national deliverance.

›4.161 OSTROV, CHURCH OF THE TRANS-FIGURATION (PREOBRAZHENIYA), from c. 1550, building history obscure: east elevation.

4.162a @ 1:1000   4.162d @ 1:1000

›4.162 MOSCOW, TENT ROOF VARIANTS: (a–c) Medvedkovo, Church of the Intercession (from 1634), plan, west elevation, north flank; (d, e) Putinki, Church of the Nativity of the Virgin (Bogoroditsa, from 1644), plan and general view from the south-west.

Built on the estate of General Dmitri Pozharski, leader of national resistance to the Poles at the advent of the Romanovs, the stone structure of Medvedkovo replaced a wooden one (of c. 1620) commemorating national liberation.

Transfiguration at Ostrov (both after 1550), the Dormition in the Aleksei Monastery at Uglich (from 1628), the Intercession at Mevedkovo (from 1634), the Nativity of the Virgin in the Moscow district of Putinki and the chapel of the Deposition in the Elijah complex at Yaroslavl (both of c. 1650). **4.158–4.163**

4.162b

4.162c

4.162e

The Putinki church was built at the command of Tsar Aleksei Romanov to replace a wooden one destroyed in 1648: the main volume is crowned with the three shatior (embellished in S. Basil's manner); offset before it (to the north of the entrance and vestibule) are the bell-tower with the largest shatior and a chapel (with minor shatior over superimposed kokoshniki).

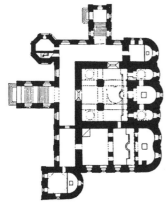

4.163a @ 1:1000

›**4.163** YAROSLAVL, CHURCH OF THE PROPHET ELIJAH, from 1647: (a) plan, (b) general view from the west, (c) detail of iconostasis, (d) gallery.

A wealthy trading town on the route north to the White Sea and Siberia, Yaroslavl is distinguished by the lavish embellishment of its churches. Commissioned by a fur-trading family, the church of the Prophet Elijah followed the quincunx tradition in plan and elevation (originally with zakomari projections) but added a gallery leading to a subsidiary church and a chapel with a shatior in asymmetrical extension from the line of the bell-tower. The fresco cycles date from c. 1680.

4.163b

4.163d

4.163c

At mid-century the tent roof was declared inappropriate as a secular intrusion into the ecclesiastical field by the reassertive patriarchate bent on puritanical Church reform. It had been adopted for the votive church in which arresting external mass rather than commodious internal space was the main concern, as we have seen. Orthodox metropolitan, parish and monastic congregational purposes were fulfilled by the traditional quincunx with one or five domes over a cube extending into eastern apses: the church of the Prophet Elijah at Yaroslavl may be taken as representative of myriad examples. The great exception to that – and to the observation of ecclesiastical stricture – is the cathedral of the New Jerusalem Monastery at Istra.**4.164**

›**4.164 ISTRA, NEW JERUSALEM (NOVI IER-YSALIMSKI) MONASTERY, CATHEDRAL OF THE RESURRECTION (VOSKRESENSKI),** from 1658: (a) plan, (b) section, (c) view from the south-east (restored).

The huge complex was commissioned by Patriarch Nikon (1605–81) who was elevated to the head of the Muscovite Church under Tsar Aleksei in 1652: he dedicated his ministry to the reassertion of the prestige of his office and counter the incursion of both Polish Catholicism and Swedish Lutheranism with reformed Orthodoxy. The perceived threat to the secular power of these ambitions led to his fall (1658) but not before he had reasserted orthodoxy in evocation of the prime monument of Christianity in the Holy City, the Anastasis (church of the Resurrection) on the banks of the Istra to the west of the capital. And that furthered Ivan IV's ideal relocation of the Holy City and its most sacred shrine on Muscovite soil, away from infidels. The shatior is quite inconsistent with the patron's own proscription of the form as an inappropriate secular intrusion into ecclesiastical building. The Patriarch was assisted in the design by the architect Sergei Turchaninov.

4.164c

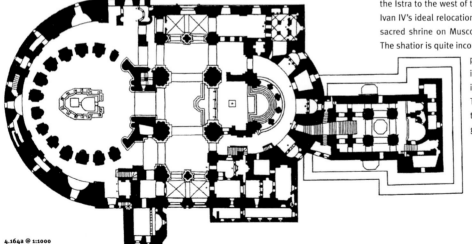

4.164a @ 1:1000

4.166a

›4.166 MOSCOW, THE KOKOSHNIKI PYRA-MID AND THE VOTIVE CHURCH: (a) Nativity (Rozhdestvenski) Convent, Nativity cathedral (c. 1500); (b) Donskoi Monastery, Small Cathedral of the Don icon of the Mother of God (from 1593), general view from the south-west and elevation; (c–e) Rubtsovo, church of the Intercession (from 1619), elevation (after V. Suslov), section and plan.

4.166b

4.165

A ubiquitous alternative superstructure for the small-scale commemorative or private church recalled the form of such prestigious works as the cathedral of the Transfiguration in Moscow's Andronikov Monastery, with its single tall cupola raised over diminishing tiers of kokoshniki. The Small Cathedral of the Don Mother of God in Moscow's Donskoi Monastery is a prominent example from the short reign of Boris Godunov (1593). The persistence of the form is well represented by the churches of the Intercession, Rubtsovo, of the Trinity, Nikitniki (Moscow, 1619 and 1628 respectively) and of S. Lazarus at Suzdal (1667). **4.165, 4.166**

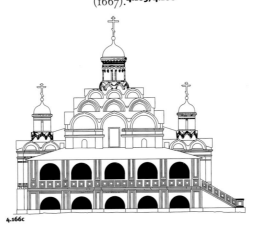

4.166c

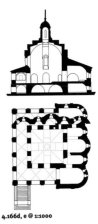

4.166d, e @ 1:1000

4.167c

After the reassertion of tradition in church design, the tent roof continued to be seen as most suitable for the bell-tower. This might be joined to the main building by an elongated vestibule in an informal way, as at the cathedral of the Intercession at Suzdal and the Elijah complex at Yaroslavl.**4.154c, 4.163b left** Or it might be erected over the monastery gate for visual and aural orientation.**4.166** However, the tower is often freestanding like the greatest example of the type in the Moscow Kremlin or in the Alexander Nevski Monastery at Suzdal, or again in the compound of S. John Chrysostom at Korovniki (from c. 1680). Detachment, of course, preserved the symmetry of the quincunx in the development of planning for the main body of the church, at least on the axis of the entrance: U-shaped galleries typically terminate in chapels to either side of the apsidal east end. Examples range from the Trinity at Viaziomi (from the end of the 16th century) to S. John Chrysostom, Korovniki (c. 1650).**4.167**

Profusion of ornament complemented formality in planning and massing but was certainly not foreign to the more pervasive informal mode of composition. Like the proscribed tent roof, that too might be seen as resulting from cross-reference to the secular tradition but was not to succumb to the puritanism of the mid-century church reformers.

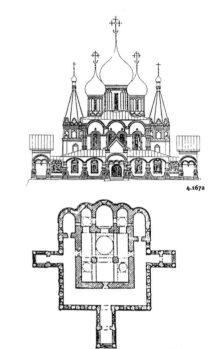

4.167a

4.167b @ 1:1000

4.167d

›4.167 YAROSLAVL: (a–c), Korovniki, church of S. John Chrystostom (after 1650), elevation and plan (after A. Pavlinov), general view with main church (left), and detached bell-tower (from c. 1680); (d) Nativity Convent, gate church and bell-tower (from 1658), general view.

A gallery once connected the gate structure to the main body of the Nativity church.

4.168c

4.168a

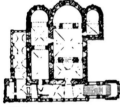
4.168b @ 1:1000

4.168d

›4.168 MUSCOVITE OPULENCE IN THE EARLY ROMANOV ERA: (a–d) Nikitniki, Church of the Trinity (c. 1630–50), elevation and plan (after Suslov), general view from the west and window detail; (e) Ostankino, Church of the Trinity (from 1678), general view from the north.

Large for an estate church, the work of the Cherkasski magnates at Ostankino is also exceptionally rich in the combination of carved limestone and brick moulded with bizarre abandon.

The patron of the Nikitniki church, Grigori Nikitniki, was sometime imperial banker. The work of architects borrowed from the imperial court marks the intrusion of secular motifs – and eclectic, essentially decorative motive – into church design: cusped arches of Islamic derivation below pediments of Western Classical ori-

4.168e

Even when church articulation is tectonic rather than architectonic – abstract in its panelled ordonnance – it is relieved with intricately cut brick or moulded terracotta and/or inset with coloured tiles: even in stone the frames of doors and windows may be startling in their profuse eclecticism. There were many permutations and many exceptions but the main modes of decorative development are well represented in mid-17th-century Moscow and later especially in Yaroslavl. The churches of the Nativity in Putinki, of the Trinity in Nikitniki and at Ostankino are outstanding early Muscovite examples. The mode in Yaroslavl fashioned the Church of the Epiphany and the churches of S. John Chrysostom and S. John the Baptist at Korovniki and Tolchkovo.**4.169**

gin, arches with or without central pendants combined with pseudo-Classical Orders of pilasters or engaged columns with a wide range of variation from the canonical in detail.

›4.169 DECORATIVE EXUBERANCE AT YARO-SLAVL: (a) church of S. John the Baptist at Tolchkovo (c. 1680), view from the south; (b) church of the Epiphany (Bogoyavleniya, from 1684), view from the south-west.

Inspired by developments in Moscow but asserting the individuality of their own rich heritage, the local merchants sustained their patronage of traditional church forms but now relished the extension of embellishment to intricate patterns in cut brick and inlaid ceramic tiles. Beyond that, the Epiphany church shows further advance towards the secularization of form in its unusually generous fenestration.

4.169a

4.169b

4.170a

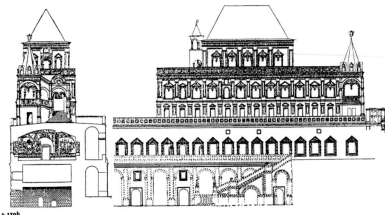

4.170b

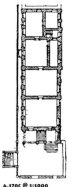

4.170c @ 1:1000

›4.170 EARLY ROMANOV SEATS: (a–c) Moscow, Kremlin, Tarem Palace of Tsar Michael (from 1635), exterior detail, elevation, section and plan (after F. Rikhter); (d) Kolomenskoe, palace rebuilt for Tsar Aleksei (from 1667), late-18th-century engraved record.

The Tarem architects recorded include Antip Konstantinov, Bazhen Ogurtsov, Trefil Sharutin and Larion Usharkov – some of whom, at least, were borrowed from the tsar by Grigori Nikitniki.

The hanging keystone (or boss) appears here before its intrusion into the porches of 'Basil's' cathedral. It was to be characteristic of the 'Russian National Style' – especially when that was rediscovered in the 19th century.

The tsars had led the development of Renaissance opulence since Ivan III commissioned the Faceted Palace in the Kremlin in 1487. A century and a half later Franco-Italian mannerisms had been translated to the Kremlin Tarem Palace of the first of the Romanovs: native floridity combined with traditional Russian elements, particularly the tent-roofed portico. And the complexity of the native timber tradition still invited rambling eclecticism as late as 1667 when the second of the Romanovs rebuilt the palace at Kolomenskoe. **4.170**

4.170d

As monasteries expanded in the 17th century with improved facilities for their inmates, the florid style of the ruler's palace was borrowed for the articulation of the façades of major structures. The great refectory of the S. Sergius-Trinity Monastery at Sergiev Posad elaborates on the rustication of the Kremlin's Faceted Palace and applies to it a regularly spaced, but irregularly proportioned, Order beneath an expansive scallop-shell frieze. As there, typically, elaboration distinguishes the window frames.**4.171**

That scallop-shell motif and something of a palatial aspect recur in the S. Sergius-Trinity gate church: both were common in the 'progressive' modification to church design in general. A regular cornice line asserted the cubic nature of the main volume at the expense of the

4.171b

4.171a

›**4.171 SERGIEV POSAD, S. SERGIUS-TRIN-
ITY MONASTERY:** (a) refectory church of S. Sergius,
exterior (from 1686); (b) gate church of S. John the Baptist (1513, rebuilt from 1692), view from the west.

The monastery was well endowed with votive offer-
ings and substantaial donations in recognition of its
role as a base for the forces engaged on repulsing the
Polish invaders. It also gained special favour for having sheltered the young co-tsar Peter from rebels in
Moscow and, later, from the machinations of his sibling
rivals. The result was enhanced walls and lavish new
building at the tsar's expense, above all the replacement of the refectory church – a quasi-secular facility of
c. 1560/1620 – on an unprecedented scale. The rebuilding of the gate church, with essentially decorative articulation, was at Strogonov expense.

›**4.172 KOLOMENSKOE, CHURCH OF THE
KAZAN ICON OF THE MOTHER OF GOD,** from
1649.

›**4.173 MOSCOW, MONASTIC FACILITIES AND
THEIR LATE-MANNERIST EMBELLISHMENT:**
(a) Simonov Monastery, refectory, west front (from
1677); (b–d) Novodevichi Convent, gate church of the
Transfiguration (from 1687), refectory of the Dormition
(from 1685), bell-tower (c. 1690).

The 14th-century Simonov Monastery was rebuilt
and refortified after the consolidation of Romanov
power in the mid-17th century: the objective was the
defence of the south-eastern approach to the capital
against resurgent Tatars. Ironically, perhaps, the memory of intrusion from the West is perpetuated in the
stepped gable of the refectory whose Netherlandish
style was transmitted through Poland.

zakomari which, no longer imposing their undulations
on eaves in definition of the structure of vaulting, were
reduced to the purely decorative scallop-shell valance.
Over that the canonical five domes usually rise from a
lightly pitched roof.**4.172** Unusually, the Dutch gable as
elaborated after Vredeman de Vries distinguishes the
refectory of Moscow's Simonov Monastery.

As a natural corollary of geometric regularity in planning, the cornice and its valance may be sustained by an
Order reinforcing the corners of the cube or dividing it
into regular bays: in addition to the refectory at Sergiev
Posad Monastery, the latter may be represented by the
church of the Kazan Mother of God at Kolomenskoe
(from 1649); selective articulation orders the refectories of
Moscow's Novodevichi and Simonov communities.**4.173**

4.172

4.173a

As under Tsar Boris Gudonov at the end of the 16th century, the monastery benefitted from imperial patronage in recognition of vital support: in the 1680s this was to Tsarevna Sophia during her regency for her brother Peter I. The depth of the gratitude may be measured by the height of the tower: at 72 metres it was the highest in the realm except for the great structure begun by Ivan the Great in the Kremlin (81 metres): the articulation in stages remains essentially decorative Mannerist rather than Baroque in scale. The style of the palatial refectory reflects the Western Classical taste of the patroness's adviser Prince Vasili Galitsin.

›4.174 MOSCOW, CHAMBERS OF THE BOYAR VOLKOV, 1690.

4.174

4.173b

4.173c

4.173d

Formal planning, extended elevation and profuse embellishment come together in the genres of the monastic gate church and the private estate chapel towards the end of the century. The former was inevitably restricted in the superficial area covered by its basic cube but, like its secular equivalents, needed elevation to serve its purpose as a marker which usually incorporated a belfry. Always the principal vertical element in the ecclesiastical complex, the latter's ground plan was often polygonal: a splendid example is presented by that in Moscow's Novodevichi Convent (from 1690). Polygonal drums were also invariably piled on a basic cube to achieve gate-church elevation. The repertory of decorative detail, pseudo-Classical in the attenuated Orders and scallop-shell zakomari, eclectic in the window frames, was deployed for maximum attraction.

The ordering of the stages of belfries and gate churches marked the advance of Classicism in Russian church architecture in the last decades of the century. As in the monastic refectory, this manifested itself in the noble town house – such as the 'chambers' of the Boyar Volkov, in part at least.**4·174** It was most spectacular in the Muscovite estate church which often followed the belfry in the ordonnance of its tiered elevation. The development is sometimes credited to influence transmitted through the eastern Polish regions of the Ukraine, won for Russia under the second Romanov tsar Aleksei (1645–76). However, its landed patrons may well have been informed by travel abroad and study of Western architectural treatises – to a degree of sophistication exceeding that of the average monastic- or parish-church builder.

The planning of the estate church typically surpassed the basic square in varied exploitation of centralization and its articulation occasionally conformed to Vitruvian precept for the superimposition of the Orders. However, the patrons were also aware of the extremes of elaboration favoured by French, Dutch, German and even English aristocratic builders in the Mannerist age, even if the followers of the du Cerceau, Vredeman de Vries or Dietterlin conveyed little of the wit of the original Italian mode. Departing perhaps from relatively restrained, canonical works like the church of the Icon of the Sign at Perovo, increasing excess culminated in the church of the same dedication at Dubrovitsi via multi-tiered extravaganzas like the church of the Intercession at Fili (all three from the early 1690s).

4.175a

>**4.175 REPRESENTATIVES OF THE ESTATE CHURCH IN THE VICINITY OF MOSCOW:** (a) the Icon of the Sign at Perovo (Znamineya Bogoma-teri, from 1690 to 1701); (b, c) the Intercession at Fili (Pokrovo Bogoroditsi, from 1690), plan and view from south; (d–f) the Icon of the Sign at Dubrovitsi (from c. 1690 to 1704), plan, section, view from south-west; (g–h) the Archangel Gabriel (Menshikov Tower, from 1701), exterior and elevation.

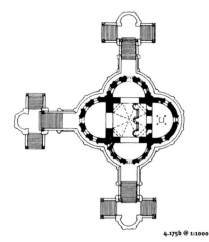

4.175c

4.175b @ 1:1000

The genre may be dated back to commemorative works like the church of the Metropolitan Peter at Moscow's Petrovski Monastery (see page 728). With the bell-tower forming the superstructure of a chapel for limited congregations of estate hands, was developed by landed magnates who had often travelled west and/or equipped themselves with Western handbooks of decorative Mannerism. The architectural detail is elaborate in embellishment but in the main it is confined to Orders applied to define bays rather more regularly than hitherto and to aedicular window frames, as in the Golitsyn work at Perovo or Narishkin Fili. Several contemporary examples include the bilobed churches of the Smolensk Mother of God on the Saltikov estate at Safarino (from 1691) and Boris Lykov's Trinity at Troitse-Lykovo (1698). The work on the estate of the tsar's tutor Boris Golitsyn at Dubrovitski is exceptional in its floridity but the vigorously sculpted ornament still rises from or is contained within architectonic ordonnance.

The combination of Western-inspired centralized planning and canonical ordonnance as the regulatory context for prolix detail – mannered if not Mannerist, still – is somewhat misleadingly identified as 'Narishkin Baroque' after Peter I's uncle Lev Narishkin who commissioned the church of the Intercession at Fili. The articulation of the distinct storeys in this 'wedding-cake' confection counters the colossal scale typical of the Baroque. Opulence in embellishment is, of course, a Baroque characteristic but it is not definitive of the style without a dynamic to its

4.175e

4.175d @ 1:1000

4.175f

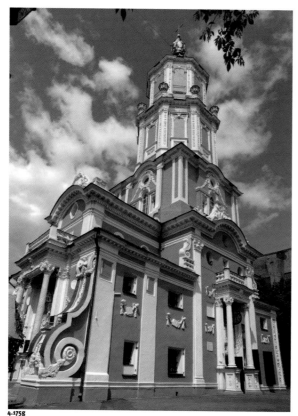

4·175g

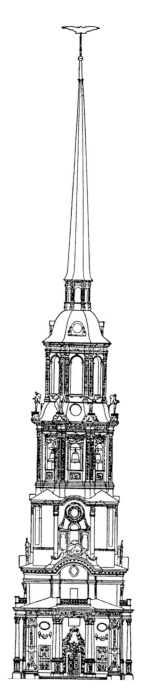

deployment. Curvature in plan is typical of these Muscovite works but it is either static or fragmented in elevation, not undulating: nor is there co-ordinated progression in plane and the plasticity of an Order to central climax. Russia knew nothing of the Baroque mode in its true Roman sense until a new wave of Italians came to dominate architectural activity in the new capital well into the new century.

Meanwhile, the canonical and the excessive achieve some sort of reconciliation in the extraordinary church of the Archangel Gabriel built by the tsar's chief minister, Aleksandr Menshikov (1673–1729) at the outset of the new century – just before the patron and his master were to embark on the project of a new capital in the north.**4·175**

4·175h

Attributed to Ivan Zarudni, the Menshikov tower is un-Classical in elevation but follows the northern Protestant mode of articulating the post-medieval steeple in Classical guise: thus regularly planned – especially octagonal – tempietti are superimposed over a basic cuboid vestibule; none of the elements is Baroque in scale. Here the western entrance to the lateral extension of the church is famed by massive volutes of a scale which none of the Dutch, British or Prussian exponents of the prototypical tower form ever contemplated. On the Moscow estate of Aleksandr Menshikov, the tsar's close associate, this work clearly follows developments in the genre of the estate church: it also anticipates the first ecclesiastical work of the new capital to which patron and master departed while it was under construction.

›4.176 SAINT PETERSBURG, ORIGIN AND NUCLEUS: (a, b) development of the city from 1706 until the end of the reign of Peter the Great in 1725; (c–e) Peter and Paul Fortress, overview (19th-century lithographic record), general view from south and-

4.176c

SAINT PETERSBURG

The Terem Palace in the Kremlin, and especially the wooden one at Kolomenskoe, could hardly contrast more spectacularly with the first palace built in his new seat for Peter I (the Great, 1682–1725) – despite the perseverance of Italians whose compatriots had been involved in the building service of the tsars for at least two centuries. Fundamentally, moreover, the sea change in the order of building began with the founding of the settlement itself

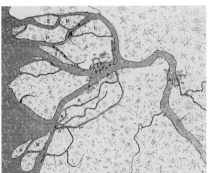

4.176a

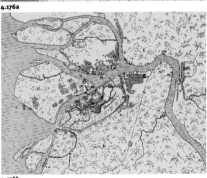

4.176b

4.176d

in 1703. Opening to the West through the Gulf of Finland – if only for the limited period of the Baltic's summer thaw – it was designed for favourable comparison with the Western capitals which the tsar had visited incognito (from 1697, see pages 22ff): with the rival imperial capital of the Habsburgs in principle; with the London of Wren in magnificence, if not in the lapse back into medieval organicism of post-Fire reconstruction; with Berlin and Dresden, where order had been extended from medieval organicism at the will of the ruler; and, more particularly, with Amsterdam where the radial order of post-medieval development embraced waterways.

In the tsar's absence, the developments at the mouth of the Neva were supervised by Menshikov and first directed by the Ticinese architect Domenico Trezzini (1670–1734). The former had already made a particular mark as a patron of Western-influenced architecture in the old capital, as we have seen. Trezzini was disappointed in the service of the Danish King Frederick IV by the promotion of Wilhelm Friedrich von Platen – who began Staldmestergarden and the Frederiksberg summer palace in the same year, as we have also seen. Among other talents imported to supplement or supplant Trezzini, Andreas Schlüter was followed from Berlin by the rather more obscure Theodor Schwertfeger in 1714. Georg Johann Mattarnovi came from Dresden on Schlüter's recommendation and two years later Jean-Baptiste-Alexandre Le Blond came from the Versailles of Robert de Cotte. Except for Schwertfeger they soon succumbed to the climate but Trezzini survived his patron by ten years in tandem with his Russian pupil Mikhail Zemstov, Schlüter's assistant Johann Braunstein and newcomers including Gaetano Chiaveri from the Saxon service of Augustus II/III and Niccolò Michetti from the Roman circle of Carlo Fontana.**1.76, 1.77**

4.176f

Evolution of the new capital

Bent on securing his control over Lake Lagoda and the basin of the River Neva after halting Swedish incursions early in 1703, Tsar Peter ordered the construction of a fortress on the innermost atoll of the fragmented archipelago at the river's outlet to the Gulf of Finland. The fort of Ss. Peter and Paul was completed in earthworks by the end of the year and within months – if not from the outset – it was seen as the guardian of a commercial settlement and naval base orientated to the West and called Saint Petersburg. Massive conscription of labourers – peasants and prisoners of war – was required to drain marshes, found shipyards and begin the imposition of habitation on the shores of the estuary for the first wave of artisans and traders settled there at the imperial will. A Department of Construction was established within three years of the first work but it could proceed with confidence only after the tsar's decisive victory over the Swedes at Poltava in 1709.

4.176e
Peter's Gate (from 1715), detail; (f) ideal urban scheme of Alexandre Le Blond c. 1717 (published by I.N. Bozherianov); (g–i) Cathedral of S. Peter and S. Paul (from 1712), half plan and section, west front and interior;

In 1710 the Monastery of S. Alexander Nevski was founded to enshrine the relics of the hero who had repulsed the Swedes half a millennium earlier: the settlement thus endowed with the religious significance essential to a tsarist seat, the court was moved from Moscow within two years. Wood was replaced with stone as the statutory building material – at least for embanking waterways and for public buildings. The aquatic environment naturally recommended Amsterdam as the urban model: the expansion of the settlement to Vasilevski Island, the largest land mass at the mouth of the river, was planned accordingly with a grid of streets parallel to canals. That was the tsar's own vision in contrast to the organicism of the primitive developments on the islands to the north of the fortress and to the south of Vasilevski, around the putative Admiralty whose shipyards were defended with earthworks from c. 1706, augmented in timber from 1711 and first expanded in masonry from 1732.

In 1716 Trezzini produced a draft of comprehensive order, extending grid planning to the zoning and grading of accommodation in accordance with the occupation and status of the inhabitants. His main legacy, however, is the citadel of S. Peter and S. Paul, rebuilt in stone from 1706 with stellar bastions in the mode currently prevalent in the West and (from 1715) a ceremonial portal of the type descended from Serlio through many rusticated triumphal arches in Germanic lands, Italy and France. Within, the cathedral (from 1712) departs decisively from the Orthodox tradition in its basilican plan, generous fenestration, illusionist vault painting and strictly canonical Doric ordonnance, even in the triumphal-arch motif of the iconostasis separating the nave and high-domed transept from the sanctuary. Like many churches in the orbit of the western empire and beyond its bounds in the Protestant north, where medieval elevation was not to be forgotten, it has a single western tower: however, that is surmounted by the type of tall, attenuated spire which was not alien to the Russian tradition most prominently represented at the Kremlin and, most recently, by Moscow's multi-storey Menshikov church tower. It was soon to be reiterated for the Admiralty building on the Neva's south-western shore.

Schlüter, out of favour in Berlin despite his distinguished contribution to the new order there, accepted the tsar's invitation to assume control of Saint Petersburg's development in 1714 but he died shortly after his arrival. He was ultimately replaced by Le Blond who produced his ideal revision of Trezzini's urban order in 1717. Before his death two years later that had been discarded as impractical: Trezzini's simpler grid was ultimately to be imposed on Vasilevski in the masterplan evolved before his death in 1734. However, radial avenues – like those of Versailles – governed development

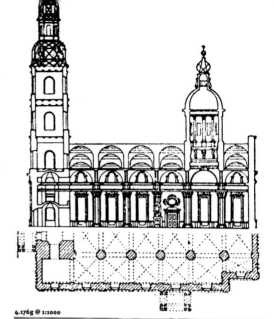

4.176g @ 1:1000

4.176i

4.176h

4.176j

4.176k

(j, k) Domenico Trezzini's revised urban order c. 1720 (drawn by J. Covens and published in Amsterdam by J.B. Homann in 1726) and development to 1737 (published by Matthäeus Seutter in Augsburg).

›**4.177 SAINT PETERSBURG, EARLY PUBLIC BUILDINGS:** (a) Twelve Colleges (from 1722), mid-18th century record (engraved by E. Vnukov after M. Makhaev) and detail of principal front; (b, c) Kunstkammer, engraved section (G. Kachalov, 1741) and general view of river front.

The first building to house the administration charged with ordering the new capital and its empire was a terrace of twelve eleven-bay units, each articulated with a colossal Order over a rusticated basement: each projects into a three-bay frontispiece crowned with a convoluted pediment at the level of the mansards.

south of the river, perhaps at Le Blond's instigation though they were not part of his masterplan and the French ideal order was to be moderated by traditional Russian accommodation to the nature of the site. In fact much of the city's definitive order is due to Zemstov and his Russian colleague, Pyotr Europkin (died 1740) who had studied in Rome at the instigation of the tsar: practitioner and theorist working in tandem, they were the principal operatives of the Commission for the Construction of Saint Petersburg established after fires destroyed the major south-bank settlement on Admiralty Island in 1736–37. That cleared the way for the first phase of the city's determined expansion south along the radial avenues which already existed in embryo – the main one, the Nevski Prospekt, leading to the Moscow road.

4.177a

Work on the fortress and church preoccupied Trezzini for most of his career. He was also commissioned to build the Alexander Nevski Monastery: his symmetrical distribution of its elements – a radical departure from the informal Russian tradition – survives but the central cathedral was rebuilt in the 1770s. Trezzini's major secular work was the complex of ecclesiastical and state administrative buildings known as the 'Twelve Colleges' (from 1722): the first element in the formal organization of Vasilevski, the extended elevation was revised by Schwertfeger. Meanwhile, in 1718, work began further east along Vasilevski's shore on the tsar's Kunstkammer – 'cabinet of curiosities' – to Mattarnovi's designs: the composition is in distinct parts, like the Twelve Colleges, but unlike the latter it is centralized on a tower: that may follow the late Muscovite estate church in its superimposition of octagonal entities but which is Baroque in scale at base and energized by the confrontation of concavity and convexity.

Mattarnovi – recommended by Schlüter – died in 1719, less than a year after construction of the Kunstkammer had begun: his multi-storey design for the tower may have been inspired by Schlüter's work on the Berlin Mint tower (see page 690) but was certainly not foreign to recent Muscovite practice. Over the next fifteen years modifications were introduced – to the tower and the internal arrangements – by Chiaveri and Zemtsov as well as Schwertfeger. The building was to be a centre of learning with a library and a museum, largely devoted to natural history, and an observatory over an anatomy theatre in the tower. The building was restored by Savva Chevakinski (from c. 1750) after extensive fire damage.

4.177b

4.177c

4.178a

4.178b

**›4.178 SAINT PETERSBURG, EARLY DOMES-
TIC BUILDINGS**: (a) Menshikov Mansion (from
1710); (b) Kikin Chambers (from 1714); (c) the imperial
summer town house (1711) in its garden setting.

For Aleksandr Menshikov, Fontana was assisted by
Gottfried Johann Schädel (of Hamburg) who arrived in
Russia with Schlüter. Before his untimely death the latter contributed little but did provide the panels which
relieve the façades of the tsar's summer palace. The
author of the Kikin house is unidentified: the patron
was implicated in intrigue with the crown prince and
executed in 1718; the palace was sequestered and
enlarged to house exhibits from the Kunstkammer.

4.178c

The town houses of the tsar's favourites, Aleksandr
Menshikov and Admiral Aleksandr Kikin, were the new
capital's premier grand domestic buildings. On Vasilevski, the former was begun in 1710 by the Italian Giovanni Maria Fontana in an elementary late-Renaissance
style with Dutch gables and a French roof. Kikin was
served by a bolder architect with a stronger sense of proportion which approximates the Baroque only insofar as
the abstract ordonnance of the frontispiece rises through
two storeys. The tsar himself was rather more modestly
accommodated by Trezzini in winter and summer quarters (from 1710): the latter survives in striking simplicity in its garden context as the best representative of its
author's secular style; its winter counterpart was replaced
at several reprises, first for Peter himself in 1721.**4.178**

Modesty is sustained in the conception of Tsar Peter's
retreat, Mon Plaisir, by the shore of the Gulf of Finland
at Peterhof. Inspired by the Trianon de Porcelaine at Versailles, it was begun before the demise of Le Blond in 1719
and completed by Braunstein in an essentially Dutch style:
a pavilion at the other end of the putative formal garden
would soon be inspired by Marly. On the site's eminence
parallel to the shore, however, the immigrant from Versailles
initiated work on the grand scale for the first in the series
of summer palaces conceived to rival the Sun King's palace

4.179a

4.179b

4.179d

4.179c

4.179e

itself – like those of the Habsburg emperor and the major
German potentates who we have encountered above. After
Le Blond the project was furthered by Michetti over the
four years before his return to Rome in 1723: he seems to
have respected the French formal garden design with Le

4.179g   4.179h

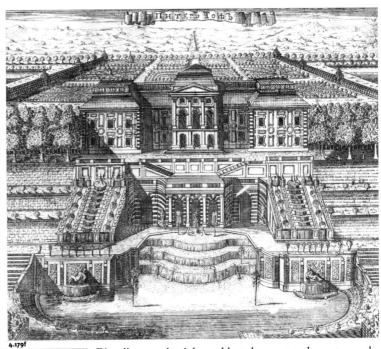

4.179f

›4.179 PETERHOF, THE SUMMER RETREAT OF PETER THE GREAT AND HIS SUCCESSORS: (a–d) Mon Plaisir (from c. 1716), south front, hall, gallery and cabinet details, (e) formal garden view along principal axis to Marly (right) with cascade (left), (f–h) Great Palace after Alexandre Le Blond and Niccolò Michetti (mid-18th-century engraving) and details of Pineau's cabinet, (i–s) post-Rastrelli (from 1745) entrance front, chapel, staircase, picture hall, ballroom, garden

front and fountains viewed from the north canal at two reprises, stepped fountain and canal from palace terrace, details of western garden fountain and cascade, site plan (1914).

Blond's central axial canal but the spectacular waterworks of the cascade at its head are due to his expertise in hydraulic engineering. He also respected the academic Classical style of the palace itself: the whole was transformed in the vast expansion of the next generation. There is the usual range of apartments to either side of formal core reception spaces with the appropriate gradations of semi-formal and free-ranging Rococo ornament. For the cabinets, Le Blond's compatriot Nicolas Pineau took the first steps towards the *genre pittoresque* with which he was to shock the champions of academic discipline in Paris (see page 331).**4.179**

Peter the Great's relatively austere style was first superceded by Trezzini for his grandson Peter II, who called for the rebuilding of the second Winter Palace in 1727. Thereafter Baroque opulence prevailed for the empresses Anna Ivannovna (1730–40) and Elizabeth Petrovna (1741–60) with Bartolomeo Rastrelli (1700–71). The principal impe-

rial architect of the century's median years was the son of a sculptor (also called Bartolomeo) who came to Saint Petersburg from Paris in 1716 – at the same time as, if not necessarily with, Le Blond. The son was sent abroad to further his education – certainly to Vienna, probably on to Italy – but the influence of the father persisted in a highly sculptural approach to the articulation of façades. Not the last of the Italians to play a formative role in the development of Saint Petersburg, he was certainly responsible for taking Russian building to its Baroque apogee.

The transformation of Peterhof (from 1745) was not Rastrelli's first imperial commission: he had worked with his father in Moscow, Saint Petersburg and Kurland (Latvia) under the German-orientated Anna who elevated him to Principal Architect. The two Rastrellis first worked together in Saint Petersburg on a vast summer palace to the east of the Petrine Summer Garden (destroyed in 1797) and a fourth Winter Palace on the southern shore of the Neva,

4.179j

4.179i   4.179m

4.179k

4.179l

4.179n

4.179o

4.179p

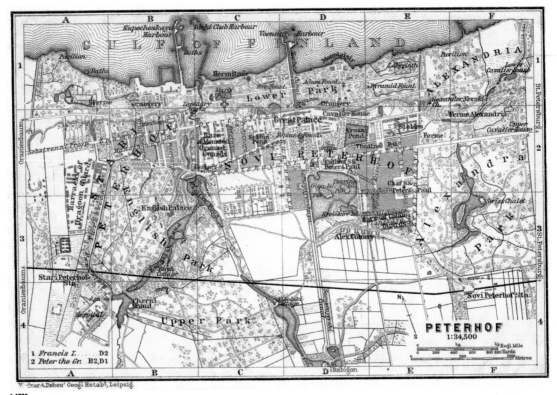

4.179s

4.179q

4.179r

next to the Admiralty (to which we shall return). However, Peterhof is the earliest complex on which the younger Rastrelli's intervention has left a major mark. This extended to galleries terminating in pavilions crowned with Rococo transmogrifications of the traditional Russian cluster of five cupolas. Rising over the cascade enhanced with sculpture by the elder Rastrelli, the central façades were articulated only with pilasters in the manner of Le Blond's more restrained French academic colleagues. However, they were enlivened by a variety of convoluted window frames, zakomari pediments and incurved mansard roofs which depart from the Mansartian legacy towards the Hildebrantian. Inside, the refurbishment achieved its apogee in the progression to the ballroom from the great staircase.

While Braunstein was still working under Le Blond at Peterhof in 1717, he was deployed at the 'Imperial Village' – Tsarskoe Selo – to build a modest country house for Tsar Peter's second wife, Catherine: her daughter, who had lived there, embarked on enlargements on a scale comparable to Michetti's Peterhof when she succeeded to the throne as Empress Elizabeth. The commission was let to Zemstov, who was also called on for a Hermitage in the park (1743): after his death within three years both projects were furthered by his protégé Andrei Kvasov (1717–82)and Savva Chevakinski (1709–c. 1775) who began the hunting pavilion of Mon Bijou on an X-shaped plan (from 1747). Rastrelli was called on to rework the Hermitage and Mon Bijou in 1748 and then to add a lakeside 'grotto': three years later he was commissioned to demolish most of the new palace and start again, the empress's ambitions having abandoned constraint.**4.180**

4.180b

4.180c

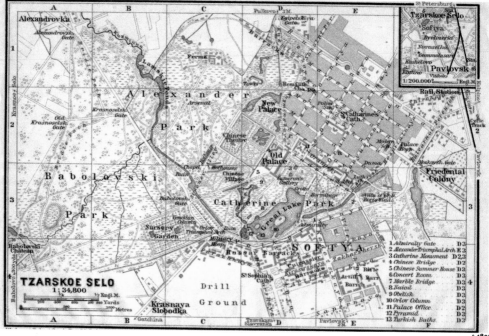

4.180a

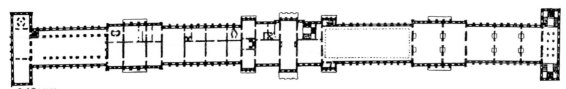

4.180d @ 1:2000

›4.180 THE PRINCIPAL PALACES OF THE
EMPRESS ELIZABETH: (a–j) Tsarskoe Selo, Ekaterinski Palace (named for the patroness's mother,
Catherine I), site plan, Hermitage (from 1743, transformed from 1748), Grotto (from 1749), Great Palace,
plan, garden-front central pavilions, general view
and corps de logis, Great Hall, Amber Room and
chapel; (k–p) Saint Petersburg, Winter Palace, third
development from the north-west and from the south
with the Admiralty (left, engraved by Vinogradov and
Kachalov respectively, after Makhaev), fourth phase
plan, from the north-west and south-west, Jordan
staircase.

The original Ekaterinski scheme was similar in
extent to the original Peterhof, with a central block
(consisting of three three-bay pavilions framing four-
bay corps de logis) linked to side blocks by wooden

The palace unconstrained

The extent of Rastrelli's response to his patroness's conception of imperial grandeur has rarely been precedented or exceeded. Closing a forecourt
defined only by one-storey galleries and service ranges, its great uni-axial
range is treated to division into nine units: a pair of three-bay terminal
pavillons (one for the chapel), two pairs of eleven-bay corps de logis separated by two nine-bay intermediate pavillons and a seventeen-bay central
block. In determination to provide invigorating incident with alternating
systems of articulation, Rastrelli applied his colossal Order of engaged columns to the three-bay frontispieces of the central block and pavillons but
extended it throughout the recessed corps de logis. There, in contrast to the
rustication of the pavillon basements, it is carried on atlante whose smaller
relatives support the arcaded windows of the piano nobile: the anthropo-

4.180e

4.18of

4.18oh

galleries: Krasov began the curved buildings defining the forecourt; Chevakinski completed the central block, rebuilt the galleries in masonry and extended the scheme to a chapel (east) and an orangery (west); Rastrelli replaced the galleries with the intermediate ranges flanking the median blocks and added a third storey throughout. Like Peterhof, the walls were painted yellow (rather than the present blue) and the articulating agents white – except for the gilded anthropomorphic members (which were removed by Catherine II but revived by the Soviet restorers).

morphism has rarely if ever been matched since the great Temple of Zeus at Agrigento in Sicily – which Rastrelli is unlikely to have known – and it certainly trumps even its most vigorous manifestation in the works of the Austrian imperial masters. Thus, however, the secondary eclipses the primary constituent elements of a composition which has failed to convince all observers that its author's objective of avoiding monotony was achieved with essential coherence: yet even Jules Hardouin-Mansart has failed to satisfy all critics of his extended scheme for Versailles precisely because they perceive its essential coherence as monotonous.

4.18og

4.18oi

4.18oj

4.18ok

Empress Elizabeth called on the younger Rastrelli for comprehensive revision of the scheme he had pursued for Anna: this involved the vast expansion of the fourth, definitive complex from 1754. The recessed range perpendicular to the southern shore of the Neva, facing west towards the Admiralty, survives in profile and some detail but the mansards of the 1730s were rejected in favour of low-pitched roofs behind continuous balustrades. Extending beyond anything imaginable in Rome, the new multi-bay north and south fronts – facing the river and the palace square respectively

The original project for the fourth Winter Palace was an extension of the third to incorporate the neighbouring Apraksin Palace, which Anna occupied after her accession in 1730. After work had begun Rastrelli per-

4.18on

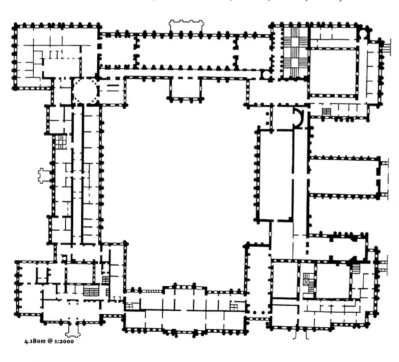

4.18om @ 1:2000

4.18oo

suaded the empress that her needs could be met only with rebuilding over the existing foundations. She died in her provisional accommodation before her ambitions were realized: Elizabeth exceeded them.

4.18ol

– project and recede in rhythmic counterpoint. Europe's last great Baroque compositions, unlike Peterhof they are variously articulated with Orders of engaged columns – colossal over regular – in denial of the grand French approach to the integration of projections but with somewhat greater consistency than the confection at Tsarskoe Selo. Exceeding even the Louvre in scale, comparable exercises may best be sought in Austria or Germany after Fischer and Hildebrandt. Colossal Orders, even of engaged columns, and convoluted pediments were favoured by many palatial builders in the

orbit of the western empire and the articulating agents were often offset in white against yellow. Yellow was favoured in Russia too – as a 'modern' alternative to the traditional red – but unique to Rastrelli's Baroque is the range of colours from blue to green, via turquoise in particular.

4.180p

Most of the Winter Palace's original interiors were destroyed by fire in 1837: the great Jordan staircase in the river range is the spectacular exception. Empress Elizabeth's Summer Palace at Tsarskoe Selo suffered no such

›4.181 RASTRELLI AND HIS COLLEAGUES
HOUSING THE NOBILITY: (a) Anchikov (from 1741),
mid-18th-century record (engraved by Vasilev after
Makhaev); (b) Stroganov (from 1752), Nevski Prospekt
front; (c) Sheremetev (from c. 1750), Fontanka Canal
front.

4.181a

fate until the cataclysm of the Nazi onslaught in World
War II. Reconstruction after total devastation has reproduced the extreme opulence of the patroness's principal
reception rooms and the sager style with which much
else was transformed under her Enlightened successor,
Catherine II (1762–96) – but that is beyond our remit here.

Rastrelli's prestige at court inevitably attracted commissions from grandees, such as Count Sergei Grigoriyevich
Stroganov who developed his large site at the corner of
the Nevski Prospekt and the Moika Canal from 1752.
Earlier, Empress Elizabeth called on her architect to finish the former Anichkov Palace for her favourite, Count
Aleksei Razumovski: facing the Fontanka at the corner of

4.181b

4.181c

4.182b

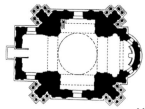

4.182a @ 1:1000

›**4.182 RASTRELLI AND THE CHURCH:** (a, b) Kiev, S. Andrew's cathedral (from 1745, revised 1748), plan and general view from the south-west; (c–g) Saint Petersburg, New Convent of the Resurrection (Voskresenski Novodevichi, from 1748, known as Smolni, 'tar', because of its site near naval storeyards), plan, lateral section, model of complex and of church opened to reveal interior, general view from the west.

The foundation was to cater for the education of the daughters of the nobility – and perhaps the patroness's retirement in suitable splendour. She instructed Rastrelli to base the design of the centrally placed cathedral on the Moscow Kremlin's Uspenski: he adopted the quincunx plan but his mass and its articulation honoured the instruction more in the breach than the letter. The model was ready in 1756, seven years after the first planning phase. Construction of the enclosing fabric took another four years. The Seven Years' War

the Nevski Prospekt, it had been left unfinished by Zemstov on his death in 1743. Among other Russians active in the domestic field in mid-century, Savva Chevakinski contributed the Sheremetev Palace: further west on the Fontanka, it retains much of its original aspect despite repeated refurbishment.**4.181**

Rastrelli's career was overwhelmingly secular: indeed, the secular eclipsed the religious in architectural activity throughout the Petrine era at Saint Petersburg, if not in Moscow where the Narishkin mode persisted.**4.182** However, the principal architect of the Elizabethan reign was entrusted with two important ecclesiastical projects. The

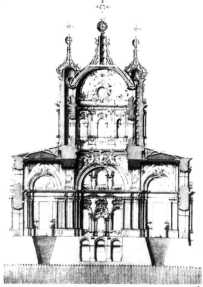

4.182d

4.182f
and the empress's death in 1761 halted progress. Therafter the bell-tower was eliminated and the interior was not decorated until the 1830s.

4.182e

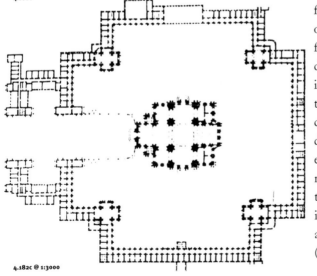

4.182c @ 1:3000

first was the cathedral of S. Andrew at Kiev, the centre of the Ukrainian homeland of the empress's Razumovski favourite: the result was a hybrid essay, expressing the traditional Russo-Byzantine quincunx in the massing but not in the cruciform space. The second commission was for the Smolni Convent on the south-eastern outskirts of the capital, conceived to reassert the centrality of the Orthodox Church to the imperial monarchy – and mark the empress's nationalist rejection of her predecessor's Germanic bent. Outside and in, this time, Rastrelli translated the traditional quincunx form of the Orthodox Church into the idiom of the Baroque as the formal, but exuberant, centrepiece of a vast symmetrical monastic scheme (from 1748).

4.182g

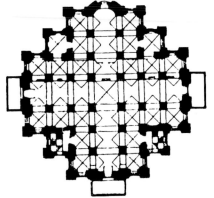

4.183a @ 1:1000

The realization of the Kiev cathedral project was entrusted to a local architect on Rastrelli's return to work in Saint Petersburg, Peterhof and Tsarskoe Selo. Given his commitments to the Crown, moreover, the non-imperial commissions in the capital went to his Russian colleagues who proved themselves adept at working in his hybrid mode – traditional in plan and section, modern in elevation. Of these, outstanding is the cathedral of S. Nikolai built for the naval community to the designs of Savva Chevakinski (from 1753). At the core is the canonical quincunx but it is expanded in stages into the arms of a Greek cross on two separate levels. The elevation through the colossal

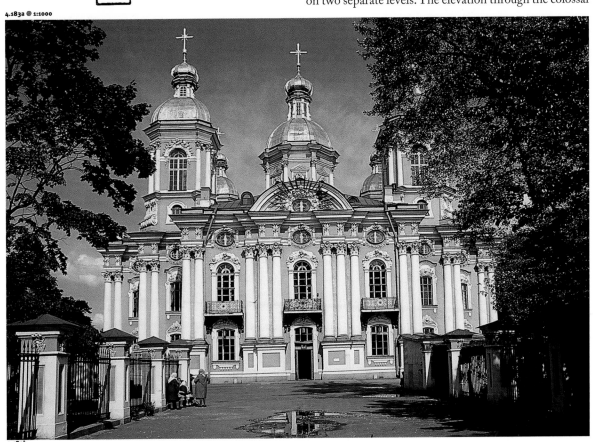

4.183b

4.183c

Corinthian columns of the four similar fronts to the five domes and onion cupolas is resplendent in blue, white and gold.**4.183**

Of course there were various permutations of the Elizabethan style in the churches of Moscow and elsewhere but none eclipses Chevakinski's great work. In height and complexity, however, the latter's detached bell-tower cedes to several of its equivalents in or about the old capital, not least in the S. Sergius-Trinity Monastery at Sergiev Posad. These adjuncts apart, the Saint Petersburg complex of S. Nikolai was to be the last exercise of its kind before the Baroque style, taken to its apogee by Rastrelli, ceded to the so-called Neoclassical.

4.183d

4.183e

5.1a

5.1c

PART 5 THE CATHOLIC SOUTH AND ITS NEW WORLDS

5.1d

5.1b

**›5.1 IBERIA AND THE IBERIAN AMERICAN
COLONIES:** (a, b) maps by Johann Baptist Homann
(Amsterdam 1730 and London 1711 respectively); (c,
d) the insignia of the kingdoms of Spain and Portugal.

1 HABSBURG TO BOURBON IN NAPLES AND SICILY

Domenico Fontana had taken his conservative Roman style to Naples and made a rather more impressive – if still monotonous – mark with the vice-regal seat there than he had with his Sistine palaces (AIC5, page 279). As late as 1620, his assistant Bartolomeo Picchiatti was still perpetrating his dry academicism in works like S. Giorgio dei Genovesi.**5.2** The Neapolitan subjects of the Spanish king were not content with monotony but Spain was not the source of their relief.

When Fontana settled in Naples in 1596, other immigrants from Rome were already engaged on important projects for ecclesiastical clients. Foremost among these was the renovation of the Certosa di S. Martino by Giovanni Antonio Dosio (1533–1609). This embraced the refashioning of the 14th-century church, sacristy and treasury, and the construction of a grand, arcaded cloister within the medieval perimeter: begun in 1591, these principal elements in the scheme were advanced, but incomplete, on Dosio's demise.**5.3, 5.7c**

›5.2 DOMENICO FONTANA AND HIS CIRCLE IN NAPLES: (a) Palazzo Reale, piazza front (from c. 1600); (b) S. Giorgio dei Genovesi, façade (Bartolomeo Picchiatti, c. 1620).

The palace's arcaded basement (reinforced in the 19th century with grand niches containing statues of Neapolitan kings), the Ionic pilasters of the piano nobile and the abstract grid of the top floor all help modulate the monotony of the Sistine palaces.

5.2b

5.3a

**›5.3 GIOVANNI ANTONIO DOSIO AND COL-
LABORATORS AT THE CERTOSA DI S. MAR-
TINO:** (a, b) details of vaulting in the adjuncts to the
sacristy, (c) general view of cloister.

Born in San Gimignano, Dosio trained as a goldsmith and engraver but, in Rome from 1548, he was
soon associated with the circle of Michelangelo. He
worked on the cloister of S. Maria degli Angeli (inconclusively sometimes attributed to the master) which
seems to have inspired his work for the Neapolitan Car-
thusians – though the terrace and second storey of the
latter have no precedent in the former. Mainly active
in Florence in the 1580s, he was in Naples from 1590
where his late-Mannerist style is best exemplified in
the designs for the stucco framework of the vaulting in
S. Martino's church and its ancillary spaces: the Cavalier d'Arpino (Giuseppe Cesari) was responsible for the
frescoes in the choir vault and sacristy; the Cavalier
Massimo (Massimo Stanzione) contributed those of
the vestibule.

5.3b

5.3c

FABRIZIO GRIMALDI AND HIS
NEAPOLITAN CIRCLE

Before Fontana's arrival, moreover, several grand schemes
had been launched by richly endowed Counter-Reformation orders which matched their Roman works in
scale and magnificence – if not always in plan. Foremost
among these is the Gesù Nuovo begun by the Jesuit father
Giuseppe Valeriano (1542–96) who had worked in Spain
and Genoa but came via Rome: the grand Corinthian
Order is that of the Jesuit's Roman mother church but
the plan departs from Vignola's formula in favour of Bramante's centralized one extended west by one set of nave
and aisle bays: the intermediary is Galeazzo Alessi's S.
Maria di Carignano (Genoa; AIC5, page 261).

A decade before Carlo Maderno transformed S. Pietro,
the latter's extended basilican plan is preceded to greater
extent by the Theatine father Fabrizio Grimaldi (1543–1613):
he had worked on the mother church of his order in Rome,
S. Andrea della Valle. Like the latter, S. Maria della Sapienza and Santi Apostoli have interconnected side chapels
in the Vignolan manner instead of full aisles; S. Paolo Mag-

giore, the principal church of the Neapolitan Theatines, was rebuilt over existing foundations but Grimaldi's wholly original S. Maria degli Angeli a Pizzofalcone is an aisled basilica which rivals all contemporary Roman work in the grandeur of its tunnel-vaulted volumes.**5·4, 5·5**

The first generation of architects wholly active in the 17th century were clearly impressed by Grimaldi's achievement: they included two Neapolitans, Dosio's protégé Giovanni Giacomo di Conforto (1569–1630) and the Dominican Fra Giuseppe Nuvolo (1570–1643). The latter first followed Valeriano's Gesù Nuovo with another variant on Galeazzo Alessi's S. Maria di Carignano type for S. Maria della Sanità (1602): he went on, via renovation of Latin-cross works, to experiment with elliptical plans for S. Sebastiano and S. Carlo all'Arena (1631).

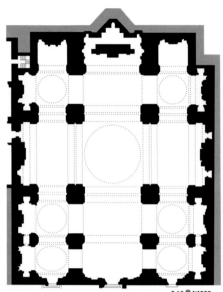

5.4a @ 1:1000

5.4c

5.4b

›5.4 GIUSEPPE VALERIANO AND THE NEA-POLITAN GESÙ NUOVO, from 1593, decorated from 1601, refurbished from 1639 after fire damage: (a) plan, (b) exterior on piazza with the Guglia dell'Immacolata (from 1747), (c) interior.

The church was built on the site of the Palazzo di Salerno (1470s) and incorporates the 'diamond' stone rustication of the latter's façade. Contrary to Valeriano's relatively austere intention – which honoured the original ethos of his Order – the interior was embellished in accordance with the fashion for rich chromaticism which flourished in the first decades of the 17th century. The plan derives from Alessi's great Genoses church of S. Maria in Carignano, itself a revision of Bramante's centralized scheme for S. Pietro (AIC5, pages 261, 275).

›5.5 FABRIZIO GRIMALDI AND THE NEAPOLITAN BASILICA: (a) S. Maria degli Angeli a Pizzofalcone (from 1600), crossing; (b, c) Ss. Apostoli (from 1610 and 1626), view from nave to sanctuary and plan.

Grimaldi's most popular work in Naples, the Cappella di S. Gennaro in the cathedral, has been transformed

5.5a

5.5b

5.5c @ 1:1000

in response to its very venerability. His first great work in his adopted city, the basilican S. Paolo Maggiore, was constrained by existing work: the body, with its traditional coffered ceiling, was added to a refurbished transept within the perimeter of an antique temple. The vertical lines of Grimaldi's Ss. Apostoli's Vignolan nave elevation are asserted by breaking the entablature over the pilasters in the manner of Giacomo della Porta at S. Maria ai Monti. Stepped pilasters proliferated at Pizzofalcone, as in Rome at S. Andrea della Valle.

While Grimaldi was expanding his work on S. Paolo, the basilican form was being perpetuated by Dionisio Nencione for the Oratorians' church of the Gerolomini with coffered ceiling and clerestory over a nave arcade carried on columns – but that was the last of the type.

Conforto was more prolific if less experimental, as in his Latin-cross exercises for S. Francesco Saverio (now S. Ferdinando) and S. Maria delle Anime del Purgatorio. Involvement in both these works began the career of the most prominent artist of High Baroque Naples, Cosimo Fanzago (1591–1678): a sculptor from Bergamo, he came south in 1608 with a taste for the mordant informed by his encounter with Bernardo Buontalenti on his passage through Florence. The degree of that involvement is elusive, beyond the façades at least: a clue is provided by the skulls with which the Purgatorio is festooned and, certainly, his first works elsewhere in Naples are sculptures in marble.**5.6**

COSIMO FANZAGO

Fanzago's architectural career emerged from the commission to complete the cloister of the Certosa di S. Martino, begun by Dosio c. 1591 and continued by Conforto: busts of saintly figures were required over the doors in the corners

5.6b

5.6a

but the convoluted framework, mannered in the mode of Buontalenti, came first and was complete in 1631. Contemporary is the balustrade of the monks' cemetery, ingenious in its oscillation between architectural and floral motifs under laurel-crowned skulls. Next came the decoration of the church which Dosio had begun refashioning: Fanzago's mark is stamped in the richly chromatic marble inlay on the limited planar surfaces of the elevation and the vast expanse of the floor. Emergent at the Certosa, Fanzago's decorative style is rich in relief, unorthodox in detail, and intricate in patterning with richly coloured marble inlay (*pietra dura*) on plane surfaces.

›5.6 GIOVANNI GIACOMO DI CONFORTO AND THE NEAPOLITAN CHURCH WITH EMBELLISH-MENT IN THE STYLE OF COSIMO FANZAGO: (a, b) S. Maria delle Anime del Purgatorio (from 1616), interior and exterior detail; (c, d) S. Francesco Saverio (from c. 1628, rededicated to S. Ferdinando after the suppression of the Jesuits in 1767), exterior detail and interior.

Conforto is reputed to have collaborated with Cola di Franco on the earlier of these two churches: the high altar and Mastrilli family monument in the sanctuary are attributable to Fanzago. The embellishment of the façade is Fanzagan too – the winged skulls of Limbo and pomegranates of regeneration touchingly relevant to the dedication of th e church in sympathy with the souls in Purgatory (as Blunt notes).

The attribution of S. Francesco Saverio has been disputed between the supporters of Conforto and Fanzago. However, a drawing inscribed *Confortus* (at S. Martino) asserts that its author provided the initial plans late in life: Fanzago revised them for execution some two years later. The embellishment is, therefore, largely due to the immigrant – though the choir was enlarged in 1685. The lower level of the façade (from c. 1660), with its richly framed niches, is attributed to Fanzago: the upper level, with pediment instead of balustrade, dates from less inspired 18th-century alterations.

5.6d

5.6c

›5.7 COSIMO FANZAGO AND THE NEAPOLI-TAN CHURCH: (a–c) Certosa di S. Martino, monks' cemetery detail, cloister portal and interior of church; (d) S. Lorenzo Maggiore, detail of Cappella Cacace (from 1643); (e, f) S. Maria Ascensione a Chiaia (begun 1626 but incomplete until 1662), plan and interior; (g) S. Giuseppe delle Scalze a Pontecorvo (from 1643), axonometric (after Blunt); (h, i) S. Maria della Sapienza, axonometric (after Blunt) and detail of exterior (from c. 1638); (j) S. Maria Egiziaca a Pizzofalcone (from 1651, completed in 1717 by Arcangelo Guglielmelli), plan.

Characteristic of Fanzago is the crisp assertion of the decorative framework and the range of the latter between High Renaissance Classicism and complex Mannerism. Characteristic of Naples in façade type is termination with a balustrade rather than a pediment. In contrast to such an external stair, with the façade as backdrop, the Sapienza and Pontecorvo churches have stairs within the portico: in contrast to the latter, the earlier of these two works is unique in Fanzago's œuvre in its abstinence from Mannerist detail as a foil to Classical severity but the triple serliana does not express the reality of ascension within.

5.7a   5.7d

Fanzago's radical inventiveness as a decorator is manifest in his many altar and chapel designs but was not characteristic of his church planning.**5·7** Often constrained by existing work or altered by others in extended execution, the range of his ecclesiastical building embraces the Greek cross with extended sanctuary (the Ascensione a Chiaia, his first

5.7b   5.7c

5.7f

independent work, begun in 1626, or S. Maria Maggiore, his late masterpiece, begun in 1653), the elongated Greek cross (S. Giuseppe delle Scalze a Pontecorvo, from 1643) and, ultimately, the purely centralized imposition of cross on octagon (S. Teresa a Chiaia and S. Maria Egiziaca a Pizzofalcone, both from c. 1651). The disparate spaces of these works manifest preference for a measure of centralization but no consistent recognition of developments in Rome is apparent until their author returned from two years there in 1650: both his late centralized works recall S. Agnese in Piazza Navona and S. Maria Maggiore develops the type of

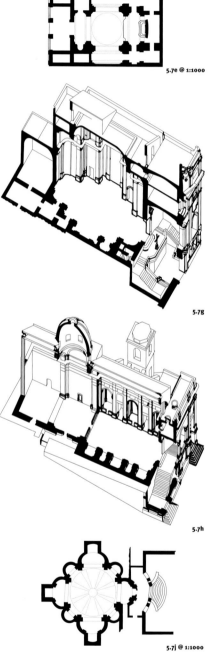

5.7e @ 1:1000

5.7g

5.7h

5.7j @ 1:1000

5.1i

›5.8 COSIMO FANZAGO'S CIVIC AND DOMES-

**›5.8 COSIMO FANZAGO'S CIVIC AND DOMES-
TIC LEGACY:** (a) Guglia di S. Gennaro (base from 1637, column and statue by 1660), general view; (b) Palazzo Donn'Anna (from c. 1642), engraved view (18th century); (c) Palazzo Maddaloni (renovated for Diomede Carafa, Duca di Maddaloni, who acquired the building in 1652 and proceeded immediately with the aggrandizement of the entrance sequence), portal; (d) Palazzo Reale (from c. 1650, as recorded before 1837).

The *guglia* type of columnar monument, dedicated to a saint, was usually erected ex voto in a prominent urban space: this one is dedicated to the patron saint of Naples, the dedicatee of the adjacent cathedral – where pilgrims witness the miraculous liquefaction of his reliquary blood on the anniversary of his martyrdom. The monument, petrifying a portable festival pole, set a precedent much followed in the kingdom of Naples and elsewhere in Catholic Europe.

The Palazzo Donn'Anna was commissioned by the Duke of Medina, the Spanish viceroy, and his very wealthy Carafa wife c. 1642 but work stopped two years later when the duke was recalled to Spain.

5.8a

Valeriano's Gesù Nuovo in reference to S. Carlo ai Catinari (see page 57). However, working on churches raised above street level by the city's hilly topography, Fanzago was masterly in his provision of staircase access in or before a portico behind a specifically Neapolitan type of screen façade.

Apart from several portals and the Guglia di S. Gennaro, Fanzago's major surviving contribution to secular architecture in Naples is the grandiose Palazzo Donn'Anna which, unfinished, lowers over the beautiful bay at Posillipo like a vast hulk. In conception it was a hybrid palazzo-villa, its crypto-portico open to the bay, its first-floor court open to access from the north and to the view of the bay through the loggia above the portico to the south: separated by the double-height loggia, the waterfront range with the patrons' twin apartments is surmounted by terraces between pavilions. The grandest surviving Neapolitan secular work of Fanzago's time is the imperial staircase in the vice regal (later royal) palace: execution, at least, is uncertainly attributed to Francesco Antonio Picchiatti who otherwise has yet to emerge from Fanzago's shadow.**5.8**

5.8b

5.8c

5.8d

5.9

The younger Picchiatti, who lived on until 1694, was prolific but little of outstanding quality survives time and decay. Indeed, after Fanzago's death in 1678 there was a generation before Neapolitans achieved new significance, mainly with the reassertion of the role of the column in the internal articulation of churches. This was the contribution, notably, of Dionisio Lazzari (1617–89)for S. Maria dell'Aiuto, Arcangelo Guglielmelli (1648–1723) for S. Angelo a Nilo and the Rosario al largo delle Pigne, and Giovan Battista Nauclerio (1666–1740) for S. Francesco delle Cappuccinelle and S. Maria delle Grazie. The typical Neapolitan portico façade persisted with either applied columns or pilasters – in one notable case at least, with Guarinesque trefoil openings in the side bays and a Borrominesque pediment.**5.9–5.11**

›**5.9 DIONISIO LAZZARI:** S. Maria dell'Aiuto (begun 1674), the near-Greek-cross interior towards the polygonal sanctuary apse.

›**5.10 GIOVAN BATTISTA NAUCLERIO:** S. Maria delle Grazie a Mondragone, Greek-cross interior towards sanctuary (before 1724).

›**5.11 MARCELLO GUGLIELMELLI:** S. Giuseppe dei Ruffi, portico façade (from c. 1715) to Dionisio Lazzari's Latin-cross church.

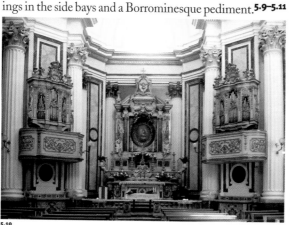

5.10

5.11

(a, b) S. Croce and the adjacent
Celestine convent, façades (first and second halves of
the 17th century respectively), interior detail; (c) S. Giovanni Battista (Rosario), north front (from 1690); (d, e)
S. Matteo, plan and façade (completed c. 1700).

S. Croce was begun in 1353 but little progress had
been made by the mid-16th century: thereafter the
lower storey of the façade was embellished (reputedly
under the direction of one Gabriele Riccardi except
for the portal); the upper storey (attributed to Cesare
Penna and Giuseppe Zimbalo) is dated 1646; the conventual buildings were added in the second half of
the 17th century (to designs claimed for Zimbalo). The
eclecticism typical of the style extends to Romanesque
reminiscence in S. Croce's circular window and stocky
freestanding Order – especially in the archaic basilican
interior. The model was the actual Romanesque church

LECCE

In a style very different to that of the early 18th-century
Neapolitan masters, the column was reasserting itself in
the basilican churches of Apulia – if, indeed, the strength
of the Romanesque tradition had ever waned there.
Represented most notably at Lecce, the region's peculiar
style is essentially peripheral. Its over-riding characteristic is mannered decorative detail, often recalling the
Romanesque – even applied to Romanesque buildings.
Overblown in the rich plasticity encouraged by the easily
worked local stone, it was elaborated as in a Renaissance
pattern book from early in the 17th century. Prominent
examples include S. Croce and the attached Celestine
convent. That complex was worked on throughout the

5.12b

5.12a

17th century but the church had been finished by 1650. Elsewhere thereafter, rampant plasticity of ornament was pruned back but applied sculpture still masked a lack of either kind of Baroque movement from a base plane through curvature or progression in mass. The most prominent examples include the north fronts of the cathedral and the Dominican Rosario church. The exception which proves the rule is the façade added to the church of S. Matteo towards the end of the century.**5.12**

of Ss. Niccolò e Cataldo to which the post-Renaissance repertory of pattern-book detail was also applied.

The long-lived local architect Giuseppe Zimbalo (1617–1710) may be seen to have exerted increasing control over sculptural embellishment: his progress may be measured from the cathedral (which he finished between 1659 and 1682) to the Dominican Rosario (from c. 1690, completed 1728), where the colossal Order prevails over the still-prolix superficial ornament but no progression is developed from the sides to the applied columns in the centre.

S. Matteo, begun in 1667 to plans attributed to Giovanni Andrea Larducci, is highly exceptional in its context for the curvature and counter-curvature of its façade: however, rather than an ellipse which may be understood to have sent the fabric bellying outwards, the interior is a rectangular hall with rounded corners.

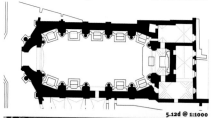

5.12d @ 1:1000

5.12c

5.12e

FERDINANDO SANFELICE AND HIS CONTEMPORARIES

It was not until the new century that significant new talent emerged in Naples. Among those born there about the time of the past master's death and embarking on their careers in their twenties, Ferdinando Sanfelice (1675–1748) and Domenico Antonio Vaccaro (1678–1745) may be singled out. They complemented one another. The latter was active primarily in the ecclesiastical field but is credited with one of the largest schemes for a Neapolitan noble seat: the Palazzo Spinelli di Tarsia, with its convoluted approach oversailing the garden, would have overlooked the city from the Salita Pontecorvo had it been realized. On the other hand, though Sanfelice's prolific œuvre includes distinguished churches based on unorthodox plans, it was in the genre of the palazzo that his originality is best demonstrated.

In his ecclesiastical work, much of it surviving, Vaccaro enjoyed planning in regular geometry but he excelled in the masking of structure with purely decorative forms: thus anti-architectonic, his work has little in common with French

›5.13 NEAPOLITAN ROCOCO IN THE CIRCLE OF DOMENICO ANTONIO VACCARO: (a) Certosa di S. Martino, altar-rail detail (c. 1700); (b, c) S. Chiara, cloister pergola and detail (c. 1740); (d) Palazzo Spinelli di Tarsia, project drawing (1739); (e) S. Maria delle Grazie (Calvizzano), detail of dome (late-1730s); (f, g) S. Maria della Concezione a Montecalvario, axonometric drawing (after Blunt), dome detail.

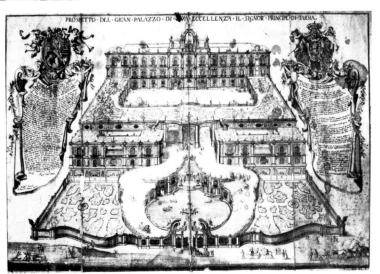

5.13e

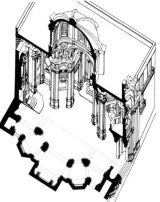

5.13f

5.13g

Rococo. Apart from the pictorial majolica revetment of the forest of pergola columns in the cloister of S. Chiara, the most spectacular example is the florid canopy floated in the dome of the presbytery he added to S. Maria delle Grazie at Calvizzano. In church furnishings, richly inlaid altars and their rails in particular, he and his follower Giuseppe Sammartino (1720–93) eliminated the structural elements which the Baroque masters had delighted in manipulating. More particularly, they may well be seen to have invented a Rococo mode of somewhat sinister, abstract dimension for rocaille motifs which is quite distinct from its usually more playful French counterpart.**5.13**

Doubtless under the influence of Borromini, Sanfelice experimented with various centralized forms in his planning of both ecclesiastical and secular buildings: S. Maria della Consolazione of Villanova (from 1737) is a hexagonal example, the project for S. Giovanni delle Dame, Capua (before 1718) is based on a square with canted corners. Most of his surviving churches are more conventional, at least in plan: the Nunziatella, Pontecorvo, sustains the influence of Grimaldi but the conservatism of the basilican façade is countered by the canting of the corners of the central block and the variations on the theme of the broken pediment as

5.14a

›5.14 ECCLESIASTICAL WORKS OF FERDI-NANDO SANFELICE: (a) Capua, S. Giovanni delle Dame, project section (c. 1718); (b, c) altar project and design for a triumphal arch (Museo Nazionale di Capodimonte); (d, e) Naples, Villanova, S. Maria della Consolazione (from 1737), plan, detail of vault; (f) Nardò, cathedral façade project (c. 1715); (g) Pontecorvo, Nunziatella (Santissima Annunziata, from 1713), façade.

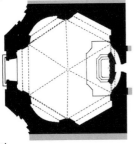

5.14b

5.14c

5.14d

5.14e

a backdrop to a street scene. Similarly, urban scenography seems to have prompted Sanfelice's idiosyncratic variation on the standard format for the façade of Nardò's medieval basilica. This is not uncommon in the era, of course, but Sanfelice had a special facility for the theatrical.**5.14**

Like the Sicilian Juvarra, the Neapolitan Sanfelice first made his mark in the invention of ephemeral props for festive occasions and stage sets. Thus his theatrical facility revived the characteristically Mannerist quality of *sprezzatura* for the late Baroque age of his native city with work rich in diverse decorative detail but more especially rich in the unorthodox layering of space and dramatic lighting effects – again like Juvarra. Hardly less than Giulio Romano, he enjoyed games of rhythmic variation in the incidence of an articulating Order – as on the façade of the Palazzo Serra di Cassano. It is within, in the realm of the staircase, that this facility is most spectacularly

The Capua project probably dates from after 1718: it would have been contemporary with Vaccaro's preferred project which itself post-dates that master's Concezione church, Montecalvario, of 1718. Sanfelice began the Nunziatella planning process with a star.

5.14f

5.14g

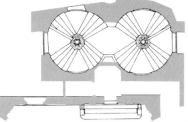

5.15a

5.15b

5.15c

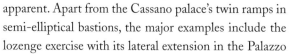

apparent. Apart from the Cassano palace's twin ramps in semi-elliptical bastions, the major examples include the lozenge exercise with its lateral extension in the Palazzo

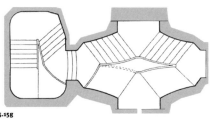

5.15g

›**5.15 SANFELICE AND THE NEAPOLITAN PALAZZO:** (a–c) Palazzo Sanfelice (from 1724), street front, left court stair cage and inner spiral plan; (d–f) Palazzo Serra di Cassano (1725), plan, court front, staircase; (g) Palazzo Bartolomeo di Maio, staircase plan (c. 1726).

Sanfelice devised two exercises for his own family palace. One, enclosed, enjoyed the junction of contiguous spiral ramps in lozenge-shaped landings. The other revitalized the open type of staircase favoured

5.15e

5.15f

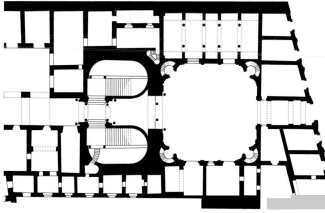

5.15d @ 1:1000

by the Neapolitans and reversed the Spanish imperial type (with its central flight ascending to a landing from which twin flights double back to a platform
above the entrance vestibule): the lateral flights start
from the vestibule and rise parallel to their cage front
on no less than three levels; meeting them at the first
of the central landings and echoed above, the first in
the sequence of central flights serves the raised garden
behind the structure and is fronted by a grotto.

In a great arcade opposite the entrance, the twin
parallel flights of the Serra di Cassano staircase turn on
semi-circular half-landings whose convex curve is presented to the line of approach like a medieval bastion,
and then rise through a square landing to a bridge over
the carriageway at the level of the piano nobile portal.
Elaboration on the theme for a palace in the Via Foria
extended to a series of central flights in place of the
carriageway. The approach has its parallel in the palace
built by Fischer von Erlach for Prince Eugene in Vienna

Bartolomeo di Maio and those in Sanfelice's own family
palace with diagonal ramps in open cages facing the court
beyond a double spiral inside.**5.15**

If rhythmic vitality was the hallmark of Sanfelice's style
in the genre of the palazzo façade, his successors opted
for an extreme simplicity which is usually received by
modern critics as monotony. On his death in 1748, Ferdinando Fuga and Luigi Vanvitelli were called from Rome
by the Bourbon King Charles III, bent on reforming his
Neapolitan kingdom. The ruler was an advanced product
of the Enlightenment which would characterize a new
age in Europe's cultural – and political – life and reason
was to rule the king's endeavours. Nowhere is the result
more worthy – or more stultifying – than in Fuga's hugely
extensive design for the Real Albergo dei Poveri which
was executed from 1752 on what were then the outskirts
of Naples. At the same time at Caserta, to the north,
Vanvitelli was engaged in realizing the king's ambitions
for a complex vast enough to house the royal family, its
entourage and the reformed, centralized administration:
we shall view that tremendous work in the context of
late-Baroque palatine building for both branches of the
southern Bourbons (see below, pages 848f).

The Mannerist rustication is, of course, the typical
product of local architects armed with Serlio or a derivative pattern book. The author of the Palazzo S. Ninfa
portal has been identified as Giuseppe Giacalone. The
author of the Messina citadel portal is unlikely to have
been the military engineer imported from service to
the Habsburgs in the north to build the complex itself
(under the Italianized name Carlo Norimbergo).

SICILY

A conservative late-Romanesque reminiscence persisted
in the island well into the era of the Renaissance. A conservative late-Renaissance style persisted there well into
the 17th century, occasionally with Michelangelesque
or Vignolan motifs. Thus, on the one hand, Serlio
had informed the work of Giuseppe Giacalone on the
Palazzo S. Ninfa in Palermo from 1588 and was exceeded
in complexity a century later by the anonymous architect of the Porta Grazia in Messina. On the other hand,
the Spanish master-mason Giovanni Vermexio drew on
Vignola for the portal of the Palazzo del Senato of Siracusa (from 1629).**5.16** Sculptural embellishment in high

5.16c   5.16b   5.16d

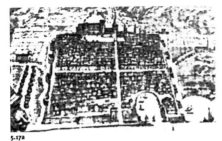

›**5.17 PALERMO, QUATTRO CANTI,** 1608–20: (a) ideal view of the urban fabric as reformed under the viceroys Toledo in the 1560s and Maqueda in the 1590s (Paolo Amato, festive altarpiece engraved in 1686), (b) general view, (c) detail.

The Cassaro was renamed Via Toledo after the viceroy who initiated its reformation. Likewise, the cross-axis was named Via Maqueda after the late-16th-century viceroy who commissioned its construction.

5.17c
The crossing was transformed under Viceroy Vigliena and named accordingly: as the stage for presenting statues of the four Spanish kings (Charles I and Philips II–IV), the four patron saints of the city and the four seasons on their four fountains, it was called 'Teatro del Sole' but the popular designation simply as 'Quattro Canti' has outlived the dynastic pretensions.

relief, often masking architectural ordonnance, was to be popular throughout the island well into the 18th century.

In the capital in the last four decades of the 16th century, conservatism led in the ordering of the urban fabric with the widening of the ancient arterial Cassaro, which led from the palace to the port, and the construction of a new cross-axis: the canting of the corners at the crossing, the 'Teatro del Sole' or Quattro Canti (from 1608), was inspired by the Quattro Fontane in Rome. The elementary articulation of the lightly concave façades with superimposed Orders provided a frame on which to hang the celebration of the Spanish monarchy which was furthering Philip II's promotion of urban reform throughout the empire at the time, primarily with the Plaza Mayor of Madrid.**5.17**

5.17b

The architects practising in 17th-century Sicily were often priests of the Counter-Reformation orders, particularly the Theatines and the Jesuits, who had studied at their Roman headquarters well before the end of the previous century: the occasional elliptical exercises paid remote homage to the Vatican church of S. Anna dei Palafrenieri but, naturally, the main thrust was proliferation of the Counter-Reformation type evolved by Vignola for the Roman Gesù. A notable example is the Jesuit father Natale

5.18b

5.18a

>5.18 TRAPANI, JESUIT COLLEGE, from c. 1614 but unfinished in the late-1630s: (a) detail of church façade, (b) engraved elevation of complex (from Arcangelo Leanti, *Lo stato presente della Sicilia*, 1761).

The college building's abstract ordonnance frames bays with paired windows of no great complexity: it is startlingly offset by the portal with pediments which add elaboration to Giacomo della Porta's variants on Michelangelo (over the upper window) but seem even to be aware of Pietro da Cortona's earliest work at the Palazzo Barberini c. 1630 (page 63). On the other hand, the basilican façade (attributed to Marco Nobile and Tommaso Blandino) reveals none of the proto-Baroque subtlety projected by Vignola for the Jesuits' seminal Roman headquarters.

Masuccio (1568–1619) who, having studied architecture in Rome from 1597, built his order's college in Trapani.**5.18** A notable exception is the Theatine priest Giacomo Besio who reverted to the Norman type of the colonnaded basilica for his order's S. Giuseppe dei Teatini in Palermo (from 1612).**5.20a** The most celebrated heterodox example, also Theatine, is Guarino Guarini who went to Messina in 1660 to work on the Santissima Annunziata for his order and also projected the church of the Padri Somaschi – but his contribution was lost to the earthquake of 1908, like much else in eastern Sicily (see page 143).**5.19**

5.19
>5.19 MESSINA, PADRI SOMASCHI, c. 1660, unexecuted: half plan and section.

5.20a

›5.20 THE 17TH-CENTURY PALERMITAN CHURCH AND ITS EMBELLISHMENT: (a) S. Giuseppe dei Teatini (built by Giacomo Besio between 1612 and 1645, late-17th-century interior decoration by Antonio Manno and Paolo Corso), interior; (b) S. Teresa alla Kalsa (begun 1686), façade (c. 1700); (c–e)

5.20b

Baroque flowered in Sicily in the early 18th century: architecture was then being reinvigorated in Naples but the connection between the two was negligible. Throughout the previous century Palermitans had continued to draw their inspiration from Rome: by its end, however, the island had its own distinct style – or, rather, range of styles. Leaders in the development were the Palermitans Paolo and Giacomo Amato (1633–1714 and 1643–1732 respectively). Yet, despite insular contempt for the peninsula, the other two most prominent architects active in Sicily in the decades before and after 1700 are called Angelo Italia (1628–1700) and Tommaso Napoli (1655–1725).

Paolo Amato developed the specifically Sicilian type of façade which culminates in an open belfry for Santissimo Salvatore in Palermo (from c. 1682). Giacomo Amato unsurprisingly promoted Roman style in the island's capital on returning there in 1685 after twelve years of study and work in Rome. As completed by Rainaldi and Fontana, the façade of Maderno's S. Andrea della Valle is revised, contracted, for the façades of S. Teresa alla Kalsa and the Pietà (1686 and 1689 respectively) with broken and undulating pediments but without the clear gradations in the plasticity of the Orders which Maderno deployed elsewhere.**5.20b** At the same time, Angelo Italia's most celebrated Palermitan church, S. Francesco Saverio (from 1684), is even less subtle in the application of freestanding columns to its façade but far more adventurous internally: rather than the post-Vignolan hall type, it recalls Borromini in its Greek-cross and octagonal plan but, more particularly, in the hexagonal chapels fitted into the corners like the subsidiary spaces of S. Carlo alle Quattro Fontane – except for their penetration up into open tribunes.**5.20c–e** The vertical perspectives of S. Francesco Saverio are vital but the effect of the interior also depends on white marble architectural detail offset against coloured marble panelling.

5.20c

5.20e

S. Francesco Saverio (begun 1684, consecrated 1711), exterior from south-east, interior to sanctuary and detail of organ gallery; (f–h) S. Caterina (from 1566, structure finished thirty years later), nave to sanctuary and details of revetment (from c. 1720, attributed to Giacomo Amato and his Palermitan colleague Andrea Palma who predeceased him by two years in 1730).

5.20d

5.20g

5.20h

5.20f

5.21c

Intricate coloured marble inlay in plane surface is most characteristic of Palermitan revetment. Flourishing by mid-century also in Messina, where much has been lost, this mode obviously has its parallel in Cosimo Fanzago's Naples but rarely as the context for three-dimensional decorative sculpture. At that the Sicilians excelled, in marble and stucco: outstanding Palermitan examples range from the marble relief of S. Caterina to the stuccowork of the Oratorio del Rosario of S. Zita.**5.20f–h** Unexcelled in the medium in scale, texture, depth of relief – and its impact on architecture – the astonishing revetment in S. Zita's Rosario chapel (from c. 1685) is due to the stuccador Giacomo Serpotta who, with his son Procopio, was employed in the last decade of the century to embellish several other oratories in the capital. And they took their extraordinary talent to Santo Spirito at Agrigento.**5.21**

Well before the end of the 17th century, the magnates of Sicily had largely turned their backs on their vast landed estates, preferring to remain near the centre of viceregal

›5.21 SERPOTTA STUCCOWORK: (a, b) Palermo, S. Zita, Oratorio del Rosario (1685–1717), end wall with dioramas of the mysteries of the Rosary and the Christian naval victory at Lepanto, detail of side fenestration; (c) Agrigento, Santo Spirito: interior (dated to c. 1695 on the circumstantial evidence that Giacomo Serpotta was not recorded in Palermo at the time).

5.21a

5.21b

5.22c

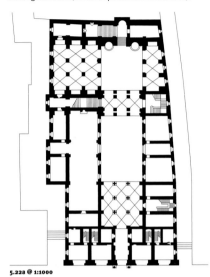

5.22a @ 1:1000

5.22b

power. The phenomenon was certainly not unique to the island, except perhaps in degree: the Mafia was one consequence; ruinous palace building was another. In that field Giacomo Amato may be credited with an innovative role in introducing scenography to the extended cortile – if not, as yet, in awarding a major dramatic role to the staircase: that followed in the second half of the 18th century.**5.22a, b**

Palermitan palace façades might be articulated with an abstract or a canonical Order over a basement but usually the main architectural impact derived from the portal, the window frames and convoluted wrought-iron balconies: the Palazzo del Principe di Cattolica retains a Vignolesque portal in an otherwise unrusticated basement, dispenses with even an abstract ordonnance and is relatively staid in its ironwork but enjoys the convolution of its piano nobile window pediments. The Palazzo del Senato also well represents the elaboration of the window aedicule but that complements an ordonnance of abstract pilaster strips and there was originally no convoluted ironwork.**5.22c** The full repertory is on display in mid-century works like the Palazzo S. Croce and the later Palazzo Belmonte Riso: the former represents culmination towards the end of the reign of Charles III which is beyond us here.

While the Amato were busy in town, their slightly younger contemporary Tommaso Napoli – a Dominican monk born in Palermo – was engaged beyond its walls. When the denizens of the vice regal court left their city palaces for relief from oppressive heat in high summer, it was for their suburban villas rather than their feudal seats. Bagheria, on the sea front to the east of the capital, was

›5.23 BAGHERIA, VILLAS: (a–e) Palagonia (from 1705), axonometric perspective, entrance and garden fronts, perimeter wall with grotesque figures, interior of salone; (f) Valguarnera (from c. 1710), entrance front.

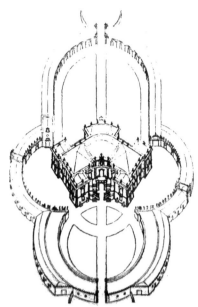

5.23b

5.23a

5.23c

5.23d

5.23e

The Villa Palagonia, bent around the concave entrance front which uncomfortably embraces the multiple rectilinear returns of the external staircase, was begun by Tommaso Napoli for Francesco Ferdinando Gravina, Prince of Palagonia (died 1736) and furthered by his son Ignazio Sebastiano (died 1746) and grandson Francesco Ferdinando II. The last was responsible for the grotesque sculptures of the exterior perimeter wall and for the eccentric decoration of the interior's many varied spaces (perhaps employing the architect Agatino Daidone).

The Valguarnera villa was commissioned by Donna Marianna del Bosco e Gravina, Duchessa della Cattolica e Gravina; the attribution to Tommaso Napoli is based on later 18th-century records as well as on stylistic grounds shared by the Palazzo del Principe di Cattolica. The convex cubicle was later inserted on the landing of the external staircase in the concave front.

one of several favoured resorts but its collection of villas is outstanding – despite dilapidation and overwhelming urban sprawl. Tommaso Napoli is credited with the least compromised survivor, the Valguarnera, and also with the most spectacular, the multi-curved Palagonia, which was later to be beset notoriously with grotesque figures on its protective wall.**5.23**

5.23f

5.24a

5.24b

Napoli deployed curve and counter curve to enliven his villa façades – as the corollary of plastic mass. In church architecture, on the other hand, variations in applying columns to plain surfaces were long sustained: they range across the island from Angelo Italia's Marsala cathedral or S. Francesco Saverio in Palermo (c. 1700), where the base plane was unvaried, to the cathedral in Siracusa (c. 1728), where the pilasters gain weight towards the centre, thrusting the columns to progressive advance under parallel spurs of entablature to the dramatic enhancement of *chiaroscuro*. Little more than a decade elapsed before the outbreak of full-blooded Baroque dispute between

›**5.24 ORDER AND MOVEMENT IN THE EARLY 18TH-CENTURY CHURCH FAÇADE:** (a) Marsala, cathedral of S. Tommaso (S. Thomas of Canterbury; Norman foundation built with materials destined for the latter), façade (attributed to Angelo Italia from 1726); (b) Siracusa, cathedral of S. Maria del Piliero (6th-century BCE Temple of Athena converted 7th century CE, rebuilt after the earthquake of 1693), façade (Andrea Palma, from 1728); (c, d) Trapani, cathedral of S. Lorenzo (15th century, rebuilt from 1635), façade (Giovanni Biagio Amico, from c. 1740) and Anime in Purgatorio, façade (Don Giovanni Friend, from 1712); (e) Palermo, S. Anna (built to reduced Counter-Reformation plan with linked side chapels by Mariana Smiriglio from c. 1630), façade (rebuilt after the earthquakes of 1726 and 1736 by Giovanni Biagio Amico).

5.24c

5.24e

5.24d

5.25a

undulating mass and articulating Orders. The initiative was taken by Giovanni Biagio Amico (1684–1754) most notably for the cathedral in his native town of Trapani and for S. Anna in Palermo (mid-1730s): curve counters curve but, instead of pilasters masked by an arcaded portico as in the Trapani work, S. Anna's columns march boldly forth between the convexity and the central concavity though the interior is rectilinear.**5.24** The contrast with the rebuilding of Siracusa's S. Lucia at the end of the old century could hardly be greater.**5.25a**

An architect from Trapani, in the far west of the island, took momentum to Palermitan masonry: a Palermitan took it to Catania in the far east where devastation in the earthquake of 1693 offered encouraging prospects to a budding architect. So too did Siracusa.**5.25b**

Giovanni Battista Vaccarini (1702–68) had studied in Rome from the early 1720s and returned south with no marked inclination towards the Classicizing intention of Fontana's followers but, rather, a preference for the more volatile style of Filippo Raguzzini and his contemporaries. Across a busy career – which takes us beyond the scope of this volume in the main – his most important commissions in Catania were to finish the huge Palazzo Municipale (from 1732) and build the cathedral of S. Agata (late-1740s).**5.26, 5.27** The whole façade of the latter undulates through curve and counter-curve but unfathomable is the generation of the momentum in a rectangular box. For the Palazzo Municipale he promoted the Palermitan contrast between abstract panelling and assertive aedicules: beyond the Palermitan norm, however, the pediments of the latter are deflected at obtuse angles from the orthogonal plane

5.25b

›5.25 SIRACUSA: (a) S. Lucia alla Badia (Luciano Caracciolo, from c. 1695 to mid-18th century); (b) Palazzo Beneventano del Bosco (Luciano Ali, 1778, incorporating earlier work) in the extension to the Piazza del Duomo in Ortigia, courtyard.

›5.26 CATANIA, CHANGING FASHION IN PALAZZO DESIGN: (a–c) Biscari, terrace front facing the harbour, window detail and salone vault (anonymous, early 18th century); (d) Municipale (from 1695, fenestration by Giovanni Battista Vaccarini from 1732) with elephant fountain (also attributed to Vaccarini).

›5.27 CATANIA, MOVEMENT IN THE CHURCH FRONT: cathedral of S. Agata (Giovanni Battista Vaccarini, from 1748).

The plan derives from Borromini's S. Agnese in Agone in Piazza Navona, Rome, and the movement in the façade is of similar inspiration – if ungenerated by internal incident. Borrominian influence had hitherto not been pronounced in Sicily.

5.26a

5.26b

5.26d

5.26c

5.27

5.28a

5.28b

5.28e

of their context in the willful manner not uncharacteristic of post-Borrominian Rome. Hitherto Catanians had overwhelmed structural framework with rampant florid ornament embracing anthropomorphic motifs in the manner of the grotesque but in coarse relief – not unlike the excesses of Lecce.

Curvature and the especially vigorous projection of grouped Orders in several tiers are highly characteristic of ecclesiastical works in south-eastern Sicily – some probably predating Vaccarini's Catanian cathedral. The array of columns in organpipe-like series at the outset of convex surfaces is well represented by several churches in the vicin-

5.28c

5.28d

›5.28 THE FAÇADES OF ROSARIO GAGLIARDI AND HIS CONTEMPORARIES IN THE RUGGED TERRAIN OF THE SOUTH-EAST: (a, b) Modica, S. Pietro (attributed to Mario Spada and Rosario Boscarino, early 18th century) and S. Giorgio (attributed to Gagliardi, 1702–38); (c, d) Ragusa Ibla, S. Giorgio (Gagliardi, dated 1746 in the porch); (e) Noto, S. Domenico (Gagliardi, c. 1735).

ity of Noto, notably S. Giorgio at both Modica and Ragusa Ibla (rebuilt between 1702–38, the latter completed c. 1745): due to the Syracusan Rosario Gagliardi, like several other churches in the area, these belong to belfries and the dramatic effect of three diminishing tiers is greatly enhanced by the steps ascending their hilly sites.**5.28**

Destroyed by the earthquake of 1693, not-far-distant Noto was rebuilt with celebrated consistency of style and substance but the work extended beyond the period covered by this volume. Meanwhile, the influence of Sicily's idiosyncratic tradition was clearly felt across the sea in the island of Malta.**5.29**

5.29b

5.29a

›5.29 MALTA, VALLETTA: (a–c) Grand Harbour and its fortification, plan c. 1800 and general views; (d, e) Quarry Wharf with its chapel and the related façade of S. Maria Liesse (founded 1620, rebuilt to the order of the French chapter in the mid-18th century); (f) Alberge d'Italie, church of S. Caterina (Cassar, 1576, remodelled in the mid-18th century possibly by Belli); (g) Alberge de Castile, Léon e Portugal (Gerolamo Cassar, 1574, remodelled by Andrea Belli, 1741); (h–j) Grandmaster's Palace (founded c. 1580, remodelled in the mid-18th century), portal, courtyard and corridor.

The Knights of S. John had been settled on Malta by the king-emperor Charles V in 1530, after the loss of Rhodes to the Turks in 1522: they moved their principal seat from Vittoriosa to Valletta in 1571. Having withstood the Turkish siege of 1565, the French grandmaster Jean Parisot de la Vallette appealed to Pope Pius V and Phillip II of Spain for help in fortifying the Grand Harbour on the island's southern tip as a base for defence of the western Mediterranean against Ottoman incursion and Barbary piracy.

Though much restored and improved since the turn of the 17th century, fortification is due in the main to the Italian military engineer Francesco Laparelli (1521–70) sent by the pope: he produced the grid plan and devised the system of bastions on which work began in 1566. On his return to Italy in 1571, Laparelli was replaced by his assistant Gerolamo Cassar (1520–86) who had studied in Rome: his post-Mannerist style is best represented by the co-cathedral of S. John, the Grandmaster's Palace and several of the auberges (inns of residence) – most notably those of the Italians and Spaniards.

Caravaggio's visit revolutionized the island's art but the major development was due to the Calabrese

5.29d

5.29e

artist Matteo Preti who transformed Cassar's austere cathedral with Baroque illusionism. Luca Giordano and Francesco Solimena followed from Naples with comparable impact. Their architectural contemporaries, Cassar's followers in his establishment, seem to have been local in origin but will have known Sicily – at least.

5.29g

5.29h

5.29i

5.29j

5.29f

5.29c

2 HABSBURG TO BOURBON IN SPAIN

Economic decline and political atrophy in the late decades of Philip IV and the protracted impotence of his unfortunate son, Charles II, curtailed royal commissions: major works, royal and ecclesiastical, awaited the consolidation of Bourbon rule and renewed prosperity in the third decade of the 18th century. The last signifcant Habsburg project was Buen Retiro: great in extent and in some of the pictures it housed, that was hardly great as architecture. Even the church was relatively reticent as a monumental builder in the last fifty years of the 17th century. Work continued on many projects

5.30a

5.30c

5.30b @ 1:1000

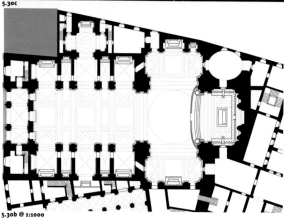

5.30d

›5.30 PROTO-BAROQUE JESUIT WORKS: (a) Toledo, S. Ildelfonso (from 1629), entrance front; (b–d) Madrid, S. Isidro el Real (former Jesuit church, from the 1620s), plan, interior and exterior.

Like the Salamanca Clerecía (see below, pages 832f), the flat plane of the Toledo façade is relieved with superimposed Orders: ignoring progression in the manner developed by Maderno to lend movement to the masonry, they follow the façade formula evolved by Francesco and Juan Gómez de Mora first for the Jesuits of Alcalá. The model was Roman but the Spanish Jesuit architects seem also to have been seduced by the Parisian Jesuit variant of S.-Paul-S.-Louis: the essentially architectonic approach of the former is compromised by ornament applied in the Flemish manner derided by the French.

The Jesuit church in Madrid was built to a design of the Gesù type by Pedro Sanchez who was responsible for construction until 1633: thereafter Francesco Bautista and Melchor de Bueras saw it to completion by 1664. Nearly a century later Ventura Rodriguez installed a new presbytery retable. That was destroyed, with much else, in a fire of 1936. The façade, largely due to Bautista, departs radically from the Roman prototype observed to varying degrees by the Mora: it is of the 'palace' type with towers favoured by Terzi and other post-Herreran architects (AIC5, pages 761f); instead of following Maderno's progressive articulation for S. Pietro, it has colossal Corinthian colums in antis to pilasters in a single plane. The church served as the cathedral from 1885 until 1993.

›5.31 JAEN, CATHEDRAL OF THE ASSUMPTION: façade (from 1667).

The architect was Eufrasio López de Rojas who succeeded Juan de Arandaa (after 1654) and Pedro del Portillo (who completed the dome from 1660). The various Roman references include, foremost, the façade to Maderno's S. Pietro with towers – as projected there – but without the movement introduced by increasing the substance of the colossal Corinthian Order in concert with the projection of the wall plane: instead, the attic is set back beyond a terrace and the pediment transferred to it – as was not uncommon in retables.

started many years before: the Jesuit churches of Salamanca, Toledo and Madrid are not the least in significance for their proto-Baroque façades: the first two acknowledge the project recently completed by their brothers in Paris at S.-Paul-S.-Louis; in Madrid, on the other hand, the Jesuits sustained the Iberian palace façade tradition with modified reference to Maderno's S. Pietro in Rome (see pages 54f and 182).**5.30** However, the cathedrals of Valladolid and Jaen were to be among the most influential – the former in its contracted form, the latter as completed with its multi-storey, twin-towered façade (AIC5, page 738).**5.31**

5.31

Much effort in the era was concentrated on embellishing interiors with retables and exteriors with façades. Their purpose was to accommodate painted and sculpted icons, but several of the former promote the architectural frame to prominence with High Renaissance superimposition of Orders after the Herreran model at S. Lorenzo del Escorial. It was to be supplemented by Colossal Orders and gravitas was tempered by Mannerist spiral fluting c. 1615 and first ceded to Solomonic bravura a generation later.**5.32**

›5.32 THE EARLY 17TH-CENTURY RETABLE: (a) Plasencia, Catedral de la Asunción (Gregorio Fernández with unidentified assemblers, 1626); (b) Valladolid, Convento de las Descalzas Reales (Juan de Muniátegui with 'Calvary' and Franciscan saints by Fernández, paintings by Santiago Morán, from c. 1610); (c) Seville, Iglesia de la Anunciación, Inmaculada (Montañés c. 1618, inner frame by Juan Vázquez el Moro, c. 1585); (d) Seville, Convento de la Merced, Inmaculada (now in Seville, Museo de Bellas Artes; Montañés, c. 1633); (e) Seville, S. Leandro, S. John Evagelist on Pat-

The early 17th-century retable

The High Renaissance clarity of the mode with regular tiers framed by canonical Orders was sustained well into the 17th century. The sculptor Gregorio Fernández (1576–1636) was one of its most distinguished participants in collaboration with various painters and 'assemblers'.**5.32a, b**

Complexity supervened as the display of the sacrament was promoted to a principal purpose of the exercise and prompted emphasis on the architecture of the tabernacle and/or the aedicule in which it was set – especially in Andalusia. Martínez Montañés (1568–1649) led the way to more structural gravitas, guided by Vignola and Palladio in particular, but not without elaboration elaborated: he introduced spiral fluting; he varied the size and shape of recesses for sculpture of differing scales; he emphasized the central niche behind the tabernacle as locus of the major icon and occasionally echoed its arch as an outer framing element. In contrast to the relative simplicity of the later Inmaculada retable from Seville's Merced convent (1633), the Inmaculada formerly in Seville's church of the Annunciation is presented in a late-16th- and early 17th-century confection of somewhat Venetian Mannerist frameworks with columns of different sizes.**5.32c, d**

The central system was susceptible of much variation. The altarpiece of S. Juan in S. Leandro, Seville (1621), has panels of different sizes, the lower ones oversailing the framework.**5.32e** The next step was to eliminate superimposed Orders, as in the Merced Inmaculada. In this mode the sculpture of Martínez was accommodated by the brothers Gaspar, Felipe and Francisco de Ribas (1611–58, 1609–48 and 1616–79 respectively) for Seville's S. Paula: collaborating there also with the painter-sculptor Alonso Cano, they

5.32a

5.32b   5.32c   5.32i

5.32d   5.32e   5.32f   5.32g   5.32h

mos (Montañés, 1632); (f–h) Seville, S. Paula, S. Juan Evangelista (Montañés, 1635 with Alonso Cano), S. Juan Bautista and Cristo de Coral (Montañés with the Ribas brothers, late-1630s); (i) Seville, Santa Cruz, Chapel of S. Ana (Pedro Roldán, 1672).

enhanced three-dimensionality of frame and content, maintained spiral fluting and amplified the central niche or enclosed it in a tabernacle.**5.32f–h**

Credit for the introduction of the Solomonic style to the Andalusian retable is shared by Bernardo Simón de Pineda (1638– 1702), whose great work of c. 1670 in the chapel of the Hospital de la Caridad, Seville, we shall view in context, and Pedro Roldán (1629–99) who provided for S. Ana in Seville's Iglesia de Santa Cruz c. 1672.**5.32i** The style was adopted for the main retable of the Jesuit church in Salamanca in 1673 by the designer identified only as Juan Fernández, who was presumably an heir to Gregorio (AIC5, page 753).

The Solomonic Order is thought first to have appeared in the upper storey of the frontispiece devised by Pedro de Ambuesa for S. Miguel de los Reyes in Valencia (c. 1640).**5·33ª** As there, the formula derived from France for Classicizing medieval elevation (AIC5, pages 307f and 330) was elaborated for several later Philippine façades as far apart as the Benedictine monastery of S. Salvador at Celanova in Galicia and the Cartuja at Jerez de las Frontera.**5·33ᵇ** Cartuja at Jerez de las Frontera and An entirely different approach to a similar objective was adopted for the new façade of Granada cathedral, perhaps the greatest single work of the end of Philip IV's reign.

Commissioned to complete Siloe's Grenadine masterpiece in 1664, Alonso Cano (1601–67) deleted the superstructural elements of the triumphal-arch motif projected for the lower storey and sent the arches up to the full height of nave and aisles but rounded off the medieval aspiration in Classical style.**5·34** The abstract ordonnance in terms of of attenuated shafts and tectonic panelling recalls the *estilo desornamentado*: the applied ornament derives from the strapwork of the school of Fontainebleau and its Flemish elaboration (AIC5, pages 321ff and 416ff). Never lost to the south, sculptural ornament would prevail over tectonic order.

The greatest work initiated in Charles II's reign was the cathedral-basilica of Nossa Senhora del Pilar in Zaragoza. First projected by Felipe Sanchez c. 1675, it was begun by Francesco de Herrera el Mozo (1622–85, first royal architect from 1677) to a plan derived from that of Valladolid cathedral. Inevitably altered after Herrera's death in 1685, it was largely vaulted by 1718 but further important alterations were made to the interior when the aspect of the chapel housing the sacred icon was changed by Ventura Rodríguez c. 1750. The striking multi-towered, multi-domed silhouette was not finally realized until the 19th century.**5·35**

5·33ª

›5.33 CLASSICIZING ELEVATION: (a) Valencia, S. Miguel de los Reyes (from c. 1640); (b) Jerez de la Frontera, Cartuja, façade (from c. 1665).

Rebuilding Valencia's Cistercian abbey church of S. Bernard under dedication to S. Michael was begun in 1623. Construction of the later façade is credited to Pedro de Ambuesa. The work at Jerez is attributed to the Carthusian brother Pedro del Pinar. Of these two architects little else is known through publication.

5·33ᵇ

5.34b

›**5.34 GRANADA, CATHEDRAL:** (a, b) west front (from 1664).

Diego Siloe had completed the lower storey of the great cathedral's north transept, the Puerta del Perdón, in the form of a triumphal arch and had projected a development of the theme on both levels of the west front: only the pedestals establishing the varied widths of the centre and the sides had been built at his death in 1563. The work was furthered by Juan de Maena and Juan de Orea between 1563 and 1590: under Ambrosio de Vico thereafter, it lapsed after the death of Philip II. Court painter and architect to Philip IV, Alonso Cano was appointed chief architect in 1654: in the execution of his scheme for the façade at the end of his life, he was assisted by Gaspar de la Peña. Funds were never found to complete the project with twin towers rising to 81 metres.

5.34a

5.35c

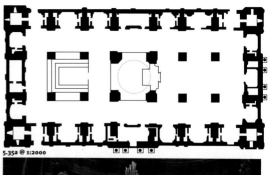

5.35a @ 1:2000

5.35d

5.35b

›5.35 ZARAGOZA, BASILICA OF NUESTRA SEÑORA DEL PILAR, from 1681, altered c1750, completed 1872: (a) plan, (b) exterior, (c, d) general view of interior and detail of main chapel.

S. James the Great, patron of Spain, is reputed to have witnessed the Virgin descending by the banks of the Ebro on a pillar carried by angels. Destroyed by fire in 1434, a Romanesque chapel was replaced on a larger scale to enshrine the Aragonese capital's iconic image. Rebuilding due again two centuries later, the project initiated by Felipe Sanchez was modifiied by Francisco Herrera the younger in 1681. Ventura Rodriguez furthered the completion of the exterior from the 1750s.

The other great work of the last Habsburg reign in Spain, also long in realization, was the reformation of the exterior of the cathedral of Santiago de Compostela. Directed by the Salamancan architect José Peña de Toro (1614–76), work began in 1667 on the royal portal facing east over the Plaza da Quintana and on the transformation of the Romanesque south-western tower. The elaboration of bell towers was to be a favoured exercise of the age throughout Spain. Of the three with which Santiago's sanctuary was to be endowed, the south-western one initiated the project to endow that great pilgrimage centre with a new façade: apart from protecting the supreme Romanesque achievement of the Porta del Gloria, that would assert the supremacy of S. James in the kingdom's hierarchy of holy patrons with supreme contemporary opulence (AIC4, page 193). Peña did not live to realize this but he set the terms for his successor, Domingo de Andrade (c. 1639–1712) who improved upon them and, in particular, provided a prime example for belfry builders elsewhere in his transformation of the Reloj tower. The culmination came with Andrade's pupil Fernando de Casas y Novoa (c. 1670–1794).**5.36**

5.36a

›5.36 SANTIAGO DE COMPOSTELA CATHEDRAL: (a) royal portal in east front to Plaza da Quintana (from 1667), (b) west front (1667–c. 1750), (c) Reloj tower (from c. 1690), (d) sanctuary baldachin (designed c. 1658, revised c. 1730).

The twin towers are Romanesque in origin: Peña de Toro began by rearticulating the mass of the southern tower (Torre das Campás), as the solid base for his square, double-arched cupola. Statues of S. James's parents (Zebedee and Maria Salome) are displayed on the northern and southern towers respectively: the apostle himself is at the apex of the façade above a representation of his tomb and the star that led to its discovery. He is attended by his disciples Athanasius and Theodomir dressed as pilgrims, identified by their scallop shells.

Santiago and El Obradoiro

Peña's east front is at base a triumphal arch, emblazoned with the royal arms, but the superstructure introduces the volutes, pinnacles and broken pediment mouldings to which Wendel Dietterlin and his fellow northern Mannerists were addicted. Andrade refaced the bulk of the adjacent medieval Reloj tower with attenuated pilasters and extended the articulation to a new belfry and cupola: this rises with limited Mannerist flourishes from its square base on an octagonal plan with tempietti in the corners.

The regularity – if not orthodoxy – of the Reloj articulation contrasts with the debased Classicism applied by Peña to the rather Gothic profile of his extended Campas tower, to the south on the west front, which was later copied for its twin, the Carraca tower to the north-west: the

5.36b

5.36c

The canopy above the high altar and the object of pilgrimage, the shrine of Santiago, was designed by Canon José de Vega y Verdugo (c. 1658) under the distant inspiration of Bernini. It was executed somewhat clumsily by sculptors working under the direction of Domingo de Andrade in the late 1670s.

5.36d

attenuated pier pilasters are panelled but, though wildly uncanonical, they become engaged columns in the centre and to the sides of the main bulk; rising from the relatively orthodox belfry pavilions, the spires are tempietti elevated over exaggerated volutes of distant endebtedness to Longhena.

The base storey of the central façade is clearly related to the same stage of the Quintana façade: the articulation in the rhythm of a triumphal arch is with columns, as there, but here they project to assert verticality and buttress the arch derived from the tunnel-vaulted nave. A riot of variations on the Quintana volute motif ramps through the frontispiece and its extensions across the second storey of the towers. There they bridge aedicules housing the images of S. James's progenitors below sepulchral versions of the much deployed urn motif. Towards the apex they buttress the great aedicule sheltering the dedicatee: an extrusion of the form emerging from the broken Quintana pediment, that in turn carries another broken pediment and the crowning tabernacle. The confection thus assembled under the inspiration – and over the base – provided by Peña, was due to the obscure local architect Fernando de Casas y Novoa: the conception surpasses even the Flemish in complexity but is more readily comparable to the façade of a northern civic building than to a church.

5.37c

5.37b

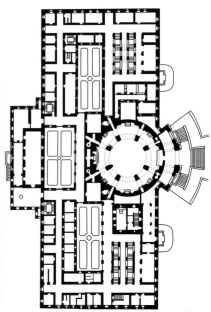

The 'Obradoiro' of Santiago was rare for its time in its application to a Romanesque basilica: it could hardly be called conservative except insofar as it presented itself as sectioning the volumes of nave and portico. Stark in contrast, the other great work begun under Charles II – and completed to revised plans under Philip V half a century later – is the Collegium Regium of Loyola: originally projected by Bernini's protégé Carlo Fontana, it is an early representative of the academic, Classicizing conservatism which would characterize the mainstream of development in Rome about the turn of the century. The purity of the rotunda is compromised by ornament applied superficially.**5.37**

Highly eclectic in derivation and increasingly rampant, as we shall see, ornament was the default mask of conservative designers. The hall-church type was occasionally recalled, not least by Francisco de Herrera in his scheme for the Pilar of Zaragoza (c. 1685). However, the Mora and their contemporaries had established

5.37a @ 1:2000

›**5.37 LOYOLA, COLEGIO**, from 1688: (a) plan, (b, c) general view of church from the south-east and interior.

Native to the locality, founder of the Jesuit order, Iñigo Lopez-Recalde (1491–1556) was canonized as S. Ignacio in 1622. Work on the monastery and college, begun under the patronage of the queen mother Mariana of Austria, was executed by José de la Incera and Martin Zaldua under the direction of the Flemish Jesuit Jean Begrand. Halted by the War of the Spanish Succession, work was begun again in 1717 by Sebastián de Lecuona under the direction of the Spanish architect Ignacio de Ibero: it was finished in 1738.

›**5.38 SALAMANCA CLERECÍA**, as augmented in the mid-18th century by Andrés García de Quiñones: (a) entrance front, (b) main cloister.

The two main storeys of the façade, executed by the Jesuit father Mato, follow the plans of Juan Gómez and the structural work begun in 1617 (AIC5, pages 752f). Completed with dome and crossing at much the same time, construction of S. Idelfonso at Toledo followed the initial work at Salamanca (see page 812).

5.38b

5.38a

Quiñones's octagonal towers, with their crocketed obelisks rising from incurving buttresses, reputedly follow the model originally projected for the ayuntamiento. His attic, with its broken pediments and multiple pilasters, is embellished with a relief of the Holy Spirit and an icon of the Virgin Mary flanked by the royal founders (Philip III and Margarita of Austria).

preference for the modified form of basilica with chapels instead of aisles – as developed by Vignola from Alberti and established as the Counter-Reformation type (AIC4, pages 748f, AIC5, pages 184f). Prominent examples include the Jesuit churches in Alcalá de Henares, Madrid, Toledo and Salamanca.

Juan Gómez de Mora's Clerecía at Salamanca was completed in the mid-18th century with the twin towers of the church's eastern entrance front by Andrés García de Quiñones: his too is the spectacular grand cloister (Patio de los Estudios). With its astonishing ordonnance of colossal Composite columns countering its two storeys, the latter is unique in the context of a religious foundation – indeed, it is scarcely matched in the grandest secular architecture of the era.**5.38** The towers well represent the form of the age after Andrade's Compostela: extending to the threshold of the Neoclassical era, variations across Spain include the detached belfry beside the cathedral of S. Domingo de la Calzada (1767).

A decade or so before García began work on completing the façade of the Salamanca Clerecía, the Valencian sculptor-architect Jaime Bort y Meliá was adding the west front to the Gothic body of Murcia cathedral: rather than S.-Paul-S.-Louis, he recalls the façade of the Parisian S. Gervais – if not the Nicchione of the Vatican Belvedere – but the conflict between the severe Classicism of Salomon de Brosse – or Metezeau – and Flemish prolixity is even more striking than in García's exercise.**5.39** As we shall see, 18th-century Spanish church fronts had already been – and would certainly go on to be – even richer in applied sculptural detail under the influence of developments in the design of the altar retable.

›5.39 MURCIA, CATHEDRAL OF S. MARÍA: façade (1736–54).

King Jaime I ordered the conversion of the Great Mosque or Aljamía and its consecration to the Virgin Mary: the original building was replaced between 1391 and 1467. Renovation after extensive damage in a flood of 1735 extended to the entirely new façade credited to the Valencian master Jaime Bort y Meliá (died 1754).

›5.40 GUADIX, CATHEDRAL OF S. MARÍA DE LA ENCARNACIÓN: façade.

A Visigothic church, extant in the 10th century and converted to a mosque, was reconverted in 1489. Plans to rebuild it were delayed until 1549 when Diego Siloe was commissioned: reflecting his great work at Granada, his project had been executed from apse to crossing when work stopped in 1574. Resumed after twenty years, it was furthered principally by Francisco Roldán and Francisco Antero. Still incomplete at the end of the Habsburg era, building work on the dome and façade was resumed under the patronage of Philip V and the successive direction of Blas Antonio Delgado (before 1714), Vicente Acero (until 1722) and Cayón de la Vega: when the latter left for Cádiz in 1731, the vaulting, the dome and the west front were under construction on plans variously amended by all three architects.

›**5.41 CÁDIZ, CATHEDRAL OF SANTA CRUZ,** from 1722: (a) entrance front, (b, c) plan and section, (d) interior.

Begun by Vicente Acero y Arebo c. 1722 on a plan derived from Siloe's Granada project, the entirely new cathedral replaced the original built c. 1260 and rebuilt from 1602 after it was burned in the English sack of 1596. Gaspar Cayón replaced Acero in 1729 and was succeeded by his nephew Torcuato Cayón in 1759:

5.40

5.41a

Before Bort's intervention at Murcia, the most prominent southern excursions into the animation of a façade with curvature were devised by Vicente Acero y Arebo for the cathedrals of Guadix and Cadiz: neither is generated by dynamic planning. The earlier of the two, for Guadix, is essentially planar but the three bays are defined by triangular projection with slightly curved facets from which fragments of pediment cascade to the sides: it was applied to a Gothic hall church project whose realization in Renaissance style is attributed to Diego Siloe.**5·40**

Siloe is also present at Cádiz, in the circular choir beyond the crossing of a basilica. Acero devised the plan, as well as the façade, but the latter responds to the space arising from the former only in section: triangular projections, deriving from Guadix, frame convex side bays in wilful contrast to a great concave central 'nicchione' which recalls the Vatican Belvedere via Murcia cathedral – with far less severity than the former and far less sculptural exuberance than the latter due to the late date of its completion.**5·41**

5.41c

5.41b @ 1:1000

on his demise in 1783 various other contributors culminated in Juan Daura (1832–53). The façade follows Acero's design as modified by the Cayon under whom construction had reached just over half height above the portal and to below the entablature on the flanking towers.

5.41d

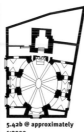

5.42c

5.42d

›5.42 THE ELLIPSE IN PLAN AND ELEVATION AT VALENCIA: (a) Cathedral of the Blessed Virgin, façade (from 1703); (b–d) church of the Desamparados, plan, exterior and interior (from 1652).

The church is dedicated to one of the city's two patron saints (Our Lady of the Helpless) whose early-15th century image was removed in 1489 from the Hospital of the Innocent Martyrs to a chapel in the cathedral. The proliferation of devotion to it after the plague of 1647 required a more ample theatre for its display: the unusual design of the new basilica, an ellipse inserted into a roughly-rectangula enveloped like Vignola's S. Anna dei Palafraneiri (AIC5, page 183), was produced by Urrana Ponce de Diego Marinez c. 1652 and realized by 1667. The embellishment of the innovative camarín behind the high altar seems not to have been completed until the early 1690s.

The cathedral was built between 1252 and 1482 on the site of an earlier mosque. The sanctuary was reworked from 1674, the nave after Rudolf had inserted his façade early in the 18th century.

5.42a

Movement of masonry in the Roman Baroque manner either of Maderno or Borromini was rare in 18th-century Spain. The most convincing example – preceding Acero's exercise at Cadiz by nearly a generation – was devised by the German Conrad Rudolf for the façade of Valencia cathedral. Introduced to a medieval basilica built over a mosque, however, it responds to no dynamic development of internal space – like Borromini's exercise for S. Carlino, to take a supreme example: instead, the semi-elliptical convexity seems to result from its squeezing to buckling between pre-existing towers.**5.42a** Even in wholly new work concordance between elliptical exterior and interior remained elusive.

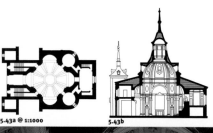

5.43a @ 1:1000

5.43b

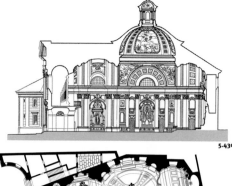

5.43c

5.43e

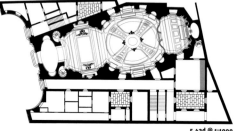

5.43d @ 1:1000

›5.43 CENTRALIZED GEOMETRY IN MADRID:
(a, b) Virgen del Puerto (Pedro de Ribera from 1718 and
1725), plan and section; (c–e) S. Marcos, section, plan
and interior (Ventura Rodríguez from 1749); (f, g) S.
Miguel, exterior and interior (Teodoro Ardemans from
1739, furthered by Santiago Bonavía).

5.43g

5.43f

›5.44 FIGUEROA AND COLLEAGUES ON ECCLE-
SIASTICAL COMMISSIONS IN SEVILLE: (a, b) La
Caridad, façade (after 1663) and retable (1670–75);

5.44a

5.44b

Nearly a century before Rudolf's intervention in Valencia, the elliptical space devised by Juan Gómez de Mora for the Bernadas of Alcalá da Henares was masked by a planar façade (AIC5, page 750). Half a century after that, Diego Martínez Ponce de Urrana's Desamparados church in Valencia is also a boxed ellipse: its chapels are less varied but its significance derives from the introduction of a raised chamber (*camarín*) behind the altar with a window on to the main space for the display of the sacred icon.**5.42b–d**

The bold convex façade projecting directly from the twin towers of S. Miguel in Madrid is attributed to Santiago Bonavía a generation after Rudolf's Valencian exercise. As there, however, the elliptical geometry was not followed through to the cruciform interior – despite the canted corners and central projection of the nave bays.**5.43f, g** Another generation on, elliptical geometry was translated from the interior to the exterior by Ventura Rodríguez for S. Marcos in Madrid: instead of Borrominesque undulation throughout the facade, however, only the wings were curved in the manner of Bernini at S. Andrea al Quirinale.**5.43c–e**

Despite the precocious resort to Serlian example by Diego de Riaño for the sacristy of Seville cathedral – and the latter-day flirtation with curvature in façades – elliptical planning was rare in Habsburg or Bourbon Spain: after the works of Juan Gómez's generation, Rodríguez's S. Marcos is the most notable exception. Apart from Bonavía's S. Antonio at Aranjuez (1748), small in scale and sheathed in an undulating portico, the large-scale circular planning of Loreto had no Spanish equal either – until the restoration of Classical principles in the late 18th century.

Conventional in Rome, not unknown in Naples, the octagon in a Greek cross was occasionally adopted by Spanish architects. Pedro de Ribera deployed it for dedication to the Virgen del Puerto in Madrid.**5.43a, b** That may be seen as a reduced version of S. Agnese on the Piazza

Navona in Rome (see pages 91 and 111). An enlarged variant of the same forms was adopted for the Jesuit church of S. Luis in Seville by Leonardo da Figueroa (1650–1730). In contrast to that master's earlier work in the city, such as his revision of El Salvador or the Caridad, S. Luis is at least as notable for the rampage of prolixity in ornament.**5.44a–g**

Figueroa crowned the career that led from S. Luis

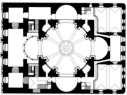

(c–g) S. Luis de los Franceses (1699–1730), plan, façade, detail of dome outside and in, crossing; (h) Seminario de S. Telmo: main frontispiece (from 1724).

The reconstruction of the Caridad church, dilapidated by 1644, was begun by Pedro Sánchez Falconete but revised in 1663 by Figueroa. The façade is of the 'palace' type: unusual despite the rich Mujédar tradition, the tiled panels represent the patrons S. Jorge and Santiago with allegories of Faith, Hope and Charity. The city's patrons, S. Fernando (Ferdinand III of Castile) and S. Hermenegildo, guard the door. The single volume of the interior is dominated by the great Solomonic retable by Bernardo Simón de Pineda with sculpture by Pedro Roldán: the interment of Christ in the centre, Faith, Hope, Charity accompanying S. Roque and S. Jorge above.

Augmenting the Jesuit complex – with its Casa Profesa and noviciate church of the Annunciation – the grander church dedicated to S. Luis was commissioned by Archbishop Luis de Salcedo y Azcona. Over the Greek-cross plan, the Solomonic ordonnance amplifies its innovative deployment to generate vitality in the retables of Pineda and his contemporaries. Dome and apses are treated to a stunning confection of architectural and celestial illusionism supplemented by flagrantly lush variations on early Rococo permutations of grotesque motifs. The retables are by Duque Corejo, with paintings – of S. Luis in the centre supported by Jesuit saints – are by the school of Zurbarán and Domingo Martínez (1743–50).

The construction of the Seminary School of the University of Navigators began in 1682 outside the walls of the city, on property belonging to the Tribunal of the Holy Office (the 'Inquisition'). It is built on a rectangular plan, with several interior courtyards, towers on the four corners, a chapel, and gardens. Figueroa designed the chapel: the outer portal was completed from 1754 by the master's son and grandson, Matias and Antonio Matias: it is supported by atlante, with aspects of indig-

5.44d

5.44e

5.44f

5.44g

with flagrant flair in the chapel of S. Telmo in Seville. The frontispiece, completed by his filial followers, may instructively be compared with its counterpart at the university of Valladolid designed by the Carmelite brother Pedro de la Visitation. Strictures of a seminal Classicist like de l'Orme are subverted by an eclectic diversity of ornament which exceeds the Plateresque in excess – and in bulk.**5.44h, 5.45a**

The Obradoiro and its Flemish counterparts notwithstanding, the taste for prolix ornament is essentially southern, not only in Spain: there, the early 18th-century manifestation may be seen as a revival of the Plateresque mentality with spectacular flourish. In the process, an

enous Americans, inhabited by allegories of the nautical arts and sciences and presided over by S. Telmo (or Elmo), patron saint of sailors, flanked by S. Fernando and S. Hermenegild, patrons of the city. Among the plethora of infuences on the subversion of the Classical ordonnance, Wendel Dietterlin may be credited with the mesmerizing fluting of the Ionic Order, at least.

›5.45 THE EXUBERANCE OF NARCISO TOMÉ: (a) University of Valladolid, frontispiece (in collaboration with Fray Pedro de la Visitation from 1715); (b–d) Toledo cathedral, Trasparente (from 1729), longitudinal section through ambulatory, general view of retable, detail of occulus.

The University of Valladolid was founded in the mid-14th century. By the beginning of the 16th century it was housed in one quadrangular building with a late-Gothic chapel. Two centuries later this was supplemented by another quadrangle entered from the then Plaza Santa María (now Plaza Univesidad) through its spectacular frontispiece.

Commissioned by Diego de Astorga y Céspedes, archbishop of Toledo, to illuminate the Sacrament on the high altar, the Trasparente was executed in three years by Tomé and his four sons – two of whom were architects, one a painter and the other a sculptor. In the central bay of the ambulatory, it takes it name from the transmission of light for that purpose from an interpolated dormer window through apertures cut in the sanctuary wall and the great altar retable. In the representation of angels revelling in this manifestation of the divine, the arts are fused under the influence of Bernini – though its architect is not known to have visited Rome. Borromini is recalled by the false perspective of the concave theatre in which a heavenly host celebrates the glory of their empyrean above a niche sheltering the Madonna and Child and below the performance of the Last Supper in a sort of exposed camarín.

5.44h

5.45a

5.45d

extraordinary role was played at the heart of the kingdom by the elder Figueroa's younger contemporary Narciso Tomé (1690–1742). He first emerges c. 1715 as a sculptor assisting his brother Diago on the Valladolid University's frontispiece. His most celebrated achievement is the Trasparente in Toledo cathedral (c. 1721). Behind the high altar, across and above the ambulatory, this astonishing confection penetrates ornamental delirium with spatial illusionism worthy of Borromini: as the arena for sacred drama lit with high theatricality, it is worthy of Bernini.**5.45b–d**

5.45b

5.45c

5.46b

Tomé apart, no Spanish architect was more riotous in embellishment than Figueroa and his heirs. Prolixity was certainly not their uncontested preserve but several of their colleagues were comparatively reserved. The contrast between the main front of the Seminario de S. Telmo and the contemporary tobacco factory – now the main building of Seville University – is no less striking for its appropriateness. Begun on royal command in 1725 by the Spanish military engineer Ignacio Sala, that exceptional industrial building was finished by the Flemish engineer Sebastián van de Borcht in 1758.**5.46**

›5.46 SEVILLE, INSTITUTIONAL BUILDINGS: (a) tobacco factory (from 1728–71, converted for the University of Seville in 1953); (b) Archbishop's Palace (from 1704 and later, by Lorenzo Fernández de Iglesias and Diego Antonio Díaz).

Seville had a monopoly on trade with the Americas where tobacco had been encountered in 1492. The first factories were established in the city early in the new century: initially dispersed, they were eventually concentrated on the site outside Puerta de Jerez facing the church of S. Pedro – for sanitary reasons and to facilitate state control. The vast complex, the largest industrial building in Spain and hardly exceeded elsewhere in Europe, was constructed between 1728 and 1771 under the direction of military engineers from Spain and the Netherlands. These included Ignacio Sala, who initiated the scheme in 1725, and Sebastián van der Borcht, in charge from 1750, who pursued the definitive work in collaboration with local master-masons Vicente Catalán Bengochea, Pedro de Silva and Lucas Cintora.

5.46a

5.47

›5.47 UMBRETE: Nuestra Señora de la Consolación
(from 1725), entrance front.

›5.48 SANTIAGO DE COMPOSTELA, MAN-
NERED BAROQUE: (a) Casa do Cabildo, screen
façade closing the Plaza de Platerías as veiwed from the
cathedral's southern portal (from 1750); (b) Convento di
S. Clara, entrance (Simón Rodríguez, from c. 1750).

5.48a

5.48b

Well before engineers embarked on the tobacco factory, a much less conventional mode of reaction to prolix
ornament may be detected in the work of home-grown
architects. At Umbrete, for instance, Diego Antonio Diaz
(1680–1748) effected the transition from floridity to tectonics: he assembled fragmented architectural motifs with
marginally less licentiousness than the examples propa-
gated by the pattern books of northerners like Vredeman
de Vries or Wendel Dietterlin – or indeed the Santiago
Obradoiro.**5.47** And the link back to José de la Peña through
that great work is revealed by the extreme example of this
inorganic mode, the gatehouse of S. Clara in Santiago de
Compostela (c. 1750).**5.48**

Inorganic, organic or both, baffling complexity of form
was the norm for much of the first half of the 18th century,
especially in retables – if there was anything normal about
a style which may be called neo-Mannerist but is best seen
as *sui generis*. Essential ingredients were the Solomonic
column and the estípite pilaster as the residue of support
on the multi-layered, foliage-entwined stage for dramatically disposed icons. The former, of eminent lineage
ascending from its revival by Raphael to its apotheosis at

the instigation of Bernini, is potentially infinite in its spiral dynamic. The estípite, extracted from the deconstructive dementia of Dietterlin, is fragmentary and static, tapering downwards contrary to the logic of structure which it further subverts with multiple interpolated capital or cornice mouldings and adventitious panelling. The juxtaposition of these two alternative forms of post is manifestly schizophrenic but that indulgence was actually rare: they usually constitute alternative contexts for equally virile sculpture, though the incontinent estípite was in great danger of succumbing to rampant floridity.

As we have seen, the Solomonic style was favoured in Iberia at least from the 1640s when it appears in Ambuesa's façade of Valencia's S. Miguel de los Reyes (see page 816): within a generation it had been promoted to a leading role in the main retable of the Seville Caridad, devised by Bernardo Simón de Pineda (c. 1670, page 829) as a proscenium framing an innovative scenographic perspective, and of the Salamanca Clerecía by Juan Fernández (1673; AIC5, page 753). The estípite came later, in the lost retable of Jeronimo de Balbas in the Sagraio of Seville cathedral (1706, destroyed 1824) and, earlier, in José Benito Churriguera's work in S. Esteban, Salamanca.**5·49a, b**

Rather than Figueroa, the name of the Churriguera brothers of sculptors-cum-set designers is usually associated with the uniquely Spanish anti-architectonic retable style, in which the estípite plays its ephemeral supporting role, though their building styles were conservative. José Benito and Joaquín vied with the most fantastic of their southern contemporaries in translating their retable style to Castille.

Joaquín resorted to estípete in 1714 for his Vera Cruz retable in Salamanca. His older brother had preferred the Solomonic style for S. Esteban in Salamanca in the last decade of the previous century, for S. Salvador de Leganés

5·49a

›5·49 THE DIVERSIFIED TALENTS OF THE CHURRIGUERA: (a) Salamanca, José Benito's retable in S. Esteban (1692); (b) Madrid, Joaquín's retable in the Colegio Calatrava (from 1717); (c) Nuevo Baztán, view of east side of plaza with cathedral, right, palace left; (d, e) Salamanca, Colegio de Calatrava, portal, Alberto's Plaza Mayor (from 1725), north range.

5·49b

An exceptional variant on the Gesù formula, the church of Nuevo Baztán was built to the plans of José Benito Churriguera c. 1710: framed by twin towers and attached to a palace in the context of rational planning, the two-storey façade may be seen as a latter-day reduction of the Escorial type but with an Order of full columns projecting through two planes to shelter the portal.

in Madrid at the beginning of the new century, and for the Sagrario chapel of the Segovian cathedral but preferred to festoon regular shafts with garlands for the Calatrava church in Madrid towards the end of his life.

José Benito (1665–1725) recalls the sobriety of Juan de Herrera's successors in the context of the informally related squares of his Nuevo Baztán.**5.49c** The major surviving work of Joaquín, the Colegio de Calatrava in Salamanca (from 1717), pays homage to Rodrigo Gil de Hontañón and the residue of his Colegio Anaya may be seen as neo-Plateresque. The youngest brother Alberto (1676–1750) worked mainly in Salamanca, above all on introducing a nucleus of grand formality with his Plaza Mayor inspired by Gómez de Moya's Madrid project (from 1725): the central elements of the latter, appropriately richer than at Nuevo Baztán in detail, may also be seen as neo-Plateresque but they are eclipsed by a fantastic exercise in pediment contortion.**5.49d, e**

5.50a

5.50b

Prominent early essays in estípite style include the Santiago and Virgin de la Antigua altarpieces in Granada cathedral (after 1710) by Francisco Hurtado Izquierdo (1669–1725) and Pedro Duque Cornejo (1678–1757) respectively.**5·50** Pedro de Ribera applied the motif on the Hospicio de S. Fernando in Madrid (c. 1722).**5·51** Thereafter it appears occasionally on façades, as at Córdoba's S. Hipólito (from 1729), and numerous retables – at which Duque Cornejo and Cayetano da Costa (1711–80) excelled. The apogee, reached by Hurtado or a close follower, is represented in S. José, Seville, which demolishes even the estípite's insubstantial pretension to structural significance in the proscenium to a dramatically lit inner sanctum. After that there was gradual reassertion of architectonic logic, notably by Cayetano da Costa in Seville.

A special position must be reserved for Francisco Hurtado who extrapolated the neo-Mannerist plethora of contortion from the plane to the round. Beyond the retable, Hurtado's all-embracing masterpieces are the richly chro-

5.51

›**5.52 HURTADO AND THE CARTHUSIAN SAGRARIO:** (a, b) Granada, Cartuja (Charterhouse), Sagrario (sacramental tabernacle chapel beyond the high altar of the church, from 1709) and sacristy (from 1727), detail of baldacchino; (c) monastery church of El Paular (from 1718), sacristy chapel.

matic Sagrario chapels of the Carthusian monasteries in Granada and at El Paular (of 1713 and 1718 respectively): in the earlier work, a riot of Solomonic columns supports the veritable surf of broken waves into which the entablature is dissolved and from which organic amorphids emerge; waves also engulf the sanctuary screen in the later work but the Solomonic style, reserved for the sacramental tabernacle within, is banished from the vestibule in favour of a Composite Order of unfluted coloured marble columns; the recognizable entablature is overwhelmed by rampant gilt stucco only above the intervening niches.**5·52**

The masterpiece of Hurtado's school is the sacristy of the Granada Cartuja: as yet unattributed, it was begun some five years after the master's death. The undulating cornice is typical of the style but exceeding all precedent is the multiplicity of frame mouldings, oozing like lava into the shallow exedrae of the lateral window bays. Even more sensational, however, is the multiplicity of architrave, capital, volute and fragmentary pediment mouldings from which the estípites might be defined as constituted if that word did not imply cohesion. The fantasy of a hyperactive – if not neurotic – imagination, naturally this work had no successors – though the luxuriantly florid camarín chapel of Nuestra Señora del Rosario in the Grenadine church of S. Domingo and the relatively tame retreat from ingenuity in the Sagrario of La Asunción parish church at Priego are sometimes referred to in this connexion, despite their late dates (1774 and 1784 respectively). By then Classical precept reigned again but when the Granada Cartuja's sacristy was first penetrated, forty years earlier, the most enticing way out from its agitated anti-architectural deconstructivism was into the thoroughly anti-architectonic human, animal and vegetal organicism essential to the Rococo. And of that, Hipólito Rovira Brocandel's portal of the palace of the Marqués de Dos Aguas knows no equal.**5·53**

5.53a

›**5.53 ROCOCO EPILOGUE:** (a) Granada, S. Domingo, Rosario Chapel, detail of vault (from 1726); (b) Valencia, Palacio de Dos Aguas, portal (from 1740).

5.52c

5.53b

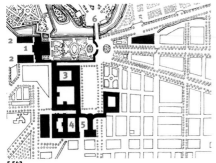

›**5.54 ARANJUEZ, ROYAL PALACE:** (a) site plan with (1) original block of Juan-Bautista Toledo and Juan de Herrera, (2) late-16th-century extensions, (3) wings added in 1771, (4) extended dependencies with (5) chapel of S. Antonio, (6) Tagus bridge, (7) new axial approach to east front skirting extended town grid, (b) general view from west.

Philip II's hunting lodge was begun to plans of Bautista Toledo but furthered by Hererra and Juan Gómez de Mora (AIC5, page 757): it was largely destroyed by two fires in the 1660s but the celebrated gardens survived to be continuously augmented under the later Habsburgs and their Bourbon successors. The reconstruction was not advanced under Philip IV. Philip V, keen to assert continuity with his Habsburg ancestors, took up the challenge and called for plans from his Spanish architects' office in 1715: work began in 1727 on the north wing. The Italian painter and decorator Giacomo Bonavia (Santiago Bonavía, 1700–60), in charge from 1731, was commissioned by Ferdinand VI to restore the palace and the town after another disastrous fire in 1748: he raised the height of the central block by a storey, relieved the Herreran severity with a new frontispiece of superimposed pilasters rising through a portico with balcony facing over the forecourt to the park, inserted an imperial staircase, extended the dependencies to the south, added the circular chapel of S. Antonio to their east and was probably responsible for building the bridge across the Tagus to the northern hunting alleys. Continuing his brother's work in 1771, King Charles III commissioned the wings flanking the forecourt from his Sicilian architect Francesco Sabatini (1722–97) who had worked for him at Caserta – as we shall see.

3 PALACES OF THE SOUTHERN BOURBONS

Philip V's idea of a grand country seat may have been formed in his childhood at Versailles but, married first to Maria Louisa of Savoy, then to the assertive Isabel Farnese, he turned to Italians to realize his architectural ambitions within and beyond Madrid. He employed the painter and decorator Giacomo Bonavia to further a scheme of great restoration and enlargement at Aranjuez.**5.54** At that time too, Andrea Procaccini, the new queen's Roman protégé, was called on to work at San Ildefonso: Sempronio Subisati followed him there in the mid-1730s. In the first decade of the reign, however, he called on his grandfather's first architect, Robert de Cotte, for advice on what to do with Buen Retiro but war inhibited action until 1712.

The extensive and architecturally unexceptional exercise of developing the Buen Retiro retreat on the eastern outskirts of the capital had been promoted with great expense by the count-duke Olivares for Philip IV (AIC5, page 757). However, the decay of the economy – and of the Habsburg line in the lamentable person of Charles II – obviated major palace building for the rest of the century. The new king and queen, Philip V and Maria Louisa Gabriella of Savoy, first focused on the amelioration of the dilapidated complex inherited from the Habsburgs which, though badly built to no consistent programme, was far more agreeable than the cold and gloomy Alcázar.

At the end of the war of succession, the assistant French royal architect René Carlier was sent to Madrid with plans for the rehabilitation of Buen Retiro. These were rejected as inadequate and impractical. Over the

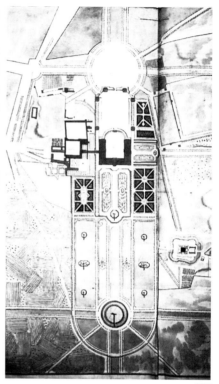

›5.55 MADRID, THE BUEN RETIRO OF ROBERT DE COTTE, 1714–15: (a–d) site plan, ground-floor plan, entrance and garden fronts of first project, (e, f) plan and section of second project.

Robert de Cotte's entirely new palace was to be sited to the east of the old one and linked to it by a gallery. The first project would have accommodated the royal couple in similar apartments on the ground and first floors of three doubled wings (the king to the southwest, the queen to the south-east) about a galleried and moated court. Except insofar as it satisfies specific Spanish court etiquette, the planning is comparable to the French Premier Architecte's other modern, convenient but eminently decorous revisions of the basic Versailles scheme or, more particularly, the Grand Trianon. The elevation recalls the French academic Classical revisions of the Italian schemes for the Louvre: the entrance front retains Bernini's engaged columns, but spaces them canonically; the garden side recalls the

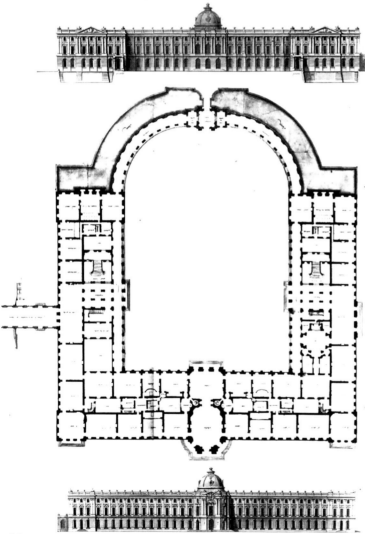

new Louvre's south front but the projection of the salon follows current French fashion enhanced by the addition of an elliptical dome.

The second scheme ranges the great rooms en enfilade – but backed by the private rooms, as at Versailles – around a square court subdivided by axial cross-wings with superimposed octagonal vestibules in the centre serving an imperial staircase in the southern arm. The façades were to be similar in style to those of the first scheme – though considerably reduced. The immediate precedent for the cross-in-square plan is Marly, where the *petit appartements* span the corners between the perpendicular enfilades of great rooms – though the scale is vastly different. The Spanish tradition, culminating in El Escorial, is obviously also relevant.

5.55f

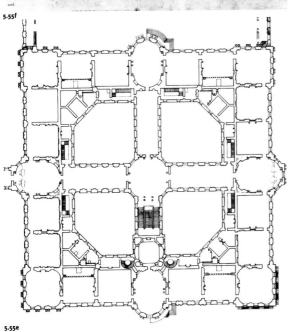

5.55e

two years thereafter, de Cotte dispatched two alternative projects for a totally new palace on the site: one was U-shaped, like Trianon, the other centralized on a cross in a square, like the Château de Marly but considerably greater in scale (see pages 276f). Before money could be found for work to begin on a definitive project there was a new queen: Isabel Farnese reacted against French influence in favour of her Italian entourage and, in any case, turned her back on the suburban complex.[5.55]

Though de Cotte's ideas for Buen Retiro found no favour with Queen Isabel, they apparently informed the major project undertaken nearly forty years later by her son, the future Charles III – as we shall see. Meanwhile, emulating his Bourbon grandfather in developing a grand seat well beyond the capital, Philip V diverted his attention from Aranjuez and turned north to the conversion of monastic buildings at San Ildefonso into an entirely new rural royal retreat which did find favour with the new queen.

While work was underway beyond the capital, Buen Retiro continued to fulfil its purpose as a resort from the overbearing Alcázar but the latter remained the principal metropolitan seat of the monarchy until it was devastated by fire in 1734. Philip V then called on Pedro de Ribera, principal royal architect, to project its replacement: he responded with a vast cruciform scheme of five courts in which grandiose formality took precedence over any semblance of economy.[5.58a] Looking for greater practical experience of large-scale palace building, the king called on Filippo Juvarra who had been working on such projects in Piedmont for Amadeus II of Savoy, king of Sardinia, father of the late French dauphine and Spanish Queen Maria Louisa (see pages 160ff): he had also worked on festive facilities for Messina's celebration of Philip's accession.[5.56] He was permitted to answer the call to Madrid in 1735, when his final great Turinese project was well on the way to completion.

ADVENT OF JUVARRA

Called in primarily to redesign the Alcázar, Juvarra was also asked to complete the transformation of San Ildefonso into the palace of La Granja. The nucleus was a 16th-century cloister around which were ranged four domestic wings, with towers at the corners (from 1721): in this initial stage the king was emulating his grandfather's retreat at Marly – at least in scale. From 1727, however, courts were added to the east and west of the cloister in much reduced emulation of Versailles. Formal gardens were already being developed in André Le Nôtre's style.

The final phase of work on La Granja followed Juvarra's intervention in the year of his death, 1736. In accordance with the revised royal ambitions for the complex, he provided the key element in linking the three courts: the grand block of state rooms addressing the garden. If the Madrid elevations recalled Cortona's Louvre – in the manner of the Turinese Palazzo Madama – the new La Granja façade was articulated with a colossal Order rising from the ground in the manner of Le Vau's Louvre – or, indeed, Boffrand's second project for Malgrange (see page 298). However, the most decidedly French element was the garden.**5.57**

5.56
›5.56 FILIPPO JUVARRA AND EPHEMERAL SCENOGRAPHY: theatre erected in Messina in 1701 for the festivities marking the accession of Philip V to the thrones of Spain, Naples and Sicily.

›5.57 SAN ILDEFONSO, LA GRANJA: (a) plan, (b) west front, (c) plan of gardens, (d) garden front.

The site was developed with a hunting lodge and a cloister dedicated to S. Ildefonso by Henry IV in the middle of the 15th century: a generation later Queen Isabella consigned it to monks from Segovia. Philip V bought it back in 1720. In the following year the initial work on framing the cloister with royal apartments was

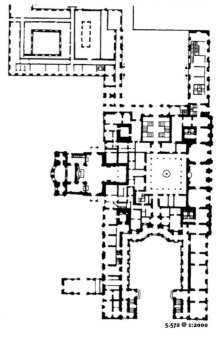

5.57b

5.57a @ 1:2000

entrusted to the Spanish architect Teodoro Ardemans. He kept the towers traditional to an alcázar but remodelled the chapel and gave it an undulating west front (facing the line of approach to the complex through the stable court): the composition recalls Fischer von Erlach's Salzburg Kollegienkirche. Andrea Procaccini began the east and west wings in 1727: after his death in 1734 the work was continued by his assistant, Sempronio Subisati, until the advent of Juvarra in 1736. On his death in that same year, Sacchetti took over – as on the Alcázar site in Madrid – but here he was able to implement Juvarra's scheme.

The formal gardens were designed by René Carlier and Étienne Boutellier: pupils of Robert de Cotte and André Le Nôtre respectively, they had been invited to transform the palace and garden at Buen Retiro shortly after Philip was confirmed in his kingdom but shortage of funds delayed that project until they were redeployed to San Ildefonso in 1720 at the instigation of Queen Isabel. Development continued well into the reign of Charles III.

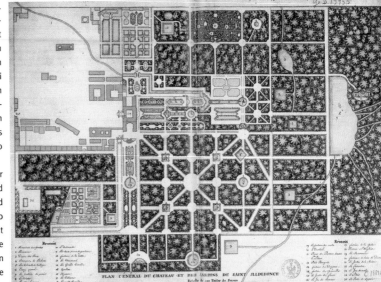

5·57c

5·57d

In Madrid Juvarra quickly produced an ideal scheme of stupendous grandeur for a new royal palace on the Alcázar site. It exceeded Pedro de Ribera's conception in scale, though reduced from five courts to four: it remained cruciform but not rigorously symmetrical about both axes. Of these the longitudinal one embraced an entrance court flanked by administrative blocks with a chapel to the right, as at Versailles, and an inner ceremonial court extruded from Bernini's third scheme for the Louvre. The extensive porticoes and staircases which open and close this

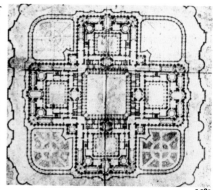

5.58a

›5.58 MADRID, PALAZZO REALE: (a) Pedro de Ribera's scheme, (b–d) Juvarra's ground-floor plan and elevations, (e) Sacchetti's plan (Madrid, Biblioteca Nacional), (f) view from forecourt.

Reduced to one court from quadripartite Juvarra's impossible ideal, Sacchetti's project rose to seven floors on the west front where the site rises steeply from the river flats. Though reverting to Bernini in plan, he retained Juvarra's doubled apartment ranges rather than an outmoded single enfilade. Juvarra's twin staircases mounted opposite one another from the grand vestibule in the left (west) range of the central court where they served twin apartments in the north and south ranges of the western court: access to similar apartments flanking the eastern court was via the galleries which enclosed the central court to north and south or a subsidiary staircase in the right (east) range. Sacchetti's compacted scheme has one staircase of parallel flights disposed laterally but linked longitudinally between the intermediate landings. Juvarra's chapel – similar in plan to S. Uberto at La Venaria Reale in Piedmont (page 162) – was to the west of the loggias separating the two ceremonial courts: Sacchetti originally placed his chapel in the entrance wing but moved it to the opposite side where it is associated with the main ceremonial rooms serving the twin royal apartments (in the east and west wings) and where its dome provides the appropriate climax to the whole composition. Construction lasted from 1738 to 1755 but the palace was not fully ready for occupation by King Charles III until 1764. Sacchetti died in Rome in that year: he had been succeeded in Madrid by Francesco Sabatini who had assisted Vanvitelli at Caserta and was translated from Naples to Spain in the train of the king.

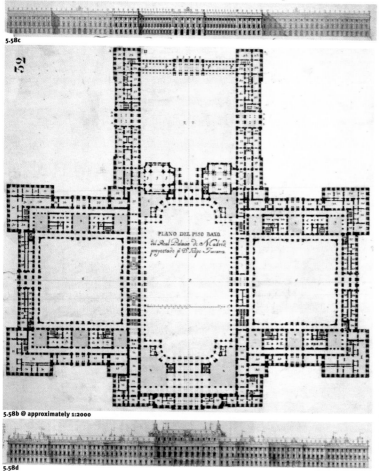

5.58c

5.58b @ approximately 1:2000

PLANO DEL PISO BAXO
del Real Palacio de Madrid
proyectado p.^r D.ⁿ Filipe Juvarra

5.58d

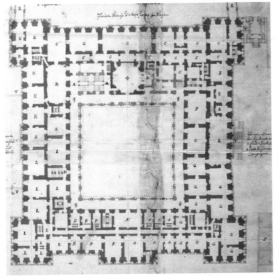

5.58e

ceremonial space serve the twin royal apartments ranged around the lateral pair of courts: these were to be square like Bernini's Louvre. Much in the elevation derived from Cortona's fourth Louvre scheme but it extended to sixty-nine bays on the fronts and seventy on the sides.**5.58a–d**

Juvarra died within a year of his advent to Madrid, before he and his scheme could be tamed. As his successor he had recommended Gian-Battista Sacchetti, who he had trained in Turin. The style subsisted but the scheme was trimmed by three-quarters.**5.58e** The vast central ceremonial court, with its extravagant porticoes, was eliminated and the lateral courts were conflated as one. The forecourt was enclosed by arcaded galleries, rising no higher than the palace basement but punctuated by isolated administrative blocks, corner pavilions and a suitably grand portico.**5.58f**

5.58f

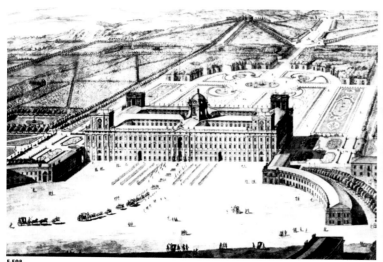

5.59a

5.59c

ADVENT OF VANVITELLI

The last and grandest palace of the southern Bourbons, another of the many responses to Versailles, was commissioned by the future Charles III of Spain when he was king of Naples. Sited in the vicinity of hunting grounds at Caserta, to the north-east of the venerable but vulnerable seaside capital below Vesuvius, it was begun in 1752.**5·59** Fourteen years earlier the king had resorted to a constricted site on a hill commanding a view of the city for his first exercise in palace design, Capodimonte, but he aborted construction in frustration with progress, cost and the architect, Giovanni Antonio Medrano.

For his new scheme, the king called on Luigi Vanvitelli (1703–60): born in Naples to the Dutch topographical painter Gaspar van Vittel (hence his Italianized name), he had trained in Rome where the Classicizing followers of Carlo Fontana were intent on taming Baroque exuberance – and where he had recently completed his masterpiece for João V of Portugal and reoriented Michelangelo's S. Maria degli Angeli in the Baths of Diocletian (AIC5, page 162, and see above, pages 116f and below, page 865).

›5·59 CASERTA, REGGIA, from 1752: (a, b) engraved overview and plan of main floor, (c) south front, (d) chapel, (e, f) staircase and central vestibule at the level of the piano reale, (g) Queen's Boudoir, detail, (h, i) general views of garden looking south from the top of the cascade and north from the Fountain of Ceres to the Grotto of Juno and Aeolus and the cascade, (j–l) sculpture groups in the basin of Diana and Acteon at the source of the cascade.

5.59d

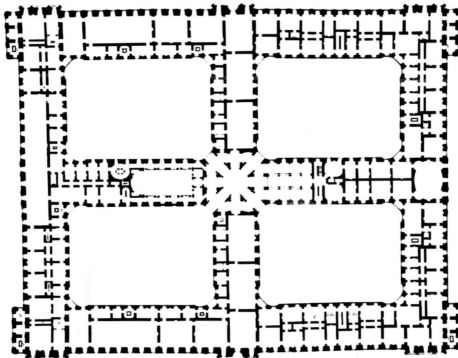

5.59b @ 1:2000

Caserta

The Reggia of Caserta was conceived to accommodate the king, his family and his government, like Versailles, but instead of extended wings for
the diversified occupants all was to be contained in one vast quadrangular structure divided internally into four huge courts by cross-wings. The
inspiration may well have been Robert de Cotte's second scheme for Buen
Retiro: that had been rejected by the patron's mother in the year before he
was born but the young Charles was trained in architectural drawing and as
king took a close interest in the development and execution of his architectural projects – like his cousin, Louis XV.

As in the abortive Madrid scheme, if with more constraint, the impact
of the axial wings on the four fronts expresses the internal organization
on the exterior: foremost, the main central range asserts itself with pedimented entrance and garden frontispieces articulated with engaged columns; these are echoed only at the corners where the perimeter wings

5·598

The perimeter is a rectangle of 183 x 152 metres: corner towers and a central dome were projected in the ideal but not executed. The five levels contain about two thousand rooms. The garden axis is about 3 kilometres long. The great sculpture groups of Diana and Actaeon are due to Paolo Persico assisted by Angelo Brunelli and Pietro Solari.

The building had been finished and roofed by 1773 when Vanvitelli died, despite the failing interest in the project of the patron's son and heir, Ferdinand IV: Vanvitelli had designed the main interiors but only those of the principal royal apartments facing south were ever to be finished – the earlier ones after his death in general to his designs under the supervision of his son Carlo.

Preoccupied with his work at Caserta until King Charles left for Spain, Vanvitelli had little time for private practice. He hoped for a call to Madrid but his assistant, Francesco Sabatini, went instead – perhaps in the interest of leaving the realization of the Caserta project to its originator. Thereafter, he worked extensively in his home city on secular and religious projects. His masterpiece is the great domed church of the Annunziata with its internal Order of freestanding and embedded Corinthian columns (from 1760): like the master's palace interiors, especially the theatre, this important work is best considered in the context of the style unsatisfactorily known as 'Neoclassicism'.

similarly penetrate one another and emerge as pavilions. Over the rusticated basement, pilasters were deployed only between the pavilions of the garden front, as on the river front of the new Louvre, on de Cotte's first project for Buen Retiro, on several of Juvarra's Savoy palace projects and on the palace currently being built for the king's brother in Madrid to Sacchetti's revision of Juvarra's designs. The strict discipline of geometry is unrelaxed in the plan and no whim moderates severity in the elevations: designed around three square courts and articulated only with Doric pilaster groups over rusticated piers, Capodimonte set the immediate precedent for rational planning and severity of repetitive order but not for scale, proportion or extended axial site lines.

The cross-wings are the axes of communication to the main parts of the palace at all its five levels: at their junction are octagonal vestibules, as in de Cotte's second scheme for Buen Retiro. The base one provides access diagonally – theatrically – into the courts and orthogonally north to the garden, or east to an imperial staircase opposite a statue of Hercules in the niche closing the western side. Surpassing de Cotte's similar scheme in grandeur, the return flights issued on the piano reale in the stunning spectacle of another octagonal vestibule with multiple columns flanking the door to the chapel to the west, opposite the stairs, and framing vistas along the routes south and north to the royal apartments – the king's to the south, the queen's to the north and their heirs' accommodation to the east beyond vestibules centred on the two main fronts. If not the stage sets of Bibiena, with their dramatic diagonal lines countering the orthogonals, the nuclear geometry recalls that elaborated by Juvarra for Stupinigi (see pages 126ff, 167ff). The chapel (from 1768) is modelled on Hardouin-Mansart's exemplar at Versailles. The articulation of the theatre with a colossal Composite Order (from 1768 to 1772) will be discussed elsewhere in the context of the French Enlightenment.

Vanvitelli projected an elliptical parade ground, surrounded by stables and barracks, before the south front. The north front addressed the extremely extended axis of the formal garden, continuing the main line of communication through the palace of course. Conceived under the inspiration of Versailles, executed to French prescription by Martin Biancourt, the scheme embraces a broad parterre nearest the palace and subsidiary zones in bosquets – including, ultimately, an informal 'Eng-

5.59h

5.59i

5.59j

ish' garden – to either side of the extended axis. The main thrust of the latter is through elongated tanks and gently rising ground to a grand cascade: fountains and a grotto with Olympian statuary ease the trajectory – as they do in the far less extensive 16th-century Italian 'riverine' garden type best represented in the grounds of the Villa Lante at Bagnaia (AIC5, pages 189f). Reversing the thrust, the cascade issues from a broad pool with superb sculpture groups representing Diana and her nymphs at their bath, observing the fatal metamorphosis of intruding Actaeon.

5.59k

5.59l

Not Versailles, not the palaces of Maria Theresa nor even Catherine the Great rival Caserta as a manifestation of the enlightened absolutism which its founder exemplified to the full. Yet Charles of Bourbon, who monitored the planning and oversaw the initial stages of construction, was not to witness the realization of his vast rationalist exercise: he progressed from Naples to Spain only seven years after building began and it was not finished until the middle of the next century. Absolutist in its overbearing scale, dynamic in its axes, rich in its marble staircase, scenographic at its heart, it may be seen as the last great achievement of the Baroque era: rationalist in its plan, strictly disciplined in its Classical order, it may also be seen as the first great exercise of the so-called Neoclassical era of Enlightenment – the subject of another volume.

›5.60 JOHN V: high-value gold 'royals' issued in limited edition from 1732.

5.60

4 THE GOLDEN AGE OF PORTUGAL AT HOME AND ABROAD

The great age of Portuguese Baroque began with the reign of John V (1706–50) following the discovery of gold in Brazil (1693).**5.60** It was catastrophically curtailed by the great earthquake which followed his death within five years. However, architectural activity spanned Portugal in distinct southern and northern schools. Initially exuberant in superficial embellishment to articulation inherited from the *estilo chão*, the northern style extended its development from Oporto and Braga in particular. The southern style is more overtly architectonic in the late Roman Baroque mode of Carlo Fontana and his heirs: it is well represented by survivals or reconstructions in and around Lisbon, and in regional centres like Coimbra.

Preoccupied with consolidation after the expulsion of the Spaniards, straitened in circumstance, John V's Braganza predecessors left a relatively meagre legacy – in Portugal, at least. In the colonies, the religious orders remained busy.

At Goa, the mid-century Theatine church of S. Cajetan follows Maderno's massive addition to the Vatican basilica. Moreover, it was furnished in sumptuous Solomonic style after Bernini's intervention in S. Pietro but in timber and to a relatively modest scale.**5.61a.b** That style, popular in Iberia at the turn of the century, was adopted for the main retable and the shrine of S. Francis Xavier in Bom Jesus.**5.61c** In

›**5.61 GOA:** (a, b) S. Cajetan (Our Lady of Divine Providence, from 1661), exterior and interior to sanctuary; (c) Bom Jesus, tomb of S. Francis Xavier (1696); (d) S. Francis of Assisi (rebuilt from 1660), view to sanctuary.

5.61c

5.61a

The last great Goan work to follow a metropolitan prototype, the Theatine church of Our Lady of Divine Providence clearly, if remotely, reflects S. Pietro in the Vatican, at least to the front. It has a sumptuous, free-standing Solomonic high altar and the domed Greek-cross volume has a Baroque sense of scale, inside and out. However, the arrangement of niches and intermediate arched doors below the roundels in the compressed façade tends to assimilate the outer bays into unsettling triads and the transition from a two- to a three-dimensional expression of the Order is prompted by no subtle gradations of plane – as in Maderno's seminal Roman masterpiece. As originally projected there, the composition is completed with twin towers.

By the end of the 17th century the sanctuaries of S. Francis of Assisi and Bom Jesus had also been endowed with gilded retables of colossal Orders – Solomonic in the latter case. In addition, the north transept of Bom Jesus was transformed into a chapel dedicated

5.61b

5.61d

contrast, the tabernacle on the high altar of S. Francis of Assisi (rebuilt from 1660) was set in a canonical triumphal arch and Solomonic columns were reserved for the minor altars at the crossing (AIC5, pages 788ff).**5.61d**

The greatest work begun in Lisbon under the early Braganzas is the church of S. Engrácia (from 1682): the centralized apsidal scheme was inspired by S. Pietro in the Vatican but without the portico projected by Michelangelo – let alone the nave of Maderno.**5.62a, b** The project was first

to S. Francis Xavier: beyond a Solomonic proscenium, the saint's remains were enshrined in a silver casket crafted by the Florentine sculptor Giovanni Battista Foggini and donated by the last Medici grand duke of Tuscany, Cosimo III, in 1696.

›5.62 LISBON, CENTRALIZED PROJECTS FURTHERED EARLY IN THE REIGN OF JOHN V: (a, b) S. Engrácia (begun 1682, completed with its dome 1966), plan and exterior; (c, d) Menino de Deus (from 1711), exterior and interior.

5.62a @ 1:1000

5.62c

5.62b

5.62d

entrusted to João Nunes Tinoco (c. 1610–89), master of works at S. Vicente de Fora from 1641 (AIC5, page 762): he was superseded by his disciple, João Antunes (1642–1712), who furthered construction until John V lost interest in favour of Mafra. Antunes was also retained for the latter's first independent project, the convent church of the Menino de Deus commissioned in 1711 to invoke grace for the birth of a royal heir. An octagonal volume behind a 'palace' façade, the building was never to be completed with its towers or dome but is a rare survivor of the 1755 Lisbon earthquake.**5.623c, d** Antunes began his exercises in centralized planning by combining a Greek cross and hexagon for the church of Bom Jesus at Barcelos (from 1701).

5.63a

Another survivor of the 1755 catastrophe is the convent church of the Madre de Deus, a 16th-century structure refurbished at royal instigation from 1730 with richly framed painted panels superimposed in antiquated manner over a high dado of blue and white tiles.**5.63a, b** The media preferred by the Portuguese for the relief of their *estilo chão* were coloured tiles (*azulejos*) in abstract patterns or figural narratives – predominantly but not exclusively blue and white – and gilt woodcarving in increasing luxuriance. The glorious revetment of the Madre de Deus church is reiterated most notably, perhaps, in S. Clara at Évora – but there are myriad variations.

5.63b

5.63c

5.63e

5.63d

›5.63 LISBON, AZULEJOS AND GILT WOOD-WORK: (a, b) Madre de Deus, interior of church and upper chapel; (c–e) S. Vicente de Fora, entrance hall, sacristy interior, cloister dado detail; (f–h) S. Roque, chapels of the Doctrine, the Sacrament and Piety.

The high altar of S. Vicente de Fora was commissioned by John V from João Frederico Ludovice, who succeeded Luis Nunes Tinoco as master of works in 1720: the tile work was begun before Tinoco's demise.

At S. Roque, the main lines of 17th-century developments in retable design may be traced from the High Renaissance sanctuary to the proto-Baroque of the dedicatee's chapel (AIC5, page 774). Of the latter's followers, the first of the series on the right flank enshrines a late-16th-century image of S. Anne instructing the Virgin Mary (hence 'Our Lady of the Doctrine'): it was redecorated early in the reign of John V with the plethora of gilt woodwork attributed to José Rodrigues Ramalho.

The range of early 18th-century azulejos embellishment is admirably demonstrated in the venerable complex of Lisbon's S. Vicente de Fora.**5.63c–e** Each bay of the severe cloisters is enlivened with a dado of tiles painted solely in blue on white to constitute unified scenes – setting fables from La Fontaine – in highly convoluted frames which depart from the horizontal base to follow the diagonal inclination of stairs. In contrast, the sacristy is entirely covered in a mosaic of many-coloured tiles forming abstract patterns. Here and even in the church's severe Herreran interior gilded woodwork is restrained – except for the latter's baldachin (AIC5, page 763). Elsewhere, as in the Madre de Deus, that medium was deployed without restraint to highlight significant zones of spatial transition and, primarily, to provide a glorious context for the dedicatees of altarpieces: unsurpassed, in Lisbon at least, is the display of the three side chapels of S. Roque completed in the first decade of the 18th century.**5.63f–h, 5.64**

5.63f

5.63g

5.63h

From Mannerism to Baroque in the Portuguese retable

The high altar of S. Vicente de Fora – the sole relief to the sanctuary's chill-ing ashlar – is covered by a gilded baldachin carried on colossal columns (AIC5, page 763). When it was installed the motif was rare: a prosecenium ordonnance of grand scale was the norm – in the motherland and the remot-est colonies, not least the ecclesiastical and administrative centre of the Portuguese East Indies at Goa, as we have just seen.

S. Roque's high altar, Classical in its restraint, is in stark contrast with the Baroque exuberance of its most spectacular side chapels. As in Spain (pages 814f), the proscenium of single orders, multiplied in depth, had superseded the superimposition of aedicular motifs by the end of the 17th century and the Solomonic prevailed at least after João Nunes Tinoco deployed it in Lisbon for the sanctuary retable of S. Justa (1661): of exam-

5.64

Further along the south flank, the chapel enshrining the image of the Assumption (now the Sacrament) was also redecorated in the late 17th century and further embellished under John V. Similar in its evolution, the chapel of the Piety (redecorated by 1711 around a sculpture of the crucifixion above the Pietà) is the most overtly theatrical of the series. On the last installation, see page 865.

5.64 AVEIRO, CONVENTO DE JESUS: church interior from nave to sanctuary.

5.65 MAFRA, PALACE MONASTERY: (a–c) interior, narthex and south side of basilica, (d) plan at base level, (e) west entrance front, (f) library.

ples too numerous to specify, the high altar of Oporto cathedral (1727) may be taken to represent the opulence of the form's northern development.

Further than the Spanish norm – but as in Brazil and even Mexico, as we shall see – profuse ornament in gilded wood or stucco often spread from the retable to the side walls and vaults of Portuguese chapels and sanctuaries through progressively expanding arches. Beyond the capital, and the splendid series in S. Roque, the mode is well represented in the Convento de Jesus at Aveiro – which also provides an outstanding example of richly framed panels over a dado of blue and white tiles. The chapel in the cathedral of Oporto is a rare example of the mode in beaten silver.

John V's reign was built on gold: of divine providence, gold was available for the lavish embellishment of his works, religious and secular, but the grateful monarch would deploy it primarily to glorify the Church Triumphant. A goldsmith was his first architect, yet the approach preferred for the royal works was architectonic – not the masking of structure with ornament in gilded wood or tiles. João Frederico Ludovice (Johann Friedrich Ludwig, 1673–1752) came from Swabia via Rome where he had worked for the Jesuits in their Gesù. He and his Italian followers imported a moderate Baroque style derived from Fontana to supplant the native *estilo chão* for their opulent royal patron.

Ludovice's role in the quasi-architectural aspects of the Gesù altarpiece was limited and his first decade in Lisbon (from 1701) also seems to have been devoted to work of immaculate craftsmanship in precious metal. However, the king charged him with responsiblity for the first great building project of the reign, the convent at Mafra decreed ex voto for an heir. Work began in 1717 to a modest scale but as it progressed the scheme was amplified to incorporate a huge basilica flanked by palatial apartments and backed by a cloister enclosed by accommodation for eighty friars. The analogy with El Escorial is obvious but here the basilica and palace were to the fore both physically and conceptually.**5.65**

5.65a

Mafra

Rather than any specifically Roman scheme – or, indeed, El Escorial – Ludovice seems to have followed contemporary developments in monastic planning in his south-west German homeland: in particular the ideal plan for Weingarten (published 1723) comes to mind and earlier Einsiedeln (from 1704) in neighbouring Switzerland, though these have no palace and their great churches thrust out from the monastic precinct. Of those churches, the morphology of Weingarten (begun 1715) is closer to that of Mafra as it emerged from the scaffolding in 1730. The plan follows Vignola's Gesù variant of the basilican type, as adapted for the Roman church of S. Ignazio but with the more pronounced transept of the German variant – and, incidentally, of Alberti's Mantuan prototype as it was about to be completed by Juvarra. Rather than an apsidal front, there is an arcaded narthex – like Maderno's S. Pietro or Herrera's S. Lorenzo del Escorial – but the towers and dome further the Swabian variations on the themes stated by Borromini for S. Agnese in

5.65c

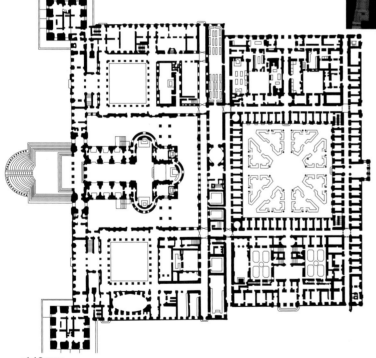

5.65d @ 1:3000

5.65b

5.65e

The original vow, made by John V at the outset of his reign, was to give thanks for the birth of a male heir with the construction of a monastery for a small community of reformed Franciscans at Mafra: after construction began in 1717, the project escalated until it ultimately accommodated 300 monks as well as the royal family when completed in 1735.

Piazza Navona (modified by Rainaldi; see pages 91 and 111). The eclecticism of the exercise ran further, to French square-domed pavilions derived from Androuet du Cerceau's Verneuil via Felipe Terzi's renovation of the main royal Portuguese residence, the riverside palace in Lisbon (AIC5, page 760).

The complex is built of brick but marble revetment was reserved for the distinction of the basilica. Extending out from the narthex, gallery wings are plastered and painted yellow. They lead to twin suites for the king and queen in the square pavilions at the extremities. The complex was long in completion and much rehabilitated in the 19th century: other than the church, the chief glory produced for its original patron is the great library which occupies the centre of the eastern range of the monastery, beyond the cloister – exactly the opposite position to that of its model at El Escorial.

5.65f

5.66a

5.66b

Ludovice translated the style of his Mafra basilica to the apse of the great Gothic cathedral at Évora. He revised the vaulting of the Mafra library for the sacristy of S. Antão in Lisbon. However, responding to the royal commission of a library for the University of Coimbra in collaboration with Claude de Laprade (1682–1738), he may well have been eclipsed by his colleague in effecting the turn from gravitas to festive display: opened illusionistically to the empyrean above an assertive cornice, repetitively emblazoned with crowned cartouches above the scenographic succession of arches, it is layered with the essential timber shelves and galleries carried on an elementary form of the estípite foreign to both its authors and, indeed, to Portugal.**5.66**

›**5.66 COIMBRA, UNIVERSITY LIBRARY** (Biblioteca Joanina), from 1717: (a, b) interior and vault.

For all its enrichment in paint, stucco and gilded carpentry, the library at Coimbra is disciplined by the geometry of its double-cube envelope and by the uncontorted entablature. Even at Mafra, despite Swabian inspiration, Baroque exuberance of line is restrained in apparent sympathy with the Classicizing tendency of Fontana and his school in the Rome of Ludovice's apprenticeship. And towards the end of his reign, John V turned to the Rome of Fontana's heirs, to the young Luigi Vanvitelli in particular, for the design of a votive chapel and its fabrication in exceptionally rich materials for importation to the venerable church of S. Roque: there this masterpiece completes the series of chapel altars in stark contrast to their prolix floridity. At the beginning of the decade the development was anticipated in polychrome marble for the chapel of S. Antonio at S. Vicente by Carlos Mardel – of whom we shall see more.**5.67**

5.67a

›5.67 LISBON, ECCLESIASTICAL WORKS OF JOHN V AND HIS SUCCESSORS: (a) S. Roque, chapel of S. John the Baptist (fabricated in lapis lazuli and gold after the design of Luigi Vanvitelli and sent from Rome in 1748); (b) Nossa Senhora de Graca (16th-century foundation extensively rebuilt and redecorated after 1755), interior; (c–f) S. Catarina (founded 1647 for the convent of S. Paul da Serra de Ossa, consecrated 1698, furnished from 1703, high altar of 1727 associated with João Frederico Ludovice, severe damage to vault in 1755 repaired with new stucco embellishment from 1763, consecrated to S. Catarina as parish church following dissolution of religious orders in 1834), exterior, interior and details of transept chapel and organ; (g) Nossa Senhora de Encarnação (late-medieval foundation destroyed 1755, completely rebuilt by 1784, like the other two great Chiado churches, Nossa Senhora dos Martires and Nossa Senhora di Loreto), interior; (h, i) S. António da Sé (1730 on early 16th-century foundations, rebuilt from 1767), exterior and interior; (j, k) Basilica da Estrela (from 1779 by Oliveira), exterior, interior.

5.67b

5.67c

5.67e

5.67f

5.67d

5.67g

Rather than prolix floridity, moreover, the style of Mafra prevailed in the main ecclesiastical commissions of the age and considerably later. During the reign of John V's son, Joseph I, several of the greatest Lisbon churches were rebuilt – or at least substantially restored – after the earthquake of 1755 with appropriate gravitas: examples include Nossa Senhora da Graça and S. Catarina, which vary the Gesù type, Nossa Senhora de Loreto, Encarnação and Martires, which vary the hall format of nearby S. Roque with or without tribunes under clerestoreys and tunnel vaulting. Mateus Vicente de Oliveira (1706–86), who had worked at Mafra under Ludovice, rebuilt S. António da Sé after the earthquake and, most notably, began the basilica of Nossa Senhora da Estrela, founded in 1779 ex voto for the birth of an heir to Maria I, John V's granddaughter.

5.67i

5.67h

5.67j

5.67k

The metropolitan – particularly the Joanaine – concern with the elaboration of an architectonic style distantly echoing developments in late-Baroque Rome was countered elsewhere: as we have already noted, the predilection for masking *estilo chão* severity with tiles and richly carved, gilded woodwork was widely popular. S. Clara at Évora apart, S. António dos Olivais at Coimbra might be singled out for the spectacular scale of its interior azulejo revetment.**5.68** Church exteriors often still displayed restraint in their basic ordonnance but enjoyed convolution in their architrave mouldings and in their cornices, attic aedicules or gables above all. The sanctuary church at Milagres, near Leiria, is a splendid example.**5.69**

5.68

›5.68 COIMBRA, S. ANTÓNIO DOS OLIVAIS: church interior (c. 1720–30).

The tiled panels of the dado, executed in the early decades of the 18th century, represent episodes in the life of S. Antony of Padua (1195–1231) who was born in Portugal and began his life as a monk there in the Franciscan monastery founded in 1217. The church and its embellishment survived the conflagration which consumed the monastic buildings in 1851.

›5.69 MILAGRES, SANCTUARY CHURCH, from 1732: west front.

José and Joaquim da Silva, father and son, revivified the Mafra basilica's format, revising the proportions for breadth rather than height, and echoing the narthex arcade along the sides: they subscribed to their compatriots' predilection for convoluted pediments, the main one breaking like waves against a central cartouche.

5.69

In the north exteriors were ordered with pilasters from the early 1690s at least, but the bays contained convoluted masonry panels: a relatively moderate example is the façade of the church of the Congredados in Oporto (before 1680); the prime example is the façade of S. Vincente at Braga (from 1690), its mouldings mixing memories of School of Fontainebleau plasterwork and the engravings of Dietterlin.**5.70** The taste for Netherlandish Mannerist flourishes – and complexity – had prevailed to various degrees in northern Portugal for much of the century, as we have seen in works like S. Lourenço dos Grillos and the first of the Carmelite churches in Oporto (AIC5, pages 771f).

Quite contrary both to the latter-day decorative Mannerism of late-17th-century Oporto, or Braga, and to the endeavours of Ludovice's circle in response to opulent royal patronage in Lisbon, is the work of the Swabian

5.70

5.71a

>5.71 NASONI AND FOLLOWERS IN OPORTO:
(a, b) episcopal palace, view from the Douro and
detail of portal; (c–f) cathedral, west portal detail,
north loggia, north transept and sanctuary altars;

5.71b

5.71e

5.71c

5.71f

5.71d

goldsmith's younger contemporary Niccolò Nazzoni (1691–1773). A Tuscan who studied in Rome, he may have passed through Calabria, Sicily and Malta on the way to Portugal. Known as Nasoni there, he was active mainly in Oporto where he is first recorded c. 1725 as decorating the cathedral with frescoes of the *quadratura* type – which he is credited with having introduced to Portugal. He is also credited with having assembled the altar in the cathedral's north transept from 17th-century silver elements. In the next decade he went on to 'modernize' the Romanesque cathedral's west portal, add the north loggia with its azulejo revetment and rebuild the bishop's palace on the bluff overlooking the river to the south (from 1736 and c. 1740 respectively).**5.71a–f**

Relatively prolific in the orbit of Oporto, Nasoni's most seductive secular work is the palace on the Quinta de Mateus – to which we shall return. His most arresting legacy to his adopted city's skyline is the six-storey campanile of S.

5.71j

5.71i

5.71h

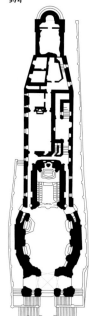

5.71g @ 1:1000

Pedro dos Clérigos (from 1732). Exceptionally high for its type, the tower is attached to its church by an exceptionally long arm penetrated by the sanctuary. The elliptical form of the congregational space has numerous Roman and southern Italian Baroque equivalents but is relatively rare in Portugal: an octagonal precedent is provided by the church of the Menino Deus in Lisbon but innovative in the Oporto work was the continuation of the sanctuary corridors as intramural passages for access to the pulpits. On the other hand, the façade is a version of the 'palace' type more common in Portugal than in Rome: disciplined at base by the triumphal-arch motif but overcome by rich sculptural detail and essentially Mannerist multiple broken pediments, its dramatic presentation at the source of a cascade of steps is not unique in Portugal.**5.71g-j** An extreme variation, in which the same rhythm of articulation may still be detected behind even more elaborate surface ornamentation and under vigorously curved cornices, was elaborated by Nasoni's pupil José de Figueiredo Seixas for the Terceiros do Carmo in Oporto (from 1756).**5.71k**

(g–j) S. Pedro dos Clérigos (from 1711), plan, tower, entrance front, interior; (k) Carmine complex (completed with the church of the third order, right, from 1756), general view of double fronts.

5.71k

Variations on the palace type of façade are the norm in the Portugal of John V, as they were in the previous century. Andres Soares (1720–69) presents a particularly striking, but atypical example in his Nossa Senhora da Consolação e Santos Passos at Guimarães: it is slender in its proportions at the top of a flight of steps, like the Clerígos church of Oporto, but the triumphal-arch motif cedes to a colossal pilaster Order framing a bold convex projection between twin towers, as at Weingarten but without the concave zone of transition. As at Weingarten, too, a central superstructure rises through concave curves but fails to find resolution in countrary curve as a pediment: instead it is cut off as the base for statues and partially eclipsed by the extraordinary frontispiece finial which emerges from a petrified valence to support the cross over a clock. In contrast, the belfries are notable for their vigorous Baroque volutes and their undulating cornices. The architectural elements are in stone, the background in blue and white tiles which, in diverse patterns, distinguish the exteriors and interiors of many Portuguese churches.**5.72a**

Soares da Silva sustained the *estilo chão* in the basic ordonnance of his Casa da Câmara at Braga but indulged in the rich elaboration of the portal and window frames in the manner we have already encountered elsewhere in contemporary Portugal.**5.73a** The pediments here and, above all, his contemporary towers at Guimarães are worthy of a latter-day Borromini – a Juvarra, even a Meissonnier. To that extent, the architecture of Portugal in the reign of John V may be categorised as Baroque in the terms with which we should now be familiar – if categorization in foreign terms is admissible at all. And with the same proviso it might be said that Soares, in particular, managed the transition from Baroque to Rococo.

5.72a

›**5.72 SOARES DA SILVA AT GUIMARÃES IN THE 1750S:** (a) Nossa Senhora de Consolação e Santos Passos, (b) Lobo-Machado house.

The masonry architectonic frame, inherited from the *estilo chão*, is enlivened with ornament in stark opposition to the plain white – or tiled – plane of the wall. The Lobo-Machado house is attributed to Soares not without contention, but it retains this approach in combination with the asymmetrical bizareries of the French genre pittoresque.

5.73 SOARES DA SILVA AT BRAGA IN THE 1750S: (a) Casa da Câmara; (b) Palácio do Raio; (c) Congregados (church of the Oratorians); (d) S. Maria Madalena do Monte da Falperra.

5.72b

5.73a

5.73b

Soares's way led to extravagant variations on Borromini's Oratory façade for the Lobo-Machado house in Guimarães and the church of the Braga Oratorians.**5.72b, 5.73c** The former draws the dislocated segments of Borromini's upper cornice into continuous undulation beyond the relative constraint of the Casa da Câmara at Braga. Like its model, the church front is articulated with pilasters on two levels but the contortion of the frames of the central voids and the pediment trade Borromini's mode of invention for that of Meissonnier. Beyond that is the façade of the extraordinary polygonal church of S. Maria Madalena on Braga's Falperra hill and the Palácio do Raio in the town centre (both from the mid-1750s): derived from the *estilo chão*, pilaster strips attempt restraint but they are etiolated in the elegant manner of French boiserie earlier in the century and the convoluted interpenetration of door, window and niche framework defies architectonic logic.**5.73b, d**

5.73c

5.73d

›5.74 FROM GOTHIC TO BAROCOCO IN
OPORTO: (a) S. Clara, interior (from 1730); (b, c) S. Francisco, sanctuary and nave detail (from c. 1750).

The gilded woodwork is by Miguel Francesco de Silva: a permutation of a persistent Christian motive, his mesmerizingly intricate denial of physical reality is alive with putti festooning their luxuriant world under simulated canopies with scalloped valences. Solomonic columns pretend to bear an ephemeral load in the sanctuary proscenium and secondary retables of S. Francisco.

5.75a

›5.75 NORTHERN PORTUGUESE CALVARY COMPLEXES: (a) Lamego, Nossa Senhora dos Remedios (from c. 1750), summit church; (b) Braga, Bom Jesus do Monte (steps from 1722), view from below.

5.75b

The identification of ornament with structural framework – not masking but vivifying it – may be seen to approximate the unrealized fluid fantasies of Meissonier's *genre pittoresque*. The motive was taken to its extreme in the gilded woodwork of Manueline complexity which encrusts the interiors of the churches of S. Clara and S. Francisco in Oporto. The latter is particularly instructive: the building is Gothic, the embellishment takes eclecticism to a Rococo extreme and the latter borrows its semblance of structural validity from the former. Strictly, that is still prolix ornament overlaid on building. However, those given to licence may see these phenomena – external and internal – as disproving the proposition that there can be no such thing as Rococo architecture.[5.74]

Though triangular at the apex, Borromini's Oratory is the ultimate source for the breaking of the pediment into contrasting curves which was particularly popular in northern Portugal – as also in Austria and southern Germany. Soares da Silva's work on the Falperro hill apart, an outstanding example crowns the façade of Nossa Senhora dos Remedios at Lamego (from c. 1750).[5.75a] A pilgrimage goal, chapels enshrining vivid realizations of the Stations of the Cross line the steps which cascade down the mountain as they did on the urban scale of the Oporto Clérigos. This simulated Calvary formula was extended on the basis of earlier flights for Bom Jesus near Braga (the first stages of the steps from 1722, the last stage and the church from 1781).[5.75b] The main façade plane is still flat in both of these churches but their styles could hardly be more diverse. A colossal Order is stamped on all five bays at Lamego and slightly projected for the nave: there is no interest in developing movement in the masonry with a progression in the weight of the Order or undulation through elliptical curves but the entablature is broken in the centre by a cartouche below the reverse curvature of the pediment and the

5.76a

convoluted frames of the doors and windows are no longer architectonic. Thirty years later, Carlos Amarante recalls the triumphal-arch motif untrammeled on two levels and reasserts Classical principles to impose discipline on the Bom Jesus façade: a new era had begun.

The new era of Neoclassicism emerged without dramatic rupture from the old one of the *estilo chão*. Congenial to the Spanish, perpetuated by the palatine office of royal buildings established under the auspices of Philip II, the so-called 'plain style' persisted beyond the restoration of Portuguese sovereignty well into the 18th century, despite the predelections of the newly affluent monarch who ruled for nearly half that age. While his grandiloquence was served by immigrant architects, the native Portuguese practitioners entrenched in the palatine office – many of them trained as engineers – remained doggedly dedicated to sobriety and taught it. Examples of their work include the church of Senhor da Pedra, built by Rodrigo Franco at a way station near Obidos on the royal route north. Outstanding, however, is the Águas Livres aqueduct and reservoir: purely utilitarian in its aesthetic, given the superior efficiency of the pointed arch, the former was constructed under the direction of the Italian engineer Antonio Canevari to carry water over the Alcantara valley to the western districts of the capital.**5.76**

5.76b

5.76c

›**5.76 ÁGUAS LIVRES:** (a) general view of the aqueduct across the Alcantara valley; (b) triumphal arch celebrating the completion of the project under the enlightened patronage of John V; (c) Chafariz da Esperança (from 1752).

5.77

›5.77 OEIRAS, PALACIO CARVALHO, from c. 1739: court front.

›5.78 MATEUS, ESTATE MANOR HOUSE, from 1739: general view from the south with entrance front (right) credited to Niccolò Nasoni.

5.78

The Águas Livres project was completed by the Hungarian military and civil engineer, Carlos Mardel: in Lisbon from 1733 after working in Central Europe and France, he forged the most decisive link between the old plain style and the new. He first took the *estilo chão* back to the Romanesque at its most austere for the reservoir. While that was under construction towards the end of the decade, he also went back beyond the prevailing manifestations of the Baroque – and beyond Serlian Mannerism – to the *estilo chão* in his design for the palace at Oeiras commissioned by Sebastião José de Carvalho (the future Marquês de Pombal): the contrast with Nasoni's Casa de Mateus, which was also under construction in 1739, could hardly be sharper.**5.77, 5.78**

The king called on Mardel for the palace known as Galvão-Mexia and approved a thirteen-bay scheme articulated simply with an Order of colossal pilasters. On completion of that project, Mardel was given charge of the principal royal residences and led his profession until his death in 1763. Among his first works in that capacity, his last as architect in charge of the Águas Livres project, was the triumphal arch erected near the reservoir in celebration of enlightened royal patronage (c. 1748): a series of fountains followed over the next decade. The adaptation of the triumphal arch's definitive motif to the grandest of those fountains, in the Rua da Esperança, necessarily responded to political motives which transcended the utilitarian: certainly not plain, the style is as much Mannerist as Baroque. An early manifestation of Neoclassicism distinguishes the last fountain of Mandel's series, in the Rua do Século where it served the town palace of the immigrant's erstwhile patron Carvalho de Pombal. Under the latter, moreover, as leading royal architect Mardel played a formative role in planning the reconstruction of Lisbon after the earthquake of 1755 and to that extent effected the transition from the eclecticism of the past to the style of the Enlightenment.

Queluz

Towards the end of the Joanine reign, a decade before the catastrophe led to the advent of a rationalist style congruous with the ideals of the French Enlightenment, the influence of an earlier phase of French architectural order had inevitably supervened in the conception of a new royal retreat in the countryside beyond the metropolis. Mateus Vicente de Oliveira – Ludovice's collaborator – began the palace at Queluz in 1747 for the king's younger son, Prince Peter, who shared his father's taste for foreign fashions. So too did his brother, the new King Joseph I (1750–77) whose first important commission was to Giovanni Carlo Sicino Galli Bibiena for an opera house near the royal palace on the Terrero do Paco: it succumbed to the earthquake.

5.79e

5.79d

5.79a @ 1:2000

>5.79 QUELUZ, ROYAL PALACE, from 1747 in development of a hunting estate confiscated in 1640 from the Marquês de Castelo Rodrigo who was dispossessed for supporting the Spanish interregnum,

completed c. 1790, much of the first floor demolished after fire damage in 1934: (a) plan with (1) Throne Room (inserted by Robillion and Colin from c. 1765 in place of several rooms behind Oliveira's façade of the early 1750s which was somewhat reworked c. 1770), (2) Music Room (Oliveira, mid-1750s, probably reformed by Robillion during his campaign in the late-1760s), (3) chapel (completed 1752 to the design of Oliveira with the woodwork of Silvestre Faria Lobo), (4) 'Façade of the Ceremonies' (refaced from 1764), (5) Ambassadors' Hall (inserted from c. 1757 by Robillion and Colin in the new western range probably in modification of the original throne room projected by Oliveira; the central ceiling painting of the court at a concert is by Francisco de Melo), (6) Don Quixote Room (begun by Robillion in 1759, initially a reception room used for dining, decorated by Manuel da Costa with the paintings which give it its name and by José António Narciso with the 'Allegory of Music' on the ceiling); (7) princess's dressing room (1760s, paintings later), (b) general view from garden to the 'Façade of the Ceremonies' (completed 1767), (c) Throne Room façade (with its Borrominian pediment and 'eared' windows), (d, e) 'Robillion Pavilion', south front and Lions Staircase (from c. 1760, completed c. 1775), (f) Throne Room, (g) Music Room, (h) chapel, (i) Tiled 'Corridor', (j) Ambassadors' Hall, (k) dressing room, (l) Don Quixote Room.

In 1760 the king's daughter (the future Queen Maria I, 1777–1816) was married to his brother (the future King Peter III, 1777–86). Closely monitored by the king, the extension and remodelling of Queluz for them was entrusted to the French goldsmith Jean-Baptiste Robillion (1704–82) as Oliveira was preoccupied with the reconstruction of Lisbon. The spectacular Throne Room was inserted in Oliveira's south-east wing centred on the pavilion whose convoluted style derives from Borromini and matches the work of Ludovice's assistant elsewhere – not least S. António da Sé in Lisbon. In contrast, the south front of Oliveira's entrance court complex, the 'Façade of the Ceremonies', was refaced by Robillion and the French sculptor Antoine Colin under the influence of Mansart's château at Marly – but the incidence of the Order was reduced and the elaboration of the window frames increased. The French immigrants pressed on, beyond the Ambassadors' Hall, to the south-western block which they articulated in a style derived from Jacques-François Blondel's *De la Distribution des maisons de plaisance, etc.* The Dutch gardener Gerald van der Kolk assisted with planting the parterres peopled from 1757 with the lead sculptures of the English master John Cheere (1709–87).

If French academic precept informs the architectonic articulation of the later façades at Queluz, subordinating Rococo detail, Baroque ordonnance is sustained in the chapel and even the Music Room but Rococo fashion infiltrates the Ambassadors' Hall and triumphs in the Throne Room. At its height in 1749 when Robillion left Paris, there Rococo was an overtly anti-architectonic mode of decoration. Questioning whether it is plausible to characterize a building style in its terms, I have suggested that the liberal case could hardly do better – beyond invoking the fantasies of a Meissonnier or André Soares – than rest on a definition of the interior of S. Francisco in Oporto. There are other examples in Oporto – and in Brazil, as we shall see – but in the greatest room of Queluz, as usual elsewhere, the style's free-ranging vegetal motifs are deployed to dissolve the tectonics of physical enclosure.

5.79i

5.79f

5.79h

5.79g

5.79k

5.79l

5.79j

5.80a

PERNAMBUCO

At Goa there were the great land powers of the Mughals and their clients in the offing with sophisticated firearms. On the other side of the world the threat was largely from rival colonialist warships: by the end of the 16th century a string of fortresses protected all the trading settlements along the long coast of Pernambuco, the easternmost extension of the Americas, east of the meridian drawn 370 leagues west of Cape Verde and therefore conceded to Portugal by the Treaty of Tordesillas (1494; AIC4, page 251). Numerous, these were not individually as impressive as the forts of Portuguese Africa or India – as those of Mombasa or Diu in particular (AIC5, pages 782ff). Urban building was modest too, of course.

The first towns, seats of the captains who laid the foundations of Portuguese empire in the west, were developed haphazardly – contrary to the norm of colonial regular planning but in conformity to the rugged terrain. The prime example is Olinda, founded in 1535 by Duarte Coe-

›5.80 OLINDA, SECULAR AND RELIGIOUS FOUNDATIONS: (a) general view; (b) detail view with S. João Batista dos Militares (from 1581); (c) plan of typical house (not to scale); (d, e) cathedral of Jesus Cristo, Salvador do Mundo (from 1584), exterior and interior; (f, g) Nossa Senhora da Graça (from 1567), exterior and interior; (h, i) Nossa Senhora do Carmo (1588), section and exterior.

Though it was sacked by the Dutch in the late-1630s, Olinda preserves Brazil's earliest houses. Usually on deep sites, these are long and narrow with living space over quarters for marketing the produce of the hinterland estates (*engenhos*). The latter were primarily

5.80b

5.80c

5.80d

5.80e

5.80f

5.80g

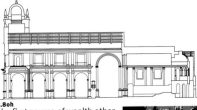

5.80h

lho Pereira on high ground to the north of the confluence of the rivers Beberibe and Capibaribe as the original
base of the Pernambuco captain. It is well preserved partly
because it was not contiguous with the riverine commercial port within the reefs to the south. The origin of Recife,
that was developed on the estuary island of Antonio Vaz by
the Dutch during their brief occupation of Pernambuco in
the years when Portugal was fighting to regain independence from Spain (1637–44): expanding on the mainland
after the Portuguese recovery, it eclipsed Olinda which
had been sacked by the intruders and rendered strategi-
cally insignificant.**5.80**

sugarcane plantations, the first source of wealth other
than mining or trade: typically, there would be a big
house with a chapel, huts and factory sheds.

In general the 16th-century style survived much
restoration after the Portugese regained control in
the late-1650s. Of the main monuments, the cathedral
was founded as a parish church by charter brought by
Duarte Coelho in 1540: it was built of wattle and daub;
in 1584 it was renovated entirely in brick; destroyed by
fire in 1631, it was restored from 1656 and inaugurated
as a cathedral in 1677.

5.80i

TO BAHIA

The first capital of the colony which would become Brazil was Salvador on the southern headland of the splendid Baía de Todos os Santos: a narrow coastal strip, developed for commerce, was overlooked by a plateau where the principals of church and state established themselves. Systematic colonization and architectural ambition waited on the first governor-general, Tomé de Sousa (1503–79), and the religious orders who accompanied him to his post in 1549: the viceroy brought his engineer/master-mason, sometimes identified as Luis Días; the Jesuits brought their architects, notably their brother Francisco Días who had worked on the church of S. Roque in Lisbon.

Unlike organic Olinda, the upper town (*cidade alta*) was built on a grid in the time-honoured manner of planned colonial settlement but not with the rigour we

>5.81 SÃO SALVADOR, SECULAR WORKS: (a, b) overviews (1626 and later 17th-century); (c, d) Forts São Antônio da Barra (from 1596 on earlier foundations) and São Marcelo (conceived c. 1605, built by 1623, reconstructed from 1650, achieved its elliptical form from c. 1670 under the direction of the engineer Antonio Correia Pinto); (e) Praca Municipal, Casa de Câmara e Cadeia (now Municipal Palace, rebuilt from 1660).

Fort São Antônio is a typically irregular polygon: the modern lighthouse has dominated the complex from the end of the 17th century, at least; it was reworked late in the 17th century. It corresponded to the more 'modern' circular Fort São Marcelo.

5.81a

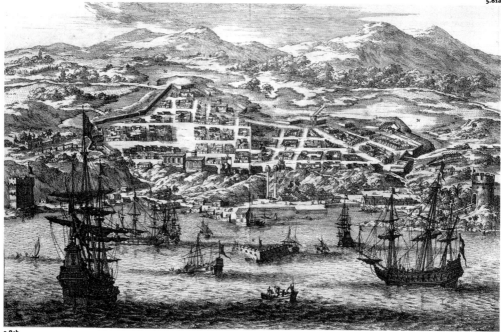

5.81b

5.81c

5.81d

shall see in Spanish America – and its order did not extend to the commercial quarters below (*cidade baixa*). If Luis or Francisco Días was responsible for laying out the new capital, the prime responsibility of the master-builder as royal engineer was, of course, to protect it: São Antônio da Barra, built on the bay's southern headland in conjunction with Fort São Felipe on the other side, is supported by the more impressive offshore installation of Fort São Marcelo.**3.81a–d**

In the civil field, priority was of course accorded to the replacement of the governor's temporary accommodation with a palace, a council chamber and a customs house addressing the main civic space: the governor's palace has been lost to later development but the town hall has been restored as rebuilt from 1660 in Serlian style, with its arcaded gallery serving the forum. Smaller than its Spanish colonial equivalents, the square – Praça Municipal – accommodates only the buildings of secular authority.**3.81e** The ecclesiastical establishment has its own larger space – Terreiro de Jesus – formed from the precincts of the Franciscans, the Dominicans and the Jesuits.

5.81e

5.82a

5.82c

5.82b

5.82d

5.82e

5.82f

›5.82 SÃO SALVATOR, CHURCHES: (a–c) Sé (former Jesuit church, from 1657), entrance front, interior, detail of vault; (d, e) Santa Casa de Misericórdia, entrance front and detail; (f) S. Teresa, entrance front.

The Jesuit church is a variant of the Portuguese hall church, best represented by Lisbon's S. Roque, with a twin-towered 'palace' façade descended from Tirzi's S. Vicente via the Jesuit seminary church in Santarém (AIC5, pages 772f). It became the cathedral after the Portuguese suppression of the Company in 1759.

São Salvator's Misericórdia represents a further variation on the theme of the hall church with 'palace' face. In contrast, the Spanish architect Macario de San Juan derived his church of S. Teresa from the precedents set for the Discalced Carmelites by Francisco de Mora in Valladolid and Madrid (AIC5, page 746) .

›5.83 RIO DE JANEIRO, S. BENTO, from 1617: (a) entrance front, (b) cloister, (c) interior to sanctuary.

In Brazil from 1603, Mesquita's sober work recalls the post-Herreran contribution to Lisbon: hall church with side chapels but no transept, fronted by a twin-towered, two-storeyed, three-bay pedimented façade with arcaded galilee and choir over narthex. The formula, imported via the Azores and widely applied elsewhere,

Except for the forts, the legacy of the first two or three centuries in the vast colonial dominion which would be Brazil is largely ecclesiastical: as there was no native architectural inheritance, the motherland provided the inspiration, at first even the architect/sculptors and often the ready-carved stone detail. As in India, the Jesuits were in the van. Introduced to Brazil in 1549 with governor Tomé de Sousa, in accordance with the royal will to convert the natives, they proselytized widely from simple adobe chapels. Their ambitions were first met by their brother Francisco Días with their collegiate churches at Olinda (1584), Rio de Janeiro (1585) and Salvador (from 1657 on earlier foundations in emulation of the order's achievements at home).**5.82**

After the Jesuits, the Benedictines were next to contribute architectural grandeur to the Brazilian colony. Extensively employed in the seat of government, Macario de San Juan was responsible for the order's complex there but that was preceded by S. Bento in Rio de Janeiro. Working on the latter from 1671, Francisco Frias de Mesquita referred back beyond brother Filippo Terzi to the *estilo chão* of Manuel Pires (AIC5, pages 762, 663): the twin-towered façade preserves its original appearance but the interior has been much altered and embellished subsequently.**5.83**

5.83a

5.83b

5.83c

is clearly drawn from the work of Pires as developed by Terzi (AIC5, pages 656ff, 760ff). The sculptural embellishment of the interior was begun in 1699 by Brother Domingos da Conceição and continued by Alejandro Machado Pereiro (from 1717): the gilding and painting are due to Caetano da Costa Coelho (from 1742).

5.84
›5.84 RIBEIRA GRANDE (AZORES), CHURCH OF ESPÍRITO SANTO (or Misericórdia, or dos Passos), founded in 1522, rebuilt from the middle of the 17th century: entrance front.

›5.85 BELÉM (City of Our Lady of Bethlehem), founded 1615: aerial view with Forte do Presépio (Castelo do Senhor Santo Cristo, from 1616, improved 1621, repaired after foreign attacks in the 1630s, rebuilt from 1728 to 1740).

5.85

JOANINE ACCRETION

Insofar as the 18th-century Portuguese developed a school of architecture which may be defined as Baroque it was exported to several coastal colonies between the Amazon and the Rio de Janeiro, via the Azores.**5.84** Its parallel development proceeded principally in four major ports and a small group of inland mining towns: there were, of course, many other sites in which comparable developments could be catalogued if we had room here.

The seat of the viceroy remained at São Salvador da Bahia until 1763: thus its art and architecture shared metropolitan significance with Lisbon and offers even more intriguing compensation than Oporto for the destruction wrought by the catastrophe of 1755. To the north, at the extremity of the continent's great eastern bluff, Pernambuco was ruled from the port of Recife after the Dutch incursion in the first half of the 17th century, as we have noted. Because of the vast distances to be defended from the Dutch and other intruders, the north-western region had been divided from central Pernambuco in 1621 as the state of Maranhão: its capital was Belém at the mouth of the Amazon.**5.85** The south was centred on the Rio de Janeiro settlement from which the French had been expelled in 1565. Apart from São Paulo, the main inland centres were the mining towns of Minas Gerais: notably Vila Rico de Ouro Preto, Mariana and São João del Rei which were constituted between 1711 and 1713. These would shift the centre of political and economic gravity in Brazil from Salvador to the estuary of the Rio de Janeiro.

The capital was established at Rio in 1703: the Benedictines had been there since 1590, had begun their great church in the early 1630s and were pursuing its lavish embellishment well before the end of the century. With the realization of the splendid harbour's importance as the

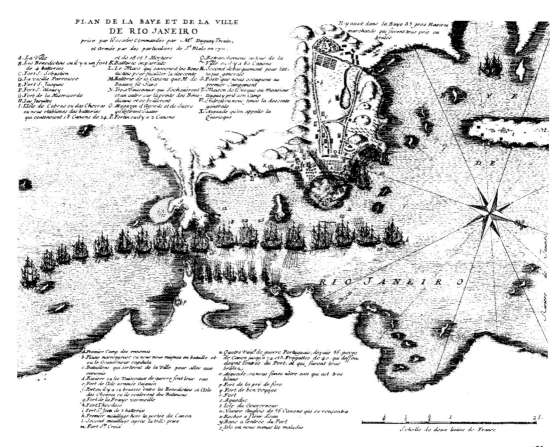

5.86a

5.86c

›5.86 RIO DE JANEIRO: (a) engraved plan of bay and settlement (1711); (b) church of the Third Order of S. Francisco da Penitência, interior to sanctuary (begun to the traditional rectangular plan, embellished from c. 1725 attributed to the sculptors Manuel and Francisco Xavier de Brito perhaps under the general direction of the painter-gilder Caetano da Costa Coelho who was also working on S. Bento at the time); (c) Joanine governor's residence (from 1738, for Gomes Freire de Andrade by the military engineer José Fernandes Pinto Alpoim), occupied by King John VI (from 1808, in flight from Napoleon), and later emperors (hence called Paço Imperial).

5.86b

maritime outlet for the lode of the hinterland mines, the settlement on the Rio de Janeiro was well protected by the opening of the 18th century: great improvements followed the devastating French incursion of 1711.**5.86**

Over the century before its eclipse, too, Salvador was further defended with forts along the lines developed from Italian precedent by Vauban for Louis XIV which prevailed throughout 18th-century Europe and its colonies. As we have seen, too, the seat of the viceroy was equipped with a cathedral and the great Jesuit church which would supplant it after the expulsion of the order in 1758.**5.82a** In the meantime it was endowed with many churches, normally rectangular but occasionally elliptical, with variously convoluted façades and a spectacular range of altar retables representing the permutations of style from later Mannerist to Baroque.

The first great additions to the city's heritage were due to the Franciscans: their definitive monastic complex succeeded the chapel of their Third Order within the decade on either side of 1700. The façade of the latter, provincial Dietterlinesque Mannerism, was unique in Brazil but echoed the Churrigueresque style soon to be developed with greater

›5.87 SALVADOR, SELECT 18TH CENTURY

ECCLESIASTICAL WORKS: (a–d) Franciscan conventual complex, Third Order chapel façade (c. 1702), First Order monastic church façade (from c. 1708), interior towards sanctuary, cloister; (e) general view from Largo do Pelourinho with Nossa Senhora do Rosário (from 1704) foreground, Nossa Senhora do Carmo and Terceira do Carmo (c. 1730) background; (f, g) S. Domingo (from 1731), exterior and illusionist ceiling; (h–j) Nossa Senhora da Conceição da Praia (from 1736), plan, exterior, interior to sanctuary.

The typical Franciscan hall, flanked by low chapel ranges, was built to the direction of Brother Vicente das Chagas and embellished by Brother Jerônimo da Graça (from 1732). The plans of the military engineer Manoel Cardoso de Saldanha for Nossa Senhora Conceição da Praia were sent to Lisbon where the stone was to be

5.87a

5.87b

5.87d

accomplishment in Mexico. Their First Order's basilican church, which faces the Jesuits beyond the extended Terreiro de Jesus (from 1708), is rather more restrained in the conservatism of its twin-towered façade: following the form of S. Bento in Rio de Janeiro, traditional in the mother country, it is Terzian in the two main storeys; beyond the Portuguese norm, however, the convolution of the gable betrays Flemish or Dutch influence. Embellished largely in the 1730s, the interior exceeds the Benedictine's Rio masterpiece even in the Baroque vigour of its comprehensively gilded relief. **5.87a–d** The mode was currently being furthered by the Third Order of the brotherhood in their basilican church on the hill of São Antônio in Rio.

5.87c

Variations on the scheme developed for the Franciscans in façade composition, if not always in rectangular hall-church planning, are represented by the churches of the first and third order of Carmelite sisters, by São Domingo of the eponymous order, by Nossa Senhora do Rosário dos Pretos (the black slave community) on the heights of Pelourinho, and by the dramatically sited parish church of Santissimo Sacramento on the Rua do Passo – to name the more prominent examples. On the other hand, Nossa Senhora Conceição da Praia is built over an extruded octagonal plan behind an *estilo chão* façade compressed between offset towers flanked by entrances to peripheral corridors.

The *estilo chão* survives in the basic ordonnance of all

5.87g

quarried for shipment with the master builder Eugenio da Mota: construction began under him in 1753 and was continued by other Portuguese masters (beyond inauguration in 1765). The illusionism evoked in the second half of the century in the churches of Salvador, notably S. Domingos and Nossa Senhora Conceição, are generally attributed to José Joachim da Rocha whose origins and training are as yet undetermined.

5.87e

5.87f

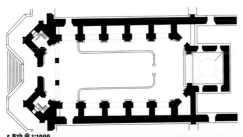

5.87h @ 1:1000

5.87i

5.87j

these façades and, as in the mother country over the first three or four decades of the century, it is relieved by increasingly convoluted architraves and pediments – though the latter are usually extruded into gables which echo the Dutch influence most apparent in the greater scale of the Franciscan work.**5.87e–j**

Naturally the old capital of Pernambuco ceded nothing in conservatism to the new one at Bahia and rarely matched its flamboyant relief patterns. The 'box' hall or basilican type of church, flat fronted and twin towered like the cathedral, persisted well beyond the post-Dutch period of Olinda's reconstruction. Its latest significant 17th-century permutation, for the Carmelites, was unusual in its applied Order but not in the substitution of domes for pyramidal roofs on the towers or for the convolution of the pediment added in the first decade of the new century (see page 885).

In Brazil, as in the mother country, the superstructure of towers would be elaborated into Baroque belfries remotely related to Borromini's Roman prototype. However, in Pernambuco the elevation of the gable between the towers would depart from Borromini's hybrid form of pediment towards the complexities of the Netherlandish north in a process of abstraction from one or other of two related sources: the attic motif with supporting volute consoles; the triangular gable fringed with volutes transposed from a substantial architectonic role to an insubstantial decorative one.

The Portuguese permutation of the former was exported from Oporto or Santarém to Salvador by the Jesuits – as we have seen. Also as we have seen, the convoluted gable was preferred by the Franciscans of Salvador: the form would have been seen as native to the tradition of the Dutch invader, as in Pernambuco where the impact was generally greater.

5.88a

5.88b

5.88c

›5.88 PERNAMBUCO OVER THE FIRST HALF OF THE 18TH CENTURY: (a, b) Olinda, general view of S. Francisco, west front of S. Bento (late 1750s); (c) Igarassu, façade of the monastery church of S. Antônio (founded c. 1670); (d–l) Recife, S. Pedro dos Clérigos (founded 1700, construction records from 1728 under the direction of Manoel Ferreira Jácome, consecrated 1782), plan, interior and exterior, Nossa Senhora Conceição dos Militares (begun c. 1710, embellishment to 1771, gilded by 1870), interior and vault detail, Rosário dos Homens Pretos (founded 1630, reconstructed 1750–71), façade detail, Nossa Senhora do Carmo (from 1687, façade dated 1767), exterior and interior and the later façade of the church of the Ordem Terceira do Carmo.

Transition to and from the culmination of gable development in Pernambuco may be traced in the façades of the Franciscan and Benedictine hall churches at Olinda, though they are both generally dated to the late-1750s. On its beautiful site by the sea, S. Francisco retains the domed form of tower which appeared at the Carmelite church at least half a century earlier but it enjoys the multiple volutes of the northern gable in bold relief like its older, greater brother in Salvador – again of nearly half a century earlier. S. Bento's builder introduced a waist to the miniature dome on his single tower, as many others had done over the previous half-century, but he was far less assertive than his Franciscan colleague in deploying the volute motive to rim his gable. In the latter respect the Franciscans of Igarassu exceed the Benedictines of Olinda in élan but, retreating from the boldness of their brothers there, the dome of their tower is compressed by a bell-shaped finial.**5.88a–c**

Several of the great churches in Recife best represent the culmination of the process in train at both the old and the new capitals. As we have seen, the trading port at the confluence of Pernambuco's Berberibe and Capiberibe rivers was founded by the Dutch and eclipsed nearby Olinda after the Dutch retreat: its affluent patrons afforded much greater elaboration of the Dutch legacy and the commerce which enriched them also transmitted knowledge of modern developments in the motherland.

The hybrid result is at its most spectacular on the façades of S. Pedro dos Clérigos and the two Carmelite churches. The rectilinear norm in planning was rejected by the architect of the former for an extruded octagon with an elongated rectangular sanctuary all encapsulated in an extensive rectangular enclosure: similarity with the general distribution of Nasoni's work for the same order at Oporto is clear but does not extend to elliptical geometry or the application of the triumphal-arch motif to the façade.**5.88d–l**

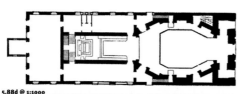
5.88d @ 1:1000

5.88e

5.88f

5.88g

5.88h

5.88i

5.88j

5.88l

5.88k

5.89

Borromini, rather than the Netherlands, prevails over the design of pediments in major churches at the extremities of our coastal spectrum: regional differences are marked across the enormous extent of the Brazilian colonies. The church builders in Belém at the mouth of the Amazon and in the settlement on the estuary of the Rio de Janeiro way to the south tend to play with pediments along Borrominesque lines – rather than constructing gables like the Pernambucans.

›5.89 BELÉM, NOSSA SENHORA DAS MER-CÊS, founded 1640, rebuilt from 1753 under the direction of the Bolognese pupil of the Bibiena, Antonio Giuseppe Landi: façade.

›5.90 RIO DE JANEIRO: (a–c) church of the Ordem Terceira do Carmo (from 1755 to plans of the Portuguese architect Manoel Alves Setúbal modified by Brother Xavier Vaz de Carvalho, façade 1761), plan, exterior, interior; (d, e) S. Pero dos Clérigos, plan, exterior; (f–h) Outeiro, Nossa Senhora da Glória (variously dated within the two decades from c. 1715 by an architect as yet inconclusively identified), plan, exterior and interior.

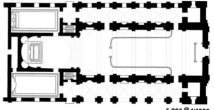

5.90a @ 1:1000

5.90b

5.90c

5.90e

5.90d @ 1:1000

At Belém, Nossa Senhora das Mercês is the outstanding work: the Bolognese architect Antonio Giuseppe Landi exceeded even Borromini in projecting a wholly convex façade. That recalls Nossa Senhora da Consolação e Santos Passos at Guimarães in the homeland and its central European predecesssors but it is recessed between giant pilasters rather than constricted by the towers.

At Rio de Janeiro, the application of pilastered frontispieces with Borrominesque pediments to the flat 'palace' façades of S. Francisco de Paula and the Terceira do Carmo, both hall churches, contrasts markedly with the Classical expression of the type for Nossa Senhora da Candelária and with the Vignolan form of the contemporary basilican Santa Cruz dos Militares. More characteristic of developments in Portugal was Rio's S. Pedro dos Clérigos, due to the engineer José Cardoso Ramalho: reitierating the elliptical plan of its Oporto namesake, rather than the extruded octagon of its brother church in Recife, that is now lost but an earlier exercise of the polygonal kind survives on the hill of Nossa Senhora da Glória.**5.89, 5.90**

5.90g

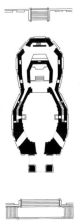

5.90f @ 1:1000

5.90h

Ramalho's excursion into elliptical planning was furthered in the second half of the 18th century by architects engaged on relatively small-scale ecclesiastical projects for the parishes of the rich mining towns of Minas Gerais. The monastic orders were excluded, but ultimately not the mendicants, and exceptional is the wealth of secular building in these towns. The main ones include Sabará, São João del Rei, Tiradentes, Mariana and the Vila Rica de Ouro Preto: of these, the last is the supreme example for its siting, its accommodation of public space and civic buildings, its private houses and its churches.**5·91**

5.91c

›**5·91 OURO PRETO:** (a) general view; (b) central square with Casa da Câmara; (c) Casa dos Contos; (d, e) Nossa Senhora da Conceição de Antônio Dias, exterior and interior.

5.89a

5.91b

5.91d

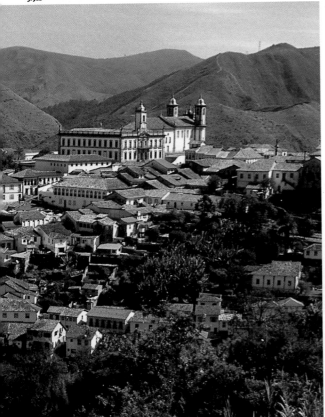

The ubiquitous hall-church formula was established from the outset of the new towns' first century: like the main church (*matriz*) of numerous parishes, S. António at Tiradentes or Manuel Francisco Lisboa's Nossa Senhora da Conceição at Ouro Preto are typical; Nossa Senhora da Conceição at Sabará and Nossa Senhora da Assunção at Mariana are exceptional in their basilican plans. The hall type was, of course, the mendicant norm too: examples include Francisco de Lima Cerquiera's Nossa Senhora do Carmo at São João del Rei (from 1759) and José Pereira dos Santos's S. Francisco and its Carmelite companion at Mariana (from 1762). The Congonhas sanctuary church of

5.91e

5.90a

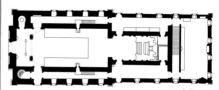

5.92b @ 1:1000

›5.92 CHURCH PLANNING IN THE NEW TOWNS OF MINAS GERAIS: (a, b) Mariana, S. Francisco (left and plan) with Nossa Senhora do Carmo; (c, d) Congonhas do Campo, Bom Jesus de Matozinhos, general view and detail of Calvary Chapel; (e, f) Ouro Preto, Nossa Senhora do Pilar, interior and plan; (g) Mariana, S. Pedro de Clérigos, plan; (h–n) Ouro Preto, Nossa Senhora Rosário dos Preos, plan and exterior; Nossa Senhora do Carmo, detail; S. Francisco de Assis, plan, section, interior, exterior.

Bom Jesus de Matozinhos, built (from 1759) in emulation of the great works near Braga, is a special – and especially prominent – example.**5.92a–d**

Antônio Francisco Pombal is among the most prominent of the architects who enriched the towns of Minas Gerais – and themselves – with multiple churches: he departed from the hall-church formula to the extent of inserting a polygonal (pseudo-elliptical) timber membrane within the masonry rectangle of his Nossa Senhora do Pilar at Ouro Preto and projecting the form through the twin towers of the façade (before 1733):**5.92e, f** except in the latter respect,

5.92d

5.92c

5.92e

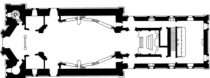

5.92f @ 1:1000

5.92g @ 1:1000

5.92h @ 1:1000

5.92i

the result recalls S. Pedro dos Clérigos at Recife. For S. Pedro dos Clérigos at Mariana, Antônio Pereira Calheiros went further to extend the elliptical form from nave to sanctuary (from 1752): except for the convex narthex – the persistent curvature, indeed – the result recalls Rio's polygonal Nossa Senhora da Glória do Outeiro.**5.90f, 5.92g** Manuel Francisco de Araújo may be credited with furthering that exercise for Nossa Senhora Rosário dos Pretos at Ouro Preto (from 1784), pushing the elliptical volume through to a narthex between cylindrical towers.**5.92h, i**

Araújo's exercise may have been prompted by distant knowledge of Guarino Guarini's church of Divina Providenza in Lisbon but it lacks the undulating movement through the ellipses of that lost masterpiece. Moreover, instead of the Borrominesque sweep of Guarini's façade, the convex projection from the towers here recalls again Weingarten, the Salzburg Kollegienkirche or, more particularly, the Wieskirche.**4.100** Soares da Silva's work at Guimarães is not irrelevant and an earlier Atlantic intermediary is to be found in the church of Espirito Santo at Ribera Grande in the Azores (second half of the 17th century): as we have seen, that façade has the simple convexity of Guimarães but it is bifurcated by bizarre relief.**5.84**

The culmination of Baroque in Brazil – certainly in Minas Gerais – is marked principally by the churches of the several mendicant orders which won through to the mining towns after the middle of the century. The extraordinary sculptor/architect to whom the most original works are attributed is identified as Antônio Francisco Lisboa (1738–1814), reputedly born in Oura Preto to Manoel Francisco and a slave: crippled (and nicknamed O Aleijadinho accordingly), his existence is sometimes thought to be mythical as there is no match for him in contemporary records. The hallmark of the œuvre is stamped with the portal: typically, it is distinguished by putti swinging on pediment fragments over multiple volutes and a didactic cartouche erupting from a crumpled lintel. Apart from the sculptural detail of Nossa Senhora do Carmo at Ouro Preto, the most celebrated examples of the œuvre are the churches of S. Francisco de Assis in Ouro Preto and S. João del Rei (from c. 1764 and 1774 respectively).**5.92j–n** The plan of the former retains corridors beside the sanctuary but widens them to beyond the perimeter of the nave: the latter is an elongated octagon preceded by a hexagonal vestibule whose concave walls project from cylindrical towers to the frontispiece. In the later work there is no vestibule but the nave walls are elliptical. In the earlier work all is planar except for the canted junction of the two main volumes and the undulating transition from the nave walls, around the towers and vestibule to the planar façade. Here at last is the type of movement in masonry – in both mass and detail – promoted by the Roman Baroque masters but in a context entirely original to whoever was Lisboa.

5.92j

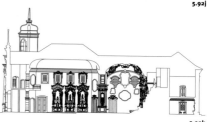

5.92k

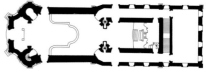

5.92l @ 1:1000

5.92n

5.92m

5.93a

5.93b

**›5.93 CARTAGENA, CASTILLO SAN FELIPE DE
BARAJAS:** (a) general view, (b) detail of ramparts.

The enlargement of the Castillo San Felipe de Barajas under Philip IV and subsequent improvements to the city's defence network as a whole in the early Bourbon era were proof against its greatest threat, the attack launched by the 25,000 British troops of Edward Vernon in 1741. Nevertheless, in 1762 the Spanish military engineer Antonio de Arévalo (1715–1800) was commissioned to extend the fortifications and, above all, to expand San Felipe to cover its entire hill: on completion later in the decade it eclipsed even the recently completed Fortaleza de San Carlos de la Cabaña half-way along the the narrow estuary of Havana Bay.

5 BOURBON AMERICA

The comprehensive programme of fortification in the Spanish Caribbean, furthered by Juan Bautista Antonelli in the 1580s, was extended to the major ports of the South American colonies and constantly expanded throughout the 17th and 18th centuries (AIC5, pages 798ff). It embraced the splendid Chilean harbour of Valdivia in one of the most impressive of all colonial systems of integrated defence works, covering the headlands, an island in the centre of the outer harbour and the mouth of the tributary river. Back in the Caribbean, however, it reached its culmination at the two poles of Spanish dominance there, Havana in Cuba and Cartagena in Colombia: of these, the latter may well claim to have been endowed with the single greatest fortress in the entire colonial world.**5.93**

ECCLESIASTICAL WORKS ACROSS TWO CONTINENTS

The perceived success of the Counter Reformation in Europe propelled the reforming orders to and through the New World with great fervour. They transmitted Tridentine reassertion of the primacy of the episcopacy, of the priest as the intermediary between the penitent worshipper and his Saviour, of the infinitely compassionate Virgin

Mary as primary intercessor, of the Eucharist as the prime instrument for the transmission of Grace. They promoted pilgrimage to shrines at the sites of the Virgin's miraculous appearance. They required many chapels for their repeated masses and, especially, an adjunct to the great church for the preservation and display of the sacrament – as in the motherland. They presented the church as the threshold of heaven and brought to its design and embellishment many of the techniques deployed after Trent to celebrate the Church Triumphant – especially those promoted by S. Carlo Borromeo in Milan (AIC5, pages 79f). However, if the characteristics of the style developed to that end in early 17th-century Rome are definitive, the term Baroque may be applied to the architecture of late-17th- and early 18th-century Spanish America – as to much in contemporary Andalusia – only with strict qualification.

5.94d

›**5.94 CÓRDOBA (ARGENTINA), CATHEDRAL,** effectively begun 1699, consecrated 1758: (a) plan, (b) general view from the south-west, (c, d) interior and detail of dome.

5.94b

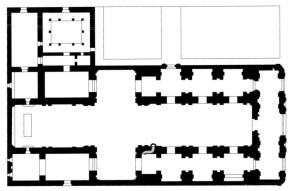

5.94a @ 1:1000

Founded in 1573 as the control post on the route from the Pacific to the Atlantic coasts of Spanish South America, Córdoba was of greater significance than Buenos Aires until late in the 18th century. It was quickly raised to a bishopric and endowed with a cathedral from 1581. Of ephemeral materials, the primitive structure was sustained until 1677. Progress on its replacement was slow: in 1699 José González Merguelte (hitherto employed on the cathedral of Sucre in Bolivia) was called in to revise the plan: the result was quasi-basilican with a narthex, an arcaded nave flanked by linked chapels and a deep rectangular chancel beyond the domed crossing.

On his death in 1710 Merguelte was replaced by the Italian Jesuit brothers Andrea Bianchi (Andrés Blanqui, 1677–1740) and Giovanni Battista (Juan Bautista) Primoli (1673–1747) who saw the work to its vaulting. Theirs is the neo-Albertian portico – recalling the hybrid temple-front triumphal-arch motif from S. Andrea in Mantua – but not the towers or dome which belong to an entirely different stylistic world. The first of the former (from c. 1734) are attributed to one José Rodríguez (and his team of native craftsmen). The mid-century dome is attributed to the Franciscan friar Vicente Muñoz of Seville – though it is strangely reminiscent of the western Spanish Romanreque forms of Zamora and Salamanca's Old Cathedral (AIC4, page 309) except for the convoluted ribbing.

5.94c

The problem of categorization is presented acutely by the cathedral of Córdoba in Argentina, which was hardly surpassed in scale in the era of Spanish South America usually defined as Baroque. The spectacular eclecticism was partly the consquence of a complex building history but even the Italian architects called in around 1710 to oversee completion failed to suppress the bizarre in belfry and dome.**5.94**

One of those Italians, Andrea Bianchi, is also credited with the Franciscan church in Buenos Aires known now as El Pilar: less problematical, perhaps, that too is eclectic with a variant on an Albertian theme for its façade, an abstract Classical internal ordonnance and a high-Solomonic Baroque retable. Certainly less problematic, on the other hand, are the cathedral and the chuch of S. Ignacio in the Argentinian capital. Though built by the Bavarian Jesuit brother Johann (Juan) Kraus (1660–1714) over a variant of the typical Jesuit plan, S. Ignacio is atypical of the florid South American norm but lacks Central European panache. The cathedral, unsoundly founded on basilican lines in a campaign beginning c. 1692, was rebuilt between 1752 and 1770 under the direction of the Savoyard architect Antonio Masella but his Classical style announces the new era which contributed its neo-Roman pronaos.**5.95**

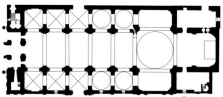

5.95a @ 1:1000

5.95b

›5.95 BUENOS AIRES, ECCLESIASTICAL
FOUNDATIONS: (a, b) S. Ignacio (from 1712), plan,
façade; (c, d) El Pilar (from 1716), exterior, interior.

The plan of S. Ignacio is a variant of the Roman prototype with rectangular sanctuary and side entrances in the
median bays of the nave: the twin-towered façade, neither Roman nor Spanish (except for the arcaded narthex),
is of Bavarian derivation – at least in profile. Juan Kraus
died two years after he had begun work on the project: his
effort was continued by his Jesuit assistants. Blanqui and
Primoli were involved, successively, in the 1720s – though
their preoccupation with Córdoba presumably meant delegation to others, notably the Jesuit brother Pedro Weger
(1693–1733). The bell tower to the left is orignal: its pendant was added in the mid-19th century.

Blanqui seems to have had prime responsibility at
least for the completion of the Franciscan church of
El Pilar. Here the triumphal-arch temple-front hybrid
recalls the façade of S. Sebastiano in Mantua – rather
than S. Andrea there. As in S. Andrea, famously, a consistent Order of pilasters relates exterior and interior
– though the latter are abstracted from the former.

5.95c

5.95d

5.96a

Argentina and beyond, Spanish South America is rich in its 18th-century legacy. In the elaboration of the latest fashions imported from the motherland, however, even Peru – innovative in its late-Mannerist era – was eclipsed by Mexico. There, as in Argentinian Córdoba, colonial buildings may be large but the scale of their ordonnance is rarely colossal. There is abundant gilding and rich ornamentation but that continues the Plateresque mentality usually in the more modern elaboration of motifs derived from the northern Mannerists, themselves inspired by the School of Fontainebleau. There is complexity, indeed contortion, of form but that continues the Mannerist mentality of pattern-book compilers – especially the northerners. There is little interest in developing complex spaces from interlocking centralized or longitudinal forms in plan and rare indulgence in expanding space illusionistically, even in paint.

Concomitantly, while there is some concern with undulation of cornice or pediment mouldings over doors or windows, that usually did not extend to developing movement in masonry mass, either through amplifying the plasticity of progressive Orders or countering concave and convex curve in elliptical undulation. Moreover, the Roman type of church façade, developed by Vignola and enlivened by Maderno, was not preferred to the French frontispiece or its more elaborate relative, the Spanish retable type. Framing a portal or backing an altar, that is the glory of the Spanish colonial church, its rampant foliage and fragmented architectural elements challenging pretence at more or less virile support in Solomonic or estípite style – as in the works of the more extreme followers of the Figueroa, the Churriguera and Hurtado in the homeland. And in the context of the timber retable before the complete emasculation of the Orders, curve was sometimes countered with curve to generate vitality.

5.96b

5.96c

Free from the responsibility of supporting anything other than its own superstructure, relatively easy to erect and carve, the timber retable was naturally the scene of freest invention. The stages on the way from tectonic logic to Mannerist ambiguity to unbridled fantasy may be traced through the altarpieces with which the great churches were endowed in the 17th and early 18th centuries onwards: the first stage is defined by works like the high altar retables of S. Bernardino at Xochimilco or S. Domingo in Oaxaca (AIC5, pages 813, 827). The Solomonic column played an essential role in the transition: the 'Churrigueresque' type was introduced from Andalusia as early as 1718 by Jerónimo de Balbás from Zamora (1680–1748). Fresh from completing the retable of the

>5.96 MEXICAN RETABLES IN THE EARLY BOURBON ERA: (a) Mexico City cathedral, Retablo de los Reyes (1718–37) by Jerónimo de Balbás; (b) Salamanca, S. Agustín, S. Anne (Pedro Joseph de Rojas, c. 1765); (c) Querétaro, S. Clara, west side altar (1770s).

5.97   5.98a

›5.97 THE RETABLE FAÇADE: Puebla, S. Francisco
(from 1743).

**›5.98 PEDRO DE ARRIETA, METROPOLITAN
CHURCHES:** (a) La Profesa (from 1597, substantially
renovated after flood and earthquake damage), main
eastern portal (from 1720); (b) Guadalupe, old basilica,
exterior (from 1695).

The Guadelupe site on the hill of Tepeyac, sacred to
the Aztec Mother Goddess (Tonantzin), achieved Christian sanctity with the repeated revelation of the Virgin
to an Indian peasant (Juan Diego) which tradition dates
to December 1531. When convinced by the miraculous
appearances at the site of roses in winter and the imprint
of the Virgin's image on the peasant's cloak, the episcopal authority permitted the construction of a chapel
dedicated to Nuestra Señora de Guadalupe whose cult
derived from the Estremadura homeland of Hernán Cortés and several of his lieutenants. The latter suggests

Seville cathedral Sagrario, he was dispatched to produce
the long-delayed furnishing of the apsidal Altar de los
Reyes in the cathedral of Mexico City:**5.96a** he went on
to close the choir with the Altar de Pedron. Fantastic dissolution is splendidly represented by the retable of S. Anne
in S. Agustín, Salamanca: abstraction by the side alars of
S. Clara, Querétaro.**5.96b, c**

Balbás promoted the estípite to prominence in his
resplendent Retablo de los Reyes and he is reputed to
have translated its style to the façade of an unexecuted
project for the new mint – but suffered from the hostility of the local profession. He was followed (c. 1730) by
Lorenzo Rodríguez who had worked on the cathedral
of Cádiz: he overcame similar prejudice to play a prime
role in the invention of the estípite façade – c. 1750 for
the cathedral Sagrario, as we shall see. Meanwhile, the
frontispiece of Puebla's S. Francisco (early 1740s) offers
a foretaste of what was to come.**5.97** Thereafter the retable may have been the preferred façade type – but the
exterior was slow to emulate the interior in freedom of
inspiration: the triumphal arch survived, if under duress.

The essentially architectonic triumphal-arch mode of
frontispiece design, derived from Siloe's unfinished project
for Granada cathedral, perfected elsewhere by Vandelvira,
or from Herrera's unfinished project for Valladolid (revised
by Nates; AIC5, pages 675f, 738f), remained popular in Mexico throughout the era in which Baroque forms of expression
might have supervened. We have already encountered variations on both themes on the south and west fronts of the
metropolitan cathedral executed over the last three decades
of the 17th century – and in other capital works. In the first
two decades of the new century, Pedro de Arrieta produced
prominent variants on the mode for the rebuilt Jesuit church
of La Profesa within the metropolis and the basilica at Guadalupe, in the northern outskirts of the capital.**5.98**

5.98b

that the cult may have been promoted officially, with or without the sanction of a miracle: be that as it may, its 'Indianization' in the terms of the miracle has been seen as the condition for the concept of a 'Chosen People' rejecting subservience to foreign masters.

The fourth basilica on the site was begun in 1695 and dedicated in 1709. The work is attributed to Pedro de Arietta, architect of the Inquisition and to the cathedral (from 1720). The interior was 'modernized' in the neo-Classical taste. The parapet over the west front is a bizarre 20th century confection instead of any recognizable form of pediment: that was obviated by the finials which resolve the vertical momentum of the triumphal arch ordonnance.

As in a plan of 1651, signed by José Durán, the church is basilican but with a central domed crossing like that of Herrera's Valladolid or Vandelvira's cathedral at Jaen. The resemblance between the frontispiece of the basilica and that of the capital's Inquisition palace (from 1736) – the ordonnance in general and the polygonal 'arches' in particular – supports the attribution of both to Arrieta (see page 937). As in most of the great religious and secular foundations of the capital, much of the effect of the articulation depends on the strong contrast between the grey volcanic stone of the frontispiece and the red brick elsewhere, except for the belfry stages of the four corner towers.

By the mid-18th century, prolix ornament is often overwhelming but beneath it the ordonnance is still essentially Classical, the Orders usually conforming to the triumphal-arch motif – though the columns may well be Solomonic. Inevitably, perhaps, the florid mode was preferred by the folk artisans of Indian – or *mestizo* – descent: the most prominent examples are intimate in scale but wide-ranging in the parochial works of central Mexico. Naturally, they retain the naive charm manifest in the iconographic reliefs on the posas and portals of the earliest missions (AIC5, page 805).**5.99**

From the echelons of ecclesiastical patronage in Mexico, there are myriad examples of scarcely sophisticated Plateresque profusion. A prominent example in the capital is the cloister of the Merced (from c. 1650–1700).**5.100**

›5.99 POPULAR RESPONSE TO METROPOLITAN PROTO-BAROQUE EMBELLISHMENT: (a) Tlacolula, Dominican convento church of La Asunción, detail of vaulting in the chapel of S. Cristo (or the Señor de Tlacolula, early 18th century); (b–d) Acatepec, S. Francisco, exterior, interior and detail of dome (c. 1730, interior redone after fire in 1939); (e) Tlacochahuaya, S. Jerónimo, interior (rebuilt from late-17th century, decorated by early 18th-century local artisans).

Popular love of ornament – and inspiration from the Rosário tradition established at Puebla and furthered at Oaxaca (AIC5, pages 825f) – promoted the profusion

5.99a

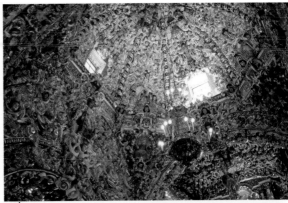

5.99d

5.99b

5.99c

of unorthodox or freely interpreted Classical mouldings: most popular were Arabesque or grotesque
motifs with zoomorphic and anthropomorphic forms
emerging from vegetation swirling in intricate low relief
around naive representation of Catholic icons. The
transition from Oaxacan Baroque – as manifest in S.
Domingo – to the popular is marked by the work in the
Tlacolula S. Cristo chapel.

›5.100 MEXICO CITY, LA MERCED: cloister
(from mid-17th century).

The church (1630–54) was demolished in the wake
of mid-19th-century anti-clerical reforms. The relatively
sober ground-floor arcade of the surviving cloister was
begun in parallel with the last phase of the church's
construction: the profusely chased and valanced upper
one, Mudéjar in inspiration, was begun c. 1700.

5.100

5.99e

5.101

5.102

5.103a

›5.101 SALAMANCA, S. BARTOLO, late-1730s: retable façade.

›5.102 ZACATECAS, CATHEDRAL OF NUESTRA SEÑORA DE LA ASUNCIÓN: west front (1740s, south tower 1904).

Attributed to Domingo Ximénez Hernández, the cathedral was built between 1729 and 1752 in place of one dating from a century earlier – which itself replaced a provisional work constructed from 1567 on a pre-Columbian temple site.

›5.103 PROLIXITY AT LARGE: (a) Guadalajara (Mexico), Augustinian church of S. Monica (from c. 1720), façade detail; (b) Arequipa (Peru), La Compañia (from 1590), façade (from c. 1700); (c) La Paz (Bolivia), S. Francisco, façade (from c. 1745).

A far-distant echo of Borromini, transmitted from Cuzco, waves through the pediment at Arequipa: the survival of pediment fragments over the outer columns of the triumphal-arch motif recurs at Puno and elsewhere in the region.

Further north, S. Bartolo in Salamanca (late 1730s) may be taken to illustrate the retable façade in the mode.**5.101** However, the most celebrated example is the west front of the cathedral at Zacatecas: the triumphal-arch motif is expanded to five bays on two levels and crowned by a neo-medieval attic of icons, no surface is left unchased, but the tectonic frame and the circularity of the voids are still appreciable.**5.102**

Extreme, the Zacatecas example is far from unique: it may also be represented by the façade of S. Monica in Guadalajara (c. 1733). It clearly ascends from the mixed style (*mestizo*) tradition which knew no frontiers in Spanish America where easily worked volcanic stone was readily available for native craftsmen to mix their interpretation of imported motifs with indigenous ones.

Beyond greater Mexico to the south the *mestizo* mode appears earlier, and rather more tamely, for La Merced in Antigua Guatemala (c. 1670; AIC5, page 829). Way off in Peru it is rampant in prolixity for the Compañia of Arequipa or the cathedrals of Puno and Cajamarca (c. 1700) or S. Lorenzo at Potosi (from c. 1730) – as for S. Francisco in the Bolivian capital of La Paz (from c. 1745).**5.103**

5.103b

5.103c

5.104

›5.104 ZACATECAS, S. DOMINGO (originally the
Jesuit Compañía), from 1746: west front.

The Jesuit church was built between 1746 and 1749
by Cayetano de Sigüenza: it was ceded to the Dominicans when the Jesuits were expelled from Mexico in the
18th century.

›5.105 HAVANA, CATHEDRAL OF THE IMMAC-
ULATE CONCEPTION (OR S. CHRISTOPHER OF
HAVANA), built from 1748: (a, b) façade and interior.
The alternative dedication acknowledges the church as
the repository of the supposed remains of Christopher
Columbus: they were removed from Hispaniola when
that island was ceded to France in 1796 and removal to
Seville in 1898 when Cuba was lost.

The church was originally designed (c.1727) to serve
the Jesuits but was incomplete on the suppression of the
Company of Jesus throughout the Spanish dominions
in 1767. After the diocese of Havana emerged from subservience to Santiago de Cuba in 1787, it was raised to
cathedral status and officially dedicated to the Virgin of
the Immaculate Conception. The towers were designed
with different dimensions to facilitate the evacuation of
water from a plaza laid out on a former swamp.

In Zacatecas, again, the mid-18th-century former Jesuit church (now S. Domingo) presents a very different
aspect to the florid cathedral: the triumphal-arch motif
asserts its authority on two levels, unchallenged by rampant ornament below a pediment fragmented in the manner of Fernando de Casas Novoa's Obradoio, but the outer
bays break forward on a semi-diagonal in far-distant
echo of Acero's Guadix. That was doubtless transmitted
via the contemporary Jesuit church in Havana, now the
cathedral: despite its conservative conformation to the

5.105b

5.105a

›5.106 GUADALAJARA, ORATORIAN CHURCH OF S. FELIPE NERI, from 1752: façade.

The church is attributed to Pedro Ciprés: the contrast between its façade and Borromini's work for the same order's headquarters in Rome is highly instructive.

›5.107 PUEBLA, FORMER JESUIT CHURCH OF ESPIRITO SANTO, from 1746: façade.

The Jesuits were established in Puebla in 1578 and began their first church almost immediately. Its replacement in the 18th century on a grander scale is attributed to José Miguel de Santa María. As elsewhere in the order's vigorous campaign of church building from the 1740s, it remained unfinished when dedicated in 1767, the year they were expelled from Spanish domains: the towers were not completed until 1804. The sumptuous style of articulation is defined as Pueblan Churrigueresque though it bears only a passing relationship to that complex mode in the mother country – or, indeed, elsewhere in Mexico.

basilican type, the façade is even more closely related to Acero's work (see page 825).**5.105**

The triumphal-arch façade admitted of rich variation – as for S. Felipe Neri in Guadalajara, for example. In Mexico, as in Guadix, that did not run to exploiting the possibility of contrasting curvature. Thus, the strictly planar façade of the Compañía in Puebla – the city's grandest church after the cathedral – breaks forward without curvature, intermediate projections or even progression in the plasticity of the Orders.**5.106, 5.107**

5.108a

In Oaxaca the two most spectacular retable façades belong to the cathedral and to the church of the Soledad.**5.108** The former is the more conservative in its wholly orthogonal projection of a triumphal-arch frontispiece still in the Siloe-Vandelvira mode: the didactic panels are echoed in the recessed side bays but the ordonnance extends across them to the inner corners of the towers and in general the sculptural enrichment does not challenge the architecture. In contrast, the church of the Soledad represents a development of the diagonally disposed projection well beyond what we have seen in contemporary Zacatecas. It emerges from a broad concave curve through which three levels of columns march to the orthogonal side

›5.108 OAXACA: (a) cathedral of the Assumption (from 1702), façade; (b) church of Nuestra Señora de la Soledad (from 1682), façade (from 1717).

The first of three cathedrals was begun in 1535 and destroyed by earthquake. The second one was consecrated in 1640, S. Juan de Dios having provided a temporary seat for the bishop. The definitive one was projected at the outset of the new century with the assistance of Pedro de Arrieta: it was consecrated in 1733. Its façade is made of the green cantera stone commonly found in Oaxaca's buildings: the central panel represents the mystery commemorated in the dedication. The interior was reformed in the 19th century.

Dedicated to the patroness of the city and conceived as the shrine of her sacred image, the basilica of the Soledad was begun in 1682 and consecrated in 1690. From that year it was associated with the convent of

bays: extending laterally like a retable, the exercise has the opulence commonly associated with the Baroque and its effect is certainly dramatic, especially in the rich contrasts of light and shade, but the complexity does not provide movement in either of the Roman Baroque modes. Nor does it in the several examples of concavity impressed in an entire façade: the amplified scallop-shell niche form is known as *puerta abocinada*.**5.109**

5.108b
Augustinian nuns founded from S. Monica in Puebla (like their sister establishment in Guadalajara). The vigorously articulated retable façade, self-assertive in screening the volume of the nave, is unique in the boldness of its projection: it was designed in part to provide earthquake-proof buttressing.

›5.109 MEXICO CITY, S. JUAN DE DOS, 1720s: façade.
The form of the *puerta abocinada* derives from the exedra – or open chapel – common to the early missionary foundations (AIC5, pages 804f). The metropolitan work is due to Miguel Custodio Durán. Another example in Cuernavaca was associated with the Franciscan convent of the Annunciation.

5.109

5.110b

5.110a

There was unarticulated movement in the advance and recession of planes. There was, too, movement in the form of individual motifs – especially the Solomonic column and the broken or undulating cornice. Imported from Seville by Juan Martínez Montalés in the middle of the 17th century, as we have noted, the spiral column effected the transition from sobriety to élan in the attic storey of the frontispieces of the cathedrals in Mexico City and Puebla. The attenuated permutation of Zacatecas cathedral apart, it was the principal agent of articulation even in the context of the triumphal arch for the parish church of S. Prisca in Taxco – as we shall see. Other Mexican examples – representative of the countless – include Querétaro's eclectic S. Agustín, where a highly mannered metamorphosis of style stages herms in support of the cloister arcades.**5.110**

Elsewhere examples of Solomonic proliferation in façades range from S. Francisco in Antigua Guatemala, and on down to the Jesuit's Compañía in Quito, Cajamarca

›**5.110 SOLOMONIC ORDERS AND ECLECTIC DIVERSITY IN QUERÉTARO:** (a, b) S. Agustín, façade (after 1731) and cloister (from c. 1745).

Authorship is disputed but it has been maintained, plausibly, that the scheme was initially devised by the Augustinian friar Luis Martínez Lucio, revised by Juan Manuel Villagomez and executed by Ignacio Mariano de las Casas: the stylistic diversity of the main parts of the complex would suggest that very different talents were brought to bear on its realization.

›**5.111 SOLOMONIC CENTRAL AND SOUTH AMERICA:** (a) Antigua Guatemala, S. Francisco, façade (c. 1700 and after 1717); (b) Quito, Compañía, façade (from 1722); (c) Lima, S. Agustín, façade (dated 1720).

The Franciscans, present at Guatemala Antigua since 1541, suffered severe damage to their church in the earthquake of 1565. Funds were not available for rebuilding on a larger scale until 1579. After the earthquakes of 1691 and 1717, there were further waves of rebuilding, but the earthquake of 1773 left the complex in ruins which have been restored only in part.

Instead of the form with superficial floral ornament common throughout the Spanish colonial world, the Franciscans at Guatemala Antigua adopted the boldly turned spirals of the original Petrine columns pillaged from Jerusalem (AIC5, pages 15f). So too did the Jesuits of Quito. The façade of the Compañía there was begun by the Franconian architect Peter Deubler in 1722 and furthered over a protracted period by the Mantuan Jesuit brother Venancio Gandolfi. The façade of S. Agustín in Lima is contemporary, at least in inception (the date is inscribed on the façade): it completed rebuilding which had begun after the earthquakes of 1681 and 1687 had destroyed the order's original foundation of 1573. The sculptor Diego de Aguirre, employed on the high-altar retable, may be assumed to have contributed to the realization of the retable façade.

5.111a

cathedral, the extraordinary bell tower of the Compañía in Potosi and the portal of S. Francisco there, S. Agustín and La Merced in Lima. On the other hand, the estípite was not popular in 18th-century New Granada or Peru – oddly, given the importance of the juxtaposition of fragmentary structural motifs in the late-17th-century Cuzco style.**5.111**

5.111c

5.111b

Around the middle of the 18th century, finally, the integrity of the triumphal-arch motif was disrupted in the façades of several prominent central Mexican churches, most notably at the Jesuit novitiate of Tepotzotlán, on the northern outskirts of the metropolis, Taxco to the south-west, at Guanajuato, further north in silver mining country, and at the centre of the capital itself. At Taxco,

5.112b

>5.112 TAXCO, S. PRISCA: (a) plan, (b) entrance front, (c) interior to sanctuary, (d) side altar.

The wealthy and philanthropic silver miner José de la Borda was granted permission in 1751 to rebuild the parish church of Taxco – *ex voto* for his immense good fortune. The identity of the cruciform exercise's author is now thought to be Cayetano de Sigüenza (who we have encountered at Zacatecas): he seems to have been assisted by Juan Caballero as master of works. Several retables are attributed to Isidoro Vicente de Balbás (adopted son of the metropolitan retable master Jerónimo de Balbás) – who may be supposed to have been consulted on the retable façade. Centred on its great relief medallion depicting the baptism of Christ, this is recessed between relatively austere twin towers: in contrast, the unusually elevated, double-height belfries are notable for exceptionally rich articulation incorporating estípites at the canted corners. The south portal, culminating in the representation of the Coronation of the Virgin, is hardly less spectacular. The cupola does not compete with the towers in the enrichment of the octagonal drum's articulation but relies for effect on the glazed tile revetment of its hemisphere.

The original interior embellishment of the usual constituent elements – choir over narthex to the west, rectangular sanctuary beyond the generous crossing – is unusually little altered. Triplicated and panelled pilasters support transverse arches between the three groin-vaulted bays of the nave and at the crossing, below the relatively unadorned octagonal drum and dome. As usual, the glory of the church is the set of nine retables which line the nave, terminate the transept and culminate in the dazzling sanctuary confection. Aspiring to reach the vaults in their complex verticality, the latter three – dedicated to the Virgin of Guadeloupe and the Rosary in the transept, to the Immaculate Conception in the sanctuary – have been distinguished from the others as the work of Balbás (whom we have encountered as a major contributor to the cathedral in Mexico City). Three more retables furnish the Chapel of the Padre Jesús which, projecting from the north side of the nave, is entered opposite the south portal.

5.112d

5.112c

5.112a @ 1:1000

in the frontispiece of S. Prisca (from c. 1750), the motif is retained at base, but it has lost its entablature to a series of little curved pediments in the service of verticality: actual or conceptual voids ascend in the profusely relieved centre through the Solomonic dissolution of the upper level.**5.112** The estípite wins in the frontispiece of S. Francisco Javier at Tepotzotlán (before 1767), but the triumphal arch motif is still distinguishable, the main cornice line is sustained at base level and regular geometry informs the main portal at least. Inside, the riot of anti-architectonic ornament is overwhelming: apart from the retables, the main glory is the Santa Casa shrine and its annexes.**5.113**

5.113b

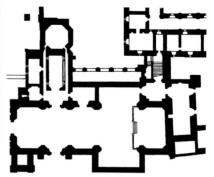

5.113a @ 1:1000

›5.113 TEPOTZOTLÁN, JESUIT NOVITIATE CHURCH OF S. FRANCISCO JAVIER, from c. 1670: (a) plan, (b) façade, (c, d) camarín chapel and vault, (e, f) sanctuary and detail of south transept retable.

The Jesuits were awarded the site of a former Franciscan mission to an Otomi Indian settlement not far from Teotihuacan in 1580 – eight years after their arrival in New Spain. The novitiate had been established by 1585 but substantial *convento* building followed the bequest of funds at the beginning of the new century: the original complex included a parish church as well as a domestic chapel. Another substantial bequest in 1670 was devoted to new accommodation for novices and to rebuilding the church on a grand scale: several generations were devoted to the completion of the façade and internal embellishment but the church was dedicated in 1682. Meanwhile work began in 1678 on a special Santa Casa shrine, inspired by the original at Loreto (AIC4, page 841) for the cult of the Virgin of Loreto to which the Jesuits were particularly devoted: amplification and embellishment, especially of the camarín for the ritual robing of the Madonna (on axis beyond the Santa Casa shrine) and the ancillary chapel of S. José, was enhanced from c. 1730 by Jesuit architects identified as Juan de Ortega and Ignacio de Paredes.

The profusely decorated camarín of the Madonna, octagonal in plan, lit through clerestory and cupola, is notable for the cross-ribbed vault of the Cordoban or Guarini type. Springing from the canted corners of the chamber, it is supported by the four archangels in the centres of the cross arms: wider and accommodating octagonal windows except where contiguous with the

5.113d

5.113c

5.113f

Santa Casa chapel, the orthogonal sides are sealed with estípite retables. These have been attributed to Isidoro Vicente de Balbás – whose other prominent works included the lost retablos mayor of the metropolitan Sagrario.

5.113e

5.114a

›5.114 GUANAJUATO: (a) La Compañía (1746–65), façade; (b, c) S. Cayetano (La Valenciana, from 1765), façade, interior to sanctuary.

Associated with a college originating from 1742, the Jesuit church was begun in 1747 under the direction of Felipe de Ureña to the plans of the Bethlemite Fray José de la Cruz. The complex was assigned to the Oratorians after the suppression of the Jesuits in 1767. The mine owners and the miners contributed to the cost of the lavish Churrigueresque façades. They did so too for the even more celebrated one built for the Theatines and dedicated to their founder, S. Cayetano – but generally called after its patron, the exceptionally rich mine-owning Conde de Valencia. This is an exceptionally refined manifestation of the style defined by the complex projection of major and minor – estípite and inter-estípite – motifs as the context for statueless niches, figural medallions and rampant floral ornament.

At Guanajuato, in the expanded frontispieces of Felipe de Ureña's Compañía (finished 1765) and the anonymous Valenciana (from 1765), the estípite progresses through diminishing planes, entablatures are broken and pediments fragmented by forms penetrating up from below but the main armature of aspiration to elevation still reverberates in tune with the High Renaissance French architectonic order.**5.114** This was not the case with Lorenzo Rodríguez's façade of the Sagrario attached to the

5.114c

5.114b

5.115c

5.115b

metropolitan cathedral from c. 1750: with its estípites repeated on two largely rectilinear levels – organ-like – it stands as the prime example of the type developed in the city. Of its major followers, the façade of S. Felipe Neri was conceived (from 1751) by Ildefonso Durán with fuller plasticity but less repetition in a semi-pyramidal format. The anonymous author of S. Francisco's Balvanera chapel opted (from 1766) for greater vertical aspiration. These and innumerable other churches are endowed with retables in the Churrigueresque style which in fact cede nothing to the most fecund of post-Hurtado fantasists.[5.115]

›5.115 MEXICO CITY, ESTÍPITE FAÇADES: (a) metropolitan parish church and cathedral, Sagrario; (b) S. Filipo Neri; (c) S. Francisco, Balvanera chapel.

First projected in 1693, work on the Sagrario was begun in 1749 with funds allocated extraordinarily without royal approval. The longitudinal basilican form proposed by Ildefonso Durán was rejected in favour of Lorenzo Rodríguez's innovative centralization – a Greek cross inscribed in a square on the quincunx principle. That was innovative in Mexico but there are Spanish precedents, such as the Sagrario attached to Granada cathedral by Hurtado (from 1704): the type descends through Serlio (Book V.14.8 or 11, for example) from Bramante – and, beyond that, Venetian sustenance of the Byzantine tradition. The interior articulation follows the style of the cathedral and has lost the dazzling contrast of the retable designed for it by Vicente de Balbás (1763). Stunning compensation is provided by the southern, eastern and northern retable façades improbably buttressed by plain spur walls with cascading cornices – beyond which are further extensions with full-blooded Baroque portals.

5.115a

5.116a

5.116c

5.116b

›5.116 TLAXCALA AND VICINITY: (a–d) Nuestra Señora de Ocotlán (from the 1720s, restored mid-19th century and again c. 1949), entrance front, interior to sanctuary, dome, plan; (e) S. José (from the mid-1770s as a parish church, now the cathedral), entrance front.

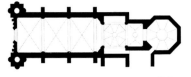

5.116d @ 1:1000

An adjunct to the Franciscan convento church of S. Lawrence, the Ocotlán shrine was founded c. 1590 to commemorate an apparition of the Virgin to an Indian convert – one Juan Diego – who was fetching medicinal water; by 1690 it housed an image of the Virgin believed to have been revealed by the apparition. Amplification began in 1670: it achieved the present form from 1717, including the white stucco Churrigueresque *puerta abocinada* façade, the proscenium to the crossing with an even more spectacular shell canopy, and the gilded Churrigueresque high-altar retable with the sacred icon in a silver niche backed by the dazzling camarín. Manuel Loayza directed the work, apparently to the designs of an Indian builder called Francisco Miguel – and to that extent it may be seen as the culmination of popular architectural activity in Mexico.

There were many regional variants on the estípite style. Among the most seductive, in main part because of its chromaticism, is that of the Puebla region. A major example is the façade of the church of Nuestra Señora at Ocotlán, near Tlaxcala: stunning is the contrast between the red tiles of the towers – the convexity of their pier buttresses countered by the concavity of the bays above – and the brilliant white stuccowork of the canopied frontispiece and superstructure. Reaction was instigated by Francisco Antonio de Guerrero y Torres (1740–92) in works like the church of S. José (now the cathedral) within Tlaxcala itself: the contrast of white and red is sustained but the Orders are restored to a measure of canonical significance despite their garlands.**5.116**

5.116e

5.117c

5.117b

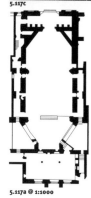

5.117a @ 1:1000

The façade of the Enseñanza in Mexico City, attributed to Guerrero, marks the advent of reform to the capital – though the Orders are not restored unembellished. The church is also exceptional in its semi-oval plan – in fact a rectangle with canted corners.**5.117a–c** Apart from semi-circular or semi-elliptical façades, curvature in planning was rare throughout the Spanish colonies. Concave and convex curvature were countered in the occasional timber retable, most notably in Pueblan S. Domingo, but the masons of Mexico rarely – if ever – emulated the carpenters. There is, however, a prominent exception close to the centre of metropolitan activity: the Pocito Chapel of the Well at Guadalupe, the minor masterpiece of Guerrero. The curvature of the juxtaposed centralized elements in the plan is entirely convex and Mannerism marks much of the detail but it would be pedantic to define the portal compositions, at least, as anything other than Baroque.**5.117d–g**

›5.117 GUERRO Y TORRES, APPROXIMATION TO CENTRALIZATION: (a–c) Mexico City, church of the Compañía de María Santísima y la Enseñanza, plan, exterior and interior; (d–g) Guadalupe, Pocito Chapel of the Well, plan compared to Serlio Book III, 4.13, general view of exterior and portal detail.

The Enseñanza convent was founded by Mother María Ignacia de Alzor of the order of Nuestra Señora María. Having obtained permission to found a convent and school for young girls on the site of two houses near the cathedral of Mexico City, she commissioned Guerrero to project a church on the restricted site: it was built between 1772 and 1778 and consecrated to Nuestra Señora el Pilar. The church of Corazón de Jesús in far-off Lima is a slightly earlier variant of this type of plan but the vaulting suggests a false oval composed of two semicircles separated by a rectangle.

The spring which watered the roses of Juan Diego's miraculous experience at Guadalupe was enshrined in Guerrero's centralized chapel from 1777: the initiative is unascribed. The programme ran to a central chamber for limited congregation at mass beyond the chamber of the well, a sacristy and four peripheral chapels dedicated to Juan Diego's apparitions. Like his older con-

5.117f

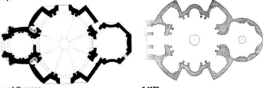

5.117d @ 1:1000   5.117e

5.117g

temporary Rodríguez, Guerrero drew inspiration for his extended centralized plan from Serlio – who drew from the imaginative reconstruction of an ancient Roman shrine (Book III, 4.13). The circular shrine of the well and the larger octagonal sacristy are juxtaposed with the elliptical congregation space on its cross-axis: the latter, of course, is a preferred Baroque form but here, entered at either end of the longitudinal axis, its integrity is not ceded to a Baroque exercise in spatial flow – as, for instance, in Ventura Rodríguez's S. Marcos in Madrid where the elements are aligned on the long axis of the elliptical central space. The interiors were altered in the 19th century.

In plan the major elements preserve their discretion but, ironically, the pure geometry of the fenestration – Mudéjar in inspiration – is compromised by curvature and cusping. Quite contrary, too, is the triangulated zig-zag pattern of the external tile revetment and the free-flowing curvature of the cornice line. Mannered variation on the Solominic theme produced the entrances to the main congregational chamber. On the other hand, the triumphal-arch motif is bent around the well chamber portal's canted corners, with reformed canonical columns, but the lintel undulates and the fimbreated upper window resembles a fountain in the lush vegetation of a Moorish garden – appropriately enough.

CAPITAL WORKS

By the end of the 17th century the sectors of the metropolitan grid inhabited by Mexicans of Spanish descent – wholly or largely – were consistent in the morphology of the broad streets: these were punctuated with some eighty churches and half that number of conventos, most of which tended colleges, hospitals or other humanitarian institution whose support was required of the rich. Social mobility, advanced by the greater opportunities for enrichment in the colonies than at home – and the venality admitted by the relaxation of royal regulation in the late Habsburg reigns – led to merchants emulating professional practitioners in aspiring to nobility. Royal authority was reasserted in centralizing administrative reforms under the Bourbons, notably Charles III, and prosperity was promoted by economic and fiscal reforms – and advances in mining technology. Despite the curtailing of noble privileges, more than a hundred families claimed social pre-eminence and most maintained palatial houses by the end of the 18th century.

Damage wrought by social unrest at the end of the Habsburg era, followed by affluence under the early Bourbons, led to so much rebuilding and renovation in the capital that little was left from its first two centuries of growth – except the grid, of course. In the centre, the greatest secular buildings address the Zócalo in the shadow of the cathedral: the viceroy's palace, which required extensive restoration after the destructive riots of 1692, was habitable again by the end of the century. The rehabilitation of the town hall opposite the cathedral awaited the settlement of the new regime c. 1720 and the archbishop's palace on the other side of the square was not begun for another decade. While that was progressing a new building for the Inquisition was begun in 1732 on the Plaza Santo Domingo where a new mint was also built. The Jesuits were busy extending their presence with the Colleges of

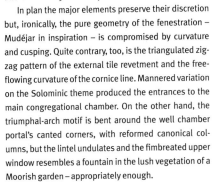

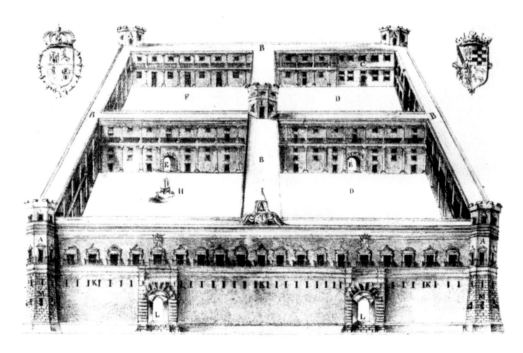

5.118a

5.118b

5.118c

5.118e

5.118d

›5.118 CAPITAL ESTABLISHMENT BUILD-
INGS: (a, b) Palacio Nacional (former viceroy's palace, from 1692 on earlier foundations, much altered),
project of 1692 and lithograph of 1860; (c) Zócalo with
the cathedral as completed c. 1800 (AIC5, pages 817f);
(d, e) Palacio de la Inquisición (from 1732), portal and
patio; (f) Las Vizcaínas, general view; (g–i) College of S.
Ildefonso, entrance portals and patio (from 1712).

The viceroy's palace, headquarters of Hernán Cortés
acquired by the Crown in 1562, was virtually rebuilt after
the riots of 1692. The 'National Palace' after Mexico won
independence in 1821, it retained the rhythm of fenestration throughout its extraordinary extent but not its architectural detail and the proportions were altered with the
addition of a third floor in the late -1920s. The Palacio de
la Inquisición fared better: it retains Pedro de Arrieta's
fenestration and frontispiece – and, therefore, the original appearance of the Guadelupe basilica's similar composition. As invariably in the secular practice of old and
New Spain, it was built around a patio but the junction of
the arcading is extraordinary.

5.118f

5.118i

5.118g

5.118h

Work on the vast complex of the Colegio de S. Ilde-fonso, incorporating earlier school buildings, was begun c. 1715 and took nearly thirty-five years to complete: the architects were the Jesuit fathers Zorella and Escobar, the latter adding the wing containing the chapel and main assembly hall. The monotony of the façades, enhanced by the extended horizontals of socle, stringcourse and cornice, is partially relieved by attenuated pilasters sepa-rating bays with two tiers of windows: the lower ones con-form to the current mode of combining circle and square in a quasi-Mudéjar manner; the upper ones have convoluted rectangular frames. The main accents are provided by the portals (one with lintels formed in the same way as the lower windows) flanked by paired Doric pilasters which support an attic articulated with a much smaller Order of Corinthian columns. As usual in the city, the detail is of grey stone set against dark-brown walls.

The Colegio de S. Ignacio (Las Vizcaínes) was founded c. 1733 as a school for orphans (of Basque descent) to be run by Jesuits: building, begun the following year to the plans of an unknown architect and largely com-plete thirty years later, was modelled on the S. Ildefonso complex. Simpler in articulation, pilasters are retained without the stringcourse and the stacking of larger, simi-larly framed windows reinforce the attempt to counter the extended horizontals; the portal is the stronger for eschewing some of its predecessor's fussy complexity.

›5.119 CAPITAL PRIVATE PALACES: (a, b) Mexico City, Casa de los Azulejos of the Condes del Valle de Orizaba (from the 1730s and 1750s) and the same family's suburban Casa de los Mascarones (from 1766); (c) Pubela, Casa del Alfeñique (c. 1790); (d–f) Mexico City, Casa de los Condes de San Mateo de Valparaíso (from c. 1770), street front, portal and patio; (g–i) Casa de los Condes de Santiago de Calimaya (from 1775), plan, street front and patio view into the staircase; (j, k) Casa de los Marqués de Jaral de Berrio (from 1779), street front.

The tile-clad Casa de Orizaba (transformed into a department store in 1919) replaced several earlier houses on the site at a date assumed to be before 1737 (when noted in a family will): more work was done by the next generation in the late-1750s but none of it is specifically identified. Attenuated pilasters of an abstract Order support the balcony cornice, the Doric pilasters of the portal give way to estípites on the piano nobile in support of an incomplete entablature and a meandering parapet: the articulating agents are in grey stone against the revetment of blue, white and yellow tiles which is unusual in Mexico City – but not in Puebla. Unique is the street front of Orizaba's single-storey villa suburbana known as the Casa de los Mascarones, begun in 1766 and unfinished on the patron's death five years later: the rusticated façade is articulated with estípites supporting atlantes (from which the house is misnamed).

S. Idelfonso and S. Ignacio from 1712 and 1734 respectively. There was a vast hospital building programme as well. The uniform morphology noted above derives in no small part from the elongated street fronts of all these projects, several returning around a whole block. Puebla and the other provincial capitals also benefited from much new building in the first half of the century but not to a similar uniform effect. A Puebla connection may explain the rare use of tiles in the capital.**5.118, 5.119**

5.119a

5.119b

5.119c

5.119e

5.119d

5.119f

The vast house of the Condes de San Mateo de Valparaiso, occupying much of a block, was rebuilt from 1769 to the plans of Francisco Guerrero y Torres: agriculture and mining paid for it, the Banco Nacional bought it in 1882 and altered the fenestration. Originally, it seems, a mezzanine was distinguished from the ground floor by windows in place of the present decorative panels. In any case the stacking of the voids between continuous frames effectively counters the extended horizontals. More imaginatively, in this – his first important work – Guerrero avoids symmetry in both the perpendicular façades: admittedly, the tower looks as though it needs a pendant at the far end of the side wing but the varied rhythm of the entrance front – stressed by the off-centre portal with its electric ribbon mouldings – is original if only in its pragmatic response to existing building. Pragmatism, however, is hardly enough to explain the most stunning coup in the whole exercise: the amazing asymmetrically crossed arcading of the patio which contradicts the axial alignment of the entrance from the street and the assertive Mannerist exit into the living quarters served by a double-flight spiral staircase.

The frontispiece of the Casa de los Condes de Santiago de Calimaya (built on agricultural wealth for one of New Mexico's most eminent families) is canonical in its ordonnance but not in the convoluted lintel to the ground-floor portal or the cusping of the balcony door in its lighly raised abstract outer frame or the flying arches of the staircase. However, Guerrero's inventiveness is nowhere less restrained by an essentially canonical ordonnance than in the portal to the chapel and here, as elsewhere in his work, much of the freedom of invention has something of the naivety of so-called 'folk Baroque'. The heteredox master's other great palace – built on an even greater scale from c. 1780 for the Conde de Santiago, who had recently been entitled Marqués de Jaral de Berrio – is distinguished by similarly bizarre embellishment to the unusual four-storey elevation. Unconstrained by existing work, Guerrero did not have to orchestrate asymmetry with his ordonnance: this manages to effect at least partial transition from the quasi-Plateresque towards the Rococo with intricate patterning which substitutes decorative virility for structural substance in its major and minor members.

The greatest private palaces might also frame a streetscape and the houses of the most successful professional practioners might combine to do so too: in either case there were portes cochères leading through to a central patio. Lower down the social scale people lived in apartments after the prototype of the ancient Roman *insula* (AICI, page 545) – obviously with varying degrees of affluence. Often simulating the palace type, they were usually built over shops like the housing of burghers – or

5.119h

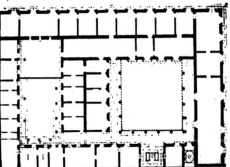

5.119g @ 1:1000

5.119i

5.119j

5.119k

landlords of traders – in all towns. Typically in the capital, at least, the detailing is in cream or grey volcanic stone against red-brown brick or stone walls.

Metropolitan preoccupation is inevitable here but it must be countered, if only with a degree of selectivity which hardly does justice to the scope of two continents in the first Bourbon half-century. Also inevitable is imbalance in the treatment of ecclesiastical and secular works: serving changing patterns of life, of course, the latter are subject to transformation and destruction to a far greater degree than the former. Yet there are fine surviving secular buildings throughout Spanish America – and, naturally, they are usually more revealing of local idiosyncracy than the churches.

5.120a

5.120b

5.120c

Spanish colonial secular practice is, of course, diverse throughout the two American continents: as in the ecclesiastical sphere, however, convolution is unsurprisingly the common factor – except in the far south. In Argentinian Córdoba, the house of the governor Rafael Sobremonte (1745–1827) could hardly be plainer before and beyond its portal.**5.120a–c** In the median zone of Peru, simplicity was modified in the manner of Vandelvira – or his Ubedan contemporaries (AIC5, page 708) – for the early

›5.120 DOMESTIC BUILDING OF VARIED STATUS ACROSS TWO CONTINENTS: (a–c) Córdoba, Palace of Rafael Sobremonte (governor of Córdoba 1783–97, viceroy of Rio de la Plata 1804–07), street front and patio; (d, e) Cuzco, Casa del Almirante, street front and exceptionally generous patio (early 17th century, now Museo Inka); (f, g) Lima, Palace of Don José

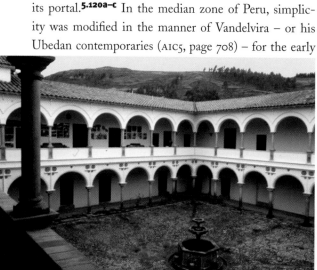

5.120e

5.120d

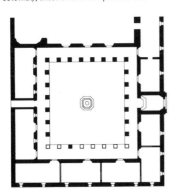

5.120f

Bernardo de Tagle y Brancho, Marques de Torre Tagle, portal flanked by enclosed balconies and patio (1735); (h, i) Antigua Guatemala, University of S. Carlos, plan and patio (early 1760s, now the Museo de Arte Colonial); (j, k) Cartagena, Palacio de la Inquisición, portal (dated 1770) and patio, modest and affluent housing (18th and early 19th century); (l–n) Havana, noble house window detail, cathedral plaza with Palacio de los Condes de Casa Bayona (1720, now the Museo de Arte Colonial), exterior and reception room.

17th-century house of Admiral Francisco Aldrete Maldonaldo in Cuzco.**5.120d, e** A century later in Lima, the Casa Torre-Tagle conforms to the ubiquitous courtyard type in plan but takes convolution to different extremes in the portal and patio arcade.**5.120f, g** The arcade has its near equivalent in the cloister of the S. Carlos University of Antigua Guatemala.**5.120h, i** And such works recall modes favoured in the Muslim world from Nasrid Granada to late-Mughal India (AIC3, pages 248f, 624ff).

5.120h

5.120i

5.120j

5.120k

The portal type recurs often, perhaps most notably for the Palacio de la Inquisición in Cartagena.**5.120j, k** Despite its official function, that building best represents early 18th-century Caribbean colonial domestic architecture at its grandest. The domestic tradition at its more modest is well represented nearer the periphery of town. The domestic tradition at the upper echelons of society is well represented in central Cartagena but nowhere more completely than by the Palacio de los Condes de Casa Bayona (1720) which faces the cathedral over the latter's plaza in Havana.**5.120l–n**

5.120l

5.120n

5.120m

The Caribbean colonial settlements with which we began are well preserved as the nuclei of extensive post-colonial developments. It may be recalled that King Philip II charged Juan de Herrera with responsibility for devising a model of urban planning to be applied throughout the empire, (AIC5, pages 740f). Essential to that was a central square – the Plaza Mayor – beyond which was a grid of streets. The latter was impossible to impose on existing urban structures like Madrid or Salamanca where the Plaza Mayor was knitted in with limited formality (AIC5, page 754, and above, page 837). It had ever been natural to the founding of colonial towns on new sites – and, fortuitously, even to the refounding of Mexico City on the basis provided by the Aztecs (AIC1, page 323). That was the precedent followed in all the major cities of New Spain which we have encountered here – all before Herrera. And Philip II's chief planner must have been at least as familiar with the Aztec basis of the urban development promoted by his compatriots in Mexico as he was with the unrealized Parisian projects of the contemporary Valois.

Santo Domingo, Havana, Veracruz and Cartagena de Indias all have something of a grid – the first two imprecise on their Caribbean islands. They were zoned for administrative, commercial and domestic buildings. The districts of the latter were themselves zoned to accommodate the distinct strata of a hierarchically ordered society. And all these cities have splendid plazas addressed by public buildings and the greatest of the houses.

In Cartagena, the governor's palace and the repository of archives face the Palacio de la Inquisición across the eponymous plaza (renamed for Bolívar after independence): the cathedral is on the diagonal, at the junction of the square with one of the grid's main arteries. The Palacio Municipal still addresses the Plaza de las Armas (the zócalo) at Veracruz: the grander merchant houses take their place on the other sides of the inner blocks of the contextual grid.**5.121a–c**

5.121a

5.121b

5.121c

5.121d

›5.121 PUBLIC AND PRIVATE FACE OF CIVIC SPACE: (a, b) Vera Cruz, El Zócalo neighbourhood, Palacio Municipal (1608, remodelled mid-18th century and 1971) and merchant housing; (c–e) Cartagena, street scenes and cathedral precinct; (f–h) Havana, Plaza de Armas, Palacio de los Capitanes Generales (projected 1773), Palacio de los Condes de Santovenia (right, projected 1784) and general view (with Castillo de la Real Fuerza, right).

5.121e

5.121h

At Havana the Plaza de la Catedral was the focus of aristocratic life in its peripheral palaces: the Plaza de Armas, originally a parade ground adjunct to the Castillo de la Real Fuerza, was transformed in the late-18th century with the construction of the Palacio de los Capitanes Generales as the hub of administration, opposite the grandest of all Havana's aristocratic residences, the Palacio de los Condes de Santovenia. Varied in style from what passes for Baroque to so-called 'Neoclassical', these buildings take us beyond the scope of this volume into the last phase of Spanish Bourbon colonial building – the first phase of a new architectural era in the wider world. **5.121d–f**

5.121f

5.121g

GLOSSARY

ADOBE mud or mud brick.

AEDICULE ornamental niche housing a sacred image, for example.

AISLE side passage of a church or temple, running parallel to the nave and separated from it by columns or piers.

ALCÁZAR any of a series of palaces built by the Moors in Spain. From Arabic *al qasr*.

ALL'ANTICA 'in the manner of the ancients'; that is, drawing on the repertoire of Classical forms in Renaissance architecture.

AMBULATORY semi-circular or polygonal arcade or walkway surrounding, for example, a sanctuary.

APSE semicircular domed or vaulted space, especially at one end of a basilica, hence **APSIDAL**, in the shape of an apse.

ARCADE series of arches supported by columns, sometimes paired and covered so as to form a walkway. Hence **BLIND ARCADE**, a series of arches applied to a wall as decoration.

ARCHITRAVE one of the three principal elements of an entablature, positioned immediately above the capital of a column, and supporting the frieze and cornice.

ARCUATE shaped like an arch. Hence (of a building) **ARCUATED**, deploying arch structures (as opposed to trabeated).

ARTESONADO coffered ceiling formed of decorative wood panels and interlaced beams.

ASHLAR masonry cut and laid to present a smooth finished surface (as opposed to, for example, Cyclopean or rubble construction).

ASTYLAR without columns.

ATLANTE element in the shape of a male figure, used in place of a column.

ATRIUM entrance-hall or courtyard, often open to the sky.

ATTIC shallow storey above the main Orders of a façade, or a wall at the top of the entablature concealing the roof.

AULA REGIA public audience chamber or throne room in a royal or imperial court.

AYUNTAMIENTO Spanish muncipal authority, hence the building housing it.

BALDACHINO canopy raised on columns over an altar or tomb.

BALUSTER short column or pillar, usually bulbous towards the base, supporting a rail.

BAPTISTRY building, adjunct to a church, dedicated to baptism.

BASILICA church, temple or other public building, consisting principally of a colonnaded rectangular space with an apse at one end, generally enclosed by an ambulatory, or having a central nave and side aisles, and lit by a clerestory.

BASTION structure projecting from the angle of a defensive wall enabling enhanced vision and mobility for a garrison.

BATTERING reinforcement of walls and column bases by building sloping supporting structure.

BAY one of a series of compartments of the interior of a building, the divisions being created by piers or columns, for example.

BEL ÉTAGE (or **ÉTAGE NOBLE**) French equivalent of piano nobile, the main floor of a large house, the location of the important reception rooms.

BELFRY bell tower or the particular room in a bell tower where the bells are hung.

BELVEDERE open-sided roofed structure, freestanding or situated on the roof of a building, placed so as to command a view.

BEMA sanctuary of a church, especially Byzantine.

BOSQUET (from Italian *boschetto*, a little wood), in French gardens, a formal arrangement of trees.

BOSS ornamental projection at the apices where the ribs of a vault meet.

BRODERIE in French formal gardening, a parterre using paths and beds to form an embroidery-like pattern.

BURGFRIED German castle keep; also, the productive area administered from a castle.

BUTTRESS support, usually stone, built against or adjacent to a wall to reinforce or take load.

CAMARÍN in a church, a chapel behind the high altar where sacred images are prepared for display and where the jewels and other ornaments used are stored.

CAMPANILE bell-tower, usually freestanding.

CANOPY roof for a niche or statue, often supported by slender poles.

CANOPY VAULT, *see* **VAULT, CANOPY**.

CAPPELLA chapel.

CAPITAL top part of a column, supporting the entablature, wider than the body of the shaft, usually formed and decorated more or less elaborately. The part of the column which, taken together with the entablature, forms the major defining element in the Greek Orders of architecture – Doric, Ionic and Corinthian.

CARYATID female figure used as a support in place of a column.

CASINA a small summer house or kiosk.

CASINO a country house, typically a house for summer occupation.

CATHEDRAL large church, serving as the focal point for a bishop in his diocese.

CAVEA the seating within a theatre.

CAVETTO concave moulding with a quarter-circular cross-section.

CENTRALIZED PLAN building design in which the structure is symmetrical in plan around the centre, allowing for reflection about both 90- and 180-degree axes.

CHANCEL part of a church where the clergy and choir are ranged, separated by screen or railing from the main body of the building.

CHANTRY CHAPEL chapel dedicated to the chanting of masses to save the soul of the sponsor.

CHAPEL subsidiary space having its own altar, situated within a larger church or cathedral.

CHAPTER HOUSE room or building within or adjacent to a monastery or cathedral, in which the chapter meets.

CHÂTEAU a large country or manor house; at one extreme, a palace.

CHEVET apse at the east end of a church wherein there is an ambulatory with chapels or miniature apses radiating off it.

CHEVRON decorative moulding composed of a zigzag pattern.

CHIAROSCURO the use of light and shadow in a painting, creating the illusions of depth and volume, often to dramatic effect.

CHOIR area of a church near the altar, in which the choir (singers) sit.

CIBORIUM canopy raised on columns so as to form a covering above an altar or tomb, for example.

CLERESTORY windowed upper level, providing light from above for a double-storey interior.

CLOISTER covered arcade, often running around the perimeter of an open courtyard.

COFFERING decoration of a ceiling or vault, for example, with sunken rectangular or other polygonal panels.

COLONNADE line of regularly spaced columns.

COLONNETTE small column, decorative and/or functional.

COLORE in art, compositional coherence achived through the painterly application of pigment, developed in Venice by Giovanni Bellini and his followers.

COLUMN vertical member, usually circular in cross-section, functionally structural or ornamental or both, comprising (usually) a base, shaft, and capital.

COLUMN, ENGAGED column which does not stand completely proud of a wall, either having stone ties or being partially sunk into the wall, though not so much as a pilaster.

CONCINNITAS beauty of style achieved through the skilful and harmonious joining of elements.

CONSOLE a **CORBEL** or bracket, often with a scroll-shaped profile.

CORBEL support bracket, usually stone, for a beam or other horizontal member. Hence **CORBELLED**, forming a stepped roof by deploying progressively overlapping corbels.

CORINTHIAN ORDER *see* **ORDER, CORINTHIAN**.

CORNICE projecting moulding forming the top part of an entablature. More generally, a horizontal ornamental moulding projecting at the top of a wall or other structure.

CORO choir in a church.

CORPS DE LOGIS principal part of a major building, as distinct from its wings, subsidiary blocks, colonnades or **PAVILLONS**, etc.

CORTILE an internal court, open to the sky and surrounded by an arcade.

COVE/COVING curved concave moulding forming or covering the junction between wall and ceiling.

CRENELLATION indentation in a parapet.

CROCKET carved ornament usually in the form of a curled leaf.

CROSSING the area where the transept of a church crosses the nave and chancel, often surmounted by a tower.

CRYPT underground chamber, often beneath the chancel of a church.

CRYPTO-PORTICUS concealed or sunken passage or arcade.

CURTAIN WALL defensive wall of a castle.

CUSP projection formed between two arcs, especially in stone tracery, hence **CUSPED**.

CYCLOPEAN masonry made up of massive irregular blocks of undressed stone.

CYMA RECTA wave-shaped moulding, usually forming all or part of a cornice, the upper part being convex and the lower concave.

CYMA REVERSA wave-shaped moulding, usually forming all or part of a cornice, the upper part being concave and the lower convex.

DADO the middle part, between base and cornice, of, for instance, a pedestal, or the lower part of a wall when treated as a continuous pedestal.

DIAPERWORK repeated pattern in brick or tile, for example, often involving diamond shapes.

DISEGNO draftsmanship; also the ability to create through drawing.

DI SOTTO IN SÙ 'from below, looking up': technique used in illusionist ceiling painting in which various spatial effects – especially drastic foreshortening – are used to produce am illusion of three-dimensional space.

DOME more or less hemispherical roof or vault, hence domical.

DONJON the keep or main tower protected by the walls of a castle.

DORIC ORDER *see* **ORDER, DORIC**.

EAVES the part of a roof which overhangs the outer face of a wall.

ENCEINTE the whole fortified area of a castle.

EN ECHELON disposed in parallel, like the rungs of a ladder.

ENFILADE a suite of rooms with their doorways aligned – thus creating a vista – and typically embodying a hierarchy from public to private.

ENGAGED COLUMN, *see* **COLUMN, ENGAGED**.

ENTABLATURE that part of the façade of a church, etc., which is immediately above the columns, and is generally composed of architrave, frieze and cornice.

ESTILO CHÃO austere Portuguese architectural style of the 16th century characterized by the use of simple Classical forms and absence of decoration.

ESTILO DESORNAMENTADO 16th- and early 17th-century Spanish architectural style reacting to the excessive decoration that characterized the **PLATERESQUE** style. In contrast, the *estilo desorna-mentado* was functional and emphasised order over ornament and symmetry – under the guidance of Vitruvius.

ESTÍPITE column or pilaster, square or rectangular in plan and broader at the top than at the base, much used in Spanish and Spanish colonial Baroque architecture.

EXEDRA recess, usually apsidal, containing seats.

EXONARTHEX extension to the narthex of a church, formed by the aisles.

FAN VAULT, *see* **VAULT, FAN.**

FILIGREE decorative work formed of a mesh or by piercing material to give the impression of a mesh.

FIMBRIATED fringed or finely striped (from heraldry).

FINIAL ornament at the top of a gable or roof, for example.

FLAMBOYANTE ARCHITECTURE highly decorative late-Gothic style developed in France in the late-14th and 15th centuries.

FLYING BUTTRESS an arch and more or less freestanding buttress which together take the load of a roof, for example.

FORUM central open space of a town, usually a marketplace surrounded by public buildings.

FRESCO method of painting done on plaster which is not yet dry, hence also the resultant artefact.

FRIEZE the middle part of an entablature, above the architrave and below the cornice. More generally, any horizontal strip decorated in relief.

FRONTISPIECE principal entrance and its surround, usually distinguished by decoration and often standing proud of the façade in which it sits.

GABLE more or less triangular vertical area formed by the ends of the inclined planes of a pitched roof.

GALLERY upper storey projecting from the interior of a building, and overlooking the main interior space.

GISANT funerary sculpture with recumbent figure of the dead person.

GOLDEN SECTION architectural proportions thought to produce an effect particularly pleasing to the eye, whereby, for example, the ratio of width to length equals the ratio of length to (width plus length).

GREEK CROSS cross with four arms of equal length.

GRISAILLE a painting in monochrome, or near monochrome, restricted to variations in tone to define form.

GROIN rib formed at the intersection of two vaults.

GROTTESCHI 'grotesques', motifs employing mixed human, animal and vegetable forms derived from the decoration of Ancient Roman grottoes rediscovered in the Renaissance.

GUTTAE projections, more or less conical in form, carved beneath the triglyphs of a Doric entablature.

HALL CHURCH church in which nave and aisles are of equal height, or nearly so, often under a single roof.

HERM sculpted pillar with a male head (usually of Hermes) and some-times his torso above a plain section. In ancient Greece these were used as markers of territory; in Renaissance architecture often applied as a decorative element.

HÔTEL PARTICULIER substantial French townhouse, often freestand-ing behind an entrance court.

ICON image of a sacred subject, often acquiring sacred significance in its own right. Hence **ICONIC**, possessing sacred significance.

ICONOSTASIS screen separating the nave from the sanctuary in a Byzantine church, latterly used for placing icons.

IGNUDO Michelangelo's term (from Italian 'nudo', 'naked') for the many seated idealized male nudes incorporated in the frescoes for the Sistine Chapel ceiling.

IMPOST structural member – usually in the form of a moulding or block – at the top of a pillar, for example, on which an arch rests.

IN ANTIS a portico in which the columns align with the flanking walls rather than projecting beyond them.

IONIC ORDER *see* **ORDER, IONIC.**

JAMB side of a doorway or window frame.

KEEP main tower of a castle, providing living accommodation.

KOKOSHNIK arched or keel-shaped decorative element in traditional Russian architecture, often assembled in tiers at the base of church cupolas.

LADY CHAPEL chapel dedicated to the Virgin Mary.

LANCET arch or window rising to a point at its apex.

LANTERN TOWER windowed structure lighting an interior, situated on a roof, often at the apex of a dome.

LATIN CROSS cross with one arm longer than the other three.

LIERNE short intermediate rib, often non-structural.

LINTEL horizontal member over a window or doorway, or bridging the gap between two columns or piers.

LOGGIA gallery open to the elements on one side.

LUNETTE semi-circular window or recess, usually at the base of a dome or vault.

LUSTGEBÄUDE garden palace or pavilion.

MACHICOLATION gallery or parapet projecting on corbels from the outside of defensive walls, with holes from which missiles might be dropped or thrown.

MANIERA literally 'style' but associated with a self-conscious style of painting that displayed technical virtuosity with value placed on qualities such as grace and innovation.

MAUSOLEUM building providing a monumental carapace for a tomb.

METOPE originally the space between the triglyphs in a Doric frieze, and subsequently the panel, often carved in relief, occupying that space.

MINSTER cathedral or major church attached to a monastery.

MONASTERY buildings providing accommodation for a community of monks or nuns.

MOSAIC decoration formed by embedding small coloured tiles (tesserae) in cement.

MULLION vertical element forming subdivisions of a window.

MULTIFOIL much subdivided basically arcuate or circular form of ornament.

NARTHEX chamber adjunct to the nave of a church.

NAVE central body of principal interior of, for example, a church.

NYMPHAEUM originally – in Classical Greece and Rome – a sanctuary dedicated to water nymphs; later a structure or area with water features treated more or less elaborately.

OCULUS circular window in a church, for example.

ORATORY small room for prayer; in a Benedictine monastery, a communal prayer room.

ORDER defining feature of Classical architecture, comprising a column – itself usually composed of base, shaft, and capital – together with its entablature.

    CORINTHIAN an evolution from the Ionic Order, characterized by the replacement of the capital volutes with a more elaborate and deeper decorative arrangement. Later Corinthian columns evolved so as to be even taller relative to their base diameters than the Ionic. The entablature retained the comparatively light characteristics of the Ionic.

    DORIC the oldest and most simply functional of the Greek Orders of architecture, characterized by a fluted and tapered column without a base, topped by a usually plain capital, surmounted by a relatively high entablature made up of architrave, frieze, and cornice.

    IONIC slightly later and more elaborate order than the Doric, featuring fluted columns with bases and characteristically topped by a capital with scrolled volutes. The columns typically are taller relative to their base diameters than are the Doric, and are correspondingly less acutely tapered. The entablature is less tall than that of the Ionic, being originally composed of architrave and cornice only, though a frieze became usual later.

ORIEL window in a projecting bay supported by a bracket or corbel.

PALATINATE area ruled by a count palatine.

PALAZZO in Italy, a mansion or other large and imposing building.

PARAPET low wall, often protecting walkway at the top of an outer wall, originally for defensive purposes.

PARTERRE gardens inspired by embroidery patterns using flat-topped hedges of uniform height to mark out a series of ornamental flowerbeds planted symmetrically. *See also* **BRODERIE**.

PATIO outdoor space; a forecourt or courtyard.

PAVILION usually a free-standing structure used for recreation and situated some distance from a house or other major building. However, the term is also often used to translate French **PAVILLON**; *see below*.

PAVILLON In a symmetrical building or range of buildings, *pavillons* are outstanding attached structures that provide emphasis at the extremes or the centre of a façade, for example.

PEDESTAL base supporting, for example, a column or statue.

PEDIMENT triangular area of wall, usually a gable, above the entablature, enclosed above by raking cornices.

PENDENTIVE curved concave triangular member used at the corners of a square or polygonal structure so as to enable reconciliation with a domed roof.

PIANO NOBILE main, usually the first, floor of a large house or palazzo, site of the important reception rooms.

PIER supporting pillar for wall or roof, often of rectangular cross-section and/or formed from a composite mass of masonry columns.

PILASTER pier of rectangular cross-section, more or less integral with and only slightly projecting from the wall it supports.

PINNACLE slender ornamental termination at the top of a gable or buttress, for example, often in the shape of a miniature turret.

PLATERESQUE intricate and decorative stonework, from the Spanish *plata* (silver).

PLINTH rectangular base or base support of, for example, a column or wall.

PODIUM continuous base or pedestal consisting of plinth, dado and cornice, to support a series of columns.

PORTA COELI entrance to a sacred building, literally 'gate of heaven'.

PORTAL doorway, usually on the grand scale.

PORTE-COCHÈRE open porch large enough to shelter a vehicle; originally an entrance to a building through which a coach could be driven to reach an enclosed courtyard.

PORTICO entrance to or vestibule of a building, often featuring a colonnade.

POSA in New Spain, etc., a small chapel at the corner of a courtyard.

PRESBYTERY area reserved for clergy, at the eastern end of a church, in which the main altar is situated.

PULPIT raised structure in church, from which the preacher addresses the congregation.

QUADRATBAU choir which is square in plan.

QUADRATURA ceiling paintings using severe perspective techniques such as foreshortening and with elaborately painted architectural settings; more generally simulated architectural features.

QUADRO RIPORTATO framed paintings in normal perspective incorporated into a ceiling fresco, often combined with illusionistic techniques.

QUATRALOBE area composed of four interlocking circular segments.

QUATREFOIL having a shape composed of four subsidiary curves.

QUINCUNX structure composed of an agglomeration of five elements, four being identical and disposed so as to form more or less a hollow square, its centre being filled by the fifth.

QUOIN external corner of a building, where the stones thereof are arranged to form a key pattern.

RAADHUIS town hall.

RAMPART defensive earthwork, usually surrounding a fortress or citadel, often with a stone parapet.

RAYONNANT style of tracery in which the pattern radiates from a central point.

REREDOS carved or painted screen in wood or stone, rising from behind an altar.

RETABLE carved screen or reredos rising above and behind the altar, especially in the Spanish tradition.

RETROCHOIR the area behind the high altar in a large church.

REVETMENT decorative reinforced facing for retaining wall.

RIB raised band on a vault or ceiling.

RICETTO a vestibule, originally a defensible area protecting a settlement.

ROCAILLE style of asymmetrical ornament developed in the mid-18th century exploiting stylized and often fantastical motifs based on natural forms such as shells and and plants.

ROTUNDA circular room or building, usually with a domed roof.

RUSTICATION exterior ornament, often but not necessarily restricted to the lowest storey of a Classical building, in which masonry is given the appearance of strength (or roughness) by the use of projection and exaggerated chamfered or otherwise recessed joints.

SACRISTY room in a church for storing valuable ritual objects.

SALA a room.

SALA TERRENA formal and extensive room, often highly decorated, with garden access through one side.

SALONE a formal room.

SALOTTO a drawing room or salon.

SANCTUARY the most sacred part of a church, usually where the altar is situated.

SARCOPHAGUS coffin or outer container for a coffin, usually of stone and decorated with carvings.

SATERI a style of Scandinavian, particularly Swedish hipped roof, often with windows.

SCAGLIOLA a composite material resembling marble and used in the manufacture of sculpture and architectural elements.

SCENAE FRONS the flat wall forming the back of the stage in a semi-circular Roman theatre.

SCENOGRAPHIC effecting a representation in perspective.

SCOTIA concave moulding on the base of a column, often between two convex torus mouldings, thus providing an apparently deep channel between them.

SCREEN partition separating one part of an interior from another.

SCREEN WALL false (i.e. non-structural) wall to the front of a building, masking the façade proper.

SÉ cathedral

SERLIANA (after Serlio but probably an innovation by Bramante) used of windows and doors (or a blind feature) in a tripartite arrangement, the central opening with a semi-circular arch supported by columns. This central feature is taller than the narrower, usually flat-topped, openings to either side of it.

SFUMATO in painting and drawing, the use of fine shading to produce subtle gradations of tone.

SGRAFFITO Italian term meaning 'to scratch', a decorative technique in which a plaster layer is scored to reveal a contrasting colour.

SHAFT more or less cylindrical element of a column rising from the base to the capital.

SLOTT (**SLOT** in Danish) Scandinavian castle.

SOCLE shallow plinth supporting, for example, a piece of sculpture.

SOFFIT the underside of an architectural element in, for example, a cornice or architrave.

SOLAR a room for sleeping or private family use; initially at the end of the great hall but later usually on the top floor of a house.

SOTOCORO below the choir.

SPANDREL triangular space formed by the outer curve of an arch and the horizontal and vertical elements of the (often virtual) rectangle within which the arch sits.

SPIRE elongated conical or pyramidal structure forming the apex of a tower.

SPRINGING the point at which an arch springs from its support.

SQUINCH arch placed across the corner of a square structure so as to form a polygon capable of being roofed with a dome.

STADTHUIS city or town hall.

STANZA a room or apartment.

STRINGCOURSE projecting horizontal course of structural elements or moulding.

STUCCO plaster, especially used where decoration is to be applied.

STUDIOLO a small room used as a more-or-less private retreat.

TABERNACLE niche or cupboard, usually housing the consecrated host or sacred relic.

TEMPIETTO a small temple.

TESSERA small tile made of marble or glass, for example, used in conjunction with others to form mosaic.

THERMAE public baths, usually divided into frigidarium, tepidarium, and calidarium.

TIE-BEAM horizontal beam preventing two other structural components from separating.

TIERCERON subordinate rib set between the main members of a rib vault.

TOITURE À L'ITALIENNE gently sloping roof concealed behind a balustrade.

TORUS large moulding, typically at base of a column, of more or less semi-circular cross-section.

TRABEATED structurally dependent on rectilinear post and beam supports.

TRACERY pattern of ribs or bars inset to ornamental effect into a window or on to a panel.

TRANSEPT that part of the interior of a large church or cathedral which crosses the nave or principal interior space at right angles.

TRANSOM cross-bar or lintel, especially of a window.

TRASCORO part of the choir behind the main body of the choir or altar (**RETROCHOIR**)

TREFOIL having a curved shape composed of three subsidiary curves.

TRIBUNE vaulted apse, often the site of an altar or throne, or a semi-circular recess behind the choir of a church, or a vaulted gallery over an aisle and commanding the nave.

TRIFORIUM arcaded corridor facing on to the nave or chancel of a church, situated immediately below the clerestory.

TRIGLYPH block carved with vertical channels, used in a Doric frieze.

TRIUMPHAL ARCH originally a monument commemorating a victory, often taking the form of a massive rectangle penetrated by an arch.

TUNNEL VAULT, *see* **VAULT, TUNNEL**.

TYMPANUM an area, usually recessed, formed by a lintel below and an arch above.

VAULT structure forming an arched roof over a space.

    BARREL enclosing a more or less hemicylindrical space.

    CANOPY creating a roof for a niche or tomb.

    DOMICAL enclosing a more or less hemispherical space.

    FAN in which ribs of equal length, spaced equidistantly, are disposed around cones whose closest point of approach creates the apex of the vault.

    GROIN enclosing a space composed of two intersecting more or less hemi-cylindrical shapes.

    RIB composed of load-bearing ribs, carrying the material which fills the spaces between them.

    TUNNEL enclosing a more or less hemi-cylindrical space.

VESTIBULE originally the courtyard in front of the entrance to a Greek or Roman house; hallway to a building; space adjunct to a larger room.

VIGNA a vineyard.

VILLA freestanding house, originally Roman country house.

VOLUTE scroll or spiral ornamental and/or support member, characteristic of Ionic capitals.

VOUSSOIR wedge-shaped stone deployed in building an arch. Hence **VOUSSOIR ARCH**, where such stones are used.

WARD castle courtyard, bailey.

WESTWORK entrance hall and superstructure at the west end of a Romanesque or Carolingian church.

XYSTUS originally the portico in front of a gymnasium, where exercise could be taken in poor weather; later a term designating the open area for promenading in front of a portico.

ZAKOMARA structural arch-like gables continuing the curve of the vaulting behind them used in traditional Russian church building.

FURTHER READING

This set of volumes, *Architecture in Context*, is based on a survey series of lectures covering the whole spectrum of architectural history developed over a quarter of a century at the Canterbury School of Architecture. It is therefore impossible, even if it were desirable, to enumerate all the books that I have consulted and, in one way or another, depended on, over that period. Beyond students of architecture, for whom this whole process was initiated, I hope that the present work will provide the general reader with a broad but also reasonably deep introduction to the way our environment has been moulded over the past five thousand years. With this in mind, rather than a bibliography, I hope it will be useful if I provide a rough guide to how I would go about developing a course in further reading, were I starting now.

First, I would consult the *Grove Dictionary of Art* and the *Macmillan Dictionary of Architecture,* as much for the bibliographies attached to each section of each subject as for the individual articles – inevitably some are better than others as different authors naturally bring different standards of scholarship to bear on their products. *A World History of Art* by Hugh Honour and John Fleming (London 1984, sixth edition 2002) is unsurpassed in the field of general introductions. Victor-L. Tapié, *The Age of Grandeur: Baroque and Classicism in Europe* (Paris 1957, English translation London 1960) is also still worth consulting. Hanno-Walter Kruft, *A History of Architectural Theory* (London 1994), is of major importance.

Second, for greater depth and breadth, I would consult the relevant volumes of *The Pelican History of Art*: now published by Yale University Press, many of these have been updated or, where the text is an historical document in itself, edited with minimal corrections. The quality in these works is in general much more even as each self-contained subject is usually given to one scholar of outstanding academic record: Wittkower's, Blunt's and Summerson's volumes are of the best. Again, the bibliographies appended to each volume will be an invaluable guide to even broader and deeper reading. Taschen (under the indefatigable editorship of Henri Stierlin) has published a lavishly illustrated multi-volume series that has perhaps been over-ambitious and therefore remains incomplete. Valuable too are Könemann's sumptuous volumes on the *Baroque* and on *Vienna* (both Rolf Toman, ed., Cologne 1998 and 1999) and the volume on *Prussia* (Gert Streidt, ed., Cologne 1999). Henry A. Millon (ed.), *The Triumph of the Baroque: Architecture in Europe 1600–1750* (Milan 1999) is the impressive catalogue of the most comprehensive exhibition on the subject ever mounted.

Third: specific histories of architecture. As any student of the subject knows, the inescapable primer is the work first published in 1896 by Sir Banister Fletcher as *A History of Architecture on the Comparative Method*: that was essentially a catalogue arranged roughly chronologically by area – starting with ancient Egypt and Mesopotamia – but as the method was gradually superseded more room was found in the later 20th-century editions for essential analysis. Beyond that, from my view in the 1970s the most useful general survey of architectural history was the multi-volume series initiated by Electa in Milan, edited by Pier Luigi Nervi and published in English by Abrams (and later by others): it had its flaws, not least in the relationship of text to illustrations especially in Christian Norberg-Schulz's two volumes devoted to Baroque and Rococo. The range of scholars involved was impressive (notwithstanding some flagrant political bias) and, despite their age, some of the material not otherwise easily available is still essential reading. From a somewhat later date, indispensible is Anthony Blunt (ed.), *Baroque and Rococo: Architecture & Decoration* (London 1978); the editor's contribution on Italy is as authoritative as his Pelican History of Art volume on France, of course: of prime importance too is the contribution of Kerry Downes on English Baroque, though that has been amplified in various formats covering the subject as a whole as well as Vanbrugh and Hawksmoor in particular; on the other hand, there is nothing in English to compete with Alastair Laing's extended essay on Central Europe and my dependence on it will be readily apparent to its author – and the attentive reader.

In particular I would recommend the following works and their bibliographies on Italians: Blunt's *Guide to Baroque Rome* (London 1982), his *Borromini* (London 1979), his *Sicilian Baroque* (London 1978) and his *Neapolitan Baroque and Rococo Architecture* (London 1975); Howard Hibbard, *Carlo Maderno* (London 1971) and *Bernini* (Harmondsworth 1965); Irving Lavin (ed.), *Gian Lorenzo Bernini: New Aspects of His Art and Thought* (Philadelphia, PA, 1985); Charles Avery, *Bernini: Genius of the Baroque* (London, 1997); Jörg Martin Merz (after Blunt) *Pietro da Cortona and Roman Baroque Architecture* (New Haven and London 2008) and Malcolm Campbell, *Pietro da Cortona at the Pitti Palace: A Study of the Planetary Rooms and Related Projects* (Princeton, NJ, 1977); Correa, Esquivas and Cantone (eds) *Filippo Juvarra e l'architetura europea* (Naples, 1998) and Enrico Castelnuovo (ed.), *La reggia de Venaria e i Savoia: arte, magnificenza e storia di una corte europea* (Turin 2007); Allen Braham (ed.), *Carlo Fontana: The Drawings at Windsor Castle* (London 1978).

The French are exhaustively introduced by Louis Hautecoeur, *Histoire de l'Architecture Classique en France*, volume 1 (Paris from 1943) and *Histoire du Louvre* (Paris n.d.); the best and most modern general studies are Jean-Marie Pérouse de Montclos, *Histoire de l'Architecture Française: De la Renaissance à la Révolution* (Paris 2003), André Chastel, *French Art: The Ancien Régime 1620–1775* (Paris 1995 and 1996) and Jean Feray, *Architecture Interieure et Décoration en France des Origines à 1875* (Paris 1988). Of the monographs, most notable are Rosalys Coope, *Salomon De Brosse & the Development of the Classical Style in French Architecture from 1565 to 1630* (London 1972); Allan Braham and Peter Smith, *François Mansart* (London 1973); Cyril Bordier, *Louis Le Vaux: Architecte* (Paris 1998) and Hilary Ballon, *Louis Le Vau: Mazarin's Collège, Colbert's Revenge* (Princeton, NJ, 1999); Robert W. Berger, *Antoine Le Pautre: A French Architect of the Era of Louis XIV* (New York 1969) and *Versailles: The Château of Louis XIV* (London 1985); Cecil Gould, *Bernini in France* (London 1981); Wolfgang Herrmann, *The Theory of Claude Perrault* (London 1963) and Michael Petzet, *Claude Perrault und die Architektur des Sonnenkönnigs* (Berlin 2000); Bertrand Jestaz, *Jules Hardouin-Mansart* (Paris 2008); Robert Neuman, *Robert de Cotte and the Perfection of Architecture in Eighteenth-Century France* (Chicago 1994); Michel Gallet *et al*, *Germain Boffrand 1667–1754* (Paris 1986); Guy Walton, *Louis XIV's Versailles* (Harmondsworth 1986).

The Flemish are covered by Hans Vlieghe, *Flemish Art and Architecture* (New Haven 1998) but the Dutch and the Danes are underrepresented in English. For Sweden there is Henrik O. Andersson and Fredric Bedoire, *Swedish Architecture: Drawings 1640–1970* (Stockholm 1986). For the general coverage of the period in England, apart from Summerson there are Giles Worsley, *Classical Architecture in Britain: The Heroic Age* (New Haven 1995), Peter Kidson and Peter Murray's introductory *A History of English Architecture* (New York 1962) and the exhaustive volume 5 of *The History of the King's Works* edited by H.M. Colvin (London 1976). Of the monographs apart from those of Downes referred to above, Margaret Whinney's *Wren* (London 1971) offers concise coverage: rather more intense are James W.P. Campbell, *Building St Paul's* (London 2007), Derek Keene *et al* (eds), *St Paul's: The Cathedral Church of London 604–2004* (New Haven 2004), and Peter Willis, *Charles Bridgeman and the English Landscape Garden* (Newcastle upon Tyne 2001).

To supplement Laing's account mentioned above, southern Germany is splendidly covered by Henry-Russell Hitchcock in *Rococo Architecture in Southern Germany* (London 1968). Of specific monographs, outstanding are Hans Aurehammer, *J.B. Fischer von Erlach* (London 1973) and Christian F. Otto, *Space into Light: The Churches of Balthasar Neumann* (New York 1979). William Craft Brumfield, *A History of Russian Architecture* (Cambridge 1993) is

indispensible but usefully supplemented by Dimitri Shvidkovsky, *Russian Architecture and the West* (New Haven 2007).

Spain is not well represented in English but there is Jay A. Levenson (ed.), *The Age of the Baroque in Portugal* (Washington and New Haven 1993). On the other hand, the Iberian American colonies fare well in works including Yves Bottineau, *Iberian-American Baroque* (New York 1970); Manuel Toussaint, *Colonial Art in Mexico* (Austin and London 1967); Joseph Armstrong Baird, Jr, *The Churches of Mexico 1530–1810* (Berkeley 1962); James Early, *The Colonial Architecture of Mexico* (Albuquerque 1994); Damián Bayón and Murillo Marx, *History of South American Colonial Art and Architecture* (Barcelona 1989); Germain Bazin, *L'Architecture Religieuse baroque au Brésil* (São Paulo and Paris, 1956–58) and Augusto Carlos do Silva Telles, *Atlas dos Monumentos Históricos e Artísticos do Brasil* (Rio de Janeiro 1975).

My own dependence on the contributors to the series cited above and to the authors of the individual monographs in the abbreviated list will be apparent to even the most cursory reader. I apologize that it is far too wide-ranging individually to acknowledge here.

Pictures

Bringing together some of the material needed for a book of this scope has been made possible by the availability of images generously published online under Creative Commons licenses. The following images are reproduced under that scheme: 0.13, 0.19a–c, 1.28c, 1.38b, 2.85b, 2.90e, 2.91b, 3.5d, 3.8b, d, 3.15c, 3.16, 3.18a, b, 3.26c, 3.28b, c, h, 3.31I, 3.33c, d, 3.39a, 3.41, 3.42b, 3.43e, 3.52a, 3.71b, 4.8a, 4.9b, d, 4.23a, 4.32d, 4.37b, 4.40b, 4.41b, 4.49g, 4.56b, c, 4.60d, 4.61a, b, d, 4.68j, 4.99b, 4.102b, 4.104a, 4.116a, 4.124c, 4.131a–c, 4.132a, b, 4.133a, b, 4.139a–d, 4.144c, 4.148a, b, 4.153b, d, 4.166b, 4.170a, 4.173d, 4.181b, 5.31, 5.43f, g, 5.44a, b, e–g, 5.54b, 5.84, 5.111a, 5.115c, 5.119i.

Images 0.8a, b and 3.52c are reproduced by permission of the Royal Collection Trust / © Her Majesty Queen Elizabeth II 2013.

Images 3.62h and l are reproduced with kind permission of His Grace, the Duke of Devonshire.

INDEX